Human Rights in the UK

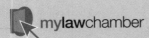 **my**law**chamber

Visit the *Human Rights in the UK*, Third Edition, Companion
Website at **www.mylawchamber.co.uk/hoffman** to find regular
updates to major changes in the law, ensuring you're up to
date with the latest developments.

University of Liverpool

We work with leading authors to develop the strongest educational materials in law, bringing cutting-edge thinking and best learning practice to a global market.

Under a range of well-known imprints, including Longman, we craft high quality print and electronic publications which help readers to understand and apply their content, whether studying or at work.

To find out more about the complete range of our publishing, please visit us on the World Wide Web at: www.pearsoned.co.uk

Human Rights in the UK

An Introduction to the Human Rights Act 1998

Third Edition

David Hoffman

MA (Oxon), BCL, Barrister

John Rowe Q.C.

MA (Oxon), Barrister

Longman
is an imprint of

Harlow, England • London • New York • Boston • San Francisco • Toronto
Sydney • Tokyo • Singapore • Hong Kong • Seoul • Taipei • New Delhi
Cape Town • Madrid • Mexico City • Amsterdam • Munich • Paris • Milan

Pearson Education Limited
Edinburgh Gate
Harlow
Essex CM20 2JE
England

and Associated Companies throughout the world

Visit us on the World Wide Web at:
www.pearsoned.co.uk

First published 2003
Second edition 2006
Third edition 2010

ISBN: 978-1-4058-7403-8

British Library Cataloguing-in-Publication Data
A catalogue record for this book is available from the British Library

Library of Congress Cataloging-in-Publication Data
Hoffman, David, 1971–
    Human rights in the UK : an introduction to the Human Rights Act 1998 / David Hoffman, John Rowe. — 3rd ed.
        p. cm.
    ISBN 978-1-4058-7403-8 (pbk.)
    1. Civil rights—Great Britain. 2. Great Britain. Human Rights Act 1998. I. Rowe, John (John Jermyn), 1936– II. Title.
    KD4080.H64 2009
    342.4108'5—dc22

                                                                    2009021448

10 9 8 7 6 5 4 3 2 1
13 12 11 10 09

Typeset in 10/12pt Minion by 35
Printed and bound in Great Britain by Henry Ling Ltd, Dorchester, Dorset

The publisher's policy is to use paper manufactured from sustainable forests.

Brief contents

Contents

Foreword to the Second Edition (2006)

The Human Rights Act was enacted in 1998 and came into force on 2 October 2000. Two and a half years later the first edition of this book was published. The second edition appears as the Act is in the course of its sixth year in operation.

The subtitle of this book is 'An Introduction to the Human Rights Act 1998'. I understand the reason for the subtitle, as the authors intended this book to be used by students embarking on law studies. However, this subtitle should not deter those who are further advanced in their legal studies, or indeed those practising law, from consulting this book. The reason for this is that, in my view, the work is in fact far more than a mere introduction to the subject. The authors have combined meticulous scholarship with an enviable ability to express matters, however complex, in clear and understandable terms. Using these skills, they cover a developing field, including matters that have come into sharp and public focus recently, such as government measures to control immigration or counter terrorism.

Before the introduction of the Human Rights Act, there was a body of opinion that regarded it as a piece of unnecessary legislation, on the grounds that the common law had developed its own means of protecting human rights. In addition, there were those who forecast that there would be an avalanche of spurious claims (or defences) based on its provisions. The latter has not occurred. As to the former, to my mind the case law in this country over the last six years has clearly demonstrated – as does this book – that the Act has provided an additional and valuable bulwark, helping in a significant way to enshrine in our domestic law the proper protection of the human rights of those in our jurisdiction. Such protection is part of the essential nature of a democratic society.

Lord Saville of Newdigate
Lord of Appeal in Ordinary
January 2006

Foreword to the First Edition (2003)

Following the election of the Labour Party in 1997, one of the first announcements by the new Government was of its intention to give people in the United Kingdom direct access to the rights contained in the European Convention on Human Rights. To say that this was a radical idea, considering the established assumption that people in the UK were adequately protected by the common law, and therefore had no need of these 'foreign' rights, is perhaps too mild a description. The keen debate that accompanied the passage of the Human Rights Bill through Parliament, in which I was involved as a Minister, then at the Home Office – the sponsor Department for the Bill – reflected the constitutional significance of the measure. Few were unmoved.

When the Human Rights Act 1998 came into effect on 2 October 2000, it was accompanied by a great deal of publicity, and a good many publications. There is no doubt that the Act presented a considerable challenge, and one that was for lawyers and the courts to deal with in the first instance. However, there was little in the wealth of new literature on the Act that was readily accessible to the interested non-lawyer. Therefore, this book will be very welcome, for not only is it very readable – owing much to the good sense and considerable experience of its authors – it is also comprehensive in its scope.

The reader will find an excellent account of the development of international protection for human rights, the unique constitutional position of the United Kingdom, including the Parliamentary process, and the history of the European Convention. Ordinarily, all of this would be enough for one book, but here it is succinctly and judiciously presented and lays the ground for the main thrust of the book which is, as the title says, *Human Rights in the UK*.

The appearance of this book some two and a half years since the Act came into force, together with all of the contextual material I have just referred to, provides the reader with a sense of perspective, as well as a ready understanding of his or her rights. Clearly, the operation of the Human Rights Act is central to this, and the book presents a balanced analysis, with useful questions at the end of each chapter for the reader to consider against what they have just read. The sections dealing with the relationship between Parliament, the Judiciary and the Executive described by the Act are as good an example as can be found anywhere.

I have no doubt that this book will contribute to the wider development of the human rights culture in the UK.

Lord Williams of Mostyn QC (1941–2003)
(Lord Privy Seal and Leader of the House of Lords 2001–2003)

Publisher's acknowledgements

We are grateful to the following for permission to reproduce copyright material:

Page 2: SGM SGM/Photolibrary.com; 10: © Imageshop/Alamy; 22: Copyright © 2009 The British Library/British Library Images Online; 38: Peter Adams/Digital Vision/Getty Images; 60: Courtesy of David Fullwood; 86: Courtesy of the authors; 108: Matt Cardy/Getty Images; 132: Science Photo Library Ltd; 170: Library of Congress (public domain); 178: Mirrorpix; 202: © Martyn Goddard/Corbis; 236: Barry Batchelor/PA Photos; 248: John Birdsall/PA Photos; 276: Chris Radburn/PA Photos; 298: Robinsa Aaron Robinson (50/50)/PA Photos; 314: © Annie Griffiths Belt/Corbis; 326: Stephen Hird/PA Photos; 336: Ganeth Fuller/PA Photos; 354: Reuters; 366: © Hubert Boesl/dpa/Corbis; 388: © Nikreates/Alamy.

Every effort has been made to trace the copyright holders and we apologise in advance for any unintentional omissions. We would be pleased to insert the appropriate acknowledgement in any subsequent edition of this publication.

Table of cases

Table of international treaties

Table of statutes

EUROPEAN LEGISLATION

 ## OTHER LEGISLATION

FRANCE

IRISH REPUBLIC

UNITED STATES

Table of statutory instruments

The home of the Council of Europe, in Strasbourg, the international body which developed the European Convention on Human Rights.

1 Introduction

'What is the use of a book,' thought Alice, 'without pictures or conversations?' (Lewis Carroll, *Alice's Adventures in Wonderland*, 1865)

Human rights are those fundamental freedoms and entitlements that each person possesses by virtue of nothing more than their status as a human being. To say that there is a right to life is to say that each person, man or woman, boy or girl, of whatever race or colour, religion or background, has the same basic entitlement to be allowed to live as every other person. Adding the word 'human' stresses that these rights are based on the basic equality of all people. They are all rights that everyone shares: no one is born with more of a right to life than anybody else.

What rights we include in a list of human rights is not an easy question, and different people throughout the centuries have come up with different lists. Some basic rights are likely to be included in any list we would make today, such as the right to life, freedom from torture and slavery, freedom of speech. Even these have not always been recognised as basic rights to which all people are entitled: for example, slavery was quite common for much of human history, and still exists in some parts of the world today. Our list should include those rights which protect the values that we hold to be most important, which set out the basic requirements of human existence with freedom and dignity.

This book is about the Human Rights Act 1998 (hereafter, 'the Act'), the Act of Parliament which brought the European Convention on Human Rights into the domestic law of the United Kingdom. The European Convention is a treaty which came into being in 1950, but it has not, until the Act, been directly a part of our law. The treaty contains a particular list of human rights, and it is these which we shall be considering, together with the legal framework for enforcing them created by the new Act. This list, which most European countries, including the United Kingdom, have long recognised as being important, should accord with our view of what basic rights we should have. If it does not, then we can criticise the law for failing to protect all those rights which should be protected.

It is also important to recognise at the outset that the Human Rights Act 1998 is one of the most important statutes ever passed in the United Kingdom. It has the scope to change the way we think about our identity as citizens of our country, in a way that only a few laws have in the past. In that sense, it can be termed a piece of constitutional legislation, which joins other significant pieces of law in making up a large part of our Constitution: for example, Magna Carta (1215), the Bill of Rights (1688), which set up our Constitutional Monarchy, the Acts of Union with Scotland (1706–7) and Ireland (1800), the European

Communities Act (1972), or the Acts granting Irish independence and, more recently, a measure of devolution to Scotland and Wales.[1]

The Human Rights Act has constitutional significance not just because it sets out clearly and in an organised manner those basic rights which must be respected, even by Parliament, but also because it applies to all law already existing and to all law that Parliament makes in the future. It therefore has great scope for remodelling many parts of our law if they do not accord proper protection to people's rights. So for the first time in the United Kingdom there is one standard for the protection of rights by which all laws are considered. This can be contrasted with the traditional approach of, for example, the English common law, which is that a citizen of the United Kingdom has the freedom to do anything which is not specifically banned, but which has never set out comprehensively what rights he or she positively possesses. Although our law has traditionally provided a fair measure of protection for a large number of basic rights, there is now scope for it to provide more such protection. Thus, our law will inevitably be more focused on the perspective of individual rights than it has been previously – and this has the potential to lead to a major shift in how we see each other as citizens of our country.

Since this book first came out there has been a steady stream of cases decided under the Act which has reinforced its importance: a search of one law database brought up several thousand 'hits', with dozens of House of Lords cases, probably more than under any other piece of legislation; and it has been crucial to the development of various areas of the law, especially the law on privacy, criminal procedure, family, immigration and terrorism. In particular, there is the pivotal case of *A* v *Home Secretary*,[2] in which the detention power which was a cornerstone of the government's anti-terrorism legislation was held by the House of Lords to infringe the Act. This unprecedented criticism by the judiciary of a statute led to prompt and extensive political debate, and the passing of new legislation within months. It can truly be said now that the Act has found a place at the heart of the constitution of the United Kingdom.

We hope that the discussion in this book will provoke thought about human rights in general and their protection in English law in particular. We will consider first the background to the Convention and the Act and set both in their political and constitutional context; then the scheme of the Act, how it implements the European Convention and how it operates in practice; then we will discuss in more detail the particular rights which the Act embodies, together with practical examples; finally we have a discussion of the particular problem area of the law's response to terrorism, a topic which raises human rights questions in a particularly acute form, and in a very current and controversial context.

We hope that the cases and other examples will help to show some of the ways in which the Human Rights Act and the implementation of the Convention rights into United Kingdom law have already affected us in some surprisingly common and everyday situations and will help you to understand the full scope of this important piece of legislation. It should also be understood at the outset that it is not the aim of this book to provide a comprehensive treatment of the case law under the Act, or in the areas of law which are affected by it, although we hope to have included all the most significant or interesting

---

[1] Government of Ireland Act 1920, Anglo-Irish Treaty Act 1922, etc.; Scotland Act 1998, Government of Wales Acts 1998 and 2006; Northern Ireland Act 1998.

[2] [2004] UKHL 56, [2005] 2 WLR 87, which we will discuss in various contexts, especially p. 376.

cases decided under the Act and the most useful in the understanding of each Convention right.

The examples we use have been taken mostly from cases decided in the United Kingdom or in Strasbourg, designed to show how the Convention works in practice. We have included the case citation but not references to academic discussion on the cases, although there is plenty to be found for those who wish to research any particular area further, and we have included some suggestions for further reading at the end of the book.[3] But those who are not studying or practising law should not need to look up any of the cases cited to understand the point that is being made. We hope that non-lawyers will not be put off by the references to British or European cases: the way one understands legislation is by considering how it works in practical situations, in cases that the courts have decided.

This book is aimed, broadly, at the law undergraduate, or other law student, or the practitioner, or for that matter, non-lawyer looking for an introduction to the subject. We also hope that it is of use for other students, or for those teaching other students, as well as of interest to anyone who would like to know more about this significant legal landmark. We have also included questions at the end of most of the chapters. These are there to provoke thought, and hopefully discussion, whether the reader is a student or not and to highlight some of the issues raised by the chapter, not as a test on the chapter. We hope that this book will encourage the reader to think about this Act and the rights it protects, and the questions are part of that aspiration. The occasional illustration will serve, we hope, the same purpose.

The Act applies throughout the United Kingdom of Great Britain and Northern Ireland. Although it is one country, the United Kingdom contains three separate legal systems[4] – those of England and Wales,[5] Scotland, and Northern Ireland. Our discussion will deal primarily with the law of England and Wales, but we hope that the general discussion of the Act will be of interest and use to readers in the other jurisdictions. As the application of the Act has developed, there have been situations where it has affected different jurisdictions differently, especially in Scotland with its distinct legal system, but the overall approach is generally consistent and applies equally to all of these systems.

The law is as at 31 January 2009, although some later matters have been able to insinuate themselves into the text at the proof stage. The first and second editions have been updated online; we hope to do the same with this third edition at reasonable intervals, so do keep an occasional eye on: http://www.pearsoned.co.uk/hoffmanrowe. In such a fast-moving subject, we hope to alleviate the risk of going out of date too soon.

ACKNOWLEDGEMENTS

This is a convenient point for the authors to acknowledge the invaluable help and assistance of the following, for proofreading, discussion, reaction and encouragement at various stages during all the three editions of this work: Matthew Butcher, Asher Dresner, Katharine Edgar, Baroness Hale of Richmond, Professor John Hoffman, Anna Short, Lord Steyn, Owain Thomas, Dave Wilkinson; for research assistance, Jenny Kumeta; and those

[3] See p. 446.
[4] There are more in the British Isles, including the Isle of Man and the Channel Islands' legal systems.
[5] Some devolved areas are the subject of different laws in Wales, but these have tended thus far not to impact on the areas discussed in this book.

who helped to steer all editions of this book towards fruition at Pearson: Pat Bond, Beth Barber, Cheryl Cheasley, David Cox, Michelle Gallagher, Owen Knight, Rebekah Taylor, and Joe Vella.

We have also retained the Foreword to the first edition, as a reminder of the privilege we still feel that the late Lord Williams of Mostyn, then leader of the House of Lords, introduced our first edition in May 2003, and we would like to express our appreciation to Lord Saville of Newdigate for his kind words in the Foreword to the second edition, which we have retained for this third edition.

None of the preceding share with the authors the responsibility for any faults or errors which remain.

 ## ABBREVIATIONS

Throughout this book we will be using the following:

'The Act'	The Human Rights Act 1998. The full text is to be found in Appendix 1, p. 393.
'The Convention'	The European Convention on Human Rights. The full text is to be found in Appendix 2, p. 415.
'The European Court'	The European Court of Human Rights, which sits in Strasbourg (not to be confused with the European Court of Justice of the European Union, which sits in Luxembourg). This is an international court and may be contrasted with the national or domestic courts of the United Kingdom or other state.
'The Commission'	The European Commission on Human Rights (and again not the Commission of the European Communities/European Union).
'The Convention rights'	The rights which are protected by the Convention and which are included in Schedule 1 to the Act.

 ## GLOSSARY OF LEGAL TERMS

The names of legal cases are given by the names of the parties, *Smith versus* (v) *Jones*, where Smith is bringing the case against Jones. Sometime a case is referred to as 'in *re*', which is Latin for 'in the matter of', where the object of the case, such as a will or a piece of land, is an easy shorthand for the case. Where the name of a case includes an initial, such as X or Y, this means that the identity of that person is being kept confidential.

Where the name of a case starts with *R*, this will usually be a criminal case, since *R* represents the crown: it stands for *Regina* (the Queen) or *Rex* (the King), in whose name all criminal prosecutions are brought.

Judicial review cases are brought as: *R versus Minister, ex parte Smith*, meaning that Smith is reviewing the decision of the Minister (*ex parte* is Latin for 'on the application of'), or for more recent cases *R (on the application of Smith)* v *Minister*, or just *R (Smith)* v *Minister*.

The following terms are used to describe the parties in a case:

In a criminal case:

Prosecution	person bringing a criminal charge at trial
Defendant	person accused of a crime in a criminal prosecution
Complainant	person against whom a crime is committed

In a civil case:

Claimant/applicant	person bringing a civil action or claim
Plaintiff	person bringing a civil action or claim (old terminology)
Defendant	person against whom a civil action has been brought

In an appeal:

Appellant	person bringing an appeal (civil or criminal)
Respondent	person against whom an application or appeal is brought

Case names sometimes also include the following acting on behalf of the state:

Attorney General (AG): the minister who is ultimately responsible for prosecutions or bringing other legal actions on behalf of the government.

Director of Public Prosecutions (DPP): the head of the Crown Prosecution Service (CPS) in whose name some prosecutions or appeals are brought.

The different judges in the courts of England and Wales (introduced in Chapter 4) are titled as follows:

The most senior judge was until recently the Lord Chancellor (abbreviated to LC). The most senior judge now is the Lord Chief Justice (LCJ).

Judges in the most senior court, the House of Lords, are referred to as Lord or Lady so-and-so, and collectively as the Law Lords. The Law Lords also sit as the Judicial Committee of the Privy Council on some appeals.

(When the Constitutional Reform Act 2005 comes fully into effect, the House of Lords, and for most purposes the Privy Council, will be replaced by the Supreme Court. The most senior judge will be the President of the Supreme Court (PSC) and the judges will be Justices of the Supreme Court (JSC).)

Judges in the Court of Appeal are titled Lord or Lady Justice so-and-so (abbreviated to LJ or LJJ in the plural). The most senior judges after the Lord Chief Justice are the Master of the Rolls (MR), Chancellor of the High Court (formerly called the Vice-Chancellor (VC)) and the Presidents of the Queen's Bench and Family Divisions (P).

In the lower courts, High Court Judges are referred to as Mr or Mrs Justice so-and-so (J or JJ) and County Court or Circuit Judges are referred to as His or Her Honour Judge so-and-so. Below them are Masters and District Judges (DJ). A reference to the Justices of a place refers to a panel of magistrates.

There are occasional references to the Court of Session. This is the Scottish equivalent of the High Court and Court of Appeal, and is the final court for appeals in Scotland, except that devolution questions (which includes human rights questions) can be appealed to the Privy Council (in due course to be replaced by the Supreme Court). The Scottish criminal judges of first instance are the Sheriffs (equivalent to District or Circuit Judges).

1

Introduction

Recent cases have a neutral citation that indicates which court is hearing the case: UKHL for the House of Lords, UKPC for Privy Council, EWCA for Court of Appeal, 'Civ' for civil and 'Crim' for criminal, EWHC for the High Court, again with a division (QB, Chanc, Fam, Admin, etc.). A list of abbreviations used for law reports and other citations can be found in 'Further reading' on p. 446.

The Statue of Liberty embodies the idea of freedom, which is a key idea in understanding rights.

Source: © Imageshop/Alamy

2 The idea of human rights

right, *noun* . . . That which is due to anyone by law, tradition or nature; a just or legal claim or title. (*Reader's Digest Illustrated Dictionary*)

 ## THE NATURE OF HUMAN RIGHTS

Before we begin our discussion in detail of the *content* of rights, and specifically the rights guaranteed by the Human Rights Act 1998, it is important to have some idea as to what we actually *mean* by rights. That is the purpose of this chapter: to set out our view on the meaning and importance of the idea of **rights** and introducing some important concepts associated with rights and human rights which will be relevant to consideration of the Act and the Convention rights: what we mean by rights, what we mean by *human* rights, what is the basis of these, and what are their limits.[1]

When we are considering the law, and what its contents should be, there is a particular benefit which comes from concentrating on rights. A focus on rights ensures that we consider the position of **individuals** under the law, as opposed to **collective interests**; and what is due to them in a positive way, as against simply the prohibition of harmful conduct.

To begin with, it is appropriate to consider what is meant by rights, because when we refer to a right we could in fact be referring to one of several types of entitlement. We could mean:

(i)   a **claim to** something (which someone else has a duty to do or provide)
      for example: an owner's right (claim) to the return of property which has been stolen (and that person has a duty to return it); *or*

(ii) a **freedom to do** something
      for example: the right to freedom of speech;
      (which is supported by other rights which are claims that other persons do not interfere with the exercise of that freedom); *or*

(iii) a **power to do** something which affects other people
      for example: a judge's right to decide a case, which affects the rights of the parties involved in the case; *or*

(iv) an **immunity from** challenge in doing something
      for example: a judge's right not to be sued for the results of a judicial decision.

---

[1] As throughout, we have not included a detailed discussion of the academic literature, but some references are contained with the Further reading at p. 446.

All of these are possible descriptions of what we mean when we talk about a right. But it may also be that when we talk about a particular right we are talking about a *bundle* of these. So, when we refer to the right to life, what we usually mean is more than just the freedom to be alive. We probably also mean the rights that protect this freedom, such as a right (claim) not to be killed. When we talk about rights over an item of property, we mean a whole bundle of things which we are free to do with that property (use it, sell it, loan it, etc.), and a whole series of claims against others that they do not interfere with that property (not steal it, damage it, destroy it, etc.). So when we talk about the '*right* to life' or 'the *right* to the property', what we mean by it is this *bundle* of rights, conveniently abbreviated by reference to the **interest** which is being protected ('life' or 'property'). Thus, it is worth bearing in mind that talk about rights could mean a variety of things – it could mean a specific claim, or freedom, or immunity. Or it could be referring to the interest being protected, in which case we need to determine what the extent of that interest is, and which more specific rights (claims, freedoms, etc.) we have to protect that interest.

When we talk about **human** rights, we are talking about a particular sort of right. We each have a variety of legal rights, for example rights under various laws to a state education or to social security benefits. However, when we talk about our human rights, we mean by this something more fundamental and more general than just those legal rights which are granted by a particular legal system. We can contrast human rights with other legal rights because of their **universality**: they are propositions as to people's general rights which they have in all situations. So, for example, a right to own property is a general right. This does not answer all specific questions about my particular rights, such as what property I in fact own, and the list of my personal property rights and the attributes and consequences of that ownership would be a very detailed one. As we move from the specific to the general, it may be that we can frame more general propositions about property rights. For example, if I own a hedge, I am entitled to trim it. We can phrase that more generally as: all owners of hedges have the right to trim them, but it is still a statement which covers a very specific situation. It may be that we can generalise further, and say that all owners of all property have the right to damage or destroy it: this is approaching a more universal proposition.

However, we would not necessarily say that the right to damage our own property is a human right. This is because human rights have a further quality in addition to their universal application, which is their **importance**. A right should be added to a list of what we consider to be *human* rights if it is important, if it protects something which is fundamental to the basic entitlements that we all possess as human beings. It is because of this that the idea of universality of application is a very important one in setting out moral principles or rights, because theories of morality derive much of their justification from whether or not they can be applied to all people in all situations. When we talk about human rights, we should mean something that is so important that it applies to all people all the time.

Thus whether or not a right really can be said to be universal in application is an important part of whether any particular list of moral or human rights is in fact correctly drawn up – and note that a right can be universal even if it is sometimes subject to exceptions or limitations. Put another way, it is a valid criticism of the inclusion of an entry in a list of human rights if it is not of universal application. Of course, that raises a very big question as to what the list of fundamental and universal rights really is, and that question will be answered differently by different people from different backgrounds. Some rights are generally agreed to be human rights, such as the protection of life and the basic freedom and security of the person. Once lists of human rights move away from these sorts of rights and start to consider social or economic rights such as the right to education, the right to withhold labour (that is, to go on strike) or a right to social security, there is less agreement about whether such rights should appropriately be considered *human* rights. Economic rights, especially those which relate to work or involve the spending of money, such as social security or paying for education, tend to be viewed in a much more culturally and politically relative manner – a right to withhold labour would make no sense in a culture where people do not work for each other – and therefore their universality is less clear.

RIGHTS UNLIMITED?

What *gives* human rights this universality is that these are rights which we consider people have from the simple fact that they are human beings, and all human beings are equally worthy of basic respect. So, a right to life is a human right because it is a fundamental part of all people's existence; freedom from torture and slavery, freedom of thought and the right to a family life, are basic attributes of human dignity.

Nonetheless, we must be aware that whilst everyone has rights which deserve respect, this does not necessarily mean that the rights of one individual deserve more respect than the rights of any other individual. To say that I have a right to something, or freedom to do something, does not mean that I have an *unlimited* right to do that or that I should *not* respect other people's rights. This comes from the same **equality** which grounds the right in the first place: because all human beings are equal, there is no legitimate basis for distinguishing between persons in respect of their basic entitlements. Thus there is an inherent scope for conflicts between rights where different individuals wish to exercise their rights in ways which conflict with each other.

Once it is appreciated that rights have limits, caused by the rights of others, it is then important to distinguish **limitations on the scope** of rights from an **interference with** that right.

A limitation on a right is inherent in the proper definition of that right: it is a way of saying that a right may not extend to all situations, or may not justify an unlimited scope for action. This is different from where there is a breach of that right, or an interference with it. There, the right does extend to that situation, it is engaged, and it is interfered with.

So, for example, freedom to associate does not extend to freedom to have a riot: that is not a part of the right, as properly understood. It is not an interference with that right to be forbidden from rioting, because that is not what the right is about. We have no entitlement to riot. But a ban on joining a trade union is an interference with the right, or at least engages it. There is no limit in the right on joining a trade union.

Another example of a series of permissible limitations on the scope of a right can be found by considering freedom of speech. If you think about freedom of speech, you will quickly realise that there are many ways in which we are *not* free to say whatever we like.

So, for example, we are not allowed to say, write, print or broadcast things which:

- make other people afraid they will be harmed (assault by threats or harassment)
- falsely insult people or harm their reputation (libel and slander)
- cause or provoke other people to commit a crime (incitement)
- are sexually or racially abusive or insulting (sex or race discrimination or harassment)

- reveal matters which are secret or confidential or infringe national security (breach of confidence and official secrets)
- infringe certain standards as to showing sex or violence (obscenity and limits on printing or showing pornography)
- invade other people's privacy without some justification (breach of confidence).[2]

You will probably broadly agree that there are good reasons for most if not all of these limitations, which is to say that they protect other rights or interests which are more important than the right of the person wishing to say or write whatever they want. Thus it is not true to say that freedom of speech is an unlimited right: it protects an important interest (self-expression) by means of a bundle of rights, but it is limited by other people's rights and interests where there is something more important to be protected than allowing unlimited self-expression.

However, there is another sort of limitation on the scope of a right which will be far less easy to justify: that is where the definition of the *persons* to whom those rights apply has been limited in a particular society. If human rights are not applied equally to all people within a society, those denied equal treatment are being denied the respect due to them *as* human beings. This means that, effectively, society, or some dominant group within it, considers the group denied equal treatment as inferior, as less than fully human. That will commonly be a minority group, for example Gypsies (Roma) or Jews in Nazi Germany, but can be a majority group, such as blacks in South Africa under apartheid. This is therefore not a legitimate way to limit rights, since it contradicts the basic equality which underlies those rights.

In addition to rights being limited in scope because of direct conflict with other individual rights, it is important that certain interests are protected for the benefit of the whole community. An example would be the physical environment we live in, whether one is thinking of rules preserving open space, wildlife and greenery, or planning controls to preserve the character or amenities of an area. This is not to say that these are somehow more or less important than the rights of individuals. On the contrary, they are the same thing: to refer to the benefit of 'the whole community' means that something benefits all the people who make up that community. So, for example, limiting the right of a person to build a factory in a residential area, or discharge chemicals into a river, by citing the common interest in a pleasant environment: this is another way of saying that the right of *all* the people in that community to live in a pleasant environment is considered sufficiently important to justify limiting the right of the property owner to build freely on his property.

To take another example, if we say that a right is limited in the interests of national security, the same calculation is going on. Here the community is broader than just a neighbourhood; it extends to the whole country. But it is still a set of individual rights, albeit a very large set, which means that we can talk about identifiable collective interests. In a community of this size, there may well be more disagreement about what those interests are. But one can say that each of us has a right to live in a safe and secure environment, and one can use the phrase 'national security' as a shorthand for the protection of this right of all those living in a particular country. Whilst we may disagree about precisely how this right should best be protected, and how it should be weighed against other rights that people

---

[2] For more detailed discussion of freedom of speech, see Chapter 16 below.

have, there is a reasonable consensus that this phrase represents a proper collective interest, that is, a set of individual rights, which deserves some protection.

But this collective interest has to justify itself in the face of any other individual right it wishes to overrule. The very need for this justification reminds us that we should not ignore the interests of people whose rights conflict with a course of action, even though we may think that this course of action is in the best interests of the whole community. An interference with rights *always* needs to be justified. Indeed, some basic rights may be such a fundamental expression of the basic dignity and autonomy of any person that there is no permissible justification for interfering with them – such as freedom from torture or freedom from slavery. In other cases, some interference may be permissible if it is justified. To use the earlier example, the factory builder's right to work to support himself by starting a business may not, in the end, justify building a factory, but his right still deserves some respect. That is why he is allowed to apply to build a factory and have an opportunity to make a case for being allowed to do so, which must be rejected for good reasons, and not just on a whim.

So one of the benefits of having a law like the Human Rights Act is that it plants a clear marker for the attention of those making or applying laws as to which basic rights they will always have to justify interfering with, even when they are acting in the common interest in doing so. A law of this sort helps to ensure that debate on particular issues, which involve possible infringements or limitations of rights, is properly focused, and does not *ignore* individual rights just because they conflict with a collective interest. In particular, we have a political system which does not provide much opportunity for individuals to have a say in the process of making political decisions at a national level – this is inevitable in any country of any size. It is in the nature of political decisions that they are likely to benefit one part of the community more than another. This may be generally beneficial – for example, taxing those who can afford it so that the state can support the poor or sick. What the Act means, however, is that such policies cannot be given such pre-eminence that no consideration is given to those who are being affected by them: there is a counterbalance to consideration of collective interests. Human rights are not unlimited; but enforceable human rights limit the scope of permissible interference with the basic requirements of a meaningful human existence.

STRIKING A BALANCE

Thus resolving questions about rights involves a **balancing** act – in most difficult situations where we are considering the exercise of rights we will have to consider not just the rights of *one* person, but how to resolve the issue where the rights of two or more persons come into conflict. We may have to consider which of these rights takes priority over the other and which interference we should allow: there are very few rights which can *never* justifiably be interfered with. In fact, the reason that the situation is a difficult one may well be *because* of this conflict and the consequent need to **balance** the different rights under consideration. This difficulty is there because it can be a hard decision as to how a particular right should be exercised or protected, and how that will affect other people and *their* rights. We have to decide which, or whose, rights are more important, and what weight we give to the different rights involved. There are some rights which we can rarely justify infringing – the right to life, for example – and some which more commonly come into conflict with other rights – for example, freedom of speech. Determining what should be done where different rights come into conflict involves considering the different rights which could apply to the situation, looking at the importance of the interests protected by the different rights and then judging which right has most weight.

This idea of balancing rights is so important to the analysis of rights we will be undertaking in this book that it is worth considering a particularly difficult case where rights came into conflict: the case of the conjoined (Siamese) twins, Jodie and Mary.

In this case, there were Siamese twins, Jodie and Mary, who shared one heart. If left joined, they were both going to die. Their parents had firm religious convictions that nature should be allowed to take its course. The doctors treating the twins wanted to separate them, because they hoped that this would allow the stronger twin, Jodie, to survive, even though it would mean the death of the weaker twin, Mary.

The case came before the Court of Appeal, who had to decide what the doctors should do, to protect the doctors from any complaint afterwards. The Court decided that the twins should be separated: Mary was going to die in any event and was incapable of independent existence, but the separation was without significant risk for Jodie who should survive the operation. The Court took into account the parents' sincere religious belief that it was God's will that the twins be born as they were and that they should be left to live their lives joined together for as long as that might be. But the Court also took into account the rights of the two twins and the views of the hospital that where one life could be saved it should be. The Court had to **balance** the welfare of each child against the other and decided that Mary could have no independent existence but Jodie could. Since Mary was only alive because she was relying on the use of Jodie's organs, removing Mary would effectively be acting in Jodie's defence, to remove a threat of fatal harm. The Court also referred to the right of each of the twins to bodily integrity and human dignity which neither of them could enjoy as they were.[3]

Examples such as this, and such as the freedom of speech example considered earlier, should make clear that questions of balancing rights can be very difficult – sometimes a matter of life and death – which is what makes it so important to realise that this is the exercise that is being undertaken. Balancing one person's right to life and another's right to a family is not balancing like with like, so there is no easy answer. But a proper decision can only be reached when it is based on a clear understanding of what is at stake – whose rights are under consideration and what weight those rights should be assigned, so that it can be determined with clarity which is more important.

THE INDIVIDUAL AND THE STATE

We have talked about human rights being founded in equality, but the discussion of limiting rights in collective interests also points to another of the key features of human rights: the content of human rights is focused on the relationship between the **individual** and society, or more precisely the **state**. A state is the highest level of organisation in a society

---

[3] [2001] 2 WLR 480; we will consider this case further on p. 141.

with the ability to control the lives of the members of that society. For present purposes, the state can also be used as a shorthand for the social order and government of a society. So, the United Kingdom is a state and our laws have the ultimate say as to what we are or are not allowed to do. The constitution of a state is that area of its law which defines how the state is structured and how the organs of the state – Parliament, government departments, the police, etc. – relate to individual citizens. Any list of basic rights will therefore have *constitutional* significance since it sets out a definitive list of rights with which the *state* is either not allowed to interfere at all, or the basis and extent to which interference with such rights is permissible.

Of course, the very existence of an organised society is itself a benefit to the individuals living within that society. There is a need for individuals living in a community of any size – even a modern city, let alone a country – to have some form of government. Individuals are entitled to what we might call moral **autonomy**, that is, their own space in which to pursue their life goals, raise a family, pursue education, a career, the enjoyment of interests, sports, hobbies, pastimes, and so on. But individuals can rarely achieve such goals by themselves. The need to have some form of government arises because cooperation between individuals is often required.

One could divide the main functions which government should perform into three broad categories. The first is to organise cooperation between individuals for their common protection and defence; this may be from each other, from other countries and from natural threats such as floods. The second is to resolve questions about how to allocate limited resources, and that includes deciding or prioritising the use of limited natural resources, such as land or water. A decision may need to be taken where these are required for different and conflicting purposes. The question of the use of resources also includes questions about if and how taxation should be used to redistribute resources. The third is to resolve disputes between individuals to prevent them resorting to force, including dealing with situations where individuals have been wronged, or where their interests or activities have come into conflict.

One of the ways in which states typically perform these functions is by having the power to use force, or other forms of coercion, to enforce resolutions to problems. Usually a state will prevent the use of force by all other persons except those authorised by the state and limit the use of force by those authorised to very specific situations. So, it is a crime to hit someone else, unless, for example, you are defending yourself against greater force, or you are a police officer who is allowed to restrain someone who is committing a crime. This use of force by states does mean, however, that it is important to define clearly the situations in which the state may use its power and resources, including coercion or force, against its citizens, to ensure that such use of force is limited to that which is strictly necessary in the circumstances. Thus a consideration of the law of human rights will be a discussion of the relationship between the individual and the state, as well as the rights of individuals against each other.

These powers which a state has for the common good – using that term broadly – for defence, allocation of resources and resolution of disputes are also open to abuse. These powers are morally justified, which is to say a morally good thing, because they are to be used for the common welfare. Once these powers are directed, to a greater or lesser extent, in favour of one group and/or against the interests of another for arbitrary, irrational or immoral reasons – for example, because one group is a different colour or sex – the use of such a power is no longer morally justified and the citizens against whom the power of the state is then applied may require the protection of the law. Thus, being ruled within the law is important because it ensures that society is not governed by the whim of those in power; and the recognition of human rights is important because it limits the ability of those in power to infringe certain basic freedoms. The consequence of both of these is that there should be a law above those in power or authority which guarantees certain basic rights and freedoms to individuals, allowing them a degree of moral autonomy.

This is made explicit in a piece of legislation such as the Human Rights Act. The Act protects basic human interests. But rights, such as the right to life or freedom from torture, slavery or arbitrary detention, also impose limits on the coercion or force which the state is allowed to use in performing all its functions. Rights such as rights to marry, to have a private and home life and to own property set limits to the state's power to reallocate resources. The right to a fair trial sets out the entitlement to have disputes properly resolved. Having a fairly run state also requires that the state allows all persons at least some participation in government, through democratic government of some sort, which implies the right to vote; and by being allowed to express their views (peacefully) on the way the state is being run, which implies freedom of belief, expression and assembly.

Of course, we might expect that in a modern, democratic society there would be no need for such protection. However, no society is ideal, and one of the key lessons of the history of the twentieth century, especially of the actions of totalitarian states like Nazi Germany or the Communist USSR, is that even states which start off as, or claim to be, democracies may be subverted for repressive or discriminatory purposes. One of the results of such events has been a greater recognition of the need to institutionalise protection of basic liberties, as we shall see when we look at the history of the European Convention itself.[4] Democracy is important to give a state legitimacy, but it is not by any means a sufficient safeguard of the rights of those who are not in the majority. Further, in a democracy, it is accepted that those in authority may not always be correct, and, certainly in this country, the days of deference to a ruling class are long gone. Constitutional limits on their power are required: an independent judiciary is one safeguard; protection of basic rights is another. This is not a new consideration – after all, the Magna Carta, signed by King John in 1215, was expressly aimed at limiting the King's powers. But it has gained momentum from the world events of the last hundred years or so, as well as from other factors, such as the greater availability of information to challenge 'official' versions of events. There has also been the increase in participation in elections and in government – for example, in the UK, full voting rights being extended to women in 1928 – which has tended to reduce the influence of any one class or group in government. In a democracy with no clear ruling group, those in government are likely one day to be no longer in government and therefore they also have an interest in preserving the rights they have as citizens against the state.

■ THE RULE OF LAW

We have touched on the principle that society should be governed by law and not by arbitrary action. This expresses the important constitutional doctrine known as the **rule of law** and it is worth exploring further. One aspect of this is that the government (and any sovereign) are subject to the same law as everybody else. This is a further consequence of

---

[4] Chapter 3 below.

the principle of equality, that the law should treat its subjects equally. The law should also treat its subjects with respect: so the rule of law requires that the law should be capable of being known, understood and obeyed by its subjects, and should be applied clearly, publicly and consistently by impartial courts. This ensures that the state allows its citizens their basic moral autonomy: the ability to plan their lives in a way which will be permitted by the state, and to know, in the case of any activity which they are planning, whether it is lawful or not.

The ideas contained in the principle of the rule of law are therefore very important; and they are a manifestation of the same ideas which lead us to consider human rights to be important. It could be said that the principle of the rule of law expresses from the point of view of the *institution* of law ideas which could equally well be expressed as individual rights. So, one could say that individuals have the right to be treated equally, to be made subject only to laws that they can know about and which are capable of being obeyed, and so on. It should therefore come as no surprise that these are ideas which will crop up in discussions of several of the Convention rights, in particular the rights under Article 5 to non-arbitrary detention, Article 6 to a fair trial, and under Article 7 to freedom from retrospective legislation. Article 7 in particular is an embodiment of an important idea which stems directly from the rule of law: that people should not be punished for something which they did which was legal when they did it. This is an aspect of being able to obey laws: you cannot obey a law which makes illegal something which you have already done. Article 7 also includes the important ideas of certainty and clarity in the law, which, as we shall see, are applied throughout the Convention rights.

On the other hand, the principle of equality before the law also contains duties. So, for example, there is the principle that 'ignorance of the law is no excuse' – what is meant by this is, in general terms, that illegal or wrongful conduct is not excused just because the actor did not know that what he or she was doing was wrong. This is an expression of equality because it makes the equal assumption that all citizens know what the law is, and an expression of fairness because all citizens should be able to rely on the law for protection. To that extent, the rule of law also imposes (or at least assumes) the duty on the part of citizens to follow the law if they can, as well as imposing duties on those who administer or uphold the law to do so fairly, publicly, consistently, and so on.

The rule of law may be contrasted with legal systems or states or governments which allow arbitrary exercises of power, based on whim or caprice, or power being exercised in private or on the basis of laws which cannot be known or followed. In that sense, the adherence by the state to the doctrine of the rule of law is a morally good thing, because it enforces and encourages respect for its subjects. But the rule of law does not guarantee that the law itself will be just or right; it does not guarantee more substantive rights such as the right to life or freedom of speech. Nonetheless, the rule of law is an important principle, since it embodies some of the key entitlements which a code of human rights should protect, and provides the framework for the protection of the others. The existence of the rule of law as a constitutional principle has now been given statutory recognition in section 1 of the Constitutional Reform Act 2005, although the section says nothing about its content: it simply confirms that the changes made by that Act do not adversely effect the existing constitutional principle of the rule of law.[5] But that Act goes on to make clear that the prime meaning of this is that the government is subject to the law, and that the judiciary

---

[5] The reforms made by this Act are discussed further, below, p. 43.

should be independent of the government.[6] Thus, the rule of law now has clear support in our constitutional legislation – which is as it should be.

 IMPLEMENTING RIGHTS

Thus we hope that this discussion has helped you to appreciate what we mean when we talk about rights. As you read on, and as we consider both the way in which the rights set out in the European Convention are implemented into our law, by the Act, and the individual Convention rights themselves, it is worth drawing on this framework to consider questions such as the following:

- When we talk about a particular right, what sort of a right is it – is it a particular claim or freedom, or is it a bundle of particular rights?

- What is the root of the right in question? Is it properly a *human* right – is it important, universal, and rooted in equality, dignity, autonomy or other basic interests?

- What is the scope of that right – when does it come up against other people's rights?

- What factors should be considered when balancing this right against others? How important is the particular right compared to others; how important is the interest it protects?

- What factors might justify interfering with the right, and, when looking at particular cases, has the balance been struck the right way?

- Does this balance also properly consider the position of the individual as against the state? Does it provide sufficient protection for the individual? Does it consider carefully the common interest?

- Does the way the right has been implemented properly apply the rule of law – is the law in question clear, comprehensible, and capable of being followed? If there is an interference with the right, is that clear, comprehensible and capable of being followed?

We will go on to consider the detail of the Act and the Convention in the next few chapters. We start, in the next chapter, with a discussion of the history of human rights in our law by way of background – when did people first start talking in terms of human rights, when did our law first protect these basic rights, how did the Convention come into being and become part of our law.

QUESTIONS

1   What rights do you think are human rights? Why? What values do they protect that you consider to be fundamental? (You might like to consider the rights set out in the European Convention in Appendix 2, and the Universal Declaration of Human Rights in Appendix 4, but you might have ideas of your own as well.)

2   Do you consider that animals have rights? Why/why not? If yes, are their rights the same as those of human beings?

---

[6] Section 3: the independence of the judiciary in our constitution is discussed below p. 18.

Magna Carta, as reissued in 1225 under the seal of Henry III: one of the first English legal statements of a series of rights.

3 The history of human rights and the Convention

We hold these truths to be self-evident, that all men are created equal, that they are endowed by their Creator with certain unalienable rights, that among these are life, liberty and the pursuit of happiness. (American Declaration of Independence, 4 July 1776)

Any law which violates the inalienable rights of man is essentially unjust and tyrannical; it is not a law at all. (Maximilien Robespierre, *Declaration of the Rights of Man*, 1789)

Prior to the Human Rights Act 1998, British law had, over the centuries, no single document which contained a comprehensive statement of individual, fundamental rights. Indeed the phrase 'human rights' was only coined in the eighteenth century: it was first used in English by the radical writer Tom Paine in 1791 in his book *The Rights of Man*, in part in translating the revolutionary French National Assembly's *Declaration of the Rights of Man*. The idea which it embodied, that each person is born with 'natural rights', was one that had only developed in those express terms in the previous century or so.

But there have still been some fundamental legal statements which have confirmed or granted individual rights. The earliest, and one of the most significant, was Magna Carta (which means 'the Great Charter'), first issued in 1215 by King John, which contains a number of important rights. Indeed, Chapter 29 of Magna Carta is still in force and states that there should be no punishment without a lawful judgment or by the law of the land, which is what we would today call a declaration of the rule of law. Likewise it states that the King will 'sell to no man [. . . and will] not deny or defer to any man either justice or right', which is a guarantee of a fair and prompt judicial process.

It is important to bear in mind that the intention behind Magna Carta was not to make a grand statement about the equality of individuals in society. On the contrary, it was meant to protect the interests of the barons who had revolted against King John and forced him to grant the Charter, and only incidentally benefited everyone else. Nonetheless, the theme of Magna Carta is that of limiting the power of the King, which is an important statement of the idea behind the rule of law, that is, that there should be government according to the law and not according to the arbitrary wishes of the ruler.

By the end of the thirteenth century, Magna Carta was recognised as an important statement of such limitations on royal power and was reissued by Henry III and Edward I to confirm its provisions. Much of Magna Carta is not relevant today because it remains rooted in the legal system of the thirteenth century. However, its general significance was not lost to later political debate, based as it is on the principle of government according to law, as opposed to unfettered royal power. It gained importance again in the early seventeenth century, when the high-handed exercise of royal power by Charles I ultimately led to the English Civil War (1642–49). The relevance of Magna Carta was brought to the fore by Chief Justice Coke, who used it as part of the political justification for the courts to try to confine royal powers.

This principle of limiting arbitrary rule also lay behind the Bill of Rights of 1688, the constitutional settlement which resulted in the modern constitutional monarchy. This governed the relationship between Parliament and the Crown, confirming the privileges of Parliament on the accession of William III and Mary after the overthrow of James II (the 'Glorious Revolution'). This guarantees such rights as free elections and the immunity of what is said in debates or proceedings in Parliament from being impeached or questioned in any court outside Parliament; it prohibits taxation without the authority of Parliament; and it removed the power which had been claimed by some previous monarchs to suspend or dispense the application of statutes. Again, therefore, there are important aspects of the Bill of Rights which support the rights of the individual, as well as rights which are still considered a basic part of having a free, democratic Parliament.

It was at this time that the idea was propounded that all people possess certain basic rights, especially by John Locke. Locke was a prominent thinker among the supporters of William III. Locke's key contribution to the theory of rights was the idea that people have a particular right to that property which is the product of their labour. This later became a crucial idea in the American Revolution, because it has the corollary that government should not be able to remove property, by way of taxes, without some form of consent on the part of those being governed – or in the phrase which the Americans settlers took to heart, 'no taxation without representation'.

There were also by this stage in English law a number of important and well-established legal protections for what we would today think of as fundamental liberties. One important example is the remedy provided by the writ of *habeas corpus*, which allows an aggrieved party to ask a court to review the reason for an imprisonment, providing some protection against arbitrary detention by ensuring some judicial supervision. This again was a remedy which was developed significantly by Chief Justice Coke and others against the exercise of arbitrary power by Charles I. The scope of *habeas corpus* has expanded further since then and it remains part of our law's protection against arbitrary or unlawful detention.[1]

Even as the idea of basic rights developed among philosophers in the seventeenth and eighteenth centuries, there was no great demand for a statement of all basic rights to be included in English law. This was in a large part because of the view of the leading English legal theorists of the day that the English common law did protect the rights of its citizens without the need for such a statement. The state of English law was defended by, in particular, William Blackstone, in his summary of English law, *Commentaries on the Laws of England* (1765–69). Blackstone considered that the law as it was did protect the rights of the citizens, especially from arbitrary government, and that all the rights which needed to be set out in a grand statement were contained within Magna Carta and the Bill of Rights, together with the Petition of Right of 1628 and Act of Settlement 1701 which further specified the limits of constitutional monarchy.

Not everyone agreed with this. We have already referred to Tom Paine, who set out views, radical by the standard of the day, as to the basic rights all men enjoy. Mary Wollstonecraft pointed out that women also enjoy these rights in her pioneering *Vindication of the Rights*

---

[1] Discussed below in the context of Article 5, p. 196.

of Woman in 1792. In places where many of those governed did not consider that their rights were being properly protected, this led to influential statements of basic rights. The most notable example was the *American Declaration of Independence* of 1776, composed primarily by Thomas Jefferson. Individual liberty was a key idea in the Declaration of Independence, as can be seen from its opening words, quoted at the start of this chapter. This was an important goal of the American War of Independence of 1775–83: the American colonists considered that they were fighting against a despotic government which did not respect their rights. The ideas embodied in the Declaration, and then in the Bill of Rights which the United States of America adopted in 1789, were founded on the ideas of individual rights and liberties talked about by Locke and Blackstone and the importance of limitations on arbitrary government, in the tradition of Magna Carta.

France likewise, following the 1789 revolution, adopted *The Declaration of the Rights of Man*. This influenced the French Civil Code, which was later propagated throughout various European countries by Napoleon. However, the declaration of such rights did not guarantee that they were respected: the revolutionary leader Robespierre presided over the Reign of Terror which followed the French Revolution, one of history's more tyrannical and bloody regimes.

In the United States of America, their Bill of Rights was given great weight, in particular after the United States Supreme Court made the landmark decision that it was empowered to declare legislation invalid if it infringed provisions of the Constitution, including the Bill of Rights – the first time basic rights could be used to defeat legislation.[2] However, important as it was, this Bill of Rights only protected a contemporary understanding of rights, and by today's standards there were some clear omissions in the law it created. So, for example, women did not in fact enjoy equal rights to men for well over a century after the Bill of Rights was adopted; and slavery was still permitted in many states, which we would now consider a fundamental infringement of basic rights, especially taken with the appalling treatment many slaves endured. It was almost one hundred years after the Declaration of Independence before the United States abolished slavery,[3] and nearly two hundred years before the Constitution was used by the American Supreme Court to strike down racist laws in individual states.[4]

In Britain, though, the ideas of those such as Blackstone remained influential – the view that there was no need for any further statutory declaration of rights, since the English common law guaranteed the rights of the individual. Additionally, any form of declaration of rights or code of law smacked of revolution and was associated with the continental systems, especially those influenced or imposed by Napoleon, and so was unpopular for that very reason. Thus in A.V. Dicey's influential *Introduction to the Study of the Law of the Constitution* of 1885, the British constitution was defended as being opposed to the arbitrary exercises of power which Dicey considered took place in continental Europe.

Even in 1950, when the European Convention on Human Rights was signed, there was no political pressure in Britain for some form of statement of basic rights to be enacted. However, as we shall discuss below, there was pressure for such a document in mainland Europe, especially because of the experience, not shared by the British,[5] of Nazi rule

---

[2] *Marbury* v *Madison* 5 US 137 (1803).
[3] 13th Amendment to the US Constitution, 1865, which followed the American Civil War.
[4] The leading case was *Brown* v *Board of Education of Topeka* [1954] 347 US 483.
[5] Only the Channel Islands, which are not constitutionally part of the United Kingdom, were occupied.

or occupation, and its abuses of governmental power and repression of the liberty of individual citizens. This was why it was not those responsible for British domestic law who were involved in the European Convention, but the Foreign Office. The reason why Britain took a leading role in the formation of the European Convention was because of the perceived importance for our relations with other countries, especially in Europe, of helping to put such an instrument into place. It is relevant therefore to consider the background to this, which is the history, such as it is, of the international protection of human rights.

INTERNATIONAL PROTECTION OF HUMAN RIGHTS

Before the Second World War there had been very little in the way of international protection of human rights. This lack of protection arose out of the nature of international law, the rules which govern relations between states. International law was traditionally considered to be law which governed only the relations between states and not individuals, and therefore as having no role in the protection of individual rights. It is based largely on treaties – agreements between states – traditionally dealing with such matters as settling disputes over borders or territories and ending wars.

However, from the mid-nineteenth century, there had been some interest in having international law make provision for humanitarian matters – that is, a basic level of protection from ill-treatment. The movement for there to be international humanitarian provisions started in the 1860s and produced the founding of the International Committee of the Red Cross in 1863[6] and the Geneva Convention of 1864.[7] This also led to the Hague Conventions on the treatment of prisoners of war,[8] which set out 'rules of war' under which states agreed that they would not permit certain conduct even in wartime. These were still viewed as matters between states, and not matters for complaint by individuals, although the benefit was not to the state itself but to its citizens. Likewise, although there was a movement against slavery during the nineteenth century, this was primarily due to the actions of individual states, in particular the Royal Navy, which played a part in confiscating slave ships.[9] The increasing recognition of the immorality of slavery did, however, lead to the Slavery Convention of 1926.

There was also a tradition of treaties settling territorial disputes or wars including guarantees of minority rights. This might include one or more states taking a role as protectors of minorities – for example, a Catholic state, such as the Austrian Empire or France, acting as notional protector for communities of Christians living in the Ottoman Turkish Empire in treaties of the seventeenth and eighteenth centuries, or in the nineteenth-century treaties which saw the creation or re-emergence of a number of European states, such as Bulgaria, Romania or Greece. However, this protection was always somewhat theoretical and rarely

---

[6] Originally the International Committee for Aid to Wounded Soldiers; one of the key figures in its founding was Henry Dunant, who was influenced by witnessing the particularly brutal consequences of the Battle of Solferino in 1859.

[7] Geneva Convention for the Amelioration of the Condition of the Wounded in Armies in the Field, 22 August 1864, signed by 12 states; now see the 1949 Geneva Conventions.

[8] Hague Conventions of 1899 and 1907.

[9] The Royal Navy was supported by the approach of the English courts since the eighteenth century and by the formal abolition of slavery in British colonies in 1838.

involved practical action, since there were no institutions to monitor compliance; nor did individuals have any rights to complain.[10]

In the same tradition, the treaties which followed the First World War (1914–18) contained provisions for the protection of minorities, with reference to some individual rights, typically to rights to life, liberty, equality before the law and non-discrimination. These were secured, in theory, by the new League of Nations and International Court of Justice, founded after the First World War to try to improve international relations. Again, although a system was devised for bringing complaints informally before the League of Nations, these provisions had very little practical effect. Only the system set up by the 1921 treaty relating to Upper Silesia, partitioned between Poland and Germany, had some effect, because it included bodies to deal with individual complaints, although without any power to enforce either decisions or negotiated compromises. There was one successful use of the treaty in 1933 to provide some (temporary) protection for the Jews of Upper Silesia from the discriminatory laws of Nazi Germany; but the treaty lapsed in 1937. Likewise the provisions under which some territories were governed after 1918 under League of Nations Mandates often had some right of individual or group petition, but not much use was made of these, although there were some investigations, which were conducted by commissioners of the League of Nations.

One final strand which involved individuals was the idea of international crimes. The first crime to be recognised as one where there was universal jurisdiction – which means that any state can prosecute any person for such a crime – was piracy, because of the international importance of unimpeded shipping. There were some attempts to extend the idea of individual international criminal responsibility in the First World War peace treaties, specifically in the Treaty of Versailles for the trial of German war criminals, but this did not have much real effect. The first real application of this concept in an international tribunal was after the Second World War with the International Military Tribunal at Nuremberg, which involved prosecutions for war crimes and crimes against humanity.

THE BACKGROUND TO THE CONVENTION: THE SECOND WORLD WAR AND THE UNITED NATIONS

The European Convention has to be set principally in the historical context of the aftermath of the Second World War (1939–45) and the atrocities committed by, in particular, Nazi Germany, which brutally tortured and murdered millions of people, including several million of its own citizens, such as Jews, Gypsies, blacks, homosexuals, the disabled and political dissidents. There was widespread shock, when the full scale of the Nazi genocide machine became known, that such a course of action could have been implemented in a supposedly civilised society. It was also clear that the traditional approach of international law, that how a state treated its own citizens was a domestic matter and not one in which other states should interfere, could no longer remain unchallenged, since this approach would not allow other states to prevent a repetition of such events.

---

[10] The first treaty which allowed for individual complaint was the Convention for the Establishment of a Central American Court of Justice which was set up in 1907 and lapsed in 1918; none of the 10 individual petitions brought were declared admissible.

It was for these reasons that protection of human rights became part of the Allied Powers' war aims in the Second World War. The first key mention of this idea was the reference by American President Franklin Roosevelt in his State of the Union address to Congress on 6 January 1941 to four freedoms – freedom of speech and expression, freedom of religion, freedom from want, and freedom from fear by reduction of armaments. He also referred to human rights, which helped to popularise the phrase. This was still, however, a general idea, and not a call for any form of specific scheme to protect human rights. As a general aim of the Allies, it was supported by the British government, and mentioned in the statement of war aims contained in the Atlantic Charter of 12 August 1941, although there the main focus was on freedom from want through a better economic system. So too in the United Nations Declaration of 1 January 1942 there is a mention of human rights in the preamble, but this was incidental to the main purpose of the declaration which was about the military alliance against Germany and Japan.

However, on the basis of these statements, as the war progressed, interest grew in having protection of human rights as a specific war aim, and various documents on the subject were issued by governments and individuals in America, Britain and Europe. For those writing in occupied Europe, the protection of human rights was part of the movement for European integration, and both human rights protection and European integration were seen as part of the protection which should be put in place for European citizens against their own governments. By 1944 there was therefore widespread interest that protection of human rights against government misconduct should be part of the new world order, especially once the full scale of atrocities perpetrated by Nazi Germany became apparent. This fed into the plans being discussed for a new international organisation to replace the League of Nations, now discredited because of its failure to prevent the Second World War, and to provide greater international security once the war was over. However, in discussions on the shape of a permanent United Nations, there was still widespread concern that such an organisation should not be able to interfere in domestic disputes between a citizen and their own government.

The United Nations Conference on International Organisation was held in June 1945 in San Francisco. At the conclusion of this conference, on 26 June 1945, the Charter of the United Nations was signed by 50 nations. The Charter and the International Court of Justice replaced the old League of Nations machinery entirely. The Charter set up the institutions of the United Nations Organisation, in particular the General Assembly and the Security Council, which has 15 members, with the United States, the United Kingdom, Russia, France and China as permanent members; and also the statute constituting the International Court of Justice, which has jurisdiction to decide any dispute between countries which those countries agree to refer to it.

The United Nations Charter includes some prominent references to human rights, as can be seen in the following extract from the preamble to the Charter:

> We the Peoples of the United Nations determined to save succeeding generations from the scourge of war, which twice in our lifetime has brought untold sorrow to mankind, and to reaffirm faith in fundamental human rights, in the dignity and worth of the human person, in the equal rights of men and women and of nations large and small, and to establish conditions under which justice and respect for the obligations arising from treaties and other sources of international law can be maintained, and to promote social progress and better standards of life in larger freedom [. . .] have resolved to combine our efforts to accomplish these aims.

The United Nations Charter then sets out its main aims in Article 1:

The Purposes of the United Nations are:

1. To maintain international peace and security, and to that end: to take effective collective measures for the prevention and removal of threats to the peace, and for the suppression of acts of aggression or other breaches of the peace, and to bring about by peaceful means, and in conformity with the principles of justice and international law, adjustment or settlement of international disputes or situations which might lead to a breach of the peace;

2. To develop friendly relations among nations based on respect for the principle of equal rights and self-determination of peoples, and to take other appropriate measures to strengthen universal peace;

3. To achieve international cooperation in solving international problems of an economic, social, cultural, or humanitarian character, and in promoting and encouraging respect for human rights and for fundamental freedoms for all without distinction as to race, sex, language, or religion; and

4. To be a center for harmonizing the actions of nations in the attainment of these common ends.

The United Nations Economic and Social Council (ECOSOC) established a Human Rights Commission in early 1946, which was under the chairmanship of Eleanor Roosevelt, the former American First Lady, until 1951. The full Commission met in 1947, and its main initial activity was to draw up an international Bill of Rights, which eventually became the Universal Declaration of Human Rights. This was the result of much work by the members of the Commission, in particular in compromising between different views about the form which the eventual document should take. The view of the British government was that a more detailed document was appropriate, in accordance with the British legal tradition of precise drafting, and would have meant that the result was a treaty imposing binding obligations. The American view was that something rather more general and declaratory should be adopted. It was in order to resolve this difference of opinion that the more detailed provisions, appropriate for a treaty rather than a declaration, became the International Covenants on Civil and Political Rights and on Economic and Social Rights: this allowed a more general declaration to be agreed sooner rather than later. A draft declaration was produced in May 1948 and was adopted by the General Assembly on 10 December 1948 as the Universal Declaration of Human Rights. The following is an extract from its preamble:

Whereas recognition of the inherent dignity and of the equal and inalienable rights of all members of the human family is the foundation of freedom, justice and peace in the world, Whereas disregard and contempt for human rights have resulted in barbarous acts, which have outraged the conscience of mankind, and the advent of a world in which human beings shall enjoy freedom of speech and belief and freedom from fear and want has been proclaimed as the highest aspiration of the common people, Whereas it is essential, if man is not to be compelled to have recourse, as a last resort, to rebellion against tyranny and oppression, that human rights should be protected by the rule of law . . .[11]

By this time it was clear that there would be difficulties in agreeing meaningful treaties to implement a detailed protection of human rights. There were differences of opinion over such issues as how these covenants should relate to states' colonies; how they would apply

---

[11] The full text of the Universal Declaration of Human Rights can be found in Appendix 4, p. 441.

in federal countries, especially the United States, where there is a constitutional balance between the individual states and the federal government; and there were Soviet objections to a system which promoted the protection of citizens against their own government. The scope for there to be any form of cooperation in the United Nations was also becoming a casualty of the growing antipathy between the Soviet Union and the United States which was developing into the Cold War. For reasons such as these, negotiations over the covenants became bogged down by the end of the 1940s and interest in effective human rights protection for Western Europe had shifted to a more regional approach. In the end the United Nations covenants were not finalised until 1966 and did not come into force until 1976.

 ## THE BACKGROUND TO THE CONVENTION: THE COUNCIL OF EUROPE

By the end of 1945, Eastern Europe had effectively fallen under the control of the Soviet Union. By 1949 it was clear, because of the international situation, that the United Nations was not going to be successful in providing effective human rights protection, or indeed collective security. The new reality of a Europe split between a communist East and a democratic West was recognised most famously by Winston Churchill in a speech given at Fulton, Missouri, on 5 March 1946 when he said 'an iron curtain has descended across the Continent'. This became clear over the next few years, especially with the division of Germany into two halves, the blockade of the West German parts of Berlin in 1948–49 and the setting up of the Berlin Wall. There was therefore a need for Western Europe to provide for its own security outside the United Nations, and this resulted in the North Atlantic Treaty of April 1949, which set up NATO. The economic well-being of Europe was supported by the United States' provision of economic aid, based on the Marshall Plan of 1947, aiming to prevent further communist expansion in Europe, which led to the creation of the Organisation for European Economic Cooperation in 1948.

Politically, there was a movement within Europe in favour of a federal European state, to promote greater peace and security, and prevent a resurgence of a militarily strong Germany. Part of this movement was for the protection of human rights, especially from those with the experience of being oppressed by their own governments. A non-governmental body, the European Federalist Movement, held a Congress in August 1947 where it adopted a proposal for a European Parliamentary Assembly, and for a European Charter of Human Rights.

The British Foreign Office, under Foreign Secretary Ernest Bevin, was a prime mover in the development of regional protection of human rights within Europe, although it was not in favour of a federal Europe. The international protection of human rights was seen as part of foreign policy because it was an important part of the security of Britain and dealings with the United Nations. It was not seen as primarily a domestic issue, since there was a general opinion within the civil service that British law adequately protected human rights. It is worth noting that the whole question of entering a human rights treaty was a matter of some debate within the government. In particular, the British Colonial Office, which at that time administered the various dominions which comprised the British Empire, was opposed to the possibility of international interference in the government of dominions. The Home Office, in charge of prisons and the police, also had concerns about a human rights treaty, when this finally loomed as a realistic prospect, as did the Lord Chancellor, who was responsible for the law courts. The Foreign Office, however, saw British participation in human rights discussions, at the United Nations and in Europe, as essential to promote a stable Europe and the formation of a coherent West European bloc, including limiting the scope for Soviet interference in European affairs.[12]

As a result of international negotiations in late 1948 and 1949, it was decided that a new organisation would be created to foster relations in spheres other than the economic or the military, with a committee of ministers from member governments and a consultative assembly, the latter being a compromise to the demands of the federalist movement. This was what became the Council of Europe, whose Statute was signed on 5 May 1949 in London. The following is an extract which sets out the aims behind the Council of Europe:

Article 1: (a) The aim of the Council of Europe is to achieve a greater unity between its members for the purpose of safeguarding and realising the ideals and principles which are their common heritage and facilitating their economic and social progress.

(b) This aim shall be pursued through the organs of the Council by discussion of questions of common concern and by agreements and common action in economic, social, cultural, scientific, legal and administrative matters and in the maintenance and further realisation of human rights and fundamental freedoms.

(c) Participation in the Council of Europe shall not affect the collaboration of its members in the work of the United Nations and of other international organisations or unions to which they are parties.

(d) Matters relating to national defence do not fall within the scope of the Council of Europe.

[...]

Article 3: Every member of the Council of Europe must accept the principles of the rule of law and of the enjoyment by all persons within its jurisdiction of human rights and fundamental freedoms, and collaborate sincerely and effectively in the realisation of the aim of the Council as specified in [Article] 1.

The treaty which became the European Convention on Human Rights was negotiated between August 1949 and September 1950. Initially the Council of Europe's Committee of Ministers was not particularly enthusiastic about the prospect of a human rights convention, but the Council's Consultative Assembly pressured the ministers into allowing this on to the agenda for the Assembly's session in August 1949. The Assembly adopted a proposal for a treaty supported by a commission and a court in September 1949.

The British government took the view that it should support the negotiations for a convention. It was opposed to the institution of a court in any event, so it was not initially intended that a treaty would lead to an international body judging British domestic law. However, its overriding concern was that there would be great political damage if negotiations for a convention failed, especially as the British government and Foreign Secretary Bevin had been largely responsible for the Council of Europe coming into existence in the

---

[12] For a more detailed discussion of the international and British internal politics surrounding the genesis of the Convention we highly recommend Professor A.W.B. Simpson's *Human Rights and the End of Empire* (Oxford, 2001).

first place: it would be very embarrassing if the Council of Europe's first major undertaking collapsed.

Again there was a difference of approach within the bodies which debated the drafting of a convention, in particular between the precise drafting typical of the English common law tradition and the civil tradition of European states which tended towards more generalised statements of principle. The difficulty was establishing a list of rights which the various countries, with their different traditions, could all sign up to as representing the basic minimum of human rights. There were also issues about the application of a convention to colonial territories.

There was also a difference of views about whether or not there should be a court of human rights. The compromise on the question of a court was that there should be a human rights court but with optional jurisdiction, which is to say that states signing up to the treaty could choose whether or not to submit to the jurisdiction of the court. There would also be a commission to act as a preliminary filter on complaints. Again by way of compromise, it was decided that it would be open to states to choose whether or not to allow individual citizens, as opposed to another state, the right to bring a complaint.

Eventually, on 4 November 1950, the European Convention for the Protection of Human Rights and Fundamental Freedoms was signed in Rome. An issue about whether or not rights relating to property, education and democratic participation should be included was resolved by continuing the negotiations about the inclusion of these rights and putting them in a separate document, the First Protocol, which was eventually signed in Paris on 20 March 1952. The United Kingdom was, however, the first country to ratify the Convention on 8 March 1951. The Convention came into force on 3 September 1953, and the European Court came into being in 1959.

The Convention was an extremely radical innovation. Never before had there been a system of international law which held states accountable to some superior court in respect of its actions against its own citizens: previous international courts and tribunals were constituted solely to settle disputes between states or, in the case of the Nuremberg Tribunal, to try individuals for their own criminal responsibility.

The system set up by the Convention has proven to have a great political attraction, especially for those countries which are keen to prove their democratic credentials. Thus, the Council of Europe has grown gradually to include most European states,[13] and their signing up to the Convention has been treated as a prerequisite of membership of the Council. So, for example, Greece, which left in 1966, rejoined in 1974 when democracy was restored after eight years of dictatorship; Portugal joined in 1976, following the removal of its dictatorship in 1974; Spain joined in 1977, following the death of General Franco in 1975.

However, the most dramatic period of growth has been in the last 20 years or so. After the countries of Eastern Europe rebelled against communist rule in the early 1990s in an extraordinary series of popular revolutions, many of them joined the Convention system within the next few years, particularly because one of the main complaints that the citizens of those countries had against those who governed them was the lack of respect that was paid to their rights. There are now 47 countries that have signed up to the Convention.[14]

---

[13] Currently all European countries except Belarus, which is still an undemocratic one-party state.
[14] See Appendix 3, p. 438, for a full list of signatories.

THE CONVENTION AND THE UNITED KINGDOM

The history of the Convention does not explain why it has only recently been incorporated into United Kingdom law. The significance of this is that under British constitutional law, until a treaty has been incorporated into domestic law by an Act of Parliament, it cannot be relied on directly in national courts by those who claim that it has been infringed by their government.

As we have seen, in 1950 the United Kingdom was opposed to giving the European Court jurisdiction over complaints from British individuals. In addition, it was not thought particularly necessary to increase human rights protection in the United Kingdom, because it was thought at that time that the law of the United Kingdom adequately protected the rights of its citizens. Indeed, the British involvement in the drafting of the Convention supported the government's view that the European Convention itself reflected the standards of protection provided by the tradition of English common law.

Britain was, however, the first country to ratify the Convention, although it did not sign up to the optional provisions, namely, submission to the jurisdiction of the European Court and the right of individual petition, which allowed individuals to complain directly to the Commission or the Court. Britain also extended the effect of the Convention (but not the First Protocol) to most of its colonies on 23 October 1953, although during the following decades before most of the colonies gained their independence a number of derogations[15] were entered in various emergency situations.

Ironically, since it was largely responsible for the Convention coming into existence, Britain was also the subject of the first inter-state case to be brought under the Convention, which was a complaint to the Commission by Greece regarding the situation in Cyprus, brought in May 1956.[16] The complaint related to British actions taken and regulations imposed in response to the actions of the Greek–Cypriot group EOKA. Greece alleged that there had been breaches of a number of articles, especially Article 3 (freedom from torture) in relation to corporal punishment and treatment of detainees and Article 5 (prohibition of arbitrary detention). After a number of hearings and a visit to Cyprus by some of the Commission members in January 1958, the Commission reported in September 1958 into the regulations and systems in place in Cyprus. The report found no human rights infringements by the United Kingdom, but did make some criticisms. Between the making of the complaint and the report being produced, some laws which might have infringed the Convention had also been repealed as a result of political pressure to avoid a finding by the Commission of a breach of human rights.[17] The Commission report was notable for introducing into the Convention jurisprudence the idea of the margin of appreciation, which is the important principle that states have some leeway to deal with, in particular, emergency situations, before they breach the Convention.[18]

---

[15] Derogations are formal statements that a provision of a treaty is to be departed from; they are discussed in more detail below at p. 113.

[16] Application 176/1956.

[17] Greece brought a second application in July 1957, which raised 49 *individual* cases of alleged torture or mistreatment. This application was overtaken by events, because there was a settlement over Cyprus in February 1959 between Greece and Turkey, so none of the complaints proceeded to a hearing by the Commission. For a more recent decision on this situation see: *Greek Cypriot land in N Cyprus* (2004) 39 EHRR 36.

[18] For a more detailed discussion of the margin of appreciation see p. 54.

The Cyprus cases did not encourage the British government to be enthusiastic to sign up to the optional provisions relating to the Court and the right of individual petition. The Colonial Office, which administered the various British territories, had always taken the view that the Convention might cause difficulties if there were too close an examination of the various legal systems in place in some of the colonies. In its view, signing up to a right of individual petition and the jurisdiction of the Court would only encourage complaints by agitators, especially those who wished to encourage the independence of the colony in question. In the early 1960s there were a number of derogations from the Convention in place in respect of various colonies, which is to say formal statements that the Convention was being disapplied in certain instances; this was precisely to cover the various legislative provisions which allowed systems of administration which might not conform to the requirements of the Convention but which were thought necessary to deal with various situations.

However, during the early 1960s, Britain was dismantling its empire in a fairly comprehensive way, and by 1964 most of the larger colonies had been granted independence. There was also some political pressure for signing up to the optional clauses; the issue was raised with the government, in particular by Lord McNair, the first British judge on the European Court, and also the first President of the Court. There was a change of government in 1964 and the new Lord Chancellor, Lord Gardiner, supported signing up to the optional clauses. By late 1965 there were even fewer colonies – the Colonial Office ceased to exist in 1966, replaced by the Commonwealth Office – and in December 1965, the Prime Minister, Harold Wilson, announced that Britain would sign up to the optional clauses, which was done in January 1966.

At this stage there was no political pressure for the Convention to be directly incorporated into United Kingdom law. This was something which developed during the 1980s and 1990s, particularly after there had been a number of findings of infringements by the United Kingdom. These put paid to the view that United Kingdom law provided adequate human rights protection without the need for the Convention. However, the European Convention was not high on the political agenda, and it was only when it was made a matter of policy by the Labour Party, in opposition, in the mid-1990s that it gained any real political relevance. The key event here was the delivery by John Smith QC, then leader of the Labour Party, of a lecture entitled 'A Citizen's Democracy' in March 1993. The Labour Party published a consultation paper in December 1996 and then, after the Labour Party became the government, it published the White Paper 'Rights Brought Home':[19] this was the start of the legislative process which resulted in the Human Rights Act 1998.

The arguments put forward for incorporation, both in the White Paper and by the government in Parliament, were based partly on the practical considerations of the cost and delay involved in taking a case to the European Court at Strasbourg, in the absence of a remedy in the local courts for an infringement of the Convention. But they were also based on the principled reason that it would allow the rights guaranteed by the Convention to more fully enter British law, in so far as they were not already protected. And it showed an acceptance that the argument used in the past, that United Kingdom law did not require the assistance of the Convention to protect people's rights, could no longer be sustained, especially in view of the number of times where the provisions or application of United

---

[19] Cm 3782, October 1997.

Kingdom law had been held by the European Court to involve a breach of the Convention rights.

Incorporating the Convention into our law would also allow our judges to contribute to the jurisprudence of the Convention, since there would now be domestic decisions on the Convention rights which could be cited before the European Court or other courts in Europe which had to consider questions of human rights. Further, it would limit the need for findings that a particular law infringed the Convention to be made by the European Court, since it would impose on our courts the duty to interpret our law in a way which is consistent with the Convention, and allow any laws which do not comply to be amended by Parliament. This should limit the number of cases taken to the European Court, and therefore the number of judgments against the United Kingdom, which would limit the political embarrassment such a judgment can cause.

Thus, after being passed by Parliament, the Human Rights Act received Royal Assent on 9 November 1998 and thereby became part of the law of the United Kingdom, 48 years after the United Kingdom signed up to the Convention. The Act has indeed meant that there has been a reduction in cases going from the UK to the Strasbourg Court, and a reduction in the findings against the UK when they get there. It has also meant, as we shall see throughout this book, that in a whole variety of areas, considerations of human rights have impacted on the rest of the law.

The Act has received institutional support in another way. In 2006, Parliament passed the Equality Act, which combined the existing anti-discrimination commissions[20] into a Commission for Equality and Human Rights. As well as taking action to enforce anti-discrimination legislation, the Commission also exists to encourage compliance with the Act, to campaign, advise and promote good practice on respecting human rights. Further, the debates sparked by the Act have, as we shall see, meant that the political debate on human rights remains topical. It has also been part of a wider review of the nature of our constitution and how it protects basic rights. Precisely how it fits into our constitution is the topic we shall consider in the next chapter.

A CONVENTION CHRONOLOGY

6 January 1941	Four Freedoms speech establishes human rights as a war aim of the Second World War
26 June 1945	United Nations Charter signed in San Francisco
14 August 1945	Second World War ends after use of nuclear weapons on Hiroshima and Nagasaki
5 March 1946	Winston Churchill speaks of an 'iron curtain' descending across Europe
4 March 1947	Britain and France sign Treaty of Dunkirk for mutual defence against Germany
12 March 1947	Truman doctrine pronounced: US economic support for reconstruction in Europe, backed by Marshall Plan in June 1947

[20] The Equal Opportunities Commission, the Commission for Racial Equality, and the Disability Rights Commission.

22 January 1948	British Foreign Secretary Bevin refers to a 'spiritual union' for Europe in the House of Commons
17 March 1948	Brussels Treaty signed between UK, France, Holland, Belgium and Luxembourg aimed at strengthening economic, social and cultural ties and includes a reference to human rights
16 April 1948	Organisation for European Economic Cooperation established
June 1948–May 1949	Berlin Blockade
9 December 1948	Genocide Convention adopted by UN General Assembly
10 December 1948	Universal Declaration of Human Rights adopted by UN General Assembly
5 May 1949	Council of Europe established
25 July 1949	North Atlantic Treaty signed, setting up NATO
4 November 1950	European Convention on Human Rights signed in Rome
8 March 1951	United Kingdom ratifies Convention
18 April 1951	European Coal and Steel Community (ECSC) formed
20 March 1952	First Protocol to Convention signed
3 September 1953	Convention comes into force
23 October 1953	UK extends Convention to 42 British dependencies
18 May 1954	European Commission for Human Rights comes into existence
1 January 1958	European Economic Community (EEC) and European Atomic Energy Community (Euratom) come into operation
18 September 1959	European Court of Human Rights established
16 September 1963	Fourth Protocol to Convention signed
13 January 1966	UK accepts jurisdiction of European court and right of individual petition
16 December 1966	United Nations Covenants signed (International Covenant on Economic, Social and Cultural Rights, entered into force 3 January 1976, and International Covenant on Civil and Political Rights, entered into force 23 March 1976)
1 July 1967	Merger of EEC with ECSC and Euratom
1 January 1973	UK joins EEC
21 February 1975	*Golder* v *UK*:[21] first finding of breach of Convention by UK
28 April 1983	Sixth Protocol to Convention signed
22 November 1984	Seventh Protocol to Convention signed
1 March 1993	John Smith QC delivers lecture 'A Citizen's Democracy'
1 November 1993	European Union replaces EEC when Maastricht Treaty comes into force

---

[21] (1979–80) 1 EHRR 524.

11 May 1994	Eleventh Protocol: reforms Convention machinery and Court (repeals or replaces Protocols which did not contain substantive rights)
24 October 1997	Labour government publishes the White Paper 'Rights Brought Home'; Human Rights Bill introduced into Parliament
1 November 1998	Single permanent European Court of Human Rights comes into being (replaces previous institutions)
9 November 1998	Human Rights Act 1998 passed
2 October 2000	Human Rights Act 1998 comes into force
4 November 2000	Twelfth Protocol opened for signature
3 May 2002	Thirteenth Protocol opened for signature
1 July 2002	International Criminal Court comes into existence (based on 1998 International Criminal Court Treaty)
13 May 2004	Fourteenth Protocol opened for signature (makes procedural amendments, not yet in force)
24 March 2005	Constitutional Reform Act 2005 expresses the rule of law
16 February 2006	Equality Act 2006 creates Commission for Equality and Human Rights
1 October 2007	Commission for Equality and Human Rights begins to operate
18 September 2008	European Court delivered its 10,000th judgment, *Takhayeva* v *Russia*

3

The history of human rights and the Convention

The Palace of Westminster, the home of the Houses of Parliament.

Source: Peter Adams/Digital Vision/Getty Images

4 Constitutional considerations

constitution: The system of fundamental laws and principles that prescribes the nature, functions, and limits of a government or other institution; the document in which this system is recorded. (*Reader's Digest Illustrated Dictionary*)

INTRODUCTION TO THE UNITED KINGDOM LEGAL SYSTEM

In order to fully understand how the Act works, it is necessary to understand the structure of the United Kingdom's constitution and legal system. This is because the Act has **constitutional** significance: it has an effect on the way Parliament passes legislation and on the relationship between the various parts of the government and machinery of the state. This chapter therefore contains an introduction to the key institutions of the state and the relationship between them, primarily for the benefit of those who are unfamiliar with our legal system and constitutional structure. This is because it is important to understand how, if at all, the Act modifies the interaction between different parts of the state machinery, and also how the Act applies to the different parts of the state.

Those who are unfamiliar with the United Kingdom's constitution or with our constitutional law may be surprised that we do not have a *written* constitution. However, we do still have a constitution, as defined in the quote above, a system of laws and principles which sets out the nature, function and limits of the different elements of the state. Our constitution is very well established and, even though it is not contained in any one document which can be described as 'the Constitution', it can be found in the constitutional law contained in a combination of statutes, judicial case law, and custom, especially customs known as constitutional conventions, which are treated as effectively binding customary rules and limitations.

The United Kingdom has a constitutional structure which is conventionally categorised in three parts: **legislative** (Parliament), **executive** (government, civil service and other parts of the administration of the country), and **judicial** (courts).

PARLIAMENT

First, **Parliament**, which is the United Kingdom's **legislature** and creates or changes the law by passing **Acts** of Parliament, also known as statutes. Parliament sits in the Palace of Westminster and is composed of two houses: the House of Commons, which is made up of elected Members of Parliament; and the House of Lords, which is made up of a mixture of appointed peers (known as life peers) and some hereditary peers. Acts of Parliament also have to be given Royal Assent, although in the modern political system, once an Act has been approved by both Houses in accordance with the proper procedure, Royal Assent is something of a formality.

Under British constitutional law, Parliament is superior to other branches of the state; this is the idea known as **Parliamentary sovereignty**. Sovereignty has two sides to it: within the United Kingdom, Parliament is the supreme law-making body, which means that measures passed by it (legislation) take precedence over what is decided by the courts or by the executive; and our Parliament is also not subject to any other national or international body, so in that sense the United Kingdom is a sovereign state.

Another aspect of the traditional theory of Parliamentary sovereignty which is relevant to the Act is the question of whether a future Parliament could repeal the Act. It is often said to be part of Parliament's sovereignty that one Parliament cannot bind its successors, since to do so would be to limit the sovereignty of that later Parliament. It was for this reason that the Act contains no attempt at what is known as entrenchment, that is a procedure to make the Act difficult to repeal, such as the need for a greater than usual majority. It was felt that any sort of entrenchment would not be in keeping with our constitutional tradition.[1] This preserves the constitutional position that Parliament could, in principle, withdraw from the Convention and repeal the Act. It should be said, though, that this would be politically unlikely, since it would amount to Parliament expressing the view that it did not respect human rights. In any event, as we will see, the Act preserves Parliament's sovereignty, so that any law passed by Parliament prevails even if it should infringe the Convention.

THE EXECUTIVE

The highest level of the **executive** branch of the state is the **government**, made up of the leading members of whichever political party has a majority in the House of Commons. The government is led by the Prime Minister, who is the leader of the majority party. The Prime Minister appoints the other Ministers, in particular the senior Ministers, who make up the Cabinet. Each of the senior Ministers is responsible for a department of state, such as the Chancellor of the Exchequer who is in charge of the Treasury, the Foreign Secretary who is in charge of the Ministry of Foreign and Commonwealth Affairs, the Justice Secretary (formerly the Home Secretary) who is in charge of the Ministry of Justice, and so on. Each ministry includes other Members of Parliament, or Members of the House of Lords, who act as junior Ministers or Parliamentary Secretaries. The staff of the ministries are then filled out by civil servants. Each ministry's senior civil servant is its Permanent Secretary; and the most senior civil servant is the Cabinet Secretary.

Therefore, for a political party, the result of winning a general election and being the party with the most Members of Parliament is that that party becomes the government and has the opportunity to organise the running of the country until the next election. By having a majority in the House of Commons, the government is usually also able to pass

---

[1] White Paper Cmd 3782, 'Rights Brought Home'.

whatever legislation it chooses, since the organisation of political parties is designed to ensure that its MPs support the party line in votes. A government with a large majority, such as Tony Blair's Labour government which was voted into office in 1997, need not be concerned by a small number of dissenters on a given issue. A government with a small majority may be severely hampered in progressing legislation; an example was John Major's Conservative government of 1992 to 1997.

The government is then able to determine what political policies will be followed in the running of the country, both through the introduction of legislation into Parliament and in the exercise of the variety of discretionary powers which the various Ministers and their departments have. Such powers are drawn from legislation or sources based on common law, in particular the **royal prerogative**. This is the name for those powers which were recognised in times past by the common law as attaching to the Crown, that is, being exercisable by the ruling monarch. These are now exercised by Ministers of state and include powers such as the capacity to represent the state in foreign affairs or the organisation of national defence.

The executive also includes all those organisations which actually run the machinery of the state: the civil service, local government and government agencies, running institutions as diverse as the health service, the armed forces and emergency services, state schools, social services and social security, the transport infrastructure of roads and airports, and so on. Constitutionally, the executive at this level carries out the wishes of Parliament, as expressed in legislation, as to how the state should be run, and where Parliament leaves a discretion or choice as to how particular matters should be decided or institutions run, this is regulated by the wishes of the government. Some matters are not regulated by Parliament at all, except in a supervisory sense. For example, sending armed forces abroad to act as peacekeepers is a decision of the government which must be politically justified in Parliament but need not be approved by it. Local government is also considered part of the executive: although those running local government are elected, local councils do not actually legislate – they implement Parliament's legislation, or act in accordance with discretion granted by Parliament. The executive also includes agencies which operate in a whole host of areas. One such is the Commission for Equality and Human Rights, created by the Equality Act 2006, which provides governmental support for encouraging respect for human rights throughout the machinery of government.

Because the government is the same as the majority in Parliament, it might be thought that the role of Parliament is limited to passing legislation in accordance with the government's wishes. However, this is not the case. Even leaving aside the occasional situation where legislation is passed against the wishes of the government, or introduced by Members of Parliament who are not part of the government (Private Members' Bills), Parliament also provides scrutiny of proposed legislation and generally of the conduct of the government and the executive. In particular, this is a major function of the House of Lords. It is also done through a series of Parliamentary Committees, which meet regularly to consider different areas of the practical government of the country. One such committee is the Joint Committee on Human Rights, which considers matters relating to human rights and matters relating to the Human Rights Act.

It is because of this supervisory role performed by Parliament that, when one is trying to understand a statute that is not entirely clear, it is sometimes relevant to consider what was said in Parliament when the wording of the statute was debated. This may help to clarify the intention behind the wording used. Statements made in Parliament can be referred to in court, if they assist in the interpretation of the statute.[2] This will only be the case if the statute is ambiguous, since the starting point for the interpretation of all statutes is the ordinary meaning of the words used, allowing for any definitions provided for by the statute being considered, or the definitions of any words with technical meanings.

THE COURTS

The third branch of the state machinery is the **judiciary**, the judges, courts and court services, which administer justice on behalf of the state for the resolution of disputes (civil law) and accusations of criminal conduct (criminal law). In England and Wales (see Figure 4.1) there are criminal courts, Crown Courts and Magistrates' Courts, which deal with the trials of those accused of criminal offences, on the basis of prosecutions brought primarily by the Crown Prosecution Service, and which impose punishments on those found guilty. Then there are civil courts, the High Court and County Courts, which deal

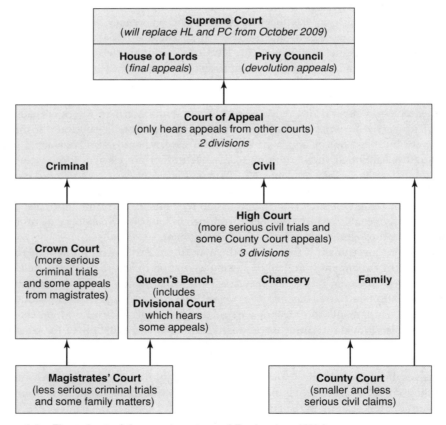

Figure 4.1 Flow chart of the court system of England and Wales

[2] *Pepper v Hart* [1993] AC 593.

mainly with actions to resolve disputes between individuals, companies or other bodies and award appropriate remedies for debts due and wrongs done, predominantly monetary compensation.

If a party considers that a court has decided a matter incorrectly, there is some scope for appealing the decision, especially on the ground that the law has been wrongly applied. This is done by bringing an appeal to the Court of Appeal, which sits primarily at the Royal Courts of Justice at the Strand in London; the Divisional Court is an equivalent court for certain sorts of appeal. The final level of appeal is to the Judicial Committee of the House of Lords. These are members of the House of Lords who are specifically appointed for that purpose, known as the Lords of Appeal in Ordinary, informally known as the Law Lords, and are generally appointed from among the appeal judges from the courts of England and Wales, Scotland and Northern Ireland, and other senior judges who hold a peerage. The Law Lords also sit as the Judicial Committee of the Privy Council, which is a body that hears appeals from jurisdictions other than the courts of England and Wales, including some appeals from Scotland and Northern Ireland. The Privy Council also remains the final court of appeal for some former colonial countries, for example a number of Caribbean countries such as Jamaica and Barbados. This appeal structure has been recently altered by the Constitutional Reform Act 2005 (CRA 2005), in order to more clearly separate the judiciary and the legislature. When the CRA 2005 comes fully into effect, both the Judicial Committee of the House of Lords and the devolution appeals jurisdiction of the Privy Council will be replaced by the new Supreme Court,[3] a body which will become wholly independent of the legislature (at the time of writing, this is expected to start operating in late 2009). Initially, the new Justices of the Supreme Court will be the previous Law Lords, so to that extent the change is one of form, not of the judges who will be deciding these appeals. There will then be a new mechanism for appointing Supreme Court Justices which will be wholly independent of the House of Lords, which will become a purely legislative body for the first time in its history.

This system of courts also sets the rules, known as the doctrine of precedent, which tells you which courts are bound by the decisions of which other courts. This operates in the same hierarchy as appeals: the House of Lords (Supreme Court) binds, but is not bound by, all other courts; the Court of Appeal is bound by the House of Lords and its own decisions but not by decisions of lower courts; the High Court is bound by both the Court of Appeal and House of Lords, but binds lower courts; below that, courts are typically bound by higher courts and not by lower courts or decisions of courts at the same level.

It is an important constitutional principle that the judiciary is independent of the government. This is grounded in considerations of legality and the rule of law, that the law is administered by people who are impartial and who are independent of those who made the law.[4] Some countries have a strict separation between the various branches of the state, known as the separation of powers. The United Kingdom had until recently some overlaps between the different sections of the state, in particular that the senior judges, who were members of the House of Lords, were able to sit in the House of Lords in its legislative capacity, and the most senior judge was the Lord Chancellor, who is also a member of the Cabinet, and therefore a political appointment. However, this has now also been changed by the CRA 2005, as part of its role to increase and formalise the separation between the judiciary,

[3] The Privy Council will remain responsible for appeals relating to its other jurisdictions.
[4] Discussed above, p. 18.

Constitutional considerations

the legislature and the executive. The present Lord Chancellor has ceased to have any judicial function[5] and his role is now combined with being the Secretary of State for Justice, so wholly a political and not judicial role; the senior judge is now the Lord Chief Justice; and the new Justices of the Supreme Court will no longer sit in the House of Lords while they are serving as Judges. Thus there is a more formal separation of powers than previously.

Even prior to the CRA 2005, the independence of the judiciary was nonetheless strictly protected, notwithstanding the partial overlap between judiciary, legislature and executive: for example, the long-standing provision that judges can only be removed from office if they commit some impropriety (such as being convicted of a crime) or by the decision of both Houses of Parliament.[6] This ensures that the government cannot sack a judge just because they issue a decision against the government or with which the government disagrees. The independence of the judiciary is now made explicit in section 3 of the CRA, covering the government's duty both to uphold the independence of the judiciary and not to seek to influence any particular judicial decision. The importance of the rule of law is also stressed (although not defined).[7]

 ## JUDICIAL REVIEW

The High Court also has a jurisdiction to supervise the acts of the executive. As mentioned above, the executive has to act in accordance with the powers granted to it, usually by Parliament, and always in accordance with the law, which means, for example, not deciding to do something illegal or which it is not authorised to do. This again is part of the principle of the rule of law, that not only should discretionary powers be exercised lawfully and properly, but also that the courts should be able to supervise any such exercise of a power and that there should be a remedy in respect of any unlawful decisions made or acts done.

When a decision is taken which is for any reason improper, this can be brought before a judge by an action called a **judicial review**. The institution of judicial review is an important element of the relationship between the courts and Parliament. The principle applied in a judicial review is that what is being reviewed is a decision which should be taken by a person appointed to take that decision. This will involve the exercise of a **discretion**, that is, that the decision-maker is given at least some degree of choice in what decision to make. This discretion has been granted to the person being challenged and in principle it is not for the courts to supplant that person's discretion by taking the decision themselves. The role of the courts is rather to police the decision-making process. Thus, in a judicial review case, the courts do not decide whether a decision or action by a public or governmental body or person is right or wrong, but whether or not it is properly within the scope of the authority or discretion which is being exercised. If the decision was improper or unlawful, it will be declared invalid (quashed).

Most of the time the discretion under scrutiny was created by a statute, but judicial review principles apply equally to non-statutory discretions exercised by servants of the

---

[5] CRA 2005 section 7 and schedule 4.

[6] Supreme Court Act 1981, section 11(3) (to be cited as the Senior Courts Act 1981 when the CRA 2005 is in force) but see now also CRA 2005, sections 108–109; CRA 2005, section 33 is the equivalent provision for Justices of the Supreme Court.

[7] Constitutional Reform Act 2005, section 1.

state, such as the powers which are part of the royal prerogative, mentioned above (although some areas of discretion are not areas which the courts will review because they fall within the exclusive jurisdiction of the executive, such as foreign policy or national security).[8] The question remains whether the decision under review is within the powers of the person making that decision. The courts also consider any allegations such as that the decision is arbitrary or unfounded, that the decision-maker is biased or that they have not allowed all relevant parties to put their case before a decision is taken.

This is where the Act comes in, since decisions taken by government ministers or officials have to take proper account of people's Convention rights. If they do not do so, if the decision infringes someone's Convention rights, it will be unlawful, an abuse of discretion, and thus one which that person has no authority to make. It will therefore be liable to be challenged and quashed on a judicial review hearing. This is what makes judicial review an important remedy in the enforcement of the Human Rights Act, especially in cases where having a decision declared invalid is a more effective remedy than payment of compensation after the event.

In one respect the Act extends the role of the court in a judicial review hearing. The traditional view of judicial review is that what is being considered is the legality and procedural propriety of the decision, to ensure that the decision falls within the scope of the statutory discretion, to ensure that it is not an improper decision because the decision-maker was biased or took into account irrelevant considerations, etc., and to ensure that all appropriate procedural steps have been followed. Under the Act, however, the courts have to consider whether the substance of the decision infringes a Convention right, especially if there is a question about whether a decision which would appear to interfere with a right can be justified. As we will be discussing later, a key idea in the question of justification is proportionality, and judging whether or not a decision is a proportionate interference with a right involves a consideration of the substantive basis of the decision, and not just the process by which it was reached.

A helpful statement of this change in approach can be found in the speech of Lord Steyn in the case of *Daly*:[9]

> The intensity of review is somewhat greater under the proportionality approach. [The] doctrine of proportionality may require the reviewing Court to assess the balance which the decision maker has struck, not merely whether it is within the range of rational or reasonable decisions. Secondly the proportionality test may go further than the traditional grounds of review in as much as it may require attention to be directed to the relative weight accorded to interests and considerations.

The House of Lords has confirmed that in human rights cases, the question for the Court is not whether the decision-maker has properly taken the applicant's rights into account, but whether they have actually been infringed by the decision that has been made – a more intense standard of review than has been traditional, and an important guide for the future.

---

[8] Considered recently in *Campaign for Nuclear Disarmament* v *Prime Minister* [2002] EWHC 2759 (QB), where the court held that it would not be proper for it to decide whether United Nations Resolution 1441 authorised states to take military action against Iraq.

[9] *R (Daly)* v *Home Secretary* [2001] UKHL 26, [2001] 2 AC 532 at 547; cited as authoritative in, e.g., *R (ProLife)* v *BBC* [2004] 1 AC 185, per Lord Walker at paras 133–5; for the facts, see below, p. 260.

In the case of *Begum*,[10] which concerned the decision of a school to exclude a pupil who refused to comply with its policy on school uniform as regards religious dress, engaging Article 9, the House of Lords upheld the school's decision. Their Lordships criticised the Court of Appeal for focusing on whether the school had taken Article 9 into account, as a procedural question, rather than addressing the substantive question of whether there was an infringement. The Lords stressed that the court must reach its own view on whether the decision or policy infringes some Convention Right. If the decision-making body has considered the Convention right carefully in its decision-making process, then that will be highly relevant and it may be harder for the court to reach a different view: but the fact that the right has or has not been considered is not decisive. In this case, Article 9 had been considered, and the Lords agreed that there was no infringement.

Again in the case of *Belfast City Council* v *Miss Behavin' Ltd*,[11] the House of Lords was considering a judicial review of the City Council to refuse to license a sex shop in a particular part of Belfast. The Court of Appeal had quashed the decision on the basis that the Council had paid insufficient attention to the applicant's Article 10 and Article 1, Protocol 1, rights in coming to its decision. The House of Lords disagreed: again, the question was whether the outcome of the decision infringed the rights of the applicant, and not the process which was followed. The governing legislation did not infringe any Convention rights, so the question was whether the right balance had been struck between the different interests being considered. The local authority was better placed to consider that balance, but where, as here, there was no indication that it had attempted to do so, the court should itself answer the question whether there was an infringement. Here, the Council's decision did not infringe the applicant's rights: the Articles were engaged, but it was appropriate to restrict them in the public interest. Thus, even though the Convention rights issues had not been considered, the result was still acceptable: the process defect did not invalidate the decision.

As Lady Hale put it:[12]

> The role of the court in human rights adjudication is quite different from the role of the court in an ordinary judicial review of administrative action. In human rights adjudication, the court is concerned with whether the human rights of the claimant have in fact been infringed, not with whether the administrative decision-maker properly took them into account.[13]

The question of how much scope should be given to an individual decision-maker within the executive when their decision is being reviewed for compliance with the Act is a topic to which we shall return later in this chapter, since this is an aspect of a larger question about the extent to which the courts should defer to Parliament. The limited nature of judicial review – ensuring the legality of decisions, but without displacing the presumption that a decision is to be taken by the person to whom Parliament has entrusted it – is itself an aspect of policing the doctrine of Parliamentary sovereignty. It is the effect of the Act on this doctrine which we shall consider next.

[10] *R (Begum)* v *Governors of Denbigh School* [2006] UKHL 15, [2007] 1 AC 100; for more detailed discussion of the facts, see below, p. 281.

[11] *Belfast City Council* v *Miss Behavin' Ltd (Northern Ireland)* [2007] UKHL 19, [2007] 1 WLR 1420.

[12] [2007] 1 WLR 1420, 1430, para 31.

[13] This applies to other appellate bodies as well as the courts, for example immigration appeals: *Huang* v *Home Secretary* [2007] UKHL 11, [2007] 2 AC 167.

THE ACT AND PARLIAMENTARY SOVEREIGN

One general question which should be considered in respect of man, cases that we will be discussing is the extent to which particular issues a. be, and are, determined by the judges or by Parliament. The Act specifica. sovereignty of Parliament: it does not allow the courts to declare that any by Parliament is unlawful and so of no effect. Thus it does not change the c relationship between Parliament and the courts or give the courts the powe example, the Supreme Court of the United States has, to declare legislation to   .valid if it is unconstitutional. The courts can only declare that the provisions of the statute are **incompatible** with the Act – that is, one or more provisions of the statute in question infringe the human rights of some person or persons.

The justification for this limitation on the scope of the Act is so that it does not interfere with the democratic process, by preventing a government being able to pursue the policies it was elected to pursue. This is an important principle. Judges are not elected: they are appointed on the basis of ability and experience,[14] and therefore they are not accountable to the general population. They cannot be elected out of office as politicians can be.

The difference in this respect between judges and politicians stems from the difference in the type of decisions which they make. It is both appropriate and desirable to have judges decide **legal disputes**, questions about what the law says in a particular area, or how the law should deal with a difficult case, since the resolution of such questions is based on expertise in the law, which is the basis of a judicial appointment. Considerations of general principles of morality and justice apply only where there is a doubt as to what the law is or a question as to what the law should be, which is not common. Usually the issue in a court case is about what really happened, i.e. a dispute about facts, and how the law applies to those facts; it is rare for the facts to be clear but the law to be vague, and it is only in those situations that the judges may have to decide what the right answer *should* be.

However, questions of human rights may well involve **political questions** of the sort which should be decided by Parliament as a matter of policy. Members of Parliament are elected on the basis of their, or their party's, political views on which policies should be adopted on a variety of important issues. They therefore have a democratic mandate to put forward certain views on contentious issues, and are accountable to the electorate for the way in which they present those views. These will be issues such as what should be done about social problems such as crime, immigration, education and the environment; how, where and when policies on such issues should be implemented; how much should be spent on defence, healthcare, social security or the police; and so on. These are political, not legal, questions, because what we are really interested in is what the state should do (if anything) to address whatever the perceived problem is – not what the law is, but what it should be. There will inevitably be a range of possible answers to such issues, and which is adopted will depend on the political viewpoint of the government which has been elected. So, it may be a worthy general principle that we should all contribute to the funding of public transport, but that does not answer the political question as to how much money should be allocated to different areas – how much on rail or bus services, how much on roads for people driving themselves, etc.

[14] A principle confirmed by CRA 2005, section 63.

...t should be emphasised that the fact that judges are not elected does not make them ...emocratic. The courts have stressed this when considering their constitutional position in relation to the Act: for example, in the words of Lord Bingham:[15]

> I do not [. . .] accept [that there is a] distinction [. . .] between democratic institutions and the courts. It is of course true that the judges in this country are not elected and are not answerable to Parliament. It is also of course true [. . .] that Parliament, the executive and the courts have different functions. But the function of independent judges charged to interpret and apply the law is universally recognised as a cardinal feature of the modern democratic state, a cornerstone of the rule of law itself. The Attorney General is fully entitled to insist on the proper limits of judicial authority, but he is wrong to stigmatise judicial decision-making as in some way undemocratic. [. . .] The Act gives the courts a very specific, wholly democratic, mandate [– to delineate] the boundaries of a rights-based democracy.

In addition to questions of democratic legitimacy, political questions are not usually appropriate to the type of process used in judicial decision-making. This is because judges are there to decide the questions that relate to the dispute between the (usually) two parties before them: the answer for that case on those facts. Political questions invariably have more than two different possible answers being put forward by (usually) a large number of persons or groups who will be affected by the solution chosen. Answering them will typically also involve much expert input. Courts have to rely on the expert evidence put before them by the parties to the dispute, whereas politicians and civil servants can be more proactive in seeking relevant information and have access to a wider variety of sources of information.

There is, of course, often no clear distinction between legal and political questions and often the question will be one of degree. For example, where the law is not clear and there is a discretion to be exercised by the judges deciding a case, because the existing cases would support more than one answer, the judges may find themselves making a 'political' decision as to what the right answer should be. This will be especially so if the law is being challenged in the highest court, the House of Lords, where it may effectively be argued that the law should be changed: the Lords will then have to consider the more general implications of the decision they are making, and the policy which they would be implementing by taking a particular view. In such cases there may well be a difference of opinion precisely on whether such a decision should be made by the courts or by Parliament, and whether or not it is appropriate for the courts to be making that sort of decision.

An example of a situation where the courts expressly considered that a policy decision was being taken, and also an example of judicial review under the Act, is the case of *Alconbury*.[16] Here, what was being challenged was a ministerial decision under statutory powers to decide a question as to whether or not planning permission should be given for a number of proposed developments. What was being argued was that the Environment Secretary was not an independent and impartial tribunal within the meaning of Article 6(1) and therefore his power to decide these questions was incompatible with the Convention.

---

[15] *A v Home Secretary* [2004] UKHL 56, [2005] 2 WLR 87, para 42.
[16] *R (Alconbury Developments Limited)* v *Secretary of State for the Environment, Transport and the Regions* [2001] UKHL 23, [2001] 2 WLR 1389.

The House of Lords rejected this argument. The role of the Secretary of State was quite appropriate since the decision at issue was one of administrative policy under the planning legislation. It would be undemocratic for the courts to determine planning questions themselves, since that was not the scheme of the legislation adopted by Parliament: the constitutional role of the Secretary of State was not a judicial role to which Article 6 applies, but involved a political, policy decision. However, overall Article 6 was complied with because the decision of the Secretary of State could be judicially reviewed, to ensure that he complied with the relevant statute, that he had followed the necessary procedural steps, and so on. There was therefore protection to ensure that the decision was *legal* and procedurally proper; but it was not for the court to say whether it was *correct*.

Questions of basic rights raised by the application of the Human Rights Act will often include such political questions – questions about what solution society should adopt to a particular problem. This means that the question of whether a particular piece of law infringes someone's rights is not an isolated question. We will see in our discussion of the various Articles of the Convention that most of them make allowances for situations where rights can be legitimately interfered with in the general interest. The way that the Act brings the Convention into our law ensures that where Parliament has adopted a particular position on a political issue, the judges will have to apply the law as Parliament has set it out, even if they consider that this statute infringes one or more Convention rights of parties affected by the legislation.

However, the fact that Parliament can pass legislation which does not conform to the Convention rights does not mean that having the Act as part of our law serves no useful purpose. On the contrary, it does ensure that Parliament, in passing legislation, has to focus directly on any issues as to potential infringements of rights which arise.[17] Thus there will be political pressure on the government and Parliament not to propose or pass laws which infringe rights and to change those that do.

The preservation of Parliamentary sovereignty has been one of the main reasons why incorporating the Convention into domestic law has been politically contentious over the years. The method adopted by the Act, that Parliament is free if it wishes to disregard the Act's provisions, preserves the existing constitutional balance between Parliament and the courts.[18] The Act has constitutional significance; it is not a new constitution.

DEVOLUTION

Another aspect of the constitution which is relevant to how the Act affects the law is how it applies in the different parts of the United Kingdom. The United Kingdom of Great Britain and Northern Ireland consists of four main constituent parts: England, Wales, Scotland and Northern Ireland. These have three different legal systems – one in England and Wales, one in Scotland and one in Northern Ireland. Whilst there are areas of the law

[17] Especially through the making of a statement of compatibility: see below, p. 75.
[18] It should be noted in *R (Jackson)* v *Attorney General* [2005] UKHL 56, [2005] 3 WLR 733, where the way in which the Hunting Act 2004 was passed by Parliament was challenged, Lords Steyn and Hope and Baroness Hale all commented in terms which suggested that, in an extreme case, the Act represented basic principles and that the courts might not enforce an attempt by Parliament to infringe them.

which apply in the same way in all three systems, there are also areas which are different. There are also distinct legal systems in the Isle of Man and the Channel Islands. The reasons for the separate legal systems are historical: in particular, the English and Scottish legal systems were entirely separate before these two countries were united by the Acts of Union.[19]

In the last few years more autonomy from the Parliament at Westminster has been granted to Scotland and Wales; this has been part of the same political interest in constitutional matters on the part of the 1997 Labour government which led to the Act being passed. The Scotland Act 1998 set up the Scottish Parliament, which sits in Edinburgh, and is empowered to pass legislation for Scotland. The Government of Wales Act 1998 set up the Welsh National Assembly which sits in Cardiff and creates subordinate legislation; its scope is expanded by the Government of Wales Act 2006. An Assembly has also been set up in Northern Ireland as part of the peace process there by the Northern Ireland Act 1998, although it has not operated continuously since its creation for political reasons. The Northern Ireland Act 1998 also set up the Northern Ireland Human Rights Commission to review the adequacy and effectiveness in Northern Ireland of law and practice relating to the protection of human rights.[20]

Each of these devolved legislative bodies has been given the power to legislate on a variety of areas. The cumulative effect of these provisions is a potentially significant decentralisation of power, certainly in those areas which have been devolved, although these vary between the different institutions. However, all of them are subject to the provisions of the Human Rights Act 1998, and any legislation passed by them which infringes the Convention rights can be declared void and of no effect.[21] In this respect, they do not have the authority that the national Parliament does to overrule the Act. Thus in each case, legislation passed by them is open to challenge on the basis that such legislation is in conflict with one of the Convention rights. Such challenges are brought before the Judicial Committee of the Privy Council, made up of a panel of Law Lords (these will in future be heard by the Supreme Court when it opens). This ensures that there is consistency where possible between the application of the Act in the legal systems of Scotland, Northern Ireland, and England and Wales.

This may not always be the case in the detail, but it should be the same in the principles which are applied. An example of this is in the law on the consequences of delay in bringing a criminal prosecution, in breach of Article 6. In the devolution appeal of *R v HM Advocate*,[22] the Privy Council held (by a majority) that, in Scottish law, once it had been established that continuing with a prosecution would be in breach of Article 6, proceedings would have to be stayed (i.e. ordered not to continue). However, when the same question

---

[19] Union with Scotland Act 1706 and Union with England Act 1707, now subject to the Scotland Act 1998.

[20] Northern Ireland Act 1998, sections 68–69; the Scottish Parliament has also created a Scottish Commission on Human Rights.

[21] Scotland Act 1998, section 29, and section 57(2) limits the Scottish Executive (and note that a claim that the Scottish Executive has acted in breach of a Convention right is not limited by the time limit which applies to the Human Rights Act: *Somerville v Scottish Ministers* [2007] UKHL 44, (2007) 1 WLR 2734, see below, p. 103); Government of Wales Act 1998, section 107(1); Northern Ireland Act 1998, section 6(2).

[22] *R v HM Advocate* [2002] UKPC D3, [2003] 2 WLR 317.

came before the House of Lords on an English appeal,[23] a nine-member panel took the view that *R* was wrong (with two dissents, who were in the majority on *R*), that a stay should not be granted automatically, but only if there could no longer be a fair trial or it was otherwise unfair to try the defendant, since some other remedy might be appropriate such as a declaration of the infringement, a reduction in sentence, or an award of damages as compensation for the delay. This left matters, to quote Lord Hope, in the 'unfortunate' position that the law was different as between England and Scotland. However, this has now been resolved by the Privy Council in the case of *Spiers* v *Ruddy*,[24] where the Privy Council chose not to follow *R*, in light of the later nine-member decision and more recent European Court cases that made clear that a delay in breach of Article 6 does not necessarily make the proceedings unsound. Thus, although it is open to the Scottish courts to apply the test differently, the basic principle is the same in both jurisdictions.

Likewise, if both English and Scottish police forces are involved in the same investigation, it makes no difference which of them is first to charge the accused for the purposes of the accused's procedural rights: they are both part of the same authority as far as the UK's international commitments to uphold the Convention are concerned, and they can be expected to cooperate in dealing fairly with a suspect.[25]

THE EUROPEAN CONVENTION IN ENGLISH LAW

As part of the background to understanding the way that the European Convention operates, it is worth explaining here what is meant by an **international treaty**, which is what the Convention is, and how a treaty fits into domestic British law. The body of law known as public international law sets out the rules that apply to relationships between states. Under international law, a state, such as the United Kingdom, can take on obligations to other states by means of a treaty, which just means a formal and binding agreement between states. Other examples of treaties apart from the European Convention itself are the treaties setting up the European Union, or the United Nations Charter. There are a host of other treaties to which the United Kingdom is a party, for example peace and territorial treaties, in some cases going back many centuries, treaties which set international standards like the Hague and Geneva Conventions, and a host of treaties that regulate international matters ranging from diplomacy between states to the status of outer space.

By entering into a treaty, confirmed if necessary by Parliament in a statute, the United Kingdom government can grant other institutions powers to make decisions about the law in the United Kingdom. So, by being a signatory to the European Convention, the United Kingdom agrees that the European Court has the authority to decide whether or not the United Kingdom has fulfilled its obligations under the Convention or not in particular cases; that is, whether or not it protects the rights of its citizens. In a similar manner, by signing up to the various treaties relating to the European Union, the United Kingdom has

---

[23] *Attorney General's Reference No. 2 of 2001* [2003] UKHL 68, [2004] 2 AC 72.
[24] *Spiers* v *Ruddy* [2007] UKPC D2, [2008] 1 AC 873.
[25] *Burns* v *HM Advocate* [2008] UKPC 63, [2009] SLT 2.

Constitutional considerations

consented to grant certain powers to European Union institutions, such as the European Commission and European Court of Justice.

It is worth noting that international bodies, set up by treaties, can interact with each other. The European Union treaties also provide for protection of basic rights. This overlaps with the Convention since all European Union countries are also members of the Council of Europe, and therefore signatories to the European Convention.[26] The European Court of Human Rights has expressed the view that it would expect valid European Union legislation to provide equivalent protection of basic rights to the Convention as otherwise it would be open to challenge on this ground before the European Court of Justice. The law would probably have to have been implemented incorrectly for there to be a breach of the Convention in its application.[27]

However, entering into a treaty does not mean that the treaty can be used to challenge the law which is laid down in an Act of Parliament. Under our constitutional law, treaties entered into with other countries have no effect in our national law unless and until they are passed as a law by Parliament.[28] That is, individuals cannot use treaty obligations as the basis for bringing a legal action until Parliament has passed a law implementing the treaty in domestic law. This again is an aspect of Parliamentary sovereignty: the government cannot simply create law by signing a treaty, but must go through the usual Parliamentary law-making process.

This limitation on the effect of treaties applied equally to the European Convention until the Human Rights Act was passed in 1998, even though the United Kingdom had been a party to the Convention since it was first signed in 1950. Until then, as with any treaty, it could be referred to in a particular dispute, but did not actually dictate how that dispute should be decided.

Thus, before the Act came into force, there were only limited ways in which the Convention could be relied on in a court case in the United Kingdom. It was certainly referred to in a number of cases which raised issues as to fundamental rights, such as freedom of speech or freedom of religion, but could only be used in limited circumstances to assist the court. The main circumstances where the Convention was used in a decision were:

- As an aid to construction of ambiguous legislation, since the courts should prefer an interpretation which allows the UK to fulfil its international obligations.

> For example, in the case of *Brind*,[29] which was about a statutory provision that allowed members of terrorist organisations to be seen but not heard on television, the Convention was referred to, although the court in the end considered that there was no ambiguity in the statute.

---

[26] There are 27 EU members out of 47 members of the Council.
[27] *Bosphorous Airways* v *Ireland* (2006) 42 EHRR 1.
[28] Some European Union legislation is directly effective: these are not new treaties, but binding under the existing European Union treaties.
[29] *R* v *Home Secretary, ex parte Brind* [1991] 1 AC 696.

- To assist with an ambiguity in the judge-made part of the common law.

> For example, in the case of *Derbyshire County Council* v *Times Newspapers*,[30] which concerned the question of whether or not a local authority could sue for libel, it was held that it could not, because this would be a restriction on freedom of speech. The Court of Appeal considered that the common law was ambiguous and relied on the Convention; the House of Lords considered that there was no ambiguity in the common law, but considered that the common law was in line with the Convention in any event.

- To assist in the exercise of judicial discretion, again to ensure that the courts uphold rather than deviate from the Convention where there is scope to do so.

> For example, regarding the application by the government for an injunction, which is a discretionary remedy, to restrain the publication of extracts of the book *Spycatcher*, members of the House of Lords made reference to the Convention and considered that it was not violated by continuing the injunctions which had been granted.[31]

THE MACHINERY OF THE EUROPEAN CONVENTION

The European Convention itself contains a machinery for the resolution of human rights disputes and allegations of infringements, including provisions to allow an individual to bring a case to the European Court to complain if the law of the country they live in does not properly protect the rights which the Convention sets out. Since 1966, individuals in the United Kingdom have been able to bring such a complaint about any alleged breach of their human rights, if they have no remedy under domestic law.

Until 1998, the Convention mechanism consisted of the European Commission and the European Court. The system was that the Commission ascertained the facts of a particular case, decided whether or not it was admissible and gave an opinion on its merits. The Court then gave a final judgment, and ordered any 'satisfaction' or remedy by way of the payment of compensation. The Council of Europe's Committee of Ministers had an overseeing role.

From 1 November 1998, the Commission was abolished, as was the judicial function of the Ministers. The present system is that the Court sits full-time, decides the facts and any questions of admissibility, and then gives judgment. The Court may sit as a Committee of three judges, or a Chamber of seven, or a Grand Chamber of seventeen. A party who is dissatisfied with a judgment of a Chamber may ask for a rehearing before a Grand Chamber, if a serious issue is raised of general importance or concerning the interpretation of the Convention, so the Grand Chamber effectively operates as an appeal court and its decisions therefore have more force than those of a Chamber.

As was the case before the Act came into force, it still remains open for a party who wishes to complain about a breach of their Convention rights to take a case to the European Court. However, in order to be allowed to do so, they must first exhaust the scope for

---

[30] *Derbyshire County Council* v *Times Newspapers* [1992] 1 QB 770, CA, [1993] AC 534, HL.
[31] *Attorney General* v *Guardian Newspapers* [1987] 1 WLR 1287, e.g. per Lord Templeman at p. 1296.

Constitutional considerations

challenging the alleged infringement in the national courts. Thus, the number of cases going from the United Kingdom to the European Court has been reduced, since allegations of infringement are likely to be dealt with, one way or another, before they get that far, and, as the European Court starts dealing with cases on facts after the Act came into force, the number of cases where there are found to be violations by the United Kingdom are also reducing.[32] This is one of the practical advantages of the Act: the European Court is now a final appeal, a last resort, and not a first stop for such complaints.

 ## THE MARGIN OF APPRECIATION

The **margin of appreciation** is an important concept in the European Court's approach to deciding cases and an important part of the European Court's view of the relationship between it and the national state authorities and state courts. The central idea of the margin of appreciation is that there are some areas where different states may legitimately take different approaches to particular rights. This is based on the principle that individual states have a certain measure of autonomy under the Convention ('appreciation' here is used in the sense of allowing a measure of understanding or leeway). This is thought appropriate because the states that are bound by the Convention cover the whole of Europe and have different cultures and histories, different dominant religions, different traditions about how people should behave and when and to what extent state interference is justified. In some areas there may be no general consensus across Europe about what should be tolerated and what should not, and that would suggest to the judges of the European Court that states should be given some scope for expressing the popular feelings of their citizens about a particular issue.

The European Court in this way accepts that different people may have different views on moral issues which are not necessarily 'right' or 'wrong'. Another way of putting this is that it is based on the principle of subsidiarity, that matters should be decided at the most local level appropriate. The principle of a margin of appreciation recognises that national legislatures or courts may be best placed to make an initial assessment of the needs and standards of their own societies; or, in some cases, that different countries have evolved different solutions to similar problems, especially on social and moral issues. But it should be emphasised that states will not be given a margin of appreciation on all issues, only where the European Court considers that there is a genuine difference of opinion across Europe on a moral issue and/or the right in question is one which permits different interpretations to be applied. There is no margin of appreciation to allow torture or slavery, for example, in breach of Articles 3 and 4. It is only on difficult moral issues that states may have a margin of appreciation.

One example is abortion: this is a difficult moral question on which people from different cultures and religions take different views. Under the Convention, the right to life contained in Article 2 is not qualified. However, different states have different laws about abortion

---

[32] For empirical discussion of the effect of the Act on the numbers of cases going before the European Court from the UK, see Amos, *The Impact of the Human Rights Act on the UK's Performance before the European Court of Human Rights* [2007] PL 655.

– taking different views about whether an unborn child is 'alive'. Some states prohibit abortion altogether, for example Ireland because of its predominantly Roman Catholic population; others, like the United Kingdom, allow abortion up to a certain stage of pregnancy. The European Court has indeed treated this as an area where the margin of appreciation applies,[33] given the wide diversity of views on the point at which life begins, of legal cultures and of national standards of protection and the legal, medical, philosophical, ethical or religious dimensions of defining the human being. There is no European consensus – indeed it is still a matter for debate even within most European states.

The principle also reflects an important aspect of the function of the European Court. The European Court will only consider whether or not the judgments of the national courts, and decisions of national governments and officials, are in accordance with the principles of the Convention. If a judgment or decision causes a citizen to suffer a breach of his or her human rights, then the Court will step in, by declaring that there has been a breach. But the European Court will not substitute its judgment for that of the national court on the application of national law – it will not reach a decision as to whether or not the national law has been applied correctly. Nor will it review the admissibility or relevance of the evidence adduced in the national court. It is in this sense a supervisory jurisdiction.

In the case of *Handyside* v *UK*,[34] the European Court was asked to consider the bringing of a prosecution in England for obscenity arising out of the publication of *The Little Red Schoolbook*, a book which was aimed at children and was prosecuted for its frank discussions of sexual matters. The publisher complained that his right to freedom of expression under Article 10 had been infringed. The United Kingdom argued that any infringement was justified in the interest of the protection of morals.

The European Court decided that, although the book had not been prosecuted in some other European countries where it had been published, it was within the margin of appreciation allowed to the United Kingdom authorities to consider that this book was unlawful in Britain. In particular, there was no uniform European conception of morals and, on this ground of justification, state authorities were better placed than the European Court to give an opinion. The Court stated that the protection established by the Convention is in that sense subsidiary to the national systems safeguarding human rights. The Court stressed, however, that allowing a margin of appreciation goes hand in hand with the Court's overall supervision, in particular the limiting requirement of proportionality between the infringement of the right and its justification.

It should also be noted that the European Court has developed its ideas over time as the popular morality of Europe has changed. This is because the European Court treats the Convention as a developing instrument. This has affected what issues are considered to be ones where states have a margin of appreciation at any one time.

---

[33] *Vo v France* (2005) 40 EHRR 259, discussed further below, p. 144.
[34] (1979–80) 1 EHRR 737, considered further below, p. 300.

A recent example of the European Court developing the margin of appreciation is in the Court's consideration of the rights of transsexuals, that is, people who undergo a sex-change operation. In the case of *Goodwin* v *UK*[35] the Court decided that there had been violations of Articles 8 (privacy) and 12 (right to marriage) in respect of two transsexuals. The Court recognised an international trend towards increased social acceptance of trans-sexuals and increased legal recognition of their new sexual identity, and came to the view that this could no longer be regarded as a matter of controversy. It was therefore no longer open to the United Kingdom to claim that their treatment of transsexuals fell within the margin of appreciation, as it had been in previous cases.[36] This was particularly so given the lack of review which appeared to have been undertaken by the United Kingdom government since previous European Court decisions on the subject, notwithstanding changes in attitudes in society. The United Kingdom did, however, retain a margin of appre-ciation as to how the rights of transsexuals should be recognised and what changes to domestic law were required as a result. The result of this case has been legal recognition of the new gender of transsexuals in various contexts.[37]

DEFERENCE TO THE LEGISLATURE

Although the margin of appreciation is an important principle for the European Court, it is important to appreciate that it has no direct application when a case is being decided by a national court. So, for example, if an English court were asked to decide whether or not an interference with freedom of association is justified by considerations of public safety, it will not apply a margin of appreciation, since it will have to either accept or reject the justification: it will have to decide whether or not there is an infringement of the right to freedom of association. Unlike the European Court, it is not being asked to consider whether it is appropriate for there to be different answers to the question in different legal systems across Europe, but what the correct answer is under English law. This difference arises out of the different roles of the national courts and the European Court, because the national court does not simply have a supervisory jurisdiction, as the European Court does.

However, the domestic courts should and do still allow some discretion as to action to those they are reviewing, although this is not strictly speaking a margin of appreciation. This will apply where, for example, the court considers that Parliament in passing a statute, or a decision-maker making a decision which is under review, is better placed to reach a proper conclusion about the matter being considered. The courts also have to consider to what extent the decision being made is based on a democratic mandate, for example in considering legislation passed by the devolved assemblies: the very fact that these are bodies elected to decide certain matters may have an effect on how much margin the courts allow them in choosing solutions to difficult questions.

This need to allow some margin for decision to Parliament (in particular) has come across clearly from the words of the judges applying the Act. In the case of *Kebilene*,[38] Lord Hope recognised that the United Kingdom courts will not expressly apply the margin of

---

[35] (2002) 35 EHRR 18. Also below, p. 330 in the context of Article 12.

[36] e.g. *Cossey* v *UK* (1991) 13 EHRR 622 and *X, Y and Z* v *UK* (1997) 24 EHRR 143.

[37] See p. 332 below for a full discussion of the changes in the law which resulted from the decision in *Goodwin*.

[38] *R* v *Kebilene* [2000] 2 AC 326, at 381, discussed further below, p. 217.

appreciation as used by the European Court. However, the rights provided by the Convention are expressions of fundamental principles, and not just a set of rules. Therefore, where there are competing interests:

> In some circumstances it will be appropriate for the courts to recognise that there is an area of judgment within which the judiciary will defer, on democratic grounds, to the considered opinion of the elected body or person whose act or decision is said to be incompatible with the Convention [. . .] It will be easier for it to be recognised where the issues involve questions of social or economic policy, much less so where the rights are of high constitutional importance or are of a kind where the courts are especially well placed to assess the need for protection.

This leeway has commonly been referred to as the principle of **deference**, picking up on the phrase of Lord Hope (and others). Lord Hoffmann, in the case of *R (ProLife) v BBC*,[39] discussed the use of the word deference and the principles which underlie it:

> [A]lthough the word 'deference' is now very popular in describing the relationship between the judicial and the other branches of government, I do not think that its overtones of servility, or perhaps gracious concession, are appropriate to describe what is happening. In a society based upon the rule of law and the separation of powers, it is necessary to decide which branch of government has in any particular instance the decision-making power and what the legal limits of that power are. That is a question of law and must therefore be decided by the courts.
>
> This means that the courts themselves often have to decide the limits of their own decision-making power. That is inevitable. But it does not mean that their allocation of decision-making power to the other branches of government is a matter of courtesy or deference. The principles upon which decision-making powers are allocated are principles of law. The courts are the independent branch of government and the legislature and executive are, directly and indirectly respectively, the elected branches of government. Independence makes the courts more suited to deciding some kinds of questions and being elected makes the legislature or executive more suited to deciding others. The allocation of these decision-making responsibilities is based upon recognised principles. The principle that the independence of the courts is necessary for a proper decision of disputed legal rights or claims of violation of human rights is a legal principle. It is reflected in [A]rticle 6 of the Convention. On the other hand, the principle that majority approval is necessary for a proper decision on policy or allocation of resources is also a legal principle. Likewise, when a court decides that a decision is within the proper competence of the legislature or executive, it is not showing deference. It is deciding the law.

The substance of the courts' approach has been summarised this way:[40] the courts must bear in mind:

- the type and status of body which is taking the decision, since more regard is to be paid to an Act of Parliament than to a decision of the executive or subordinate measure;
- the right which is under consideration and whether the European Convention allows it to be qualified or not;

---

[39] [2003] UKHL 23, [2004] 1 AC 185, paras 75–76.
[40] Laws LJ dissenting in *International Transport Roth Gmbh v Home Secretary* [2003] QB 728, 765–7, approved by Lord Walker in *Pro-Life* at [2003] UKHL 23, [2004] 1 AC 185 para 136.

- whether or not the subject matter of the case is more appropriate, constitutionally, to being considered by the decision-maker or by the courts (for example, legal procedure is constitutionally under the control of the courts); and

- whether or not the court has the appropriate expertise to reach its own view.

The following are given as some examples of situations where the courts have had to consider Parliament's view of how to address a particular issue (without going into detail, as we will be returning to all these cases later):

- In *Brown* v *Stott*,[41] the Privy Council recognised that Parliament was in as good a position as the court to decide the gravity of the problem of dangerous driving, in requiring the identity of the driver of a car to be disclosed.

- In *Poplar Housing* v *Donoghue*,[42] the Court of Appeal had to consider the statutory scheme for providing social housing, and noted that the court should pay particular attention to the intention of Parliament to prefer the needs of those dependent on social housing as a whole over those facing eviction for good cause: housing is a complex area where any decision has far-reaching consequences and decisions as to what is the right balance are more appropriate for Parliament.

- In *Marcic* v *Thames Water*,[43] the House of Lords held that a statutory scheme did not infringe individual rights as to the provision of an adequate public drainage and sewerage system: the scheme had to be considered as a whole, and not just the interests of an individual who happened to suffer from a flood.

- In *Wilson* v *First County*,[44] the House of Lords held that Parliament was entitled to legislate that some credit agreements which did not comply with certain formalities could not be enforced, to ensure consumer protection.

- In *R (Pro-Life Alliance)* v *BBC*,[45] the House of Lords considered that Parliament did not arbitrarily or unreasonably infringe rights of freedom of speech when making party political broadcasts subject to taste and decency requirements, and in the *Animal Defenders* case[46] the same applied in banning political advertising.

- In the cases challenging the statutory ban on fox hunting with hounds,[47] the House of Lords held that if there was an interference with a Convention right, it was justified as being a necessary and proportionate interference for the protection of morals. This was an issue where the courts should respect the decision of Parliament which represented the decision of a majority of the country's elected representatives, otherwise it would be subverting the democratic process; and if this were to be referred to the European Court, it would be likely to fall within the margin of appreciation.

---

[41] [2001] 2 WLR 817, Privy Council, discussed further below, p. 206.
[42] *Poplar Housing and Regeneration Community Association Ltd* v *Donoghue* [2001] 3 WLR 183 at 202; below, p. 70.
[43] [2003] UKHL 66, [2003] 3 WLR 1603, below, p. 341.
[44] [2003] UKHL 40, [2003] 3 WLR 568, below, p. 340.
[45] [2003] UKHL 23, [2004] 1 AC 185, below, p. 363.
[46] *R (Animal Defenders International)* v *Secretary for State for Culture* [2008] UKHL 15, [2008] 1 AC 1312.
[47] *R (Countryside Alliance)* v *Attorney General* [2007] UKHL 52 and *Friend* v *Lord Advocate* [2007] UKHL 53, see below p. 121.

- In *A* v *Home Secretary*,[48] however, the House of Lords held that Parliament *had* acted incompatibly with the Convention rights in enacting a power to detain persons without trial; Lord Hope in that case echoed what he said in *Kebilene* – this was not an area of social or economic policy, but a case of protecting basic constitutional rights, where the courts are entitled to intervene.

Striking the right balance is important. It is important that in complex areas, requiring political decisions as to the best of a range of permissible solutions, the courts do give weight to the decision of Parliament. However, it is also important for the courts to ensure that they do not defer to Parliament too much. Deference to Parliament should not prevent the courts from intervening in situations where Parliament has gone beyond the boundaries of what is permitted by the Convention rights. The courts have shown that they are willing to consider either conclusion – that Parliament is entitled to its view, or that it has gone too far, and it is important that they have made clear the general principle: the courts must decide what rights we have, and not just police the decisions of other parts of the state. This is one of the most important issues which arises in the application of the Act, and one which will recur as we consider the application of the Act in more detail – and especially what action the courts should take when they think that legislation infringes the Act.

QUESTIONS

1 Consider the role of judges: can you suggest the sort of matters which you think are suitable or unsuitable for being decided by a court?

2 Do you think that the Act strikes the right balance between Parliament and the courts? Does the Act go far enough to protect basic rights? Should the judges be allowed to overturn Acts of Parliament if they infringe human rights?

3 Do you agree that the European Court should allow states a margin of appreciation? Do you agree that the courts should allow Parliament a measure of deference? Do you agree with the way in which the courts have done so?

---

[48] [2004] UKHL 56, [2005] 2 WLR 87, below, p. 376.

The church at Aston Cantlow: the dispute over whether the Parish Council could enforce a right to have Mr and Mrs Wallbank pay for repairs to the church was the context for a leading decision on what is a public authority under the Act (see p. 78).

Source: Courtesy of David Fullwood

5 | The scheme of the Human Rights Act 1998

It is now plain that the incorporation of the European Convention on Human Rights into our domestic law will subject the entire legal system to a fundamental process of review and, where necessary, reform by the judiciary. (Lord Hope of Craighead, *R* v *DPP ex p. Kebilene*,[1] 2000)

The main scheme of the Act, the way in which the Convention rights are given force, is as follows:

- The decisions of the European Court and Commission are made relevant to all decisions about Convention rights (section 2).
- All United Kingdom legislation, whenever passed, must, if possible, be interpreted so as to be compatible with the Convention (section 3).
- It is made unlawful for a public authority to act in a way which is incompatible with a Convention right (section 6).
- The courts are given the power to award remedies for breaches of Convention rights (section 8).

Before the Act was passed, a citizen of the United Kingdom who felt aggrieved by a breach of their human rights could only bring a legal action in respect of such a breach directly in the European Court.[2] Since 2 October 2000, United Kingdom citizens have been able to rely on the Convention rights in the United Kingdom courts directly. We will consider in this chapter how and to what extent the Act brings the Convention into our law, and in the next chapter what remedies there are for breaches of the Convention rights and the practicalities of seeking such a remedy.

IMPORTING THE DECISIONS OF THE EUROPEAN COURT

Section 2 (1) A court or tribunal determining a question which has arisen in connection with a Convention right must take into account any: judgment, decision, declaration or advisory opinion of the European Court of Human Rights, opinion or decision of the Commission, or decision of the Committee of Ministers, whenever made or given, so far as, in the opinion of the court or tribunal, it is relevant to the proceedings in which that question has arisen.

---

[1] [2000] 2 AC 326 at 375.
[2] See p. 52, above, for discussion of the limited ways in which the Convention could be used.

Section 2 means that the law and interpretation which has been built up by the European Court and other bodies set up by the Convention must be 'taken into account' by the United Kingdom courts in deciding points under the Act. This should ensure that the way the United Kingdom courts develop the Act is consistent with the way the Convention is applied throughout the rest of Europe and by the European Court. This is important for two main reasons. The first is that having cases decided consistently is an important principle of justice – that like cases are treated alike, that rights of people in equivalent circumstances are given the same degree of respect. The second is that it should help to prevent cases having to go to Strasbourg, because the European Court law will be applied in full. This was one of the key practical reasons for bringing the Convention directly into British law. However, the consequence of this provision is to import into domestic United Kingdom law a body of case law with which lawyers have to become familiar, as will anyone else who wants to know what the effect of the Convention will be.

Note also that the wording in the Act is 'take into account'. This suggests that the European case law is not binding on the court that is considering it. The court is still likely to give any relevant European Court case law very serious consideration and in practice is likely to follow a decision of the European Court which applies to the situation it is considering. But the fact that the European case law is not strictly binding is important because European Court cases are decided in relation to a wide variety of situations arising in many different countries. The European Court also includes a wide variety of judges from different cultures and backgrounds, especially with the expansion of the Council of Europe over the last ten years or so.[3] Thus a case decided on the law in another part of Europe may not reach a result which the British court thinks is correct, even if the facts look similar to a local case. So, although European Court case law will usually be followed and given great weight, there is the opportunity for British judges to choose not to follow a particular case if there are good reasons to do so.

The other reason why it is helpful that European Court cases are not made strictly binding is that, in interpreting the Convention, one of the principles which the European Court applies is that the scope and meaning of the Convention can develop over time. Thus, there are changes and developments in moral standards, and considerations of what is generally thought of as right and wrong, or acceptable or not, and the European Court may change its views as to how to apply the Convention in particular situations.[4]

This also ties in with the way the Convention is drafted, as a series of general rights, which are open to interpretation. Since the European Court does not consider that it is strictly bound by the results it has reached in an earlier case, it is appropriate that our judges should not be bound by such a decision. If a British court decides not to follow a particular European Court decision, and the British decision is challenged so that the matter goes back before the European Court, it would be open to the European Court to prefer the British court's view to the earlier view of the European Court. Thus, the British courts can make an express contribution to the decisions of the European Court; indeed, this was seen as one of the benefits of having cases on the Convention decided in the British courts.

---

[3] A table of members showing when each joined can be found in Appendix 3.
[4] This comes across especially in the idea of the margin of appreciation, discussed above at p. 54.

The scope of this provision means that a judge is not limited by a European Court decision: it would in theory be open to the national court to go beyond the European decision, and find that there was, for example, an infringement of a right under the Act, even though in a similar case the European Court had found none. However, a dictum of Lord Bingham in the case of *Ullah*,[5] which has been widely cited, suggests that the courts should not go further than the European Court.

It was argued here that, in taking a decision to deport someone, the only relevant Convention right was Article 3, preventing ill-treatment. The House of Lords disagreed: although in the cases under review the European Court cases had not expressly relied on other Convention rights to prevent deportation, it was clear from its decisions that it might do so in a strong case. It was in that context, of considering the way in which the European Court might develop its jurisprudence, that Lord Bingham considered section 2(1) of the Act. He considered that the courts should not without good reason weaken the effect of Strasbourg case law, as this would prevent the Act serving its purpose, but he also considered that it is not for the courts to go beyond the European Court law:

> It is of course open to member states to provide for rights more generous than those guaranteed by the Convention, but such provision should not be the product of interpretation of the Convention by national courts, since the meaning of the Convention should be uniform throughout the states party to it. The duty of national courts is to keep pace with the Strasbourg jurisprudence as it evolves over time: **no more, but certainly no less**.[6] (emphasis added)

However, this approach was considered more restrictively in the case of *P*.[7] The case was about the law in Northern Ireland on whether an unmarried couple should be allowed to adopt a child. There was no European Court authority on the point, but the Lords took the view that the likelihood would be, in such a case, that the European Court would find that there was discrimination in breach of Article 14. But even if not, if the European Court should consider that the point is up to the states within a margin of appreciation, that should not inhibit the national court from finding that there was a breach of the Act. The rights protected by the Act had to be determined by the national court, based on the constitutional structure of the UK, and the court should take a principled and rational approach.

This is important: when one considers the rights protected by the Act, they are now part of our law, and must be interpreted by our courts. The European Court law provides guidance on this, and may in some cases provide a clear answer, in which case that should be followed, so that our law does not provide *less* protection than a claim directly under the Convention. But if the European Court view is not clear, or if it considers that a margin of appreciation applies, the domestic courts must then take their own view about the meaning of the rights protected by the Act. It is to be hoped that the courts do not become

[5] *R (Ullah)* v *Special Adjudicator* [2004] UKHL 26, [2004] 2 AC 323.
[6] [2004] 2 AC 323 at 350.
[7] *Re P and others* [2008] UKHL 38, [2008] 3 WLR 76.

inhibited from developing the protection of basic rights by becoming tied to the cases which the European Court has decided, not least because the European Court decisions are not always consistent. The European Court treats the Convention as a developing body of law: our courts should do the same.

There is one other issue raised by this provision, which is in the following situation. A domestic court, such as the House of Lords, could decide, on a particular set of facts, that there is no infringement of a Convention right. The European Court might disagree with that decision, in an appeal on that case, or in a later, separate case, and find that there was an infringement. This raises an issue about whether our courts should prefer the decision of the House of Lords or the European Court. We introduced the doctrine of precedence in the last chapter, the system under which courts are bound by the decisions of higher courts.[8] 'Taking into account' a European Court decision means that it is not strictly binding, it does not overrule the earlier decision, even if applying the earlier decision is now seen potentially to involve infringing the Convention. This then raises a question of *how* the courts should take into account a European Court case: follow the European Court or the House of Lords?

The courts have had to consider this in *Leeds* v *Price*, which concerned the situation where a landlord which is a public authority is seeking possession of a residential property and whether this engages the Article 8 right to a home. Here the Court of Appeal[9] was faced with a House of Lords decision (*Qazi*),[10] binding on the Court of Appeal and lower courts, which meant that the local council was entitled to evict a group of gypsies from their land. However, there had been a subsequent decision of the European Court (*Connors*)[11] which meant that *Qazi* might have to be reconsidered. The Court of Appeal took the view that it was obliged to follow the House of Lords decision – the European Court decision did not overrule the House of Lords. Given the importance of the case, however, the Court of Appeal did refer the issue back to the House of Lords to reconsider it in the light of *Connors*. The House of Lords[12] confirmed that this was the correct approach – the leading English case is binding, as this provides legal certainty, which is itself an important part of providing a just legal system. This is also appropriate because European Court decisions are often very fact-specific and may accord a margin of appreciation to the domestic authority, which includes the national court. An appeal may be appropriate to consider the inconsistency, but other than in exceptional cases, the courts should still follow binding domestic law unless and until it is reconsidered.[13]

---

[8] See above, p. 42 and Figure 4.1.

[9] *Leeds City Council* v *Price, Kay* v *Lambeth LBC* [2005] EWCA Civ 289, [2005] 1 WLR 1825.

[10] *Harrow LBC* v *Qazi* [2003] UKHL 43, [2004] 1 AC 983.

[11] *Connors* v *UK* (2005) 40 EHRR 9, this and this whole series of cases are discussed in more detail in the context of Article 8, below, p. 216.

[12] *Leeds City Council* v *Price, Kay* v *Lambeth LBC* [2006] UKHL 10, [2006] 2 AC 465, especially per Lord Bingham, paras 42–45.

[13] Note for these purposes that the Court of Appeal is able to depart from a previous Court of Appeal decision if it is inconsistent with a later European Court case, even though it is not free to depart from an inconsistent House of Lords decision barring exceptional circumstances: *R (RJM)* v *Secretary of State for Work & Pensions* [2008] UKHL 63, [2008] 3 WLR 1023.

Another area of the law where the binding authority of the House of Lords has been asserted is the law on adverse possession, which is where a claim for land is barred where someone else has had possession of it for 12 years (sometimes referred to as 'squatters' rights'). The leading case on the domestic law is that of *Pye* v *Graham*.[14] This was appealed to the European Court in *Pye* v *UK*, which was heard by a Chamber which held that the English law was in breach of Article 1-1 as being a disproportionate interference with property.[15] This resulted in some domestic decisions interpreting the law to make it compatible with *Pye*.[16] However, *Pye* was then heard by a Grand Chamber which took the opposite view, that the law on adverse possession is not in breach of Article 1, because it is proportionate to the legitimate purpose of providing a time limit on court actions.[17] The Court of Appeal has now reasserted the authority of *Pye* v *Graham* based on the decision in *Pye* v *UK*, which it has held should be treated as binding authority: where, as here, the European Court has considered the question of proportionality, there is no need for the domestic courts to revisit this.[18]

For the same reasons, the courts will not normally grant any stay of execution, to delay enforcement of a judgment, just because a claim is being brought in the European Court, since such a claim is not, strictly speaking, an appeal from the English court – the judgment of the English court will remain binding even if the European Court ruled against the United Kingdom government. The only exception might be if there was a real, imminent prospect of the decision being reversed by legislation, making immediate enforcement unfair.[19]

 ## THE ACT AND OTHER LEGISLATION

Section 3   (1) So far as it is possible to do so, primary legislation and subordinate legislation must be read and given effect in a way which is compatible with the Convention rights.

(2) This section –

(a) applies to primary legislation and subordinate legislation whenever enacted;

(b) does not affect the validity, continuing operation or enforcement of any incompatible primary legislation; and

(c) does not affect the validity, continuing operation or enforcement of any incompatible subordinate legislation if (disregarding any possibility of revocation) primary legislation prevents removal of the incompatibility.

---

[14] *JA Pye (Oxford) Ltd* v *Graham* (2002) UKHL 30, [2003] 1 AC 419.
[15] *Pye* v *United Kingdom* [2005] All ER (D) 199.
[16] In particular, *Beaulane Properties Ltd* v *Palmer* [2006] Ch 79.
[17] *JA Pye (Oxford) Ltd* v *United Kingdom* (2008) 46 EHRR 45.
[18] *Ofulue* v *Bossert* [2008] EWCA Civ 7, [2008] 3 WLR 1253; this point was not part of the appeal to the House of Lords on other aspects of the case: [2009] UKHL 16.
[19] *Locabail (UK) Limited* v *Waldorf Investment Corporation* [2000] UKHRR 592; *Westminster City Council* v *Porter* [2002] EWHC 1589 and 2179 (Ch), [2003] Ch 436.

> Section 3 is a key section . . . it is one of the primary means by which Convention rights are brought into the law of this country. (Lord Nicholls)[20]

This section is perhaps the most far-reaching in the whole Act. The consequence of section 3 is that all past and future Acts of Parliament must be made compatible with the Convention rights – that is, if a court possibly can, it must read any statute passed by Parliament so that it protects the rights granted by the Act, even if that protection does not appear on the face of the statute in question.

Even before the Act, there were cases which considered that there are some fundamental rights which can only be interfered with by Parliament on the basis of express words, which is a similar idea to section 3. This view was summarised by Lord Hoffmann in the case of *Simms*,[21] a case decided after the Act was passed, but on facts which took place before it came into force:

> Parliamentary sovereignty means that Parliament can, if it chooses, legislate contrary to fundamental principles of human rights. The Human Rights Act 1998 will not detract from this power. The constraints upon its exercise by Parliament are ultimately political, not legal. But the principle of legality means that Parliament must squarely confront what it is doing and accept the political cost. Fundamental rights cannot be overridden by general or ambiguous words. This is because there is too great a risk that the full implications of their unqualified meaning may have passed unnoticed in the democratic process. In the absence of express language or necessary implication to the contrary, the courts therefore presume that even the most general words were intended to be subject to the basic rights of the individual.

Section 3(2)(a) makes it clear that the sweeping statement in section 3(1) applies to *all* legislation, whenever enacted – so it would apply to a law passed in 1750 or one passed in 2050. This is different from almost all other legislation. Most statutes are subject to what is called the doctrine of implied repeal: this is the principle that if a later statute is inconsistent with an earlier statute, then the later statute prevails. The implication is that the later statute has repealed – revoked and replaced – the earlier statute to the extent that the two are inconsistent. This principle will not apply to this Act: if a later statute is not consistent with a provision of the Act or a Convention right, there will be no implied repeal of the Act or the Convention right. This means that the Act, or any part of it, can only be repealed by the express provisions of a later Act – Parliament would have to want to repeal it and say so.

Section 3 is complemented by section 11, which states that a person's reliance on a Convention right does not restrict any other right or freedom conferred on them by any other law or limit any claims or remedies they can pursue apart from the remedies provided by the Act. Thus the Act can only extend people's rights, and not limit rights which they already have. But it is worth noting that some such limitations may be inevitable, since any increase in the rights of a person claiming under the Act has the scope to limit the rights of a person they are claiming against – for example, Article 8 has increased rights of privacy, which may correspondingly limit a freedom that existed prior to the Act, for example to publish material that did in fact breach someone's privacy.

---

[20] *Ghaidan* v *Godin-Mendoza* [2004] UKHL 30, [2004] 2 AC 557 at para 26.
[21] *R (Simms)* v *Home Secretary* [2000] 2 AC 115 at 131, where the House of Lords upheld the right to freedom of expression at common law.

Under section 3, the courts are obliged to 'read and give effect' to the Convention rights. So where a statute may, or may not, be compatible, the courts will be required to interpret the statute being considered in such a way as to give effect to the Convention rights. They must do this 'wherever possible', which is to say that if there is more than one possible interpretation, one that complies with the Act must be chosen.

The House of Lords has emphasised in the case of *Ghaidan*[22] that a decision that there is no compatible interpretation is a drastic one and should be an uncommon result, stressing the words 'wherever possible'. In that case, the statute in issue was interpreted to mean that both homosexual and heterosexual couples should have the same rights to inherit a particular form of statutory tenancy. But since the question of a declaration of incompatibility (under section 4, which we consider below) had been raised, the House took the opportunity to consider in more general terms the question of how to recognise when a piece of legislation can be made compatible with Convention rights through interpretation.

As Lord Steyn put it, the linch-pin of the scheme to allow the enforcement of the Convention rights in our law is for interpretation under section 3 to be the main remedy, with a declaration of incompatibility a 'measure of last resort', 'an exceptional course', such that 'there is a strong rebuttable presumption in favour of an interpretation consistent with Convention rights'.

Lord Steyn was critical of what he described as a tendency in some cases to approach the task of interpretation under section 3 in 'too literal and technical a way'; what is required is a broad approach, attempting to carry out the purpose of the Act, bearing in mind the importance of the fundamental rights involved, although there is a point at which even a broad interpretation is not 'possible', when a finding of incompatibility will have to be made.[23]

Lord Nicholls also stressed the need to consider the purpose of the legislation being interpreted: the meaning imported by the application of section 3 must be compatible with the underlying thrust of the legislation being construed. Section 3 is clearly not limited to resolving ambiguities in the words of the statute, because words can be read into the statute.[24] The result of applying section 3 is not therefore dependent on the precise way that the statute is phrased: what limits it is the general intention of the legislative policy being implemented, and the need for the courts not to make decisions which require legislative deliberation,[25] or to 'go against the grain' of the statute being considered.

The case of *In re S*[26] was one where the House of Lords considered that the Court of Appeal had gone too far. Here the statute under consideration was the Children Act 1989, which gave responsibility for supervising children in care to local authorities. The Court of Appeal had decided that the statute could be interpreted to introduce a 'starring system' for prioritising cases to allow for greater judicial supervision. The House of Lords reversed this decision: to alter the system set up by the Children Act in this way would mean conferring on the courts a role which the Act had conferred on local authorities. It would be quite contrary to the 'thrust' of the Act. If a local authority failed to carry out its duties in accordance with Article 8 in particular cases, it would be open to criticism, but there was

---

[22] *Ghaidan* v *Godin-Mendoza* [2004] UKHL 30, [2004] 2 AC 557; see also below, p. 124.
[23] Lord Steyn gave the examples of *Anderson* and *Bellinger* which we consider below, p. 73.
[24] He gave as an example *R* v *A*, discussed below, p. 69.
[25] This point embodies the idea of deference, which we introduced above, p. 56.
[26] *In re S (Minors) (Care Order: Implementation of Care Plan)* [2002] UKHL 10, [2002] 2 AC 291.

no reason to suppose that the scheme set out in the statute itself needed amending to comply with the Convention. Lord Nicholls put it this way:

> For present purposes it is sufficient to say that a meaning which departs substantially from a fundamental feature of an Act of Parliament is likely to have crossed the boundary between interpretation and amendment. This is especially so where the departure has important practical repercussions which the court is not equipped to evaluate. In such a case the overall contextual setting may leave no scope for rendering the statutory provision Convention compliant by legitimate use of the process of interpretation.

This last point is an important one: it may be that there is more than one way of reading a statute so that it is compliant with the Convention, but the hearing of a dispute between two individuals does not give the court enough information or context to decide what the answer should be: this would tell against using section 3 to find a Convention-compliant interpretation.

In *Wilson* v *First County*,[27] the House of Lords considered the general principles of statutory interpretation which should apply, and in particular the use of *Hansard*, the record of Parliamentary proceedings, to assist interpretation.[28] Here too, the starting point was for the courts to identify the policy objective of the legislation and to assess whether the means employed to achieve that objective were proportionate to any interference by the legislation with any Convention rights. This might involve considering background material to the statute in question, including ministerial statements, statements made by MPs in debates in Parliament and explanatory departmental notes, but the courts should not consider the whole of the Parliamentary debates, nor treat ministerial statements as conclusive of the intention expressed in the statute. Whatever was said by ministers or in the debates, the overriding principle remains that the language used in the statute must be taken to be the expression of the will of Parliament, and that is the starting point for judging the proportionality of the measures taken by the statute.

TECHNIQUES OF INTERPRETATION

There are, in particular, three techniques which could be used to interpret statutes to make them compatible with the Convention rights; they are important in understanding how the courts approach their duty under section 3, so we shall consider them in some detail. They may be referred to as reading in, reading out and reading down: **reading in** refers to adding words to the statute, **reading out** refers to removing words from a statute, and **reading down** refers to narrowing words with potentially broad meanings so that their effect is in accordance with the Convention rights.

Reading in would refer to a situation where words needed to be added to give effect to the relevant right. The courts already do this in the context of statutes which implement European Union law. This takes priority over domestic United Kingdom law, so if the statute being considered has failed properly to implement the relevant European legislation, it may be necessary to add words to the reading of the statute which should have been

---

[27] *Wilson* v *First County Trust Limited (No. 2)* [2003] UKHL 40, [2004] 1 AC 817.
[28] Introduced above, p. 41.

included. Likewise, **reading out**, that is, effectively removing words from a statute. Both of these methods of interpretation will certainly apply to subordinate legislation (discussed below). There is a question in principle whether these techniques should apply to primary legislation because the courts are to read and give effect to the Convention rights 'so far as is possible'. It could be argued that, if words have to be added or removed to give effect to the Convention right, this is not within the bounds of what is *possible* on the basis of the words of the statute as passed by Parliament: if Parliament wanted qualifying words to be included or excluded, then they would have been. On the other hand, Lord Irvine, the then Lord Chancellor, in the Parliamentary debates on section 3, expressed the view that the courts would have this power. The courts have certainly interpreted section 3 so as to allow them to read words *in* where necessary to allow them to preserve statutes, without having to find that the statute is not consistent with the Convention rights.

An example of reading words into a statute is the case of *A*,[29] which was a rape trial. Here the House of Lords had to consider the interpretation of section 41 of the Youth Justice and Criminal Evidence Act 1999. This concerns the situation where a person accused of a sexual offence, such as rape, wishes to cross-examine the alleged victim of the offence (the complainant). Very often, in such cases, the issue is not whether or not the accused and the complainant had sexual intercourse, but whether or not the complainant consented to sex. The parties' previous sexual history *may* be relevant to this issue. The purpose of section 41 is to limit the circumstances where this can be explored in court, to prevent defendants having too much leeway to go into the detailed sexual history of complainants, since this was being abused to cause unnecessary embarrassment or humiliation of complainants. In the present case, the trial judge ruled that section 41 prevented him allowing the defendant to cross-examine the complainant about their previous sexual history. The defendant argued that this was inconsistent with his rights under Article 6 to a fair trial, since that required that he be allowed to rely on all relevant evidence.

The House of Lords' starting point was that section 41 served an entirely proper and legitimate purpose, and was not *by itself* incompatible with Article 6. But in some situations, the application of the limitations contained within section 41 *might* infringe the right to a fair trial since the section might require the exclusion of relevant evidence so as to lead to an unjust conviction. However, the House of Lords applied the interpretative obligation in section 3, and construed section 41 in the light of Article 6 as being subject to the *implied provision* that evidence or questioning of a witness which is required to ensure a fair trial under Article 6 should be allowed by the trial judge. By reading this implied provision into the statute, the House of Lords extended the discretion given to a trial judge so that it was clear it should be exercised in a way which is compatible with Article 6, as well as with the purpose of the statute. This would ensure that the discretion in section 41 would not infringe Article 6, even though this altered the effect of the statutory provision. The House then sent the matter back to the trial judge to reconsider in the light of their view of the law.

Another important example of the Act being used to read words into a statute is the case of *Middleton*.[30] After every death, there is an inquest, held by a coroner, sometimes with a

---

[29] *R v A (No. 2)* [2001] 2 WLR 1546.
[30] *R (Middleton)* v *HM Coroner for West Somerset* [2004] UKHL 10, [2004] 2 AC 182.

jury, to determine how the deceased died. In *Middleton*, the House of Lords had to consider whether the questions usually asked by a coroner of a jury at such an inquest provide for a sufficient investigation for the purposes of Article 2, since it is clear that the right to life under Article 2 also includes the right to a proper investigation of a death, where it occurs in state custody (*Middleton* itself was about a suicide in prison). The Lords held that a short verdict in the traditional form did not comply with Article 2. The Coroners Act 1988 and the Coroners Rules 1984 therefore had to be read so as to give effect to Article 2 by interpreting the word 'how' in the question 'how, when and where the deceased came by his death' – the question for the inquest – in a broad sense, meaning 'by what means and in what circumstance', rather than just as 'by what means'. This did not go as far as any finding of civil or criminal liability, which is not the proper function of an inquest, but it did involve expanding the previously understood interpretation of the statute to ensure that Article 2 was complied with.

These are just illustrations: there have been a number of cases where section 3 has been used to read words into a statute so that its interpretation is compatible with the Act. *Ghaidan*, referred to above, is another, because words were read in to make the right to succeed to the tenancy apply to the partner; others we will consider elsewhere.[31]

However, there comes a point where the suggestion that words should be read in would take the courts beyond their proper role. A case where the Court of Appeal has declined to read words into a statute was *Poplar Housing* v *Donoghue*.[32] This case concerned the procedure for bringing a particular type of lease of property (an assured shorthold tenancy) to an end by serving a notice, at which stage the court must grant possession of the property.[33] The Court of Appeal was invited to add the words 'if it is reasonable to do so' into the statute, so that the end of the lease was not automatic. The Court considered that there was no breach of Article 8, but in any event the addition of the words suggested would effectively involve legislating, because it would involve coming to a different view to Parliament about the right way to deal with a particular situation. The Court was not there to approach the matter afresh, and it should not radically alter the effect of the statutory provision.

The courts have been more reluctant to read words out of primary legislation. This is not surprising, because if the clear words of the statute state something which cannot be read in a way which gives effect to a Convention right, that suggests that the statute is incompatible with the Convention – unless words can be read *in* to create an exception to the words that are there. But it does remain a possibility, perhaps if the words in question were a minor part of the section being considered, and if removing them would give effect to a Convention right without doing damage to the statutory scheme; and it remains a technique which could be used with subordinate legislation, which we discuss below.

---

[31] Other examples include: *R* v *Holding*, below, p. 362; *Home Secretary* v *MB*, below, p. 380; *R (Baiai)* v *Home Secretary*, below, p. 328.
[32] *Poplar Housing Association Ltd* v *Donoghue* [2001] EWCA Civ 595, [2001] 3 WLR 183.
[33] Section 21(4) of the Housing Act 1988.

Reading down is a slightly different technique, where a word or phrase which could have a wide range of meanings is read so as to prefer a meaning which is in accordance with the Act. Put another way, it involves limiting the possible meanings of a statute to one which is compatible with the Convention rights. The following are examples of cases where the courts have had to consider limiting the meaning of words to enable statutes to be read so as to be compatible with the Act.

One particular situation is where a statute imposes a burden of proof on a defendant in a criminal case to prove a defence.[34] The question arises because of the presumption of innocence in Article 6(2), which is already part of our law, but which has in some situations been given a wider application by the European Court. One question which arises is whether the statutory defence imposes an *evidential* or *persuasive* burden. If it is an evidential burden, the defendant need only provide evidence to raise the statutory defence, whereupon the burden of disproving the defence is on the prosecution so that if the jury is not satisfied that the defence is disproved, the defendant should be acquitted. A persuasive burden is where the onus is on the defendant not just to raise the issue, but to satisfy the jury that the defence is made out on the balance of probabilities.

This was first considered in the case of *Kebilene*,[35] where the House of Lords took the view that the imposition of a persuasive burden *might* infringe Article 6, depending on the basis for the statute and whether or not it was a disproportionate interference with Article 6(2).

Then in the case of *R v Lambert*,[36] the House of Lords did in fact *read down* the statute being considered: their Lordships considered that to read the statute as imposing a persuasive burden would be an unjustified interference with Article 6(2), but that the statute could be read as merely imposing an evidential burden, which would not infringe Article 6(2). The statute was therefore read so as to be compatible with Article 6.

But reading down is not always necessary. For example, in the case of *Sheldrake* v *DPP*,[37] the House of Lords held that there is nothing unreasonable, unnecessary or disproportionate in requiring a person who is drunk in charge of a car to have the persuasive burden of showing that he is not likely to drive it, given the object of the statute, which is the prevention of death and serious injuries caused by dangerous driving, and the fact that whether the driver is likely to drive or not is so much a part of the driver's own state of mind at the time of the offence as to make it much more appropriate for him to prove he would not have been likely to drive. The burden was not therefore read down to be an evidential burden.

On the other hand, in the case of *AG Reference 4 of 2002*, heard at the same time as *Sheldrake*, a majority of the House considered that a presumption should be read down. The offence was that in section 11 of the Terrorism Act 2000, belonging to a proscribed organisation, and the defence was to show that the organisation was not proscribed when the person belonged to or was involved with it. The consequences of a conviction were very serious and a defendant might well have real difficulties in proving the necessary

---

[34] This is discussed further in the context of Article 6, below, pp. 217–20.
[35] *R v DPP, ex parte Kebilene* [2000] 2 AC 326; see further below, p. 217.
[36] [2001] 3 WLR 206.
[37] *Sheldrake* v *DPP; AG Reference 4 of 2002* [2004] UKHL 43, [2004] 3 WLR 976.

details about any such organisation, especially as the section did not require the defendant to have conducted any form of terrorist activity. The imposition of a persuasive burden would therefore infringe Article 6, and the section should be read down to impose an evidential burden only.

COMPATIBILITY AND PARLIAMENTARY SOVEREIGNTY

Section 4 (1) Subsection (2) applies in any proceedings in which a court determines whether a provision of primary legislation is compatible with a Convention right.

(2) If the court is satisfied that the provision is incompatible with a Convention right, it may make a declaration of that incompatibility.

[. . .]

(6) A declaration under this section ('a declaration of incompatibility') –

(a) does not affect the validity, continuing operation or enforcement of the provision in respect of which it is given; and

(b) is not binding on the parties to the proceedings in which it is made.

The limitation in section 3(2)(b) is of constitutional importance: the fact that the courts, national or European, decide that a particular statutory provision breaches, or permits a breach of, someone's Convention rights does not stop that statute being valid or enforceable. This preserves the existing constitutional position discussed earlier[38] that Parliament is superior to the courts, and the courts cannot declare an Act of Parliament to be void or of no effect. So if it is not possible for an Act of Parliament to be interpreted in a way which is compatible with the Convention rights, then the courts must still apply that Act, notwithstanding the breach of Convention rights. This may be contrasted with, for example, the Supreme Court in the United States of America, which *does* have the power to invalidate legislation if it is unconstitutional, for example if it infringes the Bill of Rights in the United States Constitution.

The House of Lords has confirmed that the Act does not affect the sovereignty of Parliament in the case of *R* v *Lyons*.[39] Here it had been decided by the European Court that compelling persons to give answers to questions in particular circumstances infringed the Article 6 right against self-incrimination. However, the procedures used had been expressly permitted by Parliament in the relevant statute. The House of Lords held that this meant that it could not be said that the evidence obtained in breach of Article 6 should have been excluded at trial. Notwithstanding that the decision of the European Court meant that the

[38] Chapter 4 above, p. 39.
[39] [2002] UKHL 44, [2003] 1 AC 976.

relevant legislative provision was in breach of the Convention, the Human Rights Act 1998 does not allow the courts to avoid giving effect to an express statutory provision. Thus, the courts have no discretion to exclude evidence obtained in a way which may be in breach of the Convention rights, if an Act of Parliament expressly permits the use of such evidence.

But our courts would not be entirely powerless in such a situation. Although they cannot refuse to enforce the offending legislation, they can make a **declaration of incompatibility**, provided for by section 4 of the Act. By doing so, the courts make clear that the legislation being considered does not comply with the European Convention: in effect, such a declaration tells Parliament that it has acted in breach of the human rights of its subjects.

The following are a few particularly notable cases where declarations of incompatibility have been made:[40]

- Perhaps the most significant and controversial decision to make a declaration of incompatibility has been *A v Home Secretary*,[41] where the House of Lords held that a power contained in the Anti-Terrorism, Crime and Security Act 2001 to detain foreign nationals, in circumstances where British nationals could not be detained, was discriminatory and breached Article 14 of the Convention. The House therefore made a declaration of incompatibility and quashed the derogation from the Convention which related to these powers. The power itself was discriminatory: there was no room for interpretation to rescue it.

- In *Bellinger*,[42] the House of Lords held that the failure of the Matrimonial Causes Act 1973 to allow for the recognition of gender reassignment for the purposes of marriage was incompatible with Articles 8 and 12 (following the European Court case of *Goodwin*).[43] The House considered that to interpret the statute governing marriage as allowing for marriage by transsexuals would involve a 'fundamental change in the traditional concept of marriage [which should] be a matter for deliberation and decision by Parliament' (per Lord Nicholls); again it was beyond the scope of interpretation.

- In *Anderson*,[44] the House of Lords held that the power of the Home Secretary to determine how long a person serving a life sentence for murder should stay in prison was incompatible with the Article 6 right to have a criminal sentence determined by an independent and impartial tribunal, being incompatible with the separation of powers between the judiciary and the executive. The statute in question gave this power to the Home Secretary: it was not possible consistently to interpret this to take the power away from him.

---

[40] We will be considering these cases in more detail, as well as other cases where declarations of incompatibility have been made, in the context of the particular Convention right(s) involved; there have been about 20 declarations made thus far, plus some which have been reversed on appeal.

[41] *A v Home Secretary* [2004] UKHL 56, [2005] 2 WLR 87; see below, p. 376.

[42] *Bellinger v Bellinger* [2003] UKHL 21, [2003] 2 AC 467; discussed further below in the context of Article 12, p. 332.

[43] *Goodwin v UK* (2002) 35 EHRR 18, below, p. 331.

[44] *R (Anderson) v Home Secretary* [2002] UKHL 46, [2003] 1 AC 837, considering section 29 of the Crime (Sentences) Act 1997; see also below, p. 198 for further discussion.

Making a declaration of incompatibility may not be necessary if action has already been taken to deal with the problem.[45] On the other hand, if no action has been taken, a declaration of incompatibility ensures that the courts make clear that the issue has not gone away.[46]

It should be noted, however, that a declaration of incompatibility does not invalidate the offending legislation any more than the fact of incompatibility does; it is not even binding on the parties who are before the court (section 4(6)), and does not provide a remedy for the breach of the Convention right in question unless there is government action following the specific case.[47] The remedy for such a breach is thus purely political, not legal – it can only be remedied by persuading Parliament to change the law, not by bringing an action before the courts.

Nonetheless, the Act clearly envisages that such breaches *will* be remedied by Parliament.[48] This was allowed for in the Act by section 10 and Schedule 2, which set up a fast-track procedure for remedying legislation which is incompatible with Convention rights: a Minister who considers there are compelling reasons, 'may by order make such amendments to the legislation as he considers necessary to remove the incompatibility' (section 10(2)). There is no definition as regards what amounts to compelling reasons. An order has to be put before Parliament, but this does not require the full process of passing a statute, so the matter can, in principle, be remedied fairly speedily.

There was some criticism of this procedure when the Act was debated in Parliament for allowing amendments by a summary process to be made to legislation passed after full Parliamentary debate. On the other hand, the concerns which led to the inclusion of the provisions for remedial orders were largely based precisely on the time it would take for the full Parliamentary process to be followed, and on the practical difficulties of enacting legislation to remedy any incompatibility. It is the case nowadays that governments tend to have substantial programmes of legislation, and Parliamentary sessions do not usually have time to deal with all of that, let alone further proposed legislation on matters which might be wholly unrelated to anything currently being considered. The making of a remedial order does not deprive Parliament of the opportunity to consider the matter because the order is still subject to being approved by Parliament before it can become law (Schedule 2, paragraph 2). The only exception to this is where the matter is considered to require urgent action (paragraph 2(b)), and, in such a case, the order still has to be approved by Parliament within 120 days, or else the order will cease to have effect (paragraph 4(4)).

Further, since the subject of the remedial order will also have been the subject of a declaration of incompatibility or a judgment of the European Court, there will already have been detailed legal arguments, and one or more judgments. To ensure that a remedial order is not made prematurely, an order can only be made where no further appeal or court proceedings are being brought (section 10(1)). The court's consideration of the matter should also have identified very precisely the incompatibility, which will define the scope of the remedial order, which can *only* be made to remove an incompatibility.

---

[45] For example, a declaration of incompatibility would have been made but for the fact that legislation had already been passed to deal with the relevant European Court decision in *Doherty* v *Birmingham City Council* [2008] UKHL 57, [2008] 3 WLR 636.

[46] In *Smith* v *Scott* [2007] CSIH 9, [2007] SLT 137 a declaration was made since more than a year had passed since the European Court decision finding an incompatibility without any legislative response.

[47] A point noted by the European Court in the case of *Burden* v *UK* (2008) 47 EHRR 38.

[48] This may be the Scottish Parliament if it relates to a devolved matter: Schedule 2, paragraph 7.

So, under this process, remedial orders have been made to alter the burden of proof relating to the discharge of a mental patient,[49] the position of a judge advocate in a court-martial,[50] and the degrees of relations who can marry.[51] In these situations, relatively technical amendments were made to address the incompatibility. On the other hand, following the declaration in *A v Home Secretary* full-blown legislation was passed (the Prevention of Terrorism Act 2005) to address the incompatibility. Likewise, following *Goodwin* and *Bellinger*, Parliament passed the Gender Recognition Act 2004 to address the incompatibility. And after the declaration in *Anderson*, the Home Secretary's role in setting the tariffs of murderers was formally ended by the Criminal Justice Act 2003. All of these were more politically controversial and required more substantive legislative amendments, justifying full-blown legislation, rather than the more summary accelerated procedure.[52]

The Act introduces one further safeguard to try to prevent an incompatibility arising: Members of Parliament, usually Ministers, who place legislation before Parliament for consideration and approval at its second reading must make a **statement of compatibility**, which states that the person proposing believes that the proposal does not infringe anyone's human rights – or, if it does, that the government still intends to proceed (section 19). The purpose of this is to ensure that attention is at least focused on whether any particular legislation is going to protect people's rights, and that Parliament is made aware if it is specifically proposed that it should infringe anyone's rights.

Following the Act, the vast majority of legislation has had a declaration of compatibility made during its presentation to Parliament, and it does indeed focus debate where a statement is not made. However, it may not always be clear whether the legislation really is compatible. A statement of compatibility was made in respect of the Anti-Terrorism, Crime and Security Act 2001 on the basis of the derogation which was in place to allow for measures which were not compatible with the Convention apart from the derogation. As we have seen, this derogation was successfully challenged in *A v Home Secretary*, which meant that the statement of compatibility was not correct, according to the court's interpretation of the statute. However, in respect of the ban on political advertising in the Communications Act 2003, the Minister stated that he was unable to make a statement of compatibility, but in fact, when the ban was challenged, the House of Lords held that it was compatible with the Act.[53]

Thus, the fact that a statement has been made in Parliament will not guarantee that the statement is correct, especially if the case is a difficult one and there is political pressure for the statute to be passed. On the other hand, the making of the statement at least ensures some scrutiny of the proposed legislation in the light of the Convention. The debates over the Prevention of Terrorism Act 2005, following *A*, as to whether it too would survive a

---

[49] Mental Health Act 1983 (Remedial) Order 2001 (SI 2001/3712) following the decision in *R (H) v Mental Health Review Tribunal* [2001] EWCA Civ 415, [2001] 3 WLR 512; see below, p. 192; the Order has since been revoked as it has been replaced by the Mental Health Act 2007.

[50] The Naval Discipline Act 1957 (Remedial) Order 2004 (SI 2004/66) following the decision of the European Court in *Grieves v UK* (2004) 39 EHRR 51, considered below, p. 213; since revoked and replaced by new Naval Courts-Martial rules: The Courts-Martial (Royal Navy) Rules 2007 SI 2007/3443.

[51] The Marriage Act 1949 (Remedial) Order 2007 (SI 2007/438) following the decision of the European Court in *B and L v UK* (2006) 42 EHRR 11, considered below, p. 330.

[52] Another solution which has been used in some cases is to make use of a proposed statute relating to the general area to include some specific extra provisions to deal with a Convention right point.

[53] *R (Animal Defenders International) v Secretary for State for Culture, Media and Sport* [2008] UKHL 15, [2008] 1 AC 1312, see below, p. 363.

challenge on the grounds of incompatibility, demonstrate the extent to which the question of protection of human rights and compatibility with the Convention is now a live part of our political debate.

SUBORDINATE LEGISLATION

Subordinate legislation refers to regulations or statutory instruments made by Ministers under powers given to them by a statute to provide further detailed provisions dealing with the precise implementation of that statute, which is known in this context as the primary or enabling Act. So, for example, an Act setting up a government agency on health may allow the Secretary of State for Health to make regulations which set out how that agency operates. Another example of subordinate legislation is the order a Minister is empowered to make by section 10(2) of the Act for remedying a statutory incompatibility with the Convention rights, as discussed above.

Subordinate legislation does not have the same immunity from judicial control as primary legislation, and the courts may strike down such regulations if they are unlawful, which includes if they are in breach of the Convention. This itself is a very wide-ranging power as very much more of the business of government is conducted by passing subordinate legislation than by passing primary legislation. This assumes, of course, that the subordinate legislation cannot be interpreted in a way which gives effect to the Convention rights, by reading words in, out or down, as illustrated above: there will be no need to strike down the subordinate legislation if it can be read in a way which is compatible with the Convention rights. It is clear that the courts have this power even without the Act: where possible, the exercise of a power under subordinate legislation should be interpreted in such a way as to make them subject to fundamental rights.[54]

The only exception to the court's power to strike down subordinate legislation under the Act is where the wording of the primary legislation prevents removal of the incompatibility. In such a case, the court may only make a declaration of incompatibility (section 4(4)). However, in such a case, the power of a Minister to make a remedial order also applies, even though the challenge was not directly to the primary legislation itself (section 10(3) and (4)). There is a list of what sorts of provisions are to be treated as primary and secondary legislation for the purposes of the Act in section 21.[55]

THE UNLAWFULNESS OF INFRINGING CONVENTION RIGHTS

Section 6   (1) It is unlawful for a public authority to act in a way which is incompatible with a Convention right.

          (6) 'An act' includes a failure to act [. . .]

---

[54] *R v Home Secretary, ex parte Simms* [2000] 2 AC 115, referred to further above, p. 66.
[55] Set out in Appendix 1, p. 393.

This is the provision of the Act which has most practical force: it means that it is unlawful for any public authority to act in a way which infringes any of the rights protected by the Convention. However, the use of the word 'unlawful' does not mean that an infringement of the Act is a crime: by section 7(8), nothing in the Act creates a criminal offence. This means that the remedy for an infringement of a Convention right is not a prosecution in the criminal courts but an action in the civil courts. Such an action would result in a decision that the act was unlawful and, if appropriate, an award of compensation. So the next question is, what bodies are covered by this obligation – what are public authorities?

DEFINITION OF PUBLIC AUTHORITIES

> **Section 6**   (3) In this section 'public authority' includes –
>
>   (a) a court or tribunal, and
>
>   (b) any person certain of whose functions are functions of a public nature
>
>   [. . .]
>
>   (5) In relation to a particular act, a person is not a public authority by virtue only of subsection (3)(b) if the nature of the act is private.

As you can see, there is no complete definition of what a **public authority** is, although sometimes this will be self-evident. So, for example, a government department or ministry or a local authority is quite clearly a public authority because that is its whole purpose: it exists to be part of the state machinery of government. This would also include any body to which a Minister's powers were delegated: it is clear from European Court law that a state remains responsible for such delegated actions. Section 6(3)(a) makes it clear that a law court or tribunal is also a public authority.

The meaning of public authority is then expanded by section 6(3)(b) to include any person 'certain of whose functions are of a public nature', but section 6(5) limits this by stating that such a person is not acting as a public authority if the nature of the act is private. So it might depend what the person is doing as to whether or not they are a public authority. 'Person' in this context does not just mean an individual: for the purposes of interpreting statutes, there is a wide definition of person, which includes not just 'real' people, but also entities that have what is called legal personality, such as companies, as well as local councils and government departments. Thus, sometimes a person, company or body is obviously a public authority, and will be so for all purposes. Sometimes it is not, such as a private individual or a private company running a commercial business. However, there is a middle ground under section 6(3)(b), where the question of whether or not a person or body is a public authority will turn on whether or not a public function is being exercised. These are sometimes referred to as 'hybrid' authorities, because they are a bit of both – sometimes public and sometimes private. In such cases, the test will always be: is the function being exercised private or public?

The main intention in using a general definition was to ensure that bodies or institutions which are treated in the Act as public authorities include all those which would be treated by the European Court as bodies for which the United Kingdom government would be answerable to the European Court for any breach by them of the Convention. This achieves the practical objective of ensuring that there is no need for a claim to be brought before the European Court only because the definition of public authority is too narrow for it to be brought domestically.

Some examples were given during the Parliamentary debates on the Act.[56] So, for example, a privatised utility company could well be a public authority when exercising public functions, although it may not count as a public authority all the time; or Railtrack, which at the time of the debates was responsible for the safety of the railway network, would be performing a public function in that context, but not if it was, say, buying a block of offices.[57] These have now been amplified by cases in a whole variety of areas. The leading case on what bodies are always public authorities is now the House of Lords decision in *Aston Cantlow PCC* v *Wallbank*.[58]

In this case, what had to be considered was the right of a parish council to enforce a right that the owners of certain land had to contribute to the maintenance of a church. The first question, though, was whether the parish council was a public authority, or performing a public function.

The Lords considered carefully the aim of section 6, which is to bring governmental bodies for which the state is accountable within the scope of the Act. Factors identified in considering whether a function is public include the extent to which the body is publicly funded, or is exercising statutory powers, or is taking the place of central government or local authorities, or is providing a public service, or is accountable to the general public for what it does or is otherwise under state supervision.

In the present case, it was held that the Church of England is a religious organisation, not a governmental one, and parochial councils related to this religious purpose, and to financial and administrative matters within the parish, which means that they are not wholly public. It was then held that whether or not parochial councils *ever* exercise public functions, the function of maintaining a parish church is *not* a public function, even though the public have certain rights in respect of their local parish church, and even though a public function could be carried out there, such as registering a wedding. Thus enforcing the liability to pay for repairs on the part of the defendants was a private law matter.

It should be noted that this was a majority decision: Lord Scott considered that a church is a public building and decisions about maintaining it are public; since the Court of Appeal had also considered that the council was a public body, this shows how finely balanced will be some of these decisions about what is a public authority.

---

[56] The main debates referred to here were the House of Commons Second Reading debate (HC Vol. 306, cols 776–778, 16 February 1998) and Committee Debate (HC Vol. 314, cols 406–433, 24 June 1998), although these were considered to have limited relevance by a number of the Lords who decided *Aston Cantlow*, considered below.

[57] The public safety function now vests in the Railway Standards Board and once this function had been passed on, Railtrack was no longer a public authority; *Cameron* v *Railtrack plc* [2006] EWHC 1133 (QB), (2007) 1 WLR 163.

[58] *Aston Cantlow Parochial Church Council* v *Wallbank* [2003] UKHL 37, [2004] 1 AC 546; the property aspect of this case is considered below, p. 347.

The next question concerns a hybrid authority, a body which is not *always* a public authority, performing a public function. The leading case on this is now *YL*.[59]

> The issue here related to a privately-owned care home to which a local council had contracted out the service of providing care for the elderly. The question was whether this was a function of a public nature. The House of Lords, by a majority, held that it was not. The majority view was that the state was not responsible for the actions of a private care home, even where it had contracted services to the state. The duty on the state, the statutory function, was the duty to arrange care. This was the public function under the Act, not the actual provision of care by the home.
>
> There were, however, strong dissents from Lord Bingham and Baroness Hale. Baroness Hale considered that there were a number of reasons why this should be considered a public function: the state had assumed responsibility for ensuring that care was provided; there is a public interest in seeing that this is achieved; the care is publicly funded; and the care may involve the use of statutory coercive powers (under the mental health legislation).

The strength of the dissent shows how difficult this issue is. Indeed, Parliament's prompt response was to reverse the result so that care homes in such cases are always public authorities.[60] This supports the view that the majority approach is somewhat restrictive and not in line with the scope of the Act as originally envisaged. It is to be hoped that the courts will not be distracted by whether the basis of the function is statute or contract so as to lose sight of the need for the protection of basic rights.

Bearing all of this in mind, and also the other cases which have been decided, here are some more examples of bodies which are, or are likely to be (at least some of the time), public authorities:

- the armed forces, police forces and other emergency services, including, for example, the Royal National Lifeboat Institution, in discharging its public function of running the lifeboat service;

- prison and immigration officers and authorities, who will all be public authorities since they act on behalf of the state, but a private security firm would only be a public authority if it was being employed to secure or patrol a public institution, such as a prison;

- the National Health Service and NHS hospitals, but not private hospitals, which may mean that a doctor is a public authority when doing NHS work but not when being paid privately;[61]

- a local authority providing care (in a home or sheltered housing) for the sick or elderly, and, as a result of the reversal of *YL* by statute, a private care home providing its services under a contract with a local authority;[62]

---

[59] *YL* v *Birmingham City Council* [2007] UKHL 27, [2008] 1 AC 95.
[60] Section 145, Health and Social Care Act 2008: someone who provides 'accommodation, together with nursing or personal care, in a care home' pursuant to the relevant statutory provisions is exercising a function of a public nature for the purposes of section 6 of the Act.
[61] *Frame* v *Grampian University Hospitals NHS Trust* (2004) Times 2.3.04: an NHS trust exercises a public function and engages state responsibility.
[62] Above, fn 60.

- a local authority when providing housing or accommodating the homeless, but not a private landlord or housing association, although a registered social landlord may be, where it is effectively a privatised section of public housing stock, or where it has had a public function in relation to housing delegated or contracted to it;[63]

- education authorities and state-funded schools, including the head teacher and governors of a state school, but not private schools, although a local authority could be liable for what is done at a private school if it has sent a pupil there in pursuance of a statutory duty;[64]

- bodies which provide a public and/or charitable welfare service may be in some or all of their functions, for example, schools run by the RNIB for the blind, but not all such bodies; for example, the RSPCA is not;[65]

- the BBC and Channel 4, which are publicly funded broadcasters, but not ITV or Five, which are privately funded, although the Independent Television Commission which regulates them would be a public authority;[66]

- utilities which have a statutory responsibility for the infrastructure of providing electricity, gas, water, sewerage, etc., but not every company which delivers utility services, so the National Grid would be but a commercial supplier of electricity would not;[67]

- bodies which do not have statutory foundations but which perform public functions in regulating certain industries or services, especially where the function is one which the state would be likely to have to perform if there were no private body to do it – examples include the Press Complaints Commission, the Advertising Standards Authority and the British Board of Film Classification – but not, for example, sports regulatory bodies such as the jockey club;[68]

- even the provision of retail services may be a public function if there is a public element, such as providing a farmers' market on public land, if connected with a local authority function;[69] but, on the other hand, the provision of a shopping mall by a private company will not usually be a public function, whatever the scale or extent of usage of the property is.[70]

Thus, as can be seen from this discussion, there will be a wide range of bodies which either are always public authorities, or which could be performing public functions at least some of the time. On the other hand, as *Aston Cantlow* makes clear, not all bodies which might appear to be part of a local or national administration which affects the public will be a

---

[63] *Poplar Housing Association Ltd* v *Donoghue* [2001] 3 WLR 183; *R (Heather)* v *Leonard Cheshire Foundation* [2002] EWCA Civ 366, [2002] 2 All ER 936; *R (Weaver)* v *London & Quadrant Housing Trust* [2008] EWHC 1377 (Admin), Times, 8.7.08.

[64] *Ali* v *Lord Grey School* [2006] UKHL 14, [2006] 2 WLR 690; *R (Begum)* v *Denbigh High School* [2006] UKHL 15, [2007] 1 AC 100; see below, p. 281 (Article 9).

[65] *RSPCA* v *Attorney General* [2002] 1 WLR 448, considered below, p. 320 (Article 11).

[66] In *R (ProLife)* v *BBC* [2003] UKHL 23, [2004] 1 AC 185, the BBC accepted that it was a public authority for the purposes of a challenge to a decision not to show a party political broadcast: see above, p. 57, and below, p. 363, for discussion of the case.

[67] *James* v *London Electricity plc* [2004] EWHC 3226 (QB), LTL 11.11.05.

[68] *R (Mullins)* v *Appeal Board of the Jockey Club* [2005] EWHC 2197 (Admin), [2006] ACD 2.

[69] *R (Beer)* v *Hampshire Farmers Market Ltd* [2003] EWCA Civ 1056, [2004] 1 WLR 233, where this used to be a council function and was non-profit making (so decisions had to comply with Article 6).

[70] *Appleby* v *UK* (2003) 37 EHRR 38: no breach of Article 10 by a private company which restricted campaigners from leafleting at a shopping mall owned by it.

public authority or performing public functions. What is important is that the scope of the Act is not unnecessarily restricted by too narrow an interpretation of 'public authority' or 'public function', especially nowadays when so many governmental functions are contracted out to agencies or private companies. The fact that a function has been contracted out should not allow the state to evade responsibility for ensuring the protection of the Convention rights, even if the initial burden has to fall on the body which has contracted out the function. If that extends the scope of hybrid authorities, so be it: any entity which has taken on a contract for performing a governmental function is free not to do so if it does not wish to be burdened with the protection of basic rights in the performance of its business.

THE COURT AS A PUBLIC AUTHORITY: HORIZONTAL EFFECT

There is another aspect to the application of the Act to public authorities, because the courts are also public authorities, as are other tribunals which decide disputes, such as an employment tribunal. This means that they have to apply the Act in reaching their decisions, even where neither party is a public authority. Where there is statute law which governs the situation, the obligation on the court to give effect to the Act is express, as we have seen. But much of the law applied by the courts is not to be found in Acts of Parliament, but in case law, the previous decisions of the courts over the years – in some cases, centuries – based on the doctrine of precedent, which we introduced above. As a result of the courts being public authorities, this case law which has built up must be applied, where necessary, to give effect to the Convention rights. Whilst many areas of law are not likely to be significantly affected by this, there are some important areas where changes have already been made, even though the law being discussed is not contained in an Act of Parliament, and so was not directly altered by the Human Rights Act, as we will see in our discussion later of individual Convention rights. This means that, in practice, there will be many areas where the standards applied to public authorities directly, and to private persons via the application of the Act by the courts, are the same and in both cases altered where necessary to ensure compliance with the Act.

> Perhaps the best example, so far, is the law on personal privacy. As we will see in our discussion of Article 8,[71] the general law on privacy before the Act did not provide much protection for individuals from the intrusion of others, and especially the press. The courts have had to apply Article 8 and the standards provided for by the cases decided by the European Court, so the protection provided by the law has been expanded. Thus the courts have used their obligation as a public authority to 'give effect' to the Convention rights to ensure that individuals' rights of privacy are protected, even where the person or company against whom the complaint of invasion of privacy is being made is not itself a public authority.

---

[71] Discussed in more detail below, Chapter 14, p. 251 onwards.

What is crucial is how they have done this: there has been no new legal cause of action created to protect privacy.[72] What the courts have done is to expand an existing cause of action, breach of confidence, which traditionally protected relatively limited categories of private information, to cover new areas, such as private information or photographs published in newspapers. In the first leading case on this, *Douglas v Hello!*, Lord Justice Sedley considered that in this area at least the courts were obliged to apply the Convention rights as between the parties to the case.[73] This approach was approved by the House of Lords in *Campbell v MGN*,[74] and by the Court of Appeal when *Douglas v Hello!*[75] came back on a further appeal. The result is that the common law remedy has been expanded to 'give effect' to the Act, whilst at the same time allowing the courts to balance privacy against freedom of expression (Article 10). In *Campbell* in particular, the House of Lords rather sidestepped the question of whether the Act itself has effect between individuals: but they did confirm the principle that, in the words of Lord Bingham, 'the values underlying Articles 8 and 10 are not confined to disputes between individuals and public authorities' – a principle presumably not limited to these particular Articles.

This process of enforcing the Act between individuals is sometimes referred to as giving the Act, and the Convention rights, **horizontal effect**, a phrase which refers to a metaphor that all citizens are on the same level as each other in the eyes of the law; as opposed to applying rights as between the citizen and the state, referred to as giving them **vertical** effect, since the state is metaphorically considered to be 'above' the citizen. The Act does not have horizontal effect in the truest sense – it cannot create a new private right of action between individual citizens, since only a public authority can be directly sued for breach of a Convention right. But the obligation on the courts has a more or less equivalent effect, since the courts have to ensure that their decisions give full effect to the Convention rights. Thus, although the courts do not have to create new causes of action to give effect to Convention rights, they may well have to adapt existing causes of action to this purpose, as happened with Article 8 and the action for breach of confidence. As Lord Bingham put it in the case of *Van Colle*,[76] where the House of Lords was considering the private law action for negligence and Article 2 rights that the state should prevent a death:[77]

> The existence of a Convention right cannot call for instant manufacture of a corresponding common law right where none exists: see *Wainwright v Home Office*.[78] On the other hand, one would ordinarily be surprised if conduct which violated a fundamental right or freedom of the individual did not find a reflection in a body of law ordinarily as sensitive to human needs as the common law, and it is demonstrable that the common law in some areas has evolved in a direction signalled by the Convention [. . .] Where a common law duty covers the same ground as a Convention right, it should, so far as practicable, develop in harmony with it.

---

[72] *Wainwright v Home Office* [2003] UKHL 53, [2003] 3 WLR 1137, where the Home Office could not be directly liable as a public authority because the Act was not yet in force.

[73] [2001] 2 WLR 992 at 1027, paragraph 133.

[74] *Campbell v Mirror Group Newspapers Ltd* [2004] UKHL 22, [2004] 2 AC 457.

[75] *Douglas v Hello! Ltd (No. 2)* [2005] EWCA Civ 595, [2005] 4 All ER 128.

[76] [2008] UKHL 50, [2008] 3 WLR 593.

[77] [2008] 3 WLR 593 at 615.

[78] [2004] 2 AC 406, where the House of Lords confirmed that the Act has not led to the creation of new private law causes of action; see below p. 258.

We will see other examples through the book of where the courts apply the Convention rights in actions between two private individuals. Although not as common as direct actions against public authorities for breach of the Act, or actions where a statute is being interpreted to give effect to the Act, this is another important respect in which the Act has the potential to have far-reaching consequences for our law, to ensure that all citizens respect each other's basic rights.

PARLIAMENTARY PRIVILEGE

Section 6   (2) Subsection (1) does not apply to an act if –

  (a) as the result of one or more provisions of primary legislation, the authority could not have acted differently; or

  (b) in the case of one or more provisions of, or made under, primary legislation which cannot be read or given effect in a way which is compatible with the Convention rights, the authority was acting so as to give effect to or enforce those provisions.

  (3) In this section 'public authority' ... does not include either House of Parliament or a person exercising functions in connection with proceedings in Parliament.

  (4) In subsection (3) 'Parliament' does not include the House of Lords in its judicial capacity.[79]

  [. . .]

  (6) 'An act' includes a failure to act but does not include a failure to –

  (a) introduce in, or lay before, Parliament a proposal for legislation; or

  (b) make any primary legislation or remedial order.

Section 6 has several provisions which tie in with the limitations we noted in the discussion of section 3, that the courts have no power to strike down or fail to enforce Acts of Parliament. By section 6(2), a public authority which implements legislation which is incompatible with the Convention is not acting unlawfully, so long as 'it could not have acted differently' – that is, it will have to show that the statute being implemented cannot be put into effect in a way which does not breach the Convention. This argument will fail if the statute can be read in more than one way, or if the court interprets the statute by reading words into it, as discussed above.

This is expanded by section 6(2)(b), which refers not to the act of complying with the legislation itself, but using other powers to enforce it. An example would be prosecuting someone for an offence – the power to bring the prosecution is not provided by the statute in issue, but it is an action to enforce that statute and so is covered by section 6(2)(b).

---

[79] This subsection will be repealed by Schedule 18 of the Constitutional Reform Act 2005 when the judicial functions of the House of Lords are transferred to the new Supreme Court, which is not part of the legislature.

Another example is found in the case of *Hooper*,[80] where the House of Lords made clear that the section was a defence to a claim against a Secretary of State who did not pay out widow's allowance to widowers, where Parliament had provided for the one but not the other. Even though this was discriminatory, in breach of Article 14, and even though he could have used common law powers to make payments, this would have involved the Secretary of State acting in a way which was not giving effect to the statute. As Lord Hope put it:

> In this way it enables the primary legislation to remain effective in the way Parliament intended. If the defence was not there the authority would have no alternative but to exercise its discretion in a way that was compatible with the Convention rights. The power would become a duty to act compatibly with the Convention, even if to do so was plainly in conflict with the intention of Parliament.[81]

This applies equally to the courts: even where exercising judicial discretion to enforce an order would contravene a Convention right, it is not a breach of the Act if doing so is required to give effect to primary legislation.[82]

Section 6 also prevents proceedings in Parliament being criticised by or made the subject of legal action in the courts. This again is in line with our existing constitutional position, known as Parliamentary privilege, which states that proceedings in Parliament cannot be made the subject of a court action, because the courts have no jurisdiction over Parliament – instead Parliament regulates its own affairs. So, for example, a Member of Parliament speaking in a debate in the House of Commons cannot be sued for slander for anything they say which may defame some person, although they may be disciplined by the House if that was appropriate. By section 6(3), the Member of Parliament could not be sued for a breach of the Convention rights if what they say or do or propose as legislation should infringe someone's rights, nor can Parliament itself be sued for implementing legislation which infringes Convention rights, whether that is known at the time or not. Not only can Members of Parliament (in either House) not be sued for proposing legislation, but also, by section 6(6), a Member of Parliament cannot be sued for failing to propose legislation, for example to correct a law which infringes a person's rights. You should note, though, that the House of Lords, when sitting as a court, is excluded from this: this is because its functions are not legislative but judicial, and the judiciary (the courts) are included in the scope of the Act.[83]

QUESTIONS

1 Do you agree with the reasons for not making the decisions of the European Court binding on our courts? Do you agree with the consequences? How far do you think our courts should be limited by European Court decisions?

---

[80] *R (Hooper)* v *Secretary of State for Work and Pensions* [2005] UKHL 29, [2005] 1 WLR 1681, discussed further below, p. 125.

[81] This defence was also held to apply in *Aston Cantlow*, considered above, p. 78.

[82] *Togher* v *Revenue & Customs Prosecution Office* [2007] EWCA Civ 686, [2008] QB 476, where the breach was of Article 7 in imposing a greater penalty than was in force at the date of the offence; see also below p. 242.

[83] This exception will no longer be required when the Constitutional Reform Act comes into effect and section 6(4) will be repealed at that stage.

2 Consider the definition of public authorities: can you think of further examples of bodies that are public or private, or which may be either depending on the function they are performing? Do you think the scope of 'public authorities' should be broader or narrower, and if so why? Do you agree with the way the courts have approached this issue?

3 Do you think it is just that the Act does not create a right for individuals to sue each other for breaches of Convention rights? Is your answer affected by the role of the courts as a public authority? Do you think that this role is an appropriate one?

The scheme of the Human Rights Act 1998

The Royal Courts of Justice in the Strand, London, home of the Court of Appeal and the Central Registry of the High Court.

Source: Courtesy of the authors

6 Remedies under the Human Rights Act

Money is coined liberty, and so it is ten times dearer to a man who is deprived of freedom. If money is jingling in his pocket, he is half consoled, even though he cannot spend it. (Fedor Dostoevsky, *House of the Dead*, 1862)

In this chapter we shall be considering what remedies are available to a person who considers that their rights have been infringed. We will not be covering the detail of the procedures for bringing an action, but will be considering the specific requirements of the Human Rights Act and other relevant provisions which affect who can bring such a claim, how they go about it and what remedies are available if a Convention right has been infringed.

WHO CAN COMPLAIN: 'VICTIMS'

Section 7 (1) A person who claims that a public authority has acted (or proposes to act) in a way which is made unlawful by section 6(1) may –

    (a) bring proceedings against the authority under this Act in the appropriate court or tribunal, or

    (b) rely on the Convention right or rights concerned in any legal proceedings, but only if he is (or would be) a victim of the unlawful act.

    [. . .]

(3) If the proceedings are brought on an application for judicial review, the applicant is to be taken to have a sufficient interest in relation to the unlawful act only if he is, or would be, a victim of that act.

    [. . .]

(7) For the purposes of this section, a person is a victim of an unlawful act only if he would be a victim for the purposes of Article 34 of the Convention if proceedings were brought in the European Court of Human Rights in respect of that act.

Article 34	The court may receive applications from any person, non-governmental organisation or group of individuals claiming to be the victim of a violation by one of the High Contracting Parties of the rights set forth in the Convention or the Protocols thereto. The High Contracting Parties undertake not to hinder in any way the effective exercise of this right.

Anyone who claims that a public authority has acted or proposes to act in a way which is incompatible with Convention rights can bring proceedings against that authority, so long as they are a 'victim' within the meaning of section 7(7); this is the effect of section 7(1)(a). Alternatively, anyone may rely on Convention rights in any legal proceedings brought by others: for example, as part of a defence to criminal or civil proceedings (section 7(1)(b)). The relevance of being a person who *would be* a victim is either if someone wants to prevent a threatened Convention right infringement from taking place or who is defending a claim, where a breach of a Convention right would occur if the claim, or prosecution, were successful. Section 7(3) ensures that the test regarding who can bring judicial review proceedings[1] is the same as for other proceedings.[2]

A **victim** is defined by reference to Article 34 of the Convention, which is the definition used by the European Court. The Convention and the Act should therefore be consistent in their effect. Article 34 in turn grants a remedy to 'any person, non-governmental organisation or group of individuals claiming to be the victim of a violation by one of the High Contracting Parties' of the Convention rights. In the context of United Kingdom law, this would include any person, non-governmental organisation or group of individuals who claimed that their Convention rights had been infringed by a public authority. However, a governmental body cannot be a 'victim' under Article 34, so will not be able to sue under the Act either.[3] That should not apply to a body which has some public functions, but is not always a public authority, which should be able to sue under the Act.

Article 34 has been discussed by the European Court in a number of cases which have clarified how it should be applied. In particular there has to have been an *actual* or *threatened* violation.[4] It is not enough for a person to allege that a particular statute or law could in theory be used to infringe his or her rights: what is complained of has to be something which has happened, or something which is likely to happen. The 'victim' could also be a family member of, or otherwise closely connected to, the person whose rights had been infringed. For example, if the complaint relates to the death of a person, a family member may have the right to bring a claim, but this will probably be limited to enforcing the duty for there to be an investigation into the death, rather than a claim for compensation.[5]

---

[1] Introduced at p. 44, above.

[2] Section 7(4) is the equivalent provision for Scotland.

[3] For example, see *Frame* v *Grampian University Hospitals NHS Trust* (2004) Times 2.3.04: NHS trust cannot be a 'victim' as defined in Article 34, since it is a governmental body and engages state responsibility; and see *Aston Cantlow* v *Wallbank* [2003] UKHL 37, [2004] 1 AC 546, e.g. per Lord Nicholls at paras 8–11.

[4] This applies to a claim for a declaration of incompatibility as well as to a claim for compensation: *Taylor* v *Lancashire County Council* [2005] EWCA Civ 284, [2005] 1 WLR 2668.

[5] A view expressed by the House of Lords in a case brought by the mother of a person who died in the care of a residential home, and in that case the duty to investigate was complied with: *Savage* v *South Essex Partnership NHS Trust* [2008] UKHL 74, [2009] 2 WLR 115.

Victims can be companies, because a company is a separate legal entity from its owners: it has legal personality. Likewise, associations or groups can bring a claim, as long as it is that group's collective interest which is affected: a trade union could not claim to be a victim because one of its members' rights are infringed, only if it is the rights of the trade union itself which have been infringed.[6] This does not prevent an interest group, such as a trade union, charity or campaigning organisation, from supporting a complainant, either with help bringing the claim, with funding or the provision of legal representation, or by applying to appear in its own right to assist the court with the issues before it, particularly if the decision will be one which decides a new or important point.

WHAT CAN THE COURT DO?

Section 7   (1) A person who claims that a public authority has acted (or proposes to act) in a way which is made unlawful by section 6(1) may –

(a) bring proceedings against the authority under this Act in the appropriate court or tribunal, or

(b) rely on the Convention right or rights concerned in any legal proceedings [. . .]

(6) In subsection (1)(b) 'legal proceedings' includes –

(a) proceedings brought by or at the instigation of a public authority; and

(b) an appeal against the decision of a court or tribunal.

Once it has been established that a person has the right to bring a complaint before the courts because they are a victim of a breach of their Convention rights, they can do so in two ways. They can bring their own legal action under section 7(1)(a), or they can rely on their Convention rights as a defence in any legal proceedings under section 7(1)(b). By section 7(6), relying on a Convention right in legal proceedings includes relying on that right as a defence to an action brought by a public authority, which will include a criminal prosecution, or in an appeal from the decision of a court or tribunal.

If the claim that a right has been infringed is established, there are then a number of ways in which the courts can deal with the matter to ensure that a proper remedy is granted. The starting point for this is section 8, which specifies that the court may grant such relief as it considers 'just and appropriate'. The courts are therefore given a very broad discretion.

The courts have a number of remedies or forms of relief which they can grant and all of these will be available, where appropriate, in cases of human rights infringements. In particular, the court can:

■ order the payment of damages, which is the term for compensation for a legal wrong, in this case the infringement of the Convention right;

---

[6] As, for example, the rights of the rail-workers' union ASLEF were breached in the case of *ASLEF* v *UK* (2007) 45 EHRR 34, discussed below p. 322.

- grant an injunction, which is an order to prevent an ongoing or threatened infringement;

- allow the Convention rights to provide a defence to a claim or a criminal prosecution;

- refuse to allow a party to rely on evidence obtained in breach of a Convention right;

- order that a governmental decision or subordinate legislation which infringes a person's rights is invalid and not to be relied on; or

- make a declaration of incompatibility.

We have already introduced the last two remedies, judicial review and declarations of incompatibility. Judicial review will usually result in an order that a decision be quashed, meaning that it has to be made again, although there are other orders open to a court: for example, an order prohibiting a person or body from taking a particular course of action. Declarations of incompatibility are the new remedy provided by section 4 of the Act where a statute is incompatible with a Convention right, and cannot be interpreted in a way which makes it compatible. The Act does not allow the court to refuse to enforce the incompatible statute, but the court can then make a declaration of incompatibility, which will indicate to Parliament that there is a potential injustice to be corrected and will allow the Parliamentary procedure for a remedial order to be implemented.[7]

Allowing a Convention right to be used as a defence is a straightforward idea. In a criminal case, this could mean an argument that the criminal charge that is being prosecuted is in breach of the Convention for some reason (for example, if the crime was being applied retrospectively in breach of Article 7). In a civil case, this would mean that what was being suggested was that the party bringing a claim was not entitled to a remedy because this would infringe the defendant's rights. In each case, the use of the Convention as a defence will depend on the substance of the law which is being argued. There are no special rules about using Convention rights in this way which are distinct from raising any other legal argument in the course of a trial.

The courts have a well-established discretion to refuse to admit evidence which has been obtained wrongfully, and this will include refusing to admit evidence obtained in breach of a Convention right. This will allow the courts, for example, to decide that the prosecution cannot rely on evidence which was obtained by infringing the defendant's right to privacy, where evidence was obtained without the proper authorisation or statutory authority. This can also apply to evidence being relied on in a civil case: for example, in a personal injury action where the defence wished to rely on video surveillance evidence which invaded someone's privacy.[8]

The most important remedies, though, will be those available where the person complaining of an infringement is bringing their own legal action, which will be for **damages**, which is monetary compensation, or an **injunction**, an order to prevent a threatened or ongoing breach. For a diagrammatic summary of the options, see Figure 6.1.

---

[7] Both of these are discussed in more detail above, p. 73.

[8] We discuss the exclusion of evidence further in the context of Article 6, below, p. 224.

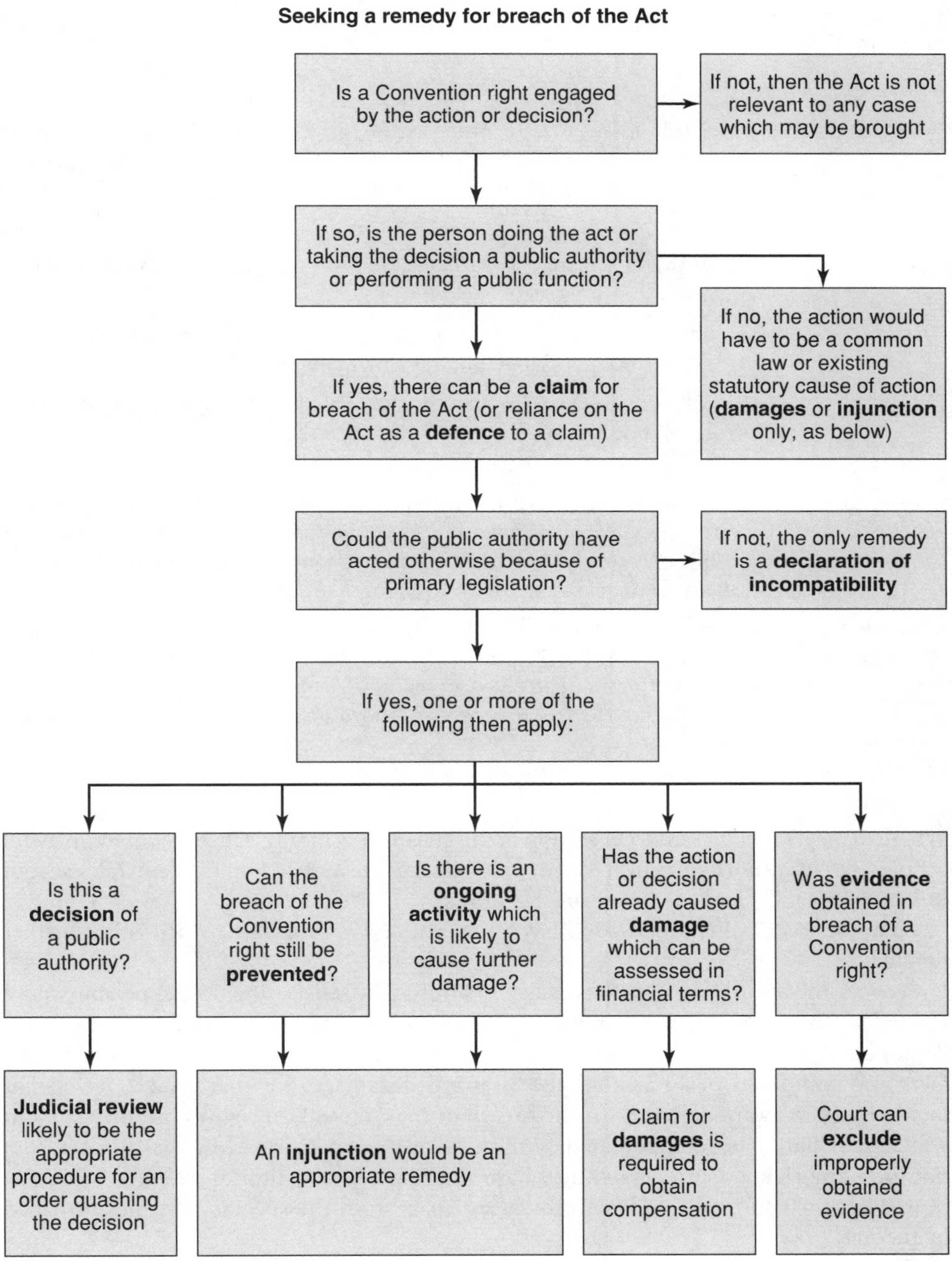

Seeking a remedy for breach of the Act

Figure 6.1 Chart illustrating remedies available in respect of the Act

■ DAMAGES

Section 8 (1) In relation to any act (or proposed act) of a public authority which the court finds is (or would be) unlawful, it may grant such relief or remedy, or make such order, within its powers as it considers just and appropriate. [. . .]

(3) No award of damages is to be made unless, taking account of all the circumstances of the case, including –

(a) any other relief or remedy granted, or order made, in relation to the act in question (by that or any other court), and

(b) the consequences of any decision (of that or any other court) in respect of that act, the court is satisfied that the award is necessary to afford just satisfaction to the person in whose favour it is made.

(4) In determining (a) whether to award damages, or (b) the amount of an award, the court must take into account the principles applied by the European Court of Human Rights in relation to the award of compensation under Article 41 of the Convention.

Article 41 If the [European] court finds that there has been a violation of the Convention or the Protocols thereto, and if the internal law of the High Contracting Party concerned allows only partial reparation to be made, the court shall, if necessary, afford just satisfaction to the injured party.

Where damages are referred to in section 8, this means specifically damages for an unlawful act of a public authority (section 8(6)). Such damages are assessed on the principles set out in section 8(1), (3) and (4). These are as follows.

First, the award of compensation has to be 'just and appropriate', which is not further defined.

Second, the award has to be 'necessary to afford just satisfaction' to the person whose rights have been infringed, bearing in mind any other remedies granted to that person. So, for example, if a person complains of a breach of a Convention right, but on the same facts also complains of an assault, and is awarded damages for that assault, it will not be necessary to award damages for the breach of the Convention right, since the claimant will already have been compensated. Section 11 of the Act makes clear that the Act does not limit any rights that a person may have to bring a legal action or claim or bring any proceedings which they could make or bring apart from the specific remedies provided by the Act.

Third, the court must also bear in mind the consequences of deciding to grant any remedy in respect of the infringement. This is because the courts have to act in a way which is consistent – this is a fundamental requirement of justice and the rule of law, that like cases are treated alike, that if one person is compensated for a particular complaint, so will another who has the same complaint. Therefore, if the courts create a new remedy in a particular case by awarding damages for a particular infringement, any other infringement of the same sort will attract the same remedy, and that might have consequences which the court has to take into account before making the award in the first place. For example, it might be feared that allowing compensation in a particular case will lead to a flood of other cases, although such fears usually turn out to be misplaced.

Finally, the court must bear in mind the principles applied by the European Court in relation to the award of compensation under Article 41 of the Convention. Of course, the courts are already obliged to apply European Court law by section 2 of the Act, but the reference here should specifically ensure that compensation is likely to be awarded by our courts to the same extent as by the European Court. This will help to prevent cases having to go to the European Court: there would be a breach of the Convention if a national court could not award an adequate remedy, where a Convention right is infringed. The principles developed by the European Court in exercising its power to award compensation under Article 41 therefore have to be considered by the court in deciding whether an award would be just and appropriate.

The basic principle applied by the European Court in awarding damages is that the injured party should be restored to the position they should have been in if the breach of the Convention had not taken place. This is the same basic principle which the United Kingdom courts already apply to claims concerning a wrong done by one person to another.

The European Court has not developed overall guidelines or principles as to how much will be awarded, but prefers to approach decisions on damages on a case by case basis. In some areas, therefore, there are inconsistencies between different cases. To this extent, there are limits on how much use the European cases will be in this area, since our courts will have to work out more definite principles for dealing with questions of quantifying losses.

Some principles do emerge from the European Court cases. In particular, it is clear that in many cases the fact that the court has found a violation of the Convention may be a sufficient remedy to provide 'just satisfaction'. This may be particularly so if the violation is not particularly serious or if it is not clear that it has caused any loss or damage of any sort, or if a remedy has been or can be provided in some other way, such as by a retrial or a pardon. This may also be appropriate if the conduct of the person bringing the claim is not very meritorious: for example, if there is a successful claim of a breach of the right to a fair trial in a criminal matter, but that does not affect the fact that the person would have been convicted anyway, it may not be just to award them monetary compensation. An example is the case of *McCann*,[9] which concerned the circumstances under which three suspected IRA terrorists were shot in Gibraltar. Although the European Court decided that there was a breach of Article 2, no compensation was awarded, since the Court was satisfied that the persons shot were planning a terrorist attack, so compensation would have been inappropriate.

This may particularly apply to cases brought under Articles 5 and 6, where there is a breach of someone's rights when they were arrested or tried, but where there is no challenge to their conviction for the crime for which they were arrested and tried. In such cases, unless the infringement is particularly serious, it may be considered that they have a sufficient remedy in the finding that their rights were infringed. This applies in our courts as well.

---

[9] *McCann* v *UK* (1996) 21 EHRR 97, considered below, p. 147.

The case of *Greenfield*[10] concerned a claim by a prisoner that there was a breach of Article 6 in the way that a breach of the prison rules was handled – by a deputy controller who refused a request for legal representation for the prisoner. Following the European Court decision in *Ezeh*,[11] the Home Secretary conceded that there were breaches of Article 6, in that the deputy controller was not an independent and impartial tribunal and that the prisoner should have been allowed legal representation.

The House of Lords held that the fact that this concession had been publicly made and resulted in a finding in the prisoner's favour was a sufficient remedy and provided just satisfaction without the need for an award of damages. Although the proceedings had breached Article 6, they had otherwise been conducted perfectly fairly. The Lords considered the European Court cases, and expressed the view that such a result would commonly be the case in claims of a breach of Article 6, unless it could be shown that the applicant had been deprived of a real chance of a better outcome; even then, any award in that respect, or for anxiety and frustration, would be modest.

The same applied to an Article 5 claim in the case of *IH*,[12] where there was held to be a breach of Article 5, but no damages were awarded because, although there had been a wrongful delay in access to a review of detention, the detention itself had not been unlawful, and there had now been a public acknowledgement of the violation and a change in the law for the future, which were sufficient for just satisfaction.

Whilst Articles 5 and 6 are the most obvious rights where a defect in process may not lead to the result being itself unjust, this can apply to other rights, especially where it is some other right which is not taken into account. Thus, in *W* v *Westminster City Council*,[13] where it was held that there was a breach of Article 8 in the disclosure of certain confidential information, the finding and the making of an apology were sufficient remedy, as no loss had been proven. Again in *Re P*,[14] the relevant authorities had acted in breach of Article 8 in failing to consult a parent before abandoning a care plan designed to rehabilitate her with her baby, but it was held that the declaration was a sufficient remedy.

But there will be some cases where the finding itself is not sufficient for there to be just satisfaction.

This applied in the case of *N*.[15] Here a Libyan citizen seeking asylum claimed a breach of Article 3 and Article 8 in the way he was treated. He was not provided with reasonable accommodation while awaiting a decision; the decision was delayed by incompetent handling; the claim was incorrectly processed; repayment of money was demanded when it should not have been; and so on. Mr Justice Silber held that N's treatment did not breach Article 3, but did breach Article 8. He was therefore entitled to claim damages, because he

---

[10] *R (Greenfield)* v *Home Secretary* [2005] UKHL 14, [2005] 1 WLR 673.
[11] *Ezeh* v *UK* (2004) 39 EHRR 1, below, pp. 228–9.
[12] *R (IH)* v *Home Secretary* [2003] UKHL 59, [2004] 2 AC 253, considered below, p. 192.
[13] [2005] EWHC 102 (QB), [2005] 4 All ER 96.
[14] [2007] EWCA Civ 2, [2007] 1 FLR.
[15] *R (N)* v *Home Secretary* [2003] EWHC 207, [2003] HRLR 20.

had shown that the breach had caused psychiatric injury and financial loss, and just satisfaction was not provided by the finding of the breach or by steps taken by the government after the breach had taken place.[16]

It may also be that there is no need for an award of damages under the Act because there is some other legal claim which provides a sufficient right to damages or other remedy, and there is nothing which is added by a claim for damages under the Act. This was the result in the case of *Dennis*,[17] where the High Court held that the existing remedy in a claim for nuisance was a sufficient remedy – there was no need for an additional award for breach of the Act. Alternatively, in some cases, there is no claim available directly for breach of the Act because the defendant is not a public authority but damages are awarded for a common law cause of action which gives effect to a Convention right. In such a case, the relevant law is that for the particular cause of action. A good example of this is *Douglas* v *Hello! Ltd*,[18] where damages were awarded for breach of confidence, giving effect to Article 8 – there was a significant award of lost revenue to *OK!* magazine and an award for distress and disruption to the Douglases.

On the other hand, if there is no other claim, and there is a real loss, and the violation is sufficiently serious, damages may be awarded. The European Court will also take into account the conduct of the state, for example if it has behaved particularly unpleasantly. So damages have been awarded to compensate for medical expenses incurred, loss of earnings or pension rights and property which has been unlawfully expropriated. Such damages for particular pecuniary losses are referred to in our law as **special** damages, and these will therefore typically be recoverable. There is no need here to consider in great detail the way in which awards of special damages are made, since they are based on providing evidence valuing the losses which have actually been suffered. An example of special damages being awarded under the Act is *Andrews* v *Reading Borough Council*,[19] where there was a breach of Article 8 because of traffic noise due to a change in the road layout. There Mr Justice Calvert-Smith awarded £2,000 as a proportion of the cost of fitting double-glazing to Mr Andrews's property.

The European Court also awards damages for non-pecuniary losses, which is to say losses that cannot be easily assessed in terms of money, such as damages to compensate for the pain and suffering caused by an injury, for distress, injury to feelings or loss of reputation – we refer to such awards as **general** damages. The basic approach which should be adopted to such awards has been set out in *Greenfield*, discussed above, where Lord Bingham, giving the leading judgment, referred to the need to award comparable sums to those which would be awarded by the European Court. He gave three particular reasons for this approach: first, that the finding of a violation will be an important part of the remedy, even where it is not the only remedy; second, that the purpose of the Act was not to provide *better* remedies than would be available from the European Court, but *the same* remedy, but without the delay and expense of going to Strasbourg; and third, as confirmed by the words of section 8(4), that the courts should look to European Court precedents. Our courts

---

[16] For further discussion of the treatment of immigrants, see below, p. 165 and p. 264.
[17] *Dennis* v *Ministry of Defence* [2003] EWHC 793 (QB), Times 6.5.03, Buckley J, below, p. 269.
[18] *Douglas* v *Hello! Ltd (No. 2)* [2007] UKHL 21, [2008] 1 AC 1, discussed above, p. 81, and below, p. 253.
[19] [2005] EWHC 256.

should therefore 'not aim to be significantly more or less generous than the [European] Court might be expected to be' – and should compare awards to the European Court cases rather than to similar English types of award.

This approach differs from the previous leading decision, that of the Court of Appeal in *Anufrijeva*,[20] where that court had approved looking to comparable English causes of action to assess how much should be awarded. In *Anufrijeva*, however, the Court had also stressed the need for awards for general damages to be modest, and this principle was approved in *Greenfield*. *Anufrijeva* was itself about a number of cases of alleged maladministration, which is an overall term for when something has gone wrong in government administration, and, although the claims in that case were all dismissed on appeal so no actual awards were made, the Court stressed that, in such cases, the costs of supporting those in need falls on the whole of society, and, if substantial damages payments are made to some, this will impact on the resources available for others. The Court also considered cases of maladministration generally: these should usually be brought in the Administrative Court, whether for judicial review or just a damages claim; internal complaints procedures or the ombudsman should be tried first; damages claims will usually be deferred until after the hearing on liability, to reduce costs and see if they can be resolved more cheaply, and, if they have to be considered by a judge, should be done in a summary manner.

Two cases which were approved in *Anufrijeva* give some guidance as to amounts of awards, but have to be considered slightly cautiously in the light of *Greenfield*. One is *R (Bernard) v Enfield LBC*,[21] where a local authority provided grossly unsuitable housing for a disabled claimant, who was awarded £10,000 damages for breach of Article 8, by reference to maladministration awards (although the reference to other UK awards might no longer be appropriate after *Greenfield*). The second is *R (KB) v Mental Health Review Tribunal*,[22] where several persons were awarded damages for breaches of Article 5, for distress; the judge made clear that, to merit an award of damages, the frustration and distress would have to be sufficiently serious to justify an award of compensation for non-pecuniary damage; awards ranged between £750 and £4,000. A similarly modest amount for general damages was awarded in the case of *Graham*,[23] where £500 was paid to a prisoner for a breach of Article 3 where he was kept in handcuffs while he received chemotherapy treatment. The European Court will not, however, award what are known as exemplary damages, which are intended to make an example of the wrongdoer. Our courts will award them in limited categories of cases, such as where there is oppressive, arbitrary or unconstitutional action by the state, or wrongdoing calculated to make a profit.[24] These are not necessary for there to be 'just satisfaction';[25] but our courts could award exemplary damages where the claimant relied on some other cause of action which was being interpreted to give effect to a Convention right: for example, a breach of confidence which infringed Article 8 and which was calculated to make a profit.

---

[20] *Anufrijeva v Southwark LBC* [2003] EWCA Civ 1406, [2004] QB 1124; the judgment was given by Lord Woolf CJ.

[21] [2002] EWHC 2282 (Admin), [2003] UKHRR 148, Sullivan J.

[22] [2003] EWHC 193 (Admin), [2003] 3 WLR 185, Stanley Burnton J.

[23] *R (Graham) v Secretary of State for Justice* [2007] EWHC 2940 (Admin).

[24] *Rookes v Barnard* [1964] AC 1129.

[25] *R (KB) v Mental Health Review Tribunal* [2003] EWHC 193 (Admin), [2003] 3 WLR 185.

The courts also have the ability to award interest on awards of damages, which compensates a person who suffered a monetary loss for the period of time they have had to wait for compensation.[26]

In all cases, a successful party may also be awarded their costs of bringing the claim, or defending the claim if the claim was unsuccessful. The courts already have a general discretion as to costs.[27] This will allow them to make whatever award is considered appropriate. It will also allow the courts to deal with questions such as who should pay the costs of a party which intervenes, such as the Crown in a case where there is a declaration of incompatibility.

PROVING THE CLAIM

In any case where damages are claimed under the Act, the burden of satisfying the court that there has been an interference with a Convention right is on the person bringing the claim. Once an interference has been proven, if it is being argued that the interference is justified, the burden of satisfying the court of this is on the state. If it is demonstrated that the interference is without justification, and amounts to a breach of a Convention right, the burden is then on the claimant to prove to the court the amount of their losses for the purposes of compensation, or that some other remedy is justified. Where there is a claim for damages, it is also necessary for the claimant to satisfy the court that any losses suffered were *caused* by the infringement of rights which has been alleged.

This question of **causation** applies to any legal claim: the point is that one should only make someone who has done something wrong pay compensation for the consequences that they have *caused*. Thus damages will not be awarded for matters which would have happened anyway, or which were caused by the person bringing the case, or by someone or something else altogether. Thus it will be important to address the question of what consequences have been caused by the breach of a right. In some cases, the relevant question will be how much *worse* were matters with the breach than without it. So, for example, a delay in bringing an accused to trial may breach Article 6, but if the person is convicted and the delay has not affected the validity of that conviction, the delay may not have *caused* that person any loss beyond the consequences of their own criminal conduct. On the other hand, if the breach of Article 6 is serious, and means that there is a *real chance* that the trial could have turned out differently, then damages may be appropriate (it does not need to be shown that the outcome would *inevitably* have been different).[28] The European Court takes a reasonably strict approach to causation, and in many cases has made no monetary award because it is not satisfied that the losses were caused by the infringement; but as with its decision on the amounts of damages, its approach does vary with the facts of the case. One unusual example of causation is the case of *Wilkinson*.[29] The House of Lords held that there was in fact no discrimination in breach of Article 14 in paying an allowance to widows only

---

[26] Supreme Court Act 1981 (Senior Courts Act), section 35A and County Courts Act 1984, section 69.
[27] Primarily by section 51(3) of the Supreme Court Act 1981 for civil cases and sections 16 and 17 of the Prosecution of Offences Act 1985 for criminal cases.
[28] *R (Greenfield)* v *Home Secretary* [2005] UKHL 14, [2005] 1 WLR 673 per Lord Bingham at para 14.
[29] *R (Wilkinson)* v *Inland Revenue Commissioners* [2005] UKHL 30, [2005] 1 WLR 1718, below, p. 125.

and not widowers. But they also considered that there would have been no remedy in any event: had Parliament paid proper regard to Article 14, the consequence would have been only that it would have abolished the offending provision sooner, rather than extend it so as to make it non-discriminatory, so no loss would have been suffered.

There is also in the European Court's decisions a limited scope for **waiver** of a right: that is, a situation where a person has agreed that they will not rely on a Convention right. However, this will only apply where there is the clearest indication that a right is being waived, so that the waiver is unequivocal, and where the waiver does not run counter to an important public interest.

> In the Scottish case of *Millar*,[30] the Privy Council had to consider a situation where it was claimed that four defendants had waived their rights to rely on Article 6. They were all tried before temporary sheriffs; but it had since been decided that the use of temporary sheriffs infringed Article 6.[31] However, the Privy Council considered that the fact that the accused did not take a point on this at their trial was not a waiver of their rights under Article 6. The accused and their representatives were unaware of their right to challenge the sheriffs, since what was reasonably understood to be the law at the time did not suggest that there was any right to be waived. To waive a right it is necessary to know that you have a right to waive. Further, a waiver must be made in an unequivocal manner, demonstrating that there was a deliberate intention not to take a point. That would usually have to be express, and for a right to be waived by not saying anything, as was suggested here, could only be inferred where the point was obvious and well-known, so that it was clear that the failure to rely on it was a conscious choice. That could not apply here, where no one realised there was a point to be taken. The public interest in the right being considered was also relevant: the more important the right, the less likely the court is to accept that it has been waived.[32]

INJUNCTIONS

The principles for awarding an injunction will be similar to those which apply to damages. The general principle is that the courts will order an injunction where damages would not be an adequate remedy. For example, if someone threatens to invade someone else's privacy, for example because they intend to publish pictures which are intrusive, then the courts may consider that the breach of privacy would not be something which could be properly assessed in monetary terms. Other examples could be where the confidentiality of information would be irretrievably lost on publication; a breach of privacy which cannot properly be assessed in monetary terms, because it is too serious; or to stop a building which would irretrievably damage a piece of land.

---

[30] *Millar* v *Dickson* [2001] UKPC D4, [2002] 1 WLR 1615.
[31] *Starrs* v *Ruxton* [2002] UKHRR 78, considered below, p. 213.
[32] For a case where it was held that the defendant *had* made a voluntary, informed and unequivocal election not to claim his Article 6 rights to be tried by an independent and impartial tribunal and to legal assistance, see *Baines* v *Army Prosecuting Authority* [2005] EWHC 1399 (Admin), DC.

When considering whether or not to grant an injunction for a threatened or continuing breach of the Act, the courts will have to consider whether to do so will be just and proportionate in all the circumstances, including whether it will be a proportionate interference with any Convention rights which could be at stake[33] – for example, a planning injunction may protect some people's rights to property but interfere with others'; an injunction to prevent publication may protect one person's Article 8 right to privacy but interfere with another's Article 10 right to freedom of expression.

In this last situation, section 12 of the Act provides some additional procedural requirements where a court is considering whether to grant any relief which might affect the exercise of the Convention right to freedom of expression under Article 10. This will apply most obviously in cases where a party seeks an injunction to prevent publication of something which is alleged to be, for example, a breach of privacy or confidentiality.[34] In particular:

- in cases of urgency, it is possible to apply for an injunction in the absence of the person against whom it is being made. However, where section 12 applies, such an injunction is not to be granted unless the court is satisfied that all practicable steps have been taken to notify that person or that there are compelling reasons why notice should not be given (section 12(2));

- an injunction to prevent publication before there has been a trial of the issues will not be granted unless the court is satisfied that the person seeking the injunction is likely to establish that publication should not be allowed (section 12(3)); and

- for journalistic, literary or artistic material, the court must have particular regard to the extent to which the material is, or is about to be, available to the public in any event, the public interest in publication of the material, and any relevant privacy code (section 12(4)).

The application of the high standard required before an injunction should be granted, set by section 12(3), has now been considered in detail by the House of Lords in *Cream Holdings Ltd v Banerjee*.[35] Section 12 reinforces the right to freedom of expression, so the party seeking the injunction must show that a claim would have to be more likely than not to succeed at trial for an order to be made to restrain publication – this is higher than the usual test for an injunction, which would be that the person applying for it need only show a real prospect of succeeding at trial. However, their Lordships recognised that there could be particular circumstances where an order was required, such as where publication could have very serious consequences – for example, in the case of threats to persons whose identity or address was being kept secret – or where an injunction for a short period of time would preserve confidentiality until there could be a full hearing of the application.

The Court of Appeal has also confirmed that, in cases of defamation (claims of libel and slander), the general principle continues to apply that there is a presumption against preventing publication unless it is clear that there would be no defence at trial to a claim for defamation.[36]

---

[33] *South Buckinghamshire District Council* v *Porter* [2003] UKHL 26, [2003] 2 AC 558.
[34] But it also applies to commercial disputes and intellectual property: *Boehringer Ingelheim Ltd* v *Vetplus Ltd* [2007] EWCA Civ 583, [2007] FSR 29.
[35] [2004] UKHL 44, [2004] 3 WLR 9.
[36] *Greene* v *Associated Newspapers* [2004] EWCA Civ 1462, [2005] 3 WLR 281.

We will consider the question of balancing competing rights in publication, and how this relates to injunctions, further in the context of Article 10.[37]

BRINGING THE CLAIM: PROCEDURE

Section 8 (2) Damages may be awarded only by a court [or tribunal] which has power to award damages, or to order the payment of compensation, in civil proceedings.

Section 9 (1) Proceedings under section 7(1)(a) in respect of a judicial act may be brought only

(a) by exercising a right of appeal;

(b) on an application (in Scotland a petition) for judicial review; or

(c) in such other forum as may be prescribed by rules.

[. . .]

(3) In proceedings under this Act in respect of a judicial act done in good faith, damages may not be awarded otherwise than to compensate a person to the extent required by Article 5(5) of the Convention.

If someone who considers that their rights have been infringed launches a legal action, this would be an example of a civil claim, as opposed to a criminal prosecution. This is confirmed by section 8(2), that damages can only be awarded by a court which will normally make an award of that sort. The effect of this is that damages cannot be awarded by a court hearing a criminal prosecution, since criminal courts do not normally make awards of damages.

The procedure for bringing a claim under the Act for damages, an injunction or any other remedy is generally the same as for any other civil claim, although there are some special provisions contained in the various court rules which apply to civil and family cases:[38]

■ There are limitations on which judges are to hear claims under the Act: actions are to be heard by High Court judges or circuit judges or recorders (who sit in the County Courts).[39] Claims under the Act arising out of anything done in court or by a judge are to be tried only in the High Court.[40] By section 4(5) of the Act, only the High Court, Court of Appeal, House of Lords and Privy Council (and when it comes into being, the Supreme Court) may grant a declaration of incompatibility.

■ Proper notice must be given that a point under the Act is going to be raised: if a claim under the Act is to be brought it must be clearly set out when the claim is brought; cases being relied on must be provided in good time for the hearing; and if a Human Rights

---

[37] Below, pp. 307–11.

[38] The Civil Procedure Rules 1998 ('CPR') and Family Proceedings Rules 1991 ('FPR'), which are the rules referred to in sections 7(2) and 9(1)(c) of the Act.

[39] Civil cases: CPR Practice Direction 2B, paragraph 7A; Family cases: President's Direction 24.7.00 [2000] 2 FLR 429, High Court and circuit judges only.

[40] Section 7(2); CPR rule 7.11.

Act point is being relied on in an appeal it must also be clearly set out in the Notice of Appeal.[41]

- There must also be proper notice (21 days or such period as the court directs) to the government if a statute is challenged as being incompatible with the Act or if a remedy is being sought in respect of a judicial act, to allow the government to make representations in defence of the statute or act being considered, and an appropriate government representative is entitled to be joined as a party.[42] If the question of a declaration of incompatibility arises during the course of proceedings, the Crown must still be given notice that this is being considered.[43]

- In addition to the court's usual duty to give reasons for its decision and to state whether or not there has been an infringement where that is the subject of the claim before it, a court should also state expressly if it finds that there has been an infringement of the Act or Convention rights in proceedings where the court orders a release from prison in an appeal from a committal to prison for breach of a court order or contempt of court, an application for *habeas corpus*, or release of a secure accommodation order for a child.[44]

- Where the court makes a decision that the claimant's Convention rights have been infringed, but the claimant is still not satisfied with the result, the court hearing the further complaint, which will usually be an appeal court, need not rehear the case, but may accept the finding of the court which heard the original complaint that there was an infringement.[45] This enables the court hearing the matter on the further complaint not to have to insist on the original claim (and all the original evidence) being heard again.

- There is also a procedure for applying for an order to restrict disclosure of the identity of children, including a procedure for service of the application on the news media if appropriate.[46]

It should also be noted that all the usual powers of the courts to manage litigation, such as ordering disclosure of documents, statements from witnesses, written arguments, etc. will all apply as necessary. In some cases, the fact that a Convention right is at stake may alter the usual procedure: it is unusual for disclosure of documents to be ordered in a judicial review, but this may be ordered more readily when considering the substantive issue of whether a right has been infringed, and whether there is a reasonable and proportionate justification for this.[47]

---

[41] CPR Practice Direction 16, paragraph 15.1 (inclusion in statements of claim), Practice Direction 39, paragraph 8.1 (authorities to be provided 3 days before hearing), Practice Direction 52, paragraph 5.1 (Notices of Appeal raising new HRA point), Practice Direction 54, paragraph 5.3 (inclusion in statement of claim in judicial review); FPR rule 10.26(2) (inclusion in originating document), President's Direction 24.7.00 [2000] 2 FLR 429 (provision of authorities).

[42] Sections 5(1), (2) and 9(4); CPR rule 19.4A and Practice Direction 19; FPR rule 10.26(4) to (21); CPR 19 is referred to as relevant to criminal proceedings by the Consolidated Criminal Practice Direction. The appropriate government representative who is entitled to be joined will be a relevant Minister of the Crown, member of the Scottish Executive, Northern Ireland Minister or department, or the Welsh Assembly: section 5(2) and National Assembly for Wales (Transfer of Functions) (No. 2) Order 2000, SI 2000/1830.

[43] Section 5(3).

[44] CPR Practice Direction 40B, paragraph 14.4; FPR rule 10.26 (22).

[45] CPR rule 33.9.

[46] President's Direction (Family) *Applications for Reporting Restriction Orders* (18 March 2005).

[47] *Tweed* v *Parades Commission for Northern Ireland* [2006] UKHL 53, [2007] 1 AC 650.

These provisions do not apply to criminal cases, although it will still be usual for notice to be given that human rights points are going to be taken. That will allow any legal argument to be dealt with in the most efficient manner: for example, by holding a preliminary hearing to consider any human rights point that is being taken.[48] There are equivalent provisions to those noted above which provide for giving notice to the government where the Court of Appeal is being invited to make a declaration of incompatibility in a criminal appeal.[49]

Where the act being complained of is a decision of a judge in court, the procedure to be used to complain about an infringement of Convention rights will be to appeal the decision which is alleged to infringe the human rights of the party: section 9(1). This is in accordance with the way the law works generally: if a party considers that a judge has decided a case in a way which is wrong, their remedy is to appeal that decision. This is a perfectly adequate remedy since the appeal court has power to decide that the result of the case should be different so that it does not infringe the party's rights, including quashing a criminal conviction. The only circumstance where this is not a sufficient remedy is that envisaged by section 9(3), where, as a result of the decision which is being appealed, a person has been detained in prison in contravention of Article 5. In this case, the state will pay compensation for the wrongful detention (section 9(4)).

TIME LIMITS AND LIMITATION

Section 7   (5) Proceedings under subsection (1)(a) must be brought before the end of –

    (a) the period of one year beginning with the date on which the act complained of took place; or

    (b) such longer period as the court or tribunal considers equitable having regard to all the circumstances, but that is subject to any rule imposing a stricter time limit in relation to the procedure in question.

Section 22   (4) Paragraph (b) of subsection (1) of section 7 applies to proceedings brought by or at the instigation of a public authority whenever the act in question took place; but otherwise that subsection does not apply to an act taking place before the coming into force of that section.

All legal proceedings are subject to **limitation** provisions. That is, there is a time limit within which legal proceedings have to be started after the occurrence of time of the action being complained of. Limitation periods serve the purpose of ensuring that claims do not relate to matters which are so long ago that the parties involved have no proper recollection or records of them, where it would be unfair for them to have to deal with a claim. They also provide a measure of certainty and finality, so that people do not have to be concerned about claims hanging over them indefinitely; so, for example, insurance against claims for

---

[48] In particular, pursuant to the parties' duties to assist the court in efficient case management: Criminal Procedure Rules 2005, especially rules 1 and 3.3.
[49] Criminal Procedure Rules 2005, rule 65.12.

business or professional liability need not be continued indefinitely. There are exceptions where the matter which is being complained of cannot be discovered at the time and only comes to light later. Limitation periods are acceptable under the Convention for these reasons, and their existence is not a breach of the Article 6 right to a fair trial, so long as the period of the limitation is reasonably proportionate to its purpose or it does not restrict or reduce a person's access to a court to such an extent that the very essence of the right of access to a court is impaired; in this respect, states enjoy a certain margin of appreciation.[50]

One recent case where the European Court has considered a limitation provision in English law is the case of *Pye* v *UK*.[51] English land law has a time limitation on claims to recover land known as adverse possession. This is where under certain circumstances an owner's claim to land which is occupied by another person (such as a squatter) is lost after 12 years. It was argued that this was a deprivation of property in breach of the right to property in Article 1-1. The Grand Chamber held that, although Article 1-1 was engaged, as this was a control of use of land, it was not disproportionate to put a time limit on such claims, even where the ownership of land is registered, as it is based on very long-standing rules, of which the landowner here was fully aware, and is within the state's margin of appreciation.

The Act itself contains a limitation provision. Under section 7(5), there is a one-year limitation period for claims for a breach of a human right, but with a discretion in (b) for the court to extend that period if there are good reasons for doing so. This might apply if, for example, the breach of human rights was not discovered until after the year was up. Another situation where the discretion could well be extended is where there was a continuing act or series of acts, some part of which was within the one-year period, but part of which was before it.

This was discussed by some of the House of Lords in *Somerville* v *Scottish Ministers*[52] although not decided since it was held that the Scottish Ministers were not liable for the acts in question. Where there is a continuing breach, Lord Hope's view[53] was that time runs from when the act ceases, and, so long as the proceedings are in time, damages can be awarded for the whole period of the continuing act, including any period more than a year before the proceedings started; Lord Scott and Lord Mance[54] took the view that the act in question should be treated as a series of acts, and the claim could be from the first act within the period of one year, but that the court would be likely to exercise discretion to extend time given the continuing nature of the complaint. This latter view would be more usual for a civil claim for damages: if there is a continuing act, the court can act to order it to cease, regardless of when it started, but can only award damages for whatever the limitation period is prior to the issue of proceedings (subject to any discretion to extend time).

---

[50] See, for example, *Stubbings* v *UK* (1997) 23 EHRR 213; *Perez de Rada Cavanilles* v *Spain* (2000) 29 EHRR 109.
[51] (2008) 46 EHRR 45, considered further above, p. 51.
[52] *Somerville* v *Scottish Ministers* [2007] UKHL 44, (2007) 1 WLR 2734.
[53] At para 51.
[54] At paras 81 and 197 respectively; Lord Rodger and Lord Walker expressed no view.

The proviso at the end of the section means that if the remedy being sought has in general a shorter time limit then that shorter time limit applies – for example, judicial review claims usually have to be brought within three months of the making of the decision which is being challenged.[55]

Note, however, that this limitation period does not apply to reliance on the Act or the Convention rights in legal proceedings which are not directly for a claim under the Act under section 7(1)(a). So if the claim that is being brought is a claim, for example, for trespass or assault, where the Act is relied on but not as the main cause of action, the usual limitation period for that type of claim will apply and not the one-year limitation period for a claim under the Act.

It is also necessary that the claim was in respect of something which happened after the Act came into force on 2 October 2000. The only limited exception to this is that section 22(4) of the Act applied section 7(1)(b) to proceedings begun before that date. That is, it allowed the Act to be used as a defence to proceedings brought by, or at the instigation of, a public authority, whenever the act or omission in question took place, even where the breach of those rights occurred before the Act came into force. This is stated to include appeals from courts and tribunals.

However, the scope of this section has been interpreted restrictively by the decisions of the House of Lords in *Lambert*[56] and *Kansal.*[57] In those cases, the House of Lords held that this section does not apply to an appeal from a conviction where the trial occurred before the Act came into force, if what is being said is that the court in reaching its decision at that trial failed to give effect to the Convention, on the basis that the Act cannot retrospectively change the application of primary legislation or make unlawful something which was done in accordance with the law as it was. However, the result would appear to be that the Act could not be used to *bring* an appeal in respect of a trial which took place before 2 October 2000, only to *defend* an appeal by a public authority from a trial before that date. This distinction is not a happy one, as recognised by the House in *Kansal*, where a majority of the judges considered that the decision in *Lambert* was not correct but the House declined to reverse it.[58] In practice, the question of the application of the Act to proceedings begun prior to October 2000 will now be of limited importance.

Thus, with the limited exception created by section 22(4), it is clear that no action can be brought for a claim under the Act based on facts which occurred prior to 2 October 2000,[59] whether an action for damages under section 6 of the Act, or for a declaration of incompatibility,[60] or for some other remedy, such as in the case of *Hurst*,[61] where the remedy sought was the resumption of an inquest, which was refused because the death occurred prior to 2 October 2000.

---

[55] Civil Procedure Rules, rule 54.5.
[56] *R v Lambert* [2001] UKHL 37, [2001] 3 WLR 206.
[57] *R v Kansal* [2001] UKHL 62, [2001] 3 WLR 1562.
[58] *Kansal* later went to the European Court where it was held that there had been a breach of Article 6: *Kansal v UK* (2004) 39 EHRR 31.
[59] *Re McKerr* [2004] UKHL 12, [2004] 1 WLR 807.
[60] *Wilson v First County Trust Limited (No. 2)* [2003] UKHL 40, [2003] 3 WLR 568, discussed also below, p. 340.
[61] *Commissioner of Police for the Metropolis v Christine Hurst* [2007] UKHL 13, [2007] 2 WLR 726.

■ WHERE DOES THE ACT APPLY: JURISDICTION

Clearly the Act applies to the United Kingdom. But can it apply elsewhere?

The territorial limits of the Act were considered in the case of *Quark Fishing*.[62] Here the question was whether the government could be liable for refusing a fishing licence in South Georgia and the South Sandwich Islands, which was argued to be in breach of Article 1 of the First Protocol. The starting point is that the Act is intended to provide a remedy to the extent that the Convention applies. Whilst there were differences of opinion in the House of Lords about whether or not the Secretary of State was a public authority for these purposes in any event, it was also clear that, since the UK had not extended the First Protocol to the territory in question, there could be no remedy under domestic law, since there would be no remedy under the Convention. The Act could not make a Convention right apply to a territory to which it did not apply under the application of the Convention itself.

But there are circumstances where the Act can apply to the actions of the British state outside its own territory. In the case of *Al-Skeini*,[63] there were a number of claims relating to the actions of United Kingdom forces in Iraq in 2003–04, which were involved in military operations and then an occupation of Iraq. The House of Lords held that the European Convention was territorial, so that it normally applied only in the territory of the UK, and Iraq was not within UK territory. Thus, claims in respect of deaths which resulted from military operations were not covered by the Act. However, an exception applies to a state's agents acting outside the UK, to areas under state control such as embassies, consulates, vessels and aircraft. In one of the cases, that of Mr Mousa, an Iraqi civilian had died as a result of treatment he received after he had been arrested and while he was in the custody of British soldiers at a military prison, so his case was covered by the Convention. His case was therefore referred back for further consideration as to whether there was a proper investigation into his death so as to comply with Article 2 (it was in fact later settled for a substantial payment).[64]

However, the effect of the Act in a situation such as that in Iraq is not unlimited. In the case of Al-Jedda,[65] it was argued that the detention of an Iraqi-born British national in Iraq by British forces breached Article 5. The detention in question was authorised by United Nations Security Council Resolution 1546, which, under international law, overrode the European Convention (by Article 103 of the United Nations Charter). Their Lordships therefore held that the detention was lawful, so long as necessary for reasons of security, although subject to the detainee's rights under Article 5 not being limited any more than was necessary to comply with the needs of security.

[62] *R (Quark Fishing) v Foreign Secretary* [2005] UKHL 57, [2005] 3 WLR 837.
[63] *R (Skeini and others) v Secretary of State for Defence* [2007] UKHL 26, [2008] 1 AC 153.
[64] The Ministry of Defence paid out some £2.8 million to 10 individuals and families in July 2008.
[65] *R (Al-Jedda) v Secretary of State for Defence* [2007] UKHL 58, [2008] 1 AC 332.

6

Remedies under the Human Rights Act

Thus, the Convention, and therefore the Act, will in principle apply to the acts of British officials overseas, where there is some form of British jurisdiction, such as an embassy or during a military occupation. But it must be given the same limits as the Convention would have in international law: either if some other international legal provision means that it does not apply, or if it has not been extended to that territory.

QUESTIONS

1 Do you think the range of remedies available for breaches of Convention rights is adequate? Are there others that you think should be available?

2 What do you think about the Courts' approach to claims for damages for breaches of the Act? Do you think that it is too generous, too mean, or about right?

3 What do you think about the issue of where the Act applies to UK overseas territories or personnel? Should it apply more widely, or less widely?

Sybil and Joyce Burden are sisters who argued, unsuccessfully, that the inheritance tax regime discriminated against them because when one of them dies, the other stands to lose her home, which is different for married couples: see p. 124.

see p. 124.

Source: Matt Cardy/Getty Images

7 Introduction to the Convention rights

We should not say that human rights, or their exercise, are subject to the common good. [. . .] On the other hand, we can appropriately say that most human rights are subject to or limited by each other and by other *aspects* of the common good. (John Finnis, *Natural Law and Natural Rights 1980*)

WHAT RIGHTS ARE PROTECTED BY THE ACT?

Section 1 (1) In this Act 'the Convention rights' means the rights and fundamental freedoms set out in –

(a) Articles 2 to 12 and 14 of the Convention,

(b) Articles 1 to 3 of the First Protocol, and

(c) Article 1 of the Thirteenth Protocol,

as read with Articles 16 to 18 of the Convention.

The Convention rights brought into our law by the Act are those provided for by the following Articles of the Convention, which are set out in full in Schedule 1 to the Act:

- Article 2, the right to life;
- Article 3, freedom from torture, and inhuman or degrading treatment or punishment;
- Article 4, freedom from slavery and forced or compulsory labour;
- Article 5, the right to personal liberty;
- Article 6, the right to a fair trial;
- Article 7, freedom from retrospective criminal law;
- Article 8, the right to respect for private and family life, home and correspondence;
- Article 9, freedom of thought, conscience and religion;
- Article 10, freedom of expression;
- Article 11, freedom of peaceful assembly and association;
- Article 12, the right to marry and found a family;
- First Protocol, Article 1, protection of property;

109

- First Protocol, Article 2, right to education;

- First Protocol, Article 3, right to free elections; and

- Thirteenth Protocol, Article 1, abolition of the death penalty.

We will be discussing these rights in detail in the following chapters. In each case, we will be considering what situations it covers, whether it is absolute or can be interfered with in some circumstances, and what the addition of the Convention right adds to our existing law. In this chapter we will be discussing certain general matters which apply to all or many of the articles, as well as a number of general provisions contained within the European Convention which relate to all the rights. As well as the articles listed above, Articles 14, 16, 17 and 18 are included within the Act. We will discuss these later in this chapter: as we will see, these are all of an ancillary nature and do not create free-standing rights.

OMISSION OF ARTICLES 1 AND 13 FROM THE ACT

Article 1: Obligation to Respect Human Rights
The High Contracting Parties shall secure to everyone within their jurisdiction the rights and freedoms defined in Section I of this Convention.

Article 13: Right to an Effective Remedy
Everyone whose rights and freedoms as set forth in this Convention are violated shall have an effective remedy before a national authority notwithstanding that the violation has been committed by persons acting in an official capacity.

It was not thought necessary to include Articles 1 and 13 in the list of rights protected by the Act. In the case of Article 1, this sets out the obligation of the state to protect the Convention rights, and this is being done by the passing of the Act itself, since the Act duplicates the Convention directly and applies it to all emanations of the state ('public authorities') to which the Convention would apply. In the case of Article 13, this is the article which secures a remedy for violations of the Convention rights. It was considered by those who drafted the Act, and by the government in Parliament[1] in proposing it, that an effective remedy is provided by section 8 of the Act, which gives the courts a general ability to provide a remedy for any breach of the Convention rights. Thus it was concluded that there was no need to have a specific separate right to an effective remedy by enacting Article 13: to include Article 13 would be a duplication. This has been borne out by the way that the Courts have applied the Act: the discussion in a case such as *Greenfield*[2] is premised on the assumption that the remedy which can be obtained under the Act is the same as that which would be available from the European Court under the Convention.

---

[1] For example, by Lord Irvine, the Lord Chancellor (*Hansard* HL Vol. 583, col. 475, 18 November 1997) and the Home Secretary, Jack Straw (*Hansard* HC Vol. 312, col. 981, 20 May 1998).

[2] *R (Greenfield)* v *Home Secretary* [2005] UKHL 14, [2005] 1 WLR 673, discussed above, pp. 94–5.

THE PROTOCOLS

The basic list of rights drawn up in the original Convention in 1950 has been supplemented by a number of protocols. We will consider here those protocols which set out additional rights; there were also a number of protocols which amended the powers and procedures for bringing a complaint under the Convention, and these have all now been replaced by the Eleventh Protocol, which is incorporated into the current text of the Convention.[3] As regards the protocols which contain additional rights, states may choose whether or not they accept these, and are therefore free to decide whether or not to sign up to any particular protocol.[4] The United Kingdom signed up to the First Protocol in 1952, and it is therefore included in the Act.

The Thirteenth Protocol prohibits the death penalty for criminal offences, and replaces the Sixth Protocol, which was the same but with a limited exception for wartime. The death penalty was largely abolished in 1965,[5] and was abolished for treason and piracy in 1998.[6] The Sixth Protocol was included in the Act as a result of an amendment to the Act during its passage through Parliament in 1998. There was a free vote, which is to say that the Members of Parliament were free to vote without the political parties taking a view, and the vote was in favour of including this Protocol. As a result, it was included in the Act and the Sixth Protocol was signed by the United Kingdom in January 1999 and ratified in May 1999. The Thirteenth Protocol was ratified in October 2003, and the Act was amended in 2004 to replace the Sixth Protocol with the Thirteenth.[7]

There are some further protocols which contain substantive rights. The Fourth Protocol contains four rights:

- the prohibition of imprisonment for debt;
- freedom of movement for a state's nationals within and between countries;
- prohibition of expulsion of people from their own country and on refusing entry to a country's own citizens; and
- the prohibition of the collective expulsion of aliens (aliens here means people who are not citizens of the country doing the expelling).

The Seventh Protocol contains five rights:

- procedural safeguards in the case of expulsion of non-nationals;
- a right of appeal in criminal cases;
- a right to compensation for wrongful conviction;
- the right not to be tried or punished twice for the same offence; and
- equality of rights and responsibilities between spouses.

---

[3] The text of the Convention, incorporating the Eleventh Protocol, can be found in Appendix 2; the current court structure under the Convention is discussed above at p. 48.

[4] These additional protocols are included in Appendix 2 and a table showing which states have signed up to which protocols may be found in Appendix 3.

[5] Murder (Abolition of Death Penalty) Act 1965.

[6] Prevention of Crime and Disorder Act 1998, section 36.

[7] Human Rights Act 1998 (Amendment) Order 2004 (SI 2004/1574).

Introduction to the Convention rights

The United Kingdom has not signed up to the Fourth Protocol and the Seventh Protocol has been signed but not ratified, and so they are not included in the rights protected by the Act. The rights contained within these protocols are considered to be largely, but not entirely, consistent with the equivalent provisions in British law. However, the government has chosen not to sign up to these protocols until the inconsistencies have been removed, so they were not included in the Act. The government's White Paper, which set out its proposals for the Act, suggested that they would be kept under review, with a view to signing up to the protocols when the inconsistencies had been removed, in particular for the Seventh Protocol; during a review in 2004, the government's view was that there were still concerns about the Fourth Protocol, but that it was intended to ratify the Seventh Protocol as soon as some legislative amendments to family law have been made.[8]

So, for example, there is already in our law a right of appeal in criminal cases and a right not to be punished twice for the same offence. On the other hand, one of the concerns about signing up to the Fourth Protocol is that there are a number of categories of British citizens, which have arisen from, for example, the de-colonisation of the British Empire, or the status of people who come from the remaining Dependent Territories. Not all the people in these categories have full rights to enter the United Kingdom itself as they wish. This was one of the areas where it was therefore thought that there could well be a problem in agreeing to the Protocol, if our current law does not comply with it. Of course, even without incorporation, the protocols can still be used as standards with which our law should seek to comply, in which case our current law can be criticised if it is inconsistent with them; for example, Article 4 of the Seventh Protocol was referred to in the case of *R v Young*,[9] where it was held that the English principle against being prosecuted twice for the same offence was held to comply with the Article.[10]

Since the Act was passed, two more substantive protocols have been drawn up: the Twelfth and Thirteenth Protocols; we have discussed the Thirteenth Protocol above, which is now in effect. The Twelfth Protocol contains a general prohibition of discrimination in respect of any legal right on the ground of sex, race, colour, language, religion, political or other opinion, national or social origin, association with a national minority, property, birth or other status. This is a more extensive protection against discrimination than the existing Article 14 of the Treaty which only prohibits discrimination in respect of the Convention rights themselves. This Protocol is in force, but the United Kingdom has not signed up to it yet, because of its potentially wide range and uncertainties about how it will be applied by the European Court, in the absence (so far) of case law, and in particular that it will be read as allowing for a defence of objective and reasonable justification,[11] although this caution has been criticised by the Parliamentary Joint Committee on Human Rights.[12] There is also now a Fourteenth Protocol, which proposes procedural changes to the working of the European Court to make it operate more efficiently. This has been ratified by all members of the Council of Europe except Russia, which is thus the only state holding up the Protocol coming into effect.[13]

---

[8] Mike O'Brien MP, Home Office Minister in the debates on the Act (*Hansard* HC Vol. 312, col. 1006); 2004 Interdepartmental Review of International Human Rights Instruments.

[9] LTL 14.10.05, CA.

[10] There are now limited exceptions to this rule in Part 10 of the Criminal Justice Act 2003.

[11] See report of Inter-Departmental Review, July 2004.

[12] See e.g. 17th Report of the 2004–05 session, 23 March 2005.

[13] We have not included it in the Appendix for the moment as it will amend the existing treaty provisions rather than establish new rights.

However, although these other protocols are not included in the rights protected by the Act, the Act does specifically provide a mechanism for these or any future protocols to be added to the Act at a later date, in section 1:

Section 1 (4) The Lord Chancellor may by order make such amendments to this Act as he considers appropriate to reflect the effect, in relation to the United Kingdom, of a protocol.

(5) In subsection (4) 'protocol' means a protocol to the Convention –

(a) which the United Kingdom has ratified; or

(b) which the United Kingdom has signed with a view to ratification.

(6) No amendment may be made by an order under subsection (4) so as to come into force before the protocol concerned is in force in relation to the United Kingdom.

Thus, under this provision, by a statutory instrument put before Parliament, rights can be added to the Act to expand the list of Convention rights where the United Kingdom ratifies a protocol; and this also applies where a protocol has been signed but not ratified. The only proviso is that the protocol has to be 'in force': this means that, for example, if a protocol needs to be ratified by 10 countries before it is effective, it is not binding until this has been done. So until then, even if the United Kingdom has ratified it, it would not be in force and so could not be added to the Act. This procedure was used to add the Thirteenth Protocol to the Act.

 ## DEROGATIONS AND RESERVATIONS

Section 1 (2) Those Articles [specifying the Convention rights] are to have effect for the purposes of this Act subject to any designated derogation or reservation.

Article 57: Reservations

1 Any State may, when signing this Convention or when depositing its instrument of ratification, make a reservation in respect of any particular provision of the Convention to the extent that any law then in force in its territory is not in conformity with the provision. Reservations of a general character shall not be permitted under this article.

2 Any reservation made under this article shall contain a brief statement of the law concerned.

Article 15: Derogation in Time of Emergency

1 In time of war or other public emergency threatening the life of the nation any High Contracting Party may take measures derogating from its obligations under this Convention to the extent strictly required by the exigencies of the situation, provided that such measures are not inconsistent with its other obligations under international law.

2 No derogation from Article 2, except in respect of deaths resulting from lawful acts of war, or from Articles 3, 4 (paragraph 1) and 7 shall be made under this provision.

3 Any High Contracting Party availing itself of this right of derogation shall keep the Secretary General of the Council of Europe fully informed of the measures which it has taken and the reasons therefor. It shall also inform the Secretary General of the Council of Europe when such measures have ceased to operate and the provisions of the Convention are again being fully executed.

A **reservation** is a declaration which allows a state to agree to a treaty, such as the Convention, where there is a particular law in force in the territory of that state which is not in conformity with the provision, which the state does not wish to alter. The reservation has to be very specific, and cannot be a general exception to one of the articles: it has to be a specific point which does not substantially detract from the protection of the article. A reservation is lodged prior to ratification of the treaty, so a state cannot add a reservation later.

A **derogation** allows for limited non-compliance with the Convention in the event of war or public emergency threatening the life of the nation. However, the derogation must only be to the extent *strictly* required by the situation and must not be inconsistent with the state's other obligations under international law – so cannot permit a law which mandated actions which would amount to war crimes or crimes against humanity. If a derogation is considered necessary, a declaration must be lodged with the Secretary General of the Council of Europe, who must also be kept informed as to when the measures requiring the derogation have ceased to operate and the provisions of the Convention are again being fully executed.

There are some articles which contain rights which are so important that no derogation from them is permissible. These are the right to life contained in Article 2, except in respect of deaths resulting from lawful acts of war, freedom from torture (Article 3), freedom from slavery (Article 4(1)) and freedom from retrospective criminal penalty (Article 7), and there can be no derogation or reservation from the abolition of the death penalty in the Thirteenth Protocol.

Under the Act, the Convention rights have effect subject to any designated derogation or reservation. This means that if the United Kingdom has entered a derogation or reservation in respect of a particular statutory position, although there may appear to be an incompatibility between that statute and the Convention rights, there is no infringement of the Convention.

'Designated reservation' for the purposes of the Act is defined in section 15. This refers at present only to the reservation to Article 2 of the First Protocol which was entered into in 1952.[14] The section also allows for the possibility that the United Kingdom might enter a reservation in the future, by permitting an order to be made by the relevant government Minister[15] designating the reservation for the purposes of the Act. Since a reservation must be entered when a treaty is signed, this could only happen if, for example, a new protocol was ratified subject to a reservation.

---

[14] Discussed in the context of the right to education, p. 257; the text can be found in Appendix 1.

[15] The designation of reservations and derogations is currently the responsibility of the Lord Chancellor: Transfer of Functions (Miscellaneous) Order 2001 (SI 2001/3500).

The detail of what is meant by a designated derogation is set out in section 14, which provides that any derogation may be designated by an order by the relevant government Minister. When the Act was passed it included the derogation from Article 5(3), which was then in force. That derogation has now been withdrawn, since the law to which it relates was replaced.[16] A further derogation was then entered to Article 5(1) in relation to powers to detain non-UK nationals who were suspected terrorists who could not be tried or deported, based on the public emergency caused by the terrorist attacks on New York in September 2001.[17] However, this derogation was quashed by the House of Lords in the case of *A* v *Home Secretary*,[18] on the basis that it discriminated against non-nationals, and as such was a disproportionate response to the situation. We consider this case in detail elsewhere;[19] the relevance here is that, following the case, the derogation was withdrawn.[20] There is therefore no current derogation in place as regards any of the Convention rights. If a derogation is amended or replaced it ceases to be a designated derogation, and a new order is required to (re)designate the new or amended derogation. By section 16, all designations of derogations expire after five years, but may be extended for a further five years; this ensures that no derogation simply continues without being reconsidered periodically. Section 17 requires that the appropriate Minister must review it and report to Parliament before the designation expires, so that Parliament can make an informed decision on any proposed order to renew the designation.

LIMITATIONS ON RIGHTS: QUALIFIED RIGHTS

As well as the specific limitations we have just discussed, which just apply to one country, many of the rights set out in the Convention contain express or implied **qualifications**. This means that there are circumstances where an action which might *appear* to be an infringement of the right is *not* an infringement because the right, as properly understood, allows for exceptions. Put another way, the drafting of the Convention expressly recognises that most human rights are not absolute: there are circumstances when it is justified to limit their application, because there is a need to protect the rights of others, where there is a conflict between the rights of different people, or because there is some common interest which requires protection, using the terms 'common interest' here as a shorthand for the general rights of others. This is what we referred to in our discussion of the nature of rights as **balancing** rights, where we considered some examples of situations where there is a need to resolve a conflict between different rights.[21]

In a very large number of the cases we will be considering, there is one party asserting a right, and a state attempting to justify an interference with it. What we will be considering here is the general approach which should be taken to such a situation, applying the European Convention, and also the guidance and principles developed by the European Court.

---

[16] Human Rights Act 1998 (Amendment) Order 2001 (SI 2001/1216).
[17] Human Rights Act 1998 (Designated Derogation) Order 2001 (SI 2001/3644); Human Rights Act 1998 (Amendment No. 2) Order 2001 (SI 2001/4032).
[18] [2004] UKHL 56, [2005] 2 WLR 87.
[19] Below, p. 376.
[20] Human Rights Act 1998 (Amendment) Order 2005 (SI 2005/1071).
[21] Above, Chapter 2, p. 15.

The European Court has developed its own way of approaching all limitations on the Convention rights. The first question is whether the right is engaged at all: does it have any application to the situation? In this context, the rights themselves are construed in a broad and purposive way. Once the right is engaged, the next question is: has it been interfered with? Do the circumstances show that there is what seems to be, on its face, a breach of the right?

If the applicant can show an interference with a right, then it is for the state to show that the interference is justified, otherwise that interference will amount to an infringement of the Convention right. In justifying the interference, the state must show that one of the limitations in the second paragraph of the Article applies; these are construed narrowly, and it is for the state to prove that the circumstances fall within it. Finally, in order to justify an interference, the action must be in accordance with the law, necessary in a democratic society and proportionate to the reason for the interference.

It is very important to distinguish between cases where a right is *not engaged*, and a case where the right is *interfered with* but *not infringed* (although note that the phraseology is not used consistently in this context). Issues such as necessity and proportionality go to the justification for an interference, whether or not there is a breach, and not the right itself.

In the case of *Austin*,[22] the courts had to consider the legality of the detention of the protesters held by police within a cordon in Oxford Circus in central London during the demonstrations on May Day 2001. The House of Lords' analysis is that Article 5(1), which prevents arbitrary detention, was not engaged, because the restrictions on movement of the protesters was not sufficiently serious to amount to a deprivation of liberty. Their Lordships also considered the purpose of the measure, and held that the measures were reasonably necessary and proportionate, and that there was no infringement. But there is a contradiction here: if the right was not *engaged*, then there is no interference with it, and no need to justify that interference. The better analysis of a situation like this is that the right is *engaged*, once there is an interference with personal freedom of movement (which there was here), but there was no infringement of Article 5 because the interference was justified by the need for crowd control for the safety of others, and it was proportionate to that need.

We will consider the specific circumstances where one applies a particular qualification in the discussion of the individual articles. The purpose of this discussion is to consider this general approach.

'IN ACCORDANCE WITH THE LAW'

This is an important requirement to ensure that the rule of law is upheld: if there are to be circumstances where what would appear to be an infringement of a right is permitted, it must be one which is clearly defined and set out by the law of the country in question. This applies equally to the phrase 'in accordance with the law' in Articles 8 to 11 or the references to 'the law' or being 'prescribed by law', for example, in Articles 2, 5 and 6.

[22] *Austin v Metropolitan Police Commissioner* [2009] UKHL 5, [2009] 2 WLR 372; discussed below in the context of Article 5, p. 189.

There are two aspects to this idea. First, there must be some basis in the national law for the provision being relied on and, second, the national law must be accessible and precise. As to the first, in most cases this is present; it is uncommon for there to be a complete absence of legal basis for official action in any of the states that are parties to the Convention. It is also not common in the European Court cases that there was a breach of national law, because if there is such a breach, there is usually a remedy under the national law; and it is necessary to exhaust the local court process before seeking a remedy from the European Court. Thus if a police officer acts in breach of the law on how to arrest someone, there will be a liability for wrongful arrest without the need to rely on any breach of Article 5 which may also have been committed.

One example where it was held that there was *no* relevant law is the *Halford*[23] case. Alison Halford was the Assistant Chief Constable of Merseyside. She complained that calls which she had made from her office and home telephones were intercepted by the police in order to gather information for use against her in sex discrimination proceedings, in breach of Article 8. At the time there was an Act of Parliament in force (the Interception of Communications Act 1985) which aimed at providing a statutory framework to ensure that the interception of communications on public systems would be authorised and controlled in a manner commanding public confidence. But it did not apply to internal communications systems operated by public authorities, such as that at Merseyside Police Headquarters, and there was no other provision in domestic law to regulate interceptions of telephone calls made on such systems. Thus it could not be said that the interference in her case was 'in accordance with the law', since there was no relevant legal framework to regulate interferences with the right to respect for privacy.

The more usual contention is the second one, that the national law is uncertain or gives too wide a discretion to officials. This is described by the European Court as meaning that there must be a 'quality of law', the law must be precise and accessible. Again, these criteria will usually be fulfilled in our law: Acts of Parliament are usually reasonably clear in their meaning, and the judgments of the courts are couched in careful and precise language. Still, this is an important test. So that everyone is treated fairly, everyone is presumed to know what the law is – this is what is meant by 'ignorance of the law is no excuse'. So everyone must be able to know what the law is which applies to any given situation.

To continue with the example of tapping a telephone, consider a situation where the police wish to tap a telephone line to prevent or detect criminal activity. Clearly it would defeat that purpose if the police were obliged to inform the citizen that their telephone conversations were being monitored. As soon as the person being monitored found out about the surveillance, they would stop using the telephone for any criminal purposes. However, in general terms, everyone is entitled to know under what circumstances it is possible or likely that an order can be made permitting the police to tap their telephone; and further, they should be able to know what safeguards exist to prevent unwarranted invasions of this privacy.

[23] (1997) 24 EHRR 523.

So in the case of *Malone*,[24] the applicant was prosecuted for offences related to the dishonest handling of stolen goods; during the trial it emerged that his telephone had been tapped by the police acting on the authority of a warrant issued by the Home Secretary. He was acquitted and sought to establish that the tapping had been unlawful, complaining of a breach of Article 8. The European Court decided that the English law did not indicate with sufficient clarity the scope and manner of exercise of the relevant discretion conferred on public authorities in the field of interception of communications. To that extent the minimum degree of legal protection to which citizens were entitled under the rule of law in a democratic society was lacking. The law should be sufficiently clear in its terms to give citizens an adequate indication as to the circumstances in which and the conditions on which public authorities are empowered to resort to their secret and potentially dangerous interference with the right to respect for privacy.[25]

A more recent example from domestic law of a failure for restrictions to be 'according to law' relates to the long-running saga of the anti-war protester Brian Haw, who has been protesting outside Parliament since June 2001 against government policy in Iraq. Section 133 of the Serious Organised Crime and Police Act 2005 required anyone intending to organise a demonstration near Parliament to apply to the police for authorisation: this was directed at Haw. One aspect of being governed by the law is for the law not to be retrospective and Haw challenged whether this statute could properly apply to his protest retrospectively, but Court of Appeal held that the Act does apply to him, from the date when it came in.[26] Authorisation was given to him in May 2006, allowing him to protest, but limiting this to an area 3m wide by 3m high and 1m deep. Haw was prosecuted for breaching these conditions, because of the size of his banners. However, at his trial, before District Judge Purdy, the Court dismissed the case on the grounds that the conditions imposed on him were not sufficiently certain and were therefore invalid. This was upheld by the Divisional Court:[27] the conditions imposed did not satisfy the test of being 'according to law'.

'NECESSARY IN A DEMOCRATIC SOCIETY'

In Articles 8 to 11, this is the second element which must be proved by the state in order to justify the interference with the right or freedom; but the idea of necessity is also found in cases on other Articles. The key idea is that the particular legal provision or official activity on the part of the state, which has caused the interference with the right or freedom, must go no further than is **necessary**. This is not the same as 'reasonable', 'ordinary' or 'desirable'. The European Court has developed this principle in accordance with the doctrine of the margin of appreciation, where it will usually be for the national authority to make the initial assessment of whether there is a pressing social need which the measure is addressing.[28] But the European Court will still review this assessment, and has established that there are three

[24] (1985) 7 EHRR 14.
[25] We discuss some more cases about what is 'in accordance with law' in the context of Article 5, below, p. 182; surveillance is considered further in the context of Article 8, below, pp. 272–4.
[26] *R (Haw) v Home Secretary* [2006] EWCA Civ 532, [2006] 3 WLR 40.
[27] *R v Haw* [2007] EWHC 1931 (Admin), [2008] 1 WLR 379.
[28] *Handyside v UK* (1979–80) 1 EHRR 737; the margin of appreciation is discussed above, pp. 54–6.

distinct matters which must be addressed. As well as answering a **pressing social need**, the measure must pursue one of the **legitimate aims** set out in the relevant Article, if it contains grounds which justify interference; and there must be a reasonable relationship of **proportionality** between the means employed and the aim which is being pursued.

One example where the European Court considered whether a restriction was 'necessary in a democratic society' was the case of *Chassagnou* v *France*.[29] This case concerned a French law which compelled certain landowners to join a hunting association and allow hunting across their land. In deciding that this was in breach of the Article 11 right to freedom of association, the European Court stated that:

> The Court reiterates that in assessing the necessity of a given measure a number of principles must be observed. The term 'necessary' does not have the flexibility of such expressions as 'useful' or 'desirable'. In addition, pluralism, tolerance and broadmindedness are hallmarks of a 'democratic society'. Although individual interests must on occasion be subordinated to those of a group, democracy does not simply mean that the views of a majority must always prevail: a balance must be achieved which ensures the fair and proper treatment of minorities and avoids any abuse of a dominant position. Lastly, any restriction imposed on a Convention right must be proportionate to the legitimate aim pursued.
>
> In the present case the only aim invoked by the Government to justify the interference complained of was 'protection of the rights and freedoms of others'. Where these 'rights and freedoms' are themselves among those guaranteed by the Convention or its Protocols, it must be accepted that the need to protect them may lead States to restrict other rights or freedoms likewise set forth in the Convention. It is precisely this constant search for a balance between the fundamental rights of each individual which constitutes the foundation of a 'democratic society'.

In this case, the aim invoked by the French government was the protection of the rights of others; but the right relied on was a right to hunt, which is not one of the Convention rights. The Court considered that in such a case only 'indisputable imperatives can justify interference with a Convention right'. The ethical objections of the applicants to hunting were sufficiently cogent and important to be worthy of respect in a democratic society. It could therefore not be said that it was *necessary*, in a democratic society, to interfere with them, and so the compulsory obligation to join a hunting society was in breach of Article 11.

PROPORTIONALITY

The idea of proportionality is an important one in all cases where there is a proviso to a right or where the European Court has had to consider any argument that an interference with a right is justified. The idea is that such interference should be proportionate: the extent of the interference covers only the purpose which justifies it, and does not go beyond it. So, for example, an interference with the right to privacy which consists of asking people questions about where they are going may be a proportionate response to a terrorist threat where arresting them without reasonable suspicion might not be. This is important because there is a point beyond which an interference with a right cannot be justified.

[29] (2000) 29 EHRR 615; the property aspect of the case is considered below, p. 345.

In considering a question of proportionality, the court must ensure that:

■ the objective of the legislation is sufficiently important to justify some interference with a basic right;

■ the measure is rationally connected with the objective in question;

■ it is not arbitrary, unfair or based on irrational considerations;

■ the limitation impairs the right as little as possible; and

■ even if these criteria are met, the interference is not so severe in effect that it outweighs the objective for which it would otherwise be permitted.[30]

One example of a case where the European Court considered that the interference with the Convention right met the criteria of being a legitimate aim, but was not necessary in a democratic society because it was disproportionate, was *Vogt* v *Germany*.[31]

Here Mrs Vogt had been dismissed from her job as a teacher for being a member of the German Communist Party, which the German tribunal considered stood for anti-constitutional aims, meaning that Mrs Vogt was infringing her duty of political loyalty as a civil servant.

The European Court considered that there was an interference with the Article 10 right to freedom of expression, which was for a legitimate aim, namely, the obligation on civil servants to actively uphold Germany's free and democratic constitution, especially given Germany's history and desire to prevent a repeat of 'the nightmare of Nazism'.

However, the Court considered that the justification put forward by the German government was not sufficient to establish that it was necessary to dismiss Mrs Vogt from her job, which was a disproportionate consequence. In particular, there were no complaints about Mrs Vogt's performance at her job, there was no evidence that Mrs Vogt had actually made any anti-constitutional statements or personally adopted an anti-constitutional stance. Nor had the Communist Party been banned.

Both considerations of what is necessary in a democratic society and what is proportionate will apply equally in every case where a justification is put forward in our domestic courts and so both will recur as we discuss the different Convention rights. There may well be differences of opinion as to what measure of response is proportionate to a particular need. To this extent, our courts will have some regard for the solution that Parliament adopts for a particular problem, although the margin of appreciation does not apply as such to the decision of United Kingdom courts.[32] However, this measure of deference should not prevent the courts from deciding that a particular provision is a disproportionate response if the court considers that it goes beyond what is justified – and the courts have indeed reached that conclusion where they thought it was justified, as we discussed above when considering declarations of incompatibility.[33]

---

[30] See, as well as the European Court discussions, *de Freitas* v *Permanent Secretary of Ministry of Agriculture* [1999] 1 AC 69; *R (Daly)* v *Home Secretary* [2001] 2 AC 532.

[31] (1996) 21 EHRR 205.

[32] The idea of deference was introduced above, pp. 56–9.

[33] Above, pp. 73–4.

One good example of our courts considering proportionality is the legislative ban on hunting, the Hunting Act 2004, which was challenged in *R (Countryside Alliance) v Attorney General*.[34] The House of Lords had to consider very carefully the way in which they should approach the question of proportionality: this involves considering the reasons for and purpose of the statute, predominantly as it appears from the words of the statute, together with any evidence of the social problem which it is addressing, set against any evidence of the likely or actual practical impact of the statute.

In this case, the House of Lords considered in detail the purpose of the legislation, which was to prevent or reduce unnecessary suffering to wild mammals, and to enact the moral position that causing suffering for sport was unethical. They also considered the evidence which was before Parliament during the passage of the statute on hunting. The Lords concluded that, on the basis of all the evidence, this was a political judgment, and the position which a majority of the House of Commons adopted, to ban hunting, was within the range of reasonably necessary and proportionate responses to the issue in a democratic society, bearing in mind that this is the sort of question which is primarily for the legislature, not the courts, to determine.

An example of case where a measure was held to be disproportionate is the case of *Baiai*.[35] Here the House of Lords had to consider an interference with right to marriage (Article 12). The statute in question regulated the rights of foreign nationals in the United Kingdom to marry in order to prevent marriages of convenience – sham marriages aimed at giving one party residential status. The House of Lords held that the statute was not disproportionate – it did not impair the right to marry. But the regulatory scheme made under the statute *was* disproportionate because there was no reasonable relationship between the objective which justified the interference with the right – namely, preventing sham marriages – and the scheme. This was because it simply imposed a blanket ban on persons with certain immigration status from getting married and did not take into account in each case whether there was any evidence that this proposed marriage was genuine or not.

WHICH RIGHTS ARE QUALIFIED?

Whether or not there are exceptions to a Convention right varies from article to article. The rights provided for by Article 3 (freedom from torture), 4(1) (prohibition of slavery) and 7 (no punishment without law) contain no exceptions – these are rights where there is no legitimate justification for an infringement. The right to life in Article 2 has some very specific and narrowly drawn exceptions for self-defence and capital punishment (and the latter is removed by the Thirteenth Protocol). Article 4(2) (prohibition of forced labour) and Article 5 (personal liberty) contain some specific exceptions. The right to a trial in public, which is part of Article 6(1), contains express exceptions; some of the other rights within the Article 6 rights to a fair trial, which have no express qualifications, are examples of where the European Court has held that some limited qualifications should be implied.

---

[34] *R (Countryside Alliance) v Attorney General* [2007] UKHL 52; see also below, p. 250 and p. 257; the equivalent challenge under Scottish law was *Friend v Lord Advocate* [2007] UKHL 53.
[35] *R (Baiai) v Home Secretary* [2008] UKHL 53, [2008] 3 WLR, see also below, p. 328.

Introduction to the Convention rights

A number of the Convention rights are qualified by the express words of an article. Thus Articles 8, 9, 10 and 11 each have a first paragraph which sets out the right in question and then a second paragraph which sets out express qualifications to that right. The qualifications set out the circumstances in which the state may interfere with the right or freedom. The right to property in Article 1 of the First Protocol also has express qualifications.

The same principles are applied to an *implied* limitation as are applied to articles where there are express qualifications: in particular, the principle that there must be proportionality between the extent of the infringement and the interest which justifies the infringement. Thus, in the case of Article 2, in respect of the very limited exceptions to the right to life, in each case it must be shown that the action being criticised was not only justified, but absolutely necessary, which sets a very high standard on the state seeking to justify the infringement. Likewise for Article 5, for the circumstances where personal liberty may be infringed, although there is no express reference in the article to the standard of justification, the principle of proportionality applies. Again, with Article 6, although most of the rights set out there contain no express qualification, they are not all treated as absolute, but any attempt to limit them must be strictly proportionate to a justifiable interest.

The qualifications for each right are not identical. One must bear in mind the different objectives of each article and the nature of the right being protected, so some of the qualifications are specific to their context. However, all of those with express qualifications do state that any limitations must be prescribed by law. So, the second paragraph of each of Articles 8 to 11 refers to this requirement and then states that limitations must be necessary in a democratic society to protect certain specified common interests. Some of these interests are common to all of these four articles: public safety, the protection of public order or prevention of disorder, the protection of health or morals, and the protection of rights of others. The first three of these are key functions of the state. The fourth expresses the point we considered above, that rights can be limited where they conflict with the rights of others, since there are many situations where two parties' rights conflict and they cannot both exercise their rights to the fullest possible extent. Other protected interests appear in most of these articles, namely national security and the prevention of crime. Article 10 has some additional limitations which relate specifically to freedom of speech. Similar ideas appear in the Article 6 right to a public trial.

Thus one must look specifically at the words of the article before one can be sure which qualifications apply. But the critical point is that, whichever article we are considering, the general principles we have set out above will apply.

NON-DISCRIMINATION

Article 14: Prohibition of Discrimination
The enjoyment of the rights and freedoms set forth in this Convention shall be secured without discrimination on any ground such as sex, race, colour, language, religion, political or other opinion, national or social origin, association with a national minority, property, birth or other status.

One further general restriction on interferences with Convention rights is that contained in Article 14. This prohibits discrimination, but only in relation to the exercise of the other Convention rights. Thus, one could imagine a case in which there was a limitation on one of the other rights, for example the Article 10 right to freedom of speech. It might be that this limitation did not infringe Article 10, if the state could show that it was reasonably necessary and proportionate. However, if the limitation was applied differently to different groups without any justification – for example, if men and women were treated differently in its application, for no good reason – although there was no breach of Article 10, there would be a breach of Article 10 taken together with Article 14. However, if *none* of the other rights is engaged, then there can be no breach of Article 14 simply because there is discriminatory conduct.

The question then is, what amounts to **discrimination**? The European Court has held that Article 14 does not prevent *all* differential treatment. What it prohibits is differential treatment which is not objectively and reasonably justified, which requires there to be a legitimate aim for the discrimination and the treatment to be proportionate to that legitimate aim. This was the view stated by the European Court in the *Belgian Linguistics* case.[36]

> Here, the Court was asked to consider the provision for the education of the children of French speakers in Belgium, which has two main languages, French and Flemish. The Court found no violation of the right to education contained in Article 2 of the First Protocol. But the Court then looked at this right taken together with Article 14, and held that the lack of provision of education in French was justified, but preventing certain children from having access to French-language schools, solely on the basis of where their parents lived, was a breach of Articles 2 and 14. There was no good reason for using this as a criterion for discriminating between some prospective students and others.

The way to decide whether there is discrimination is, first, to compare the treatment of two different groups. The applicant will have to show that they are being treated less favourably than people who are in a comparable group. The treatment will be discriminatory if it is because of one of the factors listed in the Article – sex, race, colour, language, religion, political or other opinion, national or social origin, association with a national minority, property, birth or other status. There may also be similar distinctions which are considered unjustifiable, as examples of 'other status'. So, for example, in the case of *Chassagnou* v *France*,[37] which we considered earlier, the European Court found a violation of Article 14, as well as Article 11, because the law discriminated between owners of small pieces of property, who were not allowed to object to hunting, and owners of large areas of land, who were. Other factors which have been held by the European Court not to justify differential treatment are sexual orientation, illegitimacy of birth, being a prisoner, being a conscientious objector to military service, or disability. On the other hand, the House of Lords has held that differentiating between prisoners who are serving different lengths of sentence does not engage Article 14, since that is a result of what they have done, and not who they are: it is not about their personal status.[38]

[36] (1979–80) 1 EHRR 241 & 252.
[37] (2000) 29 EHRR 615; above, p. 119; below, p. 345.
[38] *Clift* v *Home Secretary* [2006] UKHL 54, (2007) 1 AC 484, although the differential treatment was described as an 'indefensible anomaly'; see also below, p. 198.

To show discrimination, it is then necessary that the difference in treatment is *because of* the characteristic which is said to be the basis for the discrimination. If there is a real, objective difference between the two groups which are being compared, a proper reason for treating them differently, then there will not be discriminatory treatment. So, for example, treating a juvenile prisoner and an adult prisoner differently is not discriminatory;[39] nor is treating a prisoner who is a serious security risk differently from one who does not pose a security risk;[40] nor is treating differently an immigrant child who is part of a family unit from one on their own.[41]

However, where the factor is one such as sex, race or religion, the European Court has made it quite clear that the task of showing that this factor justifies differential treatment will be a difficult one. This is also the approach which our courts have taken:

In *Ghaidan* v *Godin-Mendoza*,[42] two men lived in a stable homosexual partnership; one died; the survivor claimed to be entitled to certain statutory rights to take over the protected tenancy of the home where they lived together. The deceased partner had been the tenant of the house, and under the Rent Act 1977, a surviving spouse becomes entitled to succeed to the protected tenancy. But the Rent Act goes further than just people who are married, since it allows a person living with the original tenant as his or her wife or husband to be treated as a spouse. The courts had already held that unmarried heterosexual partners could inherit a statutory tenancy.

The House of Lords, applying Article 14 and Article 8, held that the law should not discriminate on the grounds of sexual orientation and interpreted the Rent Act to give effect to this by including both homosexual and heterosexual couples. As Baroness Hale put it, homosexual couples are as much entitled to want the stability and permanence of sharing a home and life together, with or without children, as a heterosexual couple, and, in both cases, an unmarried couple whose relationship is like a marriage is equally deserving of protection.

In the case of *Burden*,[43] two sisters argued that they were discriminated against compared to a married couple in the way they were affected by inheritance tax. This tax is payable on the property left by a person who dies. No inheritance tax is paid on a jointly owned family home that passes on the death of a spouse to the other spouse, and the same applies to a civil partnership. In this case, the two sisters, who shared a family home, argued that this exemption for married couples was discriminatory, and that when one of them died, the survivor should not have to pay tax on their share of the jointly owned home. The European Court disagreed. It was permissible to treat a relationship between siblings and married couples/civil partners differently, since the relationship *is* essentially different. That the Burden sisters had chosen to live together for all their adult lives did not alter this. Marriage (or civil partnership) is a particular legal institution which confers a particular status on those who enter it. It is therefore permissible that those who do not enter into the same sort of binding commitment to each other are treated in a different way.

---

[39] *Nelson* v *UK* (1986) 49 DR 170.
[40] *X* v *UK* (9 December 1992), European Commission.
[41] *AL (Serbia)* v *Home Secretary* [2008] UKHL 42, (2008) 1 WLR.
[42] [2004] UKHL 30, [2004] 2 AC 557; see also above, p. 67.
[43] *Burden* v *UK* [2008] 47 EHRR 38.

On the other hand, in the case of *P*,[44] the House of Lords considered the position of an unmarried couple who wished to adopt children. In Northern Ireland they were not allowed to do so, because of statutory regulations. The House of Lords has held that this was discriminatory and in breach of Article 14 (with Article 8). There was no rational basis for the state to consider that in general it was better for children to be brought up by a married, rather than an unmarried, couple, and it is not an appropriate consideration where the law gives priority to the best interests of the child. The fact that the couple were unmarried might well be relevant to whether or not the court should make an order that they should be permitted to adopt the children, but it should not be taken as preventing consideration of such an adoption.

In a number of cases about alleged financial discrimination – in taxation and welfare provision, which can be of real financial importance to large numbers of people – the courts have had to consider whether there was a justification for treating some groups of people differently from others:

- In *PM* v *UK*,[45] the European Court held that tax deductions in respect of maintenance payments for children of married fathers, but not unmarried fathers, were discriminatory: the marital status of the father who takes financial responsibility for a child makes no difference to the justification for the tax relief, which is to allow the father to support a new family, and therefore can apply equally whether the father was married or not.

- In the case of *Wilkinson*,[46] the High Court granted a declaration of incompatibility in respect of the payment of a bereavement allowance which benefited widows, but not widowers; the House of Lords confirmed that the words of that provision could not be interpreted so as to read 'widow' as 'surviving spouse', so the statute was discriminatory.

- In the case of *Hooper*,[47] the House of Lords had to consider whether several provisions relating to the payment of pensions to widows, but not widowers, were discriminatory. The Lords held that there was discrimination between men and women in the payment of a widow's pension but that it had been justified: when it was instituted, married women who were widowed were not very likely to be able to earn a living; the allowance had in any event since been abolished (the timing of which had been properly a matter for Parliament) and replaced with a bereavement allowance which applied to both men and women equally.[48]

- In the cases of *Carson and Reynolds*,[49] there were two claims of discrimination. The first concerned the exclusion of pensioners resident outside the United Kingdom from

---

[44] *In re P and others* [2008] UKHL 38, [2008] 3 WLR 76.
[45] (2005) Times 15.9.05.
[46] *R (Wilkinson)* v *Inland Revenue Commissioners* [2002] STC 347 (HC), [2005] UKHL 30, [2005] 1 WLR 1718 (HL).
[47] *R (Hooper)* v *Secretary of State for Work and Pensions* [2005] UKHL 29, [2005] 1 WLR 1681; see also above, p. 84.
[48] The European Court agreed with this view in the case of *Runkee* v *UK* [2007] 2 FLR 178.
[49] *R (Carson)* v *Secretary of State for Work and Pensions* [2005] UKHL 37, [2005] 2 WLR 1369.

increases in the state retirement pension. By a majority, the Lords held that there was no discrimination on a ground which required respect under Article 14 (living abroad), and that, in any event, it was justifiable to treat people living abroad differently from those at home. The second concerned reduced payments for people out of work (Jobseeker's Allowance) who are under 25. Again, this was held to be justified: the evidence suggested that young people's necessary expenses tended to be lower than older people, there was a social policy to encourage young people out of work to stay with their parents to reduce cost, and whilst the age limit of 25 was arbitrary, a line had to be drawn somewhere. *Carson* was taken to the European Court which agreed with the House of Lords: the difference in treatment was objectively and reasonably justified.[50]

- In the cases of *Barrow*, *Pearson* and *Walker*[51] the European Court held that there was no breach of Article 14 in invalidity benefit being paid to women only to age 60, and not to age 65; in a man being paid a pension only at 65, not at 60; and in a man having to pay national insurance after age 60. In all cases, these resulted from the difference in pensionable age, which was not in breach of Article 14, given the original justification, namely the financial inequality between the sexes, the slowly evolving nature of women's working lives and the absence of a common standard among European states.

- In the case of *RJM*,[52] the House of Lords held that the exclusion of disabled homeless persons from a particular element of income support did engage Article 14, as homelessness was a personal characteristic which counted as 'other status' within Article 14, but that the discrimination was justified by the social policy it was implementing, which was to encourage homeless disabled persons to seek shelter, since this was a policy that the government were entitled to pursue in this way.

Some further examples of the application of Article 14 will be found in the discussions of some of the other articles: for example, the leading case of *A v Home Secretary*,[53] referred to above, where the decision was based in a large part on the lack of justification for discriminating between British nationals and foreign nationals. It is also important to note in this context that the lack of protection provided by Article 14, where there is no other Convention right involved, does not necessarily mean that a victim of discriminatory conduct in such a case would have *no* legal remedy: our law already contains various provisions prohibiting discrimination on the grounds of sex, race, sexuality, religion, age or disability[54] in a wide variety of situations, whether or not there is a breach of any other right.

---

[50] *Carson* v *UK* (2009) 48 EHRR 41.
[51] *Barrow, Pearson, Walker* v *UK* [2008] STC 786.
[52] *R (RJM)* v *Secretary of State for Work & Pensions* [2008] UKHL 63, [2008] 3 WLR 1023.
[53] See below, p. 376.
[54] The main legislative provisions are the Sex Discrimination Act 1975, the Race Relations Act 1976, the Disability Discrimination Act 1995, the Employment Equality (Religion or Belief) Regulations 2003 (SI 2003/1660) and the Employment Equality (Sexual Orientation) Regulations 2003 (SI 2003/1661) and 2007 (2007/1263); Employment Equality (Age) Regulations 2006 (SI 2006/1031); and the Equality Act 2006, which also combined the existing enforcement bodies into the Commission for Equality and Human Rights (there are separate Commissions for Scotland and Northern Ireland).

GENERAL PROVISIONS: ARTICLES 16–18

These articles of the Convention all also have general application. As with Article 14, none of them creates any free-standing rights. Instead they assist in the interpretation and application of the other articles which do create rights.

> ### Article 16: Restrictions on Political Activity of Aliens
> Nothing in Articles 10, 11 and 14 shall be regarded as preventing the High Contracting Parties from imposing restrictions on the political activity of aliens.

By 'aliens', what is meant is foreign nationals. It is a well-established legal principle that foreign nationals do not have the same rights as domestic nationals, in particular to reside in a country. So there is no infringement of human rights in restricting people's rights to enter into another country as such, as long as each person does have a nationality of some sort and has the right to return to that country. However, Article 16 has barely been referred to in cases under the Convention. This is because, although this was considered important when the Convention was drafted in 1950, it no longer reflects contemporary attitudes to aliens, as can be seen from the provisions for the protection of aliens in the Fourth Protocol, for example. Nowadays, there is little demand to restrict the political activities of foreign nationals: so long as they are allowed to enter the country, it is generally considered appropriate for their rights to freedom of expression and freedom of assembly to be the same as British nationals, although they will typically not be allowed to vote in elections. As Baroness Hale put it in *A v Home Secretary*:[55]

> Foreigners do not have to be given the same rights to participate in the politics and government of the country as have citizens (Article 16). Nor do they have to be given the same rights to come or to stay here; if they are here, they may be refused entry or deported [. . .] But while they are here they have the same human rights as everyone else.

In the case of *Farrakhan*,[56] there was a challenge to the decision of the Home Secretary to refuse entry to the country to Louis Farrakhan, an American black Muslim activist, because of his expression of racist and anti-Semitic views. The Court of Appeal's decision was that Article 10 was engaged by this decision, but that it was justified under Article 10(2) as an informed assessment of the risk of disorder posed by Mr Farrakhan's presence. Article 16 was referred to, but the court considered the Article to be 'something of an anachronism, half a century after the agreement of the Convention'.

As well as the massive growth in international travel during the past 50 years, making it far more common for people to be visitors in other countries, one of the most significant reasons for this is the existence and growth of the European Union. It is contrary to European Union law to refuse to allow entry to, or discriminate (for most purposes) between, citizens of different countries who are members of the European Union. So, for example, the seizure of cars from people crossing from France has been held to be subject

7

Introduction to the Convention rights

---

[55] [2004] UKHL 56, [2005] 2 WLR 87, para 229.
[56] *R (Farrakhan) v Secretary of State for the Home Department* [2002] EWCA Civ 606, [2002] 3 WLR 481.

to considerations of proportionality, and therefore potentially unlawful, under European Union law, if there are no reasonable grounds for stopping the owner or for the owner to challenge the seizure.[57] The European Court has also considered whether a citizen of the European Union qualifies as a 'foreign' national: they do not, but it is relevant.

In *Piermont* v *France*,[58] the European Court had little hesitation in holding that France could not rely on Article 16 in limiting the rights of Mrs Piermont to freedom of expression under Article 10. Mrs Piermont was a German citizen and a Member of the European Parliament (MEP). The Court considered that her Article 10 rights had been infringed in limitations placed on her when travelling to French Polynesia, and that France could not rely on Article 16 since not only was she a European citizen, but also an MEP, and therefore a member of a political body relevant to French Polynesia.

Article 17: Prohibition of Abuse of Rights

Nothing in this Convention may be interpreted as implying for any State, group or person any right to engage in any activity or perform any act aimed at the destruction of any of the rights and freedoms set forth herein or at their limitation to a greater extent than is provided for in the Convention.

Article 17 is also of relatively limited application. The purpose of Article 17 is to prevent those with extreme political views taking advantage of the Convention rights for protection, where those views are *so* extreme that they are aimed at the *destruction*, or substantial limitation, of the basic rights and freedoms set out in the Convention. It will be comparatively rare, therefore, that this article will apply. It can apply only to those rights that can be *used* to make a political point – for example, freedom of expression and freedom of assembly – and not those rights which exist solely to protect the individual – such as personal liberty and freedom from torture. Article 17 is effectively a further general limitation on some of the other articles, and, as with any other limitation, in order to rely on it, a state must show that its action is strictly necessary and proportionate to the threat.

One case which refers to Article 17 is the case of *Lawless* v *Ireland*.[59] Mr Lawless was a member of the Irish Republican Army (IRA), a terrorist organisation. His complaint was that his Article 5 rights had been infringed by a prolonged period of detention. One of the arguments that the Irish government raised was that it was entitled to rely on Article 17: the IRA was banned because its activities were aimed at the destruction of the rights and freedoms set out in the Convention and therefore Mr Lawless could not rely on his rights under Article 5 (or any other article).

---

[57] *R (Hoverspeed)* v *Commissioners of Customs and Excise* [2002] EWCA Civ 1804, [2003] QB 1041.
[58] (1995) 20 EHRR 301.
[59] *Lawless* v *Ireland (No. 3)* (1979–80) 1 EHRR 15, for Article 5, see below, p. 187.

The European Court disagreed. The Court considered that the aim of Article 17 was to prevent a person relying on a right to engage in any activity which was aimed at destroying the Convention rights, but did not positively *deprive* that person of the protection of the Convention in respect of their personal rights, such as the rights under Article 5. Whatever the goals of the IRA, in complaining about his detention, Mr Lawless was not relying on his Convention rights to justify acts aimed at destroying the Convention.

A more recent case is that of *Lehideux* v *France*.[60] In this case, the applicants had been prosecuted for paying for an advertisement which defended Marshal Petain, the governor of France's Vichy government under the Nazi occupation, who had been sentenced to death in 1945 after the Second World War for collusion with Germany.

The European Court considered that there had been a breach of Article 10 and that Article 17 did not prevent that breach. This was because the text did not claim to support the German occupation or Nazi philosophy, but argued for a sympathetic view of the actions of Petain, which the Court considered was, after 40 years, a legitimate subject of historical debate: in a democratic society, views that offend, shock or disturb may still require protection. The Court was, however, very careful to make the distinction between offering a view of the man, Petain, and an apology of Nazism. The Court stated that:

> [this] is part of an ongoing debate among historians about the events in question and their interpretation. As such, it does not belong to the category of clearly established historical facts, such as the Holocaust, whose negation or revision would be removed from the protection of Article 10 by Article 17. [. . .] There is no doubt that, like any other remark directed against the Convention's underlying values, the justification of a pro-Nazi policy could not be allowed to enjoy the protection afforded by Article 10.

Article 18: Limitation on Use of Restrictions on Rights

The restrictions permitted under this Convention to the said rights and freedoms shall not be applied for any purpose other than those for which they have been prescribed.

Finally, there is Article 18, which again has only rarely been referred to in the cases. Article 18 is only capable of being breached in conjunction with another article. It mandates that, where there is a Convention right, and a restriction on that right, a state should not abuse the legitimate scope of that restriction by limiting that right for some improper purpose.

One of the few examples where the European Court has found a breach of Article 18 is the case of *Gusinskiy* v *Russia*.[61] Here the complaint was about a breach of Article 5. The owner of a media company was detained on charges under a process which the European Court held was not 'prescribed by law' as it was not clear enough to avoid arbitrary detention, so there was a breach of Article 5(1). However, the Court went on to consider the fact that the detention had also been used to pressure Mr Gusinskiy to give up ownership of his

[60] (2000) 30 EHRR 665; for Article 10, see below, p. 301.
[61] *Gusinskiy* v *Russia* [2004] (App 70276/01).

company. Detention under Article 5(1)(c) is allowed for the purpose of bringing a person before the competent legal authority on reasonable suspicion of having committed an offence. In this case, the Court found that the detention was also being used for commercial purposes: this was a breach of Article 18, because the restriction on the personal liberty guaranteed by Article 5 was being used for a purpose other than that prescribed.

QUESTIONS

1 Consider the list of rights which are protected by the Convention and by the Act. Are there any which you consider should be excluded or any other rights which you think should be included? In particular, you may like to consider the rights set out in the protocols, and the rights protected by the Universal Declaration of Human Rights (these can be found in Appendices 2 and 4 respectively).

2 One example is a right of freedom from discrimination. Do you consider that our law should recognise a free-standing right (as in the Twelfth Protocol), as well as the Article 14 right, or do you think that the Article 14 right is sufficient?

3 Do you agree in principle that the definitions of rights should set out in what circumstances they can be interfered with (it would be relevant to consider the text of the articles in Appendix 2)? Do you think that any of the Convention rights should have more extensive – or more limited – descriptions of permissible limitations?

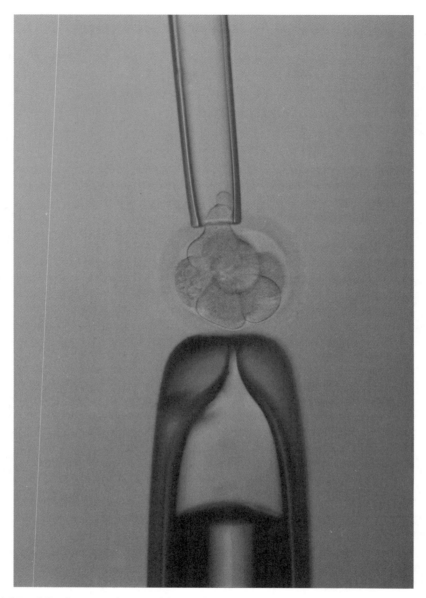

The rights of the foetus to be considered alive has been considered in cases on abortion and in vitro fertilisation (see p. 145).

Source: Science Photo Library

8 The right to life

Civilisation is nothing more than the effort to reduce the use of force to the last resort. (José Ortega y Gasset, *La Rebelión de la Masas*, 1930)

> **Article 2: Right to Life**
> 1 Everyone's right to life shall be protected by law. No one shall be deprived of his life intentionally save in the execution of a sentence of a court following his conviction of a crime for which this penalty is provided by law.
> 2 Deprivation of life shall not be regarded as inflicted in contravention of this Article when it results from the use of force which is no more than absolutely necessary:
>   (a) in defence of any person from unlawful violence;
>   (b) in order to effect a lawful arrest or to prevent the escape of a person lawfully detained;
>   (c) in action lawfully taken for the purpose of quelling a riot or insurrection.
>
> **Sixth Protocol, Article 1: Abolition of the Death Penalty**
> The death penalty shall be abolished. No one shall be condemned to such penalty or executed.

THE RIGHT TO LIFE

As a provision which not only safeguards the right to life but sets out the circumstances when the deprivation of life may be justified, Article 2 ranks as one of the most fundamental provisions in the Convention – indeed one which, in peace time, admits of no derogation under Article 15. Together with Article 3 of the Convention, it also enshrines one of the basic values of the democratic societies making up the Council of Europe. As such, its provisions must be strictly construed.

This statement is part of the European Court's judgment in the case of *McCann*,[1] which we shall consider later. It is hard to argue with the proposition it sets out – the right to life is perhaps the most basic human right, and it is appropriate that it is the first substantive right in the Convention. The very fact that it needed stating in 1950 says something about

---

[1] *McCann v UK* (1996) 21 EHRR 97, below, p. 147.

the appalling treatment, and destruction, of millions of people by various states in the previous decades.

However, one might well ask what does this statement of the right to life add to our law? In circumstances where death occurs, there are already long-established criminal offences such as murder, manslaughter, and causing death by dangerous driving. And quite apart from the criminal law, there are statutes and regulations providing for health and safety in situations where death might occur. For example, there are provisions to protect employees or visitors in shops and offices, factories and industrial premises; and there are regulations about the supply and use of potentially dangerous substances, both dangerous chemicals and germs, and everyday dangers, such as domestic electricity and gas. Police officers may use force, and sometimes death results, either accidentally or deliberately. But when that happens, the particular officer is subject to the ordinary course of the law, and he may be prosecuted or disciplined for his actions, if he acted improperly. The law is quite clear, and has been so for many years; he may not use more force than is reasonable in the circumstances, and if he does so he runs the risk of being found negligent or criminally responsible.

So what difference has Article 2 made, what has it added to our law? The answers are to be found in the surprising number of cases that have been decided by our courts which have involved Article 2. They have helped to define the duties of state agents and public authorities where death has occurred, or where there has been a risk of death.

The rights set out in Article 2 have an immediate corresponding duty. The opening words of Article 2 announce the right to life; this is everybody's right, and the state has the obligation to ensure it. There are two aspects to this obligation: first, there is a positive obligation to take steps to **protect life**; and, second, there is a negative duty to **refrain from taking life**.

The burden of these duties is on the state, through its agents, officers and departments. In practice this burden of protecting life, and not taking life, will fall most of all on those who make decisions which involve life-threatening situations, such as those responsible for security, the police and armed forces, and doctors taking life and death decisions. But this duty also falls on the courts, as a public authority and part of the state.[2] So, where there is a risk to the life of a person, the courts must provide whatever protection they can, by way of court orders to minimise such a risk, or, where death has occurred, by investigating what has occurred and awarding compensation for any breach which has occurred.

THE DUTY TO PROTECT LIFE

Dealing first with the duty to safeguard life, the duty on the state is that, where there is a real and immediate risk to the life of a specific person, there will be a breach of Article 2 if the authorities fail to take reasonable measures which are within their power to address this risk.[3] This applies to the court, where someone involved in legal proceedings is at risk of death, or very serious injury, and the court is asked to order steps which may avert that risk. An example of this is the case of *Thompson and Venables*.[4]

[2] See above, p. 81.
[3] *Osman* v *UK* (1998) 29 EHRR 243.
[4] *Thompson and Venables* v *News Group Newspapers Ltd* [2001] 2 WLR 1038; considered further below, pp. 134 and 154.

At the time of the hearing, the claimants were both 18 years of age. In 1993, when they were 10, they killed James Bulger, a two-year-old boy, and later in the same year they were convicted of his murder. The trial judge made injunctions restricting the publication of any details about them, beyond their names and background, without limit of time. At a hearing as to whether the injunctions should be lifted in 2001, there was further evidence of sustained hostility directed at them, so that they were at risk of death or serious injury if they were found. The claimants relied on Article 2, since there was a risk to their life, as well as Article 3, for the risk of serious injury, and Article 8, the right to privacy. The newspapers relied on their Article 10 right to freedom of expression.

Lady Justice Butler-Sloss, President of the Family Division, made the injunctions, so preventing the newspapers from publishing the claimants' details, on the ground that there was a real and serious risk to the claimants, under Articles 2 and 3. Notwithstanding the interference with the Article 10 rights, Article 2 required the imposition of orders to protect the claimants.

In a similar way it has been held that, where witnesses were justifiably in fear of their lives, the court may be obliged to take steps to protect them.

In the case of the Bloody Sunday inquiry,[5] into the deaths of several people in Londonderry, on 30 January 1972, there was a judicial review of the decision to hold the inquiry in Londonderry, notwithstanding the fears of soldiers due to give evidence at the inquiry that there would be a danger to their lives there. The Court of Appeal held that whilst there was not a real and immediate risk to life, account should be taken of the subjective fear of the witnesses so as to accommodate Article 2, and their evidence should be heard somewhere else.

Another case of witness protection is that of *Officer L.*[6] Here a police officer was giving evidence in the Inquiry into the death of Robert Hamill, a Catholic in Northern Ireland, whose family claimed that there was police involvement in the death. The House of Lords held that the police officers who gave evidence were entitled to have their names withheld and be screened from view during their evidence but only if there was a material increase in a real and immediate risk to them of injury or death if their identity was known. And the risk had to be objective and not just based on the officer's fear, however ill-founded.[7]

This duty applies beyond the courts. The next case is also a situation of threats to a witness in a court case, but here the question was whether the police should have acted to protect him.

---

[5] *R (A)* v *Lord Saville* [2001] EWCA Civ 2048, [2002] 1 WLR 1249.
[6] *Re Officer L* [2007] UKHL 36, [2007] 1 WLR 2135.
[7] The question of whether it is fair to the defendant on trial for witnesses to be allowed to give evidence anonymously is one we will consider in the context of Article 6, below, p. 226.

The right to life

In the case of *Van Colle*,[8] Giles Van Colle was to appear as a witness in a trial but was killed shortly before he was due to give evidence. He had reported to the police that threats had been made to him by the person against whom he was due to testify. The House of Lords considered that the test for liability under Article 2 was not met: it was not the case that the police knew or should have known that there was a real and immediate risk to the life of Mr Van Colle from the criminal acts of the accused at the trial. The murder had been committed by an unpredictable individual, with no great history of violence, so it could not reasonably have been anticipated by the police that there was a real and immediate risk to the victim's life. The test was not different because the danger to the person threatened was because they were due to give evidence, especially as the crime to which the evidence related was not a serious one. Thus there was no breach of Article 2.

The same duty applies where the state has on obligation to look after someone because they are in state custody or otherwise under state control. This applies to those in prison: even if someone is in prison because they have committed an offence, that does not mean that they forfeit rights other than their liberty. The state still owes them a duty, just as much as to any other citizen, to ensure that their right to life is protected. And the same test applies here, that the state must protect them if there is known to be a real and immediate risk to their life.

In the case of *Edwards* v *UK*,[9] Christopher Edwards was a prisoner on remand in Chelmsford Prison. He was placed in a cell with another prisoner, RL, who had been diagnosed as suffering from schizophrenia or personality disorder. RL attacked Edwards and stamped and kicked him to death, and RL later pleaded guilty to manslaughter by reason of diminished responsibility. Edwards's parents claimed that there had been a violation of Article 2, so far as their son was concerned, in that there was a failure on the part of several agencies – the doctors, police, prosecution and court – to pass on information about RL to the prison authorities, and there had been an inadequate screening of RL when he first arrived at prison.

The European Court agreed. The various agencies were part of the state system, and they had a duty to safeguard the prisoner's life. The Court heard that an inquiry had been held which reported that there had been a systematic collapse of the mechanisms which should have protected vulnerable prisoners.

But there are other reasons why someone might be in state custody or care, and the same principle applies whether the risk arises from the actions of a third party or a risk from their own conduct.

---

[8] *Van Colle* v *Chief Constable of Hertfordshire* [2008] UKHL 50, [2008] 3 WLR.
[9] (2002) 35 EHRR 487.

In the case of *Savage*,[10] a patient at a hospital suffering from mental illness had been detained under the Mental Health Act 1999, so was in the custody of the state. She escaped from the hospital and committed suicide. The House of Lords held that the same principle which applied to the police and other state bodies also applied to a health authority. Where the authority was on notice that there was a real and immediate risk to the life of a specific person, in this case by the risk of suicide, they had to take all reasonable steps to protect the patient, allowing for the resources available to them. The state does not have a duty to protect everyone against suicide, but they do where the person is in state custody and there is a known risk. This was the case here, and the hospital were in breach of Article 2.

The same could also apply where there is a failure to manage the working conditions of those for whom the state is responsible, or to impose a properly ordered system.

This comes across in the decision in *Barrett* v *UK*.[11] Mr Barrett was a naval serviceman, serving at a naval base in Norway. In one evening in June 1988, he drank 10 units of alcohol in one bar on the base, and then went to another bar and drank a further 12 units and he died from alcoholic poisoning. His widow brought a claim before the European Commission, complaining that the control and supervision of the supply and consumption of alcohol at the base, and the care and attention the deceased received following his collapse, were inadequate and such as to endanger his life in breach of Article 2.

The Commission agreed that Article 2 was engaged, where, as here, the facilities for drinking were provided by the state (because it was a naval bar). Since there was an obvious and substantial risk of excessive consumption, there needed to be measures to discourage drinking to excess and, in the event, to secure adequate care and treatment. However, on the facts of the case, the Commission considered that there were in fact adequate systems in place – orders and regulations – so there was no breach by the state.

ADEQUATE INVESTIGATION INTO LOSS OF LIFE

The second duty of the state, to refrain from taking life, means that there must be a system of law to enforce this duty – a police force which prevents criminal acts causing risk to life, and which detects criminals, and a criminal justice system which provides for the trial and punishment of those who take life. Furthermore, where death has occurred as a result of force used by agents of the state, there is an especial requirement that there should be some form of official investigation into the circumstances of the death, and an investigation which is effective.

This duty to hold a proper investigation is important. The reason for insisting on it, in the European jurisprudence, was spelled out in the case of *McCann*,[12] which we quoted at the start of this chapter, and which we consider further below. The European Court said,

---

[10] *Savage* v *South Essex Partnership NHS Trust* [2008] UKHL 74.
[11] (1997) 23 EHRR CD 185.
[12] *McCann* v *UK* (1996) 21 EHRR 97.

A general prohibition of arbitrary killing by the agents of the state would be ineffective, in practice, if there existed no procedure for reviewing the lawfulness of the use of lethal force by state authorities. The obligation to protect the right to life [taken with the state's duty to secure the Convention rights] requires by implication that there should be some form of effective official investigation when individuals have been killed as a result of the use of force by, *inter alia*, agents of the state.

In that case, the European Court found that the inquest proceedings, held in Gibraltar, had satisfied the requirement of an effective investigation. But this principle has now been applied in our law, and in some situations the result has been a fuller investigation than would have taken place prior to the Act. The following cases set out the high standard to be expected of an investigation or inquiry into a death in custody or involving a public authority.

In the case of *Manning*,[13] Mr Manning's brother, who had been remanded in police custody awaiting trial for an offence of violence, died of asphyxia while under restraint following an altercation with two officers. The death was investigated by the police and the papers were referred to the Crown Prosecution Service. At a coroner's inquest the evidence indicated that death had resulted from the manner in which one of the officers had held the deceased's head during the incident, and the jury returned a verdict of unlawful killing. A specialist case worker in the CPS undertook a detailed examination of all the available evidence, including that adduced at the inquest, and in his review note recorded his investigations. He considered a charge of the unlawful act of manslaughter, but concluded that it was only the fatal force to the deceased's neck which could be characterised as excessive, so that the only potential defendant was the officer identified as holding the head. He concluded that there was a prima facie case against that officer, but *no* realistic prospect of the prosecution being able to establish that excessive force had been used deliberately, rather than as the result of an attempt to effect proper restraint. His conclusion was that there should be no prosecution of the police officer.

The Court of Appeal held that there had been a violation of Article 2. It recognised that the right to life is the most fundamental of human rights, and that there is a duty on the state to investigate the death of a person in the state's custody, which resulted from violence inflicted by its agents. The first requirement of such an investigation was met, that the CPS should give reasons for not prosecuting the officer, which had been done. But those reasons failed to address all the specific matters, which the police officer would have to answer about the detailed circumstances of the struggle, to meet what would appear to be a strong case against him. That failure meant that the investigation had not been effective enough.

Another case about the investigation of a death arguably caused by a state authority is the case of *Wright*,[14] who was an inmate at Leeds Prison with a long history of serious asthma, and under treatment from the prison medical staff, who were arguably negligent during their treatment of him. Mr Wright suffered an asthma attack and told his cell mate that he needed a nebuliser, but although, after a delay, medical help arrived at the cell, Mr Wright died. An inquest was held, at which the prison service was represented; the family were

---

[13] *R v DPP, ex parte Manning* [2001] QB 330.
[14] *R (Wright)* v *Home Secretary* [2001] UKHRR 1399; there was also a finding of breach of Article 3, below, p. 159.

not. No reference was made at the inquest to any shortcomings in the medical treatment of Mr Wright before the night of his death. The family later read a newspaper article stating that a doctor who had treated him in prison had been guilty of serious professional misconduct, and had been suspended. The family claimed that Mr Wright's treatment had been in breach of Article 2.

The High Court found that the prison service had been negligent in their medical treatment of Mr Wright, and therefore were arguably in breach of Article 2. Further, the court found that there had not been an adequate official investigation into the death: the inquest did not meet this requirement, as the relevant witness was not called to give evidence, there was no consideration of the shortcomings of the medical treatment of Mr Wright, or of the doctor's disciplinary record, and the family was not represented.

This issue then came before the House of Lords in the case of *Amin*.[15] Here a 19-year-old prisoner, Mubarek, was battered into a coma by a fellow prisoner, Stewart, with whom he was sharing a cell at Feltham Young Offender Institution, and he died a week later. Evidence suggested that Stewart was a violent racist. A number of investigations took place; and an inquest, but it was not a full one; there was a prison service inquiry, but the family was not present; and there was an inquiry by the CRE, but the family were not allowed to participate.

The House of Lords, citing *Edwards* and *Wright*, held that the state had a duty to investigate deaths in custody to ensure that the full facts were brought to light, that culpable and discreditable wrongdoing were exposed, and that dangerous practices and procedures were rectified. The minimum standards to be met include that the investigation should be independent, effective, prompt, in public, and involve the next of kin – it has to hold the persons involved accountable for their actions. In the present case, there was a breach of Article 2 – in particular, the investigation was private, the report was not published and the family had no involvement at all, and overall the investigation was not sufficiently full or effective.

This case sets out clearly the width of the requirements of the Article 2 duty to conduct a full investigation. It is clear from these cases that the usual procedures prior to the Act coming into our law were not sufficient to discharge this duty. Indeed, the House of Lords has now expressly altered the previously understood interpretation of the Coroners Rules so that the procedure on an inquest, the investigation into a death, is made more effective to ensure compliance with Article 2: the case is *Middleton*.[16]

A prisoner hanged himself in a prison cell; he was a known suicide risk. The inquest jury gave a note of their opinion that the prison service had failed in its duty of care for prisoners; the coroner declined to record this publicly, and the prisoner's mother sought judicial review of that refusal.

The House of Lords held that since an inquest is the means by which the state ordinarily discharges its obligation to institute an effective public investigation into a death

---

[15] *R (Amin)* v *Home Secretary* [2003] UKHL 51, [2004] 1 AC 653.
[16] *R (Middleton)* v *HM Coroner for West Somerset* [2004] UKHL 10, [2004] 2 AC 182; for discussion in the context of techniques of statutory interpretation under the Act, see above, pp. 69–70.

involving a possible breach of Article 2, it should ordinarily result in the expression of a jury's conclusion on the disputed factual issues. The Coroner's Act 1988 specifies the question for the jury to answer: 'how, when and where did the deceased come by his death'. The traditional narrow meaning of the word 'how' – 'by what means' – should be expanded to 'by what means and in what circumstances' to ensure that this provision gave full effect to the enquiry required by Article 2.

Likewise, the requirements of a proper investigation compliant with Article 2 has led to alterations to the rules governing inquests to ensure the participation of all relevant parties by the provision of funding where required.

This resulted from the case of *Khan*,[17] where funding had not been made available to the father of a 3-year-old daughter, who died following grossly negligent medical treatment in hospital, to allow him to pursue a proper investigation of her death. The Court of Appeal held that the state's obligations under Article 2 required an effective inquest, not just a police and NHS investigation, and that the exceptional complexity of the case meant that the father's effective participation in the inquest required him to have expert assistance. Article 2 therefore required reasonable funding for representation for the family to ensure an adequate and proper inquiry. Following the decision, the government altered the rules, to allow for funding to be provided. This does not mean that full-scale legal representation must be provided at all inquests,[18] but it must at least be possible where necessary.

The duty to conduct an adequate investigation applies equally if, after an initial investigation has taken place, new evidence comes to light, so long as the new information is credible.[19] But the duty is not open-ended: it does not require there to be an inquiry into *any* death related to the conduct of the state. Thus, in the case of *Gentle*,[20] the House of Lords rejected an argument that Article 2 requires a public inquiry into the war in Iraq. The duty under Article 2 to investigate a death depended on there being some case that the death was itself a breach of Article 2, a failure on the part of the state to protect life. Article 2 is not a general guarantee that no one will be exposed by any state action to a risk of death, and is not infringed by deploying military personnel in a dangerous area even if there is a risk of death.[21] However, an investigation is required if there is a specific concern that the state's system for protecting the lives of its servicemen may have failed to comply with or breached Article 2, such as where a soldier serving in Iraq died of hypothermia.[22]

---

[17] *R (Khan)* v *Secretary of State for Health* [2003] EWCA Civ 1129, [2004] 1 WLR 971.
[18] *R (Main)* v *Minister for Legal Aid* [2007] EWCA Civ 1147, [2008] HRLR 8: legal aid not required for there to be a proper investigation under Article 2 in this case.
[19] *Brecknell* v *UK* (2008) 46 EHRR 42.
[20] *R (Gentle)* v *Prime Minister* [2008] UKHL 20, [2008] 2 WLR 879.
[21] For further discussion of what amounts to an adequate investigation see, in the context of Article 3, below, pp. 167–8.
[22] *R (Smith)* v *Oxfordshire Assistant Deputy Coroner* [2009] EWCA Civ 441, Times 20.5.09.

THE RIGHT TO DIE?

The converse of the protection of life is where the court is asked to decide whether a person should be allowed to die, or even *caused* to die. These are cases where there is a certainty of death, and the patient, or his doctors, or his relatives, are asking the court whether particular treatment – doing something or not doing something – which is likely to cause the patient's death, would be a breach of Article 2. There are, of course, important and agonising decisions to be made, by everybody – not least by the judge. The right to protect life has no qualifications or limitations in the words of Article 2; but the proper determination of its scope, how far the state should go to protect life, will require a balancing exercise, a consideration of competing interests, in the individual circumstances of the case. The basic principle of our law is that a patient, who is in possession of their mental faculties, has the right to refuse treatment. The real difficulty arises where the patient does not have all of their mental faculties.

In the case of two patients, *M and H*,[23] two hospitals wished to withdraw treatment from patients in their care, who were in a permanent vegetative state. The High Court's starting point was that their right to life was protected by Article 2, as well as by the same principle in English law, and Article 2 also imposed on the state the duty not to take life. However, to be an infringement of Article 2, there would have to be a positive act, resulting in death, and not simply a discontinuance of treatment. Only where the circumstances were such that there was a *positive obligation* on the state to preserve life would a failure to provide treatment amount to a breach of Article 2. Where a responsible clinical decision was made to withhold treatment because the continuation of treatment was not in the patient's best interests, the state's obligation under Article 2 was discharged. The Court also noted that it was accepted in legal systems across Europe, that there was no continuing obligation to provide treatment to those in a permanent vegetative state.

The other situation where the decision has to be taken for the patient is where the patient is a child, and too young to be asked. In such cases, the need to balance the rights of the various parties may be very acute. One case, which we referred to when introducing the idea of balancing rights,[24] is the case of *A (Children) (Conjoined Twins: Surgical Separation)*.[25]

Jodie and Mary were conjoined twins, and the separation of them would lead to the death of Mary, because her lungs and heart were too deficient to oxygenate and pump blood through her body. Had Mary been born alone, she would have died shortly after birth; she remained alive because a common artery enabled Jodie, who was stronger, to circulate the blood for both of them. Separation would involve the cutting of the artery. The parents did *not* consent to the operation of separation; they had a parental desire to keep both children alive if possible, and a religious faith in the preservation of life. The doctors, on the other hand, were convinced that if they separated the girls they would save Jodie. Without

[23] *National Health Service Trust A* v *M* [2001] 2 WLR 942.
[24] Above, p. 15.
[25] [2001] 2 WLR 480.

the operation, Jodie would die in three to six months; and thereupon, of course, so would Mary. The doctors sought a declaration that the operation might lawfully be carried out; as well as the rights of the children and of the parents, the court also had to consider the rights of the doctors, to exercise their medical skill for the purpose of saving life and to know if, by doing so, they would be acting unlawfully, if they caused the death of Mary.

The Court of Appeal held that the operation would *not* be unlawful. The interests of Jodie had to be preferred to those of Mary, because as they were, neither of them could enjoy a proper or meaningful right to life, and Mary's life could not be saved by any operation. The situation was one where the doctors could act in defence of Jodie's life, and this justified the ending of Mary's life. It was also important that the purpose of the doctors here was to save Jodie: for there to be a violation of Article 2, there would have to be an intention to kill Mary, and that required a purpose to kill, which was not present here.

This case emphasises the overall importance of the right to life in such balancing exercises; it was all the more difficult here because there were two different persons, both of whose right to life was being threatened by the other. But, suppose the person who has the right to life expresses the desire to give up life, and to abandon that right?

AK,[26] a patient aged 19, suffered from motor neurone disease. He requested his doctors to discontinue, two weeks from the date when he should lose his ability to communicate, the artificial ventilation, nutrition, and hydration which was being provided to him. He was able to communicate solely by the movement of one eyelid, but this movement would shortly cease. In communicating his wish by this means to have the ventilator removed, he had been aware that such action would lead to his death. The doctors asked the court to make a declaration that it would be lawful to comply with his wishes.

The court held that it would be lawful to do as he wished, since a patient's refusal to consent to medical treatment had to be observed and complied with, where that patient was an adult of full capacity. It was *not* an *un*lawful termination of life to cease invasive treatment; rather it would be unlawful to treat a patient in the face of a wish *not* to be treated; and there would be no breach of Article 2.

But there is no right to die; this point was made in *Pretty*.[27] Mrs Pretty was suffering pain and degradation as a result of her illness, which was terminal, and she wished to die and to have her husband's assistance in bringing about her death. That would amount to an offence on his part, of assisting a suicide. So, Mrs Pretty asked the Director of Public Prosecutions to undertake not to prosecute her husband if he did assist her. The DPP refused to give that undertaking. Mrs Pretty sought judicial review of that refusal, and her argument was that the provisions of the Suicide Act 1961 were in breach of Article 2. The House of Lords held that the right to life could not be read as a right to die, or a right to enlist the help of another in bringing about one's own death. In short, there cannot be a simple abandonment of the right to life.[28]

---

[26] *AK (Adult Patient) (Medical Treatment: Consent)* [2001] 1 FLR 129.

[27] *R (Pretty)* v *DPP* [2001] UKHL 61, [2002] 1 AC 800; see also below, p. 162.

[28] *R(Purdy)* v *DPP* [2009] EWCA Civ 92, [2009] 1 CAR 32, held that the DPP's failure to publish guidance on prosecuting for assisting suicide did not engage or infringe Article 8 either.

This view was upheld when Mrs Pretty appealed to the European Court.[29] The European Court noted that the emphasis in Article 2 cases had always been on the state to *protect* life, and Article 2 could not therefore be read as conferring the exact opposite – a right to die.

However, Article 2 does not mean that the authorities are necessarily obliged to take any and all steps to prevent someone choosing to die. This appears from the case of Z.[30] Mrs Z was diagnosed as having incurable and irreversible cerebella ataxia, a condition which attacks the part of the brain which controls the body's motor function, as well as signs of Parkinsonism, and speech and hearing difficulties. She was, however, mentally competent. Mrs Z had expressed strong views about seeking assisted suicide, and she knew that that could be arranged in Switzerland. Her husband was ready to assist her with making the necessary arrangements to visit Switzerland for this purpose. The local authority, which had various statutory duties in respect of Mrs Z's welfare, because of her vulnerability, and which had been kept fully informed, sought an injunction (which it obtained on an interim basis) to prevent Mrs Z travelling to Switzerland, on the ground that the welfare of this vulnerable person was seriously threatened by her own decision. However, Mr Justice Hedley held at trial that whilst Article 2 was clearly engaged by this action, it did not assume primacy over rights of autonomy and self-determination, and the right to choose how a person should live her own life. Mrs Z was competent to take her own decisions and act in accordance with them, and there was no obligation on the local authority to prevent her from travelling abroad in this situation.

The right to life

THE UNBORN CHILD

We have considered the state's duty to safeguard life, and how this applies to those who cannot take decisions for themselves. How does this apply to the unborn child, the foetus, and what rights does it have? The answer is that it has some rights, it must be considered, but it does not have the full right to life under Article 2: the Convention does not prohibit abortion.[31]

In the case of *Paton* v *UK*,[32] Mr Paton was married to a woman who was eight weeks pregnant, and she announced that she intended to have an abortion. The Abortion Act 1967 permits termination of a pregnancy on the ground of risk to the life of the mother or injury to the physical or mental health of the mother, and Mrs Paton's doctors certified that there was this risk. The High Court refused to grant Mr Paton an injunction to prevent the abortion, and the abortion was carried out at 10 weeks. Mr Paton applied to the European Commission, asserting that the Abortion Act denied the right to life of the foetus, and thereby violated Article 2.

[29] *Pretty* v *UK* (2002) 35 EHRR 1.
[30] *Re Z (Local Authority: Duty)* [2004] EWHC 2817 Fam, [2005] UKHRR 611.
[31] See also below, p. 257, in the context of Article 8.
[32] (1980) 19 DR 244.

The Commission declared the application to be inadmissible, and rejected it. The Commission stated that the 'life' of the foetus is intimately connected with the life of the pregnant mother, and it cannot be regarded in isolation from that life. Particular regard was given to the fact that the termination was carried out at 10 weeks, in order to save the mother, and the Commission concerned itself specifically with whether a right to life should be assumed for the initial stage of the pregnancy. The Commission recognised a wide divergence of opinion in different countries, as to whether the foetus has a right to life, but it did note that laws on abortion have tended towards liberalisation. The Commission considered that to regard a foetus at such a stage as having a right to life would prohibit all abortions, there being no express exception in the article, and this was not a general view across Europe. But the European Commission did not need to reach a decision on the principle of a right to life being protected by Article 2 at stages of pregnancy later than 10 weeks.

The Commission's view was followed by the European Court in *Vo* v *France*,[33] which concerned a woman who attended hospital for a medical examination during the sixth month of her pregnancy. Following medical negligence at the hands of her doctor, the amniotic sac was injured, so that it was necessary to terminate the pregnancy at 20–24 weeks. The doctor was charged with causing intended injury, but acquitted on the grounds that the foetus was not a human person. The applicant claimed that Article 2 had been violated by this non-recognition, which meant that there was no effective remedy for the injury caused to it in French law.

The European Court held that there was no violation of Article 2. The Court did not consider that it could take a view under the Convention on whether a foetus was entitled to Article 2 rights. Since there is a wide degree of variance on this issue in the domestic law of European states, the determination of the question of the commencement of life came within the states' margin of appreciation:[34]

> At best, it may be regarded as common ground between States that the embryo/foetus belongs to the human race. The potentiality of that being and its capacity to become a person – enjoying protection under the civil law, moreover, in many States, such as France, in the context of inheritance and gifts [. . .] – require protection in the name of human dignity, without making it a 'person' with the 'right to life' for the purposes of Article 2.

The Court also recognised that the rights of the unborn child were limited by the mother's rights and interests. The Court further considered that, in the present case, the mother did in any event have a sufficient remedy in French civil law to ensure an adequate investigation of the circumstances of the forced abortion, and compensation if appropriate, so that, even if Article 2 was engaged, it had not been violated.

The English courts have also had to consider the status of an embryo in the context of fertility treatment.

---

[33] *Vo* v *France* (2005) 40 EHRR 259.
[34] Discussed above, pp. 54–6.

In the case of *Evans*,[35] the courts had to consider whether the female claimants were entitled to use frozen embryos created by IVF treatment, after they had separated from their male partners, who had since withdrawn their consent to treatment.

Mr Justice Wall held that Article 2 was not engaged since an embryo was not a human life. He also held, and the Court of Appeal agreed, that although Article 8, respect for private life, *was* engaged, any interference was quite justified and proportionate, because it was entirely appropriate that couples taking IVF treatment should both have to consent and that either could withdraw consent before any embryos were implanted in the woman – the private life of *both* persons had to be respected.

The European Court agreed and rejected her claim. It followed *Vo* and held that whether the embryo has a right to life is within the UK's margin of appreciation, and so, since under English law the embryo does not have a right to life, there was no violation of Article 2. It also rejected the claim under Article 8: the Court was not prepared to give any privilege to Mrs Evans's wishes over those of her ex-husband, where the embryo had been created by the consent of both parties, and held that the law in the UK was also within its margin of appreciation for dealing with this situation.

This case demonstrates the difficulty of balancing rights: Mrs Evans wished to manifest her right to have children, and therefore a family, but this would impose on her ex-husband a child which he did not want, and legal responsibilities he no longer wished to undertake.

THE QUALITY OF LIFE

The duty of the state to protect life goes further than cases where literally life or death has been at stake; the ambit of Article 2 is more extensive than that. The right to life has been read as protecting a minimum **quality** of life. This is relevant to situations in which decisions are being taken, or something has happened, which threatens this quality, such as when planning decisions are taken, or where there is an incident of environmental pollution.

In the case of *LM & R v Switzerland*,[36] there was a complaint by people living in houses near a railway line. The basis of the complaint was that wagons containing nuclear waste were for a short time standing stationary on the lines nearby, and then were taken past the houses. The residents complained that they were at risk of contamination from nuclear radioactivity, with a consequent risk to health, so that there was a violation of Article 2. The European Commission's decision was that the situation could fall within Article 2, although, in the circumstances, the state had taken all necessary precautions.

---

[35] *Evans* v *Amicus Healthcare Ltd* [2003] EWHC 2161 (Fam), [2004] 2 WLR 713 Wall J, [2004] EWCA 727, [2004] 3 WLR 681, Court of Appeal: Article 2 point not allowed to proceed in the Court of Appeal; appeal to the European Court rejected: *Evans* v *UK* (2006) 46 EHRR 321.

[36] (1996) 22 EHRR CD 130.

The decision is useful for the principle which it recognises: Article 2 is relevant to circumstances where health is at risk, and is not confined to cases of death or an immediate risk of death. Then, in the case of *Guerra v Italy*,[37] one of the judges gave a clear indication that Article 2 should apply to situations where the quality of the environment is in question.

> Residents near a chemical factory complained of toxic fumes, which caused arsenic poisoning, and 150 people were taken to hospital; they complained of a violation of their rights under Article 2, as well as under Article 8 (respect for private and home life).[38]
>
> The majority of the judges of the European Court did *not* find it necessary to deal with Article 2, having found a violation of Article 8. But a minority of the judges specifically filed opinions, indicating that they considered that a violation of Article 2 was also proved, since there were on the facts real and serious risks to life. Judge Jambek specifically said that it was time for the Court to start developing Article 2 in such a situation.

This last point is an express recognition that there are, within Article 2, aspects to the right to life which may be developed: the categories of protection are not closed. And we find a similar approach in this next case, where the European Court found that environmental failures gave rise to a violation of Article 2.

> In the case of *Oneryildiz v Turkey*,[39] the applicant and his family lived in slum quarter of Istanbul, near to a tip used by local councils. There had been warnings from experts about the danger from a possible explosion, which is what happened: there was a landslip and a methane explosion causing several deaths. The European Court held that there was a violation of Article 2 on account of the lack of appropriate steps to prevent accidental death: the authorities either had known or ought to have known of a real or immediate serious risk to life, and therefore they had been under an obligation to take measures to protect individuals, especially as they had set up the site and authorised its operation. The criminal justice system had not secured the full accountability of state officials: there was therefore a breach of Article 2.

 ## THE USE OF FORCE

Article 2(2) provides limited exceptions to the duty to protect life. These are exhaustive:[40] they are the only situations where the taking of life by the agent or officer of a state is not a violation of Article 2. The situations are where the force is required for self-defence or defence of other persons (but not of property), to carry out an arrest or prevent escape, or to quash a riot or insurrection. Even in such a situation, the force used must be no more than is **absolutely necessary** and must be **strictly proportionate** to the situation. The actions taken must also be in accordance with national law; for example, laws such as those controlling the use of firearms must be properly applied.

---

[37] (1998) 26 EHRR 357.
[38] The Court's view on Article 8 is considered below, p. 269.
[39] (2004) 39 EHRR 253.
[40] *Stewart v UK* (1985) 7 EHRR 453.

When ascertaining what is 'absolute necessity', there are two questions to be asked. The first is whether the use of force met the test of being strictly proportionate to one of the situations set out in Article 2(2), bearing in mind the danger of the situation. The second is whether the operation was planned and controlled by the authorities so as to minimise, to the greatest extent possible, the use of lethal force. This two-stage test was set out and considered by the European Court in the case of *McCann*,[41] from which we have quoted previously.

In *McCann*, the relatives of three people who were killed in Gibraltar by soldiers of the SAS claimed a violation of Article 2, arising out of their deaths. Information reached the authorities that a unit of the Provisional IRA was planning a terrorist attack on Gibraltar, and three suspects were known to have entered Gibraltar. SAS soldiers were sent to assist the Gibraltar authorities to arrest the IRA active service unit. The SAS soldiers were faced with an active service unit of the IRA, composed of persons who had been convicted of bombing offences, and a known explosives expert. The soldiers shot the three suspects at very close range, believing that they were about to press remote-control devices in order to detonate a bomb. The bodies were examined, and no remote device was found. The suspects' relatives alleged that the killings violated Article 2 of the Convention.

The European Court held that there had indeed been a violation of Article 2. The Court had to judge the actions not only of the soldiers themselves, but also those in charge of the whole operation; and stated the need to consider whether the force used by the soldiers was strictly proportionate to the aim of protecting persons against unlawful violence, and whether the whole operation was planned and controlled by the authorities so as to minimise recourse to lethal force.

The European Court accepted that the soldiers honestly believed in the light of the information which they had been given that it was necessary to shoot the suspects in order to prevent them from detonating a bomb and causing serious loss of life, and the action which they took was perceived by them as absolutely necessary in order to safeguard innocent lives. The actions of the soldiers themselves did not violate Article 2.

However, the Court did consider that there was a breach of Article 2 in the control and planning of the operation. First, there was no evidence about the training or instruction of the soldiers, especially as to whether they were trained to wound rather than kill; the Court expressly considered that a degree of caution in the use of firearms is to be expected from law enforcement personnel in a democratic society. The Court stated that the soldiers' reflex action suggested a lack of instruction, and a lack of care, on the part of the authorities, in the control and organisation of the operation. The authorities had failed in two further ways: they did not stop the suspects from entering Gibraltar; and they did not stop to consider whether the intelligence information, that the suspects had a remote-controlled device, might be wrong, since it was this that led to the automatic recourse to lethal force. So the Court was *not* satisfied that the use of force was no more than was absolutely necessary, and therefore those in command had brought about a violation of Article 2(2).

---

[41] *McCann* v *UK* (1996) 21 EHRR 97.

8

The right to life

▪ THE DEATH PENALTY

Thirteenth Protocol:

Article 1: Abolition of the Death Penalty
The death penalty shall be abolished. No one shall be condemned to such penalty or executed.

Article 2, as drafted, allows for capital punishment, the death penalty, although it is careful to limit this to the execution of the sentence of a court following conviction for a crime for which this penalty is provided by law. This includes the core Convention values of legality, that there should be a proper trial, and conviction, with the penalty provided by law. However, in the United Kingdom, this has been largely academic, since the death penalty for most offences, most notably murder, was abolished in 1965.[42] It was abolished for treason and piracy in 1998.[43] Following this, the Sixth Protocol, which prohibited the death penalty except in time of war, was signed by the United Kingdom on 27 January 1999, after a free vote in Parliament. The Minister of State for the Home Office, Lord Williams of Mostyn QC, said that ratification made it impossible for Parliament to reintroduce the death penalty in the future, without denouncing the whole of the Convention.[44] The Sixth Protocol was originally included in the Act. Then on 10 October 2003, Parliament ratified the Thirteenth Protocol, which prohibits the death penalty under all circumstances. Following that Protocol coming into force in February 2004, the Act has been amended to include the Thirteenth Protocol instead of the Sixth.[45]

It is notable that there can be no derogation[46] from Article 1 of the Thirteenth Protocol: even in times of emergency, states are not allowed to suspend this Article and reintroduce the death penalty, not even in times of war.

There will be a breach of Article 1 of the Thirteenth Protocol where an individual is deported or extradited from the United Kingdom to a country where they are likely to suffer the death penalty.[47] This is clear from the case of *Aylor-Davis* v *France*.[48]

Joy Aylor-Davis was arrested in France, having false identification papers; it then appeared that she was wanted for murder in Texas, and the United States sought her extradition. She opposed the application, contending that she would suffer the death penalty, if she were to be found guilty in Texas.

France had already abolished the death penalty, and had ratified the Sixth Protocol. The American authorities gave an assurance to the French authorities that if she were to be found guilty, the death penalty would not be carried out. The French courts accepted this,

---

[42] Murder (Abolition of Death Penalty) Act 1965.
[43] Prevention of Crime and Disorder Act 1998, section 36.
[44] House of Lords debates (*Hansard*, HL Vol. 593, col. 2084); and section 21(5) of the Act.
[45] Human Rights Act 1998 (Amendment) Order 2004 (SI 2004/1574).
[46] Article 2 of the Thirteenth Protocol; derogations are explained above, pp. 113–14.
[47] Such deportations may also risk breaching Article 3, considered below, p. 163.
[48] Application no. 22742/93.

and ordered her extradition. She complained to the European Commission that the extradition was a breach of the Protocol.

The Commission agreed that if indeed there had been a likelihood of her suffering the death penalty, the extradition would have been a violation; but, on the facts, there was no such violation, because the French authorities were entitled to accept the assurance.

QUESTIONS

1 Consider the situations of medical treatment, where the courts are being asked whether or not treatment should be continued. Do you think the courts are ever right to allow treatment to be withdrawn? Do you agree or not that the patient's wishes are paramount? Do you think that the law should recognise a right to die?

2 Do you think that an unborn child does or does not have a right to life? If it does, is there any difference between its right to life and the rights of an independent child or adult? If not, what rights, if any, does it have?

3 Do you agree with the abolition of the death penalty? Does your answer apply even in times of war?

8

The right to life

Kane descend whack gosh oo gosh oo gosh.

'Kane descend whack gosh oo gosh oo gosh': corporal punishment in schools is considered (see p. 156).

Source: From Geoffery Willans and Ronald Searle (1956) Molesworth. Copyright © 1956 by Ronald Searle.

9 Freedom from torture

Is not the pleasure of feeling and exhibiting power over other beings, a principal part of the gratification of cruelty? (John Foster, *Life and Correspondence*, 1846)

Torture is not acceptable. This is a bedrock moral principle in this country. (Lord Nicholls, *A* v *Home Secretary (No 2)*,[1] 2005)

> ### Article 3: Prohibition of Torture
> No one shall be subjected to torture or to inhuman or degrading treatment or punishment.

THE IMPORTANCE OF ARTICLE 3

> Article 3 makes no provision for exceptions and no derogation from it is permissible under Article 15 in time of war or other national emergency. This absolute prohibition on torture and on inhuman or degrading treatment or punishment under the terms of the Convention shows that Article 3 enshrines one of the fundamental values of the democratic societies making up the Council of Europe. (European Court in *Soering* v *UK*)[2]

In resounding phrases, the European judges have declared the principles of this article. It embodies a fundamental right, because the right to freedom from bodily harm is second only to the right to life, and is equally based on the right which all people have to a level of basic respect and dignity as human beings. In particular, once a person has been taken into custody by the state, or is otherwise in the power, or under the control, of the state and its officials, they should be safe from the infliction of deliberate physical harm. Patients in hospital, prisoners in jail, and pupils in a school are all examples of persons in such a position, where they are under the direction of others, and the treatment applied to them – using the word in its broadest sense – engages this article, since physical mistreatment by the state machinery is something which is *never* to be tolerated in a civilised society. Likewise, the rights set out in Article 3 are so important that, as with the right to life, the state effectively has a duty to safeguard them, to protect its citizens from any foreseeable risk of such harm occurring.

That is why the rights embodied by this article may not be infringed by a state, no matter what the justification, and no matter what threat the state may be acting against. In the case

[1] [2005] UKHL 71, [2005] 3 WLR 1249.
[2] (1989) 11 EHRR 439.

of *Chahal*,[3] who was a Sikh separatist leader who was refused asylum, on the ground that he was a terrorist, and was therefore facing deportation to India from the United Kingdom, the European Court said:

> Article 3 enshrines one of the most fundamental values of democratic society. The Court is well aware of the immense difficulties faced by a state in modern times in protecting their communities from terrorist violence. However, even in these circumstances, the Convention prohibits in absolute terms torture or inhuman or degrading treatment or punishment irrespective of the victim's conduct.

Finally, emphasising the importance of this article, there is the principle that ignorance is no excuse; the state cannot plead that it was unaware of the facts. This was made clear in the case of *Ireland v United Kingdom*,[4] in which the government of the Republic of Ireland complained that the British government had used ill-treatment in the course of the interrogation of prisoners detained under the prevention of terrorism powers. The Court said:

> It is inconceivable that the higher authorities of a State should be, or at least should be entitled to be, unaware of the existence of such a practice. Furthermore, under the Convention those authorities are strictly liable for the conduct of their subordinates; they are under a duty to impose their will on subordinates and cannot shelter behind their inability to ensure that it is respected.

But what difference does Article 3 make to our law? Torture is already an offence in the criminal law, and so are ill-treatment and assault, and one would think that those offences would cover the same situation as the words 'inhuman or degrading treatment or punishment'. The answer is that Article 3 covers situations which are not necessarily criminal, and which often have nothing to do with crime. There was no crime being committed against Mr Chahal, who was facing deportation to a place where he might face persecution. And there was no crime being committed against Ms Price, a case which we shall examine later, who had her rights infringed where she was sentenced to seven days' imprisonment, but, notwithstanding that she was disabled with four-limb deficiency and kidney problems, was kept in police and prison cells which were wholly unsuitable for her physical requirements. But even where there is no crime being committed, Article 3 applies a general minimum standard for the treatment of people by the state, especially in these kinds of situations where the state is in a dominant position.

THE SCOPE OF THE ARTICLE

Article 3 deals with three separate categories of treatment which are prohibited: **torture**; punishment or treatment which is **inhuman**; and punishment or treatment which is **degrading**. One case in which the European Court has considered the definition of all of these was *Ireland v United Kingdom*.[5] This was a case in which the Court had to consider the conduct of security forces in Northern Ireland when interrogating prisoners and it arose out of the exercise by the British government of powers of arrest, detention and internment.

---

[3] *Chahal v UK* (1997) 23 EHRR 413.
[4] (1980) 2 EHRR 25.
[5] Ibid.

From 9 August 1971 onwards, numerous people in Northern Ireland were arrested and taken into custody by security forces, acting under emergency powers. Those arrested were interrogated, usually by members of the Royal Ulster Constabulary, in order to determine whether they should be interned, and also to compile information about the IRA. The interrogation took the form of 'interrogation in depth'. The methods used were described as 'disorientation', or 'sensory deprivation' techniques; and the interrogation led to the obtaining of a considerable quantity of intelligence information. These techniques gave rise to allegations of ill-treatment, and this was the substance of the complaint by the Irish government before the European Court. There were five particular methods: wall-standing, where, for long periods, the detainee was made to stand legs spread apart, on the toes, with fingers high above the head against the wall, and the weight mainly on the fingers; being hooded, with a bag over the head; being subjected to a continuous and loud hissing noise; being deprived of sleep; and being deprived of food and drink.

The European Court examined the three categories of treatment set out in Article 3, and gave the following definitions. 'Torture' the Court defined as an aggravated and deliberate form of cruel, inhuman or degrading treatment or punishment. Ill-treatment, the Court held, must attain a minimum level of severity if it is to fall within the scope of Article 3. The assessment of this minimum is in the nature of things relative; it depends on all the circumstances of the case, such as the duration of the treatment, its physical or mental effects and in some cases the sex, age and state of health of the victim.

In the *Ireland* v *UK* case itself, the Court held that the techniques did *not*, in the particular circumstances of the case, have the particular intensity and cruelty which the word 'torture' implied. However, the five techniques were applied in combination with premeditation and for several hours at a stretch; they caused, if not actual bodily injury, at least intense physical and mental suffering to the persons subjected thereto and also led to acute psychiatric disturbances during interrogation. They accordingly fell into the category of inhuman treatment within the meaning of Article 3. The Court also said that the techniques were 'degrading', since they were such as to arouse in their victims feelings of fear, anguish and inferiority, capable of humiliating and debasing the prisoners, and possibly breaking their physical or moral resistance.

Freedom from torture

It really is a matter of judgment on the facts of a particular situation whether the victim's suffering amounts to a violation of Article 3. As the court said in the *Ireland* case, the treatment of the victim must attain a minimum level of severity before it can be said that there has been a violation. Some cases will be more obvious than others. Our discussion will focus not so much on a consideration of the detail of where torture has been established and where it has not, but on distinct types of situations where Article 3 has been commonly raised. And the sort of situations where Article 3 can apply are not as unusual as you might think.

VIOLENCE AND THE THREAT OF IT

This is almost too obvious, it might be said. Violence, if it is serious, is at least a candidate to qualify as torture, or inhuman or degrading treatment. Furthermore, violence will usually amount to a criminal offence, and so will be likely to be dealt with in the criminal courts, and in that event what is the point of bringing it within the Convention jurisprudence? One particular case provides a good example of where the threat of extreme violence risked a violation of Article 3, and where the English court was able to provide protection for the potential victims. The case is one we have already referred to in the context of Article 2, that of *Thompson and Venables*,[6] in which the two applicants, both young men aged 18, claimed that they could suffer death or serious injury if they were identified.

> Thompson and Venables had been convicted of a particularly shocking murder, that of the two-year-old James Bulger. The judge made an order forbidding publication of material which might identify them, and the newspapers sought to have this removed; Thompson and Venables claimed that the order was necessary for their protection. The court heard evidence of serious threats made against them and found that there was a real and serious risk of death or serious injury to the two young men, and therefore there was a risk of violations of Article 3, as well as Article 2. The judgment does not distinguish between the threats under each Article, but it is clear that, if the threats were carried out, if death did not result, very serious harm qualifying as torture, or inhuman or degrading treatment might well do. Thus, the order restraining publication was continued, even though that would interfere with the rights of expression of the newspapers under Article 10.

For the purposes of the present discussion, this emphasises that, where there is a risk of serious physical harm, and the state is in a position to do something about it, Article 3 will be engaged. It will then be for the state to ensure that it does all it can to prevent the harm. In this case, this meant that the court ordered that the relevant information should not be disclosed. But it should also be noted that the state's responsibility is not unlimited.

> In the case of *E*,[7] it was argued that the police in Northern Ireland had failed to protect children on their way to and from a Roman Catholic school in Belfast between June and November 2001 when there were attacks by Protestant loyalists. The House of Lords held that the positive obligation to protect the children from harm was not absolute, and the test was what was reasonable and proportionate. The police were also best placed to decide what was the wisest course to take, to avoid the situation escalating, and the evidence supported the conclusion they reached.

◼ SENTENCING OF CRIMINALS

After a person has been convicted of a crime, they will be sentenced, which may involve the payment of a fine, or some form of community service order, or a prison sentence. The question in the context of Article 3 is whether a sentence can be so excessive that it can amount to an inhuman or degrading punishment. It is clear that this could be the case.

---

[6] *Thompson and Venables v News Group Newspapers* [2001] 2 WLR 1038; above, p. 134; see also below, p. 254, in the context of Article 8.
[7] *Re E (A Child)* [2008] UKHL 66, [2008] 3 WLR 1208.

In the case of *Weeks* v *UK*,[8] the European Court had to consider the following situation. Mr Weeks, at the age of 17, entered a pet shop with a starting pistol loaded with blank cartridges, pointed it at the owner and told her to hand over the till. He got 35 pence, which he dropped on the shop floor. Later, he telephoned the police station, to say he would give himself up. Two police officers met him in the street, and as they arrested him he took the pistol from his pocket, and in a struggle two blanks were fired, and one officer suffered powder burns to his wrist. He committed the robbery because he owed his mother £3, who had that day told him to find other lodgings. He was convicted of robbery. There was no evidence of mental instability; a probation officer said he was subject to mood fluctuations and was immature; he had an interest in violent literature and a fascination with guns. A psychiatric report had not been obtained. The trial judge said that the defendant was very dangerous, and that he should be detained indefinitely, and sentenced him to life imprisonment. The Court of Appeal said that life imprisonment was imposed in mercy to the defendant, as he might be released much sooner than if a longer term had been imposed because of the possibility of release on licence.

The European Court considered Article 3, and stated that having regard to Weeks's age at the time and to the particular facts of the offence he committed, had it not been for the specific reasons advanced for the sentence, one could have serious doubts as to its compatibility with Article 3, as a case of inhuman punishment.

In our legal system, the sentence imposed in any particular case is based on guidelines developed by the Court of Appeal. Save where the sentence is mandatory – such as life imprisonment for murder – a judge has a discretion as to the type and length of sentence, but if a judge imposes a sentence which is outside the guidelines, or is excessive in the circumstances of the case, the sentence is likely to be reduced by the Court of Appeal. The Court of Appeal has made clear that, where the court has a discretion, it must be exercised in accordance with the Convention, to avoid a disproportionate sentence which could infringe Article 3.

In the case of *Offen*,[9] the Court of Appeal had to consider the application of certain mandatory sentences. The statute governing the sentences required certain sentences to be applied unless there were 'exceptional circumstances'. The courts had tended to read this narrowly. The Court of Appeal considered that the statute had to be read so that it avoided imposing a sentence which infringed Article 3. This could be done by appreciating that the purpose of the sentence is to keep in prison people who are a danger to the public – so anyone who is not a danger is an exception to this. Thus, the statute could be read in a way which allowed judges fully to take into account the particular circumstances of the individual offender. The statute would not contravene Article 3 if it did not result in offenders being sentenced to life imprisonment unless they constitute a significant risk to the public.

[8] (1988) 10 EHRR 293; but the lack of review of his detention was in breach of Article 5, see below, p. 185.
[9] *R* v *Offen* [2001] 1 WLR 253, discussed in the context of Article 7, below, p. 244.

This approach has been followed again in the case of *Rehman*,[10] where the Court of Appeal made clear that a mandatory minimum offence for certain firearms offences should not be imposed if it should lead to an arbitrary and disproportionate result. Again the Court considered there was no need to import words into the statute: there was a discretion which should be exercised in accordance with the Act.

CORPORAL PUNISHMENT

Corporal punishment is no longer allowed in schools,[11] and in the United Kingdom is no longer practised as a punishment for criminals. However, the cases on it still have some relevance for the meaning of what amounts to inhuman or degrading treatment. This is because the European Court has accepted the principle that corporal punishment may be permissible, including in schools, but punishment must not reach the level of being inhuman or degrading. And it will be a matter of taking the particular circumstances of each case and judging whether that level has been reached. This is demonstrated by the case of *Costello-Roberts* v *UK*[12] where on the facts of the case it was held that there was no violation.

A seven-year-old boy at an independent school received corporal punishment from the headmaster for breaches of the school rules; he had been there only five weeks, he had collected demerit marks, for minor offences, which 'totted up' under the school rules meant that he would be punished; he was told he would get the slipper, and then had to wait three days before the execution of it; he was given three whacks of the slipper on his clothed buttocks.

The European Court reviewed the circumstances: his age, how new he was to the school, the 'totting up' procedure, the three-day wait, and then the humiliation, and the impersonal and automatic way in which the punishment had been administered. None-theless, the Court held that in the circumstances of this case it did *not* reach the level of being degrading. In order for punishment to be degrading and in breach of Article 3, the humiliation or debasement involved must attain a particular level of severity, and must in any event be other than that *usual* element of humiliation inherent in any punishment. The Court considered that the reference in Article 3 to the express prohibition of 'inhuman' and 'degrading' punishment implied a distinction between such punishment and punishment more generally.

This case therefore stands for the proposition that there was no violation simply in administering a punishment. The question of *what* level of violence is permissible before it will be characterised as 'inhuman' or 'degrading' will depend on the precise facts of the case.

---

[10] *R* v *Rehman* [2005] EWCA Crim 2056, Times 27.9.05.
[11] See below, pp. 282–4, for discussion of the belief that corporal punishment has an educational value in the context of Article 9.
[12] (1995) 19 EHRR 112; there was also no breach of Article 8.

But looking at *Costello-Roberts*, one might think that the European Court requires a high level of severity before the level is reached. One case where the European Court found that the level was attained, where there were particularly unpleasant circumstances, was *Tyrer v UK*.[13]

> Mr Tyrer, aged 15, had been sentenced to three strokes of the birch for an assault occasioning actual bodily harm. He had to wait several weeks after the announcement of the sentence. On the day, he had to wait several hours at the police station before it was done. The birching was carried out at the police station, by a police officer, by striking him on his bare backside. Two police officers held him as he bent over a table. The birch rod broke on the first stroke, but the birching continued. His father lost his self-control and tried to attack a police officer, having to be restrained.
>
> The European Court held that this was a violation of Article 3; it was a punishment which was degrading: there was an assault on the boy's dignity and physical integrity: he had to endure the mental anguish of anticipating the violence in the three-week interval, and he had the indignity of the punishment inflicted on the bare posterior; that aggravated the degrading character of the sentence. The Court said that the institutionalised character of the violence was further compounded by the 'aura of official procedure attending the punishment' and by the fact that those inflicting it were total strangers to the offender.

TREATMENT OF PRISONERS

When one person inflicts unlawful or unreasonable violence on another, that is an assault. And most fair-minded people would add this: it makes it worse if the assailant is a custodian and the victim is his prisoner. The one is at the mercy of the other. The European Court has applied this in the approach it takes in Article 3 cases. In principle, such an assault is likely to be inhuman or degrading treatment or punishment. The European Court said this in the case of *Ribitsch v Austria*.[14]

> Mr Ribitsch was a prisoner in a police station, and while in custody he was subjected to violence at the hands of police officers. The Court found that he had been treated in such a way that his rights under Article 3 had been breached.
>
> The Court said that any violence to a prisoner is 'in principle' a violation of Article 3. The precise words of the Court are interesting:
>
>> In respect of a person deprived of his liberty, any recourse to physical violence, which has not been made strictly necessary by his own conduct, diminishes human dignity and is in principle an infringement of the right set forth in Article 3 of the Convention. [The Court] reiterates that the requirements of an investigation and the undeniable difficulties inherent in the fight against crime cannot justify placing limits on the protection to be afforded in respect of the physical integrity of individuals.

---

[13] (1980) 2 EHRR 1.
[14] (1995) 21 EHRR 573.

In other words, although crime may be prevalent, and although the particular criminal investigation may require an urgent answer, these considerations will not justify violence to a prisoner, however expedient that might be. The courts have developed this beyond the standard set out in the *Ribitsch* case of simply forbidding violence. Living conditions, health and comfort are now assessed, and Article 3 is a touchstone of prisoners' rights in all these areas.

> For example, in the case of *Napier*,[15] the ordinary standard of prison life was challenged. Mr Napier, a prisoner aged 21, was on remand in Barlinnie Prison, Glasgow; his cell was grossly inadequate in living space, lighting and ventilation, particularly as he shared it with another prisoner; the sanitary arrangements consisted of slopping out, which is urinating and defecating into a vessel in the cell, which had to be emptied two or three times a day; the two prisoners were confined to the cell for excessive lengths of time; and the conditions exacerbated Napier's eczema. The government admitted that the conditions amounted to a violation of Article 3, but contended that it was impracticable to change it, as that would mean altering the conditions for every prisoner. But the Court of Session decided that Napier was entitled to have his case determined on its own merits, and the broader consequences of treating every prisoner in a similar way did not alter the balance in his favour.

This case is authority for several important propositions: first, Article 3 extends to simple living conditions; second, once a violation is proved, inconvenience and cost are irrelevant; and third, normal prison practices are called into question, something which could not have been done without reliance on Article 3 and the Act.

Whatever debate there is about the benefit of sending someone to prison – not a debate we can pursue here – there is no doubt that prison is intended by the state as a punishment. Nonetheless, that punishment must take account of the prisoner's individual weakness, and the prison authorities must consider, monitor and balance the effect of the prison system on the health of the prisoner, including the effect on them of punishment within the system. That is the effect of the case of *Keenan* v *UK*.[16]

> Mr Keenan was a prisoner serving a short prison sentence; he had mental health problems, and was known to be a suicide risk. He attacked a prison officer and, after a delay of two weeks, he was brought before a prison adjudication board, and an extra 28 days' custody was imposed, 7 days of it to be in solitary confinement. There was no possibility of appeal or review. This extra sentence was imposed 9 days before he was due to be finally released from prison. On the day after the adjudication, he committed suicide.
>
> The European Court found that there had been inadequate monitoring of his mental condition. Further, the combination and timing of the new punishment was to be regarded as inhuman; his physical and moral resistance was threatened, and the way he was treated was not compatible with what was required for a mentally ill person. The whole way in which he was treated amounted to inhuman and degrading treatment.

[15] *Napier v The Scottish Ministers* [2002] UKHRR 308.
[16] (2001) 33 EHRR 38.

Again, this is an important case. It is a signal to state authorities that there has to be a close degree of care and control in the administration of institutions such as prisons; the key, after *Keenan*, will be care for the individual. And, following *Napier*, cost and inconvenience will not be an excuse for a failure to meet this standard. Another relevant case is that of *Wright*,[17] which we considered in the context of Article 2, since death resulted. There a prisoner with serious asthma, who was not properly treated or monitored, died after an asthma attack, which he suffered when he was locked in his cell with inadequate medication, and when medical help came only after a delay. As well as engaging Article 2, his pain and suffering before he died also engaged Article 3 – to leave a sick man locked in his cell and exposed to the risk of such pain and suffering may arguably be characterised as inhuman treatment.

On the one hand, it may be said that these cases impose a high burden on the state authorities, because so much attention must be paid to individual ill-health or disabilities. On the other, the punishment to which the courts sentence the prisoner is imprisonment, not to imprisonment with risk to life or health. Furthermore, it would be quite wrong not to deal appropriately with people who have some sort of disability: prison is a punishment, but it should not provide more of a danger to people with more particular needs than other prisoners. The next case, that of *Price*,[18] aptly illustrates this. Ms Price was disabled, and was sent to prison; but the premises provided for her custody were quite unsuitable; and the Convention was engaged.

Ms Price, a four-limb-deficient thalidomide victim with numerous health problems including defective kidneys, was committed for contempt of court in civil proceedings, and she was ordered by a judge to be detained for seven days; she was in fact detained for only three nights. In police cells, she had to sleep in her wheelchair, and she could not use the toilet as it was too high; every half-hour she complained of cold, and a doctor who came recorded that the cell was cold and not adapted for her. She could not wash. When she was in prison, the nurse was unable to lift her on to the toilet, and she was obliged to submit to male officers doing so. She had become dangerously cold; there was retention of urine, and she had to be catheterised.

The European Court found that there was a violation here of Article 3. To detain a severely disabled person in these conditions – so cold that it is a danger, risk of sores when the bed is hard or inaccessible, undignified toileting, and no washing – constitutes degrading treatment. The Court also considered *intention* in the context of Article 3, that is, the intention of the person imposing the treatment or punishment. The Court stated that in considering whether treatment is degrading, one of the factors which the court will take into account is the question whether the *object* of the treatment was to humiliate and debase the person. However, there is no requirement for such a purpose, and even when it is absent there may be a finding that a violation has occurred.

---

[17] *R (Wright) v Secretary of State for the Home Department* [2001] UKHRR 1399; also see in the context of Article 2, above, pp. 138–9.
[18] *Price v UK* (2002) 34 EHRR 53.

There is an important point here, that, for there to be a breach of Article 3, there is no need to prove that there is an *intention* to inflict inhuman or degrading treatment. In *Price* itself, there was no evidence of any positive intention to humiliate or debase the applicant. Nonetheless, since that was the effect of the treatment that she suffered, there was an infringement of Article 3. The *Price* case also illustrates the kind of situation which may well develop with people with particular physical needs or disabilities. Another example is the case of *Graham*,[19] where handcuffing a prisoner while he received chemotherapy treatment was a breach of Article 3 once it became clear that he did not pose a risk to the public. The state authorities must give consideration to the kind of facilities which are required for such situations. The fact that someone can be justifiably restrained or imprisoned does not mean that they can be kept in grossly unsuitable conditions.

ILL-TREATMENT OF CHILDREN

Just as the authorities must provide for the prisoner who has a medical condition, especially a condition which may be exacerbated by the regime of prison and its discipline, so they must take account of the youthfulness of a prisoner. The European Court stated thus in the next case, but held that on the particular facts there was no violation of Article 3. The case is *MM v UK*.[20]

> M was a juvenile, aged 12, arrested by police in Northern Ireland, on suspicion of car theft and criminal damage. At 5 p.m. he was taken to a police station and interviewed; his solicitor warned that he might do harm to himself, and advised against detaining him overnight; however, he was detained. At midnight he was charged; at 1 a.m. he was taken to a juvenile centre about 72 km away. At 2.30 a.m. he arrived and was placed in a cell with no furnishings and no floor covering. At 10.30 he was taken to the magistrates' court, and released on bail. The Commission held that the detaining of a child of 12 for eight hours in such a hostile and intimidating environment was cause for concern, but the treatment was *not* sufficiently severe to raise an issue under Article 3.

It is a matter of judgment and impression whether there has been a violation, and the point of this case is that the tenderness of infancy must be a real factor in finding whether there has been inhuman or degrading treatment.

But Article 3 has a wider application than simply the custody of children. In general terms our law has a great deal of protection for the rights of children. There is a range of legislative provisions which provide a child with rights to be cared for or looked after, and, in all such cases, the interest of the child is of paramount importance. In such cases, Article 3 adds an extra ground to be considered in making sure that a child's rights are fully protected, and, in some cases, an extra remedy.

---

[19] *R (Graham)* v *Secretary of State for Justice* [2007] EWHC 2940 (Admin), [2008] ACD 29.
[20] (2002) 8 January, Application 58374/00.

In the case of *Z v UK*,[21] the European Court had to consider the case of children who had been ill-treated by their families. Z and his three siblings had been subjected to severe long-term neglect and abuse, and had sued the relevant local authority for failing in its statutory duty to safeguard them; the House of Lords had rejected the claim. Z complained that the authorities had violated Article 3. The behaviour of the family had been reported to social services on several occasions, yet they had only acted five years after the first complaint, when the children were placed in emergency care at the insistence of their mother.

The European Court held that the social services system had failed to protect the children. While the role of social services was a difficult one, the state had clearly failed in its positive obligation to protect the children from ill-treatment of which it had, or ought to have had, knowledge. There was a breach of Article 3.

Again, this is an example where the state should be protecting those who cannot protect themselves from mistreatment. The European Court found that the English system for doing so had failed, and therefore the law should have provided a remedy for the children for the invasion of their dignity and integrity. The English courts have recognised that this has altered the law of negligence to give effect to Article 3.

In *D*,[22] the courts had to consider this situation again; there was a difference, though, which was that the claims here were being brought by the parents of children where there had been unfounded accusations of abuse.

The House of Lords held that no duty was owed by the healthcare professionals to the *parents*, because if abuse was suspected the doctor had to act single-mindedly in the interests of the child. However, the House of Lords made clear that, as a result of *Z*, as Lord Bingham put it:

It is no longer legitimate to rule that, as a matter of law, no common law duty of care is owed to a child in relation to the investigation of suspected child abuse and the initiation and pursuit of care proceedings.

MEDICAL TREATMENT

What now follows is *not* a collection of cases where doctors have caused pain or prescribed inhuman treatment. The point here is that usually medical treatment is a benefit, even where it is invasive, and even compulsory treatment (for example of someone who is not mentally competent to consent) will not breach Article 3 if it is medically justified.[23] But sometimes even the best treatment and the most skilful surgery may have results which the patient does not want to suffer, and which the patient would consider degrading – even if the refusal of treatment would lead to the death of the patient. We see this in the case of *National Health Service Trust v D*.[24]

---

[21] (2002) 34 EHRR 3.
[22] *D v East Berkshire NHS Trust* [2005] UKHL 23, [2005] 2 AC 373.
[23] *R (B) v Ashworth Hospital Authority* [2005] UKHL 20, [2005] 2 WLR 695.
[24] [2000] 2 FLR 677.

Here a 19-month-old child was in a poor state of health, with an irreversible and worsening lung disease, which meant a very short expectation of life. The NHS Trust applied to the court for a declaration regarding the future: it was that in the event of future cardiac or respiratory failure, the doctors would be entitled to treat the child *without* resuscitation by artificial ventilation, but *with* full palliative care, allowing the child to die peacefully and with dignity. The doctors asked for the declaration, because a decision might have to be taken as a matter of urgency. The parents opposed the doctors' application as being premature.

The court granted the declaration, stating that the full palliative treatment, but without artificial ventilation, was in the best interests of the child; and his interests must be considered above all other views, even those of the parents, when deciding whether medical treatment should be given or withheld. The body of medical opinion was of the clear view that artificial ventilation would be an intrusive and painful process, and would not offer any lasting benefit. Provided that the suggested form of care was in the best interests of the child, such a decision could not be said to be in contravention of Article 3, or the Article 2 right to life either. Even though the avoiding of invasive and hurtful treatment would or might lead to death, if this course was in the best interest of the child, that would *not* amount to inhuman treatment.

But it is deceptively easy to say that the court will simply try to avoid imposing degrading treatment. That argument was advanced in the case of *Pretty*,[25] which we have already considered in the context of Article 2, since Mrs Pretty's primary argument was that she had the right to die.

Mrs Pretty was suffering pain and degradation as a result of a terminal illness, and she sought an assurance from the Director of Public Prosecutions that her husband would not be prosecuted for assisting her suicide, which the DPP refused to give.

In deciding that the DPP was entitled not to give such an assurance, the House of Lords examined the relation of Article 2 to Article 3, and stated that in some circumstances the state might be justified, in order to maintain the right to life, in imposing treatment which might be so invasive that it would otherwise be in breach of Article 3. But the House disposed of the Article 3 argument in this case, by pointing out that it was not the DPP's decision which was causing the pain and degradation, but her own illness.

As with the argument on the right to life, the European Court agreed with this:[26] there was no ill-treatment by the state, and, in those circumstances, Article 3 did not apply. Article 3 could not be read to oblige the state to sanction actions intended to terminate life.

Thus, the failure of Mrs Pretty's argument was not a failing in her legal rights or a decision of the court that she should be obliged to undergo pain, but because it was her illness that was causing the pain, not the treatment she was being given or anything done or decided by anybody.

[25] *R (Pretty)* v *DPP* [2001] UKHL 61, [2002] 1 AC 800; above, p. 142.
[26] *Pretty* v *UK* (2002) 35 EHRR 1.

DEPORTATION OF IMMIGRANTS

The Act, of course, extends only to the United Kingdom; it does not extend to other nations, or to public authorities of other countries, nor does it bind them.[27] So what is the position when a person is being sent to another country, outside the jurisdiction of our courts, and out of the safety of the Convention? Suppose it is obvious that this person will, in that country, suffer torture, or inhuman or degrading treatment or punishment, whether at the hands of that state's officers or from some other person?

The answer is that it will be a breach of Article 3 for the United Kingdom authority to send the person there. This is illustrated in the case of *Soering* v *UK*,[28] quoted at the start of this chapter.

> Mr Soering was the subject of a decision by the Home Secretary to extradite him to the United States to face trial in Virginia on a charge of capital murder; if he were to be convicted, and sentenced to death, he would be exposed to the so-called 'death row phenomenon'. He could expect to spend six to eight years in a stringent custodial regime, with likely attacks by fellow prisoners, and with the 'ever present and mounting anguish of awaiting execution of the death penalty'. Further, at the time of the killing, he was 18 years of age, and of a mental state which impaired his responsibility for his acts. He complained that to extradite him in these circumstances amounted to a violation, on the part of the government of the United Kingdom, of Article 3.
>
> The European Court agreed, and stated, referring to the appeal procedures in the USA:
>
> > However well intentioned and even potentially beneficial is the provision of a complex of post sentence procedures, the consequence is that the condemned prisoner has to endure for many years the conditions on death row, and the anguish and mounting tension of living in the ever present shadow of death.

In other words, however fair and careful were the legal procedures in favour of the accused, if the treatment was inhuman or degrading within the meaning of Article 3, there would be a violation of the Article to release the person to such treatment.

However, this does not require the court to be satisfied that there is *no* possibility of any treatment which could be inhuman or degrading: the test is for the deportee to show a very strong case that there would be such treatment. The House of Lords in the case of *Wellington*[29] held that a deportation to the United States to face a sentence of life imprisonment with very limited prospects of parole or release on licence was not inhuman or degrading. A majority also considered that there may be cases where there is a risk of treatment which would be forbidden as inhuman or degrading if allowed in the UK, but which would not necessarily prevent deportation: the policy in favour of extradition between countries means that a more relative standard is to be applied. Indeed, even the possibility

---

[27] Although the Convention may apply to the actions of a British official in territory under British control: see discussion of *Al-Skeina*, above, p. 105.
[28] (1989) 11 EHRR 439.
[29] *R (Wellington)* v *Home Secretary* [2008] UKHL 72, [2009] 2 WLR 48.

that the death penalty will be applied does not of itself mean that it is a breach of the Convention to transfer prisoners to a different jurisdiction.[30]

This problem is at its most acute where the people whom the government wishes to deport have committed, or are suspected of being involved in, crimes of terrorism, but there is no country which will take them where they can be free of ill-treatment: but the European Court has confirmed that their conduct does not deprive them of the protection of Article 3.[31]

The inhuman or degrading treatment may come about because the standard of life in the destination country is inferior to the standard of life in the United Kingdom. The point is that the change of standard of life may be so great, *for the particular individual*, that it bears upon him with inhumanity or degradation; and this is particularly so where a medical condition or medical treatment is at the heart of the change. We see this in the case of *D* v *UK*.[32]

D, who came from St Kitts, arrived at Gatwick Airport in possession of prohibited drugs. He was refused leave to enter the country, and he was subsequently convicted of a drug offence, and imprisoned. While in prison he was diagnosed as suffering from AIDS, and he was treated for this. After serving a term of imprisonment, and when he was due to be released on licence, the immigration authorities gave directions for his removal to St Kitts. D requested leave to remain in the United Kingdom, claiming that his removal would entail the loss of vital medical treatment, and his life would be shortened. His request was refused. He complained to the European Court that to deport him in these circumstances would be in breach of Article 3.

The European Court took account of the fact that he was receiving sophisticated treatment, and the Court was satisfied that the abrupt withdrawal of this would bring about the most dramatic consequences for him, and that his removal to St Kitts would hasten his death. It was held that to deport him would mean a violation of Article 3. But the Court noted that, in principle, aliens who serve their prison sentences and are then subject to expulsion cannot claim to remain in the territory of the expelling state in order to continue getting benefit from medical, social or other assistance. There were in this case exceptional and compelling humanitarian considerations to conclude that the removal would involve a violation of Article 3.

In the case of *N*,[33] the House of Lords distinguished *D*. N was a Ugandan citizen who sought asylum in the UK. She was very ill and was admitted to hospital with AIDS. Her claim to asylum was refused. She sought to remain in the UK on the grounds that her deportation would breach Article 3, since she would not have access to the medical treatment she needed if she were returned to Uganda.

The House of Lords held that this case did not show the exceptional circumstances found in *D*, who was unfit to travel and who would have suffered acutely at his destination. Article 3 did not oblige the UK to treat medically foreign nationals indefinitely, even if their return would expose them to inferior health treatment.

---

[30] *R (Al-Saadoon)* v *Secretary of State for Defence* [2009] EWCA Civ 7, Times 4.2.09, which concerned the transfer of prisoners in Iraq from the custody of British forces to the Iraqi authorities.
[31] *Saadi* v *Italy* [2008] 24 BHLR 123, for further discussion in the context of terrorism, see below, pp. 375–6.
[32] (1997) 24 EHRR 423.
[33] *N* v *Home Secretary* [2005] UKHL 31, [2005] 2 AC 296.

TREATMENT OF IMMIGRANTS

Article 3 may also apply to the way immigrants are treated while they are awaiting a decision about whether they will be allowed to stay in the country or not. Some immigrants are seeking political asylum – literally a place of safety – having had to flee violence or some other threat to their or their family's life, without being able to bring any means of support with them. Others are economic migrants, in search of a better life, and can be more reasonably expected to support themselves. But all people who are seeking a better life in our country, for whatever reason, deserve basic consideration of their needs while their case is considered: even though they are not citizens of the United Kingdom, they have basic human rights which our government must respect. This situation will engage Article 3 if the way in which they are treated is in fact inhuman or degrading, and this has an impact on what support they are provided by the state.

In the case of *Limbuela*,[34] Mr Wayoka Limbuela was from Angola, and had claimed asylum the day after arriving in the UK, but had been refused support for applying too late. He had spent two nights outside a police station without food before being granted temporary support. The judge who heard his case had ordered that the government provide Mr Limbuela with accommodation and support until the determination of his asylum claim. The government appealed.

The House of Lords held that shelter from the elements at night was a basic amenity and upheld the decision. In the words of Lord Bingham:

> Treatment is inhuman or degrading if, to a seriously detrimental extent, it denies the most basic needs of any human being. [To infringe Article 3 it] must achieve a minimum standard of severity, and I would accept that in a context such as this, not involving the deliberate infliction of pain or suffering, the threshold is a high one. A general public duty to house the homeless or provide for the destitute cannot be spelled out of Article 3. But I have no doubt that the threshold may be crossed if a late applicant with no means and no alternative sources of support, unable to support himself, is, by the deliberate action of the state, denied shelter, food or the most basic necessities of life.

A number of previous cases on the duty to provide support were considered. In the case of *Q*,[35] the Court of Appeal had held that the statute which governed the provision of support to refugees[36] was not being operated in a procedurally fair manner, but in principle could operate within Article 3, so long as a person claiming support was provided with it where his condition required it. However, the judges in *Limbuela* expressed continuing concerns about the way in which the support system was being operated. As Lord Hope put it:

> as soon as the asylum-seeker makes it clear that there is an imminent prospect that a breach of the article will occur because the conditions which he or she is having to endure are on the verge of reaching the necessary degree of severity the Secretary of State has the power [. . .], and the duty under [. . .] the Human Rights Act, to act to avoid it.

[34] *R (Limbuela)* v *Home Secretary* [2005] UKHL 66, [2006] 1 AC 396.
[35] *R (Q)* v *Home Secretary* [2003] EWCA Civ 364, (2003) 3 WLR 365.
[36] Section 55 of the Nationality, Immigration and Asylum Act 2002.

The question of support for immigrants is a politically controversial one, but this case shows that the Act has imposed the basic standard set by Article 3 in all such cases – whatever approach the government wishes to take to the question of immigration, it is still under a positive duty to ensure that those who arrive in the UK are treated humanely. It is also necessary that those who cannot yet be deported, perhaps because they face ill-treatment, are dealt with according to the law.

> This was the point in the case of S,[37] which hit the headlines because it concerned the rights of a number of Afghan hijackers to stay in this country. The men hijacked a plane in February 2000 to flee the Taleban regime, and forced it to fly to Stansted. They were arrested and later convicted of various offences, but the appeals were quashed because they had acted under duress and because of mistakes in the way the jury was directed at their trial. Then the government's attempt to deport them was refused because of the risk of reprisals if they were returned to Afghanistan. They were granted a form of temporary permission to stay in the UK. This was ruled to be unlawful by Mr Justice Sullivan, which was upheld by the Court of Appeal. Mr Justice Sullivan called the Home Office's refusal to abide by its own ruling, which allowed the men to stay, 'an abuse of power by a public authority at the highest level'. There was a political outcry, but the Court of Appeal agreed: the Home Secretary had had no authority to create a new category of immigrant with temporary permission to remain without legislation. The Court reaffirmed the importance of legality in executive action: government ministers cannot create new categories of immigration status as they wish but must act in accordance with the law.

 ## SEXUAL DISCRIMINATION AND HARASSMENT

Will the courts hold that sexual discrimination or harassment is capable of amounting to a violation of Article 3? Probably, if the humiliation and indignity suffered by the victim is sufficiently intense. This is important. Public authorities may have procedures which pose intrusive questions; or the state may fail to recognise sexual orientation. A case in the European Court illustrates the relevant principles in this field. It is an example of both discrimination and harassment.

> *Smith and Grady* v *UK*[38] involved two separate cases where Ms Smith and Mr Grady were discharged from the armed forces for being homosexual. Prior to their discharge, the investigation into their private lives, by service police, was of an exceptionally intrusive character. As soon as the matter was in the hands of the police, Mr Grady was obliged to leave his wife and children in the USA and return to the United Kingdom; in his absence,

---

[37] *R (S) v Home Secretary* [2006] EWHC 1111 (Admin), [2006] EWCA Civ 1157, Times 9.10.06.
[38] (2000) 29 EHRR 493.

detailed and intrusive interviews about his private life were held with his wife, a colleague, and others. His accommodation was searched. He was later interviewed, as were Ms Smith and her partner. At the interviews of Ms Smith and Mr Grady, they were each asked detailed questions of an intimate character about their particular sexual practices and preferences; they were asked about their habits, their friends, and in the case of Ms Smith about her relationship with her own foster-daughter. They were each discharged, pursuant to a Ministry of Defence policy of excluding homosexuals from the armed forces. Their discharge had a profound effect on their careers and prospects.

The European Court considered that the investigation, and discharge, together with the Ministry blanket policy, were of a particularly grave nature. And the Court accepted that the kind of treatment experienced by Ms Smith and Mr Grady, grounded on a bias of a heterosexual majority against a homosexual minority, could *in principle* fall within the scope of Article 3. But on the facts, the Court held that there was *no* breach. In short, the actual experience of Ms Smith and Mr Grady did not reach the level of degradation required by the jurisprudence of the Convention. However, the case does demonstrate how intrusion into privacy may amount to inhuman or degrading treatment.

PURSUING A CLAIM UNDER ARTICLE 3

'Fundamental' – that is how the courts regard the right under Article 3. Therefore the state must not obstruct a citizen who claims that a violation has occurred; and indeed the state has an obligation to ensure that an effective investigation takes place. This is confirmed by the case of *Green*.[39]

Mr Green was knocked off his bicycle by an unmarked car in April 1999; the car was driven by a detective sergeant; Mr Green got up, but claimed that he was knocked down again; he sustained severe injuries and he made a claim against the police officer, and this was referred to the Police Complaints Authority (PCA), which investigated the complaints in order to consider the criminal and disciplinary aspects. Mr Green sought disclosure of material from the PCA, which refused to provide it.

The House of Lords approved the principle that a complaint of police misconduct could engage Article 3 and that Article 3 then required an independent and effective investigation of such a complaint. This did not, however, go as far as to entitle a complainant, such as Mr Green, to see the full details of the evidence before the PCA. A complainant's interests were sufficiently safeguarded by his rights to contribute evidence, to be kept informed of the progress of the investigation and to see the reasoned decision at the end of the investigation. He did not have the right to participate in the investigation itself, especially if there was a possibility that a prosecution may still be brought against the police officer; nor was he entitled to disclosure of all the material before the PCA even where there was no longer an ongoing investigation in progress.

[39] *R (Green)* v *Police Complaints Authority* [2004] UKHL 6, [2004] 1 WLR 725.

Obviously, each case depends on its own facts and, had the investigation been improperly conducted, the courts could have ordered disclosure of further documents. Nevertheless, this decision shows the spirit of the Article; the European Court has always said that the rights of the Convention must be effective and not illusory, and that is the principle which our courts will seek to apply.[40]

EVIDENCE OBTAINED BY TORTURE

Suppose the claim is not directly about the torture of the individual before the court but a case where the complaint is that the state wishes to rely on evidence obtained by torture? As we have seen, Article 3 forbids the torture of prisoners in state custody. This also interfaces with Article 6 and the right to a fair trial: what should a court do if it is presented with evidence obtained by torture? The answer is that a criminal court would reject a defendant's confession wrung from him by torture, and any court will do its best to avoid making use of evidence which has been obtained by torture.

In *A v Home Secretary (No. 2)*,[41] the question arose how far it was relevant in a terrorist case that a Secretary of State's decision might be founded on evidence obtained by torture. The Secretary of State certified that the appellants were suspected international terrorists and that he had a reasonable belief that their presence in the UK was a national security risk, and so they were detained. He formed his belief and suspicion on the basis of statements and material placed before him. The question that was raised was what the court should do if there was a possibility that the evidence was obtained by torture, by the officials of some other country.

The House of Lords held that SIAC, the tribunal which hears appeals from persons who have been certified as terrorists, should not admit any evidence which had or might have been obtained by the inflicting of torture on any person. The Lords were emphatic about the exclusion of such evidence – under common law and international law as well as under the Convention – and Lord Nicholls opened his speech with the words we quoted at the start of this chapter: 'Torture is not acceptable. This is a bedrock moral principle in this country.' It is offensive in principle; it makes the evidence obtained unreliable; it cannot be justified against those not yet convicted of a crime.

There was a difference of views about whether it had to be *proved* that the evidence was obtained by torture before it was excluded: it was common ground that the defendant must provide some basis on which it can be considered that the evidence could have been obtained by torture; the majority of the Lords held that if it was more likely than not that it had been obtained by torture, it should be excluded; if not, the evidence should be admitted, but SIAC should keep any doubts in mind when considering how much weight to give to the evidence. It was also noted that ill-treatment falling short of torture might or might not need to be excluded, depending on the circumstances.

---

[40] Likewise, an effective investigation in an Article 2 case by the PCA does not require that the police officers be prevented from conferring about their evidence: *R (Saunders) v Independent Police Complaints Commission* [2008] EWHC 2372 (Admin), [2009] 1 All ER 379.

[41] *A v Home Secretary (No. 2)* [2005] UKHL 71, [2005] 3 WLR 1249; for further discussion of the exclusion of evidence in the context of Article 6, see below, pp. 264–5.

Thus our courts have been quite categorical: whatever the crime which is being investigated, there is no justification for relying on evidence obtained by torture.

QUESTIONS

1 How far should states have to go in taking responsibility for protection of the person?

2 How far should states be responsible for medical treatment?

3 Do you consider that corporal punishment in schools and/or prisons should be allowed? Why/why not?

4 Do you consider that it can ever be permissible to obtain security information by torture? What if it is to avoid an immediate threat to life, such as an imminent terrorist attack? Should such information be used in a court of law?

5 Should the state be allowed to deport people if they will face ill-treatment in their destination country? What is your answer to the issue of balancing the rights of the individual to personal safety against the rights of the community to regulate immigration?

9

Freedom from torture

An eighteenth-century advertisement for a slave market in the American colonies.

Source: Library of Congress

10 Freedom from slavery

Epitaph on a tombstone in the churchyard of the Windermere Parish Church of St Martin:
'In Memory of Rasselas Bellfield, a native of Abyssinia, who departed this life on 16th day of January 1822, aged 32 years

A slave by birth: I left my native land,
And found my Freedom on Britannia's Strand:
Blest Isle! Thou Glory of the Wise and Free!
Thy Touch alone unbinds the Chains of Slavery.'

Article 4: Prohibition of Slavery and Forced Labour

1 No one shall be held in slavery or servitude.

2 No one shall be required to perform forced or compulsory labour.

3 For the purpose of this Article the term 'forced or compulsory labour' shall not include:

   (a) any work required to be done in the ordinary course of detention imposed according to the provisions of Article 5 of this Convention or during conditional release from such detention;

   (b) any service of a military character or, in case of conscientious objectors in countries where they are recognised, service exacted instead of compulsory military service;

   (c) any service exacted in case of an emergency or calamity threatening the life or well-being of the community;

   (d) any work or service which forms part of normal civic obligations.

THE RELEVANCE OF ARTICLE 4 TODAY

A great English judge, Lord Mansfield, Chief Justice, said in 1771 that one man could not own another. This was in the case of *Somersett*[1] and that has remained our law ever since. But the slave trade continued to flourish. It still exists today: there are situations and places where people are held in subjection, where they are treated as the property of someone else.

---

[1] (1771) 20 State Trials 1.

Modern European legal systems prohibit such practices, but, sadly, that does not mean that they never take place.

Article 4 is also about people who are made to do forced labour, and questions arise about what is meant by forced labour, and whether this extends to work for long hours or for inadequate pay. This is an aspect of the same principle as the prohibition of slavery: it is a fundamental part of treating people with the basic dignity which they deserve as human beings, that they should be treated as *people* and not as *property*, or, one could add, work tools or machines.

WHAT IS SLAVERY?

To know what Article 4 is about, we must look at the definitions of the terms of the Article. The words 'slavery' and 'servitude' are not defined in the Convention. However, it can be helpful to look at other Conventions, especially those which were already part of international law in 1950, when the European Convention was drafted.

One helpful definition is that contained in the Slavery Convention of 1926, which defines **slavery** as 'the status or condition of a person over whom any or all of the powers attaching to the right of ownership are exercised'. This Convention does not define the term **servitude**: it would be fair to say that servitude means something similar to slavery, but with overtones of someone who is obliged to perform services, such as forced labour, as in the phrase 'penal servitude'. The Supplementary Convention on the Abolition of Slavery 1956 does include a definition of 'serfdom', which comes from the same Latin derivation as servitude. Serfdom is defined here as 'the condition or status of a tenant who is by law, custom or agreement, bound to live and labour on land belonging to another person and to render some determinate service to such other person, whether for reward or not, and is not free to change his status'. The key idea here, which applies equally to 'servitude', is the obligation to provide a service to someone else, without the freedom to leave that person's service – unlike when one usually provides a service as an employee, where the employee is free to leave their job, even if it is only on certain conditions, such as giving notice.

It is notable, in considering the scope of Article 4, that the 1956 Supplementary Convention on the Abolition of Slavery provides for states who sign it to take all necessary measures to bring about the abolition of a number of conditions analogous to slavery. These include serfdom, as defined above; debt bondage, where a person pledges his personal services as security for a debt, except where the scope of the services is limited to the payment of the debt; children being provided as labour; and situations where women are obliged to marry without right of refusal.

Whilst most, if not all, European states forbid these sorts of arrangements, there are certainly countries in the world today where they are permitted or where they continue, even if not legal. So, the consideration of the basic meaning of slavery has, sadly, not ceased to be relevant, nor servitude. Unfortunately, in a world where there is great economic pressure on people to move around to find jobs to support themselves and their families, there are far too many people who find themselves tricked by promises of a better life, and then bound to the service of others, which they are not in fact free to leave, especially if they are too poor or too weak to assert their legal freedoms. They are often hidden from public view, sometimes only coming to light in tragic circumstances, such as the Chinese immigrants who died when they were forced to pick cockles in Morecambe Bay and were cut off by the tide. Such cases are already criminal – Article 4 embodies the current attitude of the law and society, that such exploitation is an abomination.

An example where the European Court has had to consider the case of an immigrant worker brought to France but denied freedom when she got there is the case of *Siliadin*.[2] Ms Siliadin was from Togo and had come to Paris at the age of 15 to work. She was expecting to go to school there, but in fact was forced to work as a domestic servant, without respite, without payment and without attending school or otherwise being able to develop herself, and in addition her immigration status was never regularised. The European Court held that Ms Siliadin was being held in servitude, since she was entirely dependent on the people for whom she was working, in breach of Article 4. The Court, emphasising the fundamental nature of the obligations under Article 4, held that the French criminal law had not provided practical and effective protection against the actions of which she was a victim; that was the breach of Article 4 on the part of the French state.

This is an important, and Europe-wide, issue, especially in an age of increasing migration, and the decision emphasises that ill-treatment of workers who are in a vulnerable position may be a question which goes beyond the regulation of their employment, and may become one of their fundamental freedoms.

It is certainly not to be expected in modern European society that the *state* will keep its citizens in a state of slavery or servitude. This was argued in respect of one context where the state does control the freedom of its citizens, where they have been imprisoned for committing a crime, in the case of *Van Droogenbroeck v Belgium*.[3]

A man aged 30 was convicted of theft, and sentenced to two years' imprisonment, and the Belgian court also ordered him to 'be placed at the Government's disposal' for 10 years, under a statutory power, since he was regarded as having a persistent tendency to commit crime. He served his sentence of imprisonment, and was then put in 'semi-custodial care', which meant his attending a central heating firm as an apprentice, as well as going to intensive vocational courses on Fridays and Saturdays. He disappeared, but he then committed more offences, and he was detained again, until he had earned sufficient money to enable him to be released and rehabilitated. He complained that this sentence, and especially his being placed at the disposal of the government for 10 years, was a violation of Article 4.

The European Court rejected his claim; it stated that conduct would be regarded as servitude only if it involved a particularly serious form of denial of freedom, and that was not the case here.

[2] *Siliadin v France* (2006) 43 EHRR 16.
[3] (1982) 4 EHRR 443.

The case is instructive: it shows that Article 4 *may* be relevant when one considers the sentence imposed by a court, and the prison and penal system, even though it may be *unlikely* that this will amount to slavery or servitude.

 ## FORCED OR COMPULSORY LABOUR

Forced or compulsory labour is prohibited by Article 4(2). 'Labour' is not limited to physical work; it applies to any kind of work. Once again, some assistance in defining these terms can be found in two other Conventions. The first is the Convention Concerning Forced Labour 1930,[4] which requires the suppression of forced or compulsory labour. This defines **forced labour** as work or service which is extracted under the menace of a penalty, or for which the person has not offered himself voluntarily. The second is the Convention for the Abolition of Forced Labour 1957.[5] This was agreed in the years immediately following the Second World War, and reflects the experiences of the concentration camps, and the use of political imprisonment by totalitarian states. It prohibits forced or compulsory labour as a means of political coercion, or punishment for the expression of political or ideological views, or as a means of labour discipline, or for punishment for participation in strikes, or for racial, social, national or religious discrimination. What makes this forced or compulsory labour is thus not its physical *severity*, but its *purpose*.

The European Court has also considered the definition of what amounts to forced or compulsory labour, and has taken into account these Conventions, since they are binding on nearly all member states of the Council of Europe. The Court has held that for a person to show forced or compulsory labour, they must show that the work was not voluntary, and that it was unjustifiable or oppressive in its nature. This was set out in the case of *Van Der Mussele v Belgium*.[6]

> Mr Van Der Mussele was a Belgian lawyer, an *avocat*, in Antwerp. He was enrolled as a trainee *avocat*, and, during the course of his training, he was appointed to defend a defendant in a criminal case, and he conducted that case in court. He did so without remuneration; that was in accordance with the traditions and practice of the Belgian Bar to provide legal representation to persons of insufficient means. If he had not done so, he would have run the risk of being struck off the register of *avocats*. He complained of a violation of Article 4.
>
> The European Court rejected his claim. It defined the phrase 'forced or compulsory labour' in the manner set out above: it must be performed against the person's will, and the obligation to perform it must be unjust or oppressive, or its performance must constitute an avoidable hardship. The Court noted that the *avocat's* services did not fall outside the ambit of the normal activities of an *avocat*, and the work did not differ from the usual work of members of the Bar. Furthermore, conducting the case contributed to Mr Van Der Mussele's professional training, and gave him an opportunity to enlarge his experience and to increase his reputation. Then follows a phrase which is important: 'Finally, the burden imposed on the applicant was not disproportionate.'

[4] Treaty No. 29 of the International Labour Organisation.
[5] Treaty No. 105 of the International Labour Organisation.
[6] (1984) 6 EHRR 163.

Those final words are notable. Even in the context of a right as basic as Article 4, the European Court jurisprudence brings into play the principle of proportionality: some compulsory service for the state is not necessarily forced labour in breach of Article 4, since it is for a permissible purpose.

On the other hand, where an individual is given no choice and is simply exploited, there may be a breach of Article 4. This was the case in *Siliadin*, discussed above,[7] where the European Court also found that Ms Siliadin was subject to forced labour as she had not offered herself for work voluntarily and worked under an implied threat to her ability to stay in France.

It is worth bearing in mind that, in the usual work situation, there are a whole series of legislative provisions which govern work practices, both in British law alone, and based on European Union Directives, a number of which regulate working practices across the whole of the EU, including health and safety requirements, and conditions of work, as well as specific situations such as maternity leave. Just to give one example, the Working Time Regulations 1998, which implement the European Union's Working Time Directive: these set out minimum health and safety requirements for the organisation of working time; they apply to full-time, part-time, agency and casual workers (with some exceptions); and they provide rules for hours worked, rest breaks, and time off. Employees can enforce these rights, or any other employment rights, without needing to rely on Article 4. Where Article 4 has a role is in cases like *Siliadin*, where there are people who are not working in the regular, and regulated, job market, but have uncertain status, perhaps for reasons relating to their immigration status, and their rights to work in the UK. Even those who do not get the protection of employment law, for whatever reason, must be protected from exploitation.

PERMISSIBLE LABOUR

Article 4(3) limits the content of the right contained by Article 4(2): it provides that 'forced or compulsory labour' shall not include the activities in (a) to (d). The European Court has made it clear that Article 4(3) should be seen as setting out the scope of Article 4(2); that is, it is an exhaustive list of the only situations where forced labour is permitted, since these are the only situations which are excluded from Article 4(2). Thus Article 4(3) serves as an aid to the interpretation of Article 4(2). In the case of *Schmidt* v *Germany*,[8] the European Court said:

> The four subparagraphs of Article 4(3), notwithstanding their diversity, are grounded on the governing ideas of the general interest, social solidarity and what is normal in the ordinary course of affairs.

The activities in those sub-paragraphs reflect situations of general benefit to the whole community, and are examples of what might loosely be called community service. They are all situations where it is considered that there is a public benefit, or public service being provided, which can justify the imposition of an obligation to do the work. Although this is not expressly stated in the article, one would expect, in each case, that the labour should be provided in accordance with the relevant national law, so that it is a clear obligation.

---

[7] Above, p. 173.
[8] (1994) 18 EHRR 513.

Following *Van Der Mussele*, one would also expect that the scale of the labour should be proportionate to the necessary requirements of one of the situations set out in (a) to (d), namely, work which is compulsory in the course of lawful detention in prison, military service, service which is required in the event of an emergency, or any work or service which forms part of normal civic obligations. Work in prison, military service and normal civic obligations all fall within the description of being 'normal in the ordinary course of affairs' as well as being within the 'general interest'. The situation where there is an emergency which threatens the life or well-being of the community is a clear example of the general interest being likely to override the freedom of the individual to refuse to help out: where there is a national emergency, one would expect each person to recognise that they have a *duty* to do their part to help.

There have been some cases on the scope of these different categories. One case on Article 4(3)(b) was *Spottl v Austria.*[9]

> Thomas Spottl was called for military service in Austria, but he registered as a conscientious objector, one who has moral objections to doing military service. This was accepted, but Austrian law then required him to carry out civilian service instead. He complained that this was forced labour, and was also discriminatory, contrary to Article 14, since women were not obliged to carry out military or civilian service.
>
> The European Commission rejected his claim. The compulsory civilian service was tied to the underlying duty to perform military service, falling within Article 4(3)(b) and women were not required to perform military service. That differential treatment was justified, and many nations, while requiring military or civilian service, did not require women to carry out military service.

Finally, we shall consider the case of *Schmidt v Germany*,[10] which was quoted above. This concerned an obligation within Article 4(3)(d).

> Mr Karlheinz Schmidt's complaint was that, under the law of the state in which he lived, it was compulsory for men, but not women, to serve in the fire brigade or pay a financial contribution in lieu of this service. In so far as this fell within Article 4(3)(d), work or service which was part of normal civic obligations, Mr Schmidt's complaint was that it was discriminatory in breach of Article 14.
>
> The European Court agreed that this compulsory fire service was a part of normal civic obligations. The Court did consider that the distinction between imposing it on men and not on women was in breach of Article 14 taken with Article 4(3)(d), especially as in reality there was a sufficient number of volunteers, and so the only real duty was the obligation to pay the financial contribution, in respect of which there was no adequate justification for treating men and women differently.

[9] (1996) 22 EHRR CD 88.
[10] (1994) 18 EHRR 513.

QUESTIONS

1 It seems to be taken for granted that slavery and forced labour should not be allowed. Do you agree with this? Why? Do you think that the other specific practices covered by the Slavery Conventions should be expressly forbidden? Why?

2 Do you agree that the activities covered by Article 4(3) are not forced or compulsory labour? Do you agree that there are rights or interests of individuals or society as a whole which justify these exceptions?

10

Freedom from slavery

May Day 2001: protesters being detained in Oxford Circus by police, which was the subject of judicial consideration in the case of *Austin* (see p. 189).

Source: Mirrorpix (www.mirrorpix.com)

11 Personal liberty

No free man shall be taken or imprisoned or dispossessed, or outlawed or exiled, or in any way destroyed, nor will we go upon him, nor will we send against him except by the lawful judgment of his peers or by the law of the land. (Magna Carta, 1215)

Article 5: The Right to Liberty and Security

1 Everyone has the right to liberty and security of person.

No one shall be deprived of his liberty save in the following cases and in accordance with a procedure prescribed by law:

(a) the lawful detention of a person after conviction by a competent court;

(b) the lawful arrest or detention of a person for non-compliance with the lawful order of a court or in order to secure the fulfilment of any obligation prescribed by law;

(c) the lawful arrest or detention of a person effected for the purpose of bringing him before the competent legal authority on reasonable suspicion of having committed an offence or when it is reasonably considered necessary to prevent his committing an offence or fleeing after having done so;

(d) the detention of a minor by lawful order for the purpose of educational supervision or his lawful detention for the purpose of bringing him before the competent legal authority;

(e) the lawful detention of persons for the prevention of the spreading of infectious diseases, of persons of unsound mind, alcoholics or drug addicts or vagrants;

(f) the lawful arrest or detention of a person to prevent his effecting an unauthorised entry into the country or of a person against whom action is being taken with a view to deportation or extradition.

2 Everyone who is arrested shall be informed promptly, in a language which he understands, of the reasons for his arrest and of any charge against him.

3 Everyone arrested or detained in accordance with the provisions of paragraph 1(c) of this Article shall be brought promptly before a judge or other officer authorised by law to exercise judicial power and shall be entitled to trial within a reasonable time or to release pending trial. Release may be conditioned by guarantees to appear for trial.

4 Everyone who is deprived of his liberty by arrest or detention shall be entitled to take proceedings by which the lawfulness of his detention shall be decided speedily by a court and his release ordered if the detention is not lawful.

5 Everyone who has been the victim of arrest or detention in contravention of the provisions of this Article shall have an enforceable right to compensation.

PERSONAL LIBERTY

Article 5 embodies a fundamental part of what we mean when we say that we are free. After the rights that we should be protected from physical harm, perhaps the next most basic right is freedom of the person, the liberty to go where we please and do as we please, without interference by others or by the state, so long as we do not harm others or infringe their rights. The counterpart to this is that the conditions under which we can be deprived of this personal freedom by the state should be specified and limited, and that is the substance of Article 5. It sets out very strict limits and conditions on the ability of the state to arrest or detain its citizens.

Arrest and detention is a regular occurrence – the police make many hundreds of arrests daily. There are good reasons why an arrest or detention could be required, sometimes to deal with a crime that has been committed, sometimes to protect the public from a dangerous person, sometimes to protect a person from others or from themselves. Yet any form of arrest or detention should always be seen as something which requires strict justification.

In 1970, in the case of *De Wilde*,[1] the European Court said that the right to liberty is too important for a person to lose the benefit of the protection of the Convention for the single reason that he gives himself up to go into custody. That is remarkable: even when a man volunteers to be detained, his liberty is protected by the Convention. The European Court there emphasised the importance of liberty itself, and how it should be kept safe by the law.

Our courts have traditionally done the same, and, as we shall see, the basic principles of Article 5 are nothing new to our law. The very strong idea that liberty must be cherished, and that only the law may take it away, is one which has been prevalent in our courts for centuries. And especially, our courts have strongly resisted any invasion of liberty without lawful authority, by unauthorised acts of the executive. In the 1931 case of *Eshugbayi Eleko*,[2] it was argued that the court was prohibited from investigating the legality of an order of the Governor of Nigeria ordering Eleko to leave a specified area. The Privy Council rejected this argument, and held that the Governor had no power to make such an order. The great English judge, Lord Atkin, said, 'no member of the executive can interfere with the liberty or property of a British subject except on the condition that he can support the legality of his action before a court of justice'. As we shall see, this principle of legality, having lawful authority for action, is a key part of the application of Article 5.

---

[1] (1979–80) 1 EHRR 373.
[2] *Eshugbayi Eleko v Officer Administering the Government of Nigeria* [1931] AC 662 at 670.

THE LAW ON ARREST

We must pause a moment to consider what the law of arrest and detention is, so that we may put it in the context of the Convention rights guaranteed by Article 5. The main relevant statute is the Police and Criminal Evidence Act 1984[3] and the Codes of Practice issued under it. The basic power of arrest is straightforward: section 24 of PACE provides for a power of summary arrest in respect of all offences ('summary arrest' means arrest without a warrant) where the arrest is necessary for one of a number of reasons, including to prevent a crime or harm to any person, to prevent the person disappearing before prosecution or to allow investigation of a crime. There must be a reasonable suspicion that the person arrested has committed the offence.

As for detention, the position is that a person must not be kept in a police station for more than 24 hours without being charged, although that period may be extended for 12 hours by a senior police officer, and then further by a magistrate, up to an overall maximum of 96 hours. Codes of Practice are issued under PACE, which provide standards for the treatment of a detained person. Even within that time, as soon as the investigating police officer considers that there is sufficient evidence to successfully prosecute a detained person, they must without delay be brought before a custody officer, who will consider whether or not the detainee should be charged. Then the prisoner must be taken before a magistrate or a judge, who may, depending on the circumstances, allow them to be released on bail. Likewise, if the overall time limit expires, or there are no grounds for continuing detention, the person must be released. There are also legal proceedings which can be taken to challenge detention, such as applications for bail, or using the writ of *habeas corpus*; we will explain these in the context of Article 5(4).[4]

So, overall, our law provides rules for arrest and detention, and for bringing a suspect before a court, and for release on bail; and police officers, and the courts, must abide by those rules. So the liberty of the subject does appear to be reasonably well protected.

What then does Article 5 add? The answer is requiring that the state exercises its powers compatibly with the Convention and with fairness and proportionality, and not arbitrarily. This means considering not just the existence of the power of arrest, and whether the formal requirements for making an arrest have been complied with, although these remain crucially important. Article 5 requires an overall consideration of the necessity and proportionality of the arrest and the length of detention: even if the rules and procedures are complied with, there is still scope for a breach of Article 5 if the reasons for the arrest and detention cannot be properly justified. Thus, the Article provides for substantive scrutiny of the arrest, and not just a consideration of whether the formal requirements have been complied with.

THE SCHEME OF ARTICLE 5

The opening sentence of Article 5 announces in ringing terms the right to liberty and security of the person, and the second sentence defines the conditions under which a person may

---

[3] We shall use the common abbreviation: PACE.
[4] Below, p. 196.

Personal liberty

be deprived of his liberty. These are the grounds on which the state, or a public authority, may interfere with this right, set out in a list labelled (a) to (f). That list is exhaustive; the European Court said so in the case of *Ireland* v *United Kingdom*,[5] which involved a challenge to the forceful means of interrogation used by the British security forces in Northern Ireland. The Court noted that the wording of Article 5(1) is 'No one shall be deprived of his liberty *save in the following cases . . .*' followed by the six cases, (a) to (f). The words in italics mean this: there can be interference with liberty *only* in the circumstances set out in (a) to (f). Those circumstances cannot be extended. In addition, the arrest itself must be **lawful**, must conform to the purposes of the relevant sub-paragraph, and must **not** be **arbitrary**, because, for example, it is made in bad faith or is not a proportionate response to the situation.

THE QUALITY OF THE LAW

Pausing first on the second sentence of Article 5(1), we note that the conditions for interfering with the right must be 'in accordance with a procedure prescribed by law'. We have already considered this phrase, the idea behind which appears in a number of the Convention Articles.[6] The same idea applies to the use of the word 'lawful' in Article 5(1)(a) to (f), applied to the arrest or detention which is in question. As we discussed earlier, the phrases 'lawful' and 'in accordance with a procedure prescribed by law' mean two things: first, lawful according to national law; and, second, lawful in the Convention sense of according with the principle of legality. Thus if the arrest or detention is not lawful by the standards of the national law, there will be a breach of Article 5. On the other hand, if the arrest is lawful under the national law, it may still infringe Article 5 if the law under which the arrest is made is not accessible and precise.

These requirements are particularly important in the context of Article 5, since what is being considered is a situation where a person's personal liberty is being infringed. It is one thing where someone is arrested for doing something which they should have realised was criminal. It is quite another where they could not have known that what they were doing was against the law. This may be because the words of a statute are not precise or because the court's own order is unintelligible. To illustrate this are two cases, one where the law passed the test of being precise enough, and another where it did not.

In *Steel* v *UK*,[7] the European Court was dealing with several separate incidents. Ms Helen Steel, with about 60 other people, had attempted to obstruct a grouse shoot in Yorkshire, and she was arrested for breach of the peace, when she impeded a member of the shoot by walking in front of him as he lifted his shotgun. She was detained for 44 hours. At court she was convicted of a breach of the peace. She was ordered to be bound over to keep the peace, but she refused and she served a prison sentence. Another protester tried to stop the building of the M11 motorway, and she had broken into the site, and was arrested, for conduct likely to provoke a disturbance of the peace, whilst standing under a

[5] (1980) 2 EHRR 25, discussed above in the context of Article 3, pp. 152–3.
[6] It is discussed above, pp. 116–18.
[7] (1999) 28 EHRR 603, see also p. 301 in context of Article 10.

mechanical digger. She was detained for about 17 hours and was ordered to be bound over to keep the peace. She refused, and she too served a prison sentence. Both complained of violations of Article 5, saying that the concept of breach of the peace and the power to bind over were not sufficiently clearly defined for their detention to be 'prescribed by law'.

The European Court held that a breach of the peace was an 'offence' within Article 5(1)(c) and therefore there was a lawful arrest on reasonable suspicion of having committed an offence. It also met the requirement of being sufficiently precise to be 'lawful', with foreseeable consequences.

However, in the case of *Hashman and Harrup v UK*,[8] the applicants tried to disturb the Portman hunt, by blowing a horn and hallooing, so that the hounds were distracted and drawn out of the control of the huntsmen and the whippers-in. There was no finding by the Crown Court of a breach of the peace – which distinguishes the case from that of *Steel*. But the Crown Court found that they had behaved *contra bonos mores* (against good behaviour), and bound them over to keep the peace and not to behave *contra bonos mores*.

The European Court held that the finding of being *contra bonos mores* and the decision to bind them over was not a procedure 'prescribed by law' (in this case in breach of Article 10): the phrase *contra bonos mores* had not been defined with precision; it was not clear to the applicants what they had to refrain from doing in the future.

The contrast is therefore between where a clear crime has been committed, a breach of the peace, which was not to be repeated, as in *Steel*, and where, as in *Hashman*, there was no specific crime committed, the language of the charge against the defendants was less than clear, and they were not left in a situation where they could know what they should do or refrain from doing to avoid repeating the offence.

THE MEANING OF 'ARBITRARY'

Let us turn to the point that the arrest or detention must not be arbitrary. Pausing a moment, we should note that the requirement that an arrest should not be arbitrary is not to be found in the relevant sections of PACE, nor in the Codes of Practice. And this consideration will apply, even where the relevant arrest or detention is lawful, in the sense that it has a lawful basis: the court will still look to see if it is free from the taint of being arbitrary.

There is a good example of how our judges regard Article 5 in the case of *Evans*.[9] Mrs Evans had been convicted of robbery, burglary and assault, and she was sentenced to two years' imprisonment. Before she was sentenced, she had spent various periods in custody following her arrest for each of these offences. Then, nearing the end of her sentence, a dispute arose between herself and the prison governor as to what was her date of release. The governor relied on Home Office Guidelines, which were based on court decisions about the calculation of sentences, but those decisions were erroneous, and she spent 59 days longer in prison than she need have done. She sued for wrongful imprisonment.

---

[8] (2000) 30 EHRR 241; see also below, p. 302, in the context of Article 10.
[9] *R v Governor of Brockhill Prison, ex parte Evans (No. 2)* [2000] 3 WLR 843.

> The House of Lords held that the governor – however blameless – was liable to her for damages for wrongful imprisonment. Although the House in fact decided that the detention was unlawful in any event, so there was no need to consider Article 5, the Law Lords referred to it and decided that the governor had not acted in an arbitrary way. Lord Hope expressly considered the scope for questioning whether:
>
> > . . . assuming that the detention is lawful under domestic law, it is nevertheless open to criticism on the ground that it is arbitrary because, for example, it was resorted to in bad faith or was not proportionate.

Note those words of Lord Hope: they give examples of what may be characterised as 'arbitrary' – bad faith or lack of proportion. They are important; as we have noted, our laws of arrest and detention do not refer to bad faith or lack of proportion, so we see these ideas entering our law from the European cases.

Here is another case, which is a good example of where the court was asked to say that the provisions of a statute were disproportionate. The court looked at the surrounding circumstances in order to determine this argument; that is permissible, of course, since the concept of proportionality involves a process of measuring the means and the aim, in a context of a 'pressing social need'. The case is *Anderson, Reid and Doherty*.[10]

> The Mental Health Act 1999 had been passed to address a decision of the House of Lords under the previous law that if a patient was suffering from a psychopathic personality disorder and could not be treated, he was to be discharged. It provided that if the defendant was suffering from a mental disorder which makes it necessary to protect the public from serious harm, they would stay in hospital whether or not for medical treatment.
>
> The three applicants were all being held in a state hospital in Scotland under this provision, all having been convicted of charges of the greatest gravity (culpable homicide in two cases, kidnapping and manslaughter in the third). They contended that the Mental Health Act was in breach of Article 5.
>
> The Privy Council held that the fact that they were not susceptible to treatment did not make the system imposed by the Mental Health Act a violation of Article 5; there was nothing arbitrary or disproportionate about the circumstances. The very fact that the protection of the public was necessary was in itself a legitimate reason for detaining a person of unsound mind.

Another situation where detention must not be arbitrary is detention after conviction of an offence. One would think that, if a criminal court has passed a sentence on a prisoner, especially if the prisoner has been to the Court of Appeal and unsuccessfully challenged the sentence, it would be difficult for them to say that the sentence was an arbitrary one. But that is to leave out of account Article 5, which requires this to be considered. We see this in the next case, although the European Court was satisfied in the circumstances that it was not arbitrary. The Court was considering a case of a long sentence which had been imposed

---

[10] [2001] UKPC D5, [2002] 3 WLR 1460.

on a very young man by the English court, and the question was whether the continuing custody was still connected to the original reasons for the sentence. It is the case of *Weeks* v *UK*.[11]

> Mr Weeks, at the age of 17, entered a pet shop with a starting pistol loaded with blanks, and got 35 pence, which he dropped on the shop floor. He was convicted of robbery, and he was given an indeterminate life sentence. After 10 years in prison, he was released on licence, but then he was recalled to prison after several breaches of the licence; and then he claimed that his detention was no longer lawful.
>
> The European Court said that there had to be a sufficient causal connection between the conviction and the deprivation of liberty, and where the life sentence was imposed by reason of instability and personality disorder, his progress should be monitored, and he should be released when there was no longer a danger. Instability and personality disorder were susceptible to change and Article 5(1)(a) would be violated if a decision to keep him in custody was based on grounds inconsistent with the objectives of the sentence; a detention which had been lawful at the outset would be transferred into a deprivation of liberty that was arbitrary. However, on the facts of the case, it was a correct decision to deny him his release: in the intervals of his release on licence, he had shown that he was unstable, disturbed and aggressive.

The Court of Appeal had rejected his appeal; there was no discussion about whether the sentence was 'arbitrary' – the Act was not then part of our law. The Court of Appeal did consider whether the sentence was excessive, and so in a sense was considering whether the sentence was disproportionate; but that word was not used. What the European Court did was to emphasise that there must be a strict relationship between the offence and the penalty and a strict basis of reasoning for the length of the sentence. And what was being scrutinised – almost under a microscope – was the decision to keep the prisoner in custody. Decisions must not be arbitrary; and decisions which are based on the wrong reasons, or on no reasons, are likely to be arbitrary.

A case of an executive decision based on the wrong reasons was *Stafford* v *UK*,[12] where the European Court took the view that the prisoner was being detained unlawfully. It is a good example of the effect of the Convention on English law: before the incorporation of the Convention, it is likely that the decision would not have been challenged.

> Mr Stafford had been convicted in 1967 of murder and sentenced to life imprisonment; the Parole Board recommended his release on life licence, and the Home Secretary agreed, so he was released on licence in 1991. In 1994, however, he was convicted of a cheque fraud, and sentenced to six years' imprisonment, and his life licence was revoked by the Home Secretary. In 1996–7, when he would normally have been released from the fraud sentence, the Parole Board recommended his release on life licence, noting his previous successful transition from prison to the community without *violent* reoffending. The Home

---

[11] (1987) 10 EHRR 293, but there was a breach of Article 5(4); also considered in the context of Article 3 above, p. 155.
[12] (2002) 35 EHRR 32.

> Secretary rejected the Parole Board's recommendation, on the ground that there was a risk of *non-violent* reoffending. And when Mr Stafford challenged that in court, the House of Lords found, in favour of the Home Secretary, that he had a wide discretion. Mr Stafford was eventually released in 1998.
>
> The European Court held that the Home Secretary's decision was not justified under Article 5(1):
>
>> The Court could not accept that a decision-making power by the executive to detain him on the basis of perceived fears of future non-violent criminal conduct unrelated to his original murder conviction was in the spirit of the Convention, with its emphasis on the rule of law and protection from arbitrariness.

The point is that the Home Secretary's decision was not related to the original conviction of murder, and had no connection with the original sentence. It was simply an executive decision to keep him in custody. Again we see attention being paid to the requirement of Article 5 that a decision is not arbitrary.

 ## TYPES OF PERMISSIBLE DETENTION

We are now ready to examine each paragraph of Article 5, keeping in mind the principles we have discussed; whenever the court considers the case under one of these paragraphs, it will first determine whether the wording of the particular paragraph covers the situation, and, second, it will apply the principles of lawfulness and lack of arbitrariness.

 ## DETENTION AFTER CONVICTION

> **Article 5(1)(a):**   the lawful detention of a person after conviction by a competent court;

We have already referred to a number of cases which fall within this category, where there is a conviction for a criminal offence, by a court which has proper jurisdiction in the matter. Our legal system allows for there to be an appeal to a higher court after a conviction by a lower court, and if the appeal succeeds the conviction is quashed and any sentence of imprisonment is brought to an end. The question then arises, does that mean that the conviction was unlawful, and was the imprisonment a violation of Article 5? The answer is that the simple fact that a conviction is quashed on appeal in the domestic court does *not* mean that the conviction is unlawful. The European Court recognised this in the case of *Benham* v *UK*.[13]

---

[13] (1996) 22 EHRR 293.

Mr Benham had failed to pay his community charge, and he was summonsed to appear before the magistrates. The magistrates found that he was guilty of culpably neglecting to pay, and they imposed a prison sentence on him. He appealed to the High Court, which adjudged that Mr Benham had not been guilty of culpable neglect. Mr Benham complained to the European Court that he had been imprisoned unlawfully, in violation of Article 5, and that the only paragraph which could have justified his period of custody was Article 5(1)(a), but the High Court had found that his conviction was wrong.

The European Court examined the decision of the High Court and found that it did not necessarily mean that the magistrates' order was unlawful; an order which was erroneous in fact or law was not necessarily unlawful, and the error did not make the decision arbitrary. There was therefore no breach of Article 5.

BREACH OF A COURT ORDER

Article 5(1)(b):   the lawful arrest or detention of a person for non-compliance with the lawful order of a court or in order to secure the fulfilment of any obligation prescribed by law;

The main situation where this paragraph will apply is where a court orders a person to do, or not do, something, and the court order is disobeyed. This is the sanction where a court issues an injunction, an order that a person refrain from doing something, such as harassing another, or trespassing on someone else's property: a person who breaches an injunction is liable to be sent to prison for a period of time as a result. This is not quite the same as Article 5(1)(a): they have not acted in a way which amounts to the commission of a criminal offence as such, but they have acted unlawfully in refusing to comply with the order of the court.

The reference to securing the fulfilment of an obligation prescribed by law is intended to cover similar situations. It is not aimed at general legal obligations, which would be covered by Article 5(1)(a), but specific obligations, such as an obligation to fulfil a contractual duty, which would have to be backed up by a court order if there was a possibility of prison, or a duty to provide information in a specific situation. The lack of application of this provision to general legal obligations was considered by the European Commission in *Lawless* v *Ireland*.[14]

Mr Lawless, an Irish citizen resident in Dublin, was a member of the IRA, and he was detained for several months without trial in a military detention camp in Ireland, from July to December 1957, by order of the Irish Minister of Justice, under the Offences against the State Act 1939. The Irish government had argued that Article 5(1)(b) applied, on the basis that the detention was 'in order to secure the fulfilment of an obligation prescribed by law'.

[14] (1961) 1 EHRR 15; see also above, p. 128 for the case's reference to Article 17.

Personal liberty

> The Commission held that the detention of Mr Lawless by order of a Minister of State on suspicion of being engaged in activities prejudicial to the preservation of public peace and order or to the security of the state cannot be deemed to be a measure taken 'in order to fulfil an obligation prescribed by law' and this point was not pursued by the Irish government when the case came before the Court.

REASONABLE SUSPICION OF AN OFFENCE

Article 5(1)(c): the lawful arrest or detention of a person effected for the purpose of bringing him before the competent legal authority on reasonable suspicion of having committed an offence or when it is reasonably considered necessary to prevent his committing an offence or fleeing after having done so;

As we noted towards the start of this chapter, the general law on arrests in the United Kingdom usually requires the fulfilment of similar criteria to these. However, the precise application of our law may well be influenced by the way in which this paragraph has been applied by the European Court. *Fox, Campbell and Hartley* v *UK*[15] is one example of the consideration by the European Court of what amounts to 'reasonable suspicion of having committed an offence'.

> Mr Fox and Ms Campbell, who were married to each other but separated, were detained in Northern Ireland for periods of 30 to 44 hours, under an Act which allowed detention of persons suspected of being a terrorist. During their detention, each was questioned about their suspected membership of the Provisional IRA, and about their involvement with that organisation. They were eventually released without charge.
>
> The European Court considered that there was a violation of the Article because *no* facts were put before the Court to show that the suspicion was reasonable. The European Court said:
>
> > The reasonableness of the suspicion on which an arrest must be based forms an essential part of the safeguard against arbitrary arrest and detention which is laid down in 5(1)(c). 'Reasonable suspicion' pre-supposed the existence of facts or information which would satisfy an objective observer that the person concerned may have committed the offence. What is 'reasonable suspicion' will depend on all the circumstances.

The key idea is that the reasonableness of the suspicion is a safeguard, and therefore requires some basis. It is not enough that the arresting officer believes it to be reasonable. It is not a subjective test, but an objective one, and the court will judge whether it was reasonable. The suspicion, and the arrest, must be proved objectively to be justified.

---

[15] (1991) 13 EHRR 157; also considered below, p. 370.

Not only that, but also *an offence* must be suspected. It will not be enough that the suspicion is of some vaguely described conduct. The person making the arrest must decide what is the apparent offence that he or she is going to make the basis of the arrest. This was one of the points which arose in the case of *Brogan* v *UK*.[16]

Mr Brogan was arrested in Northern Ireland and detained for 5 days and 11 hours, then released without having been charged with any offence or taken before a magistrate or judge. In custody, he was questioned about an offence of murder of a police officer, and about suspected membership of the Provisional IRA. Brogan argued before the European Court that he had been deprived of his liberty in breach of Article 5(1)(c) in that he had not been arrested 'for having committed an offence'.

The European Court held that the definition of 'terrorism' – namely 'the use of violence for the purpose of putting the public in fear' – which was given as the basis of the arrest, was well in keeping with the idea of an offence; and, in addition, he was questioned about a specific offence. In short, there was *no* violation of Article 5.

The requirements that detention should be proportionate and not arbitrary apply equally where the detention is to prevent an offence being committed.

In the case of *Laporte*,[17] a number of demonstrators were heading for the Fairford airbase to demonstrate against the war in Iraq. Three buses were stopped 5 km from the airbase, searched and escorted back to London. The justification given for the police action was to prevent violence and to facilitate peaceful protest, on the basis that if the coaches had been allowed to continue the protesters would have had to be arrested on arrival to avoid an imminent breach of the peace.

The House of Lords held that the arrest of the buses, and the detention and confinement of the passengers, were all unlawful. It was not possible to conclude, in the circumstances of the case, that a breach of the peace was imminent when the coaches were stopped, which was a necessary requirement for a lawful arrest. In any event, the action taken was unreasonable and disproportionate and interfered with the protestors' rights to free speech and free assembly (Articles 10 and 11).

In the case of *Austin*,[18] the courts had to consider the legality of the detention of the protesters held by police in Oxford Circus in central London during the demonstrations on May Day 2001 (as illustrated at the start of this chapter). The Court held, and the House of Lords has confirmed, that there was no breach of Article 5. The Court of Appeal had held that the detention was lawful and compliant with Article 5(1)(c) because the police had a reasonable belief that limiting the freedom of a group of individuals was the only way to prevent violence or imminent violence. The House of Lords, however, went a step further, and held

---

[16] (1989) 11 EHRR 117, also considered below, p. 194.
[17] *R (Laporte)* v *Chief Constable of Gloucestershire* [2006] UKHL 55, [2007] 2 AC 105.
[18] *Austin* v *Metropolitan Police Commissioner* [2007] EWCA Civ 989, [2008] QB 660, [2009] UKHL 5, [2009] 2 WLR 372.

Personal liberty

that the crowd control measures, although a limit on freedom of movement, did not amount to detention within the meaning of Article 5(1) *at all*, since they were carried out in good faith and were reasonably necessary and proportionate to the situation, so were not *arbitrary* measures, which might make a deprivation of freedom of movement into unlawful detention.[19]

■ DETENTION OF MINORS FOR EDUCATION

Article 5(1)(d):   the detention of a minor by lawful order for the purpose of educational supervision or his lawful detention for the purpose of bringing him before the competent legal authority;

You may be surprised that the Convention contains a provision like this; it must be rare that a minor is actually detained for the purpose of making them undergo some educational training. However, the provision is wider than this. The following is an example of where Article 5(1)(d) was considered in an English case, concerning a secure accommodation order.

In *Re K*,[20] K was a 15-year-old boy, who had been convicted of a number of offences. He was diagnosed as having hyperkinetic conduct disorder and as being a serious risk to himself and others. He was made the subject of a secure accommodation order. This was challenged as being in breach of Article 5.

The Court of Appeal held that a secure accommodation order is a deprivation of liberty within Article 5, and Article 5(1)(d) applied, because the case related to the detention of a minor. For the purposes of Article 5(1)(d), 'educational supervision' did not just refer to a rigid notion of classroom teaching; in the context of local authority supervision, it covered many aspects of a local authority's exercise of parental rights for the benefit and protection of the child. Thus Article 5(1)(d) in principle allowed for the making of a secure accommodation order; it was then a question on the facts of the case as to whether its application in a particular case complied with the Convention right. In the present case K was a serious risk to others and the order was quite proper, and extended.

As usual with these grounds of detention, the key question is whether the detention is reasonable, proportionate, lawful and non-arbitrary. An example is the European Court's decision in *Bouamar* v *Belgium*.[21]

---

[19] The reasoning is considered above, p. 116.
[20] [2001] 2 WLR 1141.
[21] (1989) 11 EHRR 1.

Naim Bouamar, aged 17, had a disturbed personality due to family problems, and in 1980 he was on several occasions placed in a remand prison for periods of 15 days, on the order of the Juvenile Court, on the ground that it had been shown to be impossible to find an individual or institution which would accept him. The Belgian government's argument to the European Court was that he was detained by lawful order for purposes of educational supervision, and that Article 5(1)(c) covered the situation. But the European Court noted and emphasised that nine placements had been attempted and called it 'fruitless repetition'; they referred to the way he had been shuttled to and fro between prison and his family, and never placed in an appropriate institution, nor under the supervision of educationally trained staff; and the Court held that these circumstances had the effect of making the treatment of Naim less and less lawful.

That last word is the key to the case. The European Court will not reopen the question of whether educational supervision is in principle required, as defined by the national court, but it will look at the way in which that court has applied its own definition, judged by the test of proportionality and absence of arbitrariness.

PERSONS OF UNSOUND MIND

Article 5(1)(e): the lawful detention of persons for the prevention of the spreading of infectious diseases, of persons of unsound mind, alcoholics or drug addicts or vagrants;

Again, under this paragraph, the European Court will not interfere with a domestic definition as to what amounts to 'unsound mind', but it will enquire to see if a decision is objectively justified.

In *Ashingdane v UK*,[22] Mr Leonard Ashingdane was convicted in 1970 of offences of dangerous driving and unlawful possession of firearms; he was then 41 years of age. Medical evidence showed that he suffered from mental illness – paranoid schizophrenia – and his mental disorder was of such a degree as to warrant his detention in a psychiatric hospital, and the court made a hospital order, together with an order restricting his discharge without limit of time. He was placed in a secure special hospital, but in 1978 his condition improved, and the Home Secretary authorised his return to a local psychiatric hospital. However, the local authority for that hospital refused to accept him, because of a dispute with staff, and so the Home Secretary declined to order the transfer to proceed. Mr Ashingdane was eventually, in 1980, transferred to the local hospital, but he complained that the period, from 1978 to 1980, of continued detention in the secure hospital was unlawful.

The European Court held that to justify detention under Article 5(1)(e) the existence of a mental disorder of a sufficient degree had to be established on the basis of objective

[22] (1985) 7 EHRR 528.

Personal liberty

> medical expertise. The disorder had to persist to justify continued detention. There was no reason to doubt the medical evidence here, that it did persist; and Mr Ashingdane would still have been in detention even if he had been moved earlier to the local hospital.

The courts of the United Kingdom have now had to consider these principles in cases concerning mental health patients. We considered earlier the case of *Anderson, Doherty and Reid*, where the Privy Council held that detention necessary to protect the public from serious harm was not arbitrary or disproportionate. However, in the case of *IH*,[23] the Court of Appeal held that there was a violation of Article 5.

> The offending provision there was section 73 of the Mental Health Act 1983, which placed a burden of proof on a detained patient to show that he was no longer suffering from a mental disorder warranting detention. The Court held that this was incompatible with Article 5, and made a declaration to that effect: what Article 5 requires is for the tribunal to discharge a patient if it cannot be shown that he is currently suffering from a mental disorder which warrants detention.
>
> The result of the case was that a remedial order was made, altering the statute.[24] The law following the alteration was challenged again in the case of *IH*,[25] where the House of Lords held that it was now compatible with Article 5; and that there was no breach of Article 5(1)(e) in the patient's detention, since he had at no stage been detained when there were not grounds for doing so.

What has also been emphasised by the House of Lords is that the conditions of detention do not engage Article 5, so long as the initial detention is justified. This is so even if that involves compulsory treatment of a psychiatric patient – for example, in the case of *R (B)* v *Ashworth Hospital*,[26] where there was no breach of Article 5 because the medical criteria for detention were met and the patient was detained in an appropriate place.[27] Note also that reviewing the detention of someone being detained on this ground will also engage Article 5(4), which we consider below.[28]

ARREST FOR DEPORTATION

> **Article 5(1)(f):** the lawful arrest or detention of a person to prevent his effecting an unauthorised entry into the country or of a person against whom action is being taken with a view to deportation or extradition.

---

[23] *R (H)* v *Mental Health Review Tribunal, North and East London Region* [2001] EWCA Civ 415, [2001] 3 WLR 512.
[24] Mental Health Act 1983 (Remedial) Order 2001 (SI 2001/3712); the nature of a remedial order is discussed above, p. 74.
[25] *R (IH)* v *Home Secretary* [2003] UKHL 59, [2004] 2 AC 253.
[26] *R (B)* v *Ashworth Hospital Authority* [2005] UKHL 20, [2005] 2 AC 278.
[27] See also *R (Munjaz)* v *Mersey Care NHS Trust* [2005] UKHL 58, [2005] 3 WLR 793, where similar comments were made.
[28] In particular the case of *MH*, below, p. 197; and there *was* a breach of Article 5(4) in *IH*.

We have seen that the word 'lawful' bears two meanings: lawful according to the law of the domestic state, and lawful according to the jurisprudence of the Convention. In this next case, we see that the Convention jurisprudence is used to enable the English court to read the United Kingdom statute in a way which is lawful.

In the case of *Saadi*,[29] some Turkish Kurds claimed asylum on arrival in Britain, and they were detained at Oakington Reception Centre for up to 10 days to bring about a speedy determination of their asylum applications. This was under a Home Office fast-track procedure to deal with a large influx of applicants for asylum. This involved asylum seekers being detained for short periods of 7 to 10 days, and no longer, to ensure a speedy determination of their case by keeping them available whilst their case was decided. The detention was permitted by the terms of the Immigration Act 1971, 'pending examination and a decision to give or refuse leave to enter the country', although this does not say that this was for the *purpose* of the examination.

The House of Lords held that this detention was lawful and was not an arbitrary detention. It was not irrational to have such a policy since a short period of detention is justifiable to ensure a speedy decision on the claim for asylum, and the length of detention was not disproportionate. The European Court agreed that there was no breach of Article 5(1) in this case.[30] The short period of detention did not exceed what was reasonably required to ensure a quick and efficient determination of the asylum claim, and the conditions of the detention were satisfactory.

11

Personal liberty

PROMPT REASONS FOR ARREST

Article 5(2):   Everyone who is arrested shall be informed promptly, in a language which he understands, of the reasons for his arrest and of any charge against him.

We now move on to consider the requirements which Article 5 imposes following an arrest. The first is this: that once a person has been arrested, they are told why they have been arrested. This is an additional safeguard against arbitrary arrest: if the person making the arrest cannot say why they are doing so immediately after the arrest has been made, they are unlikely to be able to demonstrate that it is not arbitrary. This duty is already a requirement in our law,[31] that the arrested party should be told on what charge or on suspicion of what crime they are being arrested, and this applies as much to a police officer as to a private person making a citizen's arrest. If this cannot be done on arrest, it must be done at the first reasonable opportunity after the arrest. This applies to all forms of detention: in the case of *Saadi* referred to above, concerning detention pending a decision as to asylum, the European Court held that, although there was no breach of Article 5(1), there was a breach of Article 5(2) in the applicant not being told the real reason for his detention until he had already been detained for 76 hours.

---

[29] *R (Saadi) v Secretary of State for the Home Department* [2002] UKHL 41, [2002] 1 WLR 3131.
[30] *Saadi v UK* (2008) 47 EHRR 17.
[31] *Christie v Leachinsky* [1947] AC 573.

■ PROMPT APPEARANCE BEFORE A COURT

> **Article 5(3):** Everyone arrested or detained in accordance with the provisions of paragraph 1(c) of this Article shall be brought promptly before a judge or other officer authorised by law to exercise judicial power and shall be entitled to trial within a reasonable time or to release pending trial. Release may be conditioned by guarantees to appear for trial.

There are three rights in this paragraph: judicial review of detention, reasonably speedy trial, and release on bail. We shall look at the second, trial within a reasonable time, in our discussion of Article 6.[32] The other two rights are entirely within the philosophy of Article 5, which is to ensure that detention is not arbitrary. The duty to bring a detainee before a judicial authority means that a court has to authorise the continuance of detention, and the court then has the duty to consider releasing the detainee on bail; that is, releasing them from custody, pending their trial. This is usually on conditions, such as the payment of a sum of money as security; or having to report to a police station, or not leave the country, whilst on bail.

One case which provides an example of the European Court's attitude to the need for prompt judicial review is *Brogan*,[33] which we considered above.

> In this case four men had been arrested under the Prevention of Terrorism Act 1984, and they were detained for periods varying from 4 days 6 hours to 6 days $16\frac{1}{2}$ hours, without being charged or brought before a magistrate. The periods of detention had been reviewed and extended by a Minister of State, but not by any judicial officer.
>
> The European Court held that they had not been brought before a judge, promptly or at all, because the person reviewing their detention had been a member of the executive and not a judge. There was therefore a breach of Article 5(3). This provision has now been altered by the Terrorism Act 2000, and detainees are now taken before a judge.

As for bail, the European Court has made it clear that there should be nothing automatic about detention; there should be no rule of the domestic law which provides that bail is unobtainable in the case of specified offences. That would be an arbitrary policy; it would prevent the courts applying proportionality to an individual case; indeed, the converse, it would oblige the courts to refuse bail where it was proportionate to grant it.

This is the general position under United Kingdom law. The Bail Act 1976 provides that a detained person shall be granted bail unless particular circumstances exist. These are set out in the Act, and they are if the defendant might fail to surrender, might commit an offence, might interfere with witnesses or otherwise might obstruct the course of justice. The court has a discretion, with a leaning in favour of granting bail.

---

[32] See below, p. 209.
[33] (1989) 11 EHRR 117, above, p. 189.

But there was until recently a provision in an Act which prevented bail being granted, whatever the particular circumstances of the case. This was section 25 of the Criminal Justice and Public Order Act 1994, and this provided that bail could not be granted to a defendant charged with an offence of homicide or rape, who had been previously convicted of a similar offence. The discretion of the court was taken away. That provision was held to be a violation of Article 5 in the case of *Caballero v UK*.[34]

Mr Caballero had been convicted in 1987 of manslaughter, and sentenced to a term of imprisonment; he was released in August 1988. In 1996 he was arrested on suspicion of attempted rape, and although he instructed his solicitor to apply for bail, no application was made, because of section 25. He was later convicted of attempted rape, and sentenced to life imprisonment. He complained to the European Court of a violation of Article 5(3) in that he had not been brought before a judge, and indeed could not be, and he could not be released while awaiting trial. The United Kingdom government agreed that there had been a violation.

Between the trial of Mr Caballero and the decision of the European Court, the government amended the law, by the Crime and Disorder Act 1998, so that in such cases the court could grant bail if it found exceptional circumstances justifying bail. The House of Lords has since had to consider the amending provision and has held that it is compatible with Article 5(3), since it leaves the judge's discretion in place, even though it displaces the presumption that someone whose custody time limit has expired should automatically be granted bail, and so long as it is read down to impose a purely evidential burden on the accused to establish special circumstances justifying bail.[35]

The European Court has paid close attention to bail, and to the circumstances when a court may be justified in refusing it. The Court's approach can be summed up as follows: custody must be strictly justified. For example, see the case of *Letellier v France*.[36]

Mrs Monique Merdy, née Letellier, was a French national residing in France, and she took over a bar restaurant in March 1985. She was separated from her second husband, Mr Merdy, a petrol pump attendant, and she was living with a third man. On 6 July 1985, Mr Merdy was killed by a shot fired from a car. On the same day the police detained a Mr Moysan, who was found to be in possession of a pump-action shotgun. He admitted that he had fired the shot, but he said he had acted on the instructions of Mrs Merdy, and that she had agreed to pay him and a friend – who also accused her – the sum of 40,000 francs for killing her husband and that she had advanced him 2,000 francs for the purchase of the weapon. She denied the accusations, but admitted that she had seen the murder weapon, and she had given her agreement without thinking too much about it. She admitted she gave 2,000 francs to Mr Moysan to buy a car. She was charged with being an accessory to the murder.

[34] (2000) 30 EHRR 643.
[35] *O v Harrow Crown Court* [2006] UKHL 42, [2006] 3 WLR 195; an evidential burden is a burden to adduce some evidence not to persuade the court: see below, p. 216.
[36] (1992) 14 EHRR 83.

On 8 July 1985, the judge remanded her in custody. She was given bail on 24 December 1985, but on 22 January 1986 she was returned to custody, where she remained until her trial on 10 May 1988; she was sentenced to three years' imprisonment, and released on 17 May 1988, the pre-trial detention automatically being deducted from her sentence. The grounds for refusing her bail had been: the risk of pressure on witnesses, but that had diminished and disappeared; the danger of absconding, because of the severity of the likely sentence, but she had complied with her bail conditions in the time of her liberty in 1985–6; and public order, it being a murder of a husband.

The European Court found that Mrs Merdy's detention after 23 December 1986 had ceased to be based on relevant and sufficient grounds, and was a violation of Article 5(3). The European Court said:

> The persistence of reasonable suspicion that the person arrested has committed an offence is a condition *sine qua non* for the validity of the continued detention, but, after a certain lapse of time, it no longer suffices; the court must then establish whether the other grounds cited by the judicial authorities continue to justify the deprivation of liberty. Where such grounds are relevant and sufficient, the court must also ascertain whether the competent national authorities displayed special diligence in the conduct of the proceedings.

The European Court added that when the only remaining reason for continued detention – after dismissing other matters – was a fear that the accused would abscond, release on bail had to be ordered if the accused was in a position to provide adequate guarantees to ensure her appearance at her trial.

SPEEDY REVIEW OF DETENTION

Article 5(4):   Everyone who is deprived of his liberty by arrest or detention shall be entitled to take proceedings by which the lawfulness of his detention shall be decided speedily by a court and his release ordered if the detention is not lawful.

By this provision the Convention imposes a duty on states to provide a system of reviewing a detainee's custody. These again are provided for in principle by United Kingdom law in the possibility of applying for bail, on the principles we have just discussed. Another way in which detention can be reviewed is by proceedings for **habeas corpus** (literally, 'you shall have the body'). This was originally intended to ensure that the person being detained was physically brought before the court. *Habeas corpus* is available to anyone who is detained in custody. It calls upon the person keeping the prisoner in custody to justify the detention. The court enquires into whether the detention is lawful or not; the question for the court is whether the reason for the detention, given by the gaoler, is sufficient as a matter of law to justify the detention; but the court does not consider all the detail of the case to see whether the cause given is actually correct. Thus, if a statute should provide particularly wide powers of detention, perhaps without trial or without the need to show reasonable suspicion that an offence has been committed, the protection of *habeas corpus* will lessen accordingly, since the statute will have widened the scope of lawful detention.

Again, the questions of what is a speedy review and whether there has been a proper hearing raise issues which we will be considering in the context of Article 6. Again, although the principle of Article 5(4) is provided for by our law, it will be possible for it to be breached in particular cases, for example, if the review is not sufficiently speedy.

One area where review of detention has been considered is the area of mental health.

In the case of *MH*,[37] the House of Lords had to consider how a patient who is so severely mentally disordered that she cannot apply to a court or tribunal could challenge her detention in hospital. The Court of Appeal had granted a declaration of incompatibility, which the House of Lords reversed. Baroness Hale, giving the judgment in the Lords, made clear that the point was not that such detention could never breach Article 5, but that the system set up by the Act was perfectly capable of being operated compatibly with Article 5(4): there were provisions for review by a tribunal or by a county court, or via a reference from the Secretary of State to a tribunal, or via judicial review or *habeas corpus*. There were therefore ample mechanisms for review of the detention by a court.

Another area which has attracted particular attention is the review of detention of prisoners serving a life sentence. A life sentence does not mean that the person convicted spends their whole life in prison: after a period of time, they may be released on licence. Thus, where a life sentence is ordered, there is a tariff, or punitive period. This reflects the individual circumstances of the offence and the offender and represents the element of punishment, and it is followed by a preventive period. At the end of these, the prisoner ought to be released, on licence, as soon as he can satisfy the Parole Board that he no longer remains a danger. This used to be the subject of a decision by the Home Secretary, rather than a judge, although this lack of a judicial decision had caused judicial misgivings. In the case of *Stafford*,[38] which we considered above, the European Court held that Article 5(4) had been violated, because the questions of the dangerousness of and risk posed by the prisoner could change over time. Thus, new issues of lawfulness could arise which required determination by a judicial body; the Court said that:

> the continuing role of the Secretary of State in fixing the tariff and in deciding on a prisoner's release following its expiry, has become increasingly difficult to reconcile with the notion of separation of powers between the executive and the judiciary.

Then in the case of *Noorkoiv*,[39] the process of review was held to infringe Article 5(4). This case related to the review of the period of detention to be served by a life prisoner. Where a person is sentenced to detention for life, they may still be released on parole after a minimum period of time fixed by the court which sentenced them. In this case, the Parole Board did not meet to consider the continued detention of the prisoner until two months after this minimum period had expired. The Court of Appeal considered that this infringed Article 5(4): the Parole Board should have reviewed the continued detention before the end of the minimum period, since the state was required to release a life prisoner on parole when the minimum period ended unless he constituted a danger to the public. The court emphasised the importance of keeping the preventive period as short as possible.

[37] *R (MH) v Health Secretary* [2005] UKHL 60, [2005] 3 WLR 867.
[38] (2002) 35 EHRR 32, above, p. 185.
[39] *R (Noorkoiv) v Home Secretary* [2002] EWCA Civ 770, [2002] 1 WLR 3284.

This then came before the House of Lords in the case of *Anderson*,[40] where the role of the Home Secretary was considered. A seven-member panel held that the Home Secretary, in fixing the tariff element of a mandatory life sentence for murder, was not acting as an independent and impartial tribunal, and made a declaration of incompatibility. Since the case concerned the initial sentencing procedure, it was held to be a breach of Article 6, but the same considerations would apply under Article 5(4), and the Lords expressly followed the decision in *Stafford*. Following this decision, the law has now been changed to remove the Home Secretary's role in setting the tariff of murderers. Even that has been challenged by a prisoner who had been sentenced to life before the change in the law, and who then had his minimum prison term set by a judge: and the House of Lords read into the new legislation a right for prisoners to be given an oral hearing if necessary when the new minimum was set.[41]

However, in the case of *Lichniak*,[42] heard at the same time, the Lords made clear that the life sentence itself does not infringe Article 5, so long as there is independent review of the detention from time to time.

It is not just prisoners serving life sentences who have their detention reviewed. All prisoners are given the opportunity to seek to be released on parole before the end of their sentence, as long as they have behaved themselves. And there have been a series of cases which have used Article 5 to challenge the way in which detention is reviewed in such cases. There have been a number of individual cases which have been held to breach Article 5(4) because of delay or for other reasons. But there have also been challenges to the way in which decisions as to the early release of prisoners on parole are made.

In the case of *Clift*,[43] the House of Lords held that early release provisions which differentiated between those who were of foreign nationality and those of UK nationality were in breach of Article 5, taken with Article 14, and made a declaration of incompatibility. In that case their Lordships criticised the role of the Secretary of State in determining the early release of prisoners serving more than 15 years, but held that it did not breach Article 14, which was what was relied on.

On the other hand, in the case of *Black*,[44] the House of Lords held that where a prisoner has been sentenced to a specific (determinate) period, and has reached the point within that defined period where they are eligible for parole, which is to say release on conditions of good behaviour, there was no need for *judicial* involvement in this decision. Article 5 is satisfied by the fact that the original sentence is imposed by a judicial process. Article 5(4) does not require judicial involvement before the original sentence has been served. A decision to release someone on licence before their sentence has expired is an administrative decision, so it can be made by the Secretary of State with the assistance of the Parole Board.

---

[40] *R (Anderson)* v *Home Secretary* [2002] UKHL 46, [2003] 1 AC 837.
[41] *R (Hammond)* v *Home Secretary* [2005] UKHL 69, [2006] 1 All ER 219.
[42] *R* v *Lichniak* [2002] UKHL 47, [2003] 1 AC 903.
[43] *Clift* v *Home Secretary* [2006] UKHL 54, (2007) 1 AC 484.
[44] *R (Black)* v *Secretary of State for Justice* [2009] UKHL 1, [2009] 2 WLR 282.

The Parole Board plays a key role in decisions about the release of prisoners, but its position has itself been considered by the courts. It had been assumed that the Parole Board had a judicial function and therefore could provide the necessary independent review for the purposes of Article 5(4). This was held not to be infringed by the power of the Home Secretary (now the Minister of Justice) to give directions to the Parole Board as long as the directions did not seek to usurp this judicial function.[45] However, the independence of the Parole Board to perform a judicial function was itself challenged in the case of *Brooke*,[46] where the Court of Appeal held that the Parole Board is not a sufficiently independent body to satisfy Article 5(4). The relationship between the Parole Board and the Ministry of Justice, which has powers over the Board on issues such as funding, appointment, terms of office, and so on, meant that there was insufficient objective independence of the Board.

This is a very striking decision: it challenges the structure of an important institution in our penal system and will require a significant rethink of the way in which such decisions are made to ensure compliance with the right guaranteed by Article 5(4).

 ## COMPENSATION FOR WRONGFUL DETENTION

> **Article 5(5):** Everyone who has been the victim of arrest or detention in contravention of the provisions of this Article shall have an enforceable right to compensation.

Again, this is an important right, but one which is already substantially protected in United Kingdom law. There is already the right to claim compensation, by way of damages awarded by a court, for wrongful arrest and/or for false imprisonment, where the proper procedures for arrest or detention have not been followed; some of the cases we have discussed earlier were of this sort.

 ## DEROGATIONS FROM ARTICLE 5

It is appropriate to note here that Article 5 is the one article to which derogations have been entered,[47] on the basis that there were particular provisions of United Kingdom law relating to terrorism which should be retained even though it had been held that they infringed Article 5.

The initial derogation was based on the result in the case of *Brogan*,[48] where it was held by the European Court that extended periods of detention under the Prevention of Terrorism Act were in violation of Article 5(3). This was because the detention was authorised by a government Minister and not by a judge or magistrate. A derogation was therefore entered regarding Article 5, on the basis that there was an emergency in Northern Ireland by reason of terrorist activity, and that to bring a suspect before a judge for an

---

[45] *Girling* v *Home Secretary* [2006] EWCA Civ 1779, (2007) QB 783.
[46] *R (Brooke)* v *Parole Board* [2008] EWCA Civ 29, [2008] 1 WLR 1950.
[47] For discussion of derogations, see above, p. 113.
[48] *Brogan* v *UK* (1989) 11 EHRR 117, above, p. 189 and p. 194.

extension of custody would oblige the police to disclose the secret or sensitive intelligence which was the reason for the arrest. That derogation has now been lifted since the Prevention of Terrorism Act has now been repealed.

A further derogation in respect of Article 5(1)(f) was entered in respect of the Anti-terrorism, Crime and Security Act 2001.[49] This Act was passed following the terrorist attacks of 11 September 2001 in the United States. The derogation referred to an extended power to arrest and detain a foreign national indefinitely where there was considered to be a risk to national security, a suspicion that the person was an international terrorist, but where such removal or deportation was not immediately possible, for example because there was a risk of that person being ill-treated on arrival in the country to which they would be deported in breach of Article 3. However, the derogation was quashed by the House of Lords in *A* v *Home Secretary*[50] as being disproportionate and discriminatory, following which the statutory power was repealed, and there is not currently any derogation in place. We will consider this derogation in more detail in our discussion of terrorism.[51] However, the statute which replaced this power, the Prevention of Terrorism Act 2005, does contain powers which could be used if a further derogation were to be entered. This has not been done yet, but it should be noted, for the purposes of the present chapter, that if it was, that would be a situation where, even if a period of detention did *not* comply with Article 5, our courts would not be able to grant a remedy under the Convention.

QUESTIONS

1 Consider the list of permissible reasons for detention in Article 5(1). Do you agree that these should all be included? Do they all serve a justifiable purpose?

2 Do you consider that Articles 5(2) to (5) provide sufficient safeguards for persons who have been arrested? Are there any other safeguards which should be included?

---

[49] Human Rights Act 1998 (Amendment No. 2) Order 2001, SI 2001/4032.
[50] *A* v *Secretary of State for the Home Department* [2004] UKHL 56, [2005] 2 WLR 87.
[51] Below, Chapter 21.

A speed camera: the question of whether it is unfair to compel the owner of a vehicle to identify its driver when it was speeding has been considered in *Brown* v *Stott* and *O'Halloran* v *UK* (see pp. 206–7).

Source: © Martyn Goddard/Corbis

12 The right to a fair trial

My Lord Hermiston occupied the bench in the red robes of criminal jurisdiction, his face framed in the white wig. Honest all through, he did not affect the virtue of impartiality; this was no case for refinement; there was a man to be hanged, he would have said, and he was hanging him. (Robert Louis Stevenson, *The Weir of Hermiston*, 1896)

'For many years, the – a – I would say the flower of the Bar, and the – a – I would presume to add, the matured autumnal fruits of the Woolsack – have been lavished upon *Jarndyce and Jarndyce.* If the public have the benefit, and if the country have the adornment, of this great Grasp, it must be paid for in money or money's worth, sir.' 'Mr Kenge,' said Allan . . . 'Do I understand that the whole estate is found to have been absorbed in costs?' 'Hem! I believe so,' returned Mr Kenge. (Charles Dickens, *Bleak House*, 1853)

Article 6: The Right to A Fair Trial

1 In the determination of his civil rights and obligations or of any criminal charge against him, everyone is entitled to a fair and public hearing within a reasonable time by an independent and impartial tribunal established by law.

Judgment shall be pronounced publicly but the press and public may be excluded from all or part of the trial in the interest of morals, public order or national security in a democratic society, where the interests of juveniles or the protection of the private life of the parties so require, or to the extent strictly necessary in the opinion of the court in special circumstances where publicity would prejudice the interests of justice.

2 Everyone charged with a criminal offence shall be presumed innocent until proved guilty according to law.

3 Everyone charged with a criminal offence has the following minimum rights:

(a) to be informed promptly, in a language which he understands and in detail, of the nature and cause of the accusation against him;

(b) to have adequate time and facilities for the preparation of his defence;

(c) to defend himself in person or through legal assistance of his own choosing or, if he has not sufficient means to pay for legal assistance, to be given it free when the interests of justice so require;

(d) to examine or have examined witnesses against him and to obtain the attendance and examination of witnesses on his behalf under the same conditions as witnesses against him;

(e) to have the free assistance of an interpreter if he cannot understand or speak the language used in court.

THE IMPORTANCE OF A FAIR TRIAL

> . . . the object and purpose of Article 6, which, by protecting the right to a fair trial and in particular the right to be presumed innocent, is intended to enshrine the fundamental principle of the rule of law.

So runs the judgment of the European Court in the case of *Salabiaku* v *France*,[1] where criminal liability was presumed against the accused.

Article 6 contains some of the fundamental principles which underlie the idea of the rule of law, that individuals shall be treated with respect by the state: they shall not be punished unless they have committed a crime, and before they are punished it shall be proven, and not presumed, that they have done something illegal. They should be tried by a fair and impartial court which shall act on the basis of proof and the provisions of the law, and not on the basis simply of an accusation or the wishes of the state. Likewise, in deciding disputes between individuals, it is equally fundamental that the law is applied fairly and impartially, that all parties have equal access to the courts, and equal opportunities to put their case. And trials shall be in public wherever possible, so that justice may not only be done, but also it may be seen to be done, lending public confidence to the justice system.

The idea of a fair trial is by no means a new one to the British courts. Our law has over the centuries developed rules for the hearing of trials. Magna Carta, drawn up in 1215, includes a guarantee of impartial and speedy legal process.[2] For centuries, it has been the tradition that trials are held in public, so that justice can be seen to be done. Likewise, it has long been part of our law that the burden is on the prosecution of proving that a criminal offence has been committed, with the trial usually heard by a jury. Although it was only in the nineteenth century that a defendant in a criminal case was allowed to give evidence on oath, the right to put the case for the defence is a well- and long-established one, in particular the right to put questions by way of cross-examination of the witnesses for the prosecution, and the right to legal representation. Excluding unreliable evidence, such as hearsay, is also of long-standing, as is the right not to answer questions if they will incriminate the witness.

In more recent times, there have been further improvements to our system to maintain fairness, for example rules on the fair use of identification evidence or the conduct of identity parades, or the court's power to exclude evidence obtained improperly. Likewise in civil cases there are detailed rules of procedure to ensure that both parties have an equal opportunity to set out their case and put all relevant evidence before the court.

What, then, does Article 6 add to our law, if the protection of a fair trial is already such an integral part of it? Especially since the British trial tradition was an important influence on how the article was drafted in the first place, and if our law provides a higher standard of protection than the Convention, that will continue to apply.

The effect of Article 6 will not be to alter fundamentally how trials are conducted, or the basic principles which apply, or the main safeguards for fairness. However, the result of the European Court jurisprudence on Article 6 has been that changes have been made to a number of areas, where our judges have used the European cases to reconsider or review the existing rules or approach of the law and in many cases increase the protection provided to ensure a fair trial. It has not altered the basic principles of our law, but it has changed some of the ways in which these are applied.

[1] (1991) 13 EHRR 379.
[2] See above, p. 23.

And it is not in a narrow field, or in a limited kind of case, that the Convention has been applied. It has been invoked in a wide variety of situations: for example, in the criminal field, imposing a burden of proof on a defendant, drawing inferences from silence, compelling a defendant to answer incriminating questions, tempting a person to commit an offence and not allowing evidence obtained unfairly. In the civil sphere, it has been cited in questions of the conduct of hearings, the use of hearsay evidence, and the imposition of an expert witness on a party.

The addition of Article 6 to our law has therefore required the courts to consider all these areas afresh, asking the general question, is the law, or the way it is applied, fair and proportionate, or arbitrary; does our law do enough to provide a fair trial?

 ## CIVIL AND CRIMINAL CASES

There is a time-honoured division of cases into criminal and civil, because different considerations apply to how the two different categories of case are dealt with by the courts. In a civil case, the key is that both parties, being individuals, should be dealt with comparably and therefore fairly by the court, which must be impartial between them until it has heard all the evidence and argument, and then makes a decision.

In a criminal case, however, there is an imbalance from the outset: the prosecution has the resources of the state available to it, both through the police and the Crown Prosecution Service. The result is also more serious for the accused: if found guilty, they will acquire a criminal record and be liable to punishment, which will involve prison in more serious cases. It is for these reasons that the presumption of innocence is so important: before a person is deprived of their good name and liberty, it must be proved beyond reasonable doubt that they are guilty: it should not be for them to prove that they are not guilty. A court should never assume that the fact that someone is accused of something means that for that reason alone they are likely to have done it, a serious mistake too often made in the media.

The wording of Article 6 recognises that there are both civil and criminal cases in its reference to 'the determination of civil rights and obligations or of any criminal charge'. We shall follow this division when examining how the Convention affects English law, because although the general principles are the same in both sorts of trial, the way in which they are applied can be quite different. We shall consider first criminal cases.

 ## IS ARTICLE 6 UNQUALIFIED?

The first question is how much protection does Article 6 provide: is the right provided by Article 6 – the right to a fair trial – an absolute right or is it subject to any qualification? As we have seen, other rights in the Convention are expressly qualified.[3] The only such express qualification in Article 6 is to the right to have a trial in *public*, where the grounds on which this can be limited are set out.[4]

---

[3] For example, Articles 8 to 11; see above, p. 115.
[4] See *R (Mohamed) v Foreign Secretary* [2009] EWHC 152 (Admin) LTL 5.2.09 for discussion of a situation where not publishing the whole of a judgment was held to be in the public interest.

The courts have said that the overall fairness of a trial cannot be limited or qualified. There is no question of allowing a trial to be 'moderately fair' or for one kind of case to have a first-class fairness, and another a second class.

However, that is not the whole picture. Article 6 has express rights; they are expressly set out in its wording. It also has implied rights. The European Court has carried out a process of reading into the words of Article 6 a collection of other rights; they give effect to the fundamental and absolute right to a fair trial. For example, the express right to be presumed innocent includes the right to silence, and the right against self-incrimination; and those implied rights may have implied restrictions.

It will be a matter of judicial interpretation, in the circumstances of the case, whether the words of Article 6 imply a right, and whether there is any qualification of that right. The qualification will be especially gauged by the facts. Let us look at an example. There is a right to be presumed innocent; that is express. Implicit in it, according to the European Court, is the right not to incriminate oneself. But suppose an Act of Parliament permits a police officer to ask questions, and obliges the person to answer in such a way that the answers will incriminate the person being questioned. That would surely be a violation of Article 6 and the right not to incriminate oneself. On the other hand, it is in the public interest that crimes should be prevented or punished, and it may be necessary to make it obligatory to answer these questions. There will be a process of balancing the right of the individual against that of the public; and the limitation on the individual's right to a fair trial must be a proportionate one. This was the scenario in the case of *Brown* v *Stott*.[5]

Margaret Anderson Brown was at a superstore when the staff suspected that she had stolen a bottle of gin, and they called the police, who noticed that she appeared to have been drinking alcohol; the police asked her how she came to be at the store, and she answered that she had come by car, and she pointed to a car which she said was hers. She was charged with theft, and taken to a police station, where she was *required* to say who was driving the car when she used it to get to the store, and she admitted that she was the driver; she was *required* under the Road Traffic Act 1988, which obliges the keeper of a car to give information as to the identity of the driver at the time of an offence. The Privy Council held that there was no breach of Article 6. Lord Bingham said:

> The jurisprudence of the European Court very clearly establishes that while the overall fairness of a criminal trial cannot be compromised, the constituent rights comprised, whether expressly or implicitly, within Article 6 are not themselves absolute. Limited qualification of these rights is acceptable if reasonably directed by national authorities towards a clear and proper public objective and if representing no greater qualification than the situation calls for. [. . .] The high incidence of death and injury on the roads caused by the misuse of motor vehicles is a very serious problem common to almost all developed societies. The need to address it in an effective way, for the benefit of the public, cannot be doubted. [. . .] I do not for my part consider that section 172, properly applied, does represent a disproportionate response to this serious social problem, nor do I think that reliance on the respondent's admission, in the present case, would undermine her right to a fair trial.

[5] [2001] 2 WLR 817.

Thus the judges took into account the purpose of the legislation, specifically current road conditions, and carried out a balancing exercise. On the one hand, there were the rights of the individual, and on the other, the aim of the statute to punish road traffic offences, and they found that the interference with the right was proportionate to what it was trying to achieve.

The European Court has now confirmed that there is no breach of Article 6 in this provision of the Road Traffic Act.[6] That someone is compelled to give evidence does not automatically mean there is a violation of the Article. The right to a fair trial is not qualified; but the circumstances of the case are relevant to whether there is a breach. In this case, drivers of cars take on certain responsibilities when they choose to drive, and one of them is to provide the – limited – information as to the identity of the driver of a car when an offence has been committed, so long as they are reasonably able to do so. The same exercise was carried out in a drink-driving case, where the law provided that a particular fact should be presumed against a defendant, and presumed irrebuttably – he should have no right to refute it. That presumption, one may say, is in sharp conflict with another presumption – the presumption of innocence. The case was *Parker* v *DPP*.[7]

> Mr Parker had been convicted by the Magistrates' Court of driving whilst over the pre-scribed limit, contrary to section 5 of the Road Traffic Act 1988; section 15(2) of that Act provided that there was an irrebuttable presumption that the level of alcohol provided at the time of the offence could not be less than the reading given by the specimen he supplied at the police station later. Mr Parker's argument was that the section providing the presumption was incompatible with Article 6, and so should be read as *not* containing the presumption. But the Queen's Bench Divisional Court held that the presumption was reasonable in the context of the road traffic legislation as a whole, having regard to the interest at stake, which was aimed at preventing motorists from consuming alcohol before they took charge of a motor vehicle. Thus the presumption was *not* a violation of Article 6.

Once again, the court referred to the surrounding circumstances, and it undertook a balancing exercise, which took account of the importance to the public of the maintenance of road safety. And the case is a good illustration of the principle which is so important: some rights under Article 6 may be qualified, when the qualification is proportionate to its aim, in the circumstances of the particular case.[8]

A FAIR HEARING

These words are the heart of Article 6. On reading the words the first thing that we are entitled to is a **fair hearing**, and every point that is described in the wording of the remainder of the article is an ingredient of a fair hearing. For example, one aspect of a fair hearing is to be presumed innocent of accusations against you; and another is the right to examine

---

[6] *O'Halloran* v *UK* (2007) 46 EHRR 21.
[7] [2001] RTR 240.
[8] Some more cases of presumptions and the burden of proof are considered below, p. 216.

witnesses against you.[9] But even when none of those specific requirements is said to have been infringed, the court may nonetheless consider the fairness of the proceedings; it is not necessary for any of the specific ingredients of Article 6 – express or implied – to be present for the court to judge whether the hearing is fair. The word 'fair' in Article 6 has its own effect, and the courts have held that a trial may be unfair, without referring to any other words of the article. So in the case of *King*,[10] the court examined the circumstances and found that Mr King had been treated unfairly.

Mr King was disabled and had suffered a stroke; he appeared before the Crown Court for failing to carry out works at his property, when required to do so under the Housing Act 1985. At the Crown Court he was kept waiting from 10 in the morning until 4 in the afternoon; he had no legal representation, and he was not allowed to make a closing speech. The High Court held that in all these circumstances he had not had a fair trial, in breach of Article 6; and particular reference was made to the guidelines published for all judges, the Equal Treatment Bench Book, as being of assistance in achieving a 'fair' trial.

No reference was made to any specific part of Article 6, but the court had no difficulty in judging fairness without any such reference. The concept of fairness was provided by Article 6, without having to rely on one of its ingredients. And the same goes for this next case, the *International Transport Roth*[11] case, where the court held that the manner in which a penalty was imposed on lorry drivers was unfair. For there to be a fair hearing, there must *be* an actual hearing.

The question arose out of a penalty scheme imposed by the Immigration and Asylum Act 1999. This meant that lorry drivers and owners were liable to a fixed penalty of £2,000 if a person, seeking to enter the country in a clandestine way, was found concealed in such a vehicle; the driver or owner had the right to show that he acted under duress, or that he had a total lack of knowledge, or that he had an effective system to prevent such a stowaway; the vehicle meanwhile was liable to be seized by immigration officials. A group of 60 drivers complained that this was a violation of Article 6.

The Court of Appeal agreed, holding that the scheme was unfair. In particular, although the court recognised that the fixed penalty scheme was intended to deal with a social problem, that of illegal immigration, the court still considered that a substantial fixed penalty could not be reconciled with the important principle that the punishment must fit the crime, since there was no opportunity for the person being penalised to argue that the penalty should be mitigated in the particular circumstances of their case. In principle, the regime infringed the right to have the penalty determined by an independent tribunal.

The Court took into account the aims of the scheme – to prevent illegal immigration, and to promote vigilance on the part of cross-border carriers – and balanced them against the inflexibility of the statute, which imposed a penalty regardless of blameworthiness. This was what was unfair, even though it is not an express or specific requirement of Article 6 –

---

[9] See below, p. 222, for further discussion of the content of a fair trial.
[10] *R* v *King* [2001] EHRLR 14.
[11] *International Transport Roth GmbH* v *Home Secretary* [2002] EWCA Civ 158, [2002] 3 WLR 344.

in addition to references to specific points, such as the burden of proof imposed on the carriers which one judge held constituted a disproportionate and unjustifiable inroad on the right of silence.

A fair hearing also means that the judge should in fact hear what each party has to say, without undue interruption. If a proper hearing is denied to one party, there is a sense of injustice, and justice is not seen to be done. This is illustrated by the case of *CG v UK*.[12]

> CG was charged with theft, pleaded not guilty, was tried before a judge and jury and was found guilty. Her complaint was that the trial judge frequently interrupted both her defence counsel – preventing him from testing the evidence – and her own evidence. There were indeed interruptions on almost every page of cross-examination of the key prosecution witness, and on 22 out of 31 pages of her own evidence. The Court of Appeal said that there was some substance in her criticism, but the interruptions were not such as to make the conviction unsafe, and so the appeal was dismissed.
>
> The European Court took account of the fact that the Court of Appeal had examined the case. It made a careful examination of the facts, and found that some interruptions were due to misunderstandings; also, that her defence counsel had not been prevented or deterred from developing the line of defence. The European Court concluded, by a majority, that there was *no* breach of Article 6.

Nonetheless, this illustrates the principle: the way that a judge conducts a particular trial, including their interruptions, may make a trial unfair; even though on the facts of this case, that stage had not been reached.

The general obligation, that criminal trials should be fair, is now enshrined in the new Criminal Procedure Rules, which start with the overriding objective that criminal cases be dealt with justly – which includes dealing with both sides fairly, recognising the defendant's Article 6 rights, and dealing with cases in a way which is both efficient and proportionate to their gravity and complexity.[13]

WITHIN A REASONABLE TIME

We turn now to the next phrase in Article 6(1), that the trial must take place within a **reasonable time**. Here again, the criminal law has well-established rules to deal with delays in bringing proceedings. A defendant who complains of undue delay in being brought to trial may apply to the court for an order that the proceedings should be stayed, on the ground that it would be an abuse of process to permit them to continue because the trial would be unfair.

The European Court has developed its own approach to complaints of undue delay, and our courts have followed the jurisprudence of the Convention in two areas especially. The first is about the question, from what time does one measure the period of delay? The European Court has held that it is the time when the defendant is first affected by the accusation, by being interviewed, or when an investigation begins. The second area is about

---

[12] (2002) 34 EHRR 34.
[13] Criminal Procedure rules 2005, rule 1.1; the civil equivalent is discussed below, p. 235.

prejudice; must the party complaining of delay prove that they have suffered some prejudice from the delay?

The approach in the British courts until recently was that time ran from when the defendant was charged, and that he had to prove prejudice. But in a recent decision, the Privy Council reconsidered these in the light of the cases of the European Court.[14]

The Privy Council had to consider two cases. The first concerned two police officers, *Watson and Burrows*, who gave evidence at Linlithgow Sheriff Court, in April 1998, on the trial of a man charged with offences of public order, and vandalism, where at the end of the trial the Sheriff in open court announced his opinion that the two officers had committed perjury. However, after enquiries and interviews of the officers, proceedings against them were only commenced in April 2000. The other, which was quite separate, related to a boy, *JK*, aged 13, who was interviewed by the police in October 1998 about sex offences he was alleged to have committed. The indictment to commence criminal proceedings was served only in January 2001.

Each prosecution was stayed, on the grounds that there had been such a delay in bringing proceedings against the defendants as to breach the reasonable time requirement contained in Article 6. The Crown appealed to the Privy Council, which held that there *should* be a stay in the case of JK, because there had been an unreasonable delay, in a case which was not complex, but which required careful handling, and JK had not been responsible for any aspect of the delay; but there should *not* in the case of the two police officers, where the delay was 20 months, and they were not in custody. The Privy Council regarded time as starting to run in the case of the police officers when they were detained and interviewed, which is when they were seriously affected by the allegation and investigation.

This case set out the general approach to the requirement of a hearing within a reasonable time. Whilst it will not be easy to show that a case has not been heard in a reasonable time, if the period which has elapsed gives ground for real concern, the court must look into the detailed facts of the particular case; and the prosecution must explain and justify any lapse of time which appears to be excessive. The court must consider the complexity of the case, the conduct of the defendant and the manner in which the case has been dealt with by the administrative and judicial authorities. What is quite clear is that the state cannot blame an unacceptable delay on a lack of resources, whether lack of judges or prosecutors, or a general under-funding of the legal system. The obligation under Article 6 is on the state to organise its legal system to ensure that cases are prosecuted and heard within a reasonable time.

Likewise, although the question of whether or not a defendant has been prejudiced by the delay will be relevant, since the risk of prejudice by the delay is at the heart of the requirement for a prompt hearing, it is not necessary for the defendant to show that there has been prejudice to establish that there has been a breach of the requirement for a hearing within a reasonable time.

Where there has been delay which has caused prejudice, this may well lead to the proceedings being stayed or a conviction being quashed. So, for example, convictions have been declared unsafe where the delay has led to important evidence being lost[15] or where

---

[14] *Dyer* v *Watson and Burrows*; *HM Advocate* v *JK* [2002] UKPC D1, [2004] 1 AC 379.
[15] *Ali* v *CPS* [2007] EWCA Crim 691.

there was a period of 13 years between an original confiscation order and the proceedings for breach of that order.[16]

However, the fact that there is some delay which is in breach of Article 6 does not necessarily mean that a stay of the proceedings should be granted, but only if there can no longer be a fair trial or it would otherwise be unfair to try the defendant. This is because it may be that some other remedy would suffice to address the delay, such as the finding of the violation itself, a reduction in sentence, or an award of damages as compensation for the delay.[17]

AN INDEPENDENT COURT

This is a critical requirement of a fair trial. The trial cannot be fair if the court does not approach the case with an open mind. In our law this is usually expressed as comprising two fundamental principles. The first is that a person may not be a judge in his own cause: if they have an **interest in the result** of the case, it cannot be said that they are independent. Second, there must be no **bias**: a judge must not show favour to one side or another, nor have a reason to do so, nor appear to do so.

Judges in the courts of the United Kingdom are conscious of their independence; they do not hear the case if they realise they are connected with the subject matter of the case, or when there is any suggestion that they may have. Even if there is in fact no connection, a possible appearance of it may be enough for the judge to consider not hearing the case. A judge should avoid the *appearance* of partiality or bias, even if it does not actually exist. There must be complete public confidence in the impartiality of the courts in a democratic society.

AN INTEREST IN THE CASE

The question of whether or not a judge has an interest in the subject matter of the case can be illustrated by the case of the Chilean dictator, *General Pinochet*.[18]

> Senator Pinochet was a former Head of State of Chile. A judge in Spain issued warrants of arrest, alleging that Pinochet had committed various crimes against humanity during his period of office. Pinochet was therefore arrested during a visit to London under a warrant issued under the extradition law. The arrest warrants were contested and quashed in the English courts on the basis that Pinochet had immunity from arrest and extradition as a former Head of State, and the matter was appealed to the House of Lords, who held by a majority that Senator Pinochet did *not* have immunity.
>
> One of the Lords who heard the case was Lord Hoffmann, who was a member of the majority in the decision. Amnesty International, a human rights body, which had campaigned

---

[16] *R (Stone)* v *Plymouth Magistrates* [2007] EWHC 2519 (Admin).

[17] *Attorney General's Reference No. 2 of 2001* [2003] UKHL 68, [2004] 2 AC 72; *Spiers* v *Ruddy* [2007] UKPC D2, [2008] 1 AC 873 is the relevant authority for Scotland.

[18] *R* v *Bow Street Metropolitan Stipendiary Magistrate and others, ex parte Pinochet Ugarte (No. 2)* [2000] 1 AC 119.

The right to a fair trial

against the Senator, was represented at the hearing before the House of Lords. Subsequently, Senator Pinochet learned that Lord Hoffmann was an unpaid director and chairman of a subsidiary company of Amnesty International. Senator Pinochet applied to the House of Lords to set aside its decision, on the ground not that Lord Hoffmann had any actual bias but that there was *apparent* bias – a real danger or reasonable apprehension or suspicion that Lord Hoffmann *might* have been biased.

The House of Lords agreed. Once Amnesty International had been allowed to intervene, it became a party to the case. Although it was neither prosecutor nor accused, it had an interest in establishing that there was no immunity for former heads of state in relation to crimes against humanity. It therefore had an interest in procuring Pinochet's extradition, albeit a political interest, rather than, for example, a monetary interest, and *that* was an interest in promoting one of the arguments being advanced rather than another. Since Lord Hoffmann was a director of the subsidiary company, he should have been the subject of automatic disqualification: the principle is that where a judge is a party to the action or has a financial or proprietary interest in its outcome, he is automatically disqualified from hearing it, whether or not there is any likelihood or suspicion of actual bias.

BIAS

Bias is rather different. It is partiality, or a lack of objectivity, or the possible appearance of it. The incorporation of the Convention has brought about an even closer scrutiny of the notion of independence. And this appears in a case about the court-martial system, which operates where a member of the armed forces is tried for a crime under military law. Although the court-martial procedure had been in existence for a long time, this is one area where our law has been changed,[19] following the decision of the European Court in *Findlay* v *UK*.[20]

When Lance Sergeant Findlay was tried for a shooting incident, which he blamed on suffering post-traumatic stress disorder, in the then usual way, the court-martial consisted of five members of the armed forces. These members were subordinate to the convening officer of the court-martial, who himself played a significant role before the hearing, was central to the prosecution, and had power to dismiss the court-martial. The decision was confirmed by the convening officer.

The European Court held that the court-martial was not independent within the meaning of the Convention, and therefore there was a violation of Article 6, because of the overlapping roles of the convening officer between prosecution and judge. Critical questions in deciding whether a court is impartial include the manner of appointment of its members and their term of office, the existence of guarantees against outside pressures and the question whether the body presents an appearance of independence. And to be impartial, the court must not only be subjectively free of personal prejudice or bias, it must also be impartial from an objective viewpoint, that is, it must offer sufficient guarantees to exclude any legitimate doubt in this respect.

[19] Armed Forces Act 1996.
[20] (1997) 24 EHRR 221.

The House of Lords has confirmed that the court-martial system now complies with Article 6, because it has permanent presidents, with sufficient safeguards that a fair-minded observer would *not* conclude that the court was not independent or impartial.[21] However, there have been further cases about naval court-martial procedures: the European Court held in *Grieves* v *UK*[22] that naval court-martial procedures were not fair, in particular because of the absence of a full-time courts-martial judge. Naval Judge Advocates were serving officers, rather than civilians outside the chain of command. The law has now been changed to remedy this.[23] Then, in the case of *Stow*,[24] the Courts-Martial Appeals Court held that a conviction was unsafe because the prosecutor was not sufficiently independent and impartial – because he was reported on, an objective observer might well have taken the view that he could be influenced in his decisions by what he thought his superiors would think of them, coupled with factors about rank and scope for promotion. But note that it is not always necessary for a prosecutor to be impartial: in the case of *Haase*,[25] it was held that there was no breach of Article 6 in relation to prison disciplinary proceedings where the prosecution case was presented by a prison officer who might also be a witness: *Stow* was distinguished as applying to courts-martial rather than necessarily applying to all types of proceedings.

It is objective impartiality which is so important: being *seen* to be impartial. The European Court in *Findlay* states clearly the ingredients of it – manner of appointment, term of office, and guarantees of independence from pressures. But those words about independence from pressures were relevant in another case, where until the incorporation of the Convention, no thought had been given to the possibility of bias.

> In *Starrs and Chalmers* v *Ruxton*,[26] in a criminal court, the complainants appeared before a temporary sheriff, who was a judge appointed by the Secretary of State; however, the appointment was dependent on the recommendation of the Lord Advocate, and it was he who conducted the prosecution. The office of temporary sheriff was the start of a route to higher judicial office. The court held that there was an appearance of lack of objectivity, because of the manner of the appointment, and the lack of tenure of office. In these circumstances there was a violation of Article 6.

Where a judge is appointed by the government to a post which has no security of tenure, there may be an objective appearance of the judge being tempted to give a decision in favour of the government, however much it is known and accepted that the particular judge is a person of complete independence and integrity. The same applies where the person who is now judging the case was previously *part* of the government.

---

[21] *Boyd* v *Army Prosecuting Authority* [2002] UKHL 31, [2002] 3 WLR 437.
[22] (2004) 39 EHRR 51.
[23] Naval Discipline Act 1957 (Remedial) Order 2004 (SI 2004/66), see now the Courts-Martial (Royal Navy) Rules 2007 SI 2007/3443; remedial orders are discussed above, p. 75.
[24] *R* v *Stow* [2005] EWCA Crim 1157, [2005] UKHRR 754.
[25] *R (Haase)* v *Independent Adjudicator* [2008] EWCA Civ 1089, [2008] UKHRR 1260.
[26] [2000] UKHRR 78.

The right to a fair trial

In the case of *Davidson* v *Scottish Ministers*,[27] the situation was that Lord Hardie had been a government Minister involved in drafting and promoting a piece of legislation. He then became a judge, in which capacity he was required to rule on the effect of that legislation. The House of Lords held that he should not hear the case: there was a real risk of apparent bias because, without casting any aspersions on the judge's judicial integrity, he might subconsciously try to avoid a result which would undermine assurances he had given to Parliament about the effect of the legislation.

The case of *Findlay* was used in the English court case about magistrates in their capacity as licensing justices, when they are carrying out their function of granting or refusing licences to premises for alcohol or entertainment.

The relevance of Article 6 is that when a licensing decision is appealed to the Crown Court, it is heard by a judge and four magistrates, two of whom must be members of the magistrates' bench where the premises are situated which are the subject of the appeal. The idea behind this is presumably that those two magistrates will have knowledge of local conditions in the licensing field. But it means that two of the justices sitting in the Crown Court are hearing an appeal from a decision of their colleagues on the local bench. However independent and scrupulous those two magistrates are, they may be perceived to be seeking to uphold their colleagues' decision.

This was challenged in the case of *The Preston and Lincoln Crown Courts*,[28] where the High Court held that the arrangement – two magistrates sitting on the appeal from their own bench – was a violation of Article 6. The Court pointed out that the two magistrates sit on the Crown Court bench at the invitation of their own clerk, and may be asked to make an order for costs against their colleagues, and there is a danger that they may incline, even unconsciously, to conform with their colleagues.

As well as being an illustration of the way in which a judge may possibly be in a position of partiality, that is, apparent partiality, this is also a prime example of the influence of the Convention on our law. It is the wording and spirit of Article 6 which have made the courts examine again rules and procedures, which have been used over the years without question.

The test, to detect possible partiality, is a high one. It is to ask whether the circumstances would lead a fair-minded and informed observer, considering the relevant facts, to conclude that there was a real possibility that the tribunal was biased. This definition of the test was set out by the Court of Appeal after an examination of the previous English cases and after applying the Convention jurisprudence.[29]

---

[27] [2004] UKHL 34, [2004] UKHRR 1079.

[28] *R (Chief Constable of Lancashire)* v *Preston Crown Court; R (Smith)* v *Lincoln Crown Court* [2001] EWHC Admin 928, [2002] 1 WLR 1332.

[29] *In re Medicaments and Related Classes of Goods (No. 2), DGFT* v *Proprietary Association of Great Britain and Proprietary Articles Trade Association* [2001] 1 WLR 700.

The case in question concerned an application by the Director General of Fair Trading (DGFT) to the Restrictive Practices Court to discharge a 30-year-old order which had exempted branded medicines from the general ban in law on there being minimum prices on the resale of products, since the DGFT argued that this exemption could no longer be justified.

One member of the court was a doctor, and during the course of the hearing she applied to be employed by a firm which was providing expert evidence in the case, although the firm rejected her application. The trade associations defending the exemption applied for this doctor and the rest of the court to withdraw from hearing it, alleging that the court was biased. The court refused. On appeal from this decision, the Court of Appeal held that there was a violation of Article 6. After setting out the test of whether or not there is a real possibility of bias, the Court decided that, in this case, a fair-minded observer would be concerned that if the doctor esteemed the firm sufficiently to wish to be employed by them, she might consciously or unconsciously be inclined to consider them a more reliable source of expert opinion than their rivals. Thus there was a real danger that the doctor would be unable to make an objective and impartial appraisal of the expert evidence, and so she and the other members of the court should have withdrawn from the case.

One feature of the case is that the Court of Appeal, having examined the jurisprudence of the European Court, thereupon altered the English approach in cases of bias, from one in which the court decided the likelihood of the lower court being *in fact* biased, to one in which the court asks what the *fair-minded and informed observer* would have thought – that is, would they conclude that there was a real possibility that the tribunal was biased. This approach was approved by the House of Lords in the case of *Porter* v *MacGill*,[30] and then applied by the House of Lords in *Lawal* v *Northern Spirit Ltd.*[31]

This case concerned a challenge to an Employment Appeal Tribunal (EAT). An EAT is composed of a legal Chairman and two lay members. Often the Chairman was a Recorder, which is a barrister or solicitor who sits as a part-time judge. Sometimes the Recorder, on returning to his own practice as an advocate, appeared before the EAT (under another Chairman), and found himself before lay members with whom he had sat as a Chairman. This happened in Mr Lawal's case and he objected.

The House of Lords held that the fair-minded observer was likely to approach the matter on the basis that the lay members looked to the Chairman for guidance on law, and could be expected to develop a fairly close relationship of trust and confidence with them. There was no finding of the rule against bias in this specific case, but the House of Lords ruled that having barristers sit as part-time judges as EAT chairmen should be discontinued, to ensure that there was no possibility of subconscious bias on the part of the lay members in such a situation, and to ensure that public confidence in the system was not undermined.

---

[30] [2001] UKHL 67, [2002] 2 AC 357; see also *Helow* v *Advocate General for Scotland* [2008] UKHL 62, [2008] 1 WLR 2416: membership of an organisation, subscription to a journal or interest in reading matter does not establish bias, just because that reading matter might contain views opposed to those of the litigant.
[31] [2003] UKHL 35, [2004] 1 All ER.

Until the incorporation of the Convention no one had thought to question this practice, which applies more widely, since barristers and solicitors sit as Recorders with lay magistrates in the Crown Court as well, and will need to guard against appearing before these magistrates either in the magistrates' court or the Crown Court.

So far we have considered the position of judges; but where there is a jury, the parties in the case have a right to be sure that the jury is also independent. In the normal course of events, a jury is indeed independent. It is composed of individuals who have no connection with the parties, and have no knowledge of the facts of the case before it starts. When a case involves famous or notorious events or personalities, the jury is directed to ignore anything which they may have heard outside the court, and to concentrate on the evidence given in court. From time to time, it is true, efforts are made to make corrupt offers or threats to jurors, which will impair their independence; if that is discovered, the jury are discharged from giving a verdict, and the case starts again with a fresh jury. But leaving aside cases of that kind, lack of independence in a jury may arise in another way, and it has attracted the attention of the European Court. In two cases it came to the notice of the judge that the jury, or a number of them, were harbouring an attitude of racial discrimination.

In *Gregory* v *UK*,[32] the applicant, who was black, was tried at Manchester Crown Court for robbery. The jury retired to consider their verdict, and nearly two hours after retiring, a note was passed from the jury to the judge, reading, 'Jury showing racial overtones. One member to be excused.' The judge warned the jury to try the case according to the evidence and to put aside any prejudice. The jury eventually returned with a majority verdict of guilty. Relying on Articles 6 and 14, the applicant complained to the European Court that he had not had a fair trial, and that he had been discriminated against on the basis of race. The European Court found that the judge had dealt with the note firmly, and that after his direction, to try the case on the evidence, there was no further suggestion from the jury of any racial comment, and so the judge could reasonably consider that the jury had complied with the terms of his direction. He had taken sufficient steps to ensure that the jury was behaving impartially.

However, in the case of *Sander* v *UK*,[33] there were conflicting notes from the jury, and when the judge attempted to clear up what was being said, there was further contradiction. The judge allowed the jury to continue their deliberations, and they convicted the applicant. He complained that he had suffered a violation of Article 6, and the European Court agreed. The judge had not made sure that the jury were conducting themselves properly, and there remained a doubt about this.

PRESUMPTION OF INNOCENCE

In the courts of the United Kingdom, the prosecution must prove the guilt of the defendant, and there is no burden on the defendant to prove that they are not guilty. This is called the **presumption of innocence**, and it is expressly stated in Article 6(2) – a defendant is presumed to be innocent until they are proved guilty. Since this is already the courts' guiding principle, the question is whether the article has anything to add.

[32] (1998) 25 EHRR 577.
[33] (2001) 31 EHRR 44.

The answer is that it has indeed added something – especially in cases where the law has imposed a **burden of proof** on a defendant. This occurs commonly in statutes: for example, where there is a criminal offence to do something or to be in a particular place, but the statute goes on to state that the defendant may prove facts which will give him a defence – that he did not have the requisite knowledge, or that he was acting as an employee and did not have the control of the activity, for example. Modern statutes have created offences and imposed burdens on a defendant with words such as '. . . unless the defendant proves the contrary'. These words are commonly described as 'reverse onus clauses'. In time past the English courts have regarded the burden of proof on the defendant as being 'on a balance of probabilities', which is a burden lower than that resting on the prosecution, who must prove guilt so that the court is sure. It means the prosecution are taken to have proved what is necessary against the defendant, unless he satisfies the jury on a balance of probabilities to the contrary. However, this still imposes what is known as a **persuasive burden**, which is the onus of satisfying the court that the defence is proven, as opposed to an **evidential burden,** a burden simply to provide enough evidence to credibly raise the defence, which the prosecution must then disprove.

But this has now been appraised afresh, because of the influence of the Convention case law on the approach of our courts; this is aptly illustrated in the case of *Kebilene*.[34] There the House of Lords analysed the thinking behind reverse onus clauses, namely, that there may be difficulty in proving the defendant's intention or purpose, or actual possession, especially when the defendant is a terrorist and had been trained in ways of avoiding detection, or has an explanation which is a plausible one.[35] And the speeches show how a balance has to be struck between the rights of the individual, and the interest in general security represented by the state.

In 1997, officers of the anti-terrorist squad arrested Mr Kebilene and two other Algerian nationals, who were charged with offences of having articles in their possession in circumstances giving rise to a reasonable suspicion that the articles were in their possession for the purposes of terrorism. The articles in this case were chemical containers, radio equipment, manuals, credit cards and money. The statute under which they were charged provided that the defendant had a *defence* to the charge by proving that the article in question was not in his possession for the purpose of terrorism. But the statute also had a provision which assisted the prosecution to prove possession: it provided that where the prosecution proved that the defendant and the article were both present on the same premises, or the article was on premises occupied by the defendant, *that* would be sufficient evidence of his possessing the article, *unless* the defendant proved that he did not know of the article, or had no control of it.

The defendants contended that, contrary to Article 6, there was in this section no presumption of innocence; as to the two main ingredients of the offence, possession and purpose, the one could be proved by a presumption – as to the presence of the defendant and the article on the same premises – and the other by a reasonable suspicion, which is a burden lower than that normally imposed on the prosecution. After that, the burden was on the defendant.

---

[34] *R v DPP, ex parte Kebilene* [2000] 2 AC 326.
[35] For a discussion of the particular problems raised by terrorism, below, pp. 378–9.

The right to a fair trial

The House of Lords held that the statute did not necessarily violate Article 6 (it reached no final conclusion because it took the view that the decision to prosecute could not be challenged in any event). Much depended on the surrounding facts and circumstances. This was indeed a reverse onus clause, but such clauses might impose on the defendant only an evidential burden, the burden of introducing evidence on the point, which is *not* a breach of Article 6, or it might be a persuasive burden, the burden of proving the point on a balance of probabilities, which *might* be a violation, depending on the circumstances. Those circumstances have to be balanced, in this case the protection of the state against terrorism with the right of the individual to a fair trial.

The House of Lords recognised the new attitude the courts must take in the light of the Convention. Some of the relevant factors were set out by Lord Hope:

In the hands of the national courts[,] the Convention should be seen as an expression of fundamental principles rather than as a set of mere rules. The questions which the courts will have to decide in the application of these principles will involve questions of balance between competing interests and issues of proportionality. [. . .] In considering where the balance lies it may be useful to consider the following questions:

(1) what does the prosecution have to prove in order to transfer the onus to the defence?

(2) what is the burden on the accused – does it relate to something which is likely to be difficult for him to prove, or does it relate to something which is likely to be within his knowledge [or] to which he readily has access?

(3) what is the nature of the threat faced by society which the provision is designed to combat?[36]

This question of reverse burdens is one which must be considered in the context of the statute which imposes the burden, since in each case the balance between the result of the reverse burden and the underlying reason for it may be different. What the courts have stressed is that reverse burdens and presumptions are permitted by Article 6(2), so long as they are kept within reasonable limits and are not arbitrary or disproportionate, taking into accounts factors such as the opportunity which the defendant had to rebut the presumption, the importance of the interests at stake, and the evidential difficulties for both prosecution and defence. This has come back before the House of Lords on more than one occasion.

In the case of *R v Lambert*,[37] the defendant was arrested in a car park at Runcorn railway station, in possession of a duffel bag; it contained 2 kg of cocaine worth £140,000. He was charged with an offence of having in his possession a class A controlled drug with intent to supply.[38] The defendant said a man in London, for whom he was accustomed to run errands, sent him to Runcorn, with an envelope. He alighted from the train at Runcorn, and met a man he knew, who gave him a bag, saying that it was jewellery. He relied on the defence of proving that he neither believed nor suspected nor had reason to suspect that he possessed a substance which is a controlled drug.

---

[36] Discussed further below, p. 379.
[37] [2001] 3 WLR 206.
[38] Section 5(3) of the Misuse of Drugs Act 1971.

Did the defence impose an evidential or persuasive burden? There was a difference of opinion in the House of Lords, but the majority view was that it was an evidential burden only and so there was no breach of Article 6. One member of the court, Lord Hutton, considered that this was a persuasive burden, but that even so this was not a violation of Article 6, since the threat of drugs to the well-being of the community and the peculiar difficulty of proving knowledge in such cases justifies the imposition of a persuasive burden.

Then, in *Sheldrake* v *DPP; Attorney General's Reference No. 4 of 2002*,[39] two very different offences had to be considered. The general principle was considered – that presumptions were permissible so long as they were reasonable and not arbitrary or disproportionate, taking into account factors such as the opportunity which the defendant had to rebut the presumption, the importance of the interests at stake, and the evidential difficulties for both prosecution and defence.

In *Sheldrake*, it was held that there is nothing unreasonable, unnecessary or disproportionate in requiring a person who is drunk in charge of a car to have the persuasive burden of showing that he is not likely to drive it, given the object of the statute, which is the prevention of death and serious injuries caused by dangerous driving, and the fact that whether the driver is likely to drive or not is so much a part of the driver's own state of mind at the time of the offence as to make it much more appropriate for him to prove he would not have been likely to drive.

On the other hand, in the *AG's Reference*, their Lordships, by a majority, held that the breadth of the offence in section 11 of the Terrorism Act, that of belonging to a proscribed organisation, was such that the burden of disproving the defence that the organisation was not proscribed when he belonged or was involved with it should rest on the prosecution. The consequences of a conviction were very serious and a defendant might well have real difficulties in proving the necessary details about any such organisation, especially as the section did not require the defendant to have conducted any form of terrorist activity. The imposition of a persuasive burden would therefore infringe Article 6, and the section should be read down to impose an evidential burden only.

These sorts of considerations have been widely applied. Where the matter to be considered is within the defendant's knowledge, where the main offence has otherwise been proved, and where there is a strong public interest in discouraging anti-social conduct, some form of reverse burden may well be justified, as in *Sheldrake* and *Parker* (which we considered above), and similarly in the case of a driver who wishes to prove that, after being shown that they are over the limit for consumption of alcohol, they did in fact consume alcohol after the alleged offence was committed, but before providing a specimen for testing, especially as this is conduct which should be discouraged since it is likely to interfere with determining whether an offence took place.[40]

There have been a very large number of cases on reverse burdens or presumptions, because of the large number of offences which impose one. By way of further examples, to show the wide range of areas this affects, reverse burdens have also been held to be justified

---

[39] [2004] UKHL 43, [2004] 3 WLR 976.
[40] *R* v *Drummond* [2002] 2 CAR 25.

The right to a fair trial

where, in order to establish a defence a person who has been proved to have counterfeit goods (bootleg CDs, etc.) has to prove that they reasonably believed that they did not contain a registered trade mark;[41] a person convicted of drug smuggling has to show that they no longer retained all the proceeds which they had been shown to have received;[42] a bankrupt has to prove that a transaction which they had failed to disclose was not intended to defeat their creditors;[43] a director of an insolvent company who has concealed company property or debts, or who has failed to deliver up the company's books, has to show that they had no intention to defraud;[44] a landlord who has evicted a tenant has to prove that they reasonably believed that the tenant had ceased to reside in the property;[45] someone who would otherwise be a proven murderer has to show that there had been a suicide pact, which would amount to a crime of manslaughter only;[46] and a person who intimidated a witness has to prove that they had no intention of interfering with the course of justice.[47]

On the other hand, where the offence is serious and the subject of the burden is an important part of the offence, the burden is likely to be read down – in addition to section 11 of the Terrorism Act, another example of a burden read down is where a bankrupt has to prove that a gift (or other similar transaction) made within five years before bankruptcy was not intended to defraud creditors: the breadth of this offence, in terms of time and possible number of transactions covered, which may have been perfectly proper at the time, requires it to be read down as an evidential burden only.[48] Likewise, in the offence of making a damaging disclosure of secret information under the Official Secrets Act, the Court of Appeal held that putting a reverse burden on an accused to disprove the mental element of the offence would be disproportionate and unjustifiable, since the prosecution would have to advance a positive case on these elements in any event, so it was read down to an evidential burden.[49]

ADVERSE INFERENCES

The presumption of innocence means that the prosecution must prove the guilt of the defendant; he is entitled to remain silent and make the prosecution prove his guilt, if they can. This is usually referred to as the defendant's right of silence, or the privilege against self-incrimination.[50] But in English law there is a qualification to this right. By section 34 of the Criminal Justice and Public Order Act 1994, where a defendant, during his interview

---

[41] Section 92(5) of the Trade Marks Act 1994; *R v Johnstone* [2003] UKHL 28, [2003] 1 WLR 1736.
[42] *Grayson v UK* (2009) 48 EHRR 30.
[43] Section 353(1)(b) of the Insolvency Act 1986: *Attorney General's Reference No. 1 of 2004* [2004] EWCA Crim 1025, [2004] 1 WLR 2111.
[44] Sections 206 and 208 of the Insolvency Act 1986: *R (Griffin) v Richmond Magistrates Court* [2008] EWHC 84 (Admin), [2008] 1 WLR 1525.
[45] Section 1(2) of the Protection from Eviction Act 1977; *AGR 1 of 2004* op cit.
[46] Section 4(2) of the Homicide Act 1957; *AGR 1 of 2004* op cit.
[47] Section 51(7) of the Criminal Justice and Public Order Act 1994; *AGR 1 of 2004* op cit.
[48] Section 357 of the Insolvency Act 1986, also considered in *AGR 1 of 2004* op cit.
[49] *R v Keogh* [2007] EWCA Crim 528, [2007] 1 WLR 1500.
[50] Discussed above in the context of the case of *Brown v Stott* etc. p. 206.

by police officers, fails to mention something which he later relies on in his defence, the jury may draw from that failure such inferences as appear proper to them; this is usually called 'drawing adverse inferences'.

This has been considered by the European Court in the case of *Condron* v *UK*.[51] The European Court there held that when an accused has been interviewed by police officers, and maintained a silence when questioned, if the jury is allowed to infer anything adverse to him from that silence, there must be safeguards in place, and the courts have now tailored their directions to juries to meet the European Court's comments. The facts were as follows.

Both applicants were heroin addicts, and they lived at 51 Cubitt House, a large block of council flats in south London. Adjacent to their flat, at 50, lived a Mr James Curtis, and the prosecution alleged that the applicants would prepare wraps of heroin for sale, and pass them to Mr Curtis when he knocked on the back window of their flat. The wraps would be handed from the balcony of 51 to someone leaning out of the window of 50. Mr Curtis would then sell the wrap to a purchaser. When the applicants were arrested, wraps of heroin, and other material, were found in their flat. They were charged with the supply and possession of heroin with intent to supply. At a police station, they were interviewed by police officers, although their solicitor thought that they were unfit to be interviewed, because of drug withdrawal. The interviews were preceded by a warning from the interviewing officer, which stated: 'You do not have to say anything but it may harm your defence if you do not mention when questioned something which you later rely on in court. Anything you say may be given in evidence.' Each applicant said, in answer to the interviewer's questions, 'No comment'.

At their trial, both applicants gave explanations, which they had not given in interview, saying in evidence that the heroin found in their flat had been for their own personal use, that the package seen being passed between the flats was a quantity of cigarettes, and that they had said 'No comment' acting on the advice of their solicitor, who had grave doubts about their fitness to be interviewed. The solicitor gave evidence to the same effect. The trial judge, in his direction to the jury, left them with the option of drawing an inference, under section 34, which was adverse to the applicants, from their silence in interview. They were convicted; Mr Curtis was acquitted. The applicants complained to the European Court that they were entitled to remain silent at the interviews, and to draw an inference from their silence was unfair, and a violation of Article 6.

The European Court stated that the right to silence is *not an absolute right*; and whether the drawing of an adverse inference from an accused's silence infringes Article 6 is a matter to be determined in the light of all the circumstances of the particular case. But, said the Court, particular caution was required before a court could use an accused's silence against him. The Court held that the jury could draw an inference adverse to the two accused *only* if they, the jury, were satisfied that their silence at the interview must be attributed to their having no answer or none that would stand up to cross-examination. The Court of Appeal had held that it would have been 'desirable' to give that direction. But for the European Court, that was not enough: there was a breach of Article 6.

[51] (2001) 31 EHRR 1.

THE MINIMUM CONTENT OF A FAIR TRIAL

As well as the general requirement of a fair hearing, Article 6 contains a further list of minimum requirements for fairness in criminal cases. In addition to the requirements of Article 6(1) – a fair and public hearing within a reasonable time by an independent and impartial tribunal – and Article 6(2) – the presumption of innocence – there are also the specific requirements of Article 6(3). These are the rights to be informed promptly, in a language which is understood and in detail, of the nature and cause of the accusation being made; to have adequate time and facilities for the preparation of a defence; to defend oneself in person or through legal assistance, with state help in paying for this if necessary; to cross-examine witnesses; to obtain the attendance and examination of witnesses; and have the free assistance of an interpreter, if the language of the court is not understood or spoken. In broad terms, all of these further, more detailed rights are part of our law already. However, there may be specific situations where the Article will add something: for example, the requirements for the state to pay for legal assistance or for an interpreter may in some situations impose a greater burden on the state than presently. It should be noted that having an interpreter is not by itself enough to make proceedings fair: effective participation in a trial may well require legal representation as well as an interpreter.[52]

It should also be noted that there is a further 'fair trial' right, that against being tried twice for the same offence (the rule against 'double jeopardy'), which is not contained in Article 6, but in Article 4 of the Seventh Protocol.[53] This was until recently true in our law in all criminal cases; there are now limited exceptions, which allow a retrial after acquittal in relation to a limited number of the most serious crimes, where there is new and compelling evidence;[54] it remains to be seen whether, if the Seventh Protocol is incorporated into our law, this causes any incompatibility.

A number of the specific matters set out in Article 6 relate to the evidence to be called at trial and the right to challenge the evidence. There have now been a number of cases where Article 6 has been used to try to affect how evidence is provided or called at trial. Thus, Article 6 has been used to challenge the system in Scotland for the disclosure of information by the prosecution (the challenge was rejected by the Privy Council on the basis that a suitable system for disclosure is in place);[55] and to question the use of special counsel to act for a defendant where material is the subject of a claim that disclosure to the defence should be disallowed for reasons of public interest (the argument that the procedure of using special counsel who could see the confidential material is inherently a breach of Article 6 was rejected by the House of Lords).[56] It has also been used in a number of areas to challenge certain sorts of evidence, in the way it is obtained or the way it is presented at trial. We shall consider some of these next.

---

[52] *R (Matara) v Brent Magistrates' Court* [2005] EWHC 1829 (Admin).
[53] Discussed above, p. 112, and referred to in *R v Young* LTL 14.10.05 CA.
[54] Criminal Justice Act 2003, Part 10.
[55] *McDonald v HM Advocate* [2008] UKPC 46, [2008] SLT 993.
[56] *R v H* [2004] UKHL 3, (2004) 2 AC 134; the use of special counsel under the anti-terrorism legislation is considered further below in Chapter 21, pp. 380–1.

AGENTS PROVOCATEURS

In the investigation of crime, police officers have developed a technique of being proactive – of placing temptation in the way of a person, whom they suspect of committing crimes, but whom they cannot catch. When the person succumbs to the temptation, the watching police arrest him. The argument in favour of using this technique is that the secrecy in which some crime is carried out, and the consequent difficulty of detection, makes it necessary. But it is one thing to place an opportunity in the way of a person who is looking for the opportunity, and it is quite another to incite the commission of a crime, or to instigate it. Incitement or instigation will probably be an offence in itself. It is in this situation that the courts have been obliged to deal with the argument, advanced on behalf of the defendant, that the officers have acted as agents provocateurs, in the sense that they have incited the defendant to commit the crime.

Both the European Court and our own courts have grappled with the problem of deciding when such techniques are unfair. They will be unfair if they lead to an abuse of the process of the law. 'It is simply not acceptable that the state through its agents should lure its citizens into committing acts forbidden by the law and then to seek to prosecute them for doing so.' These are the words of Lord Nicholls, in the case of *R* v *Looseley*, which we are about to examine.

The English courts have dealt with unfairness by using section 78 of the Police and Criminal Evidence Act 1984 (PACE), which enables the court to exclude prosecution evidence if it would be unfair to admit it. And the courts have developed the machinery of a stay of a prosecution as being an abuse of process where they decide that it would be unfair to try the defendant, or where the trial would be unfair. In this next case the House of Lords were expressly asked to consider whether, in a case of a so-called agent provocateur, Article 6 had modified the law relating to section 78 or stay for abuse of process. The case is *R* v *Looseley*, heard with another case, referred on a point of law where there had been no conviction, *Attorney General's Reference No. 3 of 2000.*[57]

In the case of Mr Looseley, a police officer telephoned Mr Looseley and asked for 'a couple of bags'; the officer met him and bought heroin from him on this occasion, and then met him on two more occasions for two more purchases. Mr Looseley was charged with being involved in the supply of heroin. The defendant argued that he had been incited to commit the offence, which was an abuse of the legal process, and unfair. The trial judge disagreed and refused to stay the prosecution, and the House of Lords agreed, saying that the officers had *not* instigated the offence.

In the second case, undercover officers were offering contraband cigarettes for sale on a housing estate. The defendant bought cigarettes from them, and the officers then asked him if he could provide them with heroin; he said he could not get heroin at short notice, and that he was 'not really into heroin', but eventually he obtained heroin from another source, and sold it to the officers. The trial judge granted a stay of the prosecution, as the police had procured the commission of offences which the defendant would not otherwise have committed. The House of Lords agreed, saying that the police had done more than

57 [2001] UKHL 53, [2001] 1 WLR 2060.

The right to a fair trial

give the defendant an opportunity to commit an offence; they had instigated offences, because they had offered inducements. The House said:

> It would be unfair and an abuse of process if a person had been incited or pressurised by an undercover police officer into committing a crime which he would not otherwise have committed, but it would not be objectionable if the officer, behaving as an ordinary member of the public would, gave a person an unexceptional opportunity to commit a crime, and that person freely took advantage of the opportunity.

And the House stated that Article 6 had *not* modified the English approach on section 78 of PACE, or the staying of a prosecution on the ground of abuse of process.

EVIDENCE OBTAINED BY UNLAWFUL OR COVERT MEANS

Police and customs officers use covert and intrusive methods of collecting evidence against suspects; they are obliged to do so when offenders themselves use care and guile to escape detection. They listen to telephone conversations, use intrusive listening devices and long-range photography, and they adopt disguises in order to mix unobserved with the suspects. Many of these devices are capable of bringing about a violation of the suspect's right to respect for a private life, in breach of Article 8.[58] This then raises a question which is relevant to the right to a fair trial: does it make a trial unfair where evidence is relied upon which was obtained in breach of Article 8?

In English law, the fact that evidence is obtained by an underhand or even illegal method is not necessarily a reason for excluding it. The House of Lords held so in *R* v *Khan*.[59] The European Court takes the same view; in *Khan* v *UK*,[60] the European Court held that the admission of evidence obtained by means of a listening device in breach of Article 8 did *not* automatically render the proceedings unfair. There is no absolute requirement that illegally obtained evidence should be excluded, but the use of such evidence may give rise to unfairness in the particular circumstances of a case. There should be a scrutiny of the fairness and proportionality of the circumstances in each case.

On 17 September 1992, Mr Khan arrived at Manchester Airport on a flight from Pakistan, with his cousin. Both men were searched; the cousin was found to be in possession of £100,000 worth of heroin; but none was found on Mr Khan. About four months later, on 26 January 1993, he visited a friend, B, in Sheffield, who was under police investigation for dealing in heroin. Indeed, a few days before, on 12 January 1993, unknown to Mr Khan or B, the installation of a listening device on B's premises had been authorised, on the grounds that B was suspected of dealing in drugs, and conventional methods of

---

[58] Considered below, pp. 272–4.
[59] [1997] AC 558.
[60] (2001) 31 EHRR 45; see also below in the context of Article 8, p. 273.

surveillance were unlikely to provide proof. The police thereby obtained a tape recording of a conversation in which Mr Khan admitted that he was a party to the importation of the drugs by his cousin when he arrived in Manchester. Mr Khan was arrested; he was interviewed, but he made no admission. At his trial, he admitted that the voice on the tape recording was his voice. The Crown agreed that a civil trespass had been committed on B's house, with minor damage.

Mr Khan argued that the evidence of the tape conversation was obtained in violation of Article 8 and should be excluded. The trial judge ruled that it was admissible. Mr Khan thereupon pleaded guilty. Mr Khan appealed; the House of Lords held that even if there was a violation of Article 8 the evidence was admissible, and the trial was not unfair.

The European Court held that there had been a violation of Article 8, and that the United Kingdom had not satisfied Article 8(2), since there was no statutory scheme or guideline governing the use of the covert listening device, and so it was not 'in accordance with the law'. However, the European Court found that there was *no* breach of Article 6, on the basis that the surveillance was not actually unlawful, and the defendant had been able to challenge both the authenticity and admissibility of the tape, and he had spoken, in the taped conversation, voluntarily, without inducement; there was no risk, in the circumstances, that the tape was unreliable, and at each stage the court had made an assessment of the fairness of the proceedings. In these circumstances, there was no breach of the right to a fair trial.

The European Court reached a majority decision, and, as a statement of principle, it is worth considering the dissenting opinion of Judge Loucaides, who said this:

> I cannot accept that a trial can be 'fair', as required by Article 6, if a person's guilt for any offence is established through evidence obtained in breach of the human rights guaranteed by the Convention. It is my opinion that the term 'fairness', when examined in the context of the European Convention of Human Rights, implies observance of the rule of law and for that matter it presupposes respect of the human rights set out in the Convention. [. . .] If violating Article 8 can be accepted as 'fair' then I cannot see how the police can be effectively deterred from repeating their impermissible conduct.

The Court of Appeal has confirmed that the statutory discretion under section 78 of PACE and an argument under Article 6 will focus on similar considerations:[61] the exercise in both cases is to consider the proportionality and justification for the surveillance. The Court of Appeal has confirmed that similar considerations apply to civil cases.[62]

Note that there is one more serious possibility, which we have considered elsewhere, when the question is whether the evidence has been obtained, not just in breach of Article 8, by surveillance, but in breach of Article 3, by torture:[63] here, the fairness of the trial process requires that if evidence has been shown on the balance of probabilities to have been obtained by torture, it *must* be excluded.

---

[61] *R* v *Mason* [2002] EWCA Crim 385, [2002] 2 CAR 38; *R* v *Button* [2005] EWCA Crim 516.

[62] *Jones* v *Warwick University* [2003] EWCA Civ 151, [2003] 1 WLR 954, where it was held that the judge was right not to exclude the evidence but, because the evidence had been obtained improperly, the party obtaining the evidence had to pay the costs of the decision on admissibility.

[63] *A* v *Home Secretary (No. 2)* [2005] UKHL 71, [2005] 3 WLR 1249; discussed further above, p. 168.

WITNESS ANONYMITY

It is a long-standing principle of our law that a party accused of a crime should have the right to cross-examine the witnesses who are giving evidence against them. This is the heart of what is meant by an adversarial system. It is for this reason that our law has various limitations on using hearsay evidence. Hearsay evidence is evidence which is not being given in court by a person who witnessed something, but indirectly: it could be evidence of what the person who witnessed the event said about it to someone else; or their written account of what took place; or evidence from some other source, such as records, where the evidence itself is not given by a living witness. Some hearsay evidence may be perfectly reliable; sometimes there are real doubts about its veracity. The law of evidence allows for many sorts of circumstances where hearsay evidence can be relied on; and many where it cannot.

One particular situation is where a witness is to give an account of what they saw or heard in respect of a crime that was committed, but they are afraid to give their evidence in open court, for example, because they have been intimidated. Another is where the witness is no longer able to give evidence, because of illness or death, or because they have moved abroad or cannot be traced. The court have a discretion to admit hearsay evidence, under section 116 of the Criminal Justice Act 2003, in some situations such as these, and the question could be asked whether this is compatible with a fair trial.

> In the case of *Cole*,[64] the Court of Appeal held that the discretion to admit hearsay evidence is not inherently incompatible with Article 6, which does not require that the defendant has the opportunity to cross-examine all witnesses against them. The Court had two appeals before it: in one, the victim of the crime had dementia and could no longer give evidence, but had previously made a statement; in the other, the victim was dead, and evidence was to be given from people she knew about what she had told them. In both cases, the Court held that the judge was correct to allow the hearsay evidence.
>
> Again in the case of *Doherty*,[65] hearsay evidence was admitted because the witness had been subjected to intimidation by the accused. The Court had to consider the balance between allowing the evidence to be presented and protecting the witness from intimidation, and in this case, there was no unfairness in allowing the statement of the witness to be relied on, rather than the witness being called to give evidence.

One technique used to protect witnesses from intimidation, while still allowing them to give evidence, is to allow them to give evidence anonymously. This is a very useful tool for the prosecution, because it allows people who would otherwise be too afraid to give evidence to do so. On the other hand, it may deprive the defence of being able to respond effectively, since the defendant does not know who the witnesses are.

---

[64] *R v Cole* [2007] EWCA Crim 1924, [2007] 1 WLR 2716; and see also *R v Horncastle* [2009] EWCA Crim 964.
[65] *R v Doherty* [2006] EWCA Crim 2716.

The House of Lords had to consider this in the case of *Davis*.[66] This was a murder trial at which a number of witnesses, who identified him as the killer, and who were crucial to the conviction, were unwilling to testify as they would be afraid for their own lives if it was known that they had given evidence. The trial judge therefore ordered that each should be referred to under a pseudonym; details identifying them should be withheld from the defendant; the defendant's counsel should not ask questions which might allow them to be identified; and they gave evidence behind screens and with a voice distorter.

The House of Lords held that these measures went too far and made the trial unfair. It was important that the evidence against the accused was not solely dependent on anonymous witnesses, and here the defence was seriously inhibited by its inability to explore with questions the witnesses' relationship with the accused, so much as to render the trial unfair. The problem of threats of intimidation was not a new one, and the law had always found other ways of dealing with it, without having the main evidence given anonymously. The steps here sufficiently hampered cross-examination of the witnesses so as to make the trial unfair in breach of Article 6.

This caused an immediate political reaction, because it reduced the scope for the prosecution to be able to offer witnesses anonymity so as to secure convictions, and raised the risk that a number of existing trials, where such evidence had been allowed, would be reversed on appeal. Parliament responded to this case by promptly passing a particular statute to address this situation, the Criminal Evidence (Witness Anonymity) Act 2008, which regularised the law in this area, allowing witness anonymity in certain circumstances and setting out the factors which must be taken into account. The new Act also took the unusual step of applying to trials which had already taken place so that any appeal on the basis of the decision in *Davis* would not make the conviction unlawful unless even under the new law the witness would not have been allowed to remain anonymous. But the new statutory framework does still require that the trial be fair: this remains the overall test of what measures can be taken to balance the protection of the witness against the rights of the defendant to challenge the evidence against them.[67]

CIVIL PROCEEDINGS: THE SCOPE OF ARTICLE 6

Turning now to consider the effect of Article 6 in civil proceedings, the first question is, how do you determine which are civil and which are criminal proceedings? 'Civil rights and obligations' are the words in line 1 of Article 6, and it would be tempting to say that this covers whatever decisions are made which are not about criminal offences. However, not every decision will clearly fall within one or other category. It will therefore be a question to be determined from case to case, whether the proceedings are criminal or civil in substance.

---

[66] *R v Davis* [2008] UKHL 36, [2008] 3 WLR 125.
[67] The Court of Appeal gave guidance on the new law in the case of *R v Mayers* [2008] EWCA Crim 2989, [2009] 2 All ER 145, in which the overall fairness of the trial is a prime consideration.

One example which raises this question is the making of anti-social behaviour orders ('ASBOs'). The application for an order to be made is usually a civil procedure, but if it is breached by the defendant, that is a criminal offence. This therefore raises the question of whether the making of the order involves liability to a criminal penalty.

This was considered in the case of *McCann*,[68] where three brothers, aged 13, 15 and 16 years, were each made the subject of an anti-social behaviour order (ASBO), requiring them each to leave a designated area of Manchester on account of their behaviour. The order provided that if the order was breached, the brothers could be brought before the court and dealt with by way of punishment for that breach. The brothers appealed, arguing that the proceedings were criminal, so that the safeguards of Article 6(2) and (3) should be in place.

The House of Lords held that the proceedings were not criminal in nature. The obtaining of an order of this sort was merely a restriction on activities to protect the public, and not a punishment as such. There was only a punishment if there was then a breach of the order. Although the making of an order is a serious matter, involving a high standard of proof, it is still a civil proceeding. To apply the criminal standard to the process of the making of the order would defeat the object of the proceedings, which was to deal with the difficulty of persuading people to give evidence of the behaviour complained of, and the civil proceedings made it easier to prove.

If the sanction is dismissal or suspension from the person's employment, trade, profession or status, that is more likely to be a 'civil' proceeding. And sometimes, the proceedings will not fall within either category, where they are, for example, an internal procedure with a sanction falling short of dismissal or suspension from a job. Where proceedings are purely disciplinary, Article 6 may well not apply.

One example is a school disciplinary proceeding for reinstatement to a school, in the case of *B (and others)*.[69] This case concerned complaints regarding the exclusion of a number of pupils from their schools for misbehaviour. The Administrative Court considered that an independent appeal panel under the provisions of the School Standards and Framework Act 1998 was a disciplinary proceeding under a statute in a specific area and not part of the law applicable to persons generally. The determination of an application for reinstatement did not therefore engage Article 6: it did not involve the consideration of a criminal charge, nor did it determine a question which would affect the pupil's right to enjoy a reputation, since any consequences for reputation were incidental to the question of reinstatement and were not the point of the proceeding, given that there were procedural safeguards in place and the decision could be reviewed by the courts to ensure these were complied with.

Yet proceedings which are referred to as disciplinary *may* attract the provisions of Article 6. In the case of *Greenfield*[70] the Court of Appeal considered that a prison adjudication for taking a controlled drug while in prison which resulted in the addition of 21 days to Greenfield's sentence was not a criminal proceeding. However, the European Court

---

[68] *R (McCann)* v *Manchester Crown Court* [2002] UKHL 39, [2001] 1 WLR 1084.
[69] *R (B)* v *Head Teacher of Alperton Community School* [2002] LGR 132.
[70] *R (Greenfield)* v *Secretary of State for the Home Department* [2001] EWCA Civ 1224, [2001] 1 WLR 345.

then decided in the case of *Ezeh*,[71] which concerned allegations of assault and threats by prisoners, that such proceedings *are* criminal in nature, given the nature of the charges and the nature of the penalties imposed, since they render the person accused liable to an additional prison sentence, and this has now been accepted in our courts. This was then conceded when *Greenfield* went to the House of Lords.[72]

Another example is a ministerial decision suspending a care worker from working with vulnerable adults.[73] This is not a court proceeding but it does engage Article 6 because there is a determination of the rights of the care workers affected. In the case of *Wright*,[74] the House of Lords made a declaration of incompatibility since the scheme for making such decisions failed to properly protect the procedural rights of the care workers to a prompt and fair consideration of their case. The House of Lords have expressed similar views about a health authority making an urgent application which would close down a care home: there was no duty of care to the care home owner to take reasonable care in making the application because the prime duty is to protect the residents of the home, but the care home owners deserve procedural protection and if the Act had applied to the facts (it was pre-2000), there would have been a breach of Article 6.[75]

Some decisions may fall outside Article 6 for a slightly different reason: not because they are in some sense internal and not general, but because they are not in any real sense judicial, which is to say made by an independent tribunal which is constituted to find facts and apply the law. One example is a police warning: this does not involve determination of a criminal charge, since it is based on an admission of an offence.[76] Another is the decision of an immigration judge assessing whether someone has refugee status.[77] However, many decisions which affect people's rights do attract the protection of Article 6 indirectly, by way of judicial review by the courts.

One illustration of this is the *Alconbury* case,[78] which we considered in the context of the constitutional relationship between Parliament and the courts.[79] Here it was being argued that the Environment Secretary was not an independent and impartial tribunal within the meaning of Article 6(1) and therefore his power to decide these questions was incompatible with the Convention. The House of Lords rejected this argument, deciding that, since the Secretary of State's role in the planning legislation was the determination of policy and not a judicial decision as such, Article 6 did not therefore directly apply to his decision, but Article 6 *was* complied with in the procedure taken as a whole, because the decision of the Secretary of State could be judicially reviewed. There was therefore protection to ensure that the decision was *legal* and procedurally proper; but it was not for the court to say whether it was *correct*. In so far as the decision involved the finding of facts, to which Article 6 could apply, that was something which the court could consider in a judicial review application.

---

[71] *Ezeh* v *UK* (2004) 39 EHRR 1.
[72] *Greenfield* [2005] UKHL 14, [2005] 1 WLR 673, discussed above, p. 95, on remedies.
[73] Section 82 of the Care Standards Act 2000.
[74] *R (Wright)* v *Secretary of State for Health* [2009] UKHL 3, [2009] 2 WLR 267.
[75] *Trent Strategic Health Authority* v *Jain* [2009] UKHL 4, [2009] 2 WLR 248.
[76] *R (R)* v *Durham Constabulary* [2005] UKHL 21, [2005] 1 WLR 1184.
[77] *HH (Iran)* v *Home Secretary* [2008] EWCA Civ 504.
[78] *R (Alconbury Developments Limited)* v *Secretary of State for the Environment, Transport and the Regions* [2001] UKHL 23, [2001] 2 WLR 1389.
[79] Above, pp. 48–9.

Likewise, it has been held that an adjudicator, appointed by two parties pursuant to a statutory scheme to resolve a dispute arising out of a building contract, was not a public authority and was not conducting legal proceedings, so Article 6 did not apply to him; but the requirement for a public hearing of the dispute under Article 6 was satisfied by the court proceedings which would be necessary to enforce the adjudicator's decision.[80] The same has been held to apply to the statutory scheme for reviews of decisions by local councils regarding housing the homeless – the fact that there is an appeal to a county court on a point of law is enough to comply with Article 6.[81] Thus, Article 6 may not apply directly, but it may still have a role in the overall supervision of the proceedings, indirectly, through the standards applied by the court in reviewing the decision and holding it to a basic application of procedural fairness.

However, judicial review will not always be a sufficient remedy to ensure that the subject's Article 6 rights are protected.

The European Court has considered this in the case of *Tsfayo* v *UK*.[82] This case concerned an application for a social security benefit, which would be paid by the local authority. The challenge was brought because the decision as to whether the benefit should be paid was being made by a tribunal which was made up of local councillors. The European Court held that this was not an independent tribunal, because the councillors were part of the authority which would be paying the benefit. The decision was a straightforward one of fact, relating to the claimant's delay in making a claim, and not one of policy. But because the tribunal was not independent, there was no impartial decision on the claimant's factual entitlement. The claimant has an appeal to the court by way of judicial review, and the court is impartial, but the court on a judicial review will not reconsider the decision on the facts. Thus, at no stage was the question of the claimant's factual entitlement to benefit decided by an impartial and independent tribunal, and there was a violation of Article 6.

Thus it is clear that a judicial review will not be able to 'cure' all potential infringements of Article 6 where that is the only remedy.

CIVIL PROCEEDINGS: ACCESS TO JUSTICE

There is within Article 6 an implied right of access to court: it is a right to *get* to court, in order to have the fair trial promised by Article 6. This right of access applies particularly to civil proceedings, rather than to criminal cases; after all, in the latter there is no difficulty in getting access to the court, since the person who wishes to rely on Article 6 is usually brought there whether they like it or not. In civil cases, in order to have a *fair* trial, one must actually get to court, which is to say, one must have access to the process which gets one to court, by having the ability to consult a lawyer and issue a claim.

---

[80] *Austin Hall Building Ltd* v *Buckland Securities Ltd* (2002) 80 Con LR 115.
[81] *Begum* v *Tower Hamlets* [2003] UKHL 5, [2003] 2 AC 430, considering Part VII of the Housing Act 1996; *R(A)* v *Croydon LBC* [2008] EWCA Civ 1445, [2009] 1 FLR 317 considering s. 20 of the Children Act 1989; *R (Gilboy)* v *Liverpool CC* [2008] EWCA Civ 751, (2008) 4 All ER 127 on the review of demoted tenancies under the Housing Act 1996.
[82] *Tsfayo* v *UK* [2008] 48 EHRR 18.

This is nowhere stated in Article 6, which assumes that the person bringing a claim has actually reached court and got as far as a trial. But the European Court has said that there is implicit in Article 6 the right of *access* to a fair trial; the right to a fair trial is of no value if one cannot reach court, and so to give value and substance to the rights expressed in Article 6, there must be implied in Article 6 the right to have access to a court, and to the machinery of the court – the right to consult a solicitor, and to commence proceedings. This was the approach of the European Court in the case of *Golder* v *UK*.[83]

Mr Sidney Elmer Golder was serving a 15-year prison sentence. A serious disturbance occurred in a recreation area of the prison, where Mr Golder happened to be. A prison officer was attacked by prisoners, and injured, and he at first identified Mr Golder as being one of his assailants. Thereupon Mr Golder was placed in segregation, he was notified that disciplinary proceedings would be brought against him, and his letters to a Member of Parliament and a Chief Constable were stopped. The prison officer then withdrew the allegation against Mr Golder; he was returned to his normal cell, the charges were dropped, and the records were amended; but those records still bore the note about the incident. Mr Golder sought permission to consult a solicitor with a view to commencing libel proceedings against the prison officer, but permission was refused.

The European Court held that by refusing him permission to consult a solicitor, the Home Secretary hindered his right of access to the courts, and there was a violation of Article 6. The Court said:

In civil matters one can scarcely conceive of the rule of law without there being a possibility of having access to the courts. [. . .] Were Article 6(1) to be understood as concerning exclusively the conduct of an action which had already been initiated before a court, [the state] could, without acting in breach of that text, do away with its courts, or take away their jurisdiction to determine certain classes of civil actions and entrust it to organs dependent on the Government. Such assumptions, indissociable from a danger of arbitrary power, would have serious consequences which are repugnant to the aforementioned principles and which the Court cannot overlook. [. . .] It would be inconceivable, in the opinion of the Court, that Article 6(1) should describe in detail the procedural guarantees afforded to parties in a pending lawsuit and should not first protect that which alone makes it in fact possible to benefit from such guarantees, that is, access to a court.

Access to justice can include not just being able to contact a lawyer, but also being able to *afford* a lawyer – which may require legal aid – and a denial of fairness may amount to a denial of a substantive Convention right.

In *Steel and Morris* v *UK*,[84] commonly referred to as the 'Mclibel' case, two environmental campaigners had been sued for libel by McDonald's, and were not given legal aid to pay for defending the case; they successfully defended some of the case, but lost on some other grounds.

[83] (1979–80) 1 EHRR 524.
[84] (2005) 41 EHRR 403.

The European Court held that the libel trial breached the defendants' Article 6 rights to a fair trial because they were denied legal aid, especially since, under English libel law, the burden was on them to show the truth of what they were saying about McDonald's, notwithstanding the length and complexity of the trial and the detail involved. The Court went on to hold that the lack of legal aid, the burden on the defendants and the substantial damages went beyond simply being a breach of Article 6, but also impinged on the defendants' rights to freedom of expression in breach of Article 10.[85]

However, in order for rights of access to apply, there has to be a legal right which can found a claim, or about which there is an argument, and a case. If there is no such right, there is nothing to go to court for, and so no one is being prevented from claiming anything. This was the conclusion in the case of *Matthews* v *Ministry of Defence*:[86]

Mr Alan Robert Matthews had served in the Royal Navy as an electrical mechanic from 1955 to 1968; he claimed he was exposed to asbestos fibres and dust and as a result he developed asbestos-related diseases, which were not diagnosed until September 1999; he claimed damages on the ground of negligence and breach of statutory duty against the Ministry of Defence. The Ministry took the point that it was immune from liability, under the Crown Proceedings Act 1947, section 10, which deprived servicemen of their civil right to sue in negligence, and substituted an entitlement to a pension, and Mr Matthews claimed that this section prevented him from putting forward his claim, and that this was a breach of Article 6, and was incompatible with it. He was in effect prevented from having access to the court. But the House of Lords held that whether a civil right existed was a matter of substantive law. Since the effect of this Act was to deprive Mr Matthews of any right on which he could sue, there was nothing in respect of which he was being denied a fair trial. Article 6 had no impact on the substantive law; therefore there was no breach of the Article, and no right to complain that he was prevented from asserting a right.[87]

The House of Lords reached a similar result in the case of *Kehoe*.[88] Here a lone parent living apart from her husband, and caring for her children, sought maintenance for them from her husband. She applied to the Child Support Agency (CSA) which assesses and collects and enforces child maintenance. Her complaint was that there had been undue delay by the CSA in enforcing an assessment, and claimed damages for breach of Article 6 on the ground that the delay denied her access to the determination of her civil rights. But the House of Lords (by a majority) held that Mrs Kehoe and her children had no *right* to a maintenance payment, so that there was no 'right' to which Article 6 could apply. This was a matter of debate even in the Lords: Baroness Hale dissented on the grounds that the right to maintenance existed without the involvement of the CSA, which was provided by statute with the duty of enforcing this right, and had to do so in a procedurally fair manner.[89]

---

[85] For Article 10, see Chapter 16, p. 306.
[86] [2003] UKHL 4, [2003] 1 AC 1163.
[87] This approach was approved by the European Court in *Roche* v *UK* (2006) 42 EHRR 30, although the lack of access to medical records was held to breach Article 8.
[88] *R (Kehoe)* v *Secretary of State for Work and Pensions* [2005] UKHL 48, [2005] 3 WLR 252.
[89] When the case went to the European Court, it did not decide whether there was a civil right, as it found that there was no restriction on her right of effective access to a court in any event: *Kehoe* v *UK* (2009) 48 EHRR 2.

This is an area where there has been a shift in the European Court's view of the English law of negligence. To establish liability for negligence, it is necessary to show that there is a duty for one person to take reasonable care in respect of another's person or property. In the case of *Osman* v *UK*,[90] the European Court had considered that the domestic decision that the police did not owe a duty to take reasonable care towards a potential victim of a crime for the purposes of the law of negligence was a breach of Article 6. However, in *Z* v *UK*,[91] the European Court recognised that that was a misunderstanding of the way the English law of negligence works, and in that case the European Court held that a domestic decision was not a violation of Article 6 but a decision on the substantive law of negligence (the decision was that a local authority does not owe a duty of care to neglected or abused children who were not in local authority care). This makes clear that Article 6 does not apply to a substantive legal limitation, where there is no duty owed by one general class of persons to another, even if this is described as an immunity – it is not a case where there is a liability but there is no access to a court to enforce it; rather there is no liability at all, as in *Matthews*. Article 6 would apply only if the immunity was purely procedural (for example, you cannot sue without paying a large amount of money in costs first), or arbitrary (for example, all teachers owe a duty of care in negligence except for geography teachers).

CIVIL PROCEEDINGS: THE EFFECT OF THE CONVENTION

Reading through Article 6 there is a very distinct emphasis on criminal proceedings. Whilst Article 6(1) mentions both civil and criminal proceedings, Article 6(2) and (3) refer expressly to criminal proceedings and to them alone. The European Court has derived two particular principles from this. The first is that if a case is a civil one, the citizen is not permitted to rely on the express words of Article 6(2) and (3); the important rights enshrined in those paragraphs, the presumption of innocence and strict rules of evidence and procedure, are not applicable. However, the second is that Article 6(2) and (3) must still be applied to civil cases in a broad way, so that the concepts of a fair hearing in adversarial proceedings are applied. The court will look at the wording of Article 6 as a whole and apply the spirit of it to the particular facts. An example is the case of *Dombo Beheer* v *Netherlands*.[92]

Dombo Beheer was a company registered in the Netherlands, which was engaged in various commercial activities. One of the managers of the company was Mr van Reijendam. In about 1981, a dispute arose between the company and its bank about its credit limit which led to (civil) court proceedings. Dutch law did not permit Mr van Reijendam to give evidence on behalf of the company; but the bank manager could and did give evidence for the bank. The company claimed that this was unfair, and a violation of Article 6. The European Court agreed that it was a violation, saying that the company was placed at a substantial disadvantage when compared with the bank. The Court said:

[90] (1998) 29 EHRR 243.
[91] (2002) 34 EHRR 3.
[92] (1994) 18 EHRR 213.

> The requirements inherent in the concept of 'fair hearing' are not necessarily the same in cases concerning the determination of civil rights and obligations as they are in cases concerning the determination of a criminal charge [. . .] Nevertheless, certain principles concerning the notion of a 'fair trial' in cases concerning civil rights and obligations emerge from the Court's case law. Most significantly for the present case, it is clear that the requirement of 'equality of arms' in the sense of a 'fair balance' between the parties, applies in principle to such cases as well as to criminal cases. The Court agrees with the Commission that as regards litigation involving opposing private interests, 'equality of arms' implies that each party must be afforded a reasonable opportunity to present his case – including his evidence – under conditions that do not place him at a substantial disadvantage *vis-à-vis* his opponent.

This case was about the handicap of being unable to call a witness; and the Court defined that point as being a lack of equality of arms. But the actual impediment, of the witness being shut out of court, is reflected in the wording of Article 6(3)(d), 'to obtain the attendance and examination of witnesses on his behalf'. The Court did not refer to Article 6(3)(d), and simply took the benchmark of a 'fair hearing'. However, it is clear that the constituent parts of Article 6 provide guidance for what should be fair, in both a criminal and a civil trial.

In another civil case, the unfairness lay in the fact that one party did not hear all the evidence, and was not given the opportunity of commenting on it. That also is an aspect of Article 6(3)(d), 'to examine witnesses against him'. Again, the European Court has held that this was, in the circumstances, a breach of Article 6, although the Court did not refer to Article 6(3)(d) in the case of *Lobo Machado* v *Portugal*.[93]

> Mr Pedro Lobo Machado was an engineer, living in Lisbon, and he was employed by a petroleum business, which was nationalised by the Portuguese government in 1975. Having retired in 1980, he brought proceedings, against the state, in 1986, claiming that after retirement he had been wrongly classified at a lower grade for pension purposes than his entitlement. This was a civil proceeding. The case reached the Supreme Court, and the Deputy Attorney-General, representing the state, delivered to the Supreme Court an Opinion stating that the case had already been fully considered, and that the case should be dismissed. Mr Lobo Machado did not have any opportunity to see this Opinion, or to make any submissions against it. The European Court said:
>
>> Regard being had, therefore, to what was at stake for the applicant in the proceedings in the Supreme Court and to the nature of the Deputy Attorney-General's Opinion, in which it was advocated that the appeal should be dismissed, the fact that it was impossible for Mr Lobo Machado to obtain a copy of it and reply to it before judgment was given, infringed his right to adversarial proceedings. That right means in principle the opportunity for the parties to a criminal or civil trial to have knowledge of and comment on all evidence adduced or observations filed, even by an independent member of the national legal service, with a view to influencing the Court's decisions.

[93] (1997) 23 EHRR 79.

The important phrase is 'adversarial proceedings'. The usual understanding of those words is that the court will be independent, and will hear each side in the presence of the other, allowing each to challenge the other, and thereafter, applying the appropriate burden of proof, give a reasoned decision. This last sentence matches fairly well the constituent parts of Article 6. Thus, the European Court in *Lobo Machado* regarded Article 6 as applying to civil proceedings in most of its elements.

In England and Wales, the rules which govern civil procedure and the conduct of civil trials and proceedings were revised shortly before the Act came into effect, and drafted with some consideration of Article 6. In particular, for the first time, the new Civil Procedure Rules start with a general principle which should inform all procedural decisions under the rules. This is referred to as the overriding objective, which requires the court to deal with cases justly.[94] This includes ensuring that the parties are on an equal footing, which is a prime requirement of Article 6. Another requirement which echoes Article 6 is ensuring that cases are dealt with expeditiously and fairly. Other requirements are geared to the fact that the civil courts do not have unlimited time and resources, nor do litigants, and litigation which costs too much may deny some parties the ability to see their case through, especially if the costs are out of proportion to the amount in issue. But the court must also act proportionately to the importance and complexity of the case. The Court of Appeal has indicated that, in general terms, the requirements of following the Civil Procedure Rules are likely to involve similar considerations to the detail of Article 6 as it would apply to civil cases.[95]

QUESTIONS

1 Why is the impartiality of the court so important? Why should bias and interests in the case attract such attention and such a severe test be applied? Do you think the test goes far enough?

2 Why is the presumption of innocence so important? Do you consider that imposing a burden of proof on a defendant is ever justified? Does it matter how serious the burden is?

3 Consider evidence obtained in breach of someone's privacy: do you think it is fair or not that such evidence can be used in their trial for committing a crime?

4 Do you think that having juries hear serious criminal cases makes the trial more or less fair?

---

[94] Civil Procedure Rules 1998, rule 1, now mirrored in the Criminal Procedure Rules, referred to above.
[95] *Daniels* v *Walker* [2000] 1 WLR 1382.

A convicted prisoner being led away to serve a prison sentence – the application of the penalty which applied at the time of the crime is an issue we will consider (see p. 243).
Source: Barry Batchelor/PA Photos

13 Retrospective legislation

If anything is said in this court to encourage a belief that Englishmen are entitled to jump off bridges for their own amusement the next thing to go will be the Constitution. It is not for me to say what offence the appellant has committed, but I am satisfied that he has committed *some* offence, for which he has been most properly punished. (A.P. Herbert, *Uncommon Law*, 1935, per Lord Light LCJ in 'Is it a Free Country?')

Article 7: No Punishment Without Law

1 No one shall be held guilty of any criminal offence on account of any act or omission which did not constitute a criminal offence under national or international law at the time when it was committed.

Nor shall a heavier penalty be imposed than the one that was applicable at the time the criminal offence was committed.

2 This Article shall not prejudice the trial and punishment of any person for any act or omission which, at the time when it was committed, was criminal according to the general principles of law recognised by civilised nations.

THE PRINCIPLE BEHIND ARTICLE 7

One of the principles of the rule of law[1] is that criminal offences should be defined with certainty and precision. In order to have a society regulated by law, one requirement is that people should be able to obey the law; they should be able to know, at any given time, what is legal and what is illegal. And it is not possible to obey the law if at a later time Parliament or the courts change the law, so as to make something which has already been done illegal.

Article 7 deals with this. It prohibits retrospective application of the criminal law. Article 7 embodies three principles. First, the law must have been in place at the time when a person did a particular act, for a conviction to be based on that act. Second, a penalty imposed by the court must not be heavier than the penalty which was in force at the time when the crime was actually committed. Those two rules are contained in the first two sentences of Article 7(1).

The third rule is that the law – whether it be the definition of the offence or the penalty for a conviction for it – must be accessible and precise. That means it must be available and

---

[1] Introduced in Chapter 2, p. 18.

clear. The ordinary person must be able to foresee whether the court will say that any particular activity is legal or illegal; and even if this requires legal advice, that is still fair and equal treatment, because the law is still certain. But it would be unfair if the law were elastic, so that the court could stretch the wording of the law, whether it be a statute or a previous court decision, simply to enable it to cover the particular circumstances. Of course, as we know, the courts develop the law; case law itself is a means of interpreting the law, and adapting it to changing situations. Provided that the development of the law is foreseeable, it will be regarded as fair.

An example of this is the case of *Kokkinakis*.[2]

> Mr Kokkinakis was a retired businessman, of Greek nationality, and he had become a Jehovah's Witness. He had been arrested many times for the offence of proselytism, which was forbidden by Greek law. Mr Kokkinakis complained that this was not only a violation of Article 9, for infringing his freedom of belief, but also of Article 7: his complaint here was that because of the vague terms in which the offence was stated, its scope and meaning could be extended by the police. Thus he could be punished for something which was not obviously prohibited when he did it.
>
> The European Court rejected his complaint under Article 7. The Court noted that the wording of many statutes, in all nations, is not absolutely precise. There is a need to avoid excessive rigidity, and to keep pace with changing circumstances. In this instance, in Greece, there existed a body of settled national case law on this topic of proselytism. This was published and accessible. Then the European Court said this:
>
>> Article 7(1) of the Convention is not confined to prohibiting the retrospective application of the criminal law to an accused's disadvantage. It also embodies, more generally, the principle that only the law can define a crime and prescribe a penalty [and] the principle that the criminal law must not be extensively construed to an accused's detriment, for instance by analogy; it follows from this that an offence must be clearly defined in law. This condition is satisfied where the individual can know from the wording of the relevant provision and, if need be, with the assistance of the court's interpretation of it, what acts and omissions will make him liable.

In short, the law must be precise and must not be extended to any great extent without warning, that is, without legislation; but it is allowed to keep pace with developments, and, especially, it is allowed to be developed by courts, particularly in the context of the interpretation of statutes, where it is part of a court's duty to resolve uncertainties. One of the reasons for this is precisely because it is a requirement of the rule of law that the law is clear: if it is not clear, one remedy is for a court to clarify it, even if that resolves an uncertainty against an accused.

RETROSPECTIVE LAW AND OUR CONSTITUTION

In our constitutional theory, in principle there are no limits to the legislative power of Parliament.[3] Thus, in principle, Parliament may pass Acts which are retrospective in their

---

[2] (1994) 17 EHRR 397, discussed also in the context of Article 9, below, p. 288.
[3] Discussed above, Chapter 4, p. 40.

effect. And indeed Parliament has done so: the War Crimes Act 1991 and the Genocide Act 1969 are examples. But in the absence of clear provision, an Act will not be given retrospective application. Even before the incorporation of the European Convention, the approach of English law was to construe an Act of Parliament as *not* having a retrospective effect.

> In the case of *R* v *Miah*,[4] Mr Miah was charged with being an illegal immigrant, and being in possession of a false passport, contrary to the Immigration Act 1971; the Act came into force in 1973, but the events giving rise to the charge occurred before the Act came into force. His conviction was quashed: the House of Lords refused to interpret an Act of Parliament as having retrospective effect without clear words that said that that was the intention of Parliament.
>
> Lord Reid said: 'there has for a very long time been a strong feeling against making legislation, and particularly criminal legislation, retrospective'. Lord Reid then referred to the Universal Declaration of Human Rights, and Article 7 of the European Convention, which are in virtually identical terms, and he said: 'So it is hardly credible that any government department would promote or that Parliament would pass retrospective criminal legislation.'

It may therefore be a natural question to ask, what has the incorporation of the Convention added to our law, since as long ago as 1974, Lord Reid was citing the European Convention, and declaring that the practice of our courts conformed to it? The answer is, as with the other Articles, the Act enables the courts to apply the Convention directly, and so subject our law to greater scrutiny.

This scrutiny will follow the three principles of Article 7 we introduced above: what was the law in force at the time of the activity in question; what penalty followed on from that particular activity at that time; and was the law clear and precise on both of these questions? We have discussed already in other contexts the importance of this concept of precision and clarity in the law: it is the same idea reflected in requirements that something be 'in accordance with the law', which applies across all of the Convention rights.[5] The particular questions raised by this for Article 7 which we will consider are: is the law clear; what is meant by a penalty; and was a greater penalty imposed?

◼ CLARITY IN THE LAW

We are talking here of both statute law and case law, and indeed about orders made by the courts. The law must be clear and foreseeable, and the defendant must know what he must do to remain within the law. We saw this in the statement of the law in *Kokkinakis*'s case; 'an offence must be clearly defined in law'. There is a good illustration of this in the case of

---

[4] [1974] 1 WLR 683.
[5] Introduced above at p. 116.

Hashman,[6] in which hunt saboteurs were bound over to keep the peace and not to act *contra bonos mores* (against good behaviour). The European Court held that the order was not clear; the defendants could not know what it was they were forbidden to do. Thus the order of the court in imposing a penalty was unclear.

But the particular area where one might expect a defendant to claim that the law is unclear is the field of case law, where the law develops by judicial decisions. This applies to the scope of existing offences, since there are some offences (albeit relatively few) which are defined in case law: it is important that the case law is sufficiently certain about what conduct is prohibited.[7] It also applies to when the law effectively changes as a result of a new case. As was considered above in the *Kokkinakis* case, there is a real issue here if a defendant claims that he acted in accordance with what he believed the law to be: if a court later decides the law is otherwise, that is unfair and retrospective, and a breach of Article 7.

As we have seen, the European Court's answer is that it allows the law to be developed progressively, and if the judicial decision could reasonably be foreseen then the judgment is not unfair, and not a violation of Article 7. That is so long as the law has not been, in the words of the European Court in the *Kokkinakis* case, 'extensively construed to an accused's detriment, for instance by analogy'; to use our earlier phrase, 'stretching the law'.

This principle, allowing for foreseeable development, is demonstrated in the case of *SW and CR v United Kingdom*,[8] two cases heard together with different facts but a similar conclusion; we shall consider the facts of *SW*. In both, the European Court considered that the removal by the English courts of a legal rule that a husband could not be guilty of the rape of his wife did not offend Article 7.

On 18 September 1990, SW attacked his wife, and she alleged that he raped her. On the following day he was charged with rape. On 19 April 1991 he was found guilty of rape, and sentenced to a term of imprisonment.

It had long been considered part of English law that as a rule a husband could not rape his wife. However, although this had been made subject to numerous exceptions, it was only removed altogether by the decision in a separate case called *R v R*,[9] where the House of Lords held that it was no longer part of the law of England and Wales that a husband cannot rape his wife. The House stressed that the common law was capable of evolving in the light of changing social, economic and cultural developments. The old principle (dating from 1736) was out of date.

R v R was decided after the act for which SW was being prosecuted; it had reached the Court of Appeal by the time of SW's trial, so he had no defence at trial; and after his trial, *R v R* was decided by the House of Lords, on the basis of which SW withdrew his appeal against conviction, since, in short, he had no defence to the charge of rape. His complaint before the European Court was that the defence had been open to him when the rape took place and this had been taken away.

---

[6] (2000) 30 EHRR 241; considered above in the context of Article 5, p. 183.

[7] For example, the offence of causing a public nuisance, which is sufficiently clearly defined to comply with Article 7: *R v Rimmington* [2005] UKHL 63, [2005] 3 WLR 982.

[8] (1996) 21 EHRR 363.

[9] [1991] 4 All ER 481.

The European Court rejected that claim. The principle underlying Article 7 was stated to be to 'ensure that no one should be subjected to arbitrary prosecution, conviction or punishment'. In that context, the European Court's approach to the development of the criminal law was that:

> However clearly drafted a legal provision may be, in any system of law, including criminal law, there is an inevitable element of judicial interpretation. There will always be a need for elucidation of doubtful points and for adaptation to changing circumstances. Indeed, in the United Kingdom, as in the other Convention States, the progressive development of the criminal law through judicial law-making is a well entrenched and necessary part of legal tradition. [. . .] The decisions of the Court of Appeal and then the House of Lords [in this case] did no more than continue a perceptible line of case law development dismantling the immunity of a husband from prosecution for rape upon his wife. [. . .] This evolution had reached a stage where judicial recognition of the absence of immunity had become a reasonably foreseeable development of the law.

That idea that the operation of the law should not be arbitrary is one we see often in the discussion – by the European Court or our courts – of any of the Convention rights, and it is a key idea here. Behind the actual wording of Article 7 there is the requirement that the law should not be arbitrary in its application.

On the other hand, there may be cases where the development of the law is not foreseeable and then there may be a breach of Article 7. An example is the case of *Pessino* v *France*.[10] Here Mr Pessino had planning permission to build a hotel in Cannes. Following an action by local residents, the permission was suspended. The work continued, and fresh planning permission was obtained, but both planning permits were then annulled. Mr Pessino was prosecuted for carrying out construction work without planning permission, and convicted and fined.

The European Court held that there was a violation of Article 7 because there was no clear law, prior to this case, that continuing with construction work where planning permission had been granted but then suspended was a criminal offence. The suspension itself was not a judicial decision ordering the work to cease. The French Court's decision that an offence was being committed was not foreseeable and there was therefore a breach of Article 7.

WHAT IS A PENALTY?

The question may arise also in some cases as to what is a 'penalty'. This is important, because the word 'penalty' is used expressly in Article 7(1). Parliament has provided in the case of some offences that there should be a further order imposing some liability upon the defendant in addition to imprisonment, or fine, or other penal orders. In two cases in our

---

[10] *Pessino* v *France* [2006] (App no. 40403/02).

courts, Parliament had, after the criminal activity had been committed by the defendant, passed a law imposing new measures. The cases are *Welch* and *Ibbotson*.

In *Welch* v *UK*,[11] Mr Welch was arrested in 1986 for suspected drug offences. In that year the Drug Trafficking Offences Act 1986 was passed, but it came into force on 12 January 1987. Mr Welch was convicted in August 1988. The trial judge imposed a confiscation order upon him under the 1986 Act. Mr Welch complained that the confiscation order was a violation of Article 7(1), in that his drug activity had been committed before the coming into force of the Act. The question for the European Court was whether the confiscation order was a 'penalty'.

The Court found that it indeed was; it followed a conviction, it was directed to the proceeds involved in drug dealing, in default of its payment, imprisonment was a possibility, and in all these circumstances it had the appearance of a penalty. The Court said:

Looking behind appearances at the realities of the situation, whatever the characterisation of the measure of confiscation, the applicant faced more far-reaching detriment as a result of the order than that to which he was exposed at the time of the commission of the offences for which he was convicted.

It will be a matter of judgment from case to case, but the European Court there found that the far-reaching nature of the confiscation order, added to the penalty of imprisonment, was itself a 'penalty'. Thus, there was a violation of Article 7, because it was something which came into effect after the commission of the drug activity which formed the crime. The Court of Appeal has followed this in holding that a confiscation order would be a penalty, and enforcing it would breach Article 7 in a case where it was not an available sentence at the time the offence was committed.[12]

However, there was not held to be a penalty in the next case, *Ibbotson* v *UK*.[13]

In May 1996, Mr Ibbotson was convicted and sentenced to three-and-a-half years' imprisonment, regarding six charges of possession of obscene and indecent material; he was released on 20 August 1997. On 1 September 1997, the Sex Offenders Act 1997 came into force, requiring Mr Ibbotson to register with the police and to keep them informed of any change of name or home address. Thus, Parliament imposed upon him an order which had not existed at the time of his offending. He claimed that there was a violation of Article 7.

The European Court on this occasion held that this measure did *not* amount to a 'penalty'. The Court considered the case of *Welch*, but considered that the order to register was preventative rather than punitive, in the sense that inclusion on the register might help to dissuade an individual from reoffending. In short, the requirement for mere registration did not amount to a 'penalty'.

---

[11] (1995) 20 EHRR 247.
[12] *Togher* v *Revenue & Customs Prosecution Office* [2007] EWCA Civ 686, [2008] QB 476: the Court did hold that it was still entitled to impose the penalty to give effect to the relevant legislation because of section 6(2)(b) of the Act.
[13] [1999] Crim LR 153.

The Court of Appeal reached the same result in respect of a financial reporting order, in the case of *Adams*.[14] The Court held that this form of order was a preventative measure and not a penalty, and therefore could be imposed although it had not been as a possible consequence of the conduct when it took place.

CHANGES IN SENTENCING

We are talking here about the second sentence in Article 7(1), where for some reason a heavier penalty may be imposed by the court than was available at the time the offence was committed. In our courts, the level of sentencing does alter from time to time. One has only to read the newspapers to see calls for heavier sentences for particular crimes. Parliament may by statute increase the maximum sentence for a particular offence, or alternatively, the Court of Appeal deliver judgments in guideline cases, or the Sentencing Guidelines Council issues advice, where the conclusion has been reached that the general level of sentencing for a particular offence has been too low. The question then arises as to whether there is a breach of the second sentence of Article 7(1).

Our courts have analysed this point, and they have concluded that increased sentencing guidelines do not violate Article 7. This was debated in the case of *Cathra*.[15]

Mr Cathra was convicted in 2001 of one count of rape, and several counts of indecent assault committed on several members of his family between 1970 and 1983. In guideline cases the Court of Appeal had in 1986 increased the level of sentencing in such cases, so that had Mr Cathra been sentenced in, say, 1983 he would have faced lower guidelines. The maximum sentence for rape was always life imprisonment.

The Court of Appeal held that an enhanced level of sentencing which led to a higher level of sentence being imposed on Mr Cathra than was current at the time of his offence did not violate Article 7. The Court considered that Article 7 was not contravened as long as the court was entitled, at the time when the offence was committed, to impose the sentence actually passed, even though the then current guidelines might have indicated a lower sentence. What Article 7 prohibits is a court imposing a sentence which is greater than the *maximum penalty* prescribed at the time the offence was committed. The European Court does not, however, involve itself in considering the specific levels of sentencing by the national court, within the prescribed maximum. In this case, therefore, there had not been the imposition of an increased maximum penalty since the date of Mr Cathra's offences – it was simply that the guidelines had been adjusted to address public and judicial concern that sentences for rape were too low.

The same applies to other changes to the way in which the sentence is carried out, including the conditions of release from prison.

---

[14] *R v Adams* [2008] EWCA Crim 914, [2008] 4 All ER 574.
[15] *R v Cathra* [2001] EWCA Crim 2478.

In the case of *Uttley*,[16] the defendant had been convicted in 1995 of various serious sexual offences (including three rapes), all committed before 1983. There were various licence conditions on his release from prison set under the Criminal Justice Act 1991, and he argued that this involved imposing a heavier penalty than was applicable at the time of the offences.

The House of Lords rejected this argument. First of all, changes to the way in which prisoners were released, and the introduction of release on licence with conditions, did not make the sentence more severe, nor amount to a 'heavier penalty' – the maximum penalty 'applicable' when the offence had been committed had not changed from life imprisonment, and that was what had been applied when the defendant was sentenced.[17]

There is a current tendency for Parliament to provide that a criminal should receive an increased sentence for offences which are repeated: 'two strikes and out' is an example. Section 2 of the Crime (Sentences) Act 1997 provides for the imposition of an automatic life sentence on a defendant who commits a serious offence, having previously been convicted of a similar serious offence.

In *R v Offen*[18] the defendant argued that this was a breach of Article 7. He had been convicted and sentenced for one serious offence, and, after that, the 1997 Act came into force; he then committed the second offence, which the Court referred to as 'the trigger offence', and he then qualified for the life sentence. He claimed that the penalty for the earlier offence was being increased. The Court of Appeal rejected this, holding that the life sentence was imposed only for the trigger offence. The sentence for the first and earlier offence remained the same (the Court did, however, allow the appeal on the distinct question of whether the life sentence was disproportionate and thereby infringed Articles 3 and 5).[19]

CONDUCT WHICH IS ALWAYS CRIMINAL

Article 7(2) provides that there is no infringement of Article 7 if the conduct of the person being condemned was against international law or was 'criminal according to the general principles of law recognised by civilised nations'. This provision is justified because there are some acts which are wrong whether or not they are illegal under a given legal system, and punishing people for those is therefore allowed.

For example, if a law created a secret police who were allowed to shoot people for no good reason, that would be wrong and they should not act this way even if permitted to do so by law. It would therefore be morally permissible to punish them for this, and so not an infringement of the rights of any secret police who did go around shooting people. That act was 'criminal according to the general principles of law recognised by civilised nations'.

---

[16] *R (Uttley)* v *Home Secretary* [2004] UKHL 38, [2004] 1 WLR 2278.
[17] Since followed in *R v McGuigan* [2005] EWCA Crim 2861, LTL 20.10.05.
[18] [2001] 1 WLR 253.
[19] See above, p. 155, for discussion of this aspect of the case.

It is for this reason that it is considered morally acceptable to punish those who have committed war crimes, even if they acted within the law of their own country, because some acts are wrong whether or not they are permitted by law. Put another way, there are some things which cannot be made right just because they are made legal. So, the War Crimes Act 1991 provides retrospective criminal jurisdiction to courts in the United Kingdom regarding war crimes committed during the Second World War, in Germany, by persons who are British citizens or are now resident in the United Kingdom: this is not in principle contrary to Article 7 because of Article 7(2).

This was another consideration in the case of *SW* v *UK*, the marital rape case. The European Court stated:

> The essentially debasing character of rape is so manifest that the result of these decisions [. . .] cannot be said to be at variance with the object and purpose of Article 7 of the Convention. [. . .] What is more, the abandonment of the unacceptable idea of a husband being immune against prosecution for rape of his wife was in conformity not only with a civilised concept of marriage but also, and above all, with the fundamental objectives of the Convention, the very essence of which is respect for human dignity and human freedom.

Thus the Court was affirming the principle that there is no breach of Article 7 where the law allows, or appears to allow, something which is inherently and seriously wrong – and this is why, following *SW*, the Court of Appeal has confirmed that there is no breach of Article 7 in the conviction of a man for raping his wife, even when the event took place before *R* v *R*.[20] This is because it should be quite obvious to the person committing such an act that what they are doing is wrong, whether or not it is legal. It should not then be an excuse for them to hide behind a legal exception or technicality and the removal of such a legal protection does not infringe their rights, because the context is one in which they are only having to face the consequences of doing something they should not have done.

It is, however, important that the conduct in question was generally recognised to be criminal according to international law or general standards of conduct. International law and the laws of war are not constant, but develop over time – sometimes weapons or conduct are outlawed where they were considered acceptable previously. Thus, it may be necessary to consider what could have been understood to be criminal at the time.

In the case of *Kononov* v *Latvia*,[21] Mr Kononov had been a member of the Communist Resistance (a 'Red Partisan') in Latvia during the Second World War and had conducted operations against the occupying German forces. He was involved in an attack on the village of Mazie Bati on 27 May 1944 in which several civilians died. There was an issue whether those who died should have been classed as collaborators or not. Mr Kononov was prosecuted in 1998 under war crimes legislation passed by Latvia after it gained its independence from the Soviet Union. The issue for the European Court was whether there was a breach of Article 7 in this prosecution. The Court held that there was: Kononov could not have reasonably foreseen in May 1944 that his conduct was a war crime under the law of war as it then was, and any prosecution for a domestic crime would be barred by lapse of time.

---

[20] *R* v *Crooks* (2004) Times 25.3.04.
[21] *Kononov* v *Latvia* (2008) 25 BHRC 317.

RETROSPECTIVITY AND THE ACT

As we have discussed earlier,[22] the Act itself does not apply to situations before it came into force, even if they came to Court afterwards. However, there is one situation where the Act does allow for limited retrospective legislation. We discussed earlier how, where a court makes a declaration of incompatibility, stating that a statute is incompatible with a Convention right, there is a procedure whereby a remedial order can be passed through Parliament to correct the infringement.[23] Schedule 2 to the Act specifically states that the remedial order can have retrospective effect. The retrospective effect allows the order, in principle, to reverse the decision of the court which was unable to grant someone a remedy for infringement of their rights because of the incompatible legislation. Thus the retrospectivity here is designed to correct an injustice and protect the Convention rights. It is then expressly stated that such an order shall not make any person retrospectively liable to a criminal penalty.[24] This ensures that Article 7 is complied with.

QUESTIONS

1 Why are clarity and accessibility so important for the law? What rights or interests of the individual do they protect? Do they justify being the subject of a separate article?

2 Do you agree that some conduct is so wrong that it can be punished even if it was not against the law when it was done? Are categories like 'war crimes' or 'crimes against humanity' meaningful or useful?

3 What about the situation where someone is ordered to do something they know is wrong, but it is not illegal and they have no choice in the matter? Should it be a defence that they were 'just following orders'?

---

[22] Above pp. 103–4.
[23] Above, pp. 73–4.
[24] Paragraph 4 of Schedule 2.

A gypsy camp – the rights of travellers to stay on land which has become their home is a key legal and political issue under Article 8 (see pp. 266–8).

Source: John Birdsall/PA Photos

14 The right to privacy

When the sanitary inspector of the Council arrived, the appellant obstructed him with all the rights of a free-born Englishman whose premises were being invaded and defied him with a clothes prop and a spade. He was entitled to do that unless the sanitary inspector had a right to enter . . . In the opinion of this court, the appellant now succeeds because the sanitary inspector had not done that which the statute required him to do before he had a right of entry. (Lord Chief Justice Goddard, *Stroud* v *Bradbury*,[1] 1952)

Families are subversive. They nurture individuality and difference. (Lady Hale, *Countryside Alliance*,[2] 2007)

> ### Article 8: Right to Respect for Private and Family Life
> 1 Everyone has the right to respect for his private and family life, his home and his correspondence.
> 2 There shall be no interference by a public authority with the exercise of this right except such as is in accordance with the law and is necessary in a democratic society in the interests of national security, public safety or the economic well-being of the country, for the prevention of disorder or crime, for the protection of health or morals, or for the protection of the rights and freedoms of others.

THE AIMS OF ARTICLE 8

Powers of secret surveillance of citizens, characterising as they do the police state, are tolerable under the Convention only insofar as strictly necessary for safeguarding the democratic institutions . . .

This was the European Court's view of the importance of the rights protected by Article 8 in the case of *Klass* v *Germany*,[3] a case about the German state authorities opening the mail and tapping the telephone of a private citizen. This emphasises that the key aim of this Article is to protect the individual citizen against arbitrary interference in his or her private life.

---

[1] [1952] 2 All ER 76.
[2] *R (Countryside Alliance)* v *AG* [2007] 3 WLR 962, para 116.
[3] (1980) 2 EHRR 214.

In a civilised society, every person should have some freedom to be allowed to improve their life and lifestyle, to fulfil personal aims and ambitions, and to develop their individuality; we have previously referred to this as the idea of moral autonomy.[4] This is the core of what is protected by Article 8: it goes beyond the basic rights set out in the earlier parts of the Convention, which cover the physical integrity of the person from death, harm and detention without proper procedural protection. Article 8, and the Articles which follow it, expand the conception of basic human entitlements to include privacy and autonomy, having a home which is free from interference, and space to do, think, learn, and express oneself. As Lady Hale has put it:

> Article 8, it seems to me, reflects two separate but related fundamental values. One is the inviolability of the home and personal communications from official snooping, entry and interference without a very good reason. It protects a private space, whether in a building, or through the post, the telephone lines, the airwaves or the ether, within which people can both be themselves and communicate privately with one another. The other is the inviolability of a different kind of space, the personal and psychological space within which each individual develops his or her own sense of self and relationships with other people. This is fundamentally what families are for and why democracies value family life so highly. Families are subversive. They nurture individuality and difference. One of the first things a totalitarian regime tries to do is to distance the young from the individuality of their own families and indoctrinate them in the dominant view. Article 8 protects the private space, both physical and psychological, within which individuals can develop and relate to others around them.[5]

However, in a modern society, we generally consider that some interference by the state, even in one's private life, is justified. So, for example, in our houses and gardens, we may not do things which cause harm or nuisance to our neighbours or to the area where we live; at home or at work or school, we may not create health hazards to other people; and in all these cases, interferences in our privacy, which lead to detection of harm being done or crimes being committed, are to some extent permissible. But at the same time, every person should have a bare minimum of freedom, and that bare minimum is what Article 8 protects.

Thus Article 8 sets out that the state must **respect** each person's **private** and **family life**, their **home** and their **correspondence** – and that this freedom can be limited as set out in Article 8(2) in certain circumstances. We have already seen in general terms how strictly the European Court interprets the limitations set out in articles such as Article 8:[6] the state's interference must be in accordance with the law, necessary in a democratic society, must follow one of the legitimate aims listed in Article 8(2), and the interference of the right must be proportionate to the interest which motivates the interference. Even where the interference is justified, this may still tell us something about the wide scope of interests which are potentially protected by Article 8.

Article 8 has been given a wide interpretation by the European Court, so that the words 'private life' have come to include living life with individuality and satisfaction, and with a capacity to develop a personality and an ability to follow individual pursuits; and this includes the individual's wish to express their sexual orientation. Looking at all the words

---

[4] Considered above in Chapter 2.
[5] R (*Countryside Alliance*) v AG [2007] 3 WLR 962, para 116, although the activity in that case (hunting) was outside Article 8 as it not something which takes place in the home: see below, p. 257.
[6] For discussion of these general principles, see above, p. 116f.

of Article 8(1), they aim to provide protection of the home from invasion and intrusion, and allow the development of family life and relationships. This affects almost every aspect of one's personal life. And, of course, it is to a fair extent one's privacy that is being talked about, even though that word does not actually appear in the two paragraphs of Article 8; whether Article 8 does in fact create a 'right to privacy' is something we shall consider.

The wording of the right being protected by Article 8(1) bears close examination. There are four interests which paragraph (1) tells us are to be **respected**: private life, family life, home and correspondence. These are distinct ideas, although, as we shall see, they do over-lap in various situations. But before we look at those four elements of Article 8, it is worth pausing to consider the word **respect** here.

RESPECT

important

The acceptance of the idea of respect for private life means that the state has two duties: not only must the state refrain from interfering with one's private and family life, but also it must take positive steps to protect them. This connotation of the word 'respect' was considered by the European Court in the case of *Sheffield and Horsham* v *United Kingdom*:[7]

> The applicants in this case had undergone gender reassignment surgery, in this case from male to female, and their complaint was that the state refused to give legal recognition to their new status as women, or to take positive steps to modify the system of state records which they claimed operated to their detriment, in violation of Article 8. In particular, the complaint was that they were obliged to keep their original name and sex in their birth certificates, social welfare documents and other official records. Although in this case the European Court held that there was no breach of the rights granted by Article 8, it did make it clear that the word 'respect' does indeed mean that the state has a positive duty to act to protect the private life of its citizens – as opposed to a duty merely to refrain from inter-ference. The state must strike a fair balance between the community and the individual.

A RIGHT TO PRIVACY? BREACH OF CONFIDENCE

Strictly speaking, it is misleading to say that Article 8 protects a right to privacy, since, as we noted above, those words do not themselves appear in the Article. Nonetheless, privacy is an important part of all the interests protected by this Article, especially as there is a degree of overlap between them – something may be legitimately described as involving each of 'private life', 'family life' and 'correspondence'. In thinking about all of these, the questions '*Is* there a right to privacy?' or '*Should* there be a right to privacy?' are highly relevant.

For example, consider photographs being published of well-known people enjoying some private occasion. Is there, or should there be, a right to prevent one's photograph being printed in a newspaper? Does it matter in this context whether or not the person complaining about the pictures is a public figure, such as a member of the royal family or a politician, a television or film personality? Should it matter where the person is – at

[7] (1999) 27 EHRR 163.

home, at a party, in the street, doing their shopping? Should it matter how the photograph was obtained – if it was obtained surreptitiously? These are important questions which the Convention has required our judges to tackle in a way that they had not had the scope to address previously.

It used to be said that there was no right to privacy in English law, because there was no basis for suing someone who infringed the privacy of another just because they had invaded this privacy, but, as we shall see, this has changed. It is worth demonstrating how this process has occurred – although the pre-Act cases have been superseded – since it shows how the Act has led to a significant change in the protection offered by the law. First, the leading pre-Act case.

> In *Kaye* v *Robertson*,[8] the Court of Appeal had before it the case of an intrusion into a hospital ward. A newspaper reporter and photographer from the *Sunday Sport* had invaded the hospital room of the actor Gorden Kaye, well-known from the television series *'Allo, 'Allo*, when he was recovering from serious head injuries. The Court of Appeal assumed there was no right of privacy in English law and decided that there was nothing it could do to restrain publication of the pictures taken, even though it considered that they were taken in circumstances which invaded Mr Kaye's privacy. Lord Justice Glidewell said:
>
> > It is well known that in English law there is no right to privacy, and accordingly there is no right of action for breach of a person's privacy. The facts of the present case are a graphic illustration of the desirability of Parliament considering whether and in what circumstances statutory provision can be made to protect the privacy of individuals.
>
> And Lord Justice Bingham (as he then was) agreed, saying:
>
> > This case nonetheless highlights, yet again, the failure of both the common law of England and statute to protect in an effective way the personal privacy of individual citizens.

The words of the judges in that case speak for themselves: no right of privacy in English law. But in this next case we see a right developing out of the principles of an action for a breach of confidence. Breach of confidence is a well-established ground of complaint where a person wrongfully discloses information which has been given to them in confidence; for example, information about a new invention which is being kept secret, or security information about a place, or a business's lists of customers. As you can see from these examples, it has traditionally been used where the parties all appreciate, or ought to appreciate, that that information is actually confidential, or if it is the sort of information which is likely to be confidential. This was developed in the following case in particular:

> In *Hellewell* v *Chief Constable of Derbyshire*,[9] Mr Hellewell had been photographed upon his arrest for theft. He had 32 previous convictions, including 19 for theft, and was convicted on this occasion too. About three years later, an organisation of shopkeepers which was concerned about the level of local shoplifting asked the police to supply photographs of individuals known to be causing trouble in that area so that staff would recognise them.

[8] [1991] 1 FSR 62.
[9] [1995] 1 WLR 804.

The police provided a number of photographs, including one of Mr Hellewell, which had clearly been taken when he was in custody. Traders were told not to display the photos publicly, but only to show them to their staff. Mr Hellewell learnt of the use being made of his photo and applied to the court for an injunction restraining the police from disclosing his photo to the public.

Mr Justice Laws (as he then was) decided that when the police took a photo of a suspect at a police station, they might well come under a duty of confidence towards him, but that, where the photo was used reasonably for preventing or investigating crime or for catching suspects, and where the photos were distributed only to people who had reasonable need to make use of them, the police would have a public interest defence to any action for breach of confidence.

So the court here in effect held that the police had done nothing unlawful. But the case is useful in showing how the duty to keep something confidential may give the other person a right of privacy. And the judge also gave the following example: if someone with a telephoto lens were to take a picture of someone else engaged in a private act without their permission, any subsequent disclosure of the photograph would as surely amount to a breach of confidence as if he had found or stolen and published a private – and therefore confidential – letter or diary in which the act was recounted. The same defence based on the public interest which was available to the police and the shopkeepers in this case might, however, also be available.

Following the passing of the Act, this foundation was built on in the important case of *Douglas* v *Hello! Ltd*,[10] on its first visit to the Court of Appeal,[11] where the Court effectively recognised the protection of privacy in English law by adapting the existing law of breach of confidence to allow them to vindicate aggrieved parties' rights under Article 8.

This case was brought by the film stars Michael Douglas and Catherine Zeta-Jones and the publishers of *OK!* magazine. That magazine and *Hello!*, the defendant, are rivals in the same tabloid magazine market. Michael Douglas and Catherine Zeta-Jones were married at the Plaza Hotel, New York, on 18 November 2000. They had contracted with *OK!* for the exclusive publicity rights regarding the wedding. There were strict security arrangements at the wedding designed to ensure that no one, including guests and staff, could take photographs. *Hello!* knew that exclusive rights were to be granted for coverage of the wedding, and indeed had bid for those rights but had failed to get them. However, *Hello!* did manage to obtain photographs of the wedding, and was about to publish them when the High Court granted an injunction restraining the magazine publishers from doing so. The Court of Appeal, ending the injunction, still noted the need for the courts to develop the law so that it gives appropriate recognition to Article 8(1) and in doing so recognised that there was a strong argument that Douglas and Zeta-Jones have a right to privacy.

---

[10] [2001] 2 WLR 992, discussed further in the context of Article 10, below, p. 309.
[11] The second Court of Appeal decision and its appeal to the House of Lords are discussed later in this section, below, p. 255.

The *Douglas* case was promptly followed in the case of *Thompson and Venables*.[12] We have already referred to this case in the context of Articles 2 and 3: the case concerned those convicted of the shocking murder of two-year-old James Bulger, where an order was made for their identities not to be disclosed following them turning 18, for their own protection. Lady Justice Butler-Sloss, President of the Family Division, was uncertain whether the threatened breach of Article 8 would, by itself, outweigh the newspapers' right to freedom of expression under Article 10, had it not been for the threats of death or serious injury, which engaged Articles 2 and 3. However, in the present context, the case was also important for the view taken by the President as to the powers of the court to protect confidential information. The President said:

> Under the umbrella of confidentiality there will be information which may require a special quality of protection. In the present case the reason for advancing that special quality is that, if the information was published, the publication would be likely to lead to grave and possibly fatal consequences. In my judgement, the court does have the jurisdiction, in exceptional cases, to extend the protection of confidentiality of information, even to impose restrictions on the Press, where *not* to do so would be likely to lead to serious physical injury, or to death, of the person seeking that confidentiality, and there is no other way to protect the applicants other than by seeking relief from the court.[13]

Then in the case of *A v B*,[14] the Court of Appeal recognised that breach of confidence would be the appropriate cause of action where the protection of privacy was being sought, and considered that a duty of confidence would arise whenever the party subject to the duty was in a situation where he knew, or should have known, that the other person could reasonably expect his privacy to be protected. If there was an intrusion in a situation where a person could reasonably expect his privacy to be respected, that intrusion would be capable of giving rise to a liability for breach of confidence unless the intrusion could be justified. Where the person complaining of the intrusion is a public figure, their privacy should still be protected, but someone in a public position should expect a certain amount of media scrutiny, and if they courted public attention, there would be even less scope for objecting to any resulting intrusion. Thus the application here to prevent the press reporting allegations of adultery by a premier league footballer was refused, especially as it was the person with whom the extra-marital affair took place who chose to disclose the matter to a newspaper.

The House of Lords then had the opportunity to consider the interplay between the action for breach of confidence and Article 8 in the case brought by the model *Naomi Campbell*.[15] In the case of *Wainwright*,[16] the Lords had confirmed that Article 8 did not lead to the creation of a new cause of action. But in *Campbell*, the House of Lords expressly recognised that the values enshrined in Articles 8 and 10 are now part of the law on breach of confidence, and of general application; as Lord Nicholls put it (para 17):

---

[12] *Thompson and Venables* v *News Group Newspapers* [2001] 2 WLR 1038; see above in the context of Article 2, p. 134, and Article 3, p. 154 and below in the context of Article 10, p. 310.

[13] See p. 310, below, for discussion of more cases where orders have been made to prevent the disclosure of personal identities in cases where there is a risk of harm.

[14] *A v B (a company)* [2002] EWCA Civ 337, [2002] 3 WLR 542; see also, for discussion of the principles of an order to prevent publication, above, pp. 98–9, and in the context of Article 10, below, pp. 309–11.

[15] *Campbell* v *MGN Ltd* [2004] UKHL 22, [2004] 2 AC 457.

[16] [2003] UKHL 53, [2003] 3 WLR 1137, discussed below, p. 258.

The time has come to recognise that the values enshrined in Articles 8 and 10 are now part of the cause of action for breach of confidence. [. . . And] these values are of general application. The values embodied in Articles 8 and 10 are as much applicable in disputes between individuals or between an individual and a non-governmental body such as a newspaper as they are in disputes between individuals and a public authority.

In this case the Lords held (by a majority) that the publication of details of Ms Campbell's drug rehabilitation was a breach of her Article 8 rights. The fact of Ms Campbell's drug treatment was not itself confidential, since there was a legitimate story in Ms Campbell having deceived the press by stating previously that she had not taken drugs. But the details of the treatment were confidential, especially as the assurance of privacy and anonymity was important for the treatment itself to be effective, so disclosure of such details could interfere with her health. This was particularly so as photographs had been published, which were also an intrusion into her privacy, in circumstances where the newspaper accepted that the photos were private, because other people in them had had their faces pixelled out. Thus, balancing Ms Campbell's rights under Article 8 and the press' rights under Article 10, publication of the information and photographs was an unjustified interference with Article 8.

Campbell is now the leading case in UK law about the scope of privacy: if a person has a reasonable expectation of privacy, then that will engage Article 8. The European Court has gone slightly further in the case of *Von Hannover*,[17] where Princess Caroline of Monaco was awarded damages for press intrusion. This included photos taken in a public place where there were no special circumstances. The European Court made it quite clear that the scope of the private life of someone who is in the public eye is not limited just because they are in a public place. This is likely to tend the courts to a generous interpretation of *Campbell*. The following are some more cases where the scope of what counts as private life has had to be considered:

- When, following *Campbell, Douglas* v *Hello* returned to the Court of Appeal[18] on appeal from the final trial, the Court upheld the award of damages made to the Douglases, on the basis that the wedding was a private occasion and they had the right to control what photos were taken. The Court also held that, in the light of *Campbell*, that the original injunction should have been continued, as this was the appropriate remedy to prevent the breach of confidence, given the small amount of damages which were in fact recoverable.[19]

- In the case about the Prince of Wales' diaries,[20] the Prince's own journals had been supplied to a newspaper by an employee of the Prince. The Court of Appeal held that

---

[17] *Von Hannover* v *Germany* (2004) 40 EHRR 1, discussed further below, p. 307.
[18] [2005] EWCA Civ 595, [2005] 4 All ER 128.
[19] The case went to the House of Lords only on whether *OK!* could assert a claim for breach of confidence, which did not involve Article 8, as that only applied to the Douglases themselves: the Court of Appeal had held that *OK!* was not entitled to damages; this was reversed by the House of Lords which reinstated the judge's award: [2007] UKHL 21, [2008] 1 AC 1.
[20] *HRH Prince of Wales* v *Associated Newspapers Ltd* [2006] EWCA 1776, [2007] 3 WLR 222.

the information was obviously both confidential and private and that it was supplied to the newspaper in breach of confidence, and breach of the contract of employment, and that there was no public interest in its publication.

- In the case of *Ash v McKennitt*,[21] the Court of Appeal upheld a decision to prevent the publication of confidential information about the Canadian folk singer Loreena McKennitt. The book had been written by a former close friend and contained information which Ms McKennitt argued she was entitled to keep private. The judge had had particular regard to the fact that Ms McKennitt had always carefully maintained her privacy, that the information had been obtained during a close and confidential relationship, and that the information dealt with very personal matters such as the death of her fiancé, her health, and legal matters. The Court of Appeal considered that the judge had taken the correct approach, and so would not interfere with the decision.

- In the case concerning photos being taken of the son of the author JK Rowling,[22] the Court of Appeal held that intrusive press pictures of a child of someone in the public eye could amount to a breach of Article 8 (the claim was at an early stage so did not require a concluded view). The question is whether there is a reasonable expectation of privacy, and just because a child has a well-known parent does not prevent them having such an expectation.

- In the case of *Mosley*,[23] the Formula One Racing Association President, Max Mosley, complained of the printing of photographs of him involved in sexual activities, including some sado-masochistic role play. Mr Justice Eady held that there was a reasonable expectation of privacy in respect of sexual activity, even if unconventional, carried on in private between consenting adults. The fact that a participant was a public figure did not bring this into the realm of public interest and he was awarded £60,000 damages.

Thus, the courts have developed breach of confidence beyond its original limited scope to provide a full measure of protection for certain aspects of Article 8, when the alleged breach of the Article relates to the use or misuse of private information.[24] This has involved the courts engaging directly with their duty as a public authority under the Act to protect Article 8 rights, even where the complaint is not against some other public authority. And the very fact that the action for breach of confidence has expanded to provide a significant measure of protection for privacy is itself a testament to the scope and significance of the Act.

PRIVATE LIFE

Privacy, in the sense of private information, is only one aspect of the interests which Article 8(1) protects. The first of those listed is **private life**. The concept of private life starts with

---

[21] *Ash v McKennitt* [2006] EWCA Civ 1714, [2007] 3 WLR 194.
[22] *Murray v Big Pictures (UK) Limited* [2008] EWCA Civ 446, [2008] 3 WLR 1360.
[23] *Mosley v News Group Newspapers* [2008] EWHC 1777 (QB), [2008] EMLR 20.
[24] For further discussion of privacy limiting press freedom see below, pp. 307–11.

the person – Article 8 has been considered in the context of the continuance of life and safety, as we saw above in the context of cases where injunctions have been granted to prevent disclosure of information which could lead to a threat to life or limb. Article 8 has also been considered in cases of invasions of privacy in the cases of medical treatment, and in the question of abortion.[25] These raise the question of one's control over one's own body, which is an aspect of private life, although it also engages the rights of bodily integrity protected by Articles 2 and 3. However, private life goes much further than this: it covers what makes us who we are – development and expression of personality, the ability to follow a chosen lifestyle. This includes expressions of personality, such as a person's sexuality or appearance, as well as their activities.

And respect for this private life means ensuring, by positive measures, that a person's life is not made intolerable. This involves careful review of measures where the state intrudes into the private sphere, though such intrusion may be justified. Some regulation of even the private sphere can be required to protect the interests of others, such as laws that regulate sexual conduct with vulnerable groups, such as children.[26]

But it does also mean that the state has some positive obligations to ensure that the quality of a person's private life is protected. So, for example, in *Airey* v *Ireland*,[27] the European Court held that respect for private life could include a right to be parted from a spouse, with legal aid to be provided, if necessary, to ensure access to enforcement of this right.[28] And sexual fulfilment and orientation are not limited to life at home: regulation of these matters at the workplace will engage Article 8: the former policy of the armed forces not to allow homosexuals to serve was held to be an unjustified interference with Article 8 by the European Court.[29]

Likewise, private life includes personal dignity, and pride in one's own appearance, and modes of dress. Thus, Article 8 can be engaged by requirements to wear a uniform, such as apply in prison, although this may well be justified by the interests of public safety in being able to identify prisoners to prevent escape and distinguish them from visitors.[30] It can also be engaged by the need to regulate behaviour in controlled contexts, such as in prisons, schools or mental hospitals, by rules such as corporal punishment for schoolchildren,[31] or even whether mental patients are allowed to smoke.[32]

It may even include the development of one's personality, or the widening of one's horizons, although there will be limits on the state's responsibilities in this respect as one moves beyond the private sphere. This was the view of the House of Lords in the cases which challenged the ban on hunting: we quoted Lady Hale's summary from this case of what is meant by private life earlier.[33] The context of that quote was that hunting is an

---

[25] Discussed above, p. 143.

[26] Nor is there a breach of Article 8 in a child being convicted of rape of another child, rather than being labelled with some lesser offence: *R* v *G* [2008] UKHL 37, [2008] 1 WLR 1379.

[27] (1980) 2 EHRR 305.

[28] We discuss the case further below in context of Article 12, p. 333.

[29] *Smith and Grady* v *UK* (2000) 29 EHRR 493 and (2001) 31 EHRR 24; also considered above, p. 166.

[30] This was the view of the European Commission in *McFeely* v *United Kingdom* (1981) 3 EHRR 161.

[31] In *Costello-Roberts* v *UK* (1995) 19 EHRR 112, Article 8 was held to be engaged but not breached; corporal punishment in the context of Article 3 is discussed further above, p. 156.

[32] *R(G)* v *Nottinghamshire Healthcare NHS Trust* [2008] EWHC 1096 (Admin), [2008] HRLR 42: Article 8 does not include a right to facilities for smoking, although there may be rare cases where the mental health of the patient requires it.

[33] *R (Countryside Alliance)* v *AG* [2007] 3 WLR, above, p. 250; see also above, p. 121.

activity which is not part of a person's private life, because it is an activity which can only take place in public, namely, outdoors, and, in the case of organised hunts, in groups. The European Court has also held that a lack of facilities for disabled people at the seaside does not engage with a person's private life: the aspect of personality involved relates to inter-personal relationships which are too broad and indeterminate to be properly considered 'private'.[34] That said, there could be activities where Article 8 is engaged, for example in a context where facilities are provided for those being cared for by the state, such as invalids, the elderly or disabled.

SEARCHES OF THE PERSON

We are often required, for example on entering many public buildings or approaching flight departures at an airport, to submit to a personal search of the body and belongings, whether directly or by passing through an X-ray machine. That is an obvious invasion of privacy: is it allowed? The answer is that it is, on the usual conditions set out in Article 8(2) – as long as it is in accordance with the law and necessary in a democratic society for one of the aims stated there. This may well be with the consent of the person being searched, which makes a search lawful; where a search is required before a person is allowed to enter a building or area, such as when going through an airport or entering a football stadium, unless the person consents to the search they will usually not be allowed in. However, not all such searches will be necessary, or proportionate.

In *Wainwright* v *Home Office*,[35] the House of Lords had to consider the strip search of a visitor to a prison in particularly embarrassing circumstances. It was held that there was no remedy in English law, since there was no intentional invasion of privacy, although a claim under the Act was not available, because the facts of the case took place before the Act came into effect. This case was then considered by the European Court,[36] which held that there was a breach of Article 8 because the prison authorities had failed to comply with the safeguards and procedures which were in place to protect the dignity of those being searched and a further breach of Article 13 because of the lack of a remedy in English law for this breach.

Similar considerations apply to even more intrusive forms of searching for evidence of wrongdoing, such as collecting or retaining DNA samples or fingerprint evidence. Again, this is likely to be justified where it is directly connected to the detection of crime. However, what if the person who provided them has been cleared of the offence for which they were suspected? It is clear that this will engage Article 8: the question is whether it is justified.

---

[34] *Botta* v *Italy* (1998) 26 EHRR 241.
[35] *Wainwright* v *Home Office* [2003] UKHL 53, [2003] 3 WLR 1137.
[36] *Wainwright* v *UK* (2007) 44 EHRR 40.

This policy of retaining such evidence was challenged in the courts and the House of Lords held that the policy itself was justified as being necessary for the prevention of crime and the protection of the rights of others.[37] However, the European Court has disagreed.[38] Retention of fingerprints, cellular samples and DNA samples serves a legitimate purpose, but the general retention of such material is not necessary in a democratic society in respect of people who have not been convicted of an offence. In particular, the Court was concerned that this applied to people suspected of any offence, however trivial; the retention of data potentially impacted on their future rights to be presumed innocent of involvement in any particular crime; and it could be especially harmful in the case of juveniles. The interference was disproportionate and exceeded the margin of appreciation and was thus in breach of Article 8.

This case raises very difficult issues of balancing fighting crime against the protection of individual rights. It may well be that the use of stored samples can help solve cases years later. The issue, though, is whether this is necessary in a democratic society: if we want to live in a society which respects the rights of individuals, then we must be very careful what personal information we allow the state to store and use indefinitely.

THE 'PRIVATE LIFE' OF PRISONERS

The situation where discipline is most obviously a factor in the way that people are treated is in prison. Prison is a place where authority must be exercised; there is often a judgment to be made by prison staff regarding punishments and privileges and freedoms. But respect must be given to every person, regardless of his or her status, and this includes prisoners.

In *X* v *UK*,[39] a prisoner serving a life sentence in Gartree Prison applied to the governor for a visitor's order for a visit from a member of the Citizens' Commission on Human Rights, which was sponsored by the Church of Scientology, in order to examine his medical records; the governor refused, on the ground that the intended visitor had not been, before the sentence began, a relative or friend of the prisoner, and in addition there was concern about the potentially harmful effects of the Church of Scientology. The prisoner complained to the European Commission that, in violation of Article 8, he was being prevented from having contact with outside influences, which would assist his rehabilitation, and Article 8 gave him a right to a life which included relationships with other human beings, in order to develop his emotional ties and so develop his own personality. The Commission accepted that the concept of a 'private life' could include the kind of features which the prisoner was seeking for himself, although it held that on the facts there was no violation of Article 8.

---

[37] *R (S)* v *Chief Constable of South Yorkshire* [2004] UKHL 39, [2004] 1 WLR 2196.
[38] *S and Marper* v *UK* (2009) 48 EHRR 50.
[39] (1983) 5 EHRR 260.

Following the Act, the prison service, as a public authority, must give thought to the kind of facilities in prisons to give a suitable effect to the rights of a prisoner to some form of private life. A prisoner also has family relationships, even if they are physically separated from their family; when the prisoner claims to exercise them, the prison authorities or the court must balance those rights against the state's right to impose custody. Here are some of the situations which have fallen to be considered.

- Absence from cell during search of cell or correspondence: in the case of *Daly*,[40] the House of Lords held that the policy of requiring a prisoner to be absent whenever prison officers examined his privileged legal correspondence, which he had in his cell, gave rise to the possibility that an officer might improperly read it, or the belief that he would read it, so that there was an inhibiting effect on the prisoner's willingness to communicate freely with his legal adviser. This amounted to an interference with the prisoner's right to respect for his correspondence under Article 8, which was not justified, because having a routine policy was disproportionate. No account was being taken by the prison authorities of whether the particular prisoner was unruly, or likely to disrupt the search. In short, the prison authorities must take stock of each case and each situation before imposing this kind of condition.[41]

- Monitoring of phone calls: in the case of *N*,[42] a patient in a secure hospital sought to challenge a provision in the safety and security written directions which entitled the hospital authority to record and listen to a random 10 per cent of patients' telephone calls. The High Court dismissed his challenge. The court stated that while, on the one hand, it was clear that the written direction interfered with the Article 8 right to respect for private life, on the other, the hospital had a statutory duty to provide secure accommodation; abuse of the telephone system could create a security risk, and in any event the 10 per cent system went no further than was strictly necessary, and so was proportionate.

- Restrictions on visitors: in the case of *Lalley*,[43] the prisoner was serving a life sentence for murder, and had been moved to a high-security hospital. He had been visited by his child nephews, but their visits were not allowed in hospital until there had been a risk assessment. This policy was challenged, on the basis that the policy imposed a blanket ban. The High Court decided that restrictions on child visits to patients at high-security hospitals who had committed the most serious offences were wholly justified and compatible with Article 8; restricting visits to a limited category of relationship was not irrational; and no category of child was entirely excluded from visiting, as it was always possible to obtain a contact order from the court. In any case, it was not obvious that the relationship between uncles and nephews necessarily fell within the meaning of family life under Article 8. Family life is a flexible concept and depends on the facts of each case.

- Children remaining with their mother in prison: in the case of *P*,[44] two prisoners challenged the prison service's policy to allow children to remain with their mothers in prison only until they were 18 months old, arguing that the separation of mother and child was

---

[40] *R (Daly) v Home Secretary* [2001] UKHL 26, [2001] 2 WLR 1622.
[41] Some more cases about correspondence in prison are below, p. 271.
[42] *R (N) v Ashworth Special Hospital Authority* [2001] EWHC Admin 339, [2001] HRLR 46.
[43] *R (Lalley) v Secretary of State for Health* (2001) 1 FLR 406.
[44] *R (P) v Home Secretary* [2001] EWCA Civ 1151, [2001] 1 WLR 2002.

a breach of Article 8. The Divisional Court held that under Article 8 the policy was lawful because it gave sufficient respect for family life. Prisoners are sent to prison as a punishment, to deter others and for rehabilitation. The impairment of the right of family life is a consequence of the deprivation of liberty which prison involves. Thus some form of policy is necessary to ensure that mothers with babies who are in prison are treated in the same manner and to balance the interests of the mother, the interests of the child and the interference resulting from the mother being in prison. Since the policy did not preclude reconsideration in individual cases and since it was kept under review, the mother and baby policy was lawful, and there was no breach of the Convention.

■ Conceiving children while in prison: there are limits on prisoners being allowed to conceive a child by artificial insemination, and a challenge to that for failing to respect family life had been rejected.[45] However, the European Court has now held that these limits are in breach of Article 8 in the case of *Dickson*.[46] Limits on the ability to have a child is a consequence of imprisonment, but allowing for artificial insemination does not raise security issues, or unduly burden the state financially, or undermine the role of a prison sentence, especially in its aspect of rehabilitation. Having a policy which limits such facilities is not inherently in breach of Article 8, but here there was too high a burden by having to show 'exceptional circumstances' and the policy failed to fairly balance individual and public interests.

FAMILY LIFE

This is the second protected interest in Article 8(1) – the right to respect for **family life**. This concept will obviously be important in cases and disputes involving spouses and partners and children, particularly relating to the custody of children, and divorce, and financial maintenance of members of a family. It will be necessary for the courts of the United Kingdom to consider whether the Convention increases the rights of individuals who may assert a right to be consulted about the life of the family or members of it. But the Convention has a much wider effect: it will impose an obligation on public authorities to take into account a family which may be affected by a decision.

The first thing to notice is that the 'family' in Convention terms is a broad concept. The object of family life is living together in order that family relationships can develop normally and family members can enjoy one another's company, but the family exists even when the members of it are not physically living together. So in the case of *Olsson* v *Sweden*,[47] a child had been taken into the care of the state authorities. The European Court was quite clear that:

> The mutual enjoyment by parent and child of each other's company constitutes a fundamental element of family life; furthermore, the natural family relationship is not terminated by reason of the fact that the child is taken into public care.

Nor is the word 'family' in Article 8 limited to relationships dependent on marriage.

---

[45] *R (Mellor)* v *Home Secretary* [2001] EWCA Civ 742, [2001] 3 WLR 533 and see also below, p. 329.
[46] *Dickson* v *UK* (2008) 46 EHRR 41.
[47] (1989) 11 EHRR 259.

The right to privacy

14

In *Kroon v Netherlands*,[48] a child was born to a stable relationship between Mrs Kroon and Mr Zerrouk while Mrs Kroon was still married to Mr Kroon. Under Dutch law, it was impossible to obtain recognition of the biological father's paternity unless the husband denied paternity. The applicants complained that they were victims of a violation of Article 8. The Court said:

> The Court recalls that the notion of 'family life' in Article 8 is not solely confined to marriage-based relationships, and may encompass other *de facto* 'family ties' where partners are living together outside marriage. Although, as a rule, living together may be a requirement for such a relationship, exceptionally other factors may also serve to demonstrate that a relationship has sufficient constancy to create *de facto* 'family ties'; such is the case here, as since 1987 four children have been born to Mrs Kroon and Mr Zerrouk.

It has been clearly established by the European Court that Article 8 requires proper consideration to be given to preserving family relationships. So, for example, it is important that children are given proper access to their parents, and vice versa, even if the children are in the care of the state or in the process of being adopted; the child's interests are paramount, and interferences with rights of access can be justified if, but only if, they are in the child's best interests. What must be borne in mind is that in cases such as this both the child and the parents have Article 8 rights, so there is a need for balance and proportionality. So, for example, a doctor's duty of confidence to a young person, for example, when giving advice about contraception, overrides any Article 8 rights the parents might have.[49] The same balance applies to decisions about removing children from families, for example, where they are considered to be at risk of harm. This is a decision which engages Article 3 because of the risk of ill-treatment,[50] but also Article 8 because the consequence is an interference in family life. The priority here is the protection of the child, and the authorities' duty to the child is why, in English law, they do not owe a duty of care to the parents in this situation to avoid negligence in taking such decisions.

> The leading authority on this is the case of *D v East Berkshire NHS Trust*,[51] and one of the cases heard then was considered by the European Court in the case of *RK*.[52] Here a child was taken into care following a medical diagnosis that an injury to her bone was not accidental; she was later diagnosed as having brittle bone disease, and returned to her parents. The European Court held that the interim care order was a legitimate interference with Article 8: it fulfilled the authority's duty to protect the child and had acted reasonably and promptly. The fact that the original diagnosis turned out to be wrong did not make them liable or breach Article 8.[53]

---

[48] (1995) 19 EHRR 263.
[49] *R (Axon) v Secretary of State for Health* [2006] EWHC 372 (Admin), [2006] 2 WLR 1130.
[50] See above, pp. 160–1.
[51] *D v East Berkshire NHS Trust* [2005] UKHL 23, [2005] 2 AC 373, discussed above, p. 151; this has not been altered by the Act importing Article 8 into domestic law: *Lawrence v Pembrokeshire County Council* [2007] EWCA Civ 446, [2007] 1 WLR 2991.
[52] *RK v United Kingdom* (2008) (app 3000/06) LTL 2.10.08.
[53] The Court found a breach of the Convention only in the failure for there to be a remedy in domestic law, which was because the facts pre-dated the Act coming into effect.

However, it is important that in such cases the authorities pay proper attention to the rights at stake and ensure that a fair process is followed.

In *TP v UK*,[54] T lived with her daughter K, a child, in a local authority area, and the authority owed duties to the child under the Child Care Act 1980. The authority suspected that the daughter had been sexually abused. K took part in a video interview, asserting that she had been sexually abused, by a man of the same name as T's boyfriend, but denying that he was the abuser. The authority obtained a place of safety order in respect of K, on the basis that T would be unable to protect K from abuse. One year later, T and her solicitors had sight of the video interview. The European Court held that the delay in providing the video evidence amounted to a breach of Article 8, as T had not had the opportunity to participate in the decision-making procedures following K's removal from her home.

It is surprising in this case that no opportunity had been offered to her to see the video, as usually such evidence is made available. However, the principle is important and such considerations will be relevant to all cases concerning children, such as adoption decisions and child custody cases. Thus it is not just the outcome which is important: the individual must be allowed proper participation in the decision-making process, or that will itself be a breach of Article 8.

ANCESTORS OF THE FAMILY

The right to respect for family life applies equally to the cultural values of families, including values based on their ancestral histories. And there are several ways in which a family's interests in its ancestors may be affected by the activities of public authorities such as government, utilities such as railways or gas and electricity companies or building and construction authorities.

In *G & E v Norway*,[55] Lapp shepherds, fishermen and hunters claimed that the proposed flooding of a 2.8-kilometre area of their ancestral hunting grounds by a hydroelectric project would be in breach of Article 8; the Commission held that their claim was capable of being covered by Article 8, but decided that the interference was justifiable under Article 8(2). Thus, the Commission was prepared to bring family livelihood and traditional occupation within this Article.

In a decision by a comparable body, in *Hopu v France*,[56] the United Nations Human Rights Committee decided that the construction of a hotel development over an ancestral burial site was capable of being an arbitrary interference with the family life of ethnic Polynesians.

[54] (2002) 34 EHRR 2.
[55] (1983) 35 DR 30.
[56] (1983) 3 BHRC 597.

The right to privacy

Thus decisions on planning and land use and the undertaking of works by local authorities and public utilities are likely to be affected by such considerations. It has also been decided that to explore a shipwreck and enter it and remove artefacts is an interference with family privacy, when members of the family lie in the wreck.

 ## IMMIGRANTS

Nowadays, movement of people from one state to another is a regular occurrence; they become immigrants or asylum seekers, and families are affected. The right to respect to a family life must be respected by host nations, or by deporting nations, when considering how to respond to situations where there is possibility that the immigrant will no longer be allowed to stay in the country. The starting point is that the immigration appeal authorities must take into account the Article 8 rights, both of the person seeking asylum, and of their whole family unit: the House of Lords has held that there is no point in having a process which requires the immigrant and their family to have to bring separate proceedings to have their Article 8 rights considered.[57] So, for example, where the deportation of a mother would require custody of her son to be transferred to his father, who had behaved violently towards the mother and had never seen the son, this would be such a flagrant breach of Article 8 as to completely deny her rights and deportation should not take place.[58]

This also means that where there is a family unit, and especially where there are children, Article 8 will usually require the immigration process to be conducted within the UK: it will be comparatively rare for it to be more appropriate for the applicant to have to leave the UK and apply from abroad.[59] And Article 8 will have a more general impact in immigration proceedings: there does not have to be a family unit for it to be engaged, so long as the applicant has some form of relationships with the community or with others which have developed in this country these have to be considered, and delay in considering the case may itself strengthen the claim under Article 8 that they should be allowed to stay in the UK.[60] This does not mean that anyone with a family will be allowed to stay in the UK, but it does mean that the decision-making officer or tribunal will have to take proper account of the interests of that family in taking their decision. Article 8 can also apply to restrictions on the movements of UK nationals: in the case of *F*,[61] the Divisional Court held that provisions imposing travel notification requirements on certain sex offenders were incompatible with Article 8 because they lasted indefinitely without the opportunity for review.

 ## HOME

This is the third element in Article 8(1), respect for the home; and what springs to mind now is the idea of protection of the home from invasion and intrusion. 'A man's house is

[57] *B v Home Secretary* [2008] UKHL 39, [2008] 3 WLR 166.
[58] *EM (Lebanon) v Home Secretary* [2008] UKHL 64, [2008] 3 WLR 931.
[59] *C v Home Secretary* [2008] UKHL 40, [2008] 1 WLR 1420.
[60] *EB (Kosovo) v Home Secretary* [2008] UKHL 41, (2008) 3 WLR 178.
[61] *R (F) Secretary of State for Justice* [2008] EWHC 3170 (Admin), [2009] 2 CAR(S) 47.

his castle and each man's home is his safest refuge,' wrote Sir Edward Coke in 1628.[62] That is still the starting point of the modern law, and by and large the state or other public authorities may not enter private premises, unless the law permits it, as, for instance, on reasonable suspicion of crime, or under the power of a warrant. The application of Article 8 will not provide a lesser standard of protection for the individual than exists under the current law, since Article 8 itself requires that in order to be justified an invasion of privacy must be in accordance with the law. However, Article 8 may provide wider protection than previously, since it may limit the scope of a state authority to enter a home, even where it might otherwise be permitted by law.

Home has been given a broad interpretation by the European Court. So, for example, a home remains a home even though the owner may be away from the premises for a long period. In the case of *Gillow*,[63] the parties were absent from a house which they owned, but it was nonetheless held that they regarded it as their home.

> Mr and Mrs Gillow owned a house in Guernsey, which they had built for themselves and furnished with the intention of eventually living there, although after building the house they lived away from Guernsey for about 18 years. They then returned to live in their house, but were then obliged to apply for a licence to occupy it, and this licence was refused. The purpose of the legislation was to ensure that houses were available for the population of Guernsey. They complained to the European Court of a violation of Article 8, as there had been an interference with their right to respect to their home. The European Court held that they should succeed: the national court had given insufficient weight to the circumstances of the particular case.

Likewise, respect for home and home life means more than just providing some form of a dwelling or shelter: it extends to maintaining the situation to which a person has become accustomed, and the very permanence of which gives comfort. Thus, in the case of *Coughlan*,[64] where a patient who was a paraplegic had become accustomed to a particular place of residence, and the promise had been given to her that she would not be moved, the health authority which then moved her was held to have breached her rights under Article 8.

This approach will be relevant in a variety of situations where, for example, a local authority makes a decision about housing, or repossessing a property. It does not prevent such action, but suggests that due weight must be given to the facts of the case being considered. There is a public interest in local authorities having control of their housing stock, to ensure that it goes to those in most need, and that access to social housing is not abused. But when a local authority, or other public authority,[65] takes a decision to evict someone, they have to consider that person's Article 8 rights, even if they wish to use a procedure which gives the court no discretion to refuse to order possession; and if the court does have

---

[62] *Coke's Institutes of the Laws of England*, Third Part, p. 162; also *Semayne's Case*, 5 Co. Rep. 91b.
[63] (1986) 11 EHRR 335.
[64] *R (Coughlan) v N. and E. Devon Health Authority* [2000] All ER 850.
[65] See above, pp. 77–80, for discussion of what is a public authority in this context, and cases cited at p. 80 fn 63.

14

a discretion whether to order possession, it will have to consider Article 8. Where the tenant has given good grounds for eviction, such as not paying the rent,[66] or causing a nuisance, an order for possession is likely to be reasonable and not violate Article 8 because that is likely to be a fair balance between the rights of the landlord and those of the tenant. The same is likely to apply where the tenancy has simply come to an end because it was of limited duration or because notice has been served by a tenant. In general terms, the courts have held that the housing legislation strikes a fair balance between the tenant's rights to a home and the landlord's rights to their property.[67]

However, it is important that the proper process is followed and that it is not bypassed by the landlord. In the case of *McCann*,[68] the European Court held that there was a breach of Article 8 where the local authority landlord had bypassed the statutory scheme by having one co-tenant sign a notice to quit, bringing the tenancy to an end without the need to seek possession against both tenants. The breach was in failing to follow the process which would protect both tenants.

As a result of the a number of European Court cases,[69] our courts have held that there can be a challenge to a claim for possession on the grounds of Article 8, even if the statutory scheme appears to require possession to be granted to a public authority landlord. There are two circumstances where this can apply, either (a) because it could be argued that the statute itself failed to protect Article 8, so there was a question about whether a declaration of incompatibility should be made, or (b) because there was a case that the landlord, being a public authority, had acted unreasonably in seeking possession and its decision was therefore subject to challenge by way of judicial review grounds, as being outside its lawful discretion.[70] This ensures that, on the one hand, there is certainty in the law and the courts do not get clogged up by constant challenges on the basis of Article 8 every time a landlord seeks possession of a property, since usually the answer will be that the legislation strikes a fair balance. On the other hand, this does allow exceptional circumstances to be taken into account.[71]

But Article 8, as we have seen, does not provide the *right* to a home: so where someone has nowhere to live, their being granted a non-secure form of accommodation does not infringe their Article 8 rights.[72] It is also important that housing provisions and decisions do not discriminate: we referred in the context of Article 14 to the case of *Ghaidan* v *Godin-Mendoza*,[73] where a housing statute was interpreted to give a homosexual couple the same right to succeed to a tenancy as an unmarried heterosexual couple.

 ## TRADITIONAL FAMILY LIFESTYLES AND TRAVELLERS

Many people adhere to and cherish the faiths and traditions of their families. More than that, they may regard themselves as part of a culture, be proud of that and wish to live in a

---

[66] *Southwark London Borough* v *St. Brice* [2001] EWCA Civ 1138, [2002] 1 WLR 1537.
[67] *Harrow LBC* v *Qazi* [2003] UKHL 43, [2004] 1 AC 983, *Leeds City Council* v *Price* [2006] UKHL 10.
[68] *McCann* v *United Kingdom* (2008) 47 EHRR 20.
[69] Especially *Connors* v *UK* , discussed below, and *McCann* op. cit.
[70] Judicial review is introduced above, p. 44.
[71] *Kay* v *Lambeth London Borough Council, Leeds City Council* v *Price* [2006] UKHL 10, [2006] 2 AC 465; *Doherty* v *Birmingham City Council* [2008] UKHL 57, [2008] 3 WLR 636.
[72] *Sheffield City Council* v *Smart* [2002] EWCA Civ 4, [2002] LGR 467.
[73] [2004] UKHL 30, [2004] 2 AC 557, above, p. 124.

manner which is faithful to their tradition. However, sometimes this brings them into conflict with the laws of the land and a balance has to be struck. The European Court has had to consider a number of cases where gypsy families wished to pursue their traditional style of dwelling, and claimed that the law interfered with their traditions, so invading their right to respect for a private life.

In *Buckley* v *UK*,[74] Mrs Buckley and her three children were part of a family who had been gypsies for as long as they could trace back; they occupied caravans which stood on land owned by her. She applied for planning permission to have them on that land, and it was refused. The caravans were her home; yet it was apparently illegal to live in them. The local authority based their refusal on the contention that the caravans would spoil the amenity of the locality, yet there were buildings nearby, and the official gypsy site was very near. She complained to the European Court of a violation of Article 8.

The Court held that there was an interference with Mrs Buckley's family life, but (by a majority of 6 to 3) that it was justified under Article 8(2). There was a legitimate aim in limiting sites for caravans, on the grounds of public safety and economic well-being, and the health and rights of other persons; and it was necessary in a democratic society. The majority did not consider that Mrs Buckley was at any time penalised or subjected to any detrimental treatment for attempting to follow a traditional gypsy lifestyle. They did consider that the relevant national policy was aimed at enabling gypsies to cater for their own needs; a minority did, however, consider that there was a breach because of the need to protect gypsies as a vulnerable minority.

In *Chapman* v *UK*,[75] the European Court had to consider a case of gypsies who had been moved from various sites, whose applications for planning permissions had been refused, and who had been obliged to live in accommodation which they found unsuitable to their way of life. The Court found that the applicants' occupation of their caravans was an integral part of their ethnic identity as gypsies and that the enforcement measures and planning decisions interfered with their rights to respect for their private and family life. However, the Court found that the measures were in accordance with the law and pursued the legitimate aim of protecting the rights of others through preservation of the environment. The planning inspectors, in the various cases, had identified strong environmental objections to the applicants' use of their land: the Convention is not there to protect those who 'in conscious defiance of the prohibitions of the law, establish a home on an environmentally protected site'. The applicants could not occupy land where they wished just because, statistically, the number of gypsies was greater than the number of places available in authorised gypsy sites. Nor was the Court convinced that Article 8 could be interpreted to impose on the state an obligation to make available to the gypsy community an adequate number of suitably equipped sites. Article 8 did not give a right to be provided with a home, and whether the state provided funds to enable everyone to have a home was a matter for political not judicial decision.

---

[74] (1997) 23 EHRR 101.
[75] (2001) 33 EHRR 18.

The right to privacy

However, in the case of *Connors* v *UK*,[76] the European Court held that a summary eviction from a local authority gypsy caravan site was in breach of Article 8. The family had lived there, lawfully, for some 15 years (unlike *Chapman*, there was no breach of planning law). Whether the family had caused a nuisance, which would justify evicting them, had not been determined, because the local council had used a summary procedure. Overall there were insufficient procedural safeguards, and insufficient weight had been given to the rights of the persons evicted.

The ability of a public authority landlord to use a summary procedure in a case like *Connors* has been reconsidered by the House of Lords in the light of the European Court's judgment: a summary procedure can still be used in most such cases, although, as noted above, the court will consider Article 8 issues in exceptional cases.[77] The law has also been amended to ensure that there is more protection from eviction for those living in caravans or mobile homes.[78] Article 8 will also have to be taken into account when an order is sought to remove those who are living in a place without planning permission, as happened in *Chapman*. The House of Lords has confirmed that, in such situations, the court must consider whether an order is just and proportionate in all the circumstances, bearing in mind the local planning authority's assessment of public and private interests.[79] So the loss of home may be a special factor justifying not evicting a family of gypsies from green-belt land.[80] On the other hand, it has been held that discrimination in the enforcement of planning controls between those setting up mobile homes or caravans without planning permission, which can be removed, and those who build settled homes without permission is justified by the need to protect the environment.[81]

 ## QUALITY OF HOME LIFE

The enjoyment of a home may be spoilt by various forms of interference, such as noise, light, smells, fumes or other forms of pollution, and anyone who has experienced this might well refer to it as an invasion of their privacy. Aircraft noise pervades the lives of some people, and it may now be that they have a good cause of complaint under Article 8.

In *Powell and Rayner* v *UK*,[82] two families lived under the flight paths of aircraft taking off and landing at Heathrow Airport. One lived at Esher, several miles from the airport; the other lived about 1.5 miles from the runway. They had acquired their properties before the building of the runway extension, which had caused an increase in air traffic and noise. Their complaint was that the noise invaded their home life and so interfered with their private life. The European Court found, on balancing the rights of the householders and the general interest of the public in access to air travel, that there was *no* violation of Article 8.

---

[76] (2005) 40 EHRR 9E.
[77] *Kay* v *Lambeth London Borough Council, Leeds City Council* v *Price* [2006] UKHL 10, [2006] 2 AC 465.
[78] Section 4 of the Caravans Act 1968 amended by the Housing Act 2004 and section 5 of the Mobile Homes Act 1983 amended by the Housing and Regeneration Act 2008; but for these amendments, a declaration of incompatibility would have been made in *Doherty* v *Birmingham City Council* [2008] UKHL 57, [2008] 3 WLR 636.
[79] *South Buckinghamshire District Council* v *Porter* [2003] UKHL 26, [2003] 2 AC 558.
[80] *R (Wychavon District Council)* v *Secretary of State for Communities* [2008] EWCA Civ 692, [2009] 1 P&CR 15.
[81] *R (Wilson)* v *Wychavon District Council* [2007] EWCA Civ 52, [2007] 2 WLR 798.
[82] (1990) 12 EHRR 355; the Commission decision on the right to property is considered below, p. 342.

This question arose again in *Hatton* v *UK*,[83] where the complaint was as to the increase in the level of noise caused by aircraft using Heathrow Airport at night since 1993. The European Court held that this was not a breach of Article 8. The scheme for controlling aircraft noise was within the state's margin of appreciation, the state being better placed to assess such matters, and the Court accepted that the government was entitled to conclude that the economic benefits outweighed the rights of those affected.

However, not all aircraft noise will be justified in the public benefit. In the case of *Dennis* v *Minister of Defence*,[84] the claimants lived near a RAF airbase; jet aircraft produced noise which disturbed them, and they claimed damages on the ground that the noise was an actionable nuisance, and interfered with their right to private life, and the peaceful enjoyment of their possessions, since the noise had reduced the capital value of the house. The court awarded them damages; the noise was deafening, highly intrusive and frightening, and constituted a very serious interference with their enjoyment of their property. The remedy available for the common law of nuisance was held to be sufficient to dispose of the case, but the court did consider that Article 8, and Article 1 of the First Protocol, had also been violated.[85]

It is not only noise which can cause a nuisance: in *S* v *France*,[86] a nuclear power station was situated less than 300 metres from an eighteenth-century chateau on the banks of the Loire. The power station caused noise, lights at night, and the creation of a microclimate, so that the value of the property was halved. All this was held by the Commission to be an interference under Article 8, but it was justified because of its benefit to the community.

This right of respect for a private home means that the state must either take a positive line, and rectify the cause of the interference, or justify the interference under Article 8(2).

In the case of *Guerra*,[87] the court applied this standard. The town of Manfredonia, in Foggia, Italy, was near to a factory which produced fertiliser compounds, and some of the emissions from the factory contained arsenic. There was a high risk from the gases and chemicals borne on the wind and in the air, but no information had been given to the nearby townsfolk about this risk.

The European Court held that in this case there was no interference with a right as such; but the state had been guilty of a failure to take *positive steps* to give essential information, despite its knowledge of the situation over quite some time. Thus the quality of the lives of nearby people had been diminished, and their home and private lives had been affected in breach of Article 8.

In *Lopez Ostra* v *Spain*,[88] the people of a village near an industrial plant, which treated waste water, complained of fumes and smells which made their lives intolerable, and this

---

[83] (2003) 37 EHRR 28.
[84] [2003] EWHC 793 (QB), [2003] Env LR 34.
[85] *Andrews* v *Reading Borough Council* [2005] EWHC 256, LTL 21.9.06, [2006] RVR 56 is another noise case: noise from a new traffic scheme was so intrusive as to be a breach of Article 8.
[86] (1990) 65 DR 250.
[87] (1998) 26 EHRR 357; considered above in the context of Article 2, p. 146.
[88] (1995) 20 EHRR 277.

was a violation of Article 8, as damaging their private life; the state disputed that the situation was really as bad as it was described. The European Court held that severe environmental pollution may affect individuals' well-being and prevent them from enjoying their homes in such a way as to affect their private and family life adversely, even without seriously damaging their health.

Under our domestic law there are well-established remedies for people whose enjoyment of their home and property is affected by nuisances, such as noise or smells, or escaping or leaking industrial material, chemicals or waste. However, there are some limitations on these remedies under English law; in particular, they are not usually available to persons who are affected by such a nuisance where that person is not the occupier or owner of land or a house.

The leading case is *Hunter* v *Canary Wharf*,[89] where it was claimed that the building of Canary Wharf in London's Docklands had significantly interfered with the television reception of neighbouring properties. The House of Lords decided that interference with television reception, whilst it might be inconvenient, was not something which could be restrained by the courts. The House of Lords also confirmed that in order to bring a legal claim of this sort, in the tort of nuisance, it is necessary for the claimant to have property rights in the land where she lives and which are being interfered with. But this long-established restriction in English law in this sort of case may well have to be reconsidered in light of the European jurisprudence on Article 8 if complaints such as this one infringe the right to respect for private and home life of people who live in a property but do not own it, such as family members of the owner. Indeed, in *Hunter* itself, Lord Cooke, in a dissenting judgment, expressly referred to Article 8 as a possible basis for the householders' claim. As the interpretation of 'private life' in Article 8 covers this type of situation, a violation of the article will strengthen any claim and may require the domestic courts to expand the scope of those remedies which already exist.

Since the Act has been passed, the courts have recognised that the effect of Article 8 may well be to extend the existing law in this respect. In one case where there were complaints of emissions, noise pollution and invasion of privacy from a factory, the judge refused to summarily dismiss the claims, notwithstanding that the claimants were not home-owners, since there was an arguable case under Article 8, which might also require reconsideration of the law on nuisance.[90]

CORRESPONDENCE

The final category of protected interests under Article 8 is correspondence, the right to private mail. Although when this was originally drafted, only paper letters would have been in the minds of those setting out what rights Article 8 covers, this can now be applied very

---

[89] [1997] 2 WLR 684.

[90] *McKenna* v *British Aluminium Ltd* (2002) Times 25.4.02; *Dennis*, above, was a case of nuisance, but brought by the householder, so this particular question did not arise; *Dobson* v *Thames Water Utilities Ltd* [2009] EWCA Civ 28 also considered that it is possible, but unlikely, that nuisance damages for the householder might not amount to just satisfaction of a claim under the Act.

much more widely. With the growing number of forms of electronic communications, such as emails and text messages, it is a topical issue whether or not it is possible or appropriate for the state to monitor these forms of correspondence.

In a state which we like to consider a civilised democracy, it might be hard to imagine how the ordinary citizen might find the state interfering with his or her private correspondence. However, one should remember that the 'ordinary citizen' includes someone who is suspected of being involved in a crime, or who is a patient in a hospital or a prisoner in a prison. These are all situations where there might be a legitimate justification for monitoring correspondence or opening post.

> In *Herczegfalvy* v *Austria*,[91] the applicant was resident in a psychiatric hospital, where the practice was adopted of passing all letters sent by him to the curator of the hospital, who would select those which could be sent on. This was done, argued the government, to protect his health, and was done in accordance with the relevant legal requirements. In other words, the government agreed that there was an interference with the patient's right of privacy of correspondence, but contended that it was justified under Article 8(2).
>
> The European Court found that the terms of the statutes and the Civil Code were vaguely worded, and did not specify the scope of conditions of exercise of the discretionary power which was complained of: such specifications are all the more necessary in the case of detention in psychiatric institutions, because the person concerned is frequently at the mercy of the medical authorities, so that their correspondence is their only contact with the outside world. Thus, the government had failed to justify the interference and there was therefore a breach of Article 8.
>
> In *Silver* v *UK*,[92] the applicants, all convicted prisoners, complained that controls over their mail constituted a breach of their rights under Article 8. There were restrictions on correspondence other than with a relative or friend, and on correspondence with journalists, or correspondence which held the authorities up to contempt, or letters to Members of Parliament containing complaints which had not been raised with the prison authorities, or letters calculated to stimulate public agitation. The Court held that such restrictions were not necessary in a democratic society, and that there had been breaches of Article 8.

Thus it is clear that, in order to justify interference with correspondence, there must be not only a good reason for the interference, but also the rules which govern such interference must themselves be clear and available to be seen. One can put this point as a matter of principle: broad discretionary powers such as those used in the above cases do not comply with the requirement that any interference should be in accordance with the law, since the powers are too vague and discretionary to qualify properly as 'law';[93] this is an important part of the Convention's protection against arbitrary powers; and this is in addition to the need to show that the interference is reasonably necessary and proportionate.

[91] (1993) 15 EHRR 437.
[92] (1983) 5 EHRR 347.
[93] This idea is discussed more generally above, p. 116.

INTRUSION BY SURVEILLANCE

The issues raised in the context of correspondence in fact apply more generally to all the interests being protected by Article 8: in respect of all of them there is the question of the extent to which it is permissible for the state to intrude on private activities for the purposes set out in Article 8(2). There is much modern technology which can be used to intrude on people's privacy and to check up on people: closed-circuit television cameras, binoculars, video recording, photography with long-range lenses, telephone tapping and bugging devices are all part of modern methods of watching and listening. These are all used by state officials in one context or another: police officers use these devices for the detection of crime; customs officers use them to intercept smuggling or drug running; television detectors use them to catch licence evaders; local authorities rely on CCTV to prevent crime, or even to spot traffic scheme evaders; and so on. It will be easily appreciated that the use of all these devices has the potential for infringing Article 8 and their use does get challenged. In particular in criminal prosecutions, the use of evidence obtained in breach of rights of privacy or without proper legal authority may be challenged by the defence, since without that evidence a criminal prosecution may fail; but such challenges are important because it is important that all criminal convictions are founded on properly obtained and reliable evidence. Where the use of such devices is challenged, the courts, following decisions of the European Court on this topic, will look at the particular circumstances of the intrusion, to see whether there is an interference with the right of respect to a private life, and then consider whether the interference can be justified on the basis that it is in accordance with the law and necessary in a democratic society for a specified purpose: the prevention of crime and so on.

In *Kopp* v *Austria*,[94] Herr Kopp was a lawyer who was suspected of criminal activity. The President of the Austrian court had authorised a phone tap, but he placed a limitation on it that conversations connected with Herr Kopp's work as a lawyer were not to be taken into account. However, the task of supervising and managing the tapping was entrusted not to a police officer but to an official in the legal department, who was a civil servant, and all the conversations on the telephone line were listened to. The European Court held that there was a breach of Article 8, and that the tapping had not been in accordance with the law (as required by Article 8(2)). The phone tap infringed Article 8 because no care had been taken with the carrying out of the tap and it had been done in an arbitrary way.

In the case of *Hewitt* v *UK*,[95] officers of the National Council for Civil Liberties claimed that they had been the subject of telephone surveillance by the British Security Service, and that records had been kept about them, describing them as 'Communist sympathisers and subversives', based on sworn evidence from a former member of the Security Service. The European Court held that the recording and storing of information about the applicants' private lives, in a security and police register, interfered with the respect for private life. Since the rules governing this procedure were contained in non-binding and unpublished directives from the government and the Director General of the Secret Service, the framework for the surveillance was not sufficiently clear and so was not 'in accordance with the law'.

[94] (1999) 27 EHRR 91.
[95] (1992) 14 EHRR 657.

Thus it is a key requirement that surveillance be properly managed and supervised and be conducted in accordance with legal requirements and procedures. A similar type of case is *Khan* v *UK*,[96] to which we have already referred, since it raises the question of whether the reliance on evidence obtained in breach of Article 8 infringes the right to a fair trial under Article 6.

Mr Khan arrived in Britain, at Manchester Airport, from Pakistan. His cousin was on the same flight: his cousin was found to be in possession of £100,000 worth of heroin, and was charged and convicted of importing drugs. Mr Khan was not charged. However, some months later he visited a friend, who was himself under investigation for heroin dealing, at his home in Sheffield. A listening device had been fixed to the friend's house by police officers, unknown to the friend or to Mr Khan. During this visit the listening device was switched on, and Mr Khan was heard to admit that he was a party to the importing of the £100,000 worth of heroin at Manchester Airport. He was arrested and charged, and at his trial the prosecution adduced the evidence of the conversation; the prosecution admitted that the fixing of the device was a trespass on the house, which is to say that it was obtained by unlawful means. Mr Khan argued at his trial that the evidence of the telephone conversation was based on an unlawful act and that it was unfair to admit it in the trial; the judge held that it was admissible and Mr Khan was convicted. The House of Lords held that, although there was a breach of Article 8, the trial was not unfair.

The European Court held that there was indeed a violation of Article 8, although it considered that this did not mean that the trial was unfair in breach of Article 6. The Court did consider, however, that, although the trial was not unfair, the United Kingdom had not provided any remedy for the breach of Article 8 (in breach of Article 13).

This suggests that, following the Act, the United Kingdom courts must now consider very carefully whether this subject should be revisited to provide a remedy for the breach of Article 8 in such situations, whether or not the result of using such evidence makes a trial unfair.[97] Bear in mind that such evidence, although obtained improperly, may be perfectly reliable; but also that it is important that the police obey the law in all their actions and are not encouraged by the prospect of getting a conviction to obtain evidence of crime in ways which are themselves unlawful.

Since *Khan* was decided, one change to the law is that Parliament has passed the Regulation of Investigatory Powers Act 2000. This is important for our purposes because it is one of the requirements of Article 8 that, in order to be justified, conduct which would otherwise amount to a breach of Article 8 must be in accordance with the law.[98] Where a state agency carries out surveillance which is not properly regulated or adequately covered by legislation or legal principles, it runs the risk of being found to be not in accordance with the law. If there is no relevant law, it is also harder for the state to say that it is necessary in a democratic society or proportionate. Until the Regulation of Investigatory Powers

---

[96] (2001) 31 EHRR 45; also above, p. 224.
[97] This is discussed further in Chapter 12 above, pp. 224–6.
[98] Discussed above, pp. 116–18, and in particular the case of *Halford* v *UK*, which was a case of telephone tapping in breach of Article 8.

Act 2000, there were guidelines in place which applied to several forms of surveillance, but these were informal and not enshrined in statute. Thus the Regulation of Investigatory Powers Act provides a clear test for whether state surveillance is legal or illegal. This allows for a clearer assessment of whether surveillance infringes Article 8 because it is not in accordance with law, although this does not wholly answer the question of whether an infringement of privacy is justified. The Regulation of Investigatory Powers Act provides regulation of, for example, the interception of communications, the use of covert surveillance and decryption of documents, including the disclosure of an encryption key in order to have access to protected material. Authority must be obtained for the carrying out of any of this; and the granting of any authorisation under the Act must take into account 'necessity' and 'proportionality'. Any surveillance which is performed other than under this Act, or without some other statutory authority, is unlawful.[99]

QUESTIONS

1 What do you think about the development of breach of confidence to protect privacy? Do you agree with the way this has been done?

2 How private do you think public records should be? You might like to think about examples such as the electoral roll and census forms, income tax returns, fingerprints, medical records or school records.

3 What do you think about the retention of DNA samples or fingerprints? How do you strike a balance between the detection of crime and the rights of those who gave the samples? Does it make a difference if the person giving the samples was then convicted of an offence?

4 Do you think that prisoners deserve to have their rights to a private and family life respected?

5 What rights should gypsies or travellers have? How should society balance their needs against those of local landowners?

6 Do you think that people should be able to prevent others interfering with the graves of their ancestors? Does your answer change if their ancestors' burial place is of archaeological or historical importance?

7 How private should correspondence such as emails and text messages be? Does your answer change where the messages are being used to plan a crime or to cause a nuisance to someone?

---

[99] There has been further criticism of the previous law in the case of *Liberty* v *UK* (2009) 48 EHRR 1 which may have implications for similar provisions in the 2000 Act.

Shabina Begum, who unsuccessfully challenged the limits which her school's uniform policy placed on her rights to wear a jilbab to school (see p. 281).

Source: Chris Radburn/PA Photos

15 Freedom of conscience

Sapere aude – Dare to be wise (the motto of Hugh Oldham, 1450–1519, Bishop of Exeter, and of The Manchester Grammar School, which he founded).

Article 9: Freedom of Thought, Conscience and Religion
1 Everyone has the right to freedom of thought, conscience and religion; this right includes freedom to change his religion or belief and freedom, either alone or in community with others and in public or private, to manifest his religion or belief, in worship, teaching, practice and observance.

2 Freedom to manifest one's religion or beliefs shall be subject only to such limitations as are prescribed by law and are necessary in a democratic society in the interests of public safety, for the protection of public order, health or morals, or for the protection of the rights and freedoms of others.

First Protocol, Article 2: Right to Education
No person shall be denied the right to education. In the exercise of any functions which it assumes in relation to education and to teaching, the State shall respect the right of parents to ensure such education and teaching in conformity with their own religious and philosophical convictions.

 ## FREEDOM OF THOUGHT

The European Court has said:

> Freedom of thought, conscience and religion is one of the foundations of a 'democratic society' within the meaning of the Convention. It is, in its religious dimension, one of the most vital elements that go to make up the identity of believers and their conception of life, but it is also a precious asset for atheists, agnostics, sceptics and the unconcerned. The pluralism indissociable from a democratic society, which has been dearly won over the centuries, depends on it.[1]

The word 'pluralism' is defined in the *Oxford English Dictionary* as the tolerance within society of a diversity of ethnic or multicultural groups and their beliefs and attitudes. And it is notable that, in line with the fundamental importance of freedom of belief, that whilst

---

[1] *Kokkinakis v Greece* (1994) 17 EHRR 397.

there are some limitations in the Article on **manifesting** a belief, there are none on the right to **hold** a belief, which is not qualified in any way. This is because it would be wrong in principle for the state to attempt to legislate as to how people should **think**, as opposed to how they **act**. The attempt of any state to force people to think in a certain way is the hallmark of totalitarianism, and of some of the most evil regimes that have existed, such as Nazi Germany and Communist Russia. This is precisely because they attempted to stifle all freedom of thought, and not just freedom of action. This was also the enduring message of George Orwell's novel *1984*, which painted a picture of a society where the state developed technology to try to control how its citizens thought. None of the states of modern Europe are anywhere near as oppressive as these; but we will still see cases where, for example, the state has acted in a way which effectively attempts to impose on a citizen a religious attitude.

Thus, there are no qualifications at all on the primary rights contained in Article 9(1) – the freedom *of* thought, conscience and religion, that is, a right to **hold** views or beliefs, and the freedom to **change** these beliefs. However, the right to **manifest** one's religion or beliefs, how one shows or exercises them, may be limited in accordance with Article 9(2), which sets out the legitimate aims that such limitations may pursue, and also includes the familiar phrases, that such limitations should be 'prescribed by law' and 'necessary in a democratic society'.[2] This brings into play the exercise of balancing rights and, as with most of the Articles, there are a good number of cases which turn on whether or not an interference with an Article 9 right is justified under Article 9(2).

 ## THE RIGHT TO EDUCATION

We are considering Article 2 of the First Protocol[3] with Article 9, because both are aspects of the right to freedom of conscience. One of the hopes of many parents is that they will be able to bring up their children to share their fundamental beliefs about the world. This is recognised by the Convention as a legitimate aspiration in Article 2, the second sentence of which concerns just that, the right of parents to have their religious and philosophical convictions respected in the education of their children.

Yet, at the same time, children must have their own freedom of conscience, a guarantee of their ability to form their own views of the world, including their own views of basic moral and religious issues. This fundamental aspect of personal growth and development can only be guaranteed by access to education. A denial of the right to education would be to deny a person the ability to explore the world in an informed manner, as well as to deny them the chance to improve themselves intellectually, and to have the opportunity to pursue an occupation and lifestyle which will be fulfilling and worthwhile.

All these are important aspects of freedom of thought, but in a more concrete and specific context. And, as we will see, there are cases which reflect this, referring to both Articles 9 and 2. It should be noted also at the outset that, although Article 2 contains no second, qualifying paragraph, the requirement is to 'respect' the rights of parents, not to guarantee them. This is therefore not absolute, and the European Court has made clear that it can be interfered with by the state, so long as such interference is reasonably necessary and proportionate.

---

[2] Introduced above, p. 116.

[3] All references in this chapter to Article 2 should be taken to refer to this Article, not Article 2 of the Convention itself.

■ MANIFESTATION OF BELIEF

As we have noted above, only the freedom to *manifest* a belief is the subject of Article 9(2), and this is the only freedom guaranteed by Article 9 which may be limited: the right to hold or adhere to thought, conscience or religion may not be limited in any way. **Manifest** means to show and exercise something outwardly, and to demonstrate signs of it. It is therefore understandable that this is the aspect of Article 9 which may be limited, since what a person thinks is private, but how a person manifests that view may impinge on other people, and even harm them or society.

Quoting from the *Kokkinakis* case again, the European Court has referred to this distinction:

> According to Article 9, freedom to manifest one's religion is not only exercisable in community with others, 'in public' and within the circle of those whose faith one shares, but can also be asserted 'alone' and 'in private'; furthermore, it includes in principle the right to try to convince one's neighbour, for example through 'teaching', failing which, moreover, 'freedom to change one's religion or belief', enshrined in Article 9, would be likely to remain a dead letter. [. . .] The fundamental nature of the rights guaranteed in Article 9(1) is also reflected in the wording of the paragraph providing for limitations on them. Unlike the second paragraphs of Article 8, 10 and 11, which cover all the rights mentioned in the first paragraphs of those Articles, that of Article 9 refers only to 'freedom to manifest one's religion or belief'. In so doing it recognises that in democratic societies, in which several religions co-exist within one and the same population, it may be necessary to place restrictions on this freedom in order to reconcile the interests of the various groups and ensure that everyone's beliefs are respected.

We shall look now at some cases where the Court considered various limitations on manifesting belief. The Court applies the usual principles regarding such limitations – the need to examine the aims and scope of the limitation, and the principles implied in the words 'according to law', or 'necessary in a democratic society', balancing individual rights against public interests.

The case of *Pendragon* v *UK*,[4] concerned access by a modern order of Druids to Stonehenge to hold a service for the Summer Solstice. These had been prohibited because of previous disorder at such events (especially due to the attendance of non-Druids) and for fear of damage to the Stonehenge site, which is a very important national monument. But Pendragon attended anyway, in full ceremonial dress, and he was arrested. He complained that this was a violation of Article 9. The European Commission accepted that his assembly had a legitimately religious nature, but the Commission considered that the state's interference – the banning orders and the arrest – was justified, as there was a real fear of a breakdown in public order if the assembly took place.

In the case of *Taylor*,[5] Mr Paul Taylor was prosecuted and convicted of an offence of possession of cannabis, contrary to the Misuse of Drugs Act 1971. He was a Rastafarian, and it was accepted by the prosecution that this was a religion, in which drugs were used as an act of worship. Mr Taylor therefore argued that to prosecute him was a breach of Article 9. The Court of Appeal held that there was no violation. The court was entitled to consider that a ban on the possession of cannabis with intent to supply was in the interests of

---

[4] (1999) 27 EHRR Co 179.
[5] *R* v *Taylor* [2002] 1 CAR 519.

public safety to combat the health danger of drugs, supported by the United Kingdom's international commitments, such as under the Single Convention on Narcotic Drugs 1961 and the United Nations Convention against Illicit Traffic in Narcotic Drugs and Psychotropic Substances 1988. Thus although Article 9 was engaged, the interference was justified under Article 9(2). When balancing the two interests, the religious rights of Mr Taylor were outweighed by the public interest in outlawing these drugs.

Another instance where manifestation of belief came into conflict with public health is the case of *Suryananda*.[6] This concerned a Welsh Hindu Temple, which was sheltering a bullock because of Hindu religious beliefs that cows are sacred. The difficulty was that the cow had tested positive for bovine tuberculosis, which meant that there was a legal requirement for it to be killed as a protective measure. The Court of Appeal held that, although Article 9 was engaged, the decision not to exempt the bullock from slaughter was justifiable as being necessary and proportionate on the grounds of public safety.

RELIGIOUS DRESS

One area where this balancing act has hit the headlines is that of religious dress in schools, which is controversial here and across Europe, since concerns about religious fundamentalism are becoming more widespread. It has been most controversial when it concerns the dress of Muslim women and girls. Many branches of Islam mandate modest dress, but not all agree on how modest that should be; and certain forms of traditional Islamic dress raise issues about interaction with others.

The leading case in the European Court is that of *Leyla Şahin v Turkey*,[7] where the European Court held that there was no breach of Article 9 by a Turkish university in forbidding students from wearing headscarves. An important factor was the view embodied in the Turkish Constitution that official secularism is a guarantor of democratic values, of religious pluralism and of individual freedom of belief and religion, including protection for women from pressure to conform to Islamic values, and the ban applied equally to all religious symbols. This ban remains very much a live political issue in Turkey: the Turkish government, headed by an Islamic party, passed a law to allow women to wear a headscarf at university in February 2008, which was overturned by the Turkish constitutional court in June 2008.

France also has a long-established principle of secularism and has, controversially, banned all religious dress in schools. The French principle of secularism has been upheld by the European Court in the case of *Dogru v France*.[8] Here two Muslim schoolgirls were expelled from school for refusing to remove their headscarves during PE and sports classes. The European Court held that the French principle of secularism was justified because it supported the principle of respect for pluralism, so that the manifestation of religious beliefs would not be an ostentatious act that could constitute a source of pressure and exclusion for others. The reason for the expulsions was the failure to comply with school rules, which

[6] *R (Suryananda) v Welsh Ministers* [2007] EWCA Civ 893.
[7] (2005) 41 EHRR 8.
[8] *Dogru v France; Kervanci v France* (2009) 49 EHRR 8.

were justified for reasons of health and safety; and the disciplinary proceedings involving the applicants had properly taken into account their Article 9 rights.

This has come before our courts, and hit headlines, and the leading case is that of *Shabina Begum*,[9] a young Muslim woman who was a pupil at Denbigh High School. The school uniform rules allowed the wearing of a shalwar kameeze (tunic and trousers), which many Muslims consider sufficient. However, Miss Begum contended that this did *not* comply with the strict requirement of Islam as she practised it, and that she should be allowed to wear the jilbab (which covers a woman's body including the shape of her arms and legs). The school refused to allow her to attend school if she was not willing to comply with the school uniform requirements.

The House of Lords held that Miss Begum had a right under Article 9 to manifest her religion in the matter of dress at school, that the school had limited her freedom to manifest her religious belief by insisting on school uniform, but that it had not done so in a way which violated Article 9. The school had given great consideration to its uniform policy, to make it inclusive and unthreatening, it was acceptable to mainstream Muslim opinion and had contributed to harmony at the school. The school authorities were best placed to decide on an appropriate policy, and there was no reason to interfere with their decision, which was not disproportionate or unreasonable. Miss Begum was free to move to a different school if she did not want to comply with the uniform policy, as she had in fact done since the policy was enforced.

Following *Begum*, there have been a string of cases about religious dress or accessories in schools.

- In the case of *R (X) v Y School*,[10] Mr Justice Silber held that a school's policy not to allow a pupil to wear a niqab veil was reasonable and proportionate. It was justified by security considerations, to prevent pressure being applied to other pupils to wear a veil, and because the veil stopped teachers from relating well to pupils. Additionally, the pupil had been offered a place at a different school where she could have worn a niqab veil.
- A similar concern applied in the case of *Azmi*[11] where the Employment Appeal Tribunal held that a Muslim teaching assistant was not unlawfully discriminated against by being suspended when she disobeyed an instruction not to wear a veil. If there was indirect discrimination, it was justified by the need to be able to communicate clearly to a class.
- In the case of *Playfoot*,[12] a Christian student challenged her school's decision that she was not allowed to wear a purity ring, which she wished to do as an expression of her Christian faith and a sign of her belief in chastity before marriage. The High Court held that wearing a ring of this sort was not required by the student's Christianity and so she was not manifesting religious belief by wearing it; that she had accepted the school's uniform policy, which served justifiable functions, including school identity, discipline, equality and cohesion; and thus that there was no interference with her Article 9 rights.
- On the other hand, in the case of *Watkins-Singh*,[13] it was held that a school which refused to allow a Sikh pupil to wear a Kara, a steel bangle of religious significance, was religious discrimination.

[9] *R (Begum)* v *Governors of Denbigh High School* [2006] UKHL 15, [2007] 1 AC 100.
[10] *R (X)* v *Head Teachers and Governors of Y School* [2007] EWHC 298 (Admin), (2007) HRLR 20.
[11] *Azmi* v *Kirklees MBC* [2007] ICR 1154.
[12] *R (Playfoot)* v *Millais School Governing Body* [2007] EWHC 1698 (Admin), (2007) HRLR 34.
[13] *R (Watkins-Singh)* v *Aberdare Girls' High School Governors* [2008] EWHC 1865 (Admin), [2008] ACD 38.

Freedom of conscience

The key here is that there can be limitations on religious dress so long as there is a proper, reasonable and proportionate justification, which has to properly respect the religious beliefs being affected. It is a very difficult matter to find a balance between the rights of those who wish to wear such dress and what is sometimes a wider public interest, especially where some people (especially women) rely on common codes of dress to avoid pressure to dress in a way which is more modest than their own beliefs require. But what Article 9 ensures is that manifesting a belief is at least accorded a basic respect in the striking of this balance.

DO ALL BELIEFS QUALIFY FOR PROTECTION?

We have considered whether there can be limits on manifesting a belief. But what if the question which is raised is whether what is being manifested is *really* a belief, or whether it *should* be protected? Can any action count as the manifestation of a belief for the purpose of Article 9?

On the question of whether a view has to meet any basic requirements before it counts as a 'belief' or 'religion' for the purpose of Article 9, we can do no better than quote Lord Nicholls in the case of *Williamson*,[14] which makes clear that there are some basic standards which are required:

> The belief must be consistent with basic standards of human dignity or integrity. Manifestation of a religious belief, for instance, which involved subjecting others to torture or inhuman punishment would not qualify for protection. The belief must relate to matters more than merely trivial. It must possess an adequate degree of seriousness and importance. [. . .] It must be a belief on a fundamental problem. [. . .] The belief must also be coherent in the sense of being intelligible and capable of being understood. But, again, too much should not be demanded in this regard. Typically, religion involves belief in the supernatural. It is not always susceptible to lucid exposition or, still less, rational justification. The language used is often the language of allegory, symbol and metaphor. Depending on the subject matter, individuals cannot always be expected to express themselves with cogency or precision. Nor are an individual's beliefs fixed and static. The beliefs of every individual are prone to change over his lifetime. Overall, these threshold requirements should not be set at a level which would deprive minority beliefs of the protection they are intended to have under the Convention. [. . .]
>
> This leaves on one side the difficult question of the criteria to be applied in deciding whether a belief is to be characterised as religious. [But] the atheist, the agnostic, and the sceptic are as much entitled to freedom to hold and manifest their beliefs as the theist. These beliefs are placed on an equal footing for the purpose of this guaranteed freedom. Thus, if its manifestation is to attract protection under article 9, a non-religious belief, as much as a religious belief, must satisfy the modest threshold requirements implicit in this article. In particular, for its manifestation to be protected by Article 9, a non-religious belief must relate to an aspect of human life or behaviour of comparable importance to that normally found with religious beliefs.

So, first, what about the situation where a belief involves harming others? Is this a belief which does not qualify for protection when it is manifested in action? One issue raised

[14] R (Williamson) v Secretary of State for Education [2005] UKHL 15, [2005] 2 WLR 590 (paras 23–24).

by this is where there is the expression of a religious view which involves preaching that persons who belong to a different belief system should be the object of attack: here, freedom to manifest religion overlaps with freedom of speech, and we will consider this issue in that context.[15] Another example which involves consideration of a more direct infliction of harm is corporal punishment. First, the view of the European Court on those opposing corporal punishment.

In *Campbell and Cosans* v *UK*,[16] Mrs Campbell and Mrs Cosans each had children of school age attending state schools in Scotland, where, at the time, corporal punishment was used as a disciplinary measure. Mrs Campbell objected to this form of punishment, although her son was never punished in this way; Mrs Cosans' son refused to submit to a punishment and was suspended from school, and then denied readmission when his parents refused to accept the right of the school to administer corporal punishment. The European Court held that there had been a violation of 'religion and philosophical convictions' within the scope of Article 2. The Court said:

> Having regard to the Convention as a whole, including Article 17, the expression 'philosophical convictions' in the present context denotes, in the Court's opinion, such convictions as are worthy of respect in a 'democratic society' and are not incompatible with human dignity; in addition they must not conflict with the fundamental right of the child to education, the whole of Article 2 being dominated by its first sentence. The applicants' views relate to a weighty and substantial aspect of human life and behaviour, namely the integrity of the person, the propriety or otherwise of the infliction of corporal punishment and the exclusion of the distress which the risk of such punishment entails. They are views which satisfy each of the various criteria listed above; it is this that distinguishes them from opinions that might be held on other methods of discipline or on discipline in general.

But what about a belief in favour of corporal punishment? This was considered in the case of *Williamson*,[17] from which we quoted above.

Section 548 of the Education Act 1996 had removed the defence, previously available to teachers, that reasonable chastisement could be applied to pupils, and that if it was reasonable the teacher would not be guilty of assault. This section therefore meant that teachers naturally considered that they could no longer use corporal punishment, since they would be left open to a charge of assault. Some teachers and parents of children at certain Christian schools applied to the court for a ruling that the use of corporal punishment in independent schools had *not* been abolished by this section. These teachers and parents were in favour of corporal punishment; their argument was that physical discipline, admonished by teachers, was part of their Christian belief; but if that section had indeed abolished corporal punishment, that was a violation of their rights under Article 9 and Article 2.

The question of whether this belief qualified for protection was considered by the various judges who heard the case. The High Court and one of the Court of Appeal judges

---

[15] Below, pp. 306–7.
[16] (1982) 4 EHRR 293.
[17] *R (Williamson)* v *Secretary of State for Education* [2005] UKHL 15, [2005] 2 WLR 590.

had considered that the parents' view in favour of corporal punishment was not a religious conviction which warranted the protection of Article 9, because it involved violating the physical integrity of another person. The House of Lords rejected this view, considering that it was not so extreme as to fall outside the protection of Article 9. The Lords emphasised the range of views which are protected by Article 9: only quite an extreme view which involved harming others would fail to qualify for protection.

However, the House of Lords also considered that, although holding this belief was protected by Article 9, the actual manifestation of this belief could be limited by the rights of others, as it was in this case, by the rights of the children. The ban on corporal punishment was a justified and proportionate interference with that expression of a belief in the interests of protecting the welfare of the children involved. This was also part of a trend towards limiting corporal punishment – Lord Nicholls also referred to the Children Act 2004, which has restricted the extent to which parents may punish their own children.

So does any belief count? What about the threshold of importance?

In *Countryside Alliance v AG*,[18] there was a challenge to the statutory ban on hunting foxes with dogs[19] (and certain other forms of hunting) based on a number of Articles. The challenge failed on all grounds, but in reference to Article 9, the Divisional Court referred to *Williamson* on what is required for a belief to be protected under Article 9, in particular the references to the importance of the belief, and then considered whether being in favour of hunting met these criteria:[20]

> Not all opinions or convictions, however sincerely or deeply held, constitute beliefs in the sense protected by Article 9(1) of the [Convention]. The right to hunt with hounds does not have the necessary qualities identified [in *Williamson*] to qualify under Article 9. In particular, the claimants failed to persuade us that their belief in the right to hunt went beyond enjoyment of and dedication to a recreational pursuit. It cannot qualify as an aspect of human life or behaviour of comparable importance to that normally found with religious beliefs.

This shows that it will be a matter of evidence from case to case whether the view being put forward is sufficiently cogent to amount to a religious or philosophical belief, whether it relates to a sufficiently fundamental matter, whether it is capable of protection if it is being manifested, and whether it is that belief which is being manifested.

But it is worth stressing, as Lord Nicholls did in *Williamson*, that Article 9 also protects those who do not want any religious association at all, which echoes those words from *Kokkinakis*, which we quoted at the start of this chapter: the article is 'a precious asset for atheists, agnostics, sceptics and the unconcerned'. An example of this is the *Crawley Green Road Cemetery* case.[21]

---

[18] [2005] EWHC 1677 (Admin); also discussed above, p. 121 and p. 257; permission to appeal on Article 9 was refused so the point was not considered by the Court of Appeal or House of Lords: [2006] EWCA Civ 817.

[19] Hunting Act 2004.

[20] At paragraph 249.

[21] *In re Crawley Green Road Cemetery, Luton* [2001] 2 WLR 1175; we consider some more cases of freedom *not* to hold a religion below, p. 290.

Mrs S was the widow of J, and during their life together they had lived in Luton. When he died, his funeral had been conducted in the humanist tradition, but his ashes had been interred in consecrated ground at a cemetery in Luton, although neither S nor J had had any affinity with the Christian faith. Then S had moved to London. S now sought to have the ashes exhumed, so that they could be re-interred nearer her home. S told the court that if she had been aware that J's ashes had been interred in ground 'with church associations', she would have regarded it as hypocritical, and she would not have permitted it. The Church Consistory Court held that Article 9 encompassed religious beliefs such as humanism, which S sincerely held, and to refuse her would be in violation of the Article.

PRISONERS

Prisoners have human rights, including rights under Article 9, which they are entitled to exercise. But, as one might expect, prison rules may have priority. This was the situation in the case of *H v UK*.[22]

H was convicted by a court in the United Kingdom of common assault and sentenced to three years' imprisonment. In the prison where he was held, there was a policy that prisoners should spend time in the workshops, and H was told he should work in the print shop, but he refused, as he was a vegan, and he objected to working with products of animal origin, or products tested on animals – in this case the dyes in the print shop. He was disciplined for this refusal, and he complained to the European Court of a breach of Article 9.

His case came before the Commission, which agreed that veganism was a matter of conscience or belief, within Article 9. But the requirement that H should work in the print shop was a requirement which was justified under Article 9(2), as being 'prescribed by law', being provided for in the Prison Rules, which had the aim of good order in the prison. There had to be a system of allocation of work, which was fair and without favouritism, and so a prisoner could not enjoy a freedom of choice of employment. The system was a proportionate one, and there was no violation of Article 9.

Of course, one could not expect the prison authorities to act any differently in such a case, since the prison rules had to be observed, and did not allow for variations for individual prisoners. Nevertheless, even as against prisoners, it is important that such rules should still not interfere with rights except in a way which is proportionate, and should be enforced in a proportionate way, as the Commission found they were here.

CONSCIENTIOUS OBJECTORS

War, and the preparation for it, is in the eyes of many people objectionable, and one part of that objection is that it is contrary to a philosophy of peace, which may or may not be

[22] (1993) 16 EHRR CD 44.

founded on a religion or a faith; and 'conscientious objection' is a recognised belief or conviction. But the European Commission has said that conscientious objection is *not* recognised as a belief or conviction the manifestation of which is protected by Article 9. In the case of *Fadini* v *Switzerland*,[23] the Commission considered a claim that Article 9 had been violated in the case of Mr Fadini, who was required to carry out civil defence duty.

Mr Fadini, aged about 51, was required to report for compulsory civil defence duty, and in 1988, 1989 and 1991 he refused to report for duty, and was fined and imprisoned. His argument was that this civil defence duty was tantamount to the support of a war, and that his Christian conviction, which was against any form of violence, forbade him as a matter of conscience to participate in it. He therefore claimed that the punishment imposed on him by the state violated Article 9.

The Commission rejected his claim, holding that it was inadmissible; previous decisions of the Commission had held that conscientious objection to military service was not recognised as a right within Article 9, and by the same token an objection to civil defence duty could not be recognised.

Part of the reason for the Commission's view about conscientious objectors is that Article 4, which refers to compulsory labour, specifically allows for compulsory military service or the equivalent service in the case of conscientious objectors 'in countries where they are recognised': thus the Convention itself allows countries to decide whether or not to recognise the rights of conscientious objectors to be exempt from service (which is to say, they have a margin of appreciation).[24]

The position here has been considered in the case of *Khan* v *RAF*,[25] where the Divisional Court had to consider a claim to conscientious objection by a military reservist who was recalled, failed to report for duty because he objected to serving in Iraq, and was convicted of being absent without leave. The Court noted that if a reservist wished to make a claim to conscientious objection, there was a procedure for doing so, and that Mr Khan had not invoked this mechanism. This would be the correct way to manifest a claim to conscientious objection under Article 9, not by going absent without leave, so there was no interference with a manifestation of belief in his recall, arrest, prosecution or conviction.

In the UK, there is no compulsory military service, so people can choose whether or not to enlist, and, as *Khan* makes clear, they are entitled to change their view after they have signed up and register a conscientious objection, which will be respected. However, there is a situation where our courts are asked to allow conscientious objection, which is where someone wishes not to leave the country because they would have to perform military service in their own country. Usually, the law of another country is not something which our courts will rule on, including whether or not military service is compulsory, but they

---

[23] (1993) 16 EHRR CD 13.
[24] Introduced above, p. 54.
[25] *Khan* v *Royal Air Force Summary Appeal Court* [2004] EWHC 2230 (Admin).

will decline to deport someone if it can be shown that that military service is likely to involve acting in breach of the basic rules of human conduct, and that the person seeking asylum had a genuine fear that he would be punished for refusing to serve under those conditions.[26]

But the actual belief that war is wrong is a genuine belief which qualifies in principle for the protection of Article 9, even if a particular manifestation may not be permitted, or may be justifiably interfered with. This is clear from the next case, that of *Arrowsmith* v *UK*,[27] where the European Court agreed that there existed a genuine belief, but held that the state's action – a prosecution – was not in fact an interference with *that* belief, since it held that the complainant was not manifesting that belief when she was arrested and prosecuted.

> Miss Pat Arrowsmith, in September 1973, distributed leaflets at an Army centre in Warminster, where there were soldiers who were to be posted to Northern Ireland. The leaflets recounted views of ex-soldiers, and these leaflets advised the serving soldiers to go absent without leave, or to refuse to be posted to Northern Ireland. She was arrested near where the leaflets were being distributed. In May 1974, she was convicted of an offence under the Incitement to Disaffection Act 1934, and sentenced to a term of imprisonment. She was a convinced pacifist. She had campaigned in support of her views, and she was active in an organisation called the British Withdrawal from Northern Ireland Campaign.
>
> The European Commission held that pacifism, as a philosophy, *is* a belief within the scope of Article 9, and *is* therefore protected. But the question arose, was the *distribution* protected, as being the manifestation of that belief of pacifism? The leaflets emphasised the Northern Ireland question; the contents showed that the authors were opposed to the British policy in Northern Ireland. The leaflets did not express pacifist views. So, decided the Commission, her conviction and sentence did *not* interfere with the exercise of her pacifist views.

In one sense, this is an illustration of something obvious: to found a complaint of interference, the individual must show that the thing which suffered interference was the relevant belief or religion, and not something else, however nearly connected. Perhaps it is also a rather hard case: perhaps it would have made all the difference if Miss Arrowsmith had put at the top of the leaflets, 'In the name of pacifism'.

STATE REGULATION OF RELIGIOUS INSTITUTIONS

The Convention jurisprudence does not forbid or exclude the concept of a state church, that is, an official or established church, such as the Church of England. The fact that a state has established such a state church system does not violate Article 9. But a citizen must be free to join its membership, or to leave it. No one can be obliged to join it. Those are the

---

[26] *Krotov v Home Secretary* [2004] EWCA Civ 69, [2004] 1 WLR 1825; *Sepet v Home Secretary* [2003] UKHL 15, [2003] 1 WLR 856.
[27] (1981) 3 EHRR 218.

principles of the Convention, and they entirely reflect that attitude of pluralism which we mentioned earlier. And so we come to the case of *Darby* v *Sweden*,[28] which shows us how the European Commission regarded a state church and its tax laws.

Dr Peter Darby, a gentleman of British origin, and a Finnish citizen, was employed as a doctor by the Swedish State Railways, in Gavle, Sweden. He rented a flat in the town, but at weekends he lived with his family on the island of Lemland, in the Finnish archipelago of Åland. He was obliged to pay a special tax to the Lutheran Church of Sweden, which was the established church of Sweden. Membership of that church was reserved to Swedish citizens and to foreigners living in Sweden. Dr Darby was *not* a member of that church, and he complained that this tax violated his right to freedom of religion as guaranteed by Article 9.

The European Commission decided that there *was* a violation of Article 9. The Commission recognised that state church systems existed in several states that are parties to the Convention, and expressly stated that the fact that a state has established a state church system cannot in itself be considered to violate Article 9. But the Commission considered that, in order to satisfy the requirements of Article 9, a state church system must include specific safeguards for the individual's freedom of religion. It would be a breach of the Article for people to be forced to enter or be prohibited from leaving the church in question. And the Commission found that the obligation to pay a tax to the church was in effect an obligation to be a member of it, in breach of Article 9.[29]

This confirms the point we discussed above, that freedom of religion includes freedom not to hold a religion, including freedom to abstain from membership of a church and to abstain from its ceremonies, and that includes a state church.

Of course, sometimes state churches do embody an important aspect of national culture and history, and that will be relevant to the balance of whether an interference is justified.

In the case of *Kokkinakis*,[30] which we quoted earlier in this chapter, Mr Kokkinakis was a Greek national and a Jehovah's Witness, and he was invited into an Orthodox Christian's home and entered into a discussion with her; he talked of the articles of faith of the Jehovah's Witnesses sect, and sought to persuade her to join the Jehovah's Witnesses; the police were informed, and he was arrested, and convicted of the offence of proselytism, contrary to Greek law, and fined. He claimed that to prosecute him and convict him was a violation of his rights under Article 9 of the Convention.

The European Court recognised that the Christian Eastern Orthodox Church, which during nearly four centuries of foreign occupation symbolised the maintenance of Greek culture and the Greek language, took an active part in the Greek people's struggle for

---

[28] (1991) 13 EHRR 774.

[29] The European Court did not consider it necessary to decide the point under Article 9, since it found a violation of Article 14, the prohibition on discrimination, taken with Article 1 of the First Protocol: there was a discriminatory and unjustifiable difference of treatment between a resident and a non-resident in the application of a tax, which is a deprivation of property.

[30] (1994) 17 EHRR 397.

emancipation, to such an extent that Hellenism is to some extent identified with the Orthodox faith. But the Court held that by prosecuting and convicting him the state had interfered with Mr Kokkinakis's right to freedom to manifest his religion or belief; the Greek government had failed to show that the conviction was justified by any pressing social need.

Some states do grant recognition for various official and administrative purposes to religious bodies. Where they do so, it is important that this is done fairly and with respect for different religious views.

In the case of the *Supreme Holy Council Of The Muslim Community* v *Bulgaria*,[31] the European Court had to consider Bulgarian law's requirement that all those members of a particular religion willing to participate in the community's organisation should form a single governing structure, for administrative convenience. This had the consequence that different religious groups within the Muslim community of Bulgaria effectively had to compete to be the official leadership. The Court held that this was an interference with Article 9. It is not for the state to take *any* role in organising the leadership of religious groups, and certainly not necessary for the state to bring such groups under a unified leadership. The role of the state is to remain impartial as between religious groups and simply ensure that all have the opportunity to maintain their own practice. The requirement of a single religious leadership was not necessary in a democratic society for the protection of public order or the rights and freedoms of others; on the contrary, a democratic society requires pluralism and tolerance.

Another case is that of the *Religious Community of Jehovah's Witnesses* v *Austria*.[32] The complaint here was about the Austrian authorities' refusal to recognise Jehovah's Witnesses as a religious society, which involved giving them legal personality, so that they could exist as a form of corporate body. The European Court held that a delay of about 20 years in the grant of legal personality was a breach of Article 9 (on its own and as a form of discrimination in breach of Article 14). The requirement of state recognition of religious denominations pursued a legitimate aim, and allowed the religious groups to claim certain privileges, such as in respect of taxation, but it was necessary for the state authorities to act neutrally and impartially in the process of recognising such groups. Where, as here, the religious group was well-established and familiar, there was no justification for making it wait for many years for state recognition.

But it will not necessarily be a breach of Article 9 to treat different manifestations of religious belief differently. In *Gallagher* v *Church of Jesus Christ of Latter-Day Saints*,[33] the House of Lords had to consider a provision that 'places of public religious worship' are exempt from non-domestic rates. A Mormon Temple argued that it was the subject of religious discrimination because it was not exempt. The House of Lords rejected this. The

---

[31] (2005) 41 EHRR 3.
[32] (2009) 48 EHRR 17.
[33] [2008] UKHL 56, [2008] 1 WLR 1852.

reason why it was not exempt from rates was because it was not open to the public. The exemption of *public* places of worship was general and not directed at any particular groups: it was entirely up to different religious groups whether their places of worship should be open to the public or not.

 ## SECTION 13 OF THE ACT

> **Section 13** (1)   If a court's determination of any question arising under this Act might affect the exercise by a religious organisation (itself or its members collectively) of the Convention right to freedom of thought, conscience and religion, it must have particular regard to the importance of that right.

We have been discussing aspects of a state church and how Article 9 may be engaged. This is a convenient moment to mention section 13 of the Human Rights Act 1998 which refers to the rights of religious organisations generally. This section upholds and strengthens the Article 9 rights of a religious organisation and its members. It was inserted in the Act because concern was expressed, by a cross-section of society – religious leaders, the public and Members of Parliament – that the exercise of the Convention rights of others would damage the Article 9 rights of religious organisations and their members. And so the section was inserted. It requires the courts to 'have particular regard' to the importance of the Article 9 rights.

In the debates on the Act, the (then) Home Secretary gave assurances that the purpose of this section was to protect the religious organisations and their members: 'the new clause will send a clear signal to the courts that they must pay due regard to the rights guaranteed by Article 9, including, where relevant, the right of a Church to act in accordance with religious belief'.[34] And further, 'It is to reassure them against the [Act] being used to intrude upon genuinely religious beliefs or practices based on their beliefs. I emphasise the word "practices", as well as "beliefs".' The Home Secretary gave an example: 'The right of the Church, which we intend to strengthen, to refuse to marry divorced people remains protected by the Convention.' The Home Secretary's example shows how doctrinal beliefs and practices are preserved. He chose an example from the practice of the established Church, the Church of England; but it must be emphasised that section 13 extends to *any* religious organisation.

 ## FREEDOM NOT TO HOLD A BELIEF

The principle of *Darby*'s case is that there can be no obligation on a person to join a church or to pay deference to it. However, the protection provided by Article 9 goes further than this. Freedom to hold a belief means freedom *not* to hold a belief: there can be no obligation to hold a belief, or to swear by a belief, or to bow to it. That is the principle of the

---

[34]   Rt Hon. Jack Straw MP, House of Commons debates, 20 May 1998 (*Hansard* HC, Vol. 312, cols 1021–1024).

Convention, as shown in this next case of *Buscarini* v *San Marino*,[35] where members of a Parliament were obliged to swear on religious texts, contrary to their consciences.

Mr Buscarini, Mr Della Balda, and Mr Manzaroli were elected in 1993 to the General Grand Council (the Parliamentary body) of the Republic of San Marino. They asked permission to take the oath required by the Election Act, without making reference to any religious text. The Act prescribed the words of the oath as being 'I . . . swear on the Holy Gospels ever to be faithful to and obey the Constitution of the Republic . . .' At the General Grand Council session they took the oath, in writing, without reference to the Gospels, but the secretariat advised that this was invalid, and the General Grand Council resolved that they should retake the oath, on the Gospels, or else forfeit their parliamentary seats. They took the oath on the Gospels, albeit complaining that their right to freedom of religion and conscience had been infringed. The European Court agreed that this was in violation of their rights:

> That freedom entails, *inter alia*, freedom to hold or not to hold religious beliefs and to practise or not to practise a religion [. . .] In the instant case, requiring Mr. Buscarini and Mr. Della Balda to take an oath on the Gospels did indeed constitute a limitation within the meaning of the second paragraph of Article 9, since it required them to swear allegiance to a particular religion on pain of forfeiting their parliamentary seats. [. . .] Requiring the applicants to take the oath on the Gospels was tantamount to requiring two elected representatives of the people to swear allegiance to a particular religion, in a requirement which is not compatible with Article 9. [. . .] It would be contradictory to make the exercise of a mandate intended to represent different views of society within Parliament subject to a prior declaration of commitment to a particular set of beliefs.

Buscarini is an important case; there are institutions in the United Kingdom where the individual is obliged to attend an assembly, or to join in a ceremony which has some religious overtone – such as the pronouncement of a Grace – and which is objectionable to some persons attending it. And there may be occasions when one is obliged to take an oath which offends a conscientious belief. Another example is *Alexandridis* v *Greece*,[36] where the European Court held that a procedure which required the taking of an oath by a civil servant infringed Article 9 because the procedure required the applicant to specifically object to the oath. It was a breach of the freedom *not* to manifest religion to require someone to act in a way which enabled conclusions to be drawn about their religious belief.

The converse can also be true: if a particular environment is kept secular, then persons with religious convictions may be limited in their rights to object to this. This can apply to uniforms, or to work times or practices: in the case of *Copsey*,[37] an employee did not want to work on Sundays for religious reasons. The Court of Appeal held that Article 9 did not limit the power of an employer to set work times, so long as this was not being done for discriminatory reasons, since the employee was free to resign from the job to manifest his belief.[38]

---

[35] (2000) 30 EHRR 208.
[36] *Alexandridis* v *Greece* [2008] (app 19516/06).
[37] *Copsey* v *WWB Devon Clays Ltd* [2005] EWCA Civ 932, [2005] ICR 1789.
[38] Discrimination, victimisation or harassment on the basis of religion or belief in employment and vocational training is unlawful by reason of the Employment Equality (Religion or Belief) Regulations 2003 (SI 2003/1660).

CRITICISM

If the individual 'manifests' their belief or religion, they must expect the possibility of criticism; that is the approach of the European Court. There is no right to be exempt from criticism. This was clear in the case of *Otto-Preminger Institute* v *Austria*.[39]

> The Institute announced a series of public showings of a satirical film, with a religious subject matter, *The Council in Heaven*. It was a satirical tragedy, set in heaven, with trivial imagery and absurdities pointed at the Christian creed, and being a caricature of the Christian faith, and disparaging it. The Austrian Court found that it was an abusive attack on the Roman Catholic religion according to the conception of the Tyrolean public. The film was seized and forfeited, and the manager of the Institute complained that this was a violation of Article 10, the right of freedom of expression.
>
> The European Court held that the Austrian authorities had been justified in seizing the film, and the case is principally concerned with Article 10. But the Court turned to consider the attack on the religion of the Austrian public, and how far the freedom of religion carried with it the obligation to put up with criticism. The Court said,
>
>> Those who choose to exercise the freedom to manifest their religion, irrespective of whether they do so as members of a religious majority or minority, cannot reasonably expect to be exempt from all criticism. They must tolerate and accept the denial by others of their religious beliefs and even the propagation by others of doctrines hostile to their faith. However, the manner in which religious beliefs and doctrines are opposed or denied is a matter which may engage the responsibility of the State, notably its responsibility to ensure the peaceful enjoyment of the right guaranteed under Article 9 to the holders of those beliefs and doctrines.

Thus, criticism must be tolerated, since that is a fundamental part of living in a plural society, but such criticism must not be gratuitously offensive. You need not share the beliefs or views of others, but you should not be needlessly insulting to them; and you should respect the rights of others to hold beliefs with which you disagree. We will discuss in the context of Article 10 and freedom of speech the recent Racial and Religious Hatred Act 2006, which outlaws inciting religious hatred. One of the difficulties with this law is that it does not intend to outlaw criticism or dislike of a religion, but there is a grey area between criticising those who profess a particular religion for their views and attempts to stir up hatred against a religious group.[40]

RESPECT FOR BELIEFS IN EDUCATION

As we have already mentioned, one aspect of the right to respect for the beliefs of others is the right to respect for religious and philosophical convictions in education protected by Article 2. Where the education of children is concerned, the religious and philosophical convictions of parents must be respected; we have seen how the European Court has applied this in the case of *Campbell and Cosans*.[41] But what does the word 'respect' mean in

---

[39] (1995) 19 EHRR 34.
[40] See p. 292, below.
[41] (1982) 4 EHRR 293, above, p. 283.

this context? The answer is that the use of the word respect has been understood to import a balancing exercise, and proportionality in any interference with religious convictions, such as is implicit in Article 9(2). But there is still a positive requirement to respect the religious convictions of parents – as opposed to merely taking them into account.

In the case of *Kjeldsen, Busk Madsen and Pedersen* v *Denmark*,[42] the three sets of applications were six parents who had children of school age, and who objected to compulsory sex education in state schools; they could not educate the children at private schools, nor at home themselves. They argued that this compulsory sex education was contrary to the beliefs they held as Christian parents, and that the state had failed to accord respect to their religious or philosophical convictions in this regard.

The European Court held that the parents had religious and philosophical convictions, which came within Article 9; but the policy of this sex education did *not* offend them to the extent forbidden by the second sentence of Article 2, so there was no violation. First, the Court made it clear that under Convention law the state is forbidden to indoctrinate its citizens – in the sense of imposing a particular religious or moral lesson, or making it paramount; that was *not* suggested in this case. On the other hand, Article 2 does not prevent the state from importing, through teaching or education, information or knowledge of a directly or indirectly religious or philosophical kind – provided it does so in an objective critical and pluralistic way. In the present case, the Court took account of the fact that although the education involved considerations of a moral order, these were very general in character. So the education did not fail to respect the convictions of the parents who brought the complaint.

On the other hand, in *Zengin* v *Turkey*,[43] the European Court did find a breach of Article 2. Mr Zengin and his family practised a branch of Islam called Alevism, which is widespread in Turkey. The breach was that religious education in Turkey, and the textbooks used at the early stages of religious education, were focused specifically on the Sunni branch of Islam, with some teaching about the Alevi faith only at older stages. This failed to meet the criteria of objectivity and pluralism necessary for education in a democratic society. There was also no scope for Muslim students to be excused from religious classes; and in any event, religious education should be general and not aimed only at the practice of a specific religion.

Again in *Folgerø* v *Norway*,[44] the European Court upheld a complaint by some parents who were humanists about there being compulsory lessons which covered Christianity, religion and philosophy where exemption was possible only from parts. The lessons were intended to cover various faiths and intended to promote understanding and respect for Christian and humanist values, which was consistent with the principles of pluralism and objectivity embodied in Article 2. However, the predominant position given to Christianity prevented the goal of promoting understanding, respect and dialogue between those of different faiths. The limited scope for exclusion from these lessons, and the need for parents to justify such exclusion, was not sufficient to remedy this, given the intrusive nature of the justification required which was not consistent with Article 2.

---

[42] (1976) 1 EHRR 711.
[43] *Zengin* v *Turkey* (2008) 46 EHRR 44.
[44] *Folgerø* v *Norway* (2008) 46 EHRR 47.

15

Freedom of conscience

The Court in *Kjeldsen* stressed that the respect which is due from the state under Article 9 applies to the whole field of the state's functions in relation to education and training; it is not limited to religious instruction, but is required throughout the entire educational curriculum.

In a country such as the United Kingdom, where society is multi-ethnic, this duty on the state – of respect in education – is becoming more important. This appears in the next case of *K v Newham London Borough Council*.[45]

K was a parent of a girl of secondary school age. The local authority's policy was that parents were entitled to express a preference, and that a preference for a single-sex school was one of several considerations, which would be taken into account when deciding where a child would be placed. K had stated a preference for a single-sex school on the basis of being a devout Muslim. The local authority had decided that the girl would *not* be given a place at a single-sex school, and an appeal from this decision was refused. These decisions did not mention religious grounds, but stated that the decision was on the basis of efficient use of resources. K sought judicial review of the decisions in the High Court.

The High Court quashed the decisions, as being in violation of Article 2. The Court held that K's religious convictions were genuine; and they came within the meaning of Article 2. There is an obligation under the Article to recognise and take into account the religion of the parent, and the application book, provided to the parent, should have had space for this, but did not do so; the decisions had therefore been taken without the respect required by Article 2. The local authority should have taken positive steps to ensure that the religious beliefs and reasons of the parents were sought and recorded so that they could at least be considered when the decision as to placement was made.

However, this does not mean that a parent has the right to insist on a particular form of education, or education at a particular school.

In the case of O,[46] it was argued that where a religious school refused to admit a pupil on the grounds that its classes were full, this was a breach of Article 2, and also of Article 8, the right to family life, since the pupil already had a sister at the school.

The Administrative Court held that there was no breach of these rights: Article 2 did not confer any absolute right to admission to a particular school, and other considerations could also affect whether or not a pupil was allowed entry; and Article 8 did not require admission to the same school as a sibling. The requirements of the Articles were met because the school's admissions policy did have a sibling criterion, so the point would be considered when the decision was made.

THE SCOPE OF ARTICLE 2

It is important to note that Article 2 does not provide a positive right to education. This was not necessary because when the Convention was drawn up, all parties to it had education

---

[45] *R (K) v Newham London Borough Council* [2002] EWHC 405 (Admin), Times 28.2.02.
[46] *R (O) v J Roman Catholic Primary School Appeal Panel* (2001) LTL 22.10.01.

systems. What it does is require that no one shall be denied access to such education systems as exist, not that there is a positive right to any particular type of education.[47] It is in that context that respect is required for the parents' religious and philosophical convictions; that is another reason why Article 2 cannot be used to ensure education in accordance with any particular preference. Thus, where a person is unlawfully excluded from school, that will engage Article 2, but only if they are entirely excluded from the provision of education, and not just because they have been excluded from a particular school. This was the decision in the case of *Ali* v *Lord Grey School*: there was no breach of Article 2 where a child was excluded from his school because of suspected involvement in an arson attack, since he was not excluded from the provision of education, just from one particular school.[48] Likewise in *A* v *Essex County Council*,[49] there was no breach of Article 2 where there was difficulty placing a pupil who was severely disabled in an appropriate school because of the issues arising from their particular needs.

However, although the second sentence of Article 2 is phrased in terms of parents, it would be misleading to assume that the right of access to education applies only to children, or, at any rate, young students. The first sentence refers to the right to education of *every* person; this will include mature students.[50] Article 2 also extends to ensuring fairness in the provision of education, which includes how exams are dealt with: in a case where a student had passed his exams after a history of poor results, and as a result the exam board had annulled his results and refused to allow him to proceed to the next stage of his studies, the European Court found a breach of Article 2 in that there was no proper basis for this decision, since there was no evidence of cheating or other impropriety.[51]

RESERVATION TO ARTICLE 2

UK Reservation:
At the time of signing the present (First) Protocol, I declare that, in view of certain provisions of the Education Acts in the United Kingdom, the principle affirmed in the second sentence of Article 2 is accepted by the United Kingdom only so far as it is compatible with the provision of efficient instruction and training, and the avoidance of unreasonable public expenditure. Dated 20 March 1952 Made by the United Kingdom Permanent Representative to the Council of Europe.

The above is the Reservation entered by the United Kingdom with regard to Article 2.[52] The key provision is that the principle affirmed in the second sentence of Article 2 is accepted only so far as it is compatible with the provision of efficient instruction and training, and the avoidance of unreasonable public expenditure.

---

[47] *Belgian Linguistics* case (1979–80) 1 EHRR 241 and 252, considered above in the context of Article 14, p. 122.
[48] *Ali* v *Lord Grey School* [2006] UKHL 14, [2006] 2 WLR 690 (Article engaged but no entitlement to damages for unlawful exclusion).
[49] [2008] EWCA Civ 364, (2008) HRLR 31.
[50] *R (Douglas)* v *North Tyneside MBC* [2003] EWCA 1847, [2004] 1 WLR 2363: higher education covered by Article 2, but loan arrangements for mature students were not.
[51] *Eren* v *Turkey* (2007) 44 EHRR 28.
[52] The effect of a reservation is discussed above, p. 113.

The reason for this Reservation was that, at the time the Convention was signed by the United Kingdom, there was a concern that this right might not be complied with by the Education Act then in force,[53] which governed the rights to education. The Reservation still applies, although the European Commission has expressed the view that this Reservation may be questioned.[54] However, since Article 2 does not specify what sort of education the state should provide, the Reservation does not undermine the effect of the main right, since it does not inhibit access to *an* education; it is simply a further factor in considering whether the views of the parents as to the *type* of education have been respected: the United Kingdom does not accept that this requirement for respect of parents' convictions can entail unreasonable public expenditure or an inefficient use of resources. If these factors alone mean that a certain sort of education is not available, then the fact that the result may be a lack of respect for a parent's convictions should not amount to a breach of the Convention right. This is likely to be part of the proportionality calculation in any event; but, of course, when the Reservation was entered, the Court had not come into being, so none of the cases which developed the way the Court approaches such questions had been decided.

QUESTIONS

1 Freedom of conscience: are there any views which you would consider should not be protected as 'beliefs'? Do you agree that not all manifestations of beliefs should qualify for protection?

2 The right to education: should there be a positive right? You may like to compare Article 2 with Article 26 of the Universal Declaration of Human Rights (in Appendix 4), which does include a positive right to education, and goes into rather more detail, including requiring compulsory and free elementary education.

[53] Education Act 1944, see now section 9 of Education Act 1996.
[54] *SP* v *UK* (1997) 23 EHRR CD 139.

Speaker's Corner in Hyde Park, London, where anyone has been allowed to express freely any view about anything since 1872.

Source: Robinsa Aaron Robinson (50/50)/PA Photos

16 Freedom of expression

Nothing is more apt to surprise a foreigner, than the extreme liberty, which we enjoy in this country, of communicating whatever we please to the public, and of openly censuring every measure, entered into by the king or his ministers. (David Hume, *Essays Moral, Political, and Literary*, 1875)

Article 10: Freedom of Expression
1 Everyone has the right to freedom of expression. This right shall include freedom to hold opinions and to receive and impart information and ideas without interference by public authority and regardless of frontiers. This Article shall not prevent States from requiring the licensing of broadcasting, television or cinema enterprises.
2 The exercise of these freedoms, since it carries with it duties and responsibilities, may be subject to such formalities, conditions, restrictions or penalties as are prescribed by law and are necessary in a democratic society, in the interests of national security, territorial integrity or public safety, for the prevention of disorder or crime, for the protection of health or morals, for the protection of the reputation or rights of others, for preventing the disclosure of information received in confidence, or for maintaining the authority and impartiality of the judiciary.

FREE SPEECH

'The freedom of expression constitutes one of the essential foundations of a democratic society, one of the basic conditions for its progress and for the development of every man.'[1] Those are words of high principle, spoken by the European Court. They reflect the attitude of judges and statesmen, in many societies and nations, who emphasise the right of freedom of speech.

'Free speech', the words of the heading above, is a phrase used regularly: 'It's a free country', 'I can say what I like'. Article 10 certainly protects the right of free speech: but it also provides a good deal more. 'Expression' covers human activity beyond mere speech, and we shall see in this chapter what means of expression have come within the Article. Furthermore, the words of Article 10(1) are not limited to expression; they provide also a right to *receive* information.

[1] *Handyside v UK* (1979–80) 1 EHRR 737.

The judges of our courts, even before the incorporation of the Convention, recognised the right to freedom of expression. In one case, Mr Justice Laws (as he then was) in the High Court said:

> There is a general principle in our law that the expression of opinion and the conveyance of information will not be restrained by the courts, save on pressing grounds. Freedom of expression is as much a sinew of the common law as it is of the European Convention.[2]

In that case the Advertising Standards Authority had compiled a report criticising Vernons Pools, and Vernons applied to the court for an order preventing publication; the judge refused the order. These words were spoken long before the incorporation of the Convention. Note the description of the freedom of expression as a 'sinew' of the law, meaning an essential part of the common law, and a working part.

But undoubtedly the Convention has added something to the previous law: there are cases in our courts which have been decided with the Convention principles in mind, especially in the exercise of dealing with situations where there is a conflict of rights – particularly where there is a dispute over whether publication of material about someone would infringe their privacy, which we will discuss below.

 ## THE SCOPE OF THE FREEDOM

The question is this: how far may one go; how outrageous or how offensive may the content of your 'expression' be? What kind of material is actually protected by Article 10? The answer has been given by the European Court, again in *Handyside*,[3] which we quoted earlier.

Mr Handyside had published and distributed to schools and colleges a booklet entitled *The Little Red Schoolbook* which contained offensive and obscene material. It was intended to be read by schoolchildren and adolescents. He was prosecuted and convicted of distributing an obscene publication. The European Court found that the prosecution and conviction of Mr Handyside were indeed interferences with his right to impart information and ideas, within the meaning of Article 10(1). The Court in fact held that the interference was justified under Article 10(2) for the protection of morals; but the key statement of principle for our purposes is that, although the material was offensive, he had a right to publish it. The Court said:

> Subject to Article 10(2), [Article 10] is applicable not only to single 'information' or 'ideas' that are favourably received or regarded as inoffensive or a matter of indifference, but also to those that offend, shock or disturb the State or any section of the population. Such are the demands of that pluralism, tolerance and broad-mindedness without which there is no 'democratic society'.

[2] *R v Advertising Standards Authority, ex parte Vernons Organisation* [1992] 1 WLR 1289 at 1293.
[3] (1979–80) 1 EHRR 737; see also above, p. 55.

This includes the key idea of pluralism, which echoes what the European Court has said about the right to freedom of conscience and belief in Article 9. This is perfectly appropriate: freedom of expression and freedom to manifest one's belief will overlap, because the value of freedom of expression is to express what one believes. However, the focus with Article 10 is on the expression, how far one is allowed to express oneself, as opposed to the underlying belief. This will raise questions such as how far expression should be limited, if ever, if what is being said is offensive or objectionable; for example, if it is threatening, sexist, racist or pornographic. An overlapping question is how far one may be allowed to disseminate information, and this will involve considering questions such as whether this should be restricted if the information is false, or if it is confidential.

Some of these questions will be considered in our discussion of Article 10(2) below, which imposes certain limitations on the right set out in Article 10(1). However, there is one further limitation, which is worth referring to at the outset, and that is the limitation contained in Article 17.[4] This removes the protection of the Convention from those seeking to use rights, such as the right to freedom of expression, to engage in any activity or perform any act aimed at the destruction of the Convention rights. What it is important to realise is that this does not simply refer to arguments or statements which are objectionable.

So, for example, in the case of *Lehideux* v *France*,[5] a statement which was sympathetic to an individual who had been convicted of collaboration with the Nazis, the French Vichy leader, Marshal Petain, did not fall outside the protection of Article 10, since it was not expressing a pro-Nazi policy but was part of a historical debate. But the European Court was quite clear that statements seeking to justify a pro-Nazi policy or denying the Holocaust would not enjoy the protection of Article 10, because of Article 17. Such positions and statements take themselves outside Article 10, not because they are not genuinely held, but because the Convention rights are not there to protect those who wish to attack fundamentally the values on which it is based; and the Nazi regime is an example of one which clearly did not conform to even the basic standards of morality.

Freedom of expression

TYPES OF EXPRESSION

Expression clearly includes speech and the written word. It would also extend to painting, drawing and sculpture, the making of a television or radio programme or film, or even advertising:[6] these are all forms of expression. Or someone who wishes to express themselves may do it by their actions. Sometimes this will be something we might think of as artistic, such as acting in a play, cultivating a garden, using craft skills to make something. Or it may be a pastime: indulging in a hobby such as a sport or collecting something may be a means of self-expression.

But self-expression may be more political. Taking part in a protest, and simply being at a particular place, may be a means of expression, and a means of exercising the right under Article 10. This is a more contentious area, because it is in such situations that the expression of a view, or a position, or a loyalty, may reach the point where it threatens to, or does, interfere with the rights of others.

---

[4] Discussed in more detail above, p. 118.
[5] (2000) 30 EHRR 665; see also above, p. 129.
[6] *Krone Verlag GmbH* v *Austria* (2006) 42 EHRR 28.

This is what happened in the case of *Steel v UK*,[7] which concerned several protesters, at different places, who were arrested as they carried out their protests. One of them, as part of a protest against a grouse shoot, walked in front of an armed member of the shoot, thus physically preventing him from firing. Another, taking part in a protest against the building of a motorway extension, placed herself in front of machinery in order to impede the engineering works. Others, at the Queen Elizabeth Conference Centre in Westminster, where a 'Fighter Helicopter II' Conference was being held, protested against the sale of fighter helicopters, and handed out leaflets and held up banners. Each of them was arrested for a breach of the peace, and was convicted. They each complained to the European Court that their conviction was a violation of Article 10.

The European Court found that indeed they had been exercising their right of expression, and that it had been violated by being stopped, and by the prosecution. Although the Court considered that the convictions were, in the circumstances, not a disproportionate interference with the right, the important point is that their freedom of expression by way of protest was recognised as coming within Article 10.

The same applies to the case of *Hashman and Harrup v UK*.[8] The applicants acted to try to disrupt the activities of the Portman Hunt; they blew a hunting horn and engaged in hallooing, so that hounds were drawn towards them, and the hunt staff had to be deployed to recover the hounds. They also were convicted of breaches of the peace, and complained to the European Court. Here too, the Court held that they also were exercising their right of freedom of expression. The Court did not consider whether the interference was justified, because it was held not to be 'prescribed by law', given the uncertainty relating to the order made against the applicants.[9]

THE RIGHT TO RECEIVE INFORMATION

It is not really surprising that part of Article 10(1) is the right to **receive** and **impart** information: a right to impart information is of no use unless there is a right for others to receive that information. The wish to express something is accompanied by the right to hear it: without both sides of this coin, there can be no debate, and without debate, the Article would fail to protect the pluralism that is at the heart of this freedom.

A newspaper's claim that it has a right to publish information is also a claim that its readers have a right to receive it. But there may be countervailing considerations: governments or other public authorities may wish to keep something secret; yet the public, on the other hand, may wish to know about it. The principle of Article 10(1) is that access should not be denied to information that is being freely provided, and which is intended to be read. However, the right to receive information does not provide a right to freedom of information as such: it does not provide a positive right to be given information or to access to information. The following case is one where the European Court held that the individual had no right to receive information, in the particular circumstances of the case.

[7] (1999) 28 EHRR 603; for discussion in the context of Article 5, see above, p. 182.
[8] (2000) 30 EHRR 241.
[9] Discussed above, p. 183.

302

The case was *Leander* v *Sweden*.[10] Mr Leander was a carpenter by occupation, and applied for employment as a museum technician with the National Naval Museum. This involved access to certain sensitive areas. He was refused employment, after the authorities had considered secret information about him. He contended that he had a right to receive the information, and complained to the European Court.

The European Court held that Article 10 did not, in the circumstances of the case, confer on Mr Leander a right of access to the register which contained information on his personal position; the Court found that there was no violation of either Article 10 or Article 8 (respect for privacy). The Court carried out a balance of the circumstances in the case, especially bearing in mind what particular protections the state had put in place for supervising and monitoring the recording of information about employees; the Court came to the view that the citizen was sufficiently protected.

However, that is not to say that in an appropriate case there may not be a justification for access to personal files, or other information. A good example where there may be a clear public interest in access to information is where there has been a public emergency of some sort, or serious crime, and there is a clear public interest in what has happened, which may fall within the right to receive information. The following are examples of cases where what has been sought is that an inquiry into such a matter should be conducted in public.

The first case, *Wagstaff*,[11] concerned a decision to set up an inquiry following the conviction of Dr Harold Shipman for the murder of 15 of his patients. The inquiry was announced, to be chaired by Lord Laming, and the decision was that it should be held in private.

The Divisional Court held that this decision, to hold the inquiry in private, was in breach of Article 10. The reasons for holding the inquiry in private – reasons of efficiency and speed, and that witnesses might feel more free to speak in private – did not outweigh the public interest in the conduct of a medical practice, and in the question whether there had been appropriate controls and supervision. There was a breach of Article 10 because there was an interference with the reception of information which others were willing to impart.

Another case raising the same point was *Persey*.[12] In August 2001, the Secretary of State set up inquiries into the outbreak of foot and mouth disease, with the evidence to be received in private. The applicants, who were farmers, veterinary surgeons, hoteliers and media organisations applied for a court order that the Lessons Learned Inquiry should be conducted in public, because to hold it in private violated Article 10 of the Convention. They contended that an open public inquiry would restore public confidence in the government's handling of the crisis.

The Divisional Court rejected this argument. The central point of the judgment is this: Article 10 guarantees freedom of expression, and not access to information. It imposes no positive duty on a government to provide an open forum to achieve wider dissemination of views than exists already. For this reason, the Court considered that it was different from *Wagstaff*.

[10] (1987) 9 EHRR 433.
[11] *R (Wagstaff)* v *Secretary of State for Health* [2001] 1 WLR 292.
[12] *R (Persey)* v *Secretary of State for Environment, Food and Rural Affairs* [2002] EWHC 371 (Admin), [2002] 3 WLR 704.

However, what should be noted is that all citizens now have the ability to seek a wide range of official information by using the Freedom of Information Act 2000, which, although it does not allow access to *all* official information, is extremely wide-ranging. People also have rights to see information which is stored about them personally under the Data Protection Act 1998, to ensure that it is correct and so they know what is on their records. Again this right has limits, but again it is very wide-ranging. Thus, although the Convention rights do not protect access to information, there are other statutes which do so – and these could be said also to be giving effect to a basic right in a democratic society, since, without information, informed debate is not possible. Especially in an age when information can be stored and transferred so easily in vast quantity, regulation of information becomes important – both ensuring it is accessible where possible, and ensuring it is not misused.

RESTRICTIONS ON FREEDOM OF EXPRESSION

Article 10(2) is the only one of the sets of express qualifications to one of the Convention rights which expressly refers to the freedoms carrying with them **duties** and **responsibilities**, as well as setting out the interests which can justify an interference with the right. This is important: the duties and responsibilities upon the person or body who wishes to exercise their right to freedom of expression must be brought into the balance. The European Court has considered these words, for example in the case of *Handyside* again:

> Whoever exercises his freedom of expression undertakes 'duties and responsibilities' the scope of which depends on his situation and the technical means he uses. The Court cannot overlook such a person's 'duties' and 'responsibilities' when it enquires, as in this case, whether 'restrictions' or 'penalties' were conducive to the protection of morals which made them 'necessary' in a 'democratic society'.

In other words, Mr Handyside had duties and responsibilities as a publisher, since he had the power to reach a wide audience by his ability to print and publish and distribute. Those duties and responsibilities were relevant when it came to judging whether the interference with his Article 10 rights was proportionate.

Article 10(2) also includes the familiar phrase, 'prescribed by law', with its meaning that the law should be clear, foreseeable and precise:[13] this was where the state's case failed in the case of *Hashman*, discussed above. Then there is the list of grounds which may justify an interference with the right, so long as they are necessary in a democratic society and proportionate in extent. These include grounds found in comparable paragraphs of other articles, such as national security, the prevention of disorder or crime, and the protection of health or morals. It also includes some purposes which are specific to freedom of expression: preventing the disclosure of information received in confidence, which as we will see gives rise to a significant conflict of rights for the press; the protection of the reputation or rights of others; and maintaining the authority and impartiality of the judiciary.

All these grounds are already reflected in our law, which contains a variety of limitations on the right of freedom of speech, but which in principle fall within the grounds for interference in Article 10(2), depending on how they are applied in practice. Thus, there is the

---

[13] This idea is discussed above, p. 116.

law of defamation, which protects reputation from libel and slander. There are laws forbidding obscenity and certain forms of pornography, which are grounded in protecting the rights of others, especially children. The authority and impartiality of the judiciary is protected by the law of contempt of court, which, for example, prohibits the publication of information which is designed to influence improperly the outcome of a trial. It is an offence to incite another person to commit a crime or to incite racial hatred, or to use speech to foment disorder or racial divisions; all of this again is aimed at protecting the rights of others. Each of those laws will in proper circumstances fall within the 'conditions, restrictions or penalties' allowed by Article 10(2).

The courts have now had to consider a large number of these sorts of situations where different sorts of limitations on freedom of speech have had to be considered. First, a number of cases where the courts have held that the interference was justified:

■ Official secrets: in the case of *Shayler*,[14] the House of Lords held that the Official Secrets Act 1989, which limits the disclosure of documents in the interests of national security, was a justified interference with Article 10. There, a former spy alleged that the disclosures he had made were in the public interest. The Lords held that there was no such defence to the Act, but this was reasonable because there were safeguards built in, which, if properly applied, were sufficient to ensure that unlawfulness and irregularity could be reported to those who could take effective action to deal with them, that the power to withhold authorisation was not abused and that proper disclosures were not stifled. Thus there was no incompatibility with Article 10 (the same applied when the magazine *Punch* was prosecuted for contempt of court in printing material in breach of the Official Secrets Act).[15]

■ Contempt of court: in *Attorney General v Scotcher*,[16] the House of Lords held that there was no breach of Article 10 in a juror being in contempt of court for disclosing the details of jury deliberations after the trial had concluded – there had been the opportunity to do so to the judge before the end of the trial, so it was not required for the fairness of the trial process.

■ Harassment: in the case of *Silverton v Gravett*,[17] the claimants were a company, including its directors and their families, that sold furs. Their complaint was that they were being harassed by animal rights activists opposed to the selling of furs, mainly at the company's premises, but also at one of the director's homes. There had been damage to windows, offensive letters and material, obstruction of customers, and the directors' home addresses had been published. The High Court considered that, in such a situation, the claimants were entitled to the protection of the law from harassment and any interference with Article 10 was justified to prevent disorder or crime or to protect the reputation or rights of others. Likewise, in a case of someone flying offensive banners and conducting secret surveillance, the interference with Article 10 by the grant of an injunction was justified,[18] and the same applied to a conviction under the Malicious

---

[14] *R v Shayler* [2002] UKHL 11, [2003] 1 AC 247.
[15] *Attorney General v Punch* [2002] UKHL 50, [2003] 1 AC 1046.
[16] [2005] UKHL 36, [2005] 1 WLR 1867.
[17] (2001) LTL 31.10.01.
[18] *Howlett v Holding* [2006] EWHC 41 (QB), Times 8.2.06.

Communications Act 1988 where an anti-abortion campaigner sent photographs of aborted foetuses to pharmacists selling the morning-after pill.[19]

■ Insulting behaviour: in *Hammond*,[20] an evangelical Christian was preaching in public with signs which were equating homosexuality with immorality. The Divisional Court held that a conviction for insulting behaviour likely to cause harassment, alarm or distress[21] was an interference with Articles 9 and 10, but it was justified by the need to show tolerance to others. Similarly in *Norwood*,[22] an offence of causing religiously aggravated alarm or distress, by displaying material insulting to Moslems (blaming all Moslems for the September 11 attacks), was held to be a justified interference with freedom of speech, to protect the rights of others.

■ Obscenity: in *Perrin*,[23] the question was whether offences of publishing an obscene (in this case pornographic) item under the Obscenity Act 1959 infringed Article 10. The Court of Appeal held that this offence served a legitimate purpose in a democratic society, and was sufficiently certain and well defined to be 'prescribed by law'.

■ Banning harmful adverts: in the case of *British American Tobacco*,[24] the High Court held that regulations which banned advertising the sale of tobacco products[25] were a proportionate interference with Article 10 for the protection of health.

■ Banning political advertising: this has been upheld in the case of *Animal Defenders*;[26] we discuss this further in the context of Article 1–3.[27]

However, not all interferences with Article 10 will be justified.

■ Defamation: we have already considered *Steel and Morris* v *UK*,[28] the 'Mclibel' case, where two environmental campaigners had been sued for libel by McDonald's, and were not given legal aid to pay for defending the case, which they only succeeded in partially defending. The European Court held that the result of the burden of the defendants having to prove the truth of what they were saying, in the context of the enormous length, detail and complexity of the case, and without legal aid to pay for lawyers, not only breached Article 6, but was an unjustified fetter on their Article 10 rights as well.

■ Treason: in *Rusbridger* v *Attorney General*,[29] the House of Lords dismissed the suggestion that the Treason Felony Act of 1848 could be used to criminalise advocating republican government – the relevant section (section 3) was a relic of a bygone age and would not survive scrutiny under the Act.

---

[19] *Connolly* v *DPP* [2007] EWHC 237 (Admin), [2008] 1 WLR 276.
[20] *Hammond* v *DPP* [2004] EWHC 69 (Admin), LTL 13.1.04.
[21] Public Order Act 1986, section 5.
[22] *Norwood* v *DPP* [2003] EWHC 1564 (Admin), Times 30.7.03.
[23] *R* v *Perrin* [2002] EWCA Crim 747, LTL 22.3.02.
[24] *R (British American Tobacco)* v *Secretary of State for Health* [2004] EWHC 2493 (Admin).
[25] Tobacco Advertising and Promotion (Point of Sale) Regulations 2004 (SI 2004/765).
[26] *R (Animal Defenders International)* v *Secretary for State for Culture, Media and Sport* [2008] UKHL 15, [2008] 1 AC 1312.
[27] Below, p. 363.
[28] (2005) 41 EHRR 403, above, p. 231.
[29] [2003] UKHL 38, [2004] 1 AC 357.

We referred above to inciting racial hatred: this has now been expanded by the Racial and Religious Hatred Act 2006, which outlaws the stirring up of religious hatred. This has been extremely controversial because there is a distinct possibility that this new law will be incompatible with freedom of speech. Inciting *racial* hatred is already a crime,[30] and this applies to groups of persons defined by reference to colour, race, nationality or ethnic or national origins. The problem with an offence of inciting *religious* hatred is that it defines the target group by reference to religious belief or lack of religious belief. Yet these phrases, 'religious belief' and 'a group defined by reference to lack of religious belief' are not defined, and a group's religious belief, or lack of it, is much wider, and more difficult of proof, than racial or ethnic origin, which raises real questions about certainty and whether the offence is an interference 'in accordance with law', that is a law that is clear and capable of being followed.

Another issue is that the offence is not intended to catch criticism or dislike of a religion, but attempts to stir up hatred against a religious group. But it is sometimes very hard to tell the difference: if a person criticises a religion, that will likely involve criticising those who adhere to it; and if the criticism is forceful, and encourages others to dislike that religion, then there is a real question whether it would fall foul of this new offence. All religions involve believing that other religions are wrong; and an atheist believes that all religions are wrong; and saying so should not be a crime, even if it is done in a way which is provocative, and stirs up hostility in the audience. It is not right to preach hate against other people, or cause them to be afraid; but in a free society, it is not right to limit free speech except in the most extreme and clearly defined cases.

PRESS FREEDOM

'Any interference with press freedom must be justified': this was the headline in *The Times* newspaper for the report of *A* v *B*, a case about press coverage of the private life of a footballer. And the reference to duties and responsibilities, and some of the restrictions in Article 10(2), will be especially relevant when considering a claim for the exercise of freedom of expression by a newspaper or media organisation, since some of these can have real power and influence. On the other hand, this power should not be unlimited. When awarding an injunction in favour of Elizabeth Jagger to prevent publication of a film of 'sexual activities' inside the closed door of a nightclub, Mr Justice Bell considered that there is 'no legitimate public interest in the dissemination of images, which could serve only to humiliate the claimant for the prurient interest of others'.[31]

This view that there are limitations on what is properly to be considered disclosable in the public interest has been confirmed by the European Court, in the case of *von Hannover* v *Germany*.[32] In this case, the claim was brought by Princess Caroline of Monaco, who argued that German law did not protect her sufficiently from press intrusion. The European Court agreed:

> The decisive factor in balancing the protection of private life against freedom of expression should lie in the contribution that the published photos and articles make to a debate of general interest. It is clear in the instant case that they made no such contribution since the

[30] Public Order Act 1986, section 17.
[31] *Jagger* v *Darling* [2005] EWHC 683: the case is unreported; the judge was quoted in Times 10.3.05.
[32] (2004) 40 EHRR 1.

applicant exercises no official function and the photos and articles related exclusively to details of her private life. Furthermore, the Court considers that the public does not have a legitimate interest in knowing where the applicant is and how she behaves generally in her private life even if she appears in places that cannot always be described as secluded and despite the fact that she is well known to the public. Even if such a public interest exists, as does a commercial interest of the magazines in publishing these photos and these articles, in the instant case those interests must, in the Court's view, yield to the applicant's right to the effective protection of her private life.

Given the concerns expressed about press freedom, there is a particular section of the Act which is relevant here – section 12:

> **Section 12** (4) The court must have particular regard to the importance of the Convention right to freedom of expression and, where the proceedings relate to material which the respondent claims, or which appears to the court, to be journalistic, literary or artistic material (or to conduct connected with such material), to –
>
> (a) the extent to which –
>
> (i) the material has, or is about to, become available to the public; or
>
> (ii) it is, or would be, in the public interest for the material to be published;
>
> (b) any relevant privacy code.

The words of section 12 make a special point of preserving freedom of expression. The section applies only to the freedom of expression, and to no other right or freedom under the Convention. It applies if a court is considering whether to grant any relief which might affect the exercise of the right to freedom of expression; that means relief which might stifle the right, or prevent expression. The court must have particular regard to the importance of the freedom of expression; and where the court is asked to prevent publication, notice must be given to the person who has the right of expression, and an order restraining publication should be made only if the court is satisfied that publication is likely to be prevented; it is in considering such an order that the court must have 'particular regard to the importance of the Convention right to freedom of expression'.[33]

The courts have now had the opportunity to consider the effect of section 12, in the context of the desire of newspapers to publish material, when faced with a claim that such publication would infringe a right to privacy or confidentiality. We have already looked at these cases in the context of Article 8, which protects privacy.[34] We saw there how the courts have expanded the law to protect confidential or private information, which was begun in the case of *Douglas* v *Hello!*[35] and recognised by the House of Lords in *Campbell* v *MGN*.[36] In all of the cases discussed there are situations where there is a conflict between Article 8

---

[33] Section 12 is also considered above, p. 99, in the context of injunctions.
[34] Above, pp. 251–6.
[35] [2001] 2 WLR 992; see also above, p. 253.
[36] [2004] UKHL 22, [2004] 2 AC 457, above, pp. 254–5.

and Article 10. We shall consider some of them again here, from the point of view of Article 10 and section 12.

Section 12 was considered by the House of Lords in *Cream Holdings Ltd* v *Banerjee*,[37] where their Lordships stressed that Parliament had, in that section, specifically decided to reinforce freedom of expression – this meant that a claim would usually have to be more likely than not to succeed at trial before an order would be made to restrain publication, but there might be circumstances where this test was not met but there was some very good reason for preventing publication, such as threats to persons whose identity or address was being kept secret.

Section 12 was also considered by the Court of Appeal, twice, in the case of *Douglas* v *Hello!* which was the claim by the celebrity couple, Michael Douglas and Catherine Zeta-Jones, for breach of confidence in respect of pictures of their wedding. On the first appeal,[38] relating to the granting of an injunction preventing publication, the Court of Appeal recognised that Article 8 justifies a restriction on Article 10 to protect privacy. It also paid especial regard to section 12. However, on the facts of the case they declined to make an injunction, considering that there were no exceptional circumstances to justify restraining the right of freedom of expression, in particular because some photographs of the wedding would be published anyway.

However, when the case returned to the Court of Appeal,[39] this time after the trial on liability, and also after the decisions in *Cream, Campbell* and *Hannover*,[40] the Court considered that the injunction should have been left in place. The Court considered that the claim for privacy had met the test set out in *Cream*, of a case which had a high probability of success. The Court also considered that damages were not an adequate remedy, although one aspect of that was that they held that *OK!*, which had bought the rights to the photos, could not claim damages, and this finding was appealed to and reversed by the House of Lords.[41]

Some guidance as to the application of section 12 to claims of privacy has also been given in the case of *A* v *B*.[42] A was a married professional footballer (revealed to be Garry Flitcroft, then captain of Blackburn Rovers) who had sexual relationships with two women, referred to as C and D, neither of whom was his wife, who sought an injunction to prevent publication of his identity by a newspaper, after C and D disclosed details of the relationships to the press.

The Court of Appeal refused to make the injunction forbidding publication. The Court refused to accord the same protection to transient sexual relationships, such as these, as to sexual relationships within marriage, as the Court was not in a position to decide whether or not it was in the wife's interest to be kept in ignorance of the affairs. The fact that A was a professional footballer meant he was a role model and so there was a corresponding public and press interest in him. The Court also specifically referred to section 12(4): any interference with the press has to be justified because it inevitably has

---

[37] [2004] UKHL 44, [2004] 3 WLR 918; see above, p. 99, for discussion of section 12 in the context of injunctions.
[38] [2001] 2 WLR 992.
[39] *Douglas* v *Hello! Ltd (No. 2)* [2005] EWCA Civ 595, [2005] 4 All ER 128.
[40] *von Hannover* v *Germany* (2004) 40 EHRR 1, above, p. 307.
[41] [2007] UKHL 21, (2008) 1 AC 1.
[42] *A* v *B (a company)* [2002] EWCA Civ 337, [2002] 3 WLR 542; also discussed above, p. 254.

some effect on the ability of the press to perform its role in society, and because the existence of a free press is in itself desirable. Such interference can be justified by the right of privacy under Article 8, but the weaker the claim for privacy the more likely that it would be outweighed by the claim based on freedom of expression.

On the other hand, an injunction was granted in *CC v AB*.[43] The claimant had committed adultery with the defendant's wife, but the Court held that there was no rule that an adulterer could never obtain an injunction to prevent publication. If there is a legitimate expectation of privacy then Article 8 is engaged. In this case, the Court considered section 12, and held here that there was likely to be a permanent injunction, since the defendant was motivated by spite and making money, and publication would do great damage to C's family.

Of course, not all cases concern only privacy. As the Lords in *Cream* recognised, sometimes the restriction of a person's identity is more important than that, if the revelation of their identity could lead to a risk of harm, or even a risk to their life.

We have considered this situation already, in the case of *Thompson and Venables*,[44] where the identities of two convicted murderers were ordered not to be published, to protect them from a risk to their lives. Similar injunctions have been made in other cases of notorious criminals, where, once the decision is made that they can be released on licence or otherwise, they are entitled not to become a target for lynch mobs, or so that they can attempt to be rehabilitated; the most prominent have been Mary Bell, who was convicted of murder when she was a child, and was granted an injunction in light of the risk to her mental health and to her own daughter;[45] and Maxine Carr, who was an accomplice to the Soham murders, and held to be at risk of her life if her identity was revealed.[46]

The principles applicable to such a case have been considered by the House of Lords in the case of *S*.[47] This case concerned a child, CS, who was aged 8 at the time of the House of Lords hearing. His older brother, DS, had died of acute salt poisoning some two years earlier, then aged 9, and his mother had been charged with murder. Newspapers wished to publish the names and photographs of both parents and the dead boy, accepting that they should not refer to the boy CS. The boy claimed an injunction to restrain any publication of identity of the defendant in the murder trial; he relied on Article 8; the newspapers relied on Article 10.

The House of Lords held that neither Article had any precedence over the other: they had to be balanced in each case. Here, CS was not a party to the criminal trial. While it would be a deeply hurtful experience for him to be identified, he was only indirectly involved. His rights under Article 8 were in this case outweighed by the public interest

---

[43] *CC v AB* [2006] EWHC 3083 (QB), (2007) 2 FLR 301.

[44] *Thompson and Venables* v *News Group Newspapers* [2001] 2 WLR 1038; see above, in the context of Article 2, p. 134, Article 3, p. 154, and Article 8, p. 254.

[45] *X (formerly Mary Bell) and Y* v *News Group Ltd* [2003] EWHC 1101 (QB) (Dame Elizabeth Butler-Sloss (President)) (2003) EMLR 37.

[46] *Carr* v *News Group Newspapers Ltd* [2005] EWHC 971 (QB), LTL 24.2.05.

[47] *In re S (Identification: Restrictions on publication)* [2004] UKHL 47, [2005] 1 AC 593.

in the criminal process being conducted in public so that justice is open. It would be a dangerous precedent to inhibit the reporting of criminal trials, at the expense of informed debate about criminal justice.

However, in the case of W,[48] an injunction restraining publication of the identity of a parent charged with a crime was made, to protect their children. Again, the court stressed that neither Article 8 nor 10 had automatic priority. In this case, however, there were factors which weighed in favour of the children, because the crime was that the mother of the children had knowingly infected their father with HIV. It was not yet known if one of the children was HIV positive, and the very real concern was that knowledge of the children's identities would prejudice their perfectly proper placement at a nursery and with foster parents, especially given a high level of ignorance about HIV in their local community.[49]

In addition, orders to restrain publication of identity have been made, for example, to prevent the identification of a vulnerable mother on a television programme about adoption.[50] An order was also made in the case of *LM* which concerned an inquest into a the death of a murdered child: although reporting the inquest was allowed, the identity of the child's sibling was protected.[51]

JOURNALISTS' SOURCES

A 'scoop' is an exclusive piece of news for a newspaper; it means the paper is first, and ahead of its competitors. A scoop is sometimes headline-grabbing, and the newspaper's circulation figures go up. Presumably, editors and reporters dream of scoops. A reporter keeps her ear to the ground, so that she gets the information early. Some information may come to her from an informant who will extract a promise that his identity will be kept secret.

But if the newspaper publishes the information, an interested party may ask for the identity of the source. The information may be an official secret, or it may have come from company documents which are confidential, and which must remain so, and the company may consider that it is important to retrieve the documents, or to prevent any further breach of confidence. The information may reveal that there is an employee who bears a grudge, and it is important to identify him. The newspaper's answer to this is that its sources are secret, and that it must be free to publish information after giving an assurance of secrecy. It will rely upon its freedom of expression, under Article 10. The interested party, on the other hand, will rely upon Article 8 – the right to respect for a private life – and contend that its privacy has been invaded. We have seen examples of the tension between the two Articles in the discussion of the celebrity cases. In the next case, *Goodwin v UK*,[52] we see how the European Court upheld a claim of freedom of expression when the newspaper is ordered to reveal the identity of its informant.

[48] [2005] EWHC 1564 (Fam), Times 21.7.05.
[49] Reference was also made to the President's Direction 18.3.05 (Applications for Reporting Restriction Orders).
[50] *T (By her Litigation Friend the Official Solicitor) v British Broadcasting Corporation* [2007] EWHC 1683 (QB), [2008] 1 FLR 281.
[51] *Re LM (Reporting Restrictions: Coroner's Inquest)* [2007] EWHC 1902 (Fam), [2008] 1 FLR 1360.
[52] (1996) 22 EHRR 123.

William Goodwin was a British journalist on the staff of *The Engineer*. In 1989, he was telephoned by a person, 'X', who had previously supplied information to him on various companies, and X gave him information about a company, Tetra, to the effect that it had financial problems. It was sensitive information. The information was unsolicited by Mr Goodwin, and was not given in exchange for any money; it had come from a confidential memo, which had been taken from Tetra. Mr Goodwin telephoned Tetra to get assistance for an article which he planned to write for *The Engineer*. Tetra obtained an injunction restraining the publication of the article; the High Court ordered Mr G to divulge the identity of X, and he refused, and he was fined £5,000 for contempt of court. Mr G complained to the European Court that this was a violation of Article 10, contending that the public interest in disclosure outweighed the public interest in confidentiality. The Contempt of Court Act 1981 provided that a court shall not require a person to disclose their source of information unless it is satisfied that disclosure is necessary in the interests of justice, or national security, or the prevention of disorder or crime.

The European Court held that a feature to be borne in mind was that publication had been prevented; while Tetra had an interest in learning who X was and whether it was a disloyal employee, and preventing further publication, the need for a free press outweighed that. The Court said:

> Protection of journalistic sources is one of the basic conditions for press freedom, as is reflected in the laws and the professional codes of conduct in a number of Contracting States and is affirmed in several international instruments on journalistic freedoms. Without such protection, sources may be deterred from assisting the press in informing the public on matters of public interest. [. . .] Having regard to the importance of the protection of journalistic sources for press freedom in democratic society and the potentially chilling effect an order of source disclosure has on the exercise of that freedom, such a measure cannot be compatible with Article 10 of the Convention unless it is justified by an overriding requirement in the public interest. [And] The Court must look at the 'interference' complained of in the light of the case as a whole and determine whether the reasons adduced by the national authorities to justify it are 'relevant and sufficient'.

Our courts have now had to consider this, in the case of *Ashworth Hospital* v *MGN*,[53] which concerned Ian Brady, one of the Moors murderers, who was a patient at Ashworth Security Hospital. The *Daily Mirror* published an article, written by their investigations editor, Mr Gary Jones, which included verbatim extracts of the medical records of Ian Brady: he was, at the time, on a well-publicised hunger strike. The hospital sought disclosure from the newspaper of the source from which the medical records were obtained.

The newspaper relied on its rights under Article 10, and on section 10 of the Contempt of Court Act 1981 which provides that no court may order a person to disclose the source of information for a publication unless the court is satisfied that disclosing the source is 'necessary in the interests of justice or national security or for the prevention of disorder or crime'.

The House of Lords held that it was essential for the care and safety of patients and staff at Ashworth that confidentiality of records was preserved; psychiatry, more than any other branch of medicine, depends on a trusting relationship between therapists and patients. The hospital needed to ensure action could be taken to prevent further disclosure, and to discipline the person who had disclosed the material. Thus, although the journalist had rights under Article 10, the interference with those rights was proportionate.

---

[53] [2002] UKHL 29, [2002] 1 WLR 2033.

There was a sequel to that case. The *Daily Mirror* disclosed the name of Mr Ackroyd as the intermediary from whom it had received the medical records. Mr Ackroyd declined to identify *his* source, and the hospital sought a summary order identifying any employee of the hospital who was involved in his acquiring the medical records. So the Court of Appeal considered the case again.[54] But this time the circumstances were different. Times had changed: there was no longer any 'cloud of suspicion' hanging as a blight over the hospital, and there was no longer any pressing need to know the name of the perpetrator of something that had happened so long ago. Further, the Court was unwilling to shut out Mr Ackroyd from a trial of the case on a summary judgment application. The Court recognised the importance of protecting journalists' sources for press freedom. Lord Justice Ward said, in an interesting illumination of the attitude of the judiciary towards the press:

> There is today, in my view, a palpable tension between the judiciary and elements of the press. If that is right, then it is all the more important, not that judges should pander to perceived pressure from the press, but only that judges should be vigilant to protect the freedom of the press where it is legitimate to do so.

And not only did the Court of Appeal provide this protection, but so has the Court in a further hearing.[55] The Court of Appeal was considering a summary determination; the matter progressed to trial, before Mr Justice Tugendhat; he heard evidence from the reporter, and also refused to make an order for disclosure of the source. He held that there had been a disclosure of confidential information, but stressed the importance of a free press in a democratic society and, being satisfied that the journalist had acted properly and in the public interest, held that there was no pressing social need for disclosure of the source; and when this decision was itself appealed, it was upheld by the Court of Appeal.[56]

QUESTIONS

1 Freedom of speech is the only right which is expressed to carry with it duties and responsibilities. Why do you think this is? Do you agree? How does this relate to the list of limitations?

2 What do you think of the courts' approach to the various limitations on freedom of speech? Are they being too cautious or too bold in giving effect to these limitations?

3 How important is the freedom of the press, and why? What do you think of the court's approach to press freedom? Do you agree with the protection given to journalists' sources?

---

[54] *Ackroyd v Mersey Care NHS Trust* [2003] EWCA Civ 663, Times 21.5.03.
[55] *Mersey Care NHS Trust v Ackroyd* [2006] EWHC 107 (QB), Times 9.2.06.
[56] *Mersey Care NHS Trust v Ackroyd* [2007] EWCA Civ 101, (2007) 94 BMLR 84.

Freedom of expression

One of the more militant trade union strikes of recent years was the miners' strike in 1984–5, which saw clashes between police and the miners' picket lines: the picture shows a march in the West Midlands.

Source: © Annie Griffiths Belt/Corbis

17 Freedom of assembly

[In 1819] public meetings were generally prohibited. It would have been better if none had been allowed at all, for when a vast but orderly concourse of working men and women assembled on St. Peter's Fields, Manchester, to demand Parliamentary Reform, the magistrates, seized by sudden panic, let loose a charge of yeomanry which killed a dozen and seriously injured hundreds of both sexes . . . It was called 'Peterloo,' because it seemed to cancel the debt of the nation's gratitude for Waterloo. (G.M. Trevelyan, *Illustrated History of England*, on Peterloo (16 August 1819))

Article 11: Freedom of Assembly and Association

1 Everyone has the right to freedom of peaceful assembly and to freedom of association with others, including the right to form and to join trade unions for the protection of his interests.

2 No restrictions shall be placed on the exercise of these rights other than such as are prescribed by law and are necessary in a democratic society in the interests of national security or public safety, for the prevention of disorder or crime, for the protection of health or morals or for the protection of the rights and freedoms of others. This Article shall not prevent the imposition of lawful restrictions on the exercise of these rights by members of the armed forces, of the police or of the administration of the State.

THE FREEDOM DEFINED

A demonstration may annoy or give offence to persons opposed to the ideas or claims that it is seeking to promote. The participants must however be able to hold the demonstration without having to fear that they will be subjected to physical violence by their opponents; such a fear would be liable to deter associations or other groups supporting common ideas or interests from openly expressing their opinions on highly controversial issues affecting the community. In a democracy the right to counter-demonstrate cannot extend to inhibiting the exercise of the right to demonstrate.[1]

Those are the words of the European Court, and they come to this: there is a right to hold a demonstration, even though it is in favour of something unpopular or objectionable. This is part of the same group of rights as Articles 9 and 10, freedom to manifest a belief,

---

[1] *Plattform Ärzte für das Leben v Austria* (1991) 13 EHRR 204.

and freedom of expression, and there may be an overlap between them. In a tolerant and open democracy, it is important not just that people are free to hold whatever belief they choose, but also that they are free to manifest that belief, share it with others, and collectively meet to discuss, debate and demonstrate. Of course, the more that the right of freedom of association involves a physical demonstration, the more likely it is to raise questions about whether an interference with it is justified, using the principles we have seen in other Articles, for a legitimate aim, such as public order or safety, and in a way which is proportionate to that aim.

So what does Article 11 protect? Obviously, Article 11 is about demonstrations and meetings; but it goes far beyond that. Article 11 covers a wide variety of people who assemble and associate together. It is about trade unions, and political assemblies, and societies. And in a political climate, where across Europe national or ethnic minorities are making claims to recognition, it is about associations of people who claim a national identity in a larger community. For instance, protection has been given to an organisation to promote the interests of the Macedonian minority in Bulgaria, which the Bulgarian court held was divisive of national unity and was dangerous for the territorial unity of Bulgaria,[2] or the Union of People of Silesian Nationality, to promote Silesian consciousness, culture and rights in Poland.[3]

 ## WHAT IS AN ASSEMBLY?

An assembly or meeting might take place in all sorts of situations and places; assembly does not just mean something static, but includes marches and processions, as we shall see in the next case, *Plattform Arzte fur das Leben* v *Austria*.[4]

> The Plattform was an association of doctors campaigning against legalised abortion and, in 1980, it organised a march of supporters along public roads, ending in a religious service at an altar on a hillside; counter-demonstrators were expected, and indeed they came and did disrupt the march, by shouting down the Plattform members' recitation of the rosary. At the service, the counter-demonstrators used loudspeakers and threw eggs and clumps of grass at the congregation. In 1982, Plattform held a second demonstration in Salzburg Cathedral Square, and counter-demonstrators shouted opposition; police formed a protective cordon, but eventually the police cleared the square.
>
> Plattform claimed that there had been a violation of Article 11 in respect of both demonstrations, in that the police had failed to provide protection to Plattform, and had failed to ensure its members' freedom of assembly.
>
> The European Court accepted that Article 11 was applicable, to the meeting and to the march along public roads, and the Court regarded those places as legitimate places for processions and meetings which came within Article 11. But the Court rejected the claim on the facts of the situation; it dismissed the claim of Plattform that the police had remained passive; it found that the police had deployed themselves in sufficient numbers and with suitable tactics, and that no serious clashes occurred.

[2] *Stankov and United Macedonia Organisation Ilenden* v *Bulgaria* (2001) 2 October, 29221/95.
[3] *Gorzelik* v *Poland* (2005) 40 EHRR 4, although the interference with the association was held to be justified.
[4] (1991) 13 EHRR 204.

An assembly might also be static, such as a protest camp. The case of *Tabernacle*[5] concerned the Aldermaston Women's Peace Camp which has been held regularly in the vicinity of the Atomic Weapons Establishment at Aldermaston since about 1985 as a peaceful protest against nuclear weapons. Byelaws were passed which prevented camping. The Secretary of State argued that the byelaw simply regulated the manner of any protest but did not prevent it. The Court of Appeal rejected that view. Camping was not just the form of the protest; the camp was itself the protest. The byelaws were a real and substantial interference with Article 11 (and also Article 10) which was not justified in the public interest and the byelaw was quashed.

THE STATE'S DUTY

On a literal reading of Article 11(1) and (2), one might conclude that the state's duty is simply to permit the freedom to exist; there seems to be nothing more than a negative duty – to refrain from interference, except in accordance with Article 11(2). But we have already seen what the European Court said in the *Plattform* case in our quotation at the start of this chapter; there is a positive duty as well as a negative one.

In the *Plattform* case the Court was dealing with facts which brought up this point directly: had the state fulfilled its duty, by ensuring enough police and proper tactics? The Court said:

> Genuine, effective freedom of peaceful assembly cannot, therefore, be reduced to a mere duty on the part of the State not to interfere: a purely negative conception would not be compatible with the object and purpose of Article 11. Like Article 8, Article 11 sometimes requires positive measures to be taken, even in the sphere of relations between individuals, if need be.

It is not a guarantee; and the Court made that clear:

> While it is the duty of Contracting States to take reasonable and appropriate measures to enable lawful demonstrations to proceed peacefully, they cannot guarantee this absolutely and they have a wide discretion in the choice of the means to be used.

ARTICLE 10 AND ARTICLE 11

The relationship of these two Articles is close; and one finds cases where both are in issue, as part of the same claim. This is because, as we noted earlier, a person who joins an association is in effect expressing a view – that is, a view in favour of that association. Whether the particular 'assembly' is a meeting, or a procession, or a trade union association, the very fact of joining it is an expression of a view or an opinion; the person is allying himself or herself with its ideas or opinions. That is how the European Court put it in the case of *Ahmed* v *UK*.[6]

---

[5] *Tabernacle v Secretary of State for Defence* [2009] EWCA Civ 23, Times 25.2.09.
[6] (2000) 29 EHRR 1.

Messrs Ahmed, Perrin, Bentley and Brough lived in various parts of England. They were each permanently employed in different capacities by local authorities – as (respectively) solicitor, principal valuer, planning manager, and adviser to committees. Each of them wished to take part in political activities, as a candidate or assisting a constituency party. In 1990, Regulations were made so that persons holding certain posts in local authority could not participate in political activities, although they were allowed to join a political party; the posts were in a 'politically restricted' category. If they wished to continue their political activities, they were obliged to resign from their employment. The applicants were in that category. They sought exemption from the English courts, and failed, and so claimed before the European Court that there had been violations of Articles 10 and 11.

The European Court found that the creation of the restricted category was indeed a violation of both Articles 10 and 11, but that it was necessary in a democratic society to have such a restriction in order to maintain political neutrality in the local authority permanent staff.

The interesting point for us is the statement made by the Court about the relationship of the two Articles. The Court considered that:

> Notwithstanding its autonomous role and particular sphere of application, Article 11 must in the present case also be considered in the light of Article 10 having regard to the fact that the freedom to hold opinions and to receive and impart information and ideas is one of the objectives of freedom of assembly and association as enshrined in Article 11.

In short, one of the purposes of entering an association, and exercising that right, is to receive and impart information, which is at the heart of Article 10. In the *Ahmed* case, the embargo was on both expressing a political view and on taking a meaningful part in politics.

 ## POLITICAL ACTIVITIES

It is especially in the political field that one would expect the right of expression and assembly to dovetail with each other; debate, after all, is usually carried on in an assembly. Debate, however, may be forceful, and when it offers criticism, especially of the state or state agents, the state may be tempted to suppress it. We shall see in this section examples where the state has not merely forbidden participation in the particular politics, but has gone to the length of dissolving the political association or party, or outlawing it. In the United Kingdom, that is unusual; the attitude here is usually one of tolerance. That tolerance is the mark of a democratic society, which is not afraid of debate; that is the reasoning of the European Court in this next case, *The People's Party v Turkey*,[7] where the facts were as follows.

---

[7] *Yazar, Karatas, Aksoy and the People's Party (HEP) v Turkey* (2003) 36 EHRR 59.

The HEP, the People's Labour Party, was founded in 1990, and the case was brought by its Chairman, Vice Chairman, and Secretary General, all of whom were Turkish nationals. HEP stood for principles of self-determination and the recognition of language rights. The Party had severely criticised Turkey's armed forces, which had carried out an anti-terrorist campaign. The Turkish Constitutional Court dissolved the Party on the grounds that it had undermined the integrity of the state by these criticisms, on the grounds that it had lent assistance to illegal acts. Thus, these officers of HEP complained to the European Court of violations of Article 11.

The European Court held that there had been a violation of Article 11. Merely to criticise the armed forces did not mean that the Party was equivalent to the armed groups pursuing violence; and the advocating of ideas advanced by these armed groups did not mean that the Party was supporting terrorism. The state, by forbidding the propounding of those ideas, diminished the possibility of airing those questions in democratic debate.

17

Freedom of assembly

This is a strong case: there had been violence caused by terrorists in Turkey, and the Turkish courts had doubtless been concerned to see that terrorism did not flourish, and the HEP's views were unpalatable. But the European Court considered that the order dissolving the Party was disproportionate; it was in breach of Article 11.

There is a provision in our law for the proscription of an organisation. This is in the Terrorism Act 2000, which allows the banning of an organisation which the Secretary of State believes is concerned in terrorism, so that membership or support of it is unlawful. Political activity on the part of an organisation will not be enough to justify proscription; it will have to be involved in terrorism in some way, which includes elements of the planning or execution of violence and attempts to intimidate or threaten the government or the public. We will consider this again in our discussion of terrorism;[8] but it is worth noting, in the present context, that this power will raise an issue in each case as to whether such an order will be proportionate under Article 11.

 ## AN ASSOCIATION AND ITS MEMBERS

All clubs and societies wish to limit their membership in some way or other; usually, membership of the society will be based on those with a particular interest, or outlook; or a club or society may wish to have members of a certain background. Likewise, clubs and societies will usually have some form of rules, or even a legal framework, to govern their relationship with their members or would-be members. However, Article 11 may have an effect here, especially if the organisation performs a public function: for example, if it is a charity. Apart from any other considerations, if it performs a public function, it may qualify as a public authority, in which case it will be obliged to act in a way which is compatible with the Convention rights.[9] So, in making decisions, such as those about membership, associations may find that they have to apply the principles of Article 11, which means making decisions in a way which is fair, not arbitrary and where the decision is proportionate to its purpose. An example is the decision in the case of *RSPCA* v *Attorney General*.[10]

[8] See below, Chapter 21, p. 386.
[9] Section 6 of the Act, above, p. 76.
[10] [2002] 1 WLR 448.

The Royal Society for the Prevention of Cruelty to Animals (RSPCA) wished to adopt and administer a selective membership policy, so that it could freely exclude or remove from membership any individual whom the RSPCA suspected would not promote its aims and objectives – in effect, it believed certain people would damage its interests, and it wished to exclude them. The RSPCA went to the High Court and sought a declaration that its rules permitted this.

The High Court first stated that Article 11 provides freedom of association, and also of non-association. This permits the RSPCA to exclude persons who might damage its interests. However, it must do so in a non-arbitrary way; and this was so especially considering that it is a charitable organisation. Fairness here would require an opportunity for the person excluded to make representations in their defence; and any policy of exclusion should be announced on an application form for membership; if someone was excluded they had to be invited to make representations why their admission was appropriate.

Thus, although the starting point is that freedom of association includes freedom not to associate, Article 11 does require that a body which serves some public interest, such as a charity, applies some standards of fairness to its membership systems.

 ## TRADE UNIONS

Trade unions are expressly mentioned in the words of Article 11(1): the individual has the right to form and join one, for the protection of his interests. This wording is fairly wide, and might support an argument that any activity, which protects the member's interests, will fall within Article 11. However, whilst this may be the starting point, it is subject to the limitations in Article 11(2), restrictions which are prescribed by law, and necessary in a democratic society. And the next case, *UNISON* v *UK*,[11] is a good example of this.

UNISON was a union for public service employees, and it had members employed by University College London Hospital (UCLH). A substantial proportion of them were on terms of employment negotiated by UNISON at a national level. In 1998 UCLH was negotiating to transfer parts of its business, under a private finance initiative, to private companies, who would erect and run a new hospital for UCLH, and would make further transfers of staff with subcontracting to specialist companies. Some, but not all, of the UNISON members would be transferred in this way.

UNISON sought protection for its members, so there would be terms of employment on all the private companies lasting 30 years. When UCLH refused, UNISON held a pre-strike ballot, which favoured striking. UCLH then obtained a High Court injunction to prevent the strike, on the grounds that it was not in contemplation of a trade dispute, and so did not fall within the statutory protection for strikes in furtherance of a trade dispute.[12] UNISON complained to the European Court that the injunction was a breach of Article 11.

---

[11] 10 January 2002, 53574/99.
[12] Section 219 of the Trade Union and Labour Relations (Consolidation) Act 1992.

The European Court considered that the prohibition of the strike was a restriction on UNISON's power to protect its members' interests, and therefore was a restriction on freedom of association. However, the Court rejected UNISON's claim, on the grounds that the injunction was prescribed by law, and was proportionate in protecting the rights of UCLH. The principle of having private finance initiatives was an acceptable one, and UNISON remained able to take strike action if UCLH dismissed an employee, or changed their contracts; and against any private company taking over employees who threatened to dismiss an employee or threatened to 're-recognise' UNISON. In all these circumstances, the European Court found that the injunction preventing UNISON from striking was a proportionate measure.

The Court also made some interesting observations about the scope of Article 11. The Court noted that Article 11(1) did not set out any particular treatment of trade union members by the state or any particular set of powers or freedoms which a trade union should have, and left states with a choice as to how the freedom of trade unions should be safeguarded, stating:

> There is no express inclusion of a right to strike or an obligation on employers to engage in collective bargaining. At most, Article 11 may be regarded as safeguarding the freedom of trade unions to protect the occupational interests of their members. While the ability to strike represents one of the most important of the means by which trade unions can fulfil this function, there are others.

However, the lack of an obligation to treat unions a particular way does not mean that there are no limits on how unions can be treated. In the case of *Wilson*,[13] the European Court confirmed that there was no breach of Article 11 in the lack of an obligation on employers to enter into collective bargaining, but went on to hold that allowing the use of financial incentives to induce employees to surrender rights to trade union representation for collective bargaining was a breach of Article 11. Employees must not be positively discouraged from making use of union representation.

The right under Article 11 is not just to join a trade union, and for a trade union to protect its members. It is also to leave a trade union, or to refrain from membership.

In the case of *Young, James and Webster* v *UK*,[14] the three applicants were employed by British Rail, which had negotiated a closed-shop agreement between the company and trade unions, so that membership of a union was a condition of employment. The three men failed to join a union, and were dismissed from their employment. They claimed breaches of Article 11, and the European Court agreed. The Court said:

> One of the purposes of freedom of association guaranteed by Article 11 is, like Articles 9 and 10, the protection of personal opinion; and the kind of pressure exerted on the applicants to compel them to join particular unions, contrary to their convictions, strikes at the very substance of Article 11 and constitutes an interference with the rights guaranteed by it.

[13] *Wilson* v *UK* (2002) Times 5.7.02.
[14] (1982) 4 EHRR 39.

Since the events of this case, the law has been changed; it is now illegal to impose a condition of this kind on an employee.[15]

It is not just the individual who has the right under Article 11 to join, or leave, a trade union: the trade union, like any association, also has the right to regulate its membership.

In the case of *ASLEF* v *UK*,[16] ASLEF, a union representing train drivers, had expelled a member, Mr Lee, who was a member of the right-wing British National Party, on the basis that the views of the BNP were inconsistent with the views of the union. The UK courts had held that it was not entitled to do so, and ordered the union to readmit Mr Lee. The European Court held that this order was a breach of Article 11. Article 11 did not oblige a union to admit anyone who wished to join. Where an association, such as a union, espoused certain values or ideals, it would be contrary to the essence of Article 11 if that association had no control over its membership to ensure that its members did in fact hold those values. Mr Lee's interests were not prejudiced by lack of membership in the union, since not being a member did not put his job at risk. Since the union had not acted abusively or unreasonably, the union was entitled to expel Mr Lee for his political views.

Following the decision, the government has changed the law so that trade unions can apply membership rules which prohibit members from joining certain political parties, so long as they act fairly in doing so.[17]

PRIVATE ASSOCIATIONS

The terms of Article 11 are quite unlimited in their scope; an 'assembly' or an 'association' may be of any kind, public or private, so long as it is peaceful, to qualify for protection under Article 11(1). And it nonetheless may suffer interference as strictly defined by Article 11(2). We have so far been mainly considering associations or organisations which one would term 'public' – political parties, and trade unions, although the association in the *Plattform* case could be regarded as a private one. The following is a case from Italy, concerning the public scrutiny of Freemasonry,[18] which demonstrates that a purely private association will attract the protection of Article 11.

Grande Oriente D'Italia Di Palazzo Guistini was an Italian Masonic association with the legal status of an unrecognised private law association. An Italian law required candidates for certain public offices, not part of the public administration, to declare that they were not Freemasons. The Masonic Association complained to the European Court that this law breached its right to freedom of association under Article 11.

---

[15] Trade Union and Labour Relations (Consolidation) Act 1992.
[16] *Associated Society of Locomotive Engineers and Firemen (ASLEF)* v *UK* (2007) 45 EHRR 34.
[17] Employment Act 2008, section 19.
[18] (2002) 34 EHRR 22.

The European Court agreed, and held that the interference was not justified under Article 11(2). The Court said that an association of this kind was entitled to claim the protection of Article 11. The Italian law might well cause the Masonic Association to lose members, if candidates for office preferred to leave rather than make the declaration. The state had a legitimate concern to reassure public opinion at a time when activities of Freemasons in public life was under scrutiny. But a balance had to be struck, and, especially as the offices specified in the law were not part of public administration, the Italian law went too far in creating this blanket requirement to make a declaration in each and every case.

BANNING DEMONSTRATIONS

Article 11 does not prevent there being some restrictions on processions, gatherings or demonstrations, so long as they are reasonably necessary and proportionate and compliant with the limitations in Article 11(2). It is also legitimate for the state to require prior authorisation for demonstrations and to impose sanctions for holding an unauthorised demonstration, so long as the procedure is reasonable.[19]

There are often very good reasons for seeking to prevent a demonstration from taking place. It may be that the demonstration is likely to lead to violence of some sort, or at least disruption; it may be that a police presence will be required; it may be that if an unpopular organisation is allowed to hold a meeting, there will be a counter-demonstration, and a fear that the two will clash. Sometimes, it is the unpopular organisation which is allowed to hold a meeting, and a more moderate counter-demonstration which is banned, precisely for fear of disorder. It will be a matter of balancing rights, and ensuring that the relevant decision is not an arbitrary one. That was the picture in *Rai, Allmond and 'Negotiate Now' v UK*.[20]

Milan Rai and Gill Almond were members of 'Negotiate Now', which was a non-governmental organisation seeking to promote peace in Northern Ireland, and advocating a policy that the government should support peace negotiations without a prior ceasefire. In May 1994, they wished to hold a rally, in Trafalgar Square in London, to promote their views. This is a well-known venue for public demonstrations, and has been described as traditionally available to any individual or organisation who wishes to use it.

The police view was that there was no danger to public order. But the Secretary of State refused permission to hold the rally, on the grounds that the subject was controversial, being of great sensitivity, and the applicants' attempt to have the decision judicially reviewed failed. They complained of a violation of Article 11.

The Commission acknowledged that the intention of the applicants was peaceful, and found that the ban was a violation of the applicants' right to freedom of assembly. However,

[19] *Blum* v *CPS* [2006] EWHC 3209 (Admin), [2007] UKHRR 233.
[20] (1995) 19 EHRR 93.

the ban did not amount to a blanket prohibition of the holding of the rally, but only prevented the use of this high-profile location, other venues being available in central London. There were sensitive and complex issues connected with the affairs of Northern Ireland, and public order was a legitimate consideration. In these circumstances, the decision was not arbitrary, and was proportionate.

This will be the test in cases concerning such banning orders: the public authority, whether it be the police, a local authority, or whoever, will be obliged to show that the ban is proportionate.

This appears in the case of *Brehony*,[21] which concerned the exercise of a Chief Constable's power to impose conditions on any demonstration under section 14 of the Public Order Act 1986, which can be done where the Chief Constable has a reasonable belief that the demonstration may cause serious disruption to the life of the community. Breach of the conditions is a criminal offence.

Mr Brehony was a member of a pro-Palestinian group called 'Victory to the Intifada', which demonstrated regularly on a pedestrianised shopping area outside Marks & Spencer in Manchester city centre. The purpose of the demonstration was to support the Palestinian Intifada, to highlight the support given by Marks & Spencer to the government of Israel, and to urge the public to boycott goods on sale at the store. A counter-demonstration was usually held. The Chief Constable wrote to both groups of demonstrators and informed them that, in order to prevent public disorder or serious disruption to community life in the city centre during the Christmas period, their demonstrations between 29 November 2004 and 3 January 2005 would be limited to an alternative location, be of limited duration and be limited to 20 people. Mr Brehony claimed that the conditions were a violation of his right under Article 11.

The High Court held that while the conditions engaged Article 11, given the legitimate aim of preventing serious disruption and disorder in the pedestrian area of Manchester city centre on the busiest shopping days of the year, and given the temporary and limited nature of the measure, the conditions were not a disproportionate interference.[22]

STATE OFFICIALS

The final sentence of Article 11(2) refers expressly to members of the armed forces, the police, and members of the administration of the state. All of these might be described as agents of the state, and may, by Article 11(2), have restrictions placed upon them limiting their Article 11 rights. The reason for this special treatment is that because of the nature of their jobs, it may be justifiable to prevent them from joining certain associations. They may be privy to secret information, or it may be desirable that people doing certain jobs do not

[21] R (Brehony) v Chief Constable of Greater Manchester [2005] EWHC 640 (Admin), Times 15.4.05.
[22] Eight members of the group were subsequently convicted for breaching the conditions (unreported, Jewish Chronicle 11.11.05).

fall under political pressure, or are not encouraged to strike or take industrial action of certain sorts. This was the sort of situation in the *Ahmed* case, where local government officers were barred from engaging in political activity. It is likely to arise from time to time in any state, if there is a conflict between an individual's job and political interests. Once again, it will be a matter of a balance. An example is the case of *Rekvenyi* v *Hungary*.[23]

Mr Rekvenyi was a police officer and Secretary General of the Police Independent Trade Union in Hungary. In 1993, a law was passed so that from 1 January 1994 members of the police service were prohibited from joining any political activity, and a letter was sent to all police officers demanding that they refrain from political activity or leave the force. The trade union complained to the Hungarian Constitutional Court that the new law infringed the constitutional rights of career members of the police force, but the Court rejected the claim, and the trade union then complained to the European Court that the new law was a violation of both Articles 10 and 11.

The Court took particular account of the history of Hungary, which had, between 1949 and 1989, been ruled by one political party. Membership of that party was expected as a manifestation of the individual's commitment to the regime, an expectation even more pronounced in the military and the police, as the ruling party's decisions were directly implemented by the police. This was what the rules on political neutrality were designed to prevent, the police being the instruments of just one political party. On this ground, the new law was not disproportionate, and the restriction imposed on Mr Rekvenyi was not arbitrary.

17

Freedom of assembly

QUESTIONS

1 What limits do you think should be allowed on peaceful protests?

2 Why do you think that trade unions are especially mentioned as a form of association in this article? Do you think this special reference is necessary?

3 Consider the limitations allowed on the political activities of state officials. Do you think these are justified?

---

[23] (1999) 30 EHRR 519.

When Prince Charles married Camilla Parker-Bowles, Article 12 was called on to help address legal issues which were raised in connection with their marriage (see p. 329).

Source: Stephen Hird/PA Photos

18 The right to marry

It is a truth universally acknowledged, that a single man in possession of a good fortune, must be in want of a wife. (Jane Austen, *Pride and Prejudice*, 1813)

> *Article 12: Right to Marry*
> Men and women of marriageable age have the right to marry and to found a family, according to the national laws governing the exercise of this right.

THE RIGHTS PROTECTED

The right to marry and found a family is not one that has given rise to as much case law as some of the other articles. This is perhaps understandable, since it is recognised in most countries: it is not a right with which it is common for a state to interfere. On the other hand, as with so many of the other Convention rights, this does not mean that there was no point in including it in the Convention as a basic right, since the very fact of its inclusion *has* allowed challenges to previously accepted positions. At the very least, it ensures that consideration can be given to whether this right is being properly respected.

The title of Article 12 refers to the right to marry. But in fact this Article provides two quite separate rights, namely the right to marry, and the right to found a family. Both of them are expressed in fairly simple terms; there are no restrictions similar to those found in some of the other Articles, where there are express limits on the rights. The European Commission has referred to this as an 'absolute' right. But the rights do indeed have the qualification 'according to the national laws governing the exercise of this right'.

In the case of *Hamer*,[1] the Commission said:

> [the rights being absolute] does not mean that the scope afforded to the national law is unlimited. If it did, Article 12 would be redundant. The role of the national law, as the wording of Article 12 indicates, is to *govern the exercise of the right.* (original emphasis)

The Commission went on to give examples of those words in italics. National law may provide rules for such things as the notices, publicity and formalities required for solemnising marriage; and such rules may govern capacity, consent, prohibited degrees or the

[1] *Hamer v UK* (1979) 24 DR 5.

prevention of bigamy. These are the kind of national rules which the European Court will recognise; and they will obviously differ from one nation to another.

However, what the national law will not be allowed to do is to 'interfere substantially with the exercise of the right'. In other words, the national law should not prevent the marriage of someone who ought to be allowed to marry. The case of *Hamer* itself is a good example.

> Mr Hamer was a prisoner in a UK prison, and he wished to marry his fiancée, even though the ceremony would take place in prison; but the law would not permit a marriage ceremony in a prison, and the Secretary of State refused to allow him a temporary release to enable him to be married elsewhere.
>
> The Commission found this obstacle to Mr Hamer was a violation of Article 12, and it interfered with his right. The right under the Article was essentially a right to form a legal relationship, to acquire a status, and simply to allow prisoners to marry would involve no general threat to prison security, since the ceremony would take place under the supervision of prison authorities.

The strict factual result of the case of *Hamer* has been superseded by a change in the law which allows marriages to take place in prison. But the case remains a valuable analysis of the rights guaranteed by Article 12, and gives guidance about the reference to 'national laws'.

Another situation where restrictions on the right to marriage have been held to be disproportionate and unreasonable is the case of *Baiai*.[2]

> This case concerned the interplay between the right to marriage and immigration law, and statutory restrictions which exist to prevent marriages of convenience – marriages which are not genuine but only entered into so that one party can gain some advantage in residence status. The House of Lords considered this scheme in the context of Article 12. It held that there is no breach of Article 12 for there to be restrictions on the right to marry as long as the essence of the right is not impaired. It is also not necessarily a breach to prevent people taking advantage of the institution of marriage for immigration reasons. But the scheme that was in place was a disproportionate restriction of the right because the conditions that were in fact applied to prospective marriages were based purely on immigration status and not on determining whether the proposed marriage was genuine, and that is the only relevant basis for interfering with the right. The House of Lords therefore upheld a declaration of incompatibility which had been made where the statute distinguished between civil and Anglican marriages, and read words into the relevant statute so that it expressly requires compliance with Article 12.

---

[2] *R (Baiai)* v *Home Secretary* [2008] UKHL 53, [2008] 3 WLR 549.

Thus, the right is not unlimited, but interference with it must be for a reason connected with the proper scope of the right and not for extraneous reasons. Another recent, very high profile, example of Article 12 being used in the interpretation of a statute, albeit in a legal opinion rather than a court case, was when questions were raised about the legality of the marriage of Prince Charles, the Prince of Wales, and Mrs Camilla Parker-Bowles, now Duchess of Cornwall; specifically, whether a member of the royal family could get married in a civil ceremony. These were addressed by a written statement to the House of Lords by Lord Falconer, the then Lord Chancellor.[3] He took the view that the relevant law on marriages applies equally to the royal family,[4] subject to the preservation of certain procedures and the need for the sovereign's approval in some cases; but he also drew support from Article 12 (and Article 14), that if there was any doubt, the relevant provisions should be read so as to give effect to the right to marriage.

The other right given by Article 12 – the right to found a family – has been raised in another case concerning a prisoner, and the Court of Appeal looked at this right rather differently. This is the case of *Mellor*,[5] which we have already considered in the context of Article 8, since there is an overlap between the right to found a family and the right to a private and family life.

Mr Mellor was serving a life sentence for murder, and was not likely even to be released on licence – that is, on strict conditions, if he behaved in prison – until he was 35 and his wife was 31. He applied for permission for access to artificial insemination facilities to start a family. This was refused on the basis that no exceptional circumstances existed to justify the grant of such facilities. Mr Mellor challenged this refusal as a breach of his right to found a family, contrary to Article 12, as well as a failure to respect his private life, in breach of Article 8.

The Court of Appeal rejected his claim. The Court agreed that imprisonment is *not* compatible with the exercise of the full rights and liberties which a husband and wife can enjoy, in particular, the ability and freedom to start a family, so it does involve an interference with the right to found a family under Article 12. However, the interference is justifiable under Article 12, which should be read consistently with the express criteria in Article 8(2), since this also applied to this situation. One aspect of being punished by the state was the denial of precisely those rights which were now sought, which were therefore not unjustifiably infringed, so long as the interference was proportionate to the aim of operating a penal system designed for both punishment and deterrence.

Thus the Court recognised the importance of the Article 12 right to found a family, even though it considered that it was not infringed. The analysis of Article 12 as consistent with Article 8(2) is also noteworthy, and we will see that it is based on a similar analysis by the European Court.

---

[3] See, e.g., *Times* on 24 February 2005.
[4] Marriage Act 1949, Part III.
[5] *R (Mellor)* v *Secretary of State for the Home Department* [2001] 3 WLR 533; above, p. 261.

WHO CAN MARRY?

Article 12 says nothing about who can get married. This is limited by the law of incest, which prevents sexual relations between close relatives, and the law of bigamy, which prevents having more than one husband or wife. However, even limits on who can get married must be applied consistently and fairly. In the case of *B and L v UK*,[6] the European Court held that there was a breach of Article 12 in the statutory ban on marriages by certain persons already related by a previous marriage (father/daughter-in-law, son/mother-in-law). It was up to states to decide who could marry. However, English law did not apply a ban on in-laws consistently: it is not prohibited by the law on incest, so is not criminal, and such a marriage can be permitted by a private Act of Parliament, which demonstrates that the ban is not always applied. This was therefore a situation where it could not be said there was a consistent policy against such a marriage, and that resulted in a breach of Article 12. As a result of this case, the law has now been changed by a remedial order so that such marriages are allowed.[7]

THE RIGHTS OF TRANSSEXUALS

In modern times, sexual orientation and gender reassignment have become matters of public debate. All courts have been obliged to consider these matters. A particularly difficult area is the question of treatment of transsexuals, those who have undergone a sex change operation. A number of cases consider the rights of transsexuals and whether they can enter into valid marriages and found families, under Articles 12 and 8.

The first case is *Rees v UK*.[8] Mark Rees, as the applicant came to be known, was born in 1942 with female characteristics, and was registered as a female. But after exhibiting male behaviour, and receiving treatment, in 1977 he changed his name to Mark Rees, and since then he had been socially accepted as a male. He was a female to male transsexual. However, his birth certificate remained with the female registration. In the United Kingdom, a birth certificate is required to be produced from time to time, for the purposes of pensions and employment; and he would be regarded as female for the purposes of marriage. He sought to have his birth certificate altered to show his sex as male, but the Registrar General refused this request. He then complained of violations of Articles 8 and 12.

The European Court noted that different states in Europe had varying practices regarding transsexuals, so that some, unlike the United Kingdom, gave transsexuals the option of changing status to fit their new-found identity. The European Court considered there was no overall consensus, so the matter fell within the margin of appreciation, and there was therefore no violation of Articles 8 and 12. In particular, the European Court regarded Article 12 as referring to a marriage between persons of the opposite biological sex, that being the prevalent tradition.

[6] (2006) 42 EHRR 11.
[7] The Marriage Act 1949 (Remedial) Order 2007 (SI 2007/438).
[8] (1985) 7 EHRR 429.

But it is clear that the European Court was ready to consider evidence of social changes in the states of Europe as well as scientific and biological evidence, and the European Court advised nations to keep measures under review, especially having regard to scientific and societal developments.

Rees was simply a case of seeking to alter the birth certificate. But the next case sought to argue the right for a transsexual to take the further step to marry and have children.

In the case of *Cossey*,[9] Caroline Cossey, as she later became, was born in 1954, and was registered at birth as a male; she realised that psychologically she was female, and from the age of 18 dressed as a woman. At 20, she underwent gender reassignment surgery. As a transsexual, she was able to have sexual intercourse with a man. She was about to marry a man, but the Registrar General informed her that the marriage would be void. She complained that the refusal to issue a birth certificate recognising her female gender, and her inability to contract a marriage, were violations of Articles 8 and 12.

The European Court decided that there were no violations. It noted that some states would now regard as valid a marriage between a man and a person such as Caroline Cossey but still regarded the diversity of treatment, among European states, as important. Thus, it could not take a new approach to the interpretation of Article 12.

18

The right to marry

That was 1990; in a case in 1997, the factual situation was even more pronounced, as the parties entered into a marriage, and had a child. The case is *X, Y and Z* v *United Kingdom*.[10]

X was a female to male transsexual, and he had lived in a permanent relationship with Y since 1979. In 1992 after artificial insemination treatment, Y gave birth to Z, but X was not allowed to register as Z's father. They made their complaint under Article 8.

The European Court held that there was no violation of the Article, as there was no common European standard regarding transsexuals, and in this particular case the legal consequences would not cause undue hardship to Z.

This progression of cases before the European Court, whilst paying attention to the phrase in Article 12, 'according to the national laws governing the exercise of this right', and to the margin of appreciation, has also taken into account changing attitudes. The European Court has now reached the stage where it is prepared to recognise the international trend towards increased social acceptance of transsexuals and increased legal recognition of their new sexual identity, as no longer being a matter of controversy, in *Goodwin* v *UK*.[11]

---

[9] *Cossey* v *UK* (1991) 13 EHRR 622.
[10] (1997) 24 EHRR 143.
[11] (2002) 35 EHRR 447; also considered above, p. 56, as an example of the margin of appreciation.

Christine Goodwin was a post-operative male-to-female transsexual. Her particular claim related to problems with sexual harassment at work. She also faced having to pay National Insurance contributions until she was aged 65, since she was legally a man, instead of being able to stop paying in 1997 at age 60, as she would have been able to do if she was recognised as a woman. But she also complained about her inability to marry, and her legal status in general.

The European Court considered that it was artificial to assert that Ms Goodwin's right to marry had not been denied to her: legally she was a man, so could only marry a woman. Since the applicant now lived as a woman, and was denied the right to marry a man, the European Court considered that the very essence of her right to marry had been infringed. The Court considered that there was no justification for preventing the applicant from marrying under any circumstances, and so found a breach of Article 12. Changing attitudes justified considering that a state which did not recognise the rights of a transsexual was acting disproportionately.

The result of this was the decision of the House of Lords in the case of *Bellinger* v *Bellinger*,[12] where it had to consider a marriage by a transsexual.

Mrs Bellinger went to court to get a declaration that the marriage celebrated between herself and Mr Bellinger was valid. She made this application because, having been classified at birth as a male, she regarded herself as female, and she underwent gender reassignment surgery. Then followed the marriage ceremony.

The House of Lords held that English law did not recognise a marriage between two people who were of the same gender at birth, even if one of them had undergone gender reassignment treatment, and that to hold otherwise would be a major change in the law. But it did consider that, in the light of *Goodwin*, this failed to give effect to the claimant's Article 12 rights (and Article 8 rights) and made a declaration of incompatibility.

The sequel to *Goodwin* and *Bellinger* was that, less than a year later, Parliament passed the Gender Recognition Act 2004, which created a mechanism, a gender recognition certificate, which allows a transsexual person to have a change of gender legally recognised, so that they are treated as being of their new gender for all purposes.

THE RIGHT TO DIVORCE?

The 'right to marry' presumably includes the right to be in a position to marry. At any rate, that is an attractive way of putting the argument, and it would be a convenient argument when there is some obstacle which prevents one getting married. But however good that argument is in some circumstances, it is not valid when it is presented as a right to a divorce. In the case we are about to consider, one party could not exercise his right to marry

[12] [2003] UKHL 21, [2003] 2 AC 467.

because he was already married and could not obtain a dissolution of that marriage. The case is *Johnston v Ireland*.[13]

Roy Johnston was married to a woman in 1952, but by 1965 it was clear that the marriage had broken down and they decided to live separately. Mr Johnston started to live in 1971 with his partner, who then gave birth to a child. They wished to be married but, under the Irish Constitution, divorce was not permitted. They complained that the absence of any provision for divorce was a violation of Articles 8 and 12.

The European Court rejected their claims. In short, the right to marry did not include a right to a divorce. The Court paid attention to the phrase 'according to the national laws'; and the Court found that the prohibition, in the Irish Constitution, on divorce was not such an interference with the substance of the right guaranteed by Article 12. Once again, as we have seen in other cases, the Court had regard to the practices of varying nations. It referred in this case to a 'society adhering to the principle of monogamy'. In essence, a decision characterising the failure to provide a system of divorce as a violation of Article 12 would be tantamount to finding that the state must provide a system of divorce. The Court declined to do this.

But it is worth noting that if there is a system of divorce or separation of some sort in place, there may be a breach of a Convention right if there is no access to it, engaging the Article 8 right to a private life, free of a marriage which is no longer wanted.

In *Airey v Ireland*,[14] Mrs Airey was a shop assistant, from a humble family background, in Cork. She sought a decree of judicial separation from her husband but, having no private means, she could not pay for a lawyer, and no legal aid was available to her. The European Court held that this failure to provide legal aid was a violation of Article 8. The European Court stated:[15]

In Ireland, many aspects of private or family life are regulated by law. As regards marriage, husband and wife are in principle under a duty to cohabit but are entitled, in certain cases, to petition for a decree of judicial separation; this amounts to recognition of the fact that the protection of their private or family life may sometimes necessitate their being relieved from the duty to live together.

In other words, the Court was saying that respect for private life includes the right to be legally parted from one's spouse, if that is necessary for private happiness. And because the state had not provided the means for Mrs Airey to gain access to a court to seek a decree of separation – by providing free legal aid – the state had not taken proper steps to enable Mrs Airey to enforce her right.

---

[13] (1987) 9 EHRR 203.
[14] (1980) 2 EHRR 305.
[15] Paragraph 33.

QUESTIONS

1 Why should the right to marry be a legal right? Why do people have a legitimate interest in having marriage legally recognised?

2 Do you agree that transsexuals should be allowed to marry? What about homosexual couples – is there any good reason for treating such couples differently from heterosexual couples? Is any disparity addressed by the new institution of civil partnerships?

3 Should there be a right to divorce?

A fox-hunt: an activity which impinges on the use of property, fox-hunting has been the subject of more than one human rights case, especially since the Hunting Act 2004 was passed banning hunting with dogs (see p. 345).

Source: Ganeth Fuller/PA Photos

19 The right to property

Wemmick's house was a little wooden cottage in the midst of plots of garden, and the top of it was cut out and painted like a battery mounted with guns. [. . .] 'At the back, there's a pig, and there are fowls and rabbits; then I knock together my own little frame, you see, and grow cucumbers; and you'll judge at supper what sort of salad I can raise. [So,] if you can suppose the little place besieged, it would hold out a devil of a time in point of provisions.' (Charles Dickens, *Great Expectations*, 1861)

First Protocol, Article 1: Protection of Property

Every natural or legal person is entitled to the peaceful enjoyment of his possessions. No one shall be deprived of his possessions except in the public interest and subject to the conditions provided for by law and by the general principles of international law.

The preceding provisions shall not, however, in any way impair the right of a State to enforce such laws as it deems necessary to control the use of property in accordance with the general interest or to secure the payment of taxes or other contributions or penalties.

All democratic societies recognise that while there are certain basic rights which attach to the ownership of property, they are heavily qualified by considerations of the public interest. This is reflected in the terms of Article 1 of Protocol 1 to the Convention . . . Thus, under the first paragraph, property may be taken by the state, on payment of compensation, if the public interest so requires. And, under the second paragraph, the use of property may be restricted without compensation on similar grounds.

These are the words of Lord Hoffmann, in the House of Lords in the *Alconbury* case,[1] and they absolutely set the tone for this chapter. Article 1 of the First Protocol[2] provides the right to property, which may be interfered with – this right is 'heavily qualified' in Lord Hoffmann's phrase – but that interference must, following the Convention jurisprudence, be lawful, non-arbitrary, and proportionate.

This chapter will look at how a claim to the right of property may arise, and how the right may be limited. We shall consider a variety of situations, which are common enough, where the possession or use of property is limited by the state. They may occur, for example, in town and country planning, or in decisions by national or local government about the

---

[1] [2001] UKHL 23, [2001] 2 WLR 1389 at 1411; the case is considered at pp. 48 and 225, above.
[2] All references in this chapter to Article 1 should be taken to refer to this Article, not Article 1 of the Convention itself.

environment, or road building, or in some other way which has an adverse effect upon the property of an individual, as to its value, or its use, or the enjoyment they derive from it. And this will apply equally whether the person complaining is an individual or a company, which may be a large business, since a company also enjoys the right to property.

ENGLISH LAW AND THE RIGHT TO PROPERTY

In order to gauge the effect of the Convention, one must have some idea as to what is provided by the national law. First of all, what is meant by **property**? Property includes what is known in legal terminology as 'real' property, land and buildings. Then there is 'personal' property, goods such as cars and other vehicles, furniture, clothes – the whole range of things that one can buy or possess. Animals will also count as property, since they can belong to someone who is entitled to protect their rights to them, and protect them. Property does not have to be tangible, that is, it need not physically exist: so, for example, there is what is referred to as 'intellectual' property, rights such as trademarks, copyright in written material or confidential information. Money is also property, perhaps the most common example of property in court cases, whether we are talking about physical coins or, far more often, a *right* to money, such as money in a bank account, or money which is claimed from someone else as being a debt or payable for some other reason.[3] Our law provides substantial protection for people's property in a number of ways. In cases of damage to land, the owner or occupier has a number of remedies for damage to or interference with their property: trespass, nuisance and negligence. Where there is interference with or damage to goods, there are actions available of trespass, negligence or conversion. Further, a person may enter into a contract which gives them property rights, such as a sale, a hiring or a lease, and he will have an action for the breach of it. And the law of landlord and tenant provides rules which create rights of possession and property, for both the landlord and the tenant, where there is the relevant legal relationship of the lease of a property. Then there is the criminal law, which protects rights in property, through the sanction of prosecution for offences such as theft, other offences of dishonesty, robbery, burglary and criminal damage. Criminals may be ordered to return stolen money or other property, and to pay compensation for any goods taken or damage done.

However, there are also established ways in which property *can* be interfered with by the state. There is the right of the state to impose taxes, as is recognised in the words of the second paragraph of Article 1. There are also situations such as planning controls, which limit the use that can be made of land to protect the rights of other people. Then there are situations where the state seeks to deprive a person of property because it has been used to commit a crime or because it is the proceeds of crime, or where a particular use of property is prevented to avoid the commission of a crime.

Indeed, most of the cases in our discussion of this Article will involve some form of state interference, mainly because of the existing variety of protections against, and remedies for, interferences with private property, which we have mentioned above. Where the parties to a case are both individuals, arguing, for example, over who an item belongs to, the

---

[3] All of these are recognised as property for the purposes of Article 1 by the European Court: for intellectual property see, e.g., the trademark Budweiser: *Anheuser-Busch Inc v Portugal* (2007) 45 EHRR 36; for a contractual right see, e.g., an option to renew a lease: *Stretch v UK* (2004) 38 EHRR 12.

Convention right will have little, if any, application. But where the state is proposing to interfere with property, by a legislative provision, or the application of such legislation, then the general principles of Article 1 will apply. Just as we have seen in our discussion of the other Articles, the courts will now have to consider the substantive justification for any such interference, and especially whether it is proportionate, whereas previously the courts usually only had to consider whether the interference was lawful, that is, whether it complied with the relevant formal and statutory requirements.

'POSSESSIONS' AND 'PROPERTY'

Both these words are used in Article 1; what is the difference? In fact there is no real difference, and when we look at the cases we shall not be troubled by any distinction. The next case demonstrates that the phrases can be used interchangeably. More importantly, the case defines Article 1, and announces how the Convention principles – lawfulness, absence of any arbitrary decision, and proportionality – govern the whole of the Article. The case is *Marckx* v *Belgium*.[4]

> Paula Marckx had a daughter who, according to Belgian law, was 'illegitimate', and therefore could not inherit from her mother; so Paula could not leave property to her. Paula claimed that this was a violation of Article 1, since the right to property included the right to dispose of one's property. The European Court agreed that the right to dispose of one's property was part of the right to property, and said:
>
> > By recognising that everyone has the right to the peaceful enjoyment of his possessions, Article 1 is in substance guaranteeing the right of property. This is the clear impression left by the words 'possessions' and 'use of property' . . . the right to dispose of one's property constitutes a traditional and fundamental aspect of the right of property.
>
> Thus, the court drew no distinction between 'possessions' and 'property': the right to dispose of one's possessions is a right of property. The European Court's decision, on the facts of the case, was that the Belgian laws of succession regulating the right to dispose of property were not arbitrary and were permitted under the second paragraph of Article 1, which allows the control of the use of property in accordance with the 'general interest', although the European Court did find that this law was discriminatory against children, in breach of Article 14.

ANALYSIS OF THE ARTICLE

The European Court in the *Marckx* case also analysed the wording of Article 1 as being composed of three rules, each based on a sentence of the Article. The first, found in the first sentence of Article 1, is of a general nature, and sets out the principle of the **peaceful enjoyment** of property. The second, in the second sentence, covers **deprivation** of property, subject to certain conditions. The third, in the third sentence, recognises that states are

---

[4] (1980) 2 EHRR 330.

entitled to **control the use** of property for the general interest and the payment of taxes and the like. The European Court added this, and it is of the utmost importance:

> The second and third rules are concerned with particular instances of interference with the right to peaceful enjoyment of property, and should therefore be construed in the light of the general principle enunciated in the first rule.

But what is the general principle of the first rule? There is no expression of principle beyond the actual words establishing the right to peaceful enjoyment. The answer is that the European Court has read into those words the requirement that there must be a fair balance achieved between the interests of the community and the rights of the individual. We shall see the Court's expression of it in the *Air Canada*[5] case. Thus, each part of Article 1, each 'rule', is subject to the principle that any interference with the right must be **lawful, not arbitrary**, and **proportionate**. We shall repeatedly see this as we travel through examples.

 ## THE GENERAL APPROACH

We shall make some reference to this division into 'peaceful enjoyment', 'depriving of possessions' and 'control of use'. This is not always easy; sometimes it is not clear under which head the case falls, or the court does not specifically announce under which head it falls, as in the next case. But this does not greatly matter. Of greater importance are the general principles, which apply whichever classification applies.

One example of this general approach being applied in our courts is *Wilson v First County*.[6] First County were pawnbrokers, and they made an agreement with Mr Wilson which was a credit agreement for a loan; Mr Wilson provided security for the loan, and this was a BMW car. The Consumer Credit Act 1974 applied to this agreement, which required the agreement to be in a precise form; if it was not, neither the pawnbrokers nor the court could enforce it. The agreement was not in the correct form, and the Consumer Credit Act prevented enforcement of it. The pawnbrokers argued that this interfered with their right to property, in breach of Article 1, so that the section was incompatible with the Convention.

The House of Lords held that there was no breach of Article 1. The Lords expressed some doubts as to whether there was a property right involved in this case, but they considered that if there was an interference with property, it was justifiable and proportionate, and a provision which Parliament had been entitled to adopt to respond to the particular social problem in question, namely the unfair exploitation of people using credit.

The salient point is that Article 1 requires a fair balance, whichever part of the Article applies. Indeed the general approach is more important than the precise classification, the insistence on the principles that the interference is lawful, not arbitrary, and reasonably necessary and proportionate.

---

[5] (1995) 20 EHRR 150, below, p. 350.
[6] *Wilson v First County Trust Limited (No. 2)* [2003] UKHL 40, [2003] 3 WLR 568.

■ PEACEFUL ENJOYMENT

The first sentence of the Article, referring to the basic principle of peaceful enjoyment, is short, but the European Court finds in it the implication of the balancing exercise. So it is in *Iatridis* v *Greece*,[7] a case about a local authority taking over a man's property, and damaging his livelihood.

> This case concerned an open-air cinema, the Ilioupolis, built in 1950 with the appropriate permit. An open-air cinema played an important role in local cultural life in Greece, and the clientele of such cinemas was made up mainly of local residents. A dispute arose between the state and the cinema owners as to the ownership of the land. In 1978, Mr Iatridis took a lease of the cinema from the owners, and completely restored the cinema. He then operated it for 11 years, and built up the clientele, which was an asset. The town council then evicted Mr Iatridis, and assigned the cinema to itself. A judge quashed the eviction order, and that meant that the town council was in possession of the cinema, but unlawfully. The appropriate government Minister refused to revoke the assignment, so the town council remained in possession. Mr Iatridis complained of a violation of his right to property in the cinema.
>
> The European Court held in his favour. The Court expressly said that he had a right to peaceful enjoyment of his possession or property, and it was being denied him; this amounted to an interference with it; this was not an outright appropriation, only because he held a lease, which is a limited right and was properly terminated. The European Court considered whether the interference was justified by any of the grounds in the Article, and found that the interference was unlawful even by Greek law, so there was no point in looking any further; once found to be outside the national law, it could not be 'lawful' within any of the meanings of the European Convention.

So this is a case within the first sentence of Article 1. And although the 13 words of that sentence do not make any reference to 'lawful', or to any other concept of the Convention jurisprudence, that concept is to be understood as being part of the rights protected by the Article. Likewise, questions of proportionality will have to be considered.

> In the case of *Marcic* v *Thames Water*,[8] Mr Marcic's complaint was about flooding of his house and garden by sewers and drains operated by Thames Water. This was caused by heavy rain. Although the sewers had been properly constructed and maintained, they did not have the capacity to cope with large rainfall. Thames Water had not carried out the substantial works needed to reduce the risk of flooding because of the cost: Thames Water operated a system for prioritising such works, and the works required to solve Mr Marcic's problem were not therefore likely to be done for some considerable time.

[7] (2000) 30 EHRR 97.
[8] [2003] UKHL 66, [2003] 3 WLR 1603.

The right to property

19

However, the House of Lords held that there was no claim for breaches of Article 1 or Article 8 (nor any action at common law for nuisance). There was a statutory scheme in place for the regulation of the sewage system, which did not infringe those Articles because it struck a reasonable balance between competing interests, including those of householders. The scheme, considered as a whole, was a reasonable way of addressing this social issue.

DEPRIVATION OF PROPERTY

'Deprivation' is the word coming from the phrasing of the second sentence of Article 1; and it is the word used in the next case by the European Commission. It is also certainly a case of enjoyment which was not peaceful. The interest for us is the readiness of the Commission to accept that damage to the environment may be a part of a claim under this Article. The case is *Rayner v UK*.[9]

Michael Anthony Rayner was a partner with members of his family in the management of agricultural land. In 1961, he took up residence at Colnbrook, at a place which was about 1.3 miles west of Heathrow Airport north runway, and in a direct line with it. Aircraft regularly flew over the house, taking off and landing, and this produced very high noise levels. As well as a violation of Article 8, Mr Rayner claimed a violation of Protocol 1, Article 1. The Commission said:

This provision is mainly concerned with the arbitrary confiscation of property and does not, in principle, guarantee a right to the peaceful enjoyment of possessions in a pleasant environment. It is true that aircraft noise nuisance of considerable importance both as to level and frequency may seriously affect the value of real property or even render it unsaleable and thus amount to a *partial taking of property*, necessitating payment of compensation. (emphasis added)

In short, you may get a violation of Article 1 in a situation like this. However, unfortunately for Mr Rayner, he had not produced any evidence that his house had suffered any loss of value, and so on that basis the Article 1 claim failed. But the words of the Commission above are interesting, especially the words in italics. They mean that where there is proof of financial damage, because the value of the house – or other premises – is reduced, some environmental feature will be enough to come within Article 1, even though there is no 'depriving of possession' – the phrase of the second sentence – nor any 'control of use' by the state – the phrase in the last sentence. It would be loss of 'peaceful enjoyment'. This was the case in *Dennis v Ministry of Defence*,[10] where the English court awarded the claimants damages for aircraft noise, as a common law nuisance, but also on the basis that the same remedy would have been available for breach of Articles 1 and 8, since the noise was a very serious interference with their enjoyment of their property. Substantial damages were

---

[9] (1987) 9 EHRR 375, see also above, p. 268, in the context of Article 8.
[10] [2003] EWHC 793 (QB), [2003] Env LR 34, see above, p. 269.

awarded for loss of capital value, past and future loss of use and past and future loss of amenity.

 COMPENSATION

Compensation is referred to expressly at the end of the quotation from the Commission in *Rayner*; the point is that in cases where there is some taking of property – as opposed to simply a control of it – the European Court has regarded the payment of compensation, or the lack of it, as an important feature in deciding whether the act of the state was proportionate or not. The lack of compensation will lead more easily to a conclusion that there was a lack of proportionality. This will be especially relevant in cases of deprivation of property.

The next case is an example where lack of compensation was an important factor in the argument put forward. One incidental point about the case is that some of the claimants were companies, expressly provided for here by the opening words of Article 1, which mention 'every natural or legal person' – a company is a 'legal person'. The case is *James* v *UK*.[11]

> The four claimants in this case were the trustees of the will of the Second Duke of Westminster, including the Sixth Duke. In the area of Belgravia in Central London, on a site which was once farmland on the outskirts of the City of London, the Westminster family and its trustees had developed a large estate comprising about 2,000 houses which became one of the most desirable residential areas in London. By the Leasehold Reform Act 1967, occupiers of these houses who were tenants were given the right to purchase compulsorily the freehold of the house. This was called 'leasehold enfranchisement'; British governments had for nearly one hundred years sought to implement this policy, which enabled tenants to purchase the house in which they had invested money. The claimants, on the other hand, pointed out that the purchase price was often below the market value, and the tenant, having made the purchase, was able to sell again at a profit. They claimed that they were, by the compulsory sale, 'deprived of their possessions' in breach of Article 1.
>
> The European Court dealt with the phrases 'in the public interest' and 'subject to the conditions provided for by law', and said:
>
>> The Court has consistently held that the terms 'law' or 'lawful' in the Convention do not merely refer back to domestic law but also relate to the quality of the law, requiring it to be compatible with the rule of law. However, on the facts [. . .] there are *no grounds* for finding that the enfranchisement of the applicants' properties was *arbitrary* because of the terms of compensation provided for under the leasehold reform legislation. (emphasis added)

There is the reference to compensation; it was a central part of the case and, despite the claims of the applicants, the European Court found that there was nothing arbitrary about the scheme. This case is a perfect illustration of the balancing exercise the court will carry out – and a close examination of state interference. Another case about compensation, which also underlines the principle that the taking of property under Article 1 requires

[11] (1986) 8 EHRR 123.

The right to property

19

proportionality, is the case of *Pye* v *UK*,[12] where the time limitation on claims to recover land was held not to be a disproportionate deprivation of property. A third is *Lithgow* v *UK*.[13]

The applicants were shipbuilders, ship repairers, marine engineers, and aerospace manu- facturers. Their interests were nationalised by the Aircraft and Shipbuilding Industries Act 1977, which provided compensation to businesses which were nationalised. The applicants claimed that the compensation they received was grossly inadequate, and so was in violation of Article 1.

The European Court held that there had been a taking of property – a 'depriving of possessions' – within Article 1, but that on the facts the compensation was *not* so inade- quate as to be a breach. The Court stated the principle that the payment of compensation is a necessary condition for the taking of property, and to take property without it would be justifiable only in exceptional circumstances. Then the Court said:

> In this connection, the Court recalls that not only must a measure depriving a person of his property pursue, on the facts as well as in principle, a legitimate aim 'in the public interest', but there must also be a reasonable relationship of proportionality between the means employed and the aim sought to be realised.

This is the 'fair balance' point; and the amount of compensation is relevant to it. On this point of the importance of compensation, we shall consider one more case, where a company brought an action arising out of the deprivation of its property without com- pensation: the case is *Booker Aquaculture*.[14]

McConnell Salmon Ltd occupied a farm site on the island of Gigha, Scotland, and it reared turbot. In 1994, it suspected that some of the turbot were infected with a disease. It informed the Secretary of State, who then served a notice under the Disease of Fish (Control) Regulations 1994, requiring McConnell to destroy all its fish, but some fish could be slaughtered for commercial purposes on particular conditions. The Regulations were made by government to implement a European Union (EU) Directive, and so were part of the system of EU regulation. McConnell claimed compensation of over £600,000, which the Secretary of State refused. McConnell assigned its rights to Booker, who claimed a violation of Article 1.

The Inner House of the Court of Session found that McConnell's Article 1 rights had been violated – it was deprived of its property when it had to destroy its fish, and it was restricted in the use of the fish which could be used commercially on conditions; further, the court regarded the availability of compensation as relevant to the question as to whether there had been a violation, and this was also the appropriate approach under EU law.

(There was also an uncertain point of EU law involved, so the question of the deter- mination of compensation was in fact referred to the EU's court, the European Court of Justice.)

---

[12] (2008) 46 EHRR 45, above, p. 103.
[13] (1986) 8 EHRR 329.
[14] *Booker Aquaculture Limited* v *Secretary of State for Scotland* [2000] UKHRR 1.

The case is important. Government departments from time to time, and increasingly so, introduce legislation preventing the use of various types of property, on the ground of health or safety. Fur farming, for example, is to be controlled, and businesses will be affected by the regulation of it. The judgment in the *Booker* case shows that there may well be a violation of Article 1 if no proper provision is made for compensation.

CONTROL OF USE

Control of use may cover a variety of rights to use land, and this will also involve the right *not* to use property. One example of a case which involved the control of the use of land was the case of *Chassagnou v France*.[15]

19

The right to property

In this case, a French law compelled certain landowners to allow hunting across their land and to join a hunting association. The applicants all had ethical objections to hunting and so objected to the law. The European Court considered that, although the applicants had not been deprived of their right to use their property, the compulsory transfer of the hunting rights to a statutory hunting association prevented them from making use of one of the rights over their land. The fact that the applicants' intention was to make *no* use of that right – that is, the applicants wished to use their rights as landowners to *prohibit* hunting over their land – did not prevent this being a control of the use of land, and therefore an interference with their rights as owners of the property. The Court went on to consider that the law was a disproportionate interference with these rights and therefore an unjustified interference with Article 1.[16]

The same right has been invoked, but on the other side of the argument, in a challenge to the bans on fox-hunting. In the challenge to the ban instituted by the Scottish Parliament,[17] it was argued that this was an interference with the right to use of property. The Court of Session held that the ban was a control of the use of property, namely the land and hounds previously used for hunting, and so Article 1 applied. However, there was no violation: the activity of hunting was not central to the economic exploitation of the property, there was no identifiable loss, and in any event the interference was justified by the prevention of cruelty to animals. This was also the conclusion of the House of Lords when the Hunting Act 2004 was challenged in *R (Countryside Alliance) v Attorney General*.[18] Article 1 was engaged by the control of use of property, but the interference was justified as being a necessary and proportionate interference for the protection of morals, namely the prevention of cruelty to animals.

Another example of 'control of use' is the decision to designate certain land as a site of special scientific interest (SSSI),[19] which limits the use of the land in order to protect wildlife

---

[15] (2000) 29 EHRR 615.
[16] The Court also found a breach of Article 14, above, p. 119; and of Article 11, because of compulsory membership of the hunting association.
[17] *Adams v Lord Advocate* [2002] UKHRR 1189.
[18] *R (Countryside Alliance) v Attorney General* [2007] UKHL 52, [2008] 1 AC 719; see also above, p. 121.
[19] Under the Wildlife and Countryside Act 1981.

which is at risk – it gives English Nature powers to direct how the land should be managed, and obliges the owners to consult English Nature before undertaking certain activities. This has been challenged more than once, but the Court of Appeal has held that the designation provisions are not incompatible with Article 1.[20] Then in the case of *Fisher*,[21] a challenge was brought to a particular designation, land known as Breckland Farmland, which was arable and intensely farmed, but which was the habitat for an internationally important population of stone curlew. The Court of Appeal rejected the suggestion that this put unnecessary and disproportionate restrictions on the owner's enjoyment of their property.

A further example is of schemes of rent control. It is not exceptional for states to regulate the housing market to ensure that there is some control over what rent can be charged, or the way in which it can be increased. However, if such a scheme imposes a burden on landlords, it must be proportionate to what is needed to advance the social aims of the legislation. This ambit was exceeded in the case of *Hutten-Czapska v Poland*.[22] Here the Polish government had imposed a rent control scheme which unfairly impacted on landlords: property owners here had not received enough rent to cover the cost of maintaining the property, let alone actually receiving an income from the rent. The European Court held that this was a disproportionate and excessive burden: the scheme did not fairly distribute the social and financial burden involved in the reform of the housing supply.

It is notable that these are all cases where there are clear public interest factors at stake, and where it is important that governments can pursue social and economic policies in respect of property, but at the same time, there are limits which ensure that these policies do not unnecessarily disadvantage any one sector of society.

 # TAXATION

It has been said: 'Tax legislation lacks charm.'[23] Tax law can be very technical, and raises many issues of detail, rather than issues of principle. But behind it is a very important political and legal reality: the state has the power, and the right, to impose taxes; and these will interfere with the property of an individual or a business. The second paragraph of Article 1 refers expressly to taxation, in connection with the need to 'control the use' of property. But whether it is a situation of 'depriving of possessions' or 'control of use', or simply 'peaceful enjoyment', as with other interferences, it must be lawful, not arbitrary, and proportionate.[24]

---

[20] *R (Trailer & Marina (Leven) Ltd) v Secretary of State for the Environment* [2004] EWCA Civ 1580, [2005] 1 WLR 1267.
[21] *R (Fisher) v English Nature* [2004] EWCA Civ 663, [2005] 1 WLR 147.
[22] *Hutten-Czapska v Poland* (2006) 42 EHRR 15.
[23] H.H. Monroe QC, *Intolerable Inquisition? Reflections on the Law of Tax*, 1981 Hamlyn Lecture.
[24] It must also not be discriminatory: for some cases on discrimination in taxation, see above, p. 125.

The first question is whether or not the payment in question, even if to a body with some public status, is actually to be classed as a *tax*. In the case of *Aston Cantlow Parish Council v Wallbank*,[25] this was a key question. Mr and Mrs Wallbank were owners of a field. Over 250 years ago, an obligation had been attached to the field which made it rectorial property. This meant that ownership of the field made whoever owned it lay rectors of the parish where the field was located, which meant that they had an obligation to repair the chancel of the parish church, if called upon to do so. A notice requiring the Wallbanks to pay for the cost of repairing the church was served on them by the Parish Council, the cost being over £95,000. The Wallbanks argued that this infringed their Article 1 rights.

They succeeded in the Court of Appeal,[26] which held that this was a tax, and an arbitrary and discriminatory one, since it no longer had any connection with the church property itself, it might arise at any time and for any amount, and it fell on some landowners and not others.

However, the House of Lords disagreed, and allowed the Parish Council's appeal. The Lords held that the question of whether the payment was arbitrary or discriminatory did not arise: the Parish Council was not acting as a public authority when enforcing the payment,[27] but in any event this was not a tax, but a private obligation, like any other which attaches to a piece of land. This was summarised by Lord Hope as because 'the function which it is performing has nothing to do with the responsibilities which are owed to the public by the State'.

This is not a straightforward question: it could well be argued that a parish council imposing a payment on a person for the benefit of a church does certainly have a public dimension to it. And it is the very fact that the payment is only made by *one* landowner, rather than spread more widely in the community, that makes it open to the charge that it is arbitrary.[28] It is important that the courts do not focus on the form of a payment rather than the substance of the obligation which it represents.

The question of proportionality in taxation will be more difficult, since the amount and principles of any particular tax are the sort of question which a legislature is usually better placed to answer than are the courts. This is because there is a very wide range of taxes that *could* be imposed within the range of what will be proportionate: this is a very real example of a situation where the court is being asked to consider what we have described as a policy decision which is most appropriate for a democratically elected Parliament, since what taxes are imposed is often precisely the question at stake when people choose which political party to vote for in a general election. Indeed, a policy on the imposition of higher or lower taxation is often one of the key distinctions between political parties. Therefore, the courts will be slow to interfere just because a claimant happens to disagree with the amount of a particular tax, so long as it is generally applied and does not offend general principles, such as only taxing people on money upon which they are expecting to be taxed, so that they can plan their tax payments accordingly.[29]

---

[25] [2003] UKHL 37, [2003] 3 WLR 283.

[26] [2001] 3 WLR 1323.

[27] This aspect of the case is discussed above, p. 78.

[28] The bill to the Wallbanks was some £200,000 (reported *Times* 6 February 2007).

[29] The other relevant general principle is that the tax should not be discriminatory: see above, the discussion in connection with Article 14, p. 125.

Thus in the case of *National and Provincial Building Society*,[30] the property in issue was the building society's claim to repayment of tax previously paid to their investors. There was a change in the tax laws governing taxation of interest, which accidentally left a period of time for which *no* tax was payable. So regulations were passed which dealt with this gap, but which had the effect of making some tax payable twice on the same income. These regulations were successfully challenged by the Woolwich Building Society, which then recovered the money it had paid in tax under the regulations.[31]

The National and Provincial, the Leeds, and the Yorkshire Building Societies then issued proceedings to make the same claim but, before these came to trial, the government passed legislation retrospectively legalising the regulations, so the building societies' actions were barred; only the Woolwich, whose court case was over, was allowed to keep the money recovered by it. The other three societies claimed that this retrospective legislation deprived them of their 'possessions', namely their claim to the tax money which they had paid over twice, in breach of Article 1.

The European Court was prepared for the purposes of the case to proceed on the basis that these legal claims were 'possessions'. As such, it considered that they had been interfered with and went on to examine the matter as a control of the use of property in the general interest to secure the payment of tax. The Court concluded that the legislation had not acted improperly or disproportionately: if the building societies were right, they would effectively receive a windfall from the changeover in the tax regime, which would not be in the public interest; nor was the burden resulting from the regulations excessive. The balance between the protection of the building societies' claims and the public interest in the payment of taxes was not upset.

The essential point is the balancing exercise: although the retrospective application of the Act of Parliament seemed unfair to the building societies, the state is entitled to take measures to ensure that a tax is applied fairly and without the exploitation of loopholes. The 'fair balance' will sometimes involve difficult questions – and, as we have seen, can also involve claims involving very large sums of money, such as the millions of pounds at stake in the building societies' case. Likewise, there were millions of pounds in gaming licence duty claimed by Customs and Excise in the next case, *Lydiashourne Ltd*.[32]

Lydiashourne operated Maxim's Casino, where a Mr Al Shamlan was accustomed to gamble; on one occasion he obtained gaming chips or tokens to the value of £6,700,000 from the casino, by means of a banker's draft; he staked the chips and lost. The draft turned out to be forged and valueless. The casino was therefore not paid for the chips. Nonetheless Customs and Excise demanded the payment of the relevant gaming tax of £2,240,000 on the draft. The casino contended that the banker's draft was accepted by it in total and unconditional payment, which was now a bad debt, so that it was entitled to bad debt relief. The Value Added Tax and Duties Tribunal disagreed, holding that the draft was received conditionally on the bank paying it. The casino appealed to the Court of

---

[30] (1998) 25 EHRR 127.

[31] *R v Inland Revenue Commissioners, ex parte Woolwich Equitable Building Society* [1990] 1 WLR 1400.

[32] *Lydiashourne Ltd v Commissioners of Customs and Excise* (2000) LTL 2.10.00.

Appeal, contending that it was entitled to bad debt relief, and that if the statutory provisions did not allow such relief, that was a violation of Article 1, in that it was an excessive and unjustifiable interference with the casino's enjoyment of its property. It had not received payment: it should not have to pay tax on it.

The Court of Appeal considered the final sentence of Article 1, which permits the state to enforce laws to control the use of property to secure the payment of taxes; and the central question was proportionality. Lord Justice Robert Walker (as he then was) said:

> With that must be read the references [to] the need to achieve a fair balance and to the need for proportionality. Nevertheless it is plain that a challenge to tax laws as infringing Article 1 is a very steep hill to climb. It seems to me that the language of [the tax statute] is clear. I can see nothing disproportionate or exorbitant in laws which insist on the principle that gaming of this sort, conducted at casinos for very high stakes, should be carried out on a cash basis or what is tantamount to a cash basis, and that [the casino] should bear the risk of being taxed on the amount of any gaming tokens which it issues if, despite the rigours of the system, bad debts arise. Such tax laws cannot in my judgment be called devoid of reasonable foundation.

The right to property

CONFISCATION OF PROCEEDS OF CRIME

There are other situations where state officials have powers which entitle them to take property. Article 1 has also been relied on in the criminal courts, in the context of the confiscation of the proceeds of crime, and again the important principle of proportionality has been applied. Two cases, considered together, raised this issue where convicted criminals faced confiscation of their assets and claimed that this was an interference with their property. The cases are *Rezvi* and *Benjafield*.[33]

Karl Robert Benjafield was convicted of charges connected with drug supplying, and the judge made an order of confiscation of his assets to the extent of £327,971; and Syed Rezvi was convicted of offences of theft, and a confiscation order was made in his case of £214,389. The confiscation orders were made under Acts of Parliament, which empowered the court to confiscate assets following conviction of offences; the statutes permitted the court to make assumptions against the defendant that his property and expenditure originated from criminal activity, unless the defendant showed them to be incorrect.

The House of Lords considered Article 1 and agreed that these were instances of interference with property, but held that confiscation was a reasonable and proportionate reaction to the danger of drug trafficking and serious crime, so long as the court making the order did not consider that there was a risk of real or serious injustice. On the principle which justified the institution of confiscation, Lord Steyn said:

> It is a notorious fact that professional and habitual criminals frequently take steps to conceal their profits from crime. Effective but fair powers of confiscating the proceeds of crime are therefore essential. The provisions of the Criminal Justice Act 1988 are aimed at depriving

---

[33] *R v Rezvi, R v Benjafield* [2002] UKHL 1 and 2, [2002] 2 WLR 235.

such offenders of the proceeds of their criminal conduct. Its purposes are to punish convicted offenders, to deter the commission of further offences and to reduce the profits available to fund further criminal enterprises. These objectives reflect not only national but also international policy. The United Kingdom has undertaken, by signing and ratifying treaties agreed under the auspices of the United Nations and the Council of Europe, to take measures necessary to ensure that the profits of those engaged in drug trafficking or other crimes are confiscated.[34]

FORFEITURE OF GOODS – CUSTOMS AND THE PORTS

Sometimes what is to be forfeited is not property which is the proceeds of crime, but which has been used, wilfully or inadvertently sometimes, in the commission of an offence. This was considered in *Air Canada* v *UK*.[35]

Between 1983 and 1986, at Heathrow Airport, a number of incidents gave rise to concern regarding the adequacy of Air Canada's security procedures; drugs disappeared from freight or premises, or drugs were secreted in freight, and two Air Canada employees were convicted of offences connected with the importation of cannabis resin. Customs and Excise wrote letters warning that deductions could be made from the security bonds deposited by the airline. On 26 April 1987, a Tristar aircraft, worth over £60,000,000, owned and operated by Air Canada, and on a regular scheduled passenger flight, landed at Heathrow, where it discharged cargo including a container holding 331 kg of cannabis resin valued at about £800,000. The airway bill was false, and Air Canada's cargo computer did not hold any detail of the consignment. Customs officers seized the aircraft as liable to forfeiture, but the officers delivered it back on payment by Air Canada of a banker's draft of £50,000. Air Canada complained that there had been a violation of Article 1 by the seizing of the aircraft as liable to forfeiture.

The European Court regarded this as a control of use case, and so considered the case under the second paragraph of Article 1. The Court said:

According to the Court's well-established case law, the second paragraph of Article 1 must be construed in the light of the principle laid down in the Article's first sentence. Consequently, any interference must achieve a 'fair balance' between the demands of the general interest of the community and the requirements of the protection of the individual's fundamental rights. The concern to achieve this balance is reflected in the structure of Article 1 as a whole, including the second paragraph: there must therefore be a reasonable relationship of proportionality between the means employed and the aim pursued.

The Court found that, bearing in mind the history of incidents and the warnings, a fair balance had been achieved when the aircraft had been seized, and so the interference with the right of property was justified.

---

[34] *Rezvi* followed the European Court decision in *Philips* v *UK* [2001] Crim LR 817; and in the case of *Grayson* v *UK* [2008], the European Court approved the decision in *Rezvi*.
[35] (1995) 20 EHRR 150.

There have now been domestic cases, which have had to consider the forfeiture of property which has been used for illegal purposes. This has typically occurred where the vehicle has been used for smuggling: customs officials have various powers to seize goods. But such seizures are open to challenge if they are disproportionate. Further, if there is a policy in place, to make decisions faster and easier, it is important that the policy does not lead to an inflexible, or arbitrary, approach. We see that in the case of *Lindsay*.[36]

Customs and Excise officers on duty at ports check persons and vehicles for cigarettes and alcohol, on which duty is payable. In this case, they were operating a policy that in cases where a motor vehicle was seized, because duty was being evaded, Customs would return the vehicle to the owner only in exceptional circumstances; no distinction was made between large-scale, so-called 'commercial' smuggling and those bringing in goods on a non-commercial basis, for private use. Mr Lindsay, about to board a cross-Channel ferry at Calais, was stopped with substantial quantities of alcohol and cigarettes in his car. His vehicle was confiscated; the Customs officer applied the policy, and his car was not returned to him.

The Court of Appeal held there was a violation of Article 1. The question was whether there was sufficient justification for the interference with property. The deprivation of property would be justified where it was necessary and proportionate and in the public interest specifically 'to secure the payment of taxes or other contributions'. However, where, as here, no distinction was drawn between commercial and non-commercial smuggling, proportionality required that each case be considered on its facts; this included the scale of the importation, whether or not it was a first offence, whether there was any attempt to conceal the goods, the value of the vehicle, and any hardship which would be caused to the individual. Mr Lindsay was clearly importing goods for his family and friends and therefore should not have been subject to an automatic forfeiture.

Even if a policy is not applied inflexibly, individual decisions can still be unreasonable. So, in the case of *Harding*,[37] the decision to offer to restore a seized vehicle to a haulier on payment of a fee equal to its value was unreasonable and disproportionate and was set aside as being in breach of Article 1, where all that the haulier had done was fail to check that the destination warehouse was permitted to receive certain alcohol imports. In the case of *Newbury*,[38] the driver had only imported goods for his own use, and had warned his passengers to do the same. He was therefore not responsible for one of his passengers disregarding this and making an impermissible import, and it was disproportionate for him to forfeit the car and his goods to enforce another passenger's liability.[39]

---

[36] *Lindsay v Commissioners of Customs and Excise* [2002] EWCA Civ 267, [2002] 1 WLR 1766.

[37] *Nicholas Harding (T/A Nick Harding Transport) v Customs & Excise Commissioners* (2003) LTL 8.9.03.

[38] *Customs & Excise Commissioners v Newbury* [2003] EWHC 702 (Admin), [2003] 2 All ER 964.

[39] Also relevant are the *International Roth* case, considered above, p. 208, about whether the imposition of confiscation as a fixed penalty infringes Article 6; and *Hoverspeed*, above pp. 127–8, about free movement of goods within the EU.

BUSINESS AND LIVELIHOOD

We have looked at a number of cases which have concerned the business of the people claiming the protection of the right of property. However, where the alleged interference with property would have the effect of removing a person's ability to run their business, it will be particularly important to strike the right balance between the needs of that individual and the needs of the wider community. This is shown by the next case, which concerned an application for a licence of a public house. Such applications are heard daily, and the court will now have to consider whether to renew or refuse an application will be a proportionate interference with a right to property. The case is *Catscratch Ltd*.[40]

Catscratch Limited operated premises as a nightclub, under a public house licence, and had in the past enjoyed regular extensions of permitted hours until 2 a.m. from Monday to Saturday and 2.30 to 6.30 p.m. on Sundays. In June 2000, at the statutory meeting of the licensing board, Catscratch's annual application for a regular extension in relation to an entertainment licence was refused. And the same thing happened again in 2001. Although a number of objections had been lodged, none were from the police or the local authority. The company claimed it suffered loss of business as a result of the withdrawing of the licences and sought judicial review of the decision of the licensing board, complaining of a breach of Article 1.

The Court of Session accepted that the failure to obtain a permitted licensing extension, so leading to the closure of the business, amounted to a 'control of the use of the property' of the premises within Article 1, and so was an interference with Catscratch's rights. But, applying the fair balance test, there was sufficient evidence to lead the licensing board to conclude that there was a need to protect the environment, and the refusal of the licence was necessary for this purpose and not disproportionate.

A business may also be affected by having to pay workers a certain amount – the enforcement of a minimum wage – which is effectively a deprivation of the business's assets, since the business might be required to pay more than it would otherwise do. A minimum wage must therefore be reasonably necessary and proportionate – and not discriminatory.

In the case of *Middlebrook Mushrooms Ltd*,[41] the Agricultural Wages Board imposed minimum wages for various workers, split into categories. One was 'standard worker', another, with a lower minimum wage, was 'manual harvest worker'. But the definition of produce to which the lower manual harvest worker rate applied excluded mushrooms. This was challenged, and the Court agreed that this was discriminatory, in breach of Article 1 taken with Article 14: there was no good reason for excluding only mushroom pickers from an otherwise universal category of workers.

---

[40] *Catscratch Limited* v *Glasgow City Licensing Board* [2001] UKHRR 1309.
[41] *R (Middlebrook Mushrooms Ltd)* v *Agricultural Wages Board* [2004] EWHC 1447 (Admin), Times 15.7.04.

QUESTIONS

1 Why should property be protected?

2 The wording of Article 1 contains a number of limitations set out in broad and general terms. What are the general interests which these limitations protect? Are they too broad, too narrow, or about right, and why?

3 Is taxation justified? Does it matter what the purpose of the taxation is?

4 Do you consider that the law is correct to confiscate the proceeds of crime? Why?

19

The right to property

In the Iraqi election in 2005, the first since the fall of Saddam Hussein, voters had a finger stained with purple dye to ensure that they only voted once.

Source: Reuters

20 Free elections

The courts owe a special responsibility to the public as the constitutional guardian of the freedom of political debate. (Lord Justice Laws in *R (Pro-Life Alliance)* v *BBC*,[1] 2002)

Democracy is the worst form of government except all those other forms which have been tried from time to time. (Winston Churchill, speech to Parliament, 1947)

First Protocol, Article 3: Right to Free Elections

The High Contracting parties undertake to hold free elections at reasonable intervals by secret ballot, under conditions which will ensure free expression of the opinion of the people in the choice of the legislature.

THE IMPORTANCE OF DEMOCRACY

Democracy is without doubt a fundamental feature of the European public order. That is apparent, from the Preamble to the Convention,[2] which establishes a very clear connection between the Convention and democracy by stating that the maintenance and further realisation of human rights and fundamental freedoms are best ensured on the one hand by an effective political democracy and on the other by a common understanding and observance of human rights. [This emphasises] the prime importance of Article 3 of Protocol No. 1 which enshrines a characteristic principle of an effective political democracy.

This was the statement of the European Court in the case of *United Communist Party of Turkey* v *Turkey*,[3] where the Turkish Constitutional Court had made an order dissolving the Turkish Communist Party on the grounds that its programme contained statements to undermine the integrity of the state and the unity of the nation, since its programme referred to the Kurdish nation as well as the Turkish nation, and the Turkish Constitution prohibited self-determination and regional autonomy. The European Court did not in fact determine the complaint under Article 3,[4] since it found a clear breach of the Article 11 right to freedom of association.

---

[1] [2002] EWCA Civ 297, [2004] 1 AC 185.
[2] This can be found in the text of the Convention in Appendix 2, p. 415.
[3] (1998) 26 EHRR 121.
[4] All references in this chapter to Article 3 should be taken to refer to this Article, not Article 3 of the Convention itself.

355

Nonetheless, the statement of principle above is important, and it sets the scene for our examination of this Article. Democracy is something we usually consider to be one of the key features of a free society. This is partly because the right to vote has been hard-won, as has the right to be governed by elected representatives. After all, the English Civil War (1642–49) was fought over who should govern the country, and Parliament won. Likewise, the Bill of Rights 1688 was based on a forced change of sovereign, the 'Glorious Revolution', which is why it set out a number of important Parliamentary privileges and protections for democracy, including the right to free elections.[5] This right in some form has therefore been a part of our law for centuries, although, as with many other basic rights, its content and scope has developed with time – during the 'revolution' of 1688, the number of people who could actually vote was severely limited; full universal suffrage, the right of all adults to vote, cannot really be said to have been in place until 1950.[6]

It is also worth bearing in mind that what we mean by democracy, and thus what is protected by Article 3, is representative democracy. That is, the rights protected are the rights to vote for representatives to make up a legislature – in the United Kingdom, these are Members of Parliament. This is not the only possible meaning of democracy – it is a far cry from the system for which the term was invented, that of ancient Athens, where the state was the city and its territory, and government, at least in part, was by an assembly of all free adult males, which was considered at the time to be government by the people (the 'demos'). But it is the only form of democracy which is practicable in a modern country, given the number of citizens. It is therefore necessary to concentrate on how to ensure that elections are free, properly express the views of the electorate, and occur at sufficiently regular intervals so that the government never gets to the stage where it ceases to be accountable to the electorate.

THE STATE'S OBLIGATION

'The High Contracting parties . . .' – these are the opening words of this Article, and no other Article of the Convention guaranteeing a right or freedom opens in this manner. It emphasises that the Article expressly imposes an obligation on the state to ensure the right. In the case of *Mathieu-Mohin and Clerfayt* v *Belgium*[7] the European Court referred to these opening words of this Article.

> Mrs Mathieu-Mohin, a French-speaking Belgian citizen, had been elected to the Senate, one of the two Houses of the Belgian Parliament. She had taken the parliamentary oath in French, and therefore could not be a member of the Flemish Council; that was the relevant regional body for representatives elected from her area. She complained that French-speaking electors, who had elected herself, were disadvantaged in that their candidates suffered these limitations. In this sense, she complained, the 'free expression of the opinion of the people' was impaired. The European Court rejected the claim, on the facts of the case. But it did refer to these first words of Article 3:

---

[5] Discussed above, p. 24.

[6] In 1928, women were given the vote on the same terms as men; in 1950, the residence qualification was removed.

[7] (1988) 10 EHRR 1.

> The inter-State colouring of the wording of Article 3 does not reflect any difference of substance from the other substantive clauses in the Convention and Protocols. The reason for it would seem to lie rather in the desire to give greater solemnity to the commitment undertaken and in the fact that the primary obligation in the field concerned is not one of abstention or non-interference, as with the majority of the civil and political rights, but one of adoption by the State of positive measures to 'hold' democratic elections.

THE SCOPE OF ARTICLE 3

Article 3 does not contain any express limitation or restriction, such as those contained, for example, in Articles 8, 9, 10 and 11. There is no reference in the wording of Article 3 to proportionality, and no reference to any reservation.

Nevertheless, Article 3 is not absolute; that was the express statement of the European Court in the case of *Ahmed* v *UK*.[8] We have examined this case in our discussion of Article 10, the right to freedom of expression. The case concerned local government officers who were interested in taking part in the activities of political parties, but were forbidden to do so by regulations which restricted such activities of officers in 'politically restricted posts'. They claimed that their rights under Article 10 had been violated. The European Court rejected their claims, holding that there was a pressing social need for restrictions of this kind, and that these restrictions could not be said to be disproportionate. But the Court also considered Article 3:

> The Court recalls that Article 3 of Protocol No. 1 implies subjective rights to vote and to stand for election. As important as those rights are, they are not, however, absolute. Since Article 3 recognises them without setting them forth in express terms, let alone defining them, there is room for implied limitations.

This approach is consistent with the Court's treatment of other Articles: we have seen examples in other Articles of the Convention, where there are no express limitations or reservations, but where the Court has implied limitations, sometimes even where the wording appears to be absolute. As with other such implied limitations, the underlying feature of the Court's approach is the question of proportionality.

We see this perfectly illustrated in another election case. It is the case of *Robertson*.[9]

> Mr Robertson was an elector, and wished to have his name removed from an electoral register before that register was sold to a commercial concern for marketing purposes. Electoral registration officers were by statute charged with the duty of preparing and publishing each year a register of parliamentary and local government electors for their area, and were required to supply a copy to any person upon payment of a fee. Mr Robertson, although knowing it was a criminal offence to fail to return an application form duly completed, wrote to the officer in Wakefield stating that he did not intend to complete the form for inclusion on the register because he opposed the practice of selling copies of the

---

[8] (2000) 29 EHRR 1, above, p. 317.
[9] *R (Robertson)* v *Wakefield Metropolitan District Council* [2001] EWHC 915 (Admin), [2002] 2 WLR 889.

register to commercial interests. The officer replied that the compilation of the register was separate from the uses made of it, and that he intended to include the name and address of Mr Robertson.

Mr Robertson applied for judicial review on the ground that he was unlawfully being required to tolerate the dissemination of the register to commercial interests, and that his enfranchisement could not lawfully be made conditional upon acceptance of that practice. He complained of a breach of Article 8 (the right to respect for his private life) and Article 3.

The judge, Mr Justice Maurice Kay, held that the practice of selling the register to commercial concerns without affording individual electors a right of objection was a *disproportionate* way in which to give effect to the legitimate objective of retaining a commercially available register, so that there was a violation of Article 8. Further, to the extent that the relevant regulations made the right to vote conditional upon the acquiescence in that practice, with no individual right of objection, they operated in a manner which contravened Article 3 on the same reasoning of justification and proportionality that was applied in the case of Article 8.

There was a sequel to this case: as a result of this decision, the government amended the relevant regulations, to restrict the sale of the register for commercial purposes. However, credit reference agencies were still permitted to purchase the register. Mr Robertson challenged this as well.[10] Mr Justice Maurice Kay this time considered that the amended regulations did *not* infringe Article 3: this was not a marketing purpose, but pursued a legitimate aim in the facilitation of credit and the control of fraud, and the amended regulation was a reasonable and limited interference with Article 3.

Thus we see the principle of proportionality applied to this Article, here by reference also to the express limitations in Article 8; and we should bear this in mind as we turn to other aspects of elections. We shall consider first the position of the voter – systems of voting, and the franchise – and then the position of the candidate.

VOTING SYSTEMS

Possibly the two most important rights for a voter are the **system of voting**, and the **franchise**. The wording of Article 3 does not specify any particular method of voting. The election process must be 'free', and must ensure 'a secret ballot', and a 'free expression of the opinion of the people'. But that is all. There is no mention of how these should be achieved. Of course, the underlying principle is that of democracy, that there should be a true expression of the preference of the people. How that is achieved is a matter on which the European Court will allow a margin of appreciation, since the Article does not specify any particular electoral system, and since different systems are used in different countries, so long as the degree of accuracy is comparable with the systems of other European democracies.

We see this illustrated in the case of *The Liberal Party* v *UK*.[11]

[10] *R (Robertson)* v *Secretary of State* [2003] EWHC 1760 (Admin), Times 11.8.03.
[11] (1982) 4 EHRR 106.

Here, the Liberal Party (now the Liberal Democrats) was questioning the British electoral system. Our elections are run on the basis of a simple majority, known as the first past the post system. The Liberal Party was rather smaller than the two main parties, the Conservative and Labour Parties.

The Liberal Party claimed that the number of candidates elected to Parliament did not properly reflect the number of electors who voted Liberal, because it was a smaller party, and so it was disproportionately disadvantaged by the electoral system. Thus the system did not ensure the 'free expression of the opinion of the people'. The Liberal Party claimed that if one of the generally recognised systems for proportional representation had been used – such as voting for candidates on a national list, using an additional number system, or using a single transferable vote, which allows second-preference votes to count – more Liberal candidates would have been elected, which would have been a more accurate reflection of the views of the electorate. The Liberal Party therefore claimed that there were violations of Article 3, as well as Article 14 (which prohibits discrimination). The Conservative and Labour Parties opposed this, unsurprisingly, on the basis that they would lose seats.

The Commission rejected the claim. It considered that Article 3 was careful not to bind the states as to the electoral system they should use. It does not add any requirement of 'equality' to the 'secret ballot'. Furthermore, even countries with a formal requirement for equality of voting still accept that the simple majority system complies with that requirement: for example, the Federal Republic of Germany, and the United States of America.

20

Free elections

It is of interest to note that this was notwithstanding the opinion, relied upon by the Liberal Party and cited by the Commission, of Professor Wade, who has described the British electoral system of parliamentary representation as 'probably the worst that could be devised'.[12]

THE FRANCHISE

Another key aspect of elections is the **right to vote**, the franchise. In a democracy it is a valuable thing – even if some people stay away from the polling booth and so do not use it. Indeed, over the course of history, there have been long and bitter struggles by various groups to obtain the right to vote, and it was only relatively recently that it could be said that all adults have the right to vote. Article 14, which prevents discrimination in the application of the other Articles, would also be relevant here if there was ever an attempt to limit the right to vote in Article 3 on arbitrary grounds.

However, having the franchise is of no use if a person is not allowed to vote. In two cases which we will now examine, electors wished to use their franchise, and could not. Bearing in mind that the European Court accepts that the Article 3 right is not absolute, the question in both cases was whether the interference was justified and proportionate. In the first case, *Moore v UK*,[13] when Mr Moore's claim showed that the interference was not justified, Parliament changed the law.

[12] *Constitutional Fundamentals*, 1980 Hamlyn Lectures.
[13] (2000) 30 EHRR CD 90.

Mr Moore had been detained since 1993 in Colchester under the Mental Health Acts; in 1996, he wrote to the electoral registration officer asking to be entered on the electoral roll; the officer's reply was that the Representation of the People Act 1983 prevented detained patients from being resident at the place of their detention, so Mr Moore should approach the officer of his parents' area. Mr Moore did so, but that officer refused to register him, as he had not lived there for six months. Thus Mr Moore had no way of registering to vote.

He complained to the European Court of a breach of his electoral rights, claiming that he had been disenfranchised, denied his right to vote. Before the case was decided by the European Court, Parliament amended the 1983 Act to include a provision that patients could be registered for the area of the hospital where they resided. This complaint therefore brought about a change in the law, because it was realised that there was a breach of Article 3.

The European Court had to consider the equivalent ban on prisoners being disenfranchised in the case of *Hirst*.[14]

Mr Hirst was serving a term of discretionary life imprisonment for manslaughter on the ground of diminished responsibility. He had applied to the electoral registration officer for the relevant districts, to be registered on the electoral roll, and the officers had refused. He complained of violations of Article 3 of the First Protocol and Article 14 of the Convention. Section 3(1) of the Representation of the People Act 1983 provided that a convicted person detained in a penal institution was legally incapable of voting at parliamentary or local government elections. Mr Hirst had initially applied to the English courts, which had considered that the ban on prisoners' voting rights was not a disproportionate interference with Article 3.[15]

However, the European Court disagreed. Whilst limitations on the right to vote are permissible, and whilst states do have a margin of appreciation, the blanket and indiscriminate prohibition on the right to vote for *all* prisoners – irrespective of length of sentence, offence or individual circumstances – is disproportionate. It fails to give proper weight to the fact that voting is a right not a privilege.

The government's response was to propose a system categorising prisoners, banning only those imprisoned for the most serious crimes from voting, but the continued failure to implement this has led to a declaration of incompatibility being made, in the case of *Smith v Scott*.[16]

■ THE LEGISLATURE

This word is not limited to the national Parliament of the state. The word must be interpreted in the light of the constitutional structure of the nation in question. This was the attitude of the European Court in the case of *Matthews v UK*.[17]

---

[14] *Hirst* v *UK* (2005) Times 10.10.05.
[15] *R (Pearson)* v *Home Secretary*; *Hirst* v *Attorney General* [2001] EWHC 239 (Admin), [2001] HRLR 39.
[16] [2007] CSIH 9, [2007] SLT 137; for parliamentary criticism of the delay by the Joint Select Committee on Human Rights see, e.g., *Thirty-first Report*, October 2008, HL 173/HC 1078.
[17] (1999) 28 EHRR 361.

Ms Matthews was a British citizen, residing in Gibraltar; she applied to the electoral registration officer to be registered as a voter at the elections to the European Parliament, but received the reply that Gibraltar was not included in the franchise for the European parliamentary elections, so she therefore could not vote. She complained to the European Court of a violation of Article 3. The European Commission had previously found that non-national institutions, such as the European Parliament, were not to be regarded as 'the legislature' within Article 3.

> The Court noted that Gibraltar is part of the European Union, and that, according to the case law of the European Court of Justice, it is an inherent aspect of EU law that such law sits alongside, and indeed has precedence over, domestic law. The European Parliament was a legislature within the fullest sense of the word, and was indeed the European legislature for Gibraltar. The fact that a body was not envisaged by the drafters of the Convention cannot prevent that body from falling within the scope of the Convention.

And the Court added:

> The Court thus considers that to accept the Government's contention that the sphere of activities of the European Parliament falls outside the scope of Article 3 of Protocol No. 1 would risk undermining one of the fundamental tools by which 'effective political democracy' can be maintained.

One case where the English Court has had to consider the constitutional arrangements of a different system relates to the Channel Island of Sark. Sark, like all the Channel Islands, has its own system of government with the Queen as Head of State. What was complained of was a proposed electoral law which allowed for all members of the legislature to be elected except for the Seigneur of Sark and the Seneschal of Sark, and allowed for resident non-citizens of Sark to vote in the election, but not to stand for the legislature. This came before the Court in London by way of an application for judicial review of the order in council which gave royal assent to the law.[18] The Court of Appeal held that there was no infringement of Article 1-3. The Article did not require every member of a legislature to be democratically elected, and here the voting rights of the non-elected members were limited and a power of veto was also limited; and further, the legislature was free to alter its constitution on the future if it wished. Thus the legislative body was essentially democratic, although there was a breach of Article 6, the senior judge also being a member of the legislative body.

20

Free elections

THE POSITION OF CANDIDATES

The 'free expression of the opinion of the people in the choice of the legislature' is the object of this Article. But that free expression, and choice, might be impaired if some obstacle is put in the way of a candidate: the people may have voted for the candidate, but he is prevented from taking his seat. In the case of *Buscarini* v *San Marino*[19] this happened with members of the General Grand Council, which is the legislature of the Republic of

---

[18] *R (Barclay)* v *Lord Chancellor* [2008] EWCA Civ 1319, [2009] 2 WLR 1205.
[19] (2000) 30 EHRR 208, discussed in the context of Article 9, above, p. 291.

San Marino. They were obliged to swear an oath on the Gospels. They did so under protest, complaining that their right to freedom of religion and conscience had been infringed. The European Court agreed that this was in violation of their rights under Article 9. Whilst this case is primarily about freedom of conscience, it is also relevant as an example of the Convention's impact on the democratic process, which is very much what is protected by Article 3.

Of a similar kind is the case of *Bowman* v *UK*,[20] and again this is not a case under Article 3, because the complaint was of a violation of Article 10, freedom of expression; but it is instructive of the attitude of the European Court on a matter which is part of the election process – in this case, limitations on the amount that can be spent on election publicity.

Mrs Bowman was a director of SPUC, the Society for the Protection of the Unborn Child, which was opposed to abortion and human embryo experimentation and which sought to change the law which permits abortion up to 22 weeks. In the Parliamentary election of 1992, Mrs Bowman was not an election candidate; but she distributed leaflets, which assisted one of the candidates in the election. Mrs Bowman brought to the attention of electors the views and opinions of the candidates regarding abortion and related issues, by distributing leaflets in Halifax. The Representation of the People Act 1983 prohibited expenditure exceeding £5 on the conveying of information to electors with a view to promoting or procuring the election of a candidate. She was prosecuted for exceeding this figure, although she was acquitted when it was shown that the prosecution had been brought out of time. She complained to the European Court of a violation of Article 10. The Court agreed that the prosecution was a violation of Article 10; the limitation on expenditure, to so low a figure as £5, and the subsequent prosecution, were disproportionate to the legitimate aim of pursuing and securing equality between candidates.

The figure which could be spent on promoting a candidate was subsequently increased to £500. When it emerged that the drafting of the amendment to the section of the Representation of the People Act 1983 which followed the decision in *Bowman* only applied to some forms of activity covered and not to all of them, the Court of Appeal read words into the statute to ensure that the higher limit applied more generally, so as to give effect to Article 10.[21]

The picture is clear: in the context of elections, Articles 9 and 10 can be as relevant as Article 3 in ensuring that overall the electoral process is fair.

◼ PARTY POLITICAL BROADCASTS

One of the best-known modern features of general elections is the party political broadcast. It is almost an institution in itself. A broadcast of this kind is obviously 'an expression of opinion'. Again, even if Article 3 is not directly engaged, Articles 9 and 10 may well be, in a context in which they are supportive of free elections: and the European Court has

---

[20] (1998) 26 EHRR 1.
[21] *R v Holding* [2005] EWCA Crim 3185, [2006] 1 WLR 1040.

recognised the close relationship between these Articles in the democratic process.[22] This fell to be considered in a case where the BBC had refused to allow a party political broadcast.[23]

> The Pro-Life Alliance, a political party registered under the Political Parties, Election and Referendums Act 2000, campaigned for absolute respect for human life, and opposed abortion, euthanasia, destructive embryo research and human cloning. The party sought to make a party election broadcast in May 2001, but the BBC and other broadcasters declined to transmit it, on the grounds that the content did not comply with the BBC's and Independent TV's Guidelines and Code in respect of matters of taste and decency. The video was described as 'graphic and disturbing'.
>
> The House of Lords (by a majority) held that the broadcasters were entitled to refuse to show the broadcast. The fact that this was an election broadcast did not exempt the Pro-Life Alliance from taste and decency requirements. The basic right to expression, in the case of access to public media, is not to have such access denied on discriminatory, arbitrary or unreasonable grounds. Parliament, by statute, had banned offensive material, and this limit on the grounds of taste and decency was not arbitrary or unreasonable. The only question then for the broadcasters was whether the proposed broadcast was offensive, and the Lords held that the broadcasters were entitled to consider that the material was offensive.
>
> However, the importance of the issues at stake were stressed by the Lords. As Lord Nicholls put it:
>
>> Freedom of political speech is a freedom of the very highest importance in any country which lays claim to being a democracy. Restrictions on this freedom need to be examined rigorously by all concerned, not least the courts. The courts, as independent and impartial bodies, are charged with a vital supervisory role.
>
> And, quoting from the Court of Appeal's decision, the point was put this way by Lord Justice Laws:
>
>> Freedom of expression is plainly a constitutional right, and its enjoyment by an accredited political party in an election contest must call, if anything, for especially heightened protection. [Where] the context is day-to-day news reporting the broadcasters' margin of discretion may be somewhat more constrained but will remain very considerable. But the milieu, the cockpit of a general election, is inside the veins and arteries of the democratic process.

Another respect in which Article 10 has been engaged by political broadcasting is by the ban on political advertising on television and radio.

This was challenged in the *Animal Defenders* case,[24] which is a group campaigning about animal welfare. Thus the proposed adverts were not for a political party but were on a political issue. The House of Lords upheld the ban on the basis that it prevents balanced programming being subverted by political parties or interests buying broadcasting space to

---

[22] e.g. in *Bowman*, referred to above, and *TV Vest AS*, referred to below.
[23] *R (Pro-Life Alliance) v British Broadcasting Corporation* [2003] UKHL 23, [2004] 1 AC 185.
[24] *R (Animal Defenders International) v Secretary of State for Culture, Media and Sport* [2008] UKHL 15, [2008] 1 AC 1312.

advertise and thereby giving their views enhanced prominence in proportion to their resources. In that respect it is intended to be supportive of the democratic process.

However, the imposition of a blanket ban, such as that considered in *Animal Defenders*, has been rejected by the European Court in the case of *TV Vest AS* v *Norway*.[25]

Here, a ban which prevented a small special interest political party, the Pensioners' Party, from advertising was held to be a disproportionate interference with Article 10. The European Court reviewed the variety of practice across Europe and did consider that a margin of appreciation applies. However, the Pensioners' Party was not the sort of group which had the resources to obtain an unfair advantage through advertising. Although it is the sort of group which the ban was intended to protect from having its message swamped, it had not been given any opportunity to get its message across other than through paid advertising, and the sort of adverts it produced, containing a short description of the Pensioners' Party and a call to vote, were not offensive, nor did they lower the quality of political debate. The European Court held that in the circumstances of this case, fining the broadcast company for showing the adverts was a breach of Article 10.

Thus it remains to be seen if, in the light of this case, the blanket ban in the UK should be reconsidered as it might impact on smaller groups or parties which might otherwise struggle to have their voice heard as part of the political broadcast process.

QUESTIONS

1 Why is democracy important? Why should it matter that people are given the right to elect their government?

2 Are free elections all that is required by democracy? Does Article 3 provide sufficient safeguards for the democratic process? What contribution do other Articles also provide for safeguarding the democratic process? Do they go far enough?

---

[25] (2009) 48 EHRR 51.

The twin towers of the World Trade Center in New York were destroyed on
11 September 2001 by a terrorist attack which killed some 2,800 people. This prompted
a legislative reaction: the Anti-Terrorism, Crime and Security Act 2001 (see p. 372).

Source: © Hubert Boesl/dpa/Corbis

21 The problem of terrorism

Silent enim leges inter arma (In the midst of arms, the laws are dumb). (Marcus Tullius Cicero, *Pro Milone*, 52 BCE)

TERRORISM AND THE RULE OF LAW

Arms were literally surrounding the place when the Roman orator Cicero spoke those words to the court in Rome, in the midst of political crisis. The renowned general Pompey had stationed his army in the nearby Forum, and in all the temples round about. Cicero was acting as the advocate for Milo, who was charged with murdering a populist political leader and rabble-rouser, Clodius. Cicero was drawing attention to the fact that the threatening presence of Pompey's soldiers was intended to make the court forget the law and act only in accordance with the political and military pressure which was being put on them. He himself was reputed to be so afraid that he was shaking; and Milo was convicted.

Nowadays we would not expect courts to be deciding questions under siege, at least not in Britain, although there are recent examples from around the world, where state pressure has been brought to bear on courts to deal with real or perceived enemies of the state as the government wishes. But certainly, in time of war, when the state is under attack, the rule of law may come under strain. Exceptional measures may be thought necessary, to preserve the community from those using force against it, and the usual procedures of the law may have to be suspended.

In the United Kingdom there have, over the centuries, been a large number of instances where **emergency powers** have been passed to respond to a situation where the normal safeguards provided by the law were perceived as inhibiting the action which was needed to combat the threat. Indeed, as one looks at the history of particular legal safeguards, the development of exceptions to a particular safeguard in times of emergency often goes back as far as the development of the safeguard itself. So, for many centuries, one device used in a civil emergency was the suspension of *habeas corpus*, which meant that there could be no judicial scrutiny of detention of suspects; this was last used in Ireland in 1866–69. A similar measure was **martial law**, which refers to rule by military authority during a state of war. It was last used in Britain in 1780, but was invoked in Ireland in 1916 and 1920, and then in a number of colonial situations later in the twentieth century, although its use declined after the Amritsar Massacre in India in 1919, which occurred whilst martial law was in force. During both the First World War (1914–18) and the Second World War (1939–45), there were emergency powers in force in the United Kingdom.[1]

Although a terrorism campaign does not pose as grave a threat to national security and public safety as does a full-scale war, the threat of terrorism may still be a serious one. Over the last few decades, there have been a number of terrorist bombings on mainland Britain with serious consequences, especially those committed by the Irish Republican Army (IRA) and its offshoots, and even more so in Northern Ireland. Then, of course, the events of 11 September 2001, when the twin towers of the World Trade Center in New York were destroyed by terrorists using hijacked aircraft as flying bombs, demonstrated that terrorism can be carried out on a massive scale, and that a terrorist may attack any corner of the world; and this was tragically confirmed by the suicide bombings in London on 7 July 2005. Terror organisations can have the resources to do real damage, even without the backing of a state or government.

This raises the question as to whether special laws are required to deal with terrorists, and whether it is justified for these laws to interfere with human rights, if that is necessary to tackle this threat. Given the particular issues and problems of having to balance the need to combat a serious threat against the potential for infringements of human rights, the terrorism legislation is worth considering as a separate topic, as a difficult issue which applies to many of the individual Convention rights. On the one hand, extraordinary threats may require extraordinary measures to be taken; on the other hand, if we allow our basic rights to be too far restricted, even in the reasonable pursuit of security, we are in danger of giving in to terrorism – of handing the terrorists the victory they are seeking by relinquishing the very essence of our free and democratic society, which is what is being attacked.

WHAT IS TERRORISM?

The first thing we should do is to define what we mean by **terrorism**. The legal definition is that contained in section 1 of the Terrorism Act 2000, which can be distilled into: the threat or use of any action which involves **serious violence** against persons or property, **endangers life**, creates a **serious risk to public health or safety** or is designed **seriously** to interfere with or **disrupt an electronic system**, where this action has the **purpose of intimidating or coercing** a government or the public, in order to advance a **political, religious, racial or ideological cause.**

Thus, the emphasis is on serious violence or damage, or the threat of it, carried out for a particular cause, and aimed at the government or the public. The government or public which is the target need not be those of the country where the attack is carried out – for example, the bomb attacks on the United States embassy in Nairobi, Kenya, in 1998 were terrorist attacks because they were aimed at the United States government and diplomats. The reference to electronic systems has in mind what is termed cyber-terrorism, the threat of taking advantage of our reliance nowadays on technological systems for controlling safety, such as air-traffic control, or national arms-control systems.

During the passage of the Terrorism Act 2000, the (then) Home Secretary said:

---

[1] We highly recommend Chapter 2 of Professor Simpson's *Human Rights and the End of Empire* for a rather more detailed discussion of the history of emergency and martial laws in the UK and its colonies.

Terrorism is premeditated, and aimed to create a climate of extreme fear. While the direct victims may be specific or symbolic targets, they may also be selected at random. In any event, terrorism is aimed at influencing a wider target than its immediate victims. Although all crime to some degree plainly threatens the stability of the social and political order, terrorism differs from crime motivated solely by greed, in that it is directed at undermining the foundations of Government.[2]

There are some particular situations which fall outside the statutory definition. In particular, industrial or trade disputes are not intended to be caught by this definition. Although that is action for a political cause, aimed at influencing the government, it does not have the aim of causing harm. Indeed reference was made in Parliament to the fact that unions which represent those who provide essential services usually go to considerable lengths to seek to avoid serious risk to life, health and safety as a result of the way in which they pursue industrial disputes.[3]

Likewise ordinary political protest, of the sort we have discussed in the context of Articles 10 and 11,[4] will fall outside the definition, unless it involves serious violence. Much civil disobedience is without any violence, or it may involve only the risk of harm to the protesters themselves. In order that this latter situation does not qualify as terrorism, the reference to endangering a person's life, in the definition of terrorism in section 1, specifically excludes endangering the life of the person committing the action.

This tells us what we are talking about when we are considering measures to deal with terrorists. One could say that, in such cases, we are dealing with people who are willing to cause great damage to others to make a political point, and who try to intimidate a government through fear and violence. The right to express views which are opposed to a particular political view or system is itself a fundamental right. But this is the right to express those views peacefully: at meetings, in print, by public protest, or by putting pressure on politicians. Not by rejecting the democratic process itself, whether this is by bombing trains, or bombing abortion clinics, or victimising those involved in animal testing. All of these are forms of terrorism, because they are rejections of the democratic process in favour of attempts to create political change by violence. Such violence cannot be justified in a democratic society where free expression of opinion is available and so where there is ample opportunity to demonstrate how one feels about an issue or situation without harming others.

DEALING WITH THE THREAT

Most acts of terrorism involve breaches of the ordinary criminal law: for example, a terrorist who uses a firearm to kill a member of the public can be charged with the usual offence of murder. But there are two particular aspects of terrorism which make it a particular threat. The first is the scale of the threat: when terrorism strikes, it is often part of a campaign, with repeated incidents committed by an organisation. The second is the nature of the threat: terrorists may be especially dangerous because they are in the category of people who clearly do not respect the rights of others to life and physical integrity.

[2] Rt Hon. Jack Straw MP, House of Commons debates, 14 December 1999 (*Hansard* HC, Vol. 341, col. 152).
[3] Lord Bassam of Brighton, House of Lords debates, 4 July 1999 (*Hansard* HL, Vol. 614, col. 1449).
[4] See above, Chapters 16 and 17.

When a campaign of violence is being pursued by terrorists, there may be a real perception that it is necessary to subordinate human rights to extraordinary laws intended to prevent or detect terrorism. This in particular is what drives governments to pass special laws to deal with it, going beyond the ordinary law of the land, and suspending the established safeguards of the law. This is what can lead to violations of human rights; either because the law itself, by its very terms, contravenes a human right, or because the way in which the law is put into effect infringes a human right.

However, the fact that human rights are infringed does not *necessarily* mean that these laws are unjustified. The threat of terrorism may be so great, at a particular time, that extraordinary measures may be genuinely necessary to prevent them from committing outrages, or to detect the perpetrators of an attack as a matter of urgency, and this may justify some breaches of human rights. Measures may be considered necessary, such as powers of arrest without an offence being committed or suspected; detention without trial; an obligation to give incriminating answers to questioning; abolition of the right to remain silent in the face of an accusation; and the placing of a burden of proof on an accused person.

These sorts of far-reaching powers are examples of those which have been put in place in the United Kingdom. Parliament passed two Acts to deal with terrorism within a little over a year of each other – the Terrorism Act 2000 (references here to 'the Terrorism Act' refer to this Act) and the Anti-Terrorism, Crime and Security Act 2001 ('the ATCS Act') – and further legislation has followed with the Prevention of Terrorism Act 2005, the Terrorism Act 2006 and the Counter-Terrorism Act 2008 (we shall refer to these collectively as 'the Terrorism Acts').

Each of them contains powers which may give rise to breaches of human rights, raising the problem of balancing the threat against the potential or actual interference with a Convention right: even where the threat is serious, one must still consider whether the means chosen to deal with it are proportionate.

The courts have also recognised that terrorism may have to be treated as a special case. In the case of *Fox, Campbell and Hartley* v *UK*,[5] the European Court, considering the question of reasonable suspicion founding an arrest, said:

> What may be 'reasonable' will depend upon all the circumstances. In this respect, terrorist crime falls into a special category. Because of the attendant risk of loss of life and human suffering, the police are obliged to act with utmost urgency in following up all information, including information from secret sources. Further, the police may frequently have to arrest a suspected terrorist on the basis of information which is reliable but which cannot, without putting in jeopardy the source of the information, be revealed to the suspect or produced in court to support a charge [. . .] in view of the difficulties inherent in the investigation and prosecution of terrorist-type offences in Northern Ireland, the 'reasonableness' of the suspicion justifying such arrests cannot always be judged according to the same standards as are applied in dealing with conventional crime.

The Court in that case decided that, even allowing for this being a terrorist case, insufficient facts had been shown to reach a conclusion that the arresting officer's belief was reasonable. But the important point is that terrorism may be taken into account when considering whether a measure is arbitrary or proportionate.

But by the same token, it is vital that the state does not overreact to the threat – which is to say that there must be some proportionality between the threat and the interference

---

[5] (1991) 13 EHRR 157.

with human rights. Not every risk, even of terrorism, will justify every interference with rights such as freedom from arbitrary detention or the right of access to a court, and it is important, in a democratic and free society, that these rights are not interfered with without cogent justification. This warning was sounded by Lord Hoffmann, in his dissenting speech in *A v Home Secretary*, and much cited in the consequent parliamentary debates:

> I do not underestimate the ability of fanatical groups of terrorists to kill and destroy, but they do not threaten the life of the nation. Whether we would survive Hitler hung in the balance, but there is no doubt that we shall survive Al-Qaeda. [. . .] Terrorist violence, serious as it is, does not threaten our institutions of government or our existence as a civil community. [. . .] The real threat to the life of the nation, in the sense of a people living in accordance with its traditional laws and political values, comes not from terrorism but from laws such as these. That is the true measure of what terrorism may achieve. It is for Parliament to decide whether to give the terrorists such a victory.[6]

All of the Terrorism Acts raise questions about how the Convention rights might be engaged by the operation of the powers they provide. We shall consider some of the ways in which the various Convention rights may be engaged by the exercise of the various powers which have been thought necessary to combat terrorism, after a short introduction to the Acts.

THE TERRORISM LEGISLATION

The Terrorism Act 2000 completely reformed the law relating to terrorist activity. It applies, with a few exceptions, to the whole of the United Kingdom, including terrorism connected with the affairs of Northern Ireland. It also extends to terrorism abroad: it creates a wide range of offences connected with the commission of acts of terrorism outside the United Kingdom.

One of its main features is the procedure for proscribing and deproscribing an organisation. Proscription is a way of denouncing a person or organisation, by making them illegal, and is used nowadays to outlaw organisations involved in terrorism. There are also specific offences relating to fundraising for terrorist organisations, using money or property for terrorism, money laundering, and failing to disclose information about such offences. Then there are wide powers of investigation, and search procedures, including a provision requiring financial institutions to reveal details of customers and their accounts. In addition, there are specific counter-terrorist powers of stop, search, questioning and arrest.

The Terrorism Act 2000 came into force on 19 February 2001. Then on 11 September 2001 there occurred the terrorist attacks in the United States of America; these had been well planned and managed and organised, with the application of much effort and money; the terrorists who carried them out were skilled and trained, and they were supported by organisations which clearly had access to great financial resources. And they operated on an international basis. After 11 September, the general perception was that further attacks could well occur, and that they might happen anywhere in the world, and that nuclear, chemical or biological weapons might be used. Thus on 12 November 2001, the Anti-Terrorism, Crime and Security Bill was presented and read in Parliament for the first time. It was carried through Parliament with expedition: it received the Royal Assent on 14 December 2001.

---

[6] *A v Home Secretary* [2004] UKHL 56, [2005] 2 WLR 87, paras 96–97; see below, p. 376.

One of the main provisions is the power to confiscate funds used for terrorism. There are further provisions ordering financial institutions to provide information about their customers' accounts. The assets of overseas governments and persons may be frozen, where there is a threat to the economic interests of the United Kingdom.[7] There are provisions for the disclosure of information by public authorities and government departments to the security services. There are also provisions which relate to the security of various industries and activities, including the security of the nuclear and aviation industries, and the regulation of transactions with nuclear, chemical and biological weapons or hazardous material.

One of the most contentious sections in the ATCS Act was a power to detain persons suspected of being international terrorists. This provision involved a derogation from Article 5 of the Convention which was ruled to be disproportionate and quashed by the House of Lords in the case of *A* v *Home Secretary*. As a result, the Prevention of Terrorism Act 2005 was passed which repealed that part of the ATCS Act and replaced it with a power to make control orders, and the derogation was withdrawn. We will consider this in more detail below.

Further anti-terrorism legislation has followed, with the Terrorism Act 2006 and the Counter-Terrorism Act 2008. The Terrorism Act 2006 created a whole new set of terrorism offences, many of which raise potential issues about their compatibility with the Human Rights Act. In particular, there are a number which potentially interfere with freedom of expression under Article 10, especially offences of encouraging or glorifying terrorism, disseminating terrorist publications, and providing or receiving terrorist training. Even attending at a place used for terrorist training is now an offence, without being directly involved, which potentially interferes with freedom of association under Article 11, as does the extension of the grounds for proscribing organisations to include those which encourage or glorify terrorism.

The Counter-Terrorism Act 2008 was the focus for the continuing debate about how long a terrorist suspect can be questioned before they are charged with an offence, and in the end an extension to this period was dropped while the Act was passing through Parliament. However, the Act did enact a number of provisions: amongst others, it brought in notification requirements, so that persons who have been convicted of terrorism-related offences must keep the police notified of certain personal information, and may have their overseas travel restricted; it increased various powers relating to money laundering, the gathering and sharing of information in terrorism matters between state bodies; and it allows for the questioning of terrorist suspects after they have been charged.

THE RIGHT TO LIFE

Terrorism raises particular issues in the context of the right to life because it leads to situations which are on the frontier between normal policing and responding to an armed attack on society. There are therefore particular risks that decisions or actions will be taken which do not adequately protect the right to life, which in a civilised society should be extended in principle even to those who are acting to try to harm that society, subject to the right to defend against their attacks. Thus police officers and members of the armed forces are deployed from time to time in places and situations where terrorism is suspected,

---

[7] Controversially used against Iceland in the recent economic crisis.

or expected, or where it has actually occurred; and, in these situations, the use of force may bring about a death, or cause the risk of it.

Article 2 covers such situations, by imposing a twofold duty on the state: the positive obligation to take steps to protect life, as well as the duty to refrain from taking life. Article 2(2) provides that deprivation of life shall not be regarded as being in breach of Article 2(1) when it results from the use of force which is no more than absolutely necessary and strictly proportionate to protect people from violence (but *not* property), to effect an arrest, or to quell a riot or insurrection. Additionally, where death results from the acts or omissions of an agent of the state, there must be an effective official investigation into the death. It will be a matter of judging, from case to case, whether there has been effective control and management of the situation, to limit as far as possible the risk to life, in the guidance and instructions issued to the security forces, and whether there has been a proper investigation into any death which might have occurred.

> These principles were illustrated in the case of *McCann*.[8] SAS soldiers shot and killed three IRA suspects in Gibraltar. The European Court held that in order to judge whether only such force was used as was absolutely necessary, there must be proper planning, control and organisation of the operation. In this case, the Court found that the planning and control of the operation failed properly to protect the right to life of the suspects, although the Court did find that there was a sufficient investigation into the deaths.

The Terrorism Acts themselves do not regulate the use of firearms or explosives by the police or armed forces. Section 114 of the Terrorism Act 2000 provides that a police officer may use reasonable force for the purpose of exercising a power given by that Act, which means that consideration of reasonable force may additionally apply to the various powers we will be considering below. Section 95 is an equivalent provision for the armed forces in Northern Ireland.

■ FREEDOM FROM TORTURE

Article 3 provides the right to be free of torture, inhuman or degrading treatment or punishment. We have already considered the case of *Ireland* v *United Kingdom*,[9] where methods used by the security forces in Northern Ireland to try to obtain information about IRA activities were held to amount to inhuman and degrading treatment; and *A* v *Home Secretary (No. 2)*,[10] where the House of Lords held that evidence which has been obtained by torture should not be admitted in consideration of whether a person was a terrorist – and whatever the threat. The Terrorism Acts do not contain provisions which directly threaten to infringe Article 3. But there is a real temptation on the part of those investigating, or trying to prevent, serious terrorist crimes to take such steps. Again, it is the mark of a civilised society not to stoop to the level of those who do *not* respect the rights of individuals to be free from physical violence, whatever the provocation or perceived threat, including not deporting persons to face torture abroad. As President of the Israeli Supreme

---

[8] *McCann* v *UK* (1996) 21 EHRR 97, considered above, p. 147.
[9] (1980) 2 EHRR 25, discussed in detail above, pp. 152–3.
[10] [2005] UKHL 71, [2005] 3 WLR 1249, discussed above, p. 168.

Court Barak noted in a decision which ruled against the use of various physical inter-rogation methods by the Israeli security forces: 'Although a democracy must often fight with one hand tied behind its back, it nonetheless has the upper hand.'[11]

ARREST WITHOUT WARRANT

Section 41 of the Terrorism Act 2000 provides for particular powers of detention by the police of someone suspected of being a terrorist: a constable may arrest without a warrant a person who is reasonably suspected to be a terrorist. The definition of a terrorist here includes a person who is or has been concerned in the commission, preparation or instiga-tion of terrorism; but these are not of themselves criminal offences. Thus a police officer making an arrest under section 41 need have no suspicion that any particular offence has been committed.

This raises an issue under Article 5, the right to freedom from arbitrary detention. Article 5 contains an exhaustive list of circumstances in which a person may be justifiably deprived of their liberty.[12] The relevant ground here is (c), which permits the deprivation of liberty on 'the lawful arrest or detention of a person effected for the purpose of bring-ing him before the competent legal authority *on reasonable suspicion of having committed an offence . . .*' (emphasis added). Since terrorism as such is not an offence, it follows that an arrest under section 41 of a person suspected of being a terrorist may be a violation of his rights under Article 5.

> This was raised in the case of *Brogan*.[13] Mr Brogan was arrested in Northern Ireland under the Prevention of Terrorism Act then in force. He was detained for 5 days and 11 hours, and then released without having been charged with any offence, or taken before a magistrate or judge. In custody, he was questioned about an offence of murder of a police officer, and about suspected membership of the Provisional IRA. He argued that he had been deprived of his liberty in breach of Article 5(1)(c) in that he had not been arrested 'for having com-mitted an offence'.
>
> The European Court held that the definition of 'terrorism' (for which he *was* arrested) – namely 'the use of violence for the purpose of putting the public in fear' – was well in keeping with the idea of an offence; and in addition he was questioned about a specific offence. Thus there was no violation of Article 5.

Section 41 has now been considered in the case of *I*[14] by Mr Justice Collins, who held that the power to detain without warrant was compatible with Article 5. Article 5(1)(c) was satisfied because the detention was lawful and, so long as the purpose of the detention is to bring the detainee before a judicial authority on reasonable suspicion of having committed an offence, it does not require there to be reasonable suspicion of an offence to make the detention itself lawful (although arguably that is a somewhat narrow reading of

---

[11] *Public Committee Against Torture in Israel* v *Israel* (1999) 7 BHRC 31.
[12] These are discussed in detail above in Chapter 11.
[13] *Brogan* v *UK* (1989) 11 EHRR 117. For discussion of Article 5(3) see p. 194, above.
[14] *R (I)* v *City of Westminster Magistrates Court* [2008] EWHC 2146 (Admin), [2008] 105 (36) LSG 24.

Article 5(1)(c)). Article 5 is then satisfied because there is then proper judicial control over whether there should be further detention. Under section 41 and Schedule 8, there are extended periods for detention for suspected terrorists. With such measures, it will be important to ensure that the Article 5 safeguards are still applied, especially review of the detention by a proper authority. Thus, under the Terrorism Act 2000, a detainee may be held for 48 hours before being taken before a magistrate, which may be extended to 7 days; the usual periods are 36 hours and 96 hours.[15] Likewise, a person so detained may be delayed in consulting a solicitor, or having a named person informed of his arrest, for up to 48 hours; the usual period is 30 hours.[16]

There is a similar power of detention under section 53 and Schedule 7 of that Act, for detention for questioning at a port or border, which raises similar issues. They empower a police or customs officer at a port or border to stop and question a person in order to determine *whether* that person is involved in the commission, preparation or instigation of acts of terrorism. Again, the officer need entertain no suspicion at all about the person – whether of terrorism or any specific offence. The officer may require information, proof of identity, and disclosure of documents, and he may detain the person for up to nine hours, and again may suffer a delay in consulting a solicitor or having a person informed of the detention. In any of these cases, there must be at least a risk that the conditions of the detention will be such that they could amount to a violation of Article 5.[17]

There is one case where the European Commission considered that a similar provision did fall within (b), arrest or detention in order to secure the fulfilment of an obligation prescribed by law, but the case is not easy to follow;[18] it is not clear why there is a legal obligation here. The conclusion must be that there is a real risk of a violation of Article 5 in the operation of these provisions.

DETENTION OF SUSPECTED TERRORISTS

> Indefinite imprisonment without charge or trial is anathema in any country which observes the rule of law. It deprives the detained person of the protection a criminal trial is intended to afford. Wholly exceptional circumstances must exist before this extreme step can be justified. (Lord Nicholls in *A* v *Home Secretary*)

The issue of detaining suspected terrorists was an issue which Part 4 of the ATCS Act was designed to meet, which the House of Lords held was in breach of the Convention in the case of *A*, and which the Prevention of Terrorism Act 2005 was then passed to address.

Under the ATCS Act, the Secretary of State was able to certify that a person is a 'suspected international terrorist', and then that person could be detained indefinitely without trial. This was done for a number of people who were held at Belmarsh Prison. The purpose of this power, and the reason for its conflict with Article 5, was to address the concern that there could be foreign nationals present in this country suspected of being concerned in terrorism, or of having links with international terrorist groups. In such a situation there are three options. The first is to allow the suspects to leave the UK voluntarily and to return

---

[15] Police and Criminal Evidence Act 1984, sections 43(5) and 44(3).
[16] Police and Criminal Evidence Act 1984, section 58(5).
[17] These provisions have been considered by the House of Lords in the case of *Ward* v *Police Service of Northern Ireland* [2007] UKHL 50, [2007] 1 WLR 3013, but whether there was any Article 5 issue was not raised.
[18] *McVeigh* v *UK* (1982) 25 DR 15.

to their own country; the difficulty is if they do not wish to do so because they would return to a regime which is oppressive. The second is to prosecute them, which means that any detention would be in accordance with Article 5(1)(c); but that may not be possible because the evidence against them is based on sensitive intelligence which cannot be presented to a court. It may also be that there has been a prosecution, which has not resulted in a conviction for some reason, but there is still a concern that the person is a terrorist; or it may even be that they have been prosecuted and convicted and served their sentence, but there is a continuing concern about the risk they pose. The third is to deport them; detention for the purpose of deportation is permitted by Article 5(1)(f); and there is power under the Immigration Act 1971 to remove or deport them, because their presence here is not conducive to the public good, on national security grounds. However, there may be reasons why deportation is not possible, because their removal or deportation would be a violation of Article 3, if they were liable to suffer torture or inhuman or degrading treatment or punishment in the destination country,[19] or because there are practical reasons why they cannot be sent to a particular country, or reasons of international law.[20]

In addition, there is European Court authority that Article 5(1)(f) requires deportation proceedings to be taken with due diligence,[21] and that could not be guaranteed if they could not be deported.

Thus, to detain such a person may well be a violation of Article 5, if they are not being brought before a court on suspicion of having committed an offence, or deported within a reasonable time, within Article 5(1)(c) and (f) respectively.

So Parliament, by section 21 of the ATCS Act, gave the Secretary of State power to certify a person to be a 'suspected international terrorist', if he reasonably believed that the person's presence in the United Kingdom was a risk to national security, and he reasonably suspected the person was a terrorist, with no need for a specific offence to have been committed. This applied only to foreign nationals, not to British subjects. There was a right of appeal to the Special Immigration Appeals Commission (SIAC). The United Kingdom then entered a **derogation**[22] to avoid the possibility of a conflict with Article 5, on the ground of an emergency threatening the life of the nation.

However, the derogation was challenged by persons detained under this power in the case of *A v Home Secretary*,[23] which was first heard in SIAC, and went to the House of Lords.

> A number of foreign nationals had been detained under the provisions of sections 21 and 23 of the ATCS Act, and they raised several points, in particular that their detention violated Article 3 of the Convention, because no term had been fixed for their detention; and also that it violated Article 14, since the fact that British nationals were not liable to be detained meant that there was discriminatory treatment of the applicants.

---

[19] The European Court has confirmed that the fact that the potential deportee might be a danger to the deporting country cannot justify limiting the scope of Article 3 to prohibit their deportation if the deportee is at serious risk of harm: *Saadi v Italy* [2008] 24 BHLR 123.

[20] This is specifically covered by section 22 of the ATCS Act.

[21] *Chahal v UK* (1997) 23 EHRR 413.

[22] Human Rights Act 1998 (Designated Derogation) Order 2001 (SI 2001/3644); derogations are discussed above, p. 113.

[23] *A v Secretary of State for the Home Department* [2004] UKHL 56, [2005] 2 WLR 87.

SIAC rejected the arguments that the derogation was not permissible or that there was a breach of Article 3, but considered that there was discriminatory treatment in breach of Article 14. The Court of Appeal reversed the decision on Article 14; but the House of Lords agreed with SIAC that there was a breach of Article 14.

The Lords sat as a nine-member panel. The majority considered that they could not displace the conclusion that there was an emergency threatening the life of the nation; Lord Hoffmann dissented on this point, considering that this condition was not satisfied as there was no terrorist threat to the nation's existence as a civil community.[24] However, the Lords did consider that the derogation and power to imprison without trial or deportation was a disproportionate response to the threat, and discriminated against foreign nationals, since there was an equal threat from UK nationals, yet there had been no derogation from Article 14. They therefore declared section 23 incompatible with the Act and quashed the derogation.

As Baroness Hale concluded:

There is absolutely no reason to think that the problem applies only to foreigners. Quite the reverse. There is every reason to think that there are British nationals living here who are international terrorists within the meaning of the Act; who cannot be shown to be such in a court of law; and who cannot be deported to another country because they have every right to be here.[25] Yet the Government does not think that it is necessary to lock them up. Indeed, it has publicly stated that locking up nationals is a Draconian step which could not at present be justified. But it has provided us with no real explanation of why it is necessary to lock up one group of people sharing exactly the same characteristics as another group which it does not think necessary to lock up. [. . .] The conclusion has to be that it is not necessary to lock up the nationals. Other ways must have been found to contain the threat which they present. And if it is not necessary to lock up the nationals it cannot be necessary to lock up the foreigners. It is not strictly required by the exigencies of the situation.

As a result of this decision the derogation was withdrawn and Parliament passed the Prevention of Terrorism Act 2005. This replaced Part 4 of the ATCS Act, the part held to breach the Convention, and replaced it with a power to impose control orders. These apply equally to both British and foreign nationals and allow for restrictions to be placed on the activities and movements of persons reasonably suspected of being involved in activity related to terrorism. However, an order which imposes any restriction which would infringe the Act, such as house arrest, can only be made if a derogation from the Convention is in force, and then only by a court, and not by the Home Secretary, whereas other control orders can be made by the Home Secretary. At present, no derogation has been filed to replace the one quashed by the House of Lords in *A*, and those persons who were imprisoned in reliance on the derogation and the ATCS Act have been released under control orders.

The decision in *A* was therefore of great importance because it involved a politically sensitive piece of legislation being declared incompatible with the Act, because for the first time it saw the quashing of a derogation from the Convention, and because it put the provisions of the Act at the centre of the political debate. The view of Lord Hoffmann, that there could not be said to be an emergency threatening the life of the nation, although a

---

[24] Quoted above, p. 371.
[25] Proven to be all too accurate by the London bombings on 7 July 2005, which were carried out by British nationals.

The problem of terrorism

21

dissent, was widely cited in the debates in Parliament over the Prevention of Terrorism Act 2005.

contr. orders

The control orders which have been made have in turn been considered by the courts as to whether the terms of the specific order amount to a deprivation of liberty in breach of Article 5, which would be unlawful since there is no derogation in place permitting such a breach.

In the case of *JJ*,[26] the House of Lords considered a control order which set an 18-hour curfew and banned social contact except with a very limited number of people authorised by the Home Office and held (by a majority) that this amounted to a deprivation of liberty in breach of Article 5, since it amounted to solitary confinement, and as a matter of principle meant that the control order should be quashed.

However, in the case of *E*,[27] the House of Lords held that the control order did not breach Article 5: E lived in his own home with his family, he was able to leave his home for 12 hours a day and free to go where he wished, so he had a degree of freedom to engage in everyday activities and conduct a social life which did not amount to a deprivation of liberty, even though there was a curfew, restrictions on visitors, approval of visits and meetings, and police searches. This was therefore a very much less severe case than that of *JJ*.

The operation of control orders is regularly reviewed and remains a live political issue, especially since the control order provisions need to be renewed annually by Parliament. There is a continuing tension in such cases between the state, which wishes to restrict the opportunity for suspected terrorists to put the community at risk, and the rights of the individuals concerned, who have not been convicted of an offence and yet are having their liberty restrained. It remains to be seen whether Parliament will come up with a more satisfactory way of dealing with this issue.

THE PRESUMPTION OF INNOCENCE

This is the first of two aspects of Article 6 which are particularly engaged by terrorism legislation. In our discussion of Article 6, we introduced the idea of the presumption of innocence, that it is for the prosecution to prove a criminal charge and not for the defence to disprove it. We also introduced the idea of a reverse burden, where a defendant has to prove some facts which would amount to a defence to the charge, which may be evidential – a burden simply to produce some evidence raising an issue which the prosecution have to disprove – or persuasive – a burden to actually prove, as being more likely than not, that the defence is made out.[28] Such a burden is not necessarily a breach of Article 6; it depends on the particular offence.

A number of offences in the Terrorism Act 2000 put reverse burdens on defendants. One example is section 57, which creates an offence where a person possesses an article in circumstances which give rise to a reasonable suspicion that it is for terrorist purposes; note

[26] *Home Secretary* v *JJ* [2007] UKHL 45, [2008] 1 AC 385.
[27] *Home Secretary* v *E* [2007] UKHL 47, [2008] 1 AC 409.
[28] Discussed above, pp. 217–20.

that what is required here is reasonable suspicion and not proof that the item is possessed for a terrorist purpose. It is then a defence for the accused to prove that possession of the article was not for that purpose: the burden is on the defendant. Further, if the article was simply on the same premises as the defendant, or on premises occupied or used by him, the court may *assume* that he was in possession of the article, unless the defendant *proves* that he did not know or have control of the article. This is a further reverse burden: before we even get to the question of purpose, the defendant may have to prove that they were *not* in possession of the article.

This provision reproduced a previous offence, which was considered in the case of *Kebilene*,[29] a case we considered in some detail in our discussion of Article 6.

> The defendants were suspected Algerian terrorists, and they were found with maps and other documents on them, which could be useful in the planning of an attack. They argued that the burdens placed on them by the statute amounted to a breach of the presumption of innocence set out in Article 6(2). The House of Lords considered that an evidential burden would not infringe Article 6(2); a persuasive burden might do; although they did not find it necessary to decide which this section imposed. However, the House of Lords did specifically refer to the purpose of the statute, dealing with terrorism. Lord Hope referred to the principle that, in balancing the rights of the individual and the community, the court has to consider the nature of the threat faced by society which the provision is designed to combat.

Those who drafted this provision took into account the House of Lords' judgment in *Kebilene*, and section 118 expressly requires the court to read certain sections of the Terrorism Act 2000, which create offences and have a reverse burden relating to a defence, in such a way as to place upon the defendant only an evidential burden – that is, the less onerous burden. Section 57 is one such section, so the burdens imposed on a defendant by that section are burdens to adduce evidence only, not to persuade the court that the defence is made out.

For those offences to which section 118 does not apply, the court has to consider this Article 6 point, in considering what sort of burden is imposed, and in any event to ensure that the defendant has a fair trial. This is especially so where the charge is as emotive a crime as anything related to terrorism.

This has been considered by the House of Lords in relation to an offence under section 11, which makes it an offence to be a member of a proscribed organisation; this is not an offence to which section 118 expressly applies.[30] It was held that the burden should rest on the prosecution to disprove the defence that the organisation was not proscribed when the defendant belonged to or was involved with it. This was because of the breadth of the offence, the very serious consequences of a conviction, and the real difficulties which a defendant might well face in proving the necessary details about any such organisation, especially as the section did not require the defendant to have conducted any form of terrorist activity. The imposition of a persuasive burden would therefore infringe Article 6, and the section should be read down to impose an evidential burden only.

[29] *R v DPP, ex parte Kebilene* [2000] 2 AC 326; see above, p. 217.
[30] *Attorney General's Reference No. 4 of 2002* [2004] UKHL 43, [2004] 3 WLR 976, discussed above in the context of Article 6, p. 219.

UNKNOWN EVIDENCE

The second point under Article 6 is the right to know the case against you and be able to challenge it, which is enshrined in Article 6(3)(d). There are situations brought about by the Terrorism Acts where the defendant will not be allowed to know who is giving evidence against them, or what that evidence is. In the process of proscription and deproscription under the Terrorism Act 2000, the Secretary of State may act on sensitive and secret intelligence, which cannot be revealed to the individual or organisation being proscribed. The same applies to a number of other situations, such as making a control order under the Prevention of Terrorism Act 2005; and to the procedures for making orders freezing assets which are being used for terrorism.[31] In such cases an advocate can be appointed to represent the interests of the person or organisation, known as a special advocate. The special advocate may see or hear the sensitive intelligence, but may not communicate it to the person represented. Thus, they have a limited ability to challenge the evidence, since they cannot ask the person to whom it relates for their response to it.

The European Court has considered this kind of situation, where the defendant or person affected may not hear all the evidence, and the decisions of the Court have shown that it is not necessarily a violation of Article 6.[32] Provided that there is an adequate framework, or system, for monitoring the decision, it will not necessarily be unfair, even though the evidence is given against a person in their absence. Thus, the procedure is likely to be more fair if it is a court rather than an administrative or executive officer making the decision, provided the court sees or hears the whole of the evidence, and can make a fair decision about whether the subject should be informed of the sensitive information. The court will, of course, bear in mind the subject's own rights, especially the right to a fair trial and the right to respect for their private life.

The system of special advocates has also been challenged in the context of the litigation on control orders: does the procedure provide a fair hearing for the person affected?

In the case of *MB*,[33] the House of Lords considered the overall impact of the control order procedure, and in particular the lack of access by the person who is having the control order made against them to the material which is being used by the Home Secretary, and the use of special advocates. Their Lordships held that the making of a control order did not involve the making of a criminal charge, but even so Article 6 applied to ensure that the person concerned had a fair hearing. What was important was to ensure that the statutory procedure was interpreted in a way which applied Article 6, by the application of the Human Rights Act – for example relying on Article 6 to ensure that material is shown to the accused person if it is to be relied on. Their Lordships did not decide whether, in the cases they were considering, there had been a breach of Article 6, but they had grave concerns that there may have been, since the cases relied heavily on material which had not been

---

[31] Counter-Terrorism Act 2008 Part 6, applying to that Act and orders under the ATCS Act 2001 and various orders which implement United Nations measures against the funding of terrorism; special advocates could already be used before the 2008 Act to ensure compliance with Article 6: *A v HM Treasury* [2008] EWCA Civ 1187, [2009] 2 All ER 747.

[32] Considered in e.g. *Chahal v UK* (1997) 23 EHRR 413.

[33] *Home Secretary v MB* [2007] UKHL 46, [2007] 3 WLR 681.

shown to the person subject to the order, so on which they could not comment, and the cases were remitted for reconsideration.

The European Court considered this in the case of A[34]: the use of special advocates and closed material did not necessarily make proceedings unfair, but a fair trial required that the detainee is given the essence of the case against them and not just general information. It found that in some of the cases before it this had not been done. The House of Lords has followed this in the case of AF[35], holding that this level of disclosure is required in domestic law, and it was not provided in the cases before it, which were remitted for further consideration.

The courts also have general powers to order the disclosure of evidence, which is another requirement of having a fair trial: being able to collect evidence to support your case. Again, a balance must be struck between the requirements of public security and the right of the individual to know the case they have to meet in respect of very serious allegations.

The case of *Mohamed*[36] was one which has been in the headlines because it has highlighted the relationship between the United Kingdom and the United States. Here, the court ordered the disclosure of documents relating to the detention of a suspected terrorist by the United States government at Guantanamo Bay, subject to the requirements of national security, which entitle the government to claim public interest immunity from having to disclose documents. The fair trial here is that which Mr Mohamed faced in the United States. A similar balance had to be struck, in the same case, between the public interest in the publication of the judgment and national security. The Divisional Court ordered that part of its original judgment should not be made public because of the national security issue as the United States threatened that publication would impact on the sharing of security intelligence between the two countries.[37]

PRECISION IN THE LAW

Article 7 is defined in terms of freedom from punishment without law, which is primarily concerned with freedom from being held guilty under retrospective legislation. But Article 7 also underlines the principle of Convention law that the law should be clear and precise and its effect foreseeable.[38] It is upon this latter aspect that we now concentrate, because the term 'terrorist', used in the Terrorism Acts, is vague and imprecise, and therefore, at least arguably, its meaning is not foreseeable.

The essence of this point is that the definition of 'terrorism' does not refer to any specific offence, and terrorism is not itself an offence. The definition of 'terrorism' relies

---

[34] *A v UK* [2009] 26 BHRLR 1, the appeal from *A v Home Secretary*.
[35] *Home Secretary v AF* [2009] UKHL 28.
[36] *R (Mohamed) v Secretary of State for Foreign and Commonwealth Affairs* [2008] EWHC 2048 (Admin) and [2008] EWHC 2100 (Admin).
[37] [2009] EWHC 152 (Admin).
[38] See above, Chapter 13.

upon ingredients of violence or the threat of it, in order to influence the government or the public for a political or similar cause. There is no requirement of the commission of a particular offence, which makes the meaning of the term uncertain.

The Terrorism Acts then use the term 'terrorist investigation', meaning an investigation into acts of terrorism, the resources of a proscribed organisation, and so on. If an investigation is a terrorist investigation, a number of specific powers for the investigation and detection of terrorism and terrorist activity apply. Again, there is no requirement that a specific criminal offence should be investigated or even suspected, which means that this term, too, is imprecise.

So, for example, to support a terrorist investigation, the police may obtain a warrant to enter premises, or a court order for the production of documents, or the explanation of documents; this is provided by section 37 of and Schedule 5 to the Terrorism Act 2000; and there are offences connected with these powers. Likewise, for the purposes of a terrorist investigation, the police may obtain a court order under section 38 of and Schedules 6 and 6A to the Terrorism Act 2000 requiring financial institutions to give details of their customers and accounts. Section 19 of the Terrorism Act 2000 makes it an offence for a person to fail to disclose their knowledge, belief or suspicion that an offence has been committed relating to fundraising or money laundering for terrorist purposes. Under section 1 of the ATCS Act, money may be forfeited where it is intended for terrorist purposes, or was obtained by terrorism. All these powers and offences are rooted in the definition of terrorism, which requires no specific offence to be proved to substantiate the allegation that terrorism is involved.

Finally, under section 4 of the ATCS Act, the Treasury has the power to make an order to freeze the assets of persons or governments overseas, whom the Treasury reasonably believes are acting to the detriment of the economy of the United Kingdom, or constituting a threat to the life or property of nationals of the United Kingdom. It will be realised at once that the conditions allowing the making of such an order are vague, and again there is no requirement that there should be any suspicion of criminal activity, let alone that actual criminal activity be proven.

Ensuring compliance with Article 7 has been used in one case to ensure that a terrorism offence is kept within limits. In the case of K,[39] the Court of Appeal had to consider the scope of the offence under section 58 of the Terrorism Act 2000, which prohibits possessing records containing information 'likely to be useful to a person committing or preparing an act of terrorism'. The argument was that this phrase is too vague to comply with Article 7. The Court held that, so long as the phrase was given its straightforward meaning, and applied to information which, on its face, might raise a suspicion that it was intended to assist in the preparation or commission of an act of terrorism, then it did not infringe Article 7. But what the prosecution could not do was to call evidence beyond the document itself to show that a document, which appeared to be innocuous, was in fact intended for the purpose prohibited: this would expand the scope of the offence too far beyond what was certain.[40]

---

[39] *R* v *K* [2008] EWCA Crim 185, [2008] 2 WLR 1026.
[40] Note that in *R* v *G* [2009] UKHL 13 [2009] 2 WLR 724, this approach to the offence was used although *K*'s reading of the relevant defence in s. 58 was over-ruled.

A similar precision is required in relation to the offence we referred to earlier, under section 57 of the Terrorism Act, relating to possessing an object for purposes relating to terrorism: here too, there has to be a direct connection between the possession of the object and the act of terrorism.[41]

DISCLOSURE OF INFORMATION

Here we are considering the rights protected by Article 8, respect for private life. Article 8 will be engaged by some of the procedures and orders to which we have just referred – the entry, search and seizure and financial information provisions in Schedules 5, 6 and 6A to the Terrorism Act 2000 – because all of these relate to private information. The provisions on forfeiture of money and freezing orders under sections 1 and 4 of the ATCS Act will engage Article 8, and also Article 1 of the First Protocol, since they are also an interference with the enjoyment of property. In all these situations, there may be an infringement of these Articles if an order is made which is not reasonably necessary and proportionate, albeit taking into account the nature of the threat of terrorism, following the principles set out in *Fox, Campbell and Hartley* and *Kebilene*. They may also fall foul of these Articles for the same reason they may fall foul of Article 7, if they are too vague to be 'in accordance with the law': that is, if they offend the principle of legality. There is, however, some guidance for some of the provisions which involve questioning suspects, taking audio and video recordings of interviews and the forfeiture of terrorist money, because in these areas the Terrorism Act 2000 requires the issuing of codes of conduct. These will provide some standards on whether particular conduct is proper or not, whether or not it should be considered arbitrary or disproportionate.

However, there are also further provisions which engage Article 8. One is covered by those parts of the ATCS Act which deal with the retention of communications data, intrusions by the state into information on telephone, postal or electronic communications.

Communications providers – the postal or telephone authorities, or Internet service providers in the case of email – commonly maintain records relating to the use of their services. This is 'communications data' – the information on a customer's telephone bill, the address of a website visited by a customer, the date, time, and title of an email, and the identities of the sender and recipient. It does *not* include the contents of the telephone call or email message. The providers may retain it for commercial purposes, but, if it is retained for any other purpose, it must be made anonymous. Under the Regulation of Investigatory Powers Act 2000, law enforcement agencies may gain access to such data, for the purpose of protecting national security, economic well-being, public safety or health, preventing crime or preventing death or damage, or collecting taxes. There is no statutory requirement that this data should be retained for any particular period.

Sections 102 to 107 of the ATCS Act enable the Secretary of State to issue codes of practice for the retention of data on grounds of national security, or for the prevention or detection of crime or for the prosecution of offenders, when the crime or the offender affects national security. The Act provides, in the first instance, for a voluntary agreement as to the codes of practice but, if this does not operate satisfactorily, the Secretary of State may impose a regime. No violation of Article 8 arises from these sections themselves, but

---

[41] *R* v *Zafar* [2008] EWCA 184, [2008] 2 WLR 1013; though its approach to the defence under s. 57 was doubted in *R* v *G* [2009] UKHL 13, [2009] 2 WLR 724.

this is another situation where any disclosure by a communications provider may well violate its customer's right under Article 8, and therefore must be strictly justified, and must be proportionate. In order to assist in the assessment of what is proper conduct in this area, section 102 provides for a code of practice for the retention of communications data.

There is a further power in the ATCS Act which relates to the disclosure of information, and that is section 17, which extends the power of security services to obtain access to private information; it enlarges the number of sources which they may use in order to obtain intelligence.

This section inserts a new provision into the statutes which create a number of public authorities, set out in Schedule 4. For example, the Harbours Act 1964 makes provision for a National Ports Council, and the Airports Act 1986 for the Civil Aviation Authority. Each of these is authorised by the statute creating it to make enquiries, and to obtain information, in order to assist its usual functions. In each case the statute provides that this information shall not be disclosed, by the public authority, to a third person, except for particular reasons, such as for the proper functioning of the authority, or for legal proceedings, or with the consent of the person originally providing the information.

Section 17 of the ATCS Act provides that each of the statutes listed in the Schedule should be amended so as to permit disclosure for the purposes of assisting *any* criminal investigation or criminal proceedings in the United Kingdom, or abroad, or to assist in the task of deciding whether *any* investigation or proceedings should begin or end. It may be that no criminal offence has been committed, or that there is no suspicion of any offence; and disclosure is permitted even before an investigation has started. The wording of section 17(2) will cover an investigation into conduct falling within section 41 of the Terrorism Act 2000, 'a person suspected to be a terrorist', which may be conduct not even amounting to an offence.

The provisions of this section are available in terrorism cases, but they are not limited to such cases; the disclosure of information may be made for the purpose of *any* criminal proceedings. No order of the court is necessary. And there is no provision for any subsequent check by any supervisory authority.

Clearly, proportionality is essential to the exercise of the powers under this section. There will be an interference with Article 8 on any disclosure of information under section 17, and that disclosure must be justified under Article 8(2). Also, a disclosure may produce material which is later used in evidence in a trial; if the disclosure is in violation of Article 8, the use of the evidence may make the trial unfair, in breach of Article 6. All this is indeed reflected in the section itself; section 17(5) of the ATCS Act provides that no disclosure shall be made under this section unless the public authority doing so is satisfied that the making of the disclosure is *proportionate* to what is sought to be achieved by it. The policing of this power is vital to ensuring that its use is properly restrained, since, in principle, it could be a very serious invasion of privacy. This is even more so now that the state security services have additional powers to share information under Part 1 of the Counter-Terrorism Act 2008.

PERSONAL SEARCHES

This raises similar issues to those we considered in relation to detention above, but relating to Article 8, infringement of privacy. There is a power under sections 44 and 45 of the

Terrorism Act 2000 for a senior police officer to authorise police officers in an area to stop and search members of the public at random for articles which could be used in connection with terrorism, but without requiring reasonable suspicion of an offence being committed. There are safeguards: the authorisation has to be for a single purpose, for a specified, limited period, and is subject to confirmation by the Secretary of State. This power was challenged in the case of *Gillan*.[42]

An authorisation for searches had been granted for the whole of the London Metropolitan area, lasting for 28 days, the maximum period possible, as part of a programme of successive authorisations which had taken place since the Act came into force. Mr Gillan was a student who was on his way to join a demonstration against an arms fair in Docklands, East London; and a challenge was also brought by a journalist who was in the area to film the protests; both were stopped and searched by police officers pursuant to the authorisation, and nothing incriminating was found in either case.

The House of Lords held that the power in sections 44 and 45 had to be restrictively construed but did not infringe any Convention rights, especially because of all the safeguards and limitations to the power, so long as it was exercised in a way which was reasonably necessary and proportionate. The particular authorisations were justified in the context of the arms fair. The power was also sufficiently certain to conform to the principle of legality. Thus if there was any intrusion into privacy, it was justified. It was also held that the short stopping of a person for a search was not a detention within Article 5. Some notes of caution were sounded, however, in both the Court of Appeal and House of Lords, as to the importance of this power not being exercised in an arbitrary manner.

FREEDOM OF EXPRESSION

There are anti-terrorism powers which engage Article 10, in particular press freedom. These raise the sort of issues we have considered in the context of that Article. One such power is the court's power to make an order that the identity of someone who is subject to a control order should be kept anonymous,[43] where the courts have to balance the controlled person's right to privacy, given that they haven't been convicted of an offence, and the public interest.[44] Another is the court's power under schedule 5 of the Terrorism Act 2000 to order the disclosure of material, which can include journalistic material and therefore raise issues about the protection of journalists' sources. Again the courts will have to seek a balance between the public interest in combating terrorism and the Article 10 rights which include protection of sources.[45]

---

[42] *R (Gillan)* v *Commissioner of Police of the Metropolis* [2006] UKHL 12, [2006] 2 AC 307.
[43] Prevention of Terrorism Act 2005, Schedule 1 para. 5.
[44] Considered in *Times Newspapers Ltd* v *Home Secretary* [2008] EWHC 2455 (Admin), [2009] ACD 1.
[45] Considered in *Malik* v *Manchester Crown Court* [2008] EWHC 1362 (Admin), (2008) 4 All ER 403, where the court held that an order was appropriate, but too wide in the form granted.

FREEDOM OF ASSOCIATION

An order under section 3 of the Terrorism Act 2000, proscribing an organisation, makes the organisation illegal, and it is unlawful to be a member of it, or joining, supporting or funding it. That will engage Article 11; there will be an interference with the freedom of association.

The next question is whether the interference is justified under Article 11(2). The Secretary of State has power to proscribe an organisation if he 'believes that it is concerned in terrorism' (section 3(4)). The test is a subjective one; there is no condition that he must 'reasonably believe'. But an organisation or person affected by his decision may appeal to the Proscribed Organisations Appeal Commission, and the appeal will be decided in the light of the principles of judicial review (section 5(3)); therefore, the principles of the European Convention will apply.[46] Here too, at all stages, the use of the power must be proportionate and must not be arbitrary.[47]

QUESTIONS

1   Should terrorism be a special case? Do you agree with the principles which are used to justify special provisions to deal with terrorists?

2   Considering the particular measures which have been adopted, do they meet the standards of being necessary and proportionate interferences with the various Convention rights we have discussed, and why/why not? What is your overall assessment?

3   Do you agree with the decision in *A* v *Home Secretary*? What do you think about Parliament allowing indefinite detention without trial or deportation? What do you think about the control order regime that is now in place?

---

[46]   The Proscribed Organisations Appeal Commission is the correct forum for a challenge in relation to a pro-scription on human rights grounds: The Proscribed Organisations Appeal Commission (Human Rights Act 1998 Proceedings) Rules 2006 (2006/No. 2290).

[47]   See above discussion of *Attorney General's Reference No. 4 of 2002* for the burden of proof for an offence of belonging to a proscribed organisation, p. 379.

The Middlesex Guildhall, which is to be the home of the new Supreme Court.

Source: © Nikreates/Alamy

22 Conclusion

There are two things which I am confident I can do very well: one is an introduction to any literary work, stating what it is to contain, and how it should be executed in the most perfect manner; the other is a conclusion, shewing from various causes why the execution has not been equal to what the author promised to himself and to the public. (Samuel Johnson, 1755)

So there it is: the Human Rights Act 1998, and the rights set out in the European Convention on Human Rights. We hope that you now have an understanding of the basic principles of the Act, and of the way in which the Convention rights are to be analysed, as well as some understanding of the different areas in which the Act has affected United Kingdom law.

The incorporation of the Convention was a welcome step, and a fine starting point for ensuring the greater protection of individual rights. The United Kingdom helped to draft the Convention and was the first to ratify it. The delay in allowing it to be used in our courts led to a rather greater number of decisions against the United Kingdom in the European Court than there should have been. Our courts now have the opportunity to make their own contribution to the wider debate on rights, and to allow the Convention to permeate our law. And it is doing so – the number of cases decided on some Convention point, and the wide range of areas which it has affected, tell us that.

Anyone who expected the Act to work immediate and radical alterations to our law was, predictably, incorrect – realising the full potential of the Act was always going to be a gradual process. If our law had so failed in its protection of basic rights that the Act was badly needed, then there would have been a political outcry for its implementation long ago. The view of the British civil servants involved in the drafting of the Convention in 1950 was broadly correct, that it embodied, in the main, basic principles and underlying rights, which are to be found in our law – although their view that English law adequately protected all those rights in all circumstances was seriously deficient, as the European Court had shown, even prior to the Act.

However, the Act is making itself felt, both legally and politically. The Act is now an important new ground for the scrutiny of legislation and of executive action. We have seen, in our discussion of the individual Convention rights, a whole host of areas where the Convention jurisprudence has forced a reassessment of the previous law, the standards applied to everyday decisions and situations, the way in which the courts scrutinise governmental decisions and actions. Whilst the effects have been mostly incremental, that is what one would expect from the way our common law develops.

The courts have been cautious in some respects – the traditional property-based approach of cases like *Aston Cantlow* on parish councils, or the (majority) focus in *YL* on the contractual relationship in the role of care homes rather than the function served by them, or looking at the form of ASBO proceedings in *McCann* rather than the consequences for the individual, do not always sit comfortably with the more sweeping approach of the European Court. *YL* has been reversed by Parliament on its facts: this may send a signal to the courts that a broader, more purposive interpretation of the scope of the Act is appropriate. The courts have been reluctant to use the Act to expand human rights protection beyond current European Court decisions, as can be seen by the way that the dictum in *Ullah* – that the protection of the Act should be 'no more but certainly no less' than the Convention – has been cited, although again there is a signal the other way in *P* that this is not the only appropriate approach. And sometimes there is a certain timidity in interpretation, commented on by Lord Steyn in *Ghaidan*, where he drew attention to the tendency to make declarations of incompatibility rather than taking a more creative approach to interpretation.

But there have been significant departures from the previous law in some areas. Perhaps the most notable is the courts' new-found ability to protect the right to privacy, something which they had quite obviously felt unable to do before the Act was passed. The Act has resulted in a complete facelift in this area: the lack of *any* real protection of privacy prior to the Act has been remedied, and the real arguments in any particular case about what can be published in the public interest and what should be properly within the private life of individuals can be aired. And this is so even where the subjects are in the public eye, because what interests the public and what is in the public interest are not the same, and our courts can now police the distinction. There have also been milestone decisions in areas such as discrimination on grounds of gender or sexuality, the political role of the Home Secretary in setting prison terms in cases of life imprisonment, ensuring that the burden of proving a defence does not unbalance the fairness of a criminal trial, mandating that inquests conduct a full inquiry into deaths in custody, and the courts' ability to review the substantive grounds of an arrest. And, of course, the most exciting, and important, case decided under the Act is *A* v *Home Secretary*, which showed the full potential of the Act to allow our judges to scrutinise legislation from the perspective of basic rights.[1]

This is perhaps the main effect of the Act: to oblige the courts to consider cases concerning basic rights in a more substantive way than they did before, applying the principles developed by the European Court, of balance, legality and proportionality. As well as 'reasonableness' – long the touchstone of the common law – 'necessity', 'proportionality' and '(non)arbitrariness' are now also key ideas in legal discourse, whenever a discretion is exercised, a decision is scrutinised or a statute is interpreted. The government is now required to justify its laws, actions and decisions more closely. Before the Act, if a decision was lawful and within the bounds of a 'reasonable' decision, it could not be challenged. The courts now demand a more substantive justification if a Convention right is at stake.[2] There is a greater identification of issues of rights, a focus in the argument before the courts, in cases in which basic rights are at stake. This is one of the benefits we identified at the outset of this book: identifying someone's rights is not the end of the matter, since one must also consider their duties and the rights of others, but discussion in terms of rights ensures that no one's rights are ridden over roughshod.

---

[1] We cover the detail of all these cases and developments elsewhere: *Aston Cantlow*, pp. 78 and 347; *YL*, p. 79; *McCann*, p. 228; *Ullah* and *P*, p. 63; *Ghaidan*, p. 67 and p. 124; privacy in Chapter 14; discrimination in Chapter 7; life sentences in Chapter 11; reverse burdens in Chapter 12; inquests in Chapter 8; arrest in Chapter 11; *A*, especially at p. 376.

[2] *Daly, Begum*: discussed above, pp. 45–6.

But none of this means that there has been, or is likely to be, a wholesale shift in power from Parliament and the executive to the courts. Our judges are acutely aware of the potential political difficulties the Act could get them into. The Act's preservation of Parliamentary sovereignty means that the elected representatives of the people ultimately have the last word. The declaration of incompatibility has been used where the words of a statute cannot be avoided – the courts have not shown any enthusiasm for reading words out. And then there is the important idea of judicial deference, allowing that where there is a range of acceptable solutions to a problem, it may be appropriate to accept the view of Parliament or whichever person or body is best placed to consider the matter. Deference plays an important part in keeping judges from areas which are not appropriate to their form of decision-making – so long as it does not stifle the protection of basic rights, and *A* has shown that it has not compelled the judges to hold back where basic liberties are at stake.

Yet the Act is in its own way profoundly democratic. The process of getting legislation through Parliament is slow, especially for matters which may be important in principle, but are not high in political priority – so the incorporation of the Convention means that the courts now provide another forum for questions of rights affecting individuals to be aired. Questions concerning basic rights can now be argued by litigation in the public forum of the courts, and this can only enhance democratic accountability, by opening a dialogue between the branches of the state – a dialogue to which Parliament has responded, as can be seen from the changes in the law which have typically followed findings of incompatibility.[3]

This is most notable in the response to *A*. The terrorist attacks in New York on 11 September 2001, in Madrid, in Bali, and in London on 7 and 21 July 2005, amongst others, have caused some profound changes in our views on security, reflected in pressure on the government from the security forces and the public to respond to terrorist threats. It has been hugely significant for the reasoned development of these views that the courts have been able to assess the measures taken against the standard of the protection of individual rights, and take steps when they find such measures lacking by that standard. At the same time, the form of the Act means that the courts did not have the power to undo the measures that had been implemented: their incompatibility did not mean invalidity. So the consequences of the decision in *A* was not to immediately imperil security by undoing the measures in place, but to pass the issue of rights back to Parliament to find a better balance. It is greatly to the credit of the government and Parliament that the response to *A* was for the derogation to be withdrawn and the law to be changed. And in the debates which followed *A*, and led to the Prevention of Terrorism Act 2005, considerations of human rights, of necessity and reasonableness, and the Law Lords' views in *A*, were front and centre. The continuing Parliamentary concern for basic rights is clear from the debates about the Counter-Terrorism Act 2008, where the government's renewed proposal to increase the time in which persons could be detained without charge was again defeated and did not become law. In this context, it would be a wholly retrograde step if effect were given to the occasional political or tabloid suggestion that if the Convention interferes with the ability of the state to protect its citizens then it should be abrogated. That would amount to a victory for terrorism – a blow to the very democracy which is under attack. Indeed, far from considering limiting individual rights, the statutory recognition of our most fundamental rights should prompt us to consider whether other rights should be accepted in the same

[3] See above, p. 75.

way. What about economic and social rights such as a right to social security or a positive right to a free education? When, for example, the Parliamentary Joint Committee on Human Rights refers to a new bill of rights as a possibility, it has in mind something more extensive, not more limited. Indeed, when having a new or different bill of rights is suggested, it would be remarkable if it did not begin by including the same protection as the Act provides – there are sometimes calls for a 'British' bill of rights, but, as we have seen, this one *is*; it reflected the fundamental rights which the drafters found in *our* law. That it has been expanded by European Court judges does not make it 'foreign' – we have a judge in the European Court as well – and had the Convention been capable of founding decisions in our courts before 1998, there would doubtless have been fewer European Court decisions against the UK.

The Act is also part of, and underpins, a major wave of constitutional reform, which has addressed fundamental questions about the relationship between the citizen and the state, such as new laws on electronic surveillance, freedom of information and data protection; and how and where governmental decisions are made, for example with devolution. In this context, the Act has brought into focus the relationship between the executive and the judiciary: the new Constitutional Reform Act has involved a reconsideration of how judges are appointed and their democratic accountability, especially in light of their role under the Act – and so what input from the executive or Parliament is appropriate in this process. There is also the Equality Act 2006, which promises to be a real twenty-first-century statute. It combines the various anti-discrimination bodies into a joint Commission for Equality and Human Rights, whose remit is set in aspirational terms: to promote the creation of a society where there is respect for and protection of each individual's human rights, where there is respect for the dignity and worth of each individual, where there is understanding of equality and the value of diversity, and where all have equal opportunities, not limited by prejudice or discrimination. It is charged with promoting the understanding and protection of human rights – and human rights here are not limited to the Convention rights. This will help to ensure that the protection of human rights is not just a matter for Parliament or the courts, but for the whole of the machinery of government, and indeed for all of the wider society.

In many ways, the Act has been a breath of fresh air for the law. It has forced a rethink in a whole variety of areas. It provides an opportunity for the courts, the lawyers, journalists, academics, and the public as a whole to consider whether the law *really does* protect the rights that we tend to assume we have. Perhaps now it would not be stating the position too strongly to say that the courts have begun the 'fundamental process of review and, where necessary, reform by the judiciary' which Lord Hope referred to in *Kebilene*.[4] The potential is certainly there. We hope that this process will continue, and that our judges will continue gradually to review and develop our law against the benchmark of the Convention rights.

---

[4] [2000] 2 AC 326 at 375, above, p. 61 and p. 71.

The Human Rights Act 1998

An Act to give further effect to rights and freedoms guaranteed under the European Convention on Human Rights; to make provision with respect to holders of certain judicial offices who become judges of the European Court of Human Rights; and for connected purposes.

[9th November 1998]

BE IT ENACTED by the Queen's most Excellent Majesty, by and with the advice and consent of the Lords Spiritual and Temporal, and Commons, in this present Parliament assembled, and by the authority of the same, as follows: –

 ## INTRODUCTION

The Convention rights

1. – (1) In this Act 'the Convention rights' means the rights and fundamental freedoms set out in –
    (a) Articles 2 to 12 and 14 of the Convention,
    (b) Articles 1 to 3 of the First Protocol, and
    (c) Article 1 of the Thirteenth Protocol,
    as read with Articles 16 to 18 of the Convention.
(2) Those Articles are to have effect for the purposes of this Act subject to any designated derogation or reservation (as to which see sections 14 and 15).
(3) The Articles are set out in Schedule 1.
(4) The Secretary of State[1] may by order make such amendments to this Act as he considers appropriate to reflect the effect, in relation to the United Kingdom, of a protocol.
(5) In subsection (4) 'protocol' means a protocol to the Convention –
    (a) which the United Kingdom has ratified; or
    (b) which the United Kingdom has signed with a view to ratification.
(6) No amendment may be made by an order under subsection (4) so as to come into force before the protocol concerned is in force in relation to the United Kingdom.

---

[1] References to functions exercised by the Secretary of State were altered to refer to the Lord Chancellor in 2001 (Transfer of Functions (Miscellaneous) Order 2001, SI 2001/3500), and then altered back by the Secretary of State for Constitutional Affairs Order 2003 (SI 2003/1887); at present the Secretary of State for Constitutional Affairs and the Lord Chancellor are the same person.

Interpretation of Convention rights

2. – (1)   A court or tribunal determining a question which has arisen in connection with a Convention right must take into account any –

    (a) judgment, decision, declaration or advisory opinion of the European Court of Human Rights,

    (b) opinion of the Commission given in a report adopted under Article 31 of the Convention,

    (c) decision of the Commission in connection with Article 26 or 27(2) of the Convention, or

    (d) decision of the Committee of Ministers taken under Article 46 of the Convention,

whenever made or given, so far as, in the opinion of the court or tribunal, it is relevant to the proceedings in which that question has arisen.

(2)   Evidence of any judgment, decision, declaration or opinion of which account may have to be taken under this section is to be given in proceedings before any court or tribunal in such manner as may be provided by rules.

(3)   In this section 'rules' means rules of court or, in the case of proceedings before a tribunal, rules made for the purposes of this section –

    (a) by the Secretary of State, in relation to any proceedings outside Scotland;

    (b) by the Secretary of State, in relation to proceedings in Scotland; or

    (c) by a Northern Ireland department, in relation to proceedings before a tribunal in Northern Ireland –

        (i) which deals with transferred matters; and

        (ii) for which no rules made under paragraph (a) are in force.

LEGISLATION

Interpretation of legislation

3. – (1)   So far as it is possible to do so, primary legislation and subordinate legislation must be read and given effect in away which is compatible with the Convention rights.

(2)   This section –

    (a) applies to primary legislation and subordinate legislation whenever enacted;

    (b) does not affect the validity, continuing operation or enforcement of any incompatible primary legislation; and

    (c) does not affect the validity, continuing operation or enforcement of any incompatible subordinate legislation if (disregarding any possibility of revocation) primary legislation prevents removal of the incompatibility.

Declaration of incompatibility

4. – (1)   Subsection (2) applies in any proceedings in which a court determines whether a provision of primary legislation is compatible with a Convention right.

(2)   If the court is satisfied that the provision is incompatible with a Convention right, it may make a declaration of that incompatibility.

(3) Subsection (4) applies in any proceedings in which a court determines whether a provision of subordinate legislation, made in the exercise of a power conferred by primary legislation, is compatible with a Convention right.

(4) If the court is satisfied –

    (a) that the provision is incompatible with a Convention right, and

    (b) that (disregarding any possibility of revocation) the primary legislation concerned prevents removal of the incompatibility,

it may make a declaration of that incompatibility.

(5) In this section 'court' means –

    (a) the House of Lords;[2]

    (b) the Judicial Committee of the Privy Council;

    (c) the Courts-Martial Appeal Court;

    (d) in Scotland, the High Court of Justiciary sitting otherwise than as a trial court or the Court of Session;

    (e) in England and Wales or Northern Ireland, the High Court or the Court of Appeal;

    (f) the Court of Protection, in any matter being dealt with by the President of the Family Division, the Vice-Chancellor or a puisne judge of the High Court.[3]

(6) A declaration under this section ('a declaration of incompatibility') –

    (a) does not affect the validity, continuing operation or enforcement of the provision in respect of which it is given; and

    (b) is not binding on the parties to the proceedings in which it is made.

Right of Crown to intervene

5. – (1) Where a court is considering whether to make a declaration of incompatibility, the Crown is entitled to notice in accordance with rules of court.

(2) In any case to which subsection (1) applies –

    (a) a Minister of the Crown (or a person nominated by him),

    (b) a member of the Scottish Executive,

    (c) a Northern Ireland Minister,

    (d) a Northern Ireland department,

is entitled, on giving notice in accordance with rules of court, to be joined as a party to the proceedings.

(3) Notice under subsection (2) may be given at any time during the proceedings.

(4) A person who has been made a party to criminal proceedings (other than in Scotland) as the result of a notice under subsection (2) may, with leave, appeal to the House of Lords[4] against any declaration of incompatibility made in the proceedings.

(5) In subsection (4) –

'criminal proceedings' includes all proceedings before the Courts-Martial Appeal Court; and

'leave' means leave granted by the court making the declaration of incompatibility or by the House of Lords.[5]

---

[2] The House of Lords will be replaced by the Supreme Court when the Constitutional Reform Act 2005 comes into effect: CRA 2005, Schedule 9, paragraph 66.

[3] Subsection (5)(f) will be inserted by the Mental Capacity Act 2005 when it comes into effect.

[4] See footnote 2 above.

[5] See footnote 2 above.

▮ PUBLIC AUTHORITIES

Acts of public authorities

6. – (1)   It is unlawful for a public authority to act in a way which is incompatible with a Convention right.

(2)   Subsection (1) does not apply to an act if –

(a)   as the result of one or more provisions of primary legislation, the authority could not have acted differently; or

(b)   in the case of one or more provisions of, or made under, primary legislation which cannot be read or given effect in a way which is compatible with the Convention rights, the authority was acting so as to give effect to or enforce those provisions.

(3)   In this section 'public authority' includes –

(a)   a court or tribunal, and

(b)   any person certain of whose functions are functions of a public nature, but does not include either House of Parliament or a person exercising functions in connection with proceedings in Parliament.

(4)   In subsection (3) 'Parliament' does not include the House of Lords in its judicial capacity.[6]

(5)   In relation to a particular act, a person is not a public authority by virtue only of subsection (3)(b) if the nature of the act is private.

(6)   'An act' includes a failure to act but does not include a failure to –

(a)   introduce in, or lay before, Parliament a proposal for legislation; or

(b)   make any primary legislation or remedial order.

Proceedings

7. – (1)   A person who claims that a public authority has acted (or proposes to act) in a way which is made unlawful by section 6(1) may –

(a)   bring proceedings against the authority under this Act in the appropriate court or tribunal, or

(b)   rely on the Convention right or rights concerned in any legal proceedings, but only if he is (or would be) a victim of the unlawful act.

(2)   In subsection (1)(a) 'appropriate court or tribunal' means such court or tribunal as may be determined in accordance with rules; and proceedings against an authority include a counterclaim or similar proceeding.

(3)   If the proceedings are brought on an application for judicial review, the applicant is to be taken to have a sufficient interest in relation to the unlawful act only if he is, or would be, a victim of that act.

(4)   If the proceedings are made by way of a petition for judicial review in Scotland, the applicant shall be taken to have title and interest to sue in relation to the unlawful act only if he is, or would be, a victim of that act.

---

[6] This subsection will be deleted when the Constitutional Reform Act 2005 comes into effect (Schedule 9, paragraph 66 of that Act) since the judicial function and capacity of the House of Lords will cease.

(5) Proceedings under subsection (1)(a) must be brought before the end of –

    (a) the period of one year beginning with the date on which the act complained of took place; or

    (b) such longer period as the court or tribunal considers equitable having regard to all the circumstances,

but that is subject to any rule imposing a stricter time limit in relation to the procedure in question.

(6) In subsection (1)(b) 'legal proceedings' includes –

    (a) proceedings brought by or at the instigation of a public authority; and

    (b) an appeal against the decision of a court or tribunal.

(7) For the purposes of this section, a person is a victim of an unlawful act only if he would be a victim for the purposes of Article 34 of the Convention if proceedings were brought in the European Court of Human Rights in respect of that act.

(8) Nothing in this Act creates a criminal offence.

(9) In this section 'rules' means –

    (a) in relation to proceedings before a court or tribunal outside Scotland, rules made by the Secretary of State for the purposes of this section or rules of court,

    (b) in relation to proceedings before a court or tribunal in Scotland, rules made by the Secretary of State for those purposes,

    (c) in relation to proceedings before a tribunal in Northern Ireland –

        (i) which deals with transferred matters; and

        (ii) for which no rules made under paragraph (a) are in force,

    rules made by a Northern Ireland department for those purposes,

and includes provision made by order under section 1 of the Courts and Legal Services Act 1990.

(10) In making rules, regard must be had to section 9.

(11) The Minister who has power to make rules in relation to a particular tribunal may, to the extent he considers it necessary to ensure that the tribunal can provide an appropriate remedy in relation to an act (or proposed act) of a public authority which is (or would be) unlawful as a result of section 6(1), by order add to –

    (a) the relief or remedies which the tribunal may grant; or

    (b) the grounds on which it may grant any of them.

(12) An order made under subsection (11) may contain such incidental, supplemental, consequential or transitional provision as the Minister making it considers appropriate.

(13) 'The Minister' includes the Northern Ireland department concerned.

Judicial remedies

8. – (1) In relation to any act (or proposed act) of a public authority which the court finds is (or would be) unlawful, it may grant such relief or remedy, or make such order, within its powers as it considers just and appropriate.

(2) But damages may be awarded only by a court which has power to award damages, or to order the payment of compensation, in civil proceedings.

(3) No award of damages is to be made unless, taking account of all the circumstances of the case, including –

(a) any other relief or remedy granted, or order made, in relation to the act in question (by that or any other court), and

(b) the consequences of any decision (of that or any other court) in respect of that act, the court is satisfied that the award is necessary to afford just satisfaction to the person in whose favour it is made.

(4) In determining –

(a) whether to award damages, or

(b) the amount of an award,

the court must take into account the principles applied by the European Court of Human Rights in relation to the award of compensation under Article 41 of the Convention.

(5) A public authority against which damages are awarded is to be treated –

(a) in Scotland, for the purposes of section 3 of the Law Reform (Miscellaneous Provisions) (Scotland) Act 1940 as if the award were made in an action of damages in which the authority has been found liable in respect of loss or damage to the person to whom the award is made;

(b) for the purposes of the Civil Liability (Contribution) Act 1978 as liable in respect of damage suffered by the person to whom the award is made.

(6) In this section –

'court' includes a tribunal;

'damages' means damages for an unlawful act of a public authority; and

'unlawful' means unlawful under section 6(1).

9. – (1) Proceedings under section 7(1)(a) in respect of a judicial act may be brought only –

(a) by exercising a right of appeal;

(b) on an application (in Scotland a petition) for judicial review; or

(c) in such other forum as may be prescribed by rules.

(2) That does not affect any rule of law which prevents a court from being the subject of judicial review.

(3) In proceedings under this Act in respect of a judicial act done in good faith, damages may not be awarded otherwise than to compensate a person to the extent required by Article 5(5) of the Convention.

(4) An award of damages permitted by subsection (3) is to be made against the Crown; but no award may be made unless the appropriate person, if not a party to the proceedings, is joined.

(5) In this section –

'appropriate person' means the Minister responsible for the court concerned, or a person or government department nominated by him;

'court' includes a tribunal;

'judge' includes a member of a tribunal, a justice of the peace (or, in Northern Ireland, a lay magistrate)[7] and a clerk or other officer entitled to exercise the jurisdiction of a court;

'judicial act' means a judicial act of a court and includes an act done on the instructions, or on behalf, of a judge; and

'rules' has the same meaning as in section 7(9).

---

[7] Included by the Justice (Northern Ireland) Act 2002, when in force.

REMEDIAL ACTION

Power to take remedial action

10. – (1) This section applies if –
  (a) a provision of legislation has been declared under section 4 to be incompatible with a Convention right and, if an appeal lies –
    (i) all persons who may appeal have stated in writing that they do not intend to do so;
    (ii) the time for bringing an appeal has expired and no appeal has been brought within that time; or
    (iii) an appeal brought within that time has been determined or abandoned; or
  (b) it appears to a Minister of the Crown or Her Majesty in Council that, having regard to a finding of the European Court of Human Rights made after the coming into force of this section in proceedings against the United Kingdom, a provision of legislation is incompatible with an obligation of the United Kingdom arising from the Convention.
  (2) If a Minister of the Crown considers that there are compelling reasons for proceeding under this section, he may by order make such amendments to the legislation as he considers necessary to remove the incompatibility.
  (3) If, in the case of subordinate legislation, a Minister of the Crown considers –
  (a) that it is necessary to amend the primary legislation under which the subordinate legislation in question was made, in order to enable the incompatibility to be removed, and
  (b) that there are compelling reasons for proceeding under this section, he may by order make such amendments to the primary legislation as he considers necessary.
  (4) This section also applies where the provision in question is in subordinate legislation and has been quashed, or declared invalid, by reason of incompatibility with a Convention right and the Minister proposes to proceed under paragraph 2(b) of Schedule 2.
  (5) If the legislation is an Order in Council, the power conferred by subsection (2) or (3) is exercisable by Her Majesty in Council.
  (6) In this section 'legislation' does not include a Measure of the Church Assembly or of the General Synod of the Church of England.
  (7) Schedule 2 makes further provision about remedial orders.

OTHER RIGHTS AND PROCEEDINGS

Safeguard for existing human rights

11. A person's reliance on a Convention right does not restrict –
  (a) any other right or freedom conferred on him by or under any law having effect in any part of the United Kingdom; or
  (b) his right to make any claim or bring any proceedings which he could make or bring apart from sections 7 to 9.

Freedom of expression

12. – (1)   This section applies if a court is considering whether to grant any relief which, if granted, might affect the exercise of the Convention right to freedom of expression.

(2)   If the person against whom the application for relief is made ('the respondent') is neither present nor represented, no such relief is to be granted unless the court is satisfied –

    (a)   that the applicant has taken all practicable steps to notify the respondent; or

    (b)   that there are compelling reasons why the respondent should not be notified.

(3)   No such relief is to be granted so as to restrain publication before trial unless the court is satisfied that the applicant is likely to establish that publication should not be allowed.

(4)   The court must have particular regard to the importance of the Convention right to freedom of expression and, where the proceedings relate to material which the respondent claims, or which appears to the court, to be journalistic, literary or artistic material (or to conduct connected with such material), to –

    (a)   the extent to which –

        (i)   the material has, or is about to, become available to the public; or

        (ii)   it is, or would be, in the public interest for the material to be published;

    (b)   any relevant privacy code.

(5)   In this section –

'court' includes a tribunal; and

'relief' includes any remedy or order (other than in criminal proceedings).

Freedom of thought, conscience and religion

13. – (1)   If a court's determination of any question arising under this Act might affect the exercise by a religious organisation (itself or its members collectively) of the Convention right to freedom of thought, conscience and religion, it must have particular regard to the importance of that right.

(2)   In this section 'court' includes a tribunal.

 # DEROGATIONS AND RESERVATIONS

Derogations

14.[8] – (1)   In this Act 'designated derogation' means any derogation by the United Kingdom from an Article of the Convention, or of any protocol to the Convention, which is designated for the purposes of this Act in an order made by the Secretary of State.

(2)   [. . .][8]

(3)   If a designated derogation is amended or replaced it ceases to be a designated derogation.

(4)   But subsection (3) does not prevent the Secretary of State from exercising his power under subsection (1) to make a fresh designation order in respect of the Article concerned.

---

[8] The Human Rights Act (Amendment) Order 2001 (SI 2001/1216) amended this section to remove the reference to the previous derogation to Article 5(3), including the removal of subsection (2).

(5) The Secretary of State must by order make such amendments to Schedule 3 as he considers appropriate to reflect –

    (a) any designation order; or

    (b) the effect of subsection (3).

(6) A designation order may be made in anticipation of the making by the United Kingdom of a proposed derogation.

Reservations

15. – (1) In this Act 'designated reservation' means –

    (a) the United Kingdom's reservation to Article 2 of the First Protocol to the Convention; and

    (b) any other reservation by the United Kingdom to an Article of the Convention, or of any protocol to the Convention, which is designated for the purposes of this Act in an order made by the Secretary of State.

(2) The text of the reservation referred to in subsection (1)(a) is set out in Part II of Schedule 3.

(3) If a designated reservation is withdrawn wholly or in part it ceases to be a designated reservation.

(4) But subsection (3) does not prevent the Secretary of State from exercising his power under subsection (1)(b) to make a fresh designation order in respect of the Article concerned.

(5) The Secretary of State must by order make such amendments to this Act as he considers appropriate to reflect –

    (a) any designation order; or

    (b) the effect of subsection (3).

Period for which designated derogations have effect

16.[9] – (1) If it has not already been withdrawn by the United Kingdom, a designated derogation ceases to have effect for the purposes of this Act at the end of the period of five years beginning with the date on which the order designating it was made.

(2) At any time before the period –

    (a) fixed by subsection (1), or

    (b) extended by an order under this subsection,

comes to an end, the Secretary of State may by order extend it by a further period of five years.

(3) An order under section 14(1) ceases to have effect at the end of the period for consideration, unless a resolution has been passed by each House approving the order.

(4) Subsection (3) does not affect –

    (a) anything done in reliance on the order; or

    (b) the power to make a fresh order under section 14(1).

(5) In subsection (3) 'period for consideration' means the period of forty days beginning with the day on which the order was made.

---

[9] As amended by the Human Rights Act (Amendment) Order 2001 (SI 2001/1216).

(6) In calculating the period for consideration, no account is to be taken of any time during which –
    (a) Parliament is dissolved or prorogued; or
    (b) both Houses are adjourned for more than four days.

(7) If a designated derogation is withdrawn by the United Kingdom, the Secretary of State must by order make such amendments to this Act as he considers are required to reflect that withdrawal.

Periodic review of designated reservations

17. – (1) The appropriate Minister must review the designated reservation referred to in section 15(1)(a) –
    (a) before the end of the period of five years beginning with the date on which section 1(2) came into force; and
    (b) if that designation is still in force, before the end of the period of five years beginning with the date on which the last report relating to it was laid under subsection (3).

(2) The appropriate Minister must review each of the other designated reservations (if any) –
    (a) before the end of the period of five years beginning with the date on which the order designating the reservation first came into force; and
    (b) if the designation is still in force, before the end of the period of five years beginning with the date on which the last report relating to it was laid under subsection (3).

(3) The Minister conducting a review under this section must prepare a report on the result of the review and lay a copy of it before each House of Parliament.

◼ JUDGES OF THE EUROPEAN COURT OF HUMAN RIGHTS

Appointment to European Court of Human Rights

18. – (1) In this section 'judicial office' means the office of –
    (a) Lord Justice of Appeal, Justice of the High Court or Circuit judge, in England and Wales;
    (b) judge of the Court of Session or sheriff, in Scotland;
    (c) Lord Justice of Appeal, judge of the High Court or county court judge, in Northern Ireland.

(2) The holder of a judicial office may become a judge of the European Court of Human Rights ('the Court') without being required to relinquish his office.

(3) But he is not required to perform the duties of his judicial office while he is a judge of the Court.

(4) In respect of any period during which he is a judge of the Court –
    (a) a Lord Justice of Appeal or Justice of the High Court is not to count as a judge of the relevant court for the purposes of section 2(1) or 4(1) of the Supreme Court[10] Act 1981 (maximum number of judges) nor as a judge of the Supreme Court for the purposes of section 12(1) to (6) of that Act (salaries etc.);

---

[10] Reference will be amended to Senior Courts Act 1981 by the CRA 2005.

(b)   a judge of the Court of Session is not to count as a judge of that court for the purposes of section 1(1) of the Court of Session Act 1988 (maximum number of judges) or of section 9(1)(c) of the Administration of Justice Act 1973 ('the 1973 Act') (salaries etc.);

(c)   a Lord Justice of Appeal or judge of the High Court in Northern Ireland is not to count as a judge of the relevant court for the purposes of section 2(1) or 3(1) of the Judicature (Northern Ireland) Act 1978 (maximum number of judges) nor as a judge of the Supreme Court of Northern Ireland for the purposes of section 9(1)(d) of the 1973 Act (salaries etc.);

(d)   a Circuit judge is not to count as such for the purposes of section 18 of the Courts Act 1971 (salaries etc.);

(e)   a sheriff is not to count as such for the purposes of section 14 of the Sheriff Courts (Scotland) Act 1907 (salaries etc.);

(f)   a county court judge of Northern Ireland is not to count as such for the purposes of section 106 of the County Courts Act (Northern Ireland) 1959 (salaries etc.).

(5)   If a sheriff principal is appointed a judge of the Court, section 11(1) of the Sheriff Courts (Scotland) Act 1971 (temporary appointment of sheriff principal) applies, while he holds that appointment, as if his office is vacant.

(6)   Schedule 4 makes provision about judicial pensions in relation to the holder of a judicial office who serves as a judge of the Court.

(7)   The Lord Chancellor or the Secretary of State may by order make such transitional provision (including, in particular, provision for a temporary increase in the maximum number of judges) as he considers appropriate in relation to any holder of a judicial office who has completed his service as a judge of the Court.

(7A)[11] The following paragraphs apply to the making of an order under subsection (7) in relation to any holder of a judicial office listed in subsection (1)(a) –

(a)   before deciding what transitional provision it is appropriate to make, the person making the order must consult the Lord Chief Justice of England and Wales;

(b)   before making the order, that person must consult the Lord Chief Justice of England and Wales.

(7B) The following paragraphs apply to the making of an order under subsection (7) in relation to any holder of a judicial office listed in subsection (1)(c) –

(a)   before deciding what transitional provision it is appropriate to make, the person making the order must consult the Lord Chief Justice of Northern Ireland;

(b)   before making the order, that person must consult the Lord Chief Justice of Northern Ireland.

(7C) The Lord Chief Justice of England and Wales may nominate a judicial office holder (within the meaning of section 109(4) of the Constitutional Reform Act 2005) to exercise his functions under this section.

(7D) The Lord Chief Justice of Northern Ireland may nominate any of the following to exercise his functions under this section –

(a)   the holder of one of the offices listed in Schedule 1 to the Justice (Northern Ireland) Act 2002;

(b)   a Lord Justice of Appeal (as defined in section 88 of that Act).

---

[11] Subsections (7A) to (7D) will be inserted by the Constitutional Reform Act 2005, when it comes into effect.

PARLIAMENTARY PROCEDURE

Statements of compatibility

19. – (1)   A Minister of the Crown in charge of a Bill in either House of Parliament must, before Second Reading of the Bill –
  (a)   make a statement to the effect that in his view the provisions of the Bill are compatible with the Convention rights ('a statement of compatibility'); or
  (b)   make a statement to the effect that although he is unable to make a statement of compatibility the government nevertheless wishes the House to proceed with the Bill.

(2)   The statement must be in writing and be published in such manner as the Minister making it considers appropriate.

 SUPPLEMENTAL

Orders etc. under this Act

20. – (1)   Any power of a Minister of the Crown to make an order under this Act is exercisable by statutory instrument.

(2)   The power of the Secretary of State to make rules (other than rules of court) under section 2(3) or 7(9) is exercisable by statutory instrument.

(3)   Any statutory instrument made under section 14, 15 or 16(7) must be laid before Parliament.

(4)   No order may be made by the Secretary of State under section 1(4), 7(11) or 16(2) unless a draft of the order has been laid before, and approved by, each House of Parliament.

(5)   Any statutory instrument made under section 18(7) or Schedule 4, or to which subsection (2) applies, shall be subject to annulment in pursuance of a resolution of either House of Parliament.

(6)   The power of a Northern Ireland department to make –
  (a)   rules under section 2(3)(c) or 7(9)(c), or
  (b)   an order under section 7(11), is exercisable by statutory rule for the purposes of the Statutory Rules (Northern Ireland) Order 1979.

(7)   Any rules made under section 2(3)(c) or 7(9)(c) shall be subject to negative resolution; and section 41(6) of the Interpretation Act (Northern Ireland) 1954 (meaning of 'subject to negative resolution') shall apply as if the power to make the rules were conferred by an Act of the Northern Ireland Assembly.

(8)   No order may be made by a Northern Ireland department under section 7(11) unless a draft of the order has been laid before, and approved by, the Northern Ireland Assembly.

Interpretation, etc.

21. – (1)   In this Act –
  'amend' includes repeal and apply (with or without modifications);
  'the appropriate Minister' means the Minister of the Crown having charge of the appropriate authorised government department (within the meaning of the Crown Proceedings Act 1947);

'the Commission' means the European Commission of Human Rights;

'the Convention' means the Convention for the Protection of Human Rights and Fundamental Freedoms, agreed by the Council of Europe at Rome on 4th November 1950 as it has effect for the time being in relation to the United Kingdom;

'declaration of incompatibility' means a declaration under section 4;

'Minister of the Crown' has the same meaning as in the Ministers of the Crown Act 1975;

'Northern Ireland Minister' includes the First Minister and the deputy First Minister in Northern Ireland;

'primary legislation' means any –

(a)   public general Act;

(b)   local and personal Act;

(c)   private Act;

(d)   Measure of the Church Assembly;

(e)   Measure of the General Synod of the Church of England;

(f)   Order in Council –

    (i)   made in exercise of Her Majesty's Royal Prerogative;

    (ii)   made under section 38(1)(a) of the Northern Ireland Constitution Act 1973 or the corresponding provision of the Northern Ireland Act 1998; or

    (iii)   amending an Act of a kind mentioned in paragraph (a), (b) or (c);

and includes an order or other instrument made under primary legislation (otherwise than by the National Assembly for Wales, a member of the Scottish Executive, a Northern Ireland Minister or a Northern Ireland department) to the extent to which it operates to bring one or more provisions of that legislation into force or amends any primary legislation;

'the First Protocol' means the protocol to the Convention agreed at Paris on 20th March 1952;

'the Eleventh Protocol' means the protocol to the Convention (restructuring the control machinery established by the Convention) agreed at Strasbourg on 11th May 1994;

'the Thirteenth Protocol' means the protocol to the Convention (concerning the abolition of the death penalty in all circumstances) agreed at Vilnius on 3rd May 2002;

'remedial order' means an order under section 10;

'subordinate legislation' means any –

(a)   Order in Council other than one –

    (i)   made in exercise of Her Majesty's Royal Prerogative;

    (ii)   made under section 38(1)(a) of the Northern Ireland Constitution Act 1973 or the corresponding provision of the Northern Ireland Act 1998; or

    (iii)   amending an Act of a kind mentioned in the definition of primary legislation;

(b)   Act of the Scottish Parliament;

(c)   Act of the Parliament of Northern Ireland;

(d)   Measure of the Assembly established under section 1 of the Northern Ireland Assembly Act 1973;

(e)   Act of the Northern Ireland Assembly;

(f)   order, rules, regulations, scheme, warrant, byelaw or other instrument made under primary legislation (except to the extent to which it operates to bring one or more provisions of that legislation into force or amends any primary legislation);

(g)   order, rules, regulations, scheme, warrant, byelaw or other instrument made under legislation mentioned in paragraph (b), (c), (d) or (e) or made under an Order in Council applying only to Northern Ireland;

(h)   order, rules, regulations, scheme, warrant, byelaw or other instrument made by a member of the Scottish Executive, a Northern Ireland Minister or a Northern Ireland department in exercise of prerogative or other executive functions of Her Majesty which are exercisable by such a person on behalf of Her Majesty;

'transferred matters' has the same meaning as in the Northern Ireland Act 1998; and 'tribunal' means any tribunal in which legal proceedings may be brought.

(2)   The references in paragraphs (b) and (c) of section 2(1) to Articles are to Articles of the Convention as they had effect immediately before the coming into force of the Eleventh Protocol.

(3)   The reference in paragraph (d) of section 2(1) to Article 46 includes a reference to Articles 32 and 54 of the Convention as they had effect immediately before the coming into force of the Eleventh Protocol.

(4)   The references in section 2(1) to a report or decision of the Commission or a decision of the Committee of Ministers include references to a report or decision made as provided by paragraphs 3, 4 and 6 of Article 5 of the Eleventh Protocol (transitional provisions).

(5)   Any liability under the Army Act 1955, the Air Force Act 1955 or the Naval Discipline Act 1957 to suffer death for an offence is replaced by a liability to imprisonment for life or any less punishment authorised by those Acts; and those Acts shall accordingly have effect with the necessary modifications.

Short title, commencement, application and extent

22. – (1)   This Act may be cited as the Human Rights Act 1998.

(2)   Sections 18, 20 and 21(5) and this section come into force on the passing of this Act.

(3)   The other provisions of this Act come into force on such day as the Secretary of State may by order appoint; and different days may be appointed for different purposes.

(4)   Paragraph (b) of subsection (1) of section 7 applies to proceedings brought by or at the instigation of a public authority whenever the act in question took place; but otherwise that subsection does not apply to an act taking place before the coming into force of that section.

(5)   This Act binds the Crown.

(6)   This Act extends to Northern Ireland.

(7)   Section 21(5), so far as it relates to any provision contained in the Army Act 1955, the Air Force Act 1955 or the Naval Discipline Act 1957, extends to any place to which that provision extends.

SCHEDULE 1 – THE ARTICLES

Part I The Convention rights and freedoms

Article 2 Right to life

1. Everyone's right to life shall be protected by law. No one shall be deprived of his life intentionally save in the execution of a sentence of a court following his conviction of a crime for which this penalty is provided by law.

2. Deprivation of life shall not be regarded as inflicted in contravention of this Article when it results from the use of force which is no more than absolutely necessary:

    (a)   in defence of any person from unlawful violence;

    (b)   in order to effect a lawful arrest or to prevent the escape of a person lawfully detained;

    (c)   in action lawfully taken for the purpose of quelling a riot or insurrection.

Article 3 Prohibition of torture

No one shall be subjected to torture or to inhuman or degrading treatment or punishment.

Article 4 Prohibition of slavery and forced labour

1. No one shall be held in slavery or servitude.

2. No one shall be required to perform forced or compulsory labour.

3. For the purpose of this Article the term 'forced or compulsory labour' shall not include:

    (a)   any work required to be done in the ordinary course of detention imposed according to the provisions of Article 5 of this Convention or during conditional release from such detention;

    (b)   any service of a military character or, in case of conscientious objectors in countries where they are recognised, service exacted instead of compulsory military service;

    (c)   any service exacted in case of an emergency or calamity threatening the life or well-being of the community;

    (d)   any work or service which forms part of normal civic obligations.

Article 5 Right to liberty and security

1. Everyone has the right to liberty and security of person. No one shall be deprived of his liberty save in the following cases and in accordance with a procedure prescribed by law:

    (a)   the lawful detention of a person after conviction by a competent court;

    (b)   the lawful arrest or detention of a person for non-compliance with the lawful order of a court or in order to secure the fulfilment of any obligation prescribed by law;

    (c)   the lawful arrest or detention of a person effected for the purpose of bringing him before the competent legal authority on reasonable suspicion of having committed an offence or when it is reasonably considered necessary to prevent his committing an offence or fleeing after having done so;

(d) the detention of a minor by lawful order for the purpose of educational super-vision or his lawful detention for the purpose of bringing him before the competent legal authority;

(e) the lawful detention of persons for the prevention of the spreading of infectious diseases, of persons of unsound mind, alcoholics or drug addicts or vagrants;

(f) the lawful arrest or detention of a person to prevent his effecting an unauth-orised entry into the country or of a person against whom action is being taken with a view to deportation or extradition.

2. Everyone who is arrested shall be informed promptly, in a language which he under-stands, of the reasons for his arrest and of any charge against him.

3. Everyone arrested or detained in accordance with the provisions of paragraph 1(c) of this Article shall be brought promptly before a judge or other officer authorised by law to exercise judicial power and shall be entitled to trial within a reasonable time or to release pending trial. Release may be conditioned by guarantees to appear for trial.

4. Everyone who is deprived of his liberty by arrest or detention shall be entitled to take proceedings by which the lawfulness of his detention shall be decided speedily by a court and his release ordered if the detention is not lawful.

5. Everyone who has been the victim of arrest or detention in contravention of the provi-sions of this Article shall have an enforceable right to compensation.

Article 6 Right to a fair trial

1. In the determination of his civil rights and obligations or of any criminal charge against him, everyone is entitled to a fair and public hearing within a reasonable time by an inde-pendent and impartial tribunal established by law. Judgment shall be pronounced publicly but the press and public may be excluded from all or part of the trial in the interest of morals, public order or national security in a democratic society, where the interests of juveniles or the protection of the private life of the parties so require, or to the extent strictly necessary in the opinion of the court in special circumstances where publicity would prejudice the interests of justice.

2. Everyone charged with a criminal offence shall be presumed innocent until proved guilty according to law.

3. Everyone charged with a criminal offence has the following minimum rights:

(a) to be informed promptly, in a language which he understands and in detail, of the nature and cause of the accusation against him;

(b) to have adequate time and facilities for the preparation of his defence;

(c) to defend himself in person or through legal assistance of his own choosing or, if he has not sufficient means to pay for legal assistance, to be given it free when the interests of justice so require;

(d) to examine or have examined witnesses against him and to obtain the attend-ance and examination of witnesses on his behalf under the same conditions as witnesses against him;

(e) to have the free assistance of an interpreter if he cannot understand or speak the language used in court.

Article 7 No punishment without law

1. No one shall be held guilty of any criminal offence on account of any act or omission which did not constitute a criminal offence under national or international law at the time

when it was committed. Nor shall a heavier penalty be imposed than the one that was applicable at the time the criminal offence was committed.

2. This Article shall not prejudice the trial and punishment of any person for any act or omission which, at the time when it was committed, was criminal according to the general principles of law recognised by civilised nations.

Ariticle 8 Right to respect for private and family life

1. Everyone has the right to respect for his private and family life, his home and his correspondence.

2. There shall be no interference by a public authority with the exercise of this right except such as is in accordance with the law and is necessary in a democratic society in the interests of national security, public safety or the economic well-being of the country, for the prevention of disorder or crime, for the protection of health or morals, or for the protection of the rights and freedoms of others.

Ariticle 9 Freedom of thought, conscience and religion

1. Everyone has the right to freedom of thought, conscience and religion; this right includes freedom to change his religion or belief and freedom, either alone or in community with others and in public or private, to manifest his religion or belief, in worship, teaching, practice and observance.

2. Freedom to manifest one's religion or beliefs shall be subject only to such limitations as are prescribed by law and are necessary in a democratic society in the interests of public safety, for the protection of public order, health or morals, or for the protection of the rights and freedoms of others.

Article 10 Freedom of expression

1. Everyone has the right to freedom of expression. This right shall include freedom to hold opinions and to receive and impart information and ideas without interference by public authority and regardless of frontiers. This Article shall not prevent States from requiring the licensing of broadcasting, television or cinema enterprises.

2. The exercise of these freedoms, since it carries with it duties and responsibilities, may be subject to such formalities, conditions, restrictions or penalties as are prescribed by law and are necessary in a democratic society, in the interests of national security, territorial integrity or public safety, for the prevention of disorder or crime, for the protection of health or morals, for the protection of the reputation or rights of others, for preventing the disclosure of information received in confidence, or for maintaining the authority and impartiality of the judiciary.

Article 11 Freedom of assembly and association

1. Everyone has the right to freedom of peaceful assembly and to freedom of association with others, including the right to form and to join trade unions for the protection of his interests.

2. No restrictions shall be placed on the exercise of these rights other than such as are prescribed by law and are necessary in a democratic society in the interests of national security or public safety, for the prevention of disorder or crime, for the protection of health or morals or for the protection of the rights and freedoms of others. This Article

shall not prevent the imposition of lawful restrictions on the exercise of these rights by members of the armed forces, of the police or of the administration of the State.

Article 12 Right to marry

Men and women of marriageable age have the right to marry and to found a family, according to the national laws governing the exercise of this right.

Article 14 Prohibition of discrimination

The enjoyment of the rights and freedoms set forth in this Convention shall be secured without discrimination on any ground such as sex, race, colour, language, religion, political or other opinion, national or social origin, association with a national minority, property, birth or other status.

Article 16 Restrictions on political activity of aliens

Nothing in Articles 10, 11 and 14 shall be regarded as preventing the High Contracting Parties from imposing restrictions on the political activity of aliens.

Article 17 Prohibition of abuse of rights

Nothing in this Convention may be interpreted as implying for any State, group or person any right to engage in any activity or perform any act aimed at the destruction of any of the rights and freedoms set forth herein or at their limitation to a greater extent than is provided for in the Convention.

Article 18 Limitation on use of restrictions on rights

The restrictions permitted under this Convention to the said rights and freedoms shall not be applied for any purpose other than those for which they have been prescribed.

Part II The first protocol

Article 1 Protection of property

Every natural or legal person is entitled to the peaceful enjoyment of his possessions. No one shall be deprived of his possessions except in the public interest and subject to the conditions provided for by law and by the general principles of international law. The preceding provisions shall not, however, in any way impair the right of a State to enforce such laws as it deems necessary to control the use of property in accordance with the general interest or to secure the payment of taxes or other contributions or penalties.

Article 2 Right to education

No person shall be denied the right to education. In the exercise of any functions which it assumes in relation to education and to teaching, the State shall respect the right of parents to ensure such education and teaching in conformity with their own religious and philosophical convictions.

Article 3 Right to free elections

The High Contracting Parties undertake to hold free elections at reasonable intervals by secret ballot, under conditions which will ensure the free expression of the opinion of the people in the choice of the legislature.

Part III The thirteenth protocol[12]

Article 1 Abolition of the death penalty

The death penalty shall be abolished. No one shall be condemned to such penalty or executed.

 SCHEDULE 2 – REMEDIAL ORDERS

Orders

1. – (1)   A remedial order may –
    (a)   contain such incidental, supplemental, consequential or transitional provision as the person making it considers appropriate;
    (b)   be made so as to have effect from a date earlier than that on which it is made;
    (c)   make provision for the delegation of specific functions;
    (d)   make different provision for different cases.
  (2)   The power conferred by sub-paragraph (1)(a) includes –
    (a)   power to amend primary legislation (including primary legislation other than that which contains the incompatible provision); and
    (b)   power to amend or revoke subordinate legislation (including subordinate legislation other than that which contains the incompatible provision).
  (3)   A remedial order may be made so as to have the same extent as the legislation which it affects.
  (4)   No person is to be guilty of an offence solely as a result of the retrospective effect of a remedial order.

Procedure

2. No remedial order may be made unless –
    (a)   a draft of the order has been approved by a resolution of each House of Parliament made after the end of the period of 60 days beginning with the day on which the draft was laid; or
    (b)   it is declared in the order that it appears to the person making it that, because of the urgency of the matter, it is necessary to make the order without a draft being so approved.

---

[12] Amended to replace the Sixth Protocol with the Thirteenth by the Human Rights Act 1998 (Amendment) Order 2004 (SI 2004/1574).

Orders laid in draft

3. – (1)   No draft may be laid under paragraph 2(a) unless –
  (a)   the person proposing to make the order has laid before Parliament a document which contains a draft of the proposed order and the required information; and
  (b)   the period of 60 days, beginning with the day on which the document required by this sub-paragraph was laid, has ended.

(2)   If representations have been made during that period, the draft laid under paragraph 2(a) must be accompanied by a statement containing –
  (a)   a summary of the representations; and
  (b)   if, as a result of the representations, the proposed order has been changed, details of the changes.

Urgent cases

4. – (1)   If a remedial order ('the original order') is made without being approved in draft, the person making it must lay it before Parliament, accompanied by the required information, after it is made.

(2)   If representations have been made during the period of 60 days beginning with the day on which the original order was made, the person making it must (after the end of that period) lay before Parliament a statement containing –
  (a)   a summary of the representations; and
  (b)   if, as a result of the representations, he considers it appropriate to make changes to the original order, details of the changes.

(3)   If sub-paragraph (2)(b) applies, the person making the statement must –
  (a)   make a further remedial order replacing the original order; and
  (b)   lay the replacement order before Parliament.

(4)   If, at the end of the period of 120 days beginning with the day on which the original order was made, a resolution has not been passed by each House approving the original or replacement order, the order ceases to have effect (but without that affecting anything previously done under either order or the power to make a fresh remedial order).

Definitions

5.   In this Schedule –
  'representations' means representations about a remedial order (or proposed remedial order) made to the person making (or proposing to make) it and includes any relevant Parliamentary report or resolution; and 'required information' means –
  (a)   an explanation of the incompatibility which the order (or proposed order) seeks to remove, including particulars of the relevant declaration, finding or order; and
  (b)   a statement of the reasons for proceeding under section 10 and for making an order in those terms.

Calculating periods

6.   In calculating any period for the purposes of this Schedule, no account is to be taken of any time during which –

(a)   Parliament is dissolved or prorogued; or

(b)   both Houses are adjourned for more than four days.

7.[13] (1)   This paragraph applies in relation to –

   (a)   any remedial order made, and any draft of such an order proposed to be made –

      (i)   by the Scottish Ministers; or

      (ii)   within devolved competence (within the meaning of the Scotland Act 1998) by Her Majesty in Council; and

   (b)   any document or statement to be laid in connection with such an order (or proposed order).

(2)   This Schedule has effect in relation to any such order (or proposed order), document or statement subject to the following modifications.

(3)   Any reference to Parliament, each House of Parliament or both Houses of Parliament shall be construed as a reference to the Scottish Parliament.

(4)   Paragraph 6 does not apply and instead, in calculating any period for the purposes of this Schedule, no account is to be taken of any time during which the Scottish Parliament is dissolved or is in recess for more than four days.

SCHEDULE 3 - DEROGATION AND RESERVATION[14]

Part II Reservation

At the time of signing the present (First) Protocol, I declare that, in view of certain provisions of the Education Acts in the United Kingdom, the principle affirmed in the second sentence of Article 2 is accepted by the United Kingdom only so far as it is compatible with the provision of efficient instruction and training, and the avoidance of unreasonable public expenditure. Dated 20 March 1952. Made by the United Kingdom Permanent Representative to the Council of Europe.

SCHEDULE 4 - JUDICIAL PENSIONS

Duty to make orders about pensions

1. – (1)   The appropriate Minister must by order make provision with respect to pensions payable to or in respect of any holder of a judicial office who serves as an ECHR judge.

(2)   A pensions order must include such provision as the Minister making it considers is necessary to secure that –

   (a)   an ECHR judge who was, immediately before his appointment as an ECHR judge, a member of a judicial pension scheme is entitled to remain as a member of that scheme;

   (b)   the terms on which he remains a member of the scheme are those which would have been applicable had he not been appointed as an ECHR judge; and

---

[13] Inserted by the Scotland Act 1998 (Consequential Modifications) Order 2000 (SI 2000/2040).

[14] Part 1 of Schedule 3 was repealed by the Human Rights Act 1998 (Amendment) Order 2005 (SI 2005/1071) following the withdrawal of the derogation to the Convention which had been entered in respect of provisions of the Anti-Terrorism, Crime and Security Act 2005 which were repealed by the Prevention of Terrorism Act 2005: see discussion in Chapter 21.

(c) entitlement to benefits payable in accordance with the scheme continues to be determined as if, while serving as an ECHR judge, his salary was that which would (but for section 18(4)) have been payable to him in respect of his continuing service as the holder of his judicial office.

Contributions

2. A pensions order may, in particular, make provision –
   (a) for any contributions which are payable by a person who remains a member of a scheme as a result of the order, and which would otherwise be payable by deduction from his salary, to be made otherwise than by deduction from his salary as an ECHR judge; and
   (b) for such contributions to be collected in such manner as may be determined by the administrators of the scheme.

Amendments of other enactments

3. A pensions order may amend any provision of, or made under, a pensions Act in such manner and to such extent as the Minister making the order considers necessary or expedient to ensure the proper administration of any scheme to which it relates.

Definitions

4. In this Schedule –
   'appropriate Minister' means –
   (a) in relation to any judicial office whose jurisdiction is exercisable exclusively in relation to Scotland, the Secretary of State; and
   (b) otherwise, the Lord Chancellor;[15]
   'ECHR judge' means the holder of a judicial office who is serving as a judge of the Court;
   'judicial pension scheme' means a scheme established by and in accordance with a pensions Act;
   'pensions Act' means –
   (a) the County Courts Act (Northern Ireland) 1959;
   (b) the Sheriffs' Pensions (Scotland) Act 1961;
   (c) the Judicial Pensions Act 1981; or
   (d) the Judicial Pensions and Retirement Act 1993; and
   'pensions order' means an order made under paragraph 1.

---

[15] This function of the Lord Chancellor is preserved by the CRA 2005, Schedule 7.

Appendix 2

The European Convention for the Protection of Human Rights and Fundamental Freedoms[1]

The governments signatory hereto, being members of the Council of Europe,

Considering the Universal Declaration of Human Rights proclaimed by the General Assembly of the United Nations on 10th December 1948;

Considering that this Declaration aims at securing the universal and effective recognition and observance of the Rights therein declared;

Considering that the aim of the Council of Europe is the achievement of greater unity between its members and that one of the methods by which that aim is to be pursued is the maintenance and further realisation of human rights and fundamental freedoms;

Reaffirming their profound belief in those fundamental freedoms which are the foundation of justice and peace in the world and are best maintained on the one hand by an effective political democracy and on the other by a common understanding and observance of the human rights upon which they depend;

Being resolved, as the governments of European countries which are like-minded and have a common heritage of political traditions, ideals, freedom and the rule of law, to take the first steps for the collective enforcement of certain of the rights stated in the Universal Declaration, Have agreed as follows:

Article 1 – Obligation to respect human rights

The High Contracting Parties shall secure to everyone within their jurisdiction the rights and freedoms defined in Section I of this Convention.

Section I – Rights and freedoms

Article 2 – Right to life

1   Everyone's right to life shall be protected by law. No one shall be deprived of his life intentionally save in the execution of a sentence of a court following his conviction of a crime for which this penalty is provided by law.
2   Deprivation of life shall not be regarded as inflicted in contravention of this article when it results from the use of force which is no more than absolutely necessary:
    a   in defence of any person from unlawful violence;
    b   in order to effect a lawful arrest or to prevent the escape of a person lawfully detained;
    c   in action lawfully taken for the purpose of quelling a riot or insurrection.

---

[1] The text is as amended by Protocol 11.

Article 3 - Prohibition of torture

No one shall be subjected to torture or to inhuman or degrading treatment or punishment.

Article 4 - Prohibition of slavery and forced labour

1 No one shall be held in slavery or servitude.
2 No one shall be required to perform forced or compulsory labour.
3 For the purpose of this article the term 'forced or compulsory labour' shall not include:
    a any work required to be done in the ordinary course of detention imposed according to the provisions of Article 5 of this Convention or during conditional release from such detention;
    b any service of a military character or, in case of conscientious objectors in countries where they are recognised, service exacted instead of compulsory military service;
    c any service exacted in case of an emergency or calamity threatening the life or well-being of the community;
    d any work or service which forms part of normal civic obligations.

Article 5 - Right to liberty and security

1 Everyone has the right to liberty and security of person. No one shall be deprived of his liberty save in the following cases and in accordance with a procedure prescribed by law:
    a the lawful detention of a person after conviction by a competent court;
    b the lawful arrest or detention of a person for non-compliance with the lawful order of a court or in order to secure the fulfilment of any obligation prescribed by law;
    c the lawful arrest or detention of a person effected for the purpose of bringing him before the competent legal authority on reasonable suspicion of having committed an offence or when it is reasonably considered necessary to prevent his committing an offence or fleeing after having done so;
    d the detention of a minor by lawful order for the purpose of educational supervision or his lawful detention for the purpose of bringing him before the competent legal authority;
    e the lawful detention of persons for the prevention of the spreading of infectious diseases, of persons of unsound mind, alcoholics or drug addicts or vagrants;
    f the lawful arrest or detention of a person to prevent his effecting an unauthorised entry into the country or of a person against whom action is being taken with a view to deportation or extradition.
2 Everyone who is arrested shall be informed promptly, in a language which he understands, of the reasons for his arrest and of any charge against him.
3 Everyone arrested or detained in accordance with the provisions of paragraph 1.c of this article shall be brought promptly before a judge or other officer authorised by law to exercise judicial power and shall be entitled to trial within a reasonable time or to release pending trial. Release may be conditioned by guarantees to appear for trial.
4 Everyone who is deprived of his liberty by arrest or detention shall be entitled to take proceedings by which the lawfulness of his detention shall be decided speedily by a court and his release ordered if the detention is not lawful.
5 Everyone who has been the victim of arrest or detention in contravention of the provisions of this article shall have an enforceable right to compensation.

Article 6 - Right to a fair trial

1   In the determination of his civil rights and obligations or of any criminal charge against him, everyone is entitled to a fair and public hearing within a reasonable time by an independent and impartial tribunal established by law. Judgment shall be pronounced publicly but the press and public may be excluded from all or part of the trial in the interests of morals, public order or national security in a democratic society, where the interests of juveniles or the protection of the private life of the parties so require, or to the extent strictly necessary in the opinion of the court in special circumstances where publicity would prejudice the interests of justice.

2   Everyone charged with a criminal offence shall be presumed innocent until proved guilty according to law.

3   Everyone charged with a criminal offence has the following minimum rights:
    a   to be informed promptly, in a language which he understands and in detail, of the nature and cause of the accusation against him;
    b   to have adequate time and facilities for the preparation of his defence;
    c   to defend himself in person or through legal assistance of his own choosing or, if he has not sufficient means to pay for legal assistance, to be given it free when the interests of justice so require;
    d   to examine or have examined witnesses against him and to obtain the attendance and examination of witnesses on his behalf under the same conditions as witnesses against him;
    e   to have the free assistance of an interpreter if he cannot understand or speak the language used in court.

Article 7 - No punishment without law

1   No one shall be held guilty of any criminal offence on account of any act or omission which did not constitute a criminal offence under national or international law at the time when it was committed. Nor shall a heavier penalty be imposed than the one that was applicable at the time the criminal offence was committed.

2   This article shall not prejudice the trial and punishment of any person for any act or omission which, at the time when it was committed, was criminal according to the general principles of law recognised by civilised nations.

Article 8 - Right to respect for private and family life

1   Everyone has the right to respect for his private and family life, his home and his correspondence.

2   There shall be no interference by a public authority with the exercise of this right except such as is in accordance with the law and is necessary in a democratic society in the interests of national security, public safety or the economic well-being of the country, for the prevention of disorder or crime, for the protection of health or morals, or for the protection of the rights and freedoms of others.

Article 9 - Freedom of thought, conscience and religion

1   Everyone has the right to freedom of thought, conscience and religion; this right includes freedom to change his religion or belief and freedom, either alone or in

community with others and in public or private, to manifest his religion or belief, in worship, teaching, practice and observance.

2 Freedom to manifest one's religion or beliefs shall be subject only to such limitations as are prescribed by law and are necessary in a democratic society in the interests of public safety, for the protection of public order, health or morals, or for the protection of the rights and freedoms of others.

Article 10 - Freedom of expression

1 Everyone has the right to freedom of expression. This right shall include freedom to hold opinions and to receive and impart information and ideas without interference by public authority and regardless of frontiers. This article shall not prevent States from requiring the licensing of broadcasting, television or cinema enterprises.

2 The exercise of these freedoms, since it carries with it duties and responsibilities, may be subject to such formalities, conditions, restrictions or penalties as are prescribed by law and are necessary in a democratic society, in the interests of national security, territorial integrity or public safety, for the prevention of disorder or crime, for the protection of health or morals, for the protection of the reputation or rights of others, for preventing the disclosure of information received in confidence, or for maintaining the authority and impartiality of the judiciary.

Article 11 - Freedom of assembly and association

1 Everyone has the right to freedom of peaceful assembly and to freedom of association with others, including the right to form and to join trade unions for the protection of his interests.

2 No restrictions shall be placed on the exercise of these rights other than such as are prescribed by law and are necessary in a democratic society in the interests of national security or public safety, for the prevention of disorder or crime, for the protection of health or morals or for the protection of the rights and freedoms of others. This article shall not prevent the imposition of lawful restrictions on the exercise of these rights by members of the armed forces, of the police or of the administration of the State.

Article 12 - Right to marry

Men and women of marriageable age have the right to marry and to found a family, according to the national laws governing the exercise of this right.

Article 13 - Right to an effective remedy

Everyone whose rights and freedoms as set forth in this Convention are violated shall have an effective remedy before a national authority notwithstanding that the violation has been committed by persons acting in an official capacity.

Article 14 - Prohibition of discrimination

The enjoyment of the rights and freedoms set forth in this Convention shall be secured without discrimination on any ground such as sex, race, colour, language, religion, political or other opinion, national or social origin, association with a national minority, property, birth or other status.

Article 15 – Derogation in time of emergency

1   In time of war or other public emergency threatening the life of the nation any High Contracting Party may take measures derogating from its obligations under this Convention to the extent strictly required by the exigencies of the situation, provided that such measures are not inconsistent with its other obligations under international law.
2   No derogation from Article 2, except in respect of deaths resulting from lawful acts of war, or from Articles 3, 4 (paragraph 1) and 7 shall be made under this provision.
3   Any High Contracting Party availing itself of this right of derogation shall keep the Secretary General of the Council of Europe fully informed of the measures which it has taken and the reasons therefor. It shall also inform the Secretary General of the Council of Europe when such measures have ceased to operate and the provisions of the Convention are again being fully executed.

Article 16 – Restrictions on political activity of aliens

Nothing in Articles 10, 11 and 14 shall be regarded as preventing the High Contracting Parties from imposing restrictions on the political activity of aliens.

Article 17 – Prohibition of abuse of rights

Nothing in this Convention may be interpreted as implying for any State, group or person any right to engage in any activity or perform any act aimed at the destruction of any of the rights and freedoms set forth herein or at their limitation to a greater extent than is provided for in the Convention.

Article 18 – Limitation on use of restrictions on rights

The restrictions permitted under this Convention to the said rights and freedoms shall not be applied for any purpose other than those for which they have been prescribed.

Section II – European Court of Human Rights

Article 19 – Establishment of the Court

To ensure the observance of the engagements undertaken by the High Contracting Parties in the Convention and the Protocols thereto, there shall be set up a European Court of Human Rights, hereinafter referred to as 'the Court'. It shall function on a permanent basis.

Article 20 – Number of judges

The Court shall consist of a number of judges equal to that of the High Contracting Parties.

Article 21 – Criteria for office

1   The judges shall be of high moral character and must either possess the qualifications required for appointment to high judicial office or be jurisconsults of recognised competence.
2   The judges shall sit on the Court in their individual capacity.
3   During their term of office the judges shall not engage in any activity which is incompatible with their independence, impartiality or with the demands of a full-time office; all questions arising from the application of this paragraph shall be decided by the Court.

Article 22 - Election of judges

1 The judges shall be elected by the Parliamentary Assembly with respect to each High Contracting Party by a majority of votes cast from a list of three candidates nominated by the High Contracting Party.
2 The same procedure shall be followed to complete the Court in the event of the accession of new High Contracting Parties and in filling casual vacancies.

Article 23 - Terms of office

1 The judges shall be elected for a period of six years. They may be re-elected. However, the terms of office of one-half of the judges elected at the first election shall expire at the end of three years.
2 The judges whose terms of office are to expire at the end of the initial period of three years shall be chosen by lot by the Secretary General of the Council of Europe immediately after their election.
3 In order to ensure that, as far as possible, the terms of office of one-half of the judges are renewed every three years, the Parliamentary Assembly may decide, before proceeding to any subsequent election, that the term or terms of office of one or more judges to be elected shall be for a period other than six years but not more than nine and not less than three years.
4 In cases where more than one term of office is involved and where the Parliamentary Assembly applies the preceding paragraph, the allocation of the terms of office shall be effected by a drawing of lots by the Secretary General of the Council of Europe immediately after the election.
5 A judge elected to replace a judge whose term of office has not expired shall hold office for the remainder of his predecessor's term.
6 The terms of office of judges shall expire when they reach the age of 70.
7 The judges shall hold office until replaced. They shall, however, continue to deal with such cases as they already have under consideration.

Article 24 - Dismissal

No judge may be dismissed from his office unless the other judges decide by a majority of two-thirds that he has ceased to fulfil the required conditions.

Article 25 - Registry and legal secretaries

The Court shall have a registry, the functions and organisation of which shall be laid down in the rules of the Court. The Court shall be assisted by legal secretaries.

Article 26 - Plenary Court

The plenary Court shall
a elect its President and one or two Vice-Presidents for a period of three years; they may be re-elected;
b set up Chambers, constituted for a fixed period of time;
c elect the Presidents of the Chambers of the Court; they may be re-elected;
d adopt the rules of the Court; and
e elect the Registrar and one or more Deputy Registrars.

Article 27 – Committees, Chambers and Grand Chamber

1   To consider cases brought before it, the Court shall sit in committees of three judges, in Chambers of seven judges and in a Grand Chamber of seventeen judges. The Court's Chambers shall set up committees for a fixed period of time.

2   There shall sit as an *ex officio* member of the Chamber and the Grand Chamber the judge elected in respect of the State Party concerned or, if there is none or if he is unable to sit, a person of its choice who shall sit in the capacity of judge.

3   The Grand Chamber shall also include the President of the Court, the Vice-Presidents, the Presidents of the Chambers and other judges chosen in accordance with the rules of the Court. When a case is referred to the Grand Chamber under Article 43, no judge from the Chamber which rendered the judgment shall sit in the Grand Chamber, with the exception of the President of the Chamber and the judge who sat in respect of the State Party concerned.

Article 28 – Declarations of inadmissibility by committees

A committee may, by a unanimous vote, declare inadmissible or strike out of its list of cases an application submitted under Article 34 where such a decision can be taken without further examination. The decision shall be final.

Article 29 – Decisions by Chambers on admissibility and merits

1   If no decision is taken under Article 28, a Chamber shall decide on the admissibility and merits of individual applications submitted under Article 34.

2   A Chamber shall decide on the admissibility and merits of inter-State applications submitted under Article 33.

3   The decision on admissibility shall be taken separately unless the Court, in exceptional cases, decides otherwise.

Article 30 – Relinquishment of jurisdiction to the Grand Chamber

Where a case pending before a Chamber raises a serious question affecting the interpretation of the Convention or the protocols thereto, or where the resolution of a question before the Chamber might have a result inconsistent with a judgment previously delivered by the Court, the Chamber may, at any time before it has rendered its judgment, relinquish jurisdiction in favour of the Grand Chamber, unless one of the parties to the case objects.

Article 31 – Powers of the Grand Chamber

The Grand Chamber shall

1   a   determine applications submitted either under Article 33 or Article 34 when a Chamber has relinquished jurisdiction under Article 30 or when the case has been referred to it under Article 43; and

    b   consider requests for advisory opinions submitted under Article 47.

Article 32 – Jurisdiction of the Court

1   The jurisdiction of the Court shall extend to all matters concerning the interpretation and application of the Convention and the protocols thereto which are referred to it as provided in Articles 33, 34 and 47.

2   In the event of dispute as to whether the Court has jurisdiction, the Court shall decide.

Article 33 - Inter-State cases

Any High Contracting Party may refer to the Court any alleged breach of the provisions of the Convention and the protocols thereto by another High Contracting Party.

Article 34 - Individual applications

The Court may receive applications from any person, non-governmental organisation or group of individuals claiming to be the victim of a violation by one of the High Contracting Parties of the rights set forth in the Convention or the protocols thereto. The High Contracting Parties undertake not to hinder in any way the effective exercise of this right.

Article 35 - Admissibility criteria

1   The Court may only deal with the matter after all domestic remedies have been exhausted, according to the generally recognised rules of international law, and within a period of six months from the date on which the final decision was taken.
2   The Court shall not deal with any application submitted under Article 34 that
   a   is anonymous; or
   b   is substantially the same as a matter that has already been examined by the Court or has already been submitted to another procedure of international investigation or settlement and contains no relevant new information.
3   The Court shall declare inadmissible any individual application submitted under Article 34 which it considers incompatible with the provisions of the Convention or the protocols thereto, manifestly ill-founded, or an abuse of the right of application.
4   The Court shall reject any application which it considers inadmissible under this Article. It may do so at any stage of the proceedings.

Article 36 - Third party intervention

1   In all cases before a Chamber or the Grand Chamber, a High Contracting Party one of whose nationals is an applicant shall have the right to submit written comments and to take part in hearings.
2   The President of the Court may, in the interest of the proper administration of justice, invite any High Contracting Party which is not a party to the proceedings or any person concerned who is not the applicant to submit written comments or take part in hearings.

Article 37 - Striking out applications

1   The Court may at any stage of the proceedings decide to strike an application out of its list of cases where the circumstances lead to the conclusion that
   a   the applicant does not intend to pursue his application; or
   b   the matter has been resolved; or
   c   for any other reason established by the Court, it is no longer justified to continue the examination of the application.
However, the Court shall continue the examination of the application if respect for human rights as defined in the Convention and the protocols thereto so requires.
2   The Court may decide to restore an application to its list of cases if it considers that the circumstances justify such a course.

Article 38 – Examination of the case and friendly settlement proceedings

1 If the Court declares the application admissible, it shall
   a pursue the examination of the case, together with the representatives of the parties, and, if need be, undertake an investigation, for the effective conduct of which the States concerned shall furnish all necessary facilities;
   b place itself at the disposal of the parties concerned with a view to securing a friendly settlement of the matter on the basis of respect for human rights as defined in the Convention and the protocols thereto.
2 Proceedings conducted under paragraph 1.b shall be confidential.

Article 39 – Finding of a friendly settlement

If a friendly settlement is effected, the Court shall strike the case out of its list by means of a decision which shall be confined to a brief statement of the facts and of the solution reached.

Article 40 – Public hearings and access to documents

1 Hearings shall be in public unless the Court in exceptional circumstances decides otherwise.
2 Documents deposited with the Registrar shall be accessible to the public unless the President of the Court decides otherwise.

Article 41 – Just satisfaction

If the Court finds that there has been a violation of the Convention or the protocols thereto, and if the internal law of the High Contracting Party concerned allows only partial reparation to be made, the Court shall, if necessary, afford just satisfaction to the injured party.

Article 42 – Judgments of Chambers

Judgments of Chambers shall become final in accordance with the provisions of Article 44, paragraph 2.

Article 43 – Referral to the Grand Chamber

1 Within a period of three months from the date of the judgment of the Chamber, any party to the case may, in exceptional cases, request that the case be referred to the Grand Chamber.
2 A panel of five judges of the Grand Chamber shall accept the request if the case raises a serious question affecting the interpretation or application of the Convention or the protocols thereto, or a serious issue of general importance.
3 If the panel accepts the request, the Grand Chamber shall decide the case by means of a judgment.

Article 44 – Final judgments

1 The judgment of the Grand Chamber shall be final.
2 The judgment of a Chamber shall become final
   a when the parties declare that they will not request that the case be referred to the Grand Chamber; or

b three months after the date of the judgment, if reference of the case to the Grand Chamber has not been requested; or

c when the panel of the Grand Chamber rejects the request to refer under Article 43.

3 The final judgment shall be published.

Article 45 – Reasons for judgments and decisions

1 Reasons shall be given for judgments as well as for decisions declaring applications admissible or inadmissible.

2 If a judgment does not represent, in whole or in part, the unanimous opinion of the judges, any judge shall be entitled to deliver a separate opinion.

Article 46 – Binding force and execution of judgments

1 The High Contracting Parties undertake to abide by the final judgment of the Court in any case to which they are parties.

2 The final judgment of the Court shall be transmitted to the Committee of Ministers, which shall supervise its execution.

Article 47 – Advisory opinions

1 The Court may, at the request of the Committee of Ministers, give advisory opinions on legal questions concerning the interpretation of the Convention and the protocols thereto.

2 Such opinions shall not deal with any question relating to the content or scope of the rights or freedoms defined in Section I of the Convention and the protocols thereto, or with any other question which the Court or the Committee of Ministers might have to consider in consequence of any such proceedings as could be instituted in accordance with the Convention.

3 Decisions of the Committee of Ministers to request an advisory opinion of the Court shall require a majority vote of the representatives entitled to sit on the Committee.

Article 48 – Advisory jurisdiction of the Court

The Court shall decide whether a request for an advisory opinion submitted by the Committee of Ministers is within its competence as defined in Article 47.

Article 49 – Reasons for advisory opinions

1 Reasons shall be given for advisory opinions of the Court.

2 If the advisory opinion does not represent, in whole or in part, the unanimous opinion of the judges, any judge shall be entitled to deliver a separate opinion.

3 Advisory opinions of the Court shall be communicated to the Committee of Ministers.

Article 50 – Expenditure on the Court

The expenditure on the Court shall be borne by the Council of Europe.

Article 51 – Privileges and immunities of judges

The judges shall be entitled, during the exercise of their functions, to the privileges and immunities provided for in Article 40 of the Statute of the Council of Europe and in the agreements made thereunder.

Section III - Miscellaneous provisions

Article 52 - Inquiries by the Secretary General

On receipt of a request from the Secretary General of the Council of Europe any High Contracting Party shall furnish an explanation of the manner in which its internal law ensures the effective implementation of any of the provisions of the Convention.

Article 53 - Safeguard for existing human rights

Nothing in this Convention shall be construed as limiting or derogating from any of the human rights and fundamental freedoms which may be ensured under the laws of any High Contracting Party or under any other agreement to which it is a Party.

Article 54 - Powers of the Committee of Ministers

Nothing in this Convention shall prejudice the powers conferred on the Committee of Ministers by the Statute of the Council of Europe.

Article 55 - Exclusion of other means of dispute settlement

The High Contracting Parties agree that, except by special agreement, they will not avail themselves of treaties, conventions or declarations in force between them for the purpose of submitting, by way of petition, a dispute arising out of the interpretation or application of this Convention to a means of settlement other than those provided for in this Convention.

Article 56 - Territorial application

1 Any State may at the time of its ratification or at any time thereafter declare by notification addressed to the Secretary General of the Council of Europe that the present Convention shall, subject to paragraph 4 of this Article, extend to all or any of the territories for whose international relations it is responsible.
2 The Convention shall extend to the territory or territories named in the notification as from the thirtieth day after the receipt of this notification by the Secretary General of the Council of Europe.
3 The provisions of this Convention shall be applied in such territories with due regard, however, to local requirements.
4 Any State which has made a declaration in accordance with paragraph 1 of this article may at any time thereafter declare on behalf of one or more of the territories to which the declaration relates that it accepts the competence of the Court to receive applications from individuals, non-governmental organisations or groups of individuals as provided by Article 34 of the Convention.

Article 57 - Reservations

1 Any State may, when signing this Convention or when depositing its instrument of ratification, make a reservation in respect of any particular provision of the Convention to the extent that any law then in force in its territory is not in conformity with the provision. Reservations of a general character shall not be permitted under this article.
2 Any reservation made under this article shall contain a brief statement of the law concerned.

Article 58 - Denunciation

1 A High Contracting Party may denounce the present Convention only after the expiry of five years from the date on which it became a party to it and after six months' notice contained in a notification addressed to the Secretary General of the Council of Europe, who shall inform the other High Contracting Parties.

2 Such a denunciation shall not have the effect of releasing the High Contracting Party concerned from its obligations under this Convention in respect of any act which, being capable of constituting a violation of such obligations, may have been performed by it before the date at which the denunciation became effective.

3 Any High Contracting Party which shall cease to be a member of the Council of Europe shall cease to be a Party to this Convention under the same conditions.

4 The Convention may be denounced in accordance with the provisions of the preceding paragraphs in respect of any territory to which it has been declared to extend under the terms of Article 56.

Article 59 - Signature and ratification

1 This Convention shall be open to the signature of the members of the Council of Europe. It shall be ratified. Ratifications shall be deposited with the Secretary General of the Council of Europe.

2 The present Convention shall come into force after the deposit of ten instruments of ratification.

3 As regards any signatory ratifying subsequently, the Convention shall come into force at the date of the deposit of its instrument of ratification.

4 The Secretary General of the Council of Europe shall notify all the members of the Council of Europe of the entry into force of the Convention, the names of the High Contracting Parties who have ratified it, and the deposit of all instruments of ratification which may be effected subsequently.

Done at Rome this 4th day of November 1950, in English and French, both texts being equally authentic, in a single copy which shall remain deposited in the archives of the Council of Europe. The Secretary General shall transmit certified copies to each of the signatories.

Protocol to the Convention for the Protection of Human Rights and Fundamental Freedoms (as amended by Protocol No. 11) Paris, 20.III.1952

The governments signatory hereto, being members of the Council of Europe,

Being resolved to take steps to ensure the collective enforcement of certain rights and freedoms other than those already included in Section I of the Convention for the Protection of Human Rights and Fundamental Freedoms signed at Rome on 4 November 1950 (hereinafter referred to as 'the Convention'),

Have agreed as follows:

Article 1 – Protection of property

Every natural or legal person is entitled to the peaceful enjoyment of his possessions. No one shall be deprived of his possessions except in the public interest and subject to the conditions provided for by law and by the general principles of international law. The preceding provisions shall not, however, in any way impair the right of a State to enforce such laws as it deems necessary to control the use of property in accordance with the general interest or to secure the payment of taxes or other contributions or penalties.

Article 2 – Right to education

No person shall be denied the right to education. In the exercise of any functions which it assumes in relation to education and to teaching, the State shall respect the right of parents to ensure such education and teaching in conformity with their own religious and philosophical convictions.

Article 3 – Right to free elections

The High Contracting Parties undertake to hold free elections at reasonable intervals by secret ballot, under conditions which will ensure the free expression of the opinion of the people in the choice of the legislature.

Article 4 – Territorial application

Any High Contracting Party may at the time of signature or ratification or at any time thereafter communicate to the Secretary General of the Council of Europe a declaration stating the extent to which it undertakes that the provisions of the present Protocol shall apply to such of the territories for the international relations of which it is responsible as are named therein. Any High Contracting Party which has communicated a declaration in virtue of the preceding paragraph may from time to time communicate a further declaration modifying the terms of any former declaration or terminating the application of the provisions of this Protocol in respect of any territory. A declaration made in accordance with this article shall be deemed to have been made in accordance with paragraph 1 of Article 56 of the Convention.

Article 5 – Relationship to the Convention

As between the High Contracting Parties the provisions of Articles 1, 2, 3 and 4 of this Protocol shall be regarded as additional articles to the Convention and all the provisions of the Convention shall apply accordingly.

Article 6 – Signature and ratification

This Protocol shall be open for signature by the members of the Council of Europe, who are the signatories of the Convention; it shall be ratified at the same time as or after the ratification of the Convention. It shall enter into force after the deposit of ten instruments of ratification. As regards any signatory ratifying subsequently, the Protocol shall enter into force at the date of the deposit of its instrument of ratification.

The instruments of ratification shall be deposited with the Secretary General of the Council of Europe, who will notify all members of the names of those who have ratified.

Done at Paris on the 20th day of March 1952, in English and French, both texts being equally authentic, in a single copy which shall remain deposited in the archives of the Council of Europe. The Secretary General shall transmit certified copies to each of the signatory governments.

Protocol No. 4 to the Convention for the Protection of Human Rights and Fundamental Freedoms, securing certain rights and freedoms other than those already included in the Convention and in the first Protocol thereto, as amended by Protocol No. 11 Strasbourg, 16.IX.1963

The governments signatory hereto, being members of the Council of Europe,

Being resolved to take steps to ensure the collective enforcement of certain rights and freedoms other than those already included in Section I of the Convention for the Protection of Human Rights and Fundamental Freedoms signed at Rome on 4th November 1950 (hereinafter referred to as the 'Convention') and in Articles 1 to 3 of the First Protocol to the Convention, signed at Paris on 20th March 1952,

Have agreed as follows:

Article 1 - Prohibition of imprisonment for debt

No one shall be deprived of his liberty merely on the ground of inability to fulfil a contractual obligation.

Article 2 - Freedom of movement

1 Everyone lawfully within the territory of a State shall, within that territory, have the right to liberty of movement and freedom to choose his residence.
2 Everyone shall be free to leave any country, including his own.
3 No restrictions shall be placed on the exercise of these rights other than such as are in accordance with law and are necessary in a democratic society in the interests of national security or public safety, for the maintenance of *ordre public*, for the prevention of crime, for the protection of health or morals, or for the protection of the rights and freedoms of others.
4 The rights set forth in paragraph 1 may also be subject, in particular areas, to restrictions imposed in accordance with law and justified by the public interest in a democratic society.

Article 3 - Prohibition of expulsion of nationals

1 No one shall be expelled, by means either of an individual or of a collective measure, from the territory of the State of which he is a national.
2 No one shall be deprived of the right to enter the territory of the State of which he is a national.

Article 4 - Prohibition of collective expulsion of aliens

Collective expulsion of aliens is prohibited.

Article 5 - Territorial application

1   Any High Contracting Party may, at the time of signature or ratification of this Protocol, or at any time thereafter, communicate to the Secretary General of the Council of Europe a declaration stating the extent to which it undertakes that the provisions of this Protocol shall apply to such of the territories for the international relations of which it is responsible as are named therein.

2   Any High Contracting Party which has communicated a declaration in virtue of the preceding paragraph may, from time to time, communicate a further declaration modifying the terms of any former declaration or terminating the application of the provisions of this Protocol in respect of any territory.

3   A declaration made in accordance with this article shall be deemed to have been made in accordance with paragraph 1 of Article 56 of the Convention.

4   The territory of any State to which this Protocol applies by virtue of ratification or acceptance by that State, and each territory to which this Protocol is applied by virtue of a declaration by that State under this article, shall be treated as separate territories for the purpose of the references in Articles 2 and 3 to the territory of a State.

5   Any State which has made a declaration in accordance with paragraph 1 or 2 of this Article may at any time thereafter declare on behalf of one or more of the territories to which the declaration relates that it accepts the competence of the Court to receive applications from individuals, non-governmental organisations or groups of individuals as provided in Article 34 of the Convention in respect of all or any of Articles 1 to 4 of this Protocol.

Article 6 - Relationship to the Convention

As between the High Contracting Parties the provisions of Articles 1 to 5 of this Protocol shall be regarded as additional articles to the Convention, and all the provisions of the Convention shall apply accordingly.

Article 7 - Signature and ratification

1   This Protocol shall be open for signature by the members of the Council of Europe who are the signatories of the Convention; it shall be ratified at the same time as or after the ratification of the Convention. It shall enter into force after the deposit of five instruments of ratification. As regards any signatory ratifying subsequently, the Protocol shall enter into force at the date of the deposit of its instrument of ratification.

2   The instruments of ratification shall be deposited with the Secretary General of the Council of Europe, who will notify all Members of the names of those who have ratified. In witness whereof the undersigned, being duly authorised thereto, have signed this Protocol.

Done at Strasbourg, this 16th day of September 1963, in English and in French, both texts being equally authoritative, in a single copy which shall remain deposited in the archives of the Council of Europe. The Secretary General shall transmit certified copies to each of the signatory States.

Protocol No. 6 to the Convention for the Protection of Human Rights and Fundamental Freedoms concerning the abolition of the death penalty, as amended by Protocol No. 11
Strasbourg, 28.IV.1983

The member States of the Council of Europe, signatory to this Protocol to the Convention for the Protection of Human Rights and Fundamental Freedoms, signed at Rome on 4 November 1950 (hereinafter referred to as 'the Convention'),

Considering that the evolution that has occurred in several member States of the Council of Europe expresses a general tendency in favour of abolition of the death penalty,

Have agreed as follows:

Article 1 - Abolition of the death penalty

The death penalty shall be abolished. No-one shall be condemned to such penalty or executed.

Article 2 - Death penalty in time of war

A State may make provision in its law for the death penalty in respect of acts committed in time of war or of imminent threat of war; such penalty shall be applied only in the instances laid down in the law and in accordance with its provisions. The State shall communicate to the Secretary General of the Council of Europe the relevant provisions of that law.

Article 3 - Prohibition of derogations

No derogation from the provisions of this Protocol shall be made under Article 15 of the Convention.

Article 4 - Prohibition of reservations

No reservation may be made under Article 57 of the Convention in respect of the provisions of this Protocol.

Article 5 - Territorial application

1 Any State may at the time of signature or when depositing its instrument of ratification, acceptance or approval, specify the territory or territories to which this Protocol shall apply.
2 Any State may at any later date, by a declaration addressed to the Secretary General of the Council of Europe, extend the application of this Protocol to any other territory specified in the declaration. In respect of such territory the Protocol shall enter into force on the first day of the month following the date of receipt of such declaration by the Secretary General.
3 Any declaration made under the two preceding paragraphs may, in respect of any territory specified in such declaration, be withdrawn by a notification addressed to the Secretary General. The withdrawal shall become effective on the first day of the month following the date of receipt of such notification by the Secretary General.

Article 6 - Relationship to the Convention

As between the States Parties the provisions of Articles 1 to 5 of this Protocol shall be regarded as additional articles to the Convention and all the provisions of the Convention shall apply accordingly.

Article 7 - Signature and ratification

The Protocol shall be open for signature by the member States of the Council of Europe, signatories to the Convention. It shall be subject to ratification, acceptance or approval. A member State of the Council of Europe may not ratify, accept or approve this Protocol unless it has, simultaneously or previously, ratified the Convention. Instruments of ratification, acceptance or approval shall be deposited with the Secretary General of the Council of Europe.

Article 8 - Entry into force

1 This Protocol shall enter into force on the first day of the month following the date on which five member States of the Council of Europe have expressed their consent to be bound by the Protocol in accordance with the provisions of Article 7.

2 In respect of any member State which subsequently expresses its consent to be bound by it, the Protocol shall enter into force on the first day of the month following the date of the deposit of the instrument of ratification, acceptance or approval.

Article 9 - Depositary functions

The Secretary General of the Council of Europe shall notify the member States of the Council of:

a any signature;

b the deposit of any instrument of ratification, acceptance or approval;

c any date of entry into force of this Protocol in accordance with Articles 5 and 8;

d any other act, notification or communication relating to this Protocol.

In witness whereof the undersigned, being duly authorised thereto, have signed this Protocol. Done at Strasbourg, this 28th day of April 1983, in English and in French, both texts being equally authentic, in a single copy which shall be deposited in the archives of the Council of Europe. The Secretary General of the Council of Europe shall transmit certified copies to each member State of the Council of Europe.

Protocol No. 7 to the Convention for the Protection of Human Rights and Fundamental Freedoms, as amended by Protocol No. 11 Strasbourg, 22.XI.1984

The member States of the Council of Europe signatory hereto,

Being resolved to take further steps to ensure the collective enforcement of certain rights and freedoms by means of the Convention for the Protection of Human Rights and Fundamental Freedoms signed at Rome on 4 November 1950 (hereinafter referred to as 'the Convention'),

Have agreed as follows:

Article 1 - Procedural safeguards relating to expulsion of aliens

1 An alien lawfully resident in the territory of a State shall not be expelled therefrom except in pursuance of a decision reached in accordance with law and shall be allowed:

a   to submit reasons against his expulsion,

b   to have his case reviewed, and

c   to be represented for these purposes before the competent authority or a person or persons designated by that authority.

2   An alien may be expelled before the exercise of his rights under paragraph 1.a, b and c of this Article, when such expulsion is necessary in the interests of public order or is grounded on reasons of national security.

Article 2 - Right of appeal in criminal matters

1   Everyone convicted of a criminal offence by a tribunal shall have the right to have his conviction or sentence reviewed by a higher tribunal. The exercise of this right, including the grounds on which it may be exercised, shall be governed by law.

2   This right may be subject to exceptions in regard to offences of a minor character, as prescribed by law, or in cases in which the person concerned was tried in the first instance by the highest tribunal or was convicted following an appeal against acquittal.

Article 3 - Compensation for wrongful conviction

When a person has by a final decision been convicted of a criminal offence and when subsequently his conviction has been reversed, or he has been pardoned, on the ground that a new or newly discovered fact shows conclusively that there has been a miscarriage of justice, the person who has suffered punishment as a result of such conviction shall be compensated according to the law or the practice of the State concerned, unless it is proved that the non-disclosure of the unknown fact in time is wholly or partly attributable to him.

Article 4 - Right not to be tried or punished twice

1   No one shall be liable to be tried or punished again in criminal proceedings under the jurisdiction of the same State for an offence for which he has already been finally acquitted or convicted in accordance with the law and penal procedure of that State.

2   The provisions of the preceding paragraph shall not prevent the reopening of the case in accordance with the law and penal procedure of the State concerned, if there is evidence of new or newly discovered facts, or if there has been a fundamental defect in the previous proceedings, which could affect the outcome of the case.

3   No derogation from this Article shall be made under Article 15 of the Convention.

Article 5 - Equality between spouses

Spouses shall enjoy equality of rights and responsibilities of a private law character between them, and in their relations with their children, as to marriage, during marriage and in the event of its dissolution. This Article shall not prevent States from taking such measures as are necessary in the interests of the children.

Article 6 - Territorial application

1   Any State may at the time of signature or when depositing its instrument of ratification, acceptance or approval, specify the territory or territories to which the Protocol shall apply and state the extent to which it undertakes that the provisions of this Protocol shall apply to such territory or territories.

2   Any State may at any later date, by a declaration addressed to the Secretary General of the Council of Europe, extend the application of this Protocol to any other territory specified in the declaration. In respect of such territory the Protocol shall enter into force on the first day of the month following the expiration of a period of two months after the date of receipt by the Secretary General of such declaration.

3   Any declaration made under the two preceding paragraphs may, in respect of any territory specified in such declaration, be withdrawn or modified by a notification addressed to the Secretary General. The withdrawal or modification shall become effective on the first day of the month following the expiration of a period of two months after the date of receipt of such notification by the Secretary General.

4   A declaration made in accordance with this Article shall be deemed to have been made in accordance with paragraph 1 of Article 56 of the Convention.

5   The territory of any State to which this Protocol applies by virtue of ratification, acceptance or approval by that State, and each territory to which this Protocol is applied by virtue of a declaration by that State under this Article, may be treated as separate territories for the purpose of the reference in Article 1 to the territory of a State.

6   Any State which has made a declaration in accordance with paragraph 1 or 2 of this Article may at any time thereafter declare on behalf of one or more of the territories to which the declaration relates that it accepts the competence of the Court to receive applications from individuals, non-governmental organisations or groups of individuals as provided in Article 34 of the Convention in respect of Articles 1 to 5 of this Protocol.

Article 7 – Relationship to the Convention

As between the States Parties, the provisions of Articles 1 to 6 of this Protocol shall be regarded as additional Articles to the Convention, and all the provisions of the Convention shall apply accordingly.

Article 8 – Signature and ratification

This Protocol shall be open for signature by member States of the Council of Europe which have signed the Convention. It is subject to ratification, acceptance or approval. A member State of the Council of Europe may not ratify, accept or approve this Protocol without previously or simultaneously ratifying the Convention. Instruments of ratification, acceptance or approval shall be deposited with the Secretary General of the Council of Europe.

Article 9 – Entry into force

1   This Protocol shall enter into force on the first day of the month following the expiration of a period of two months after the date on which seven member States of the Council of Europe have expressed their consent to be bound by the Protocol in accordance with the provisions of Article 8.

2   In respect of any member State which subsequently expresses its consent to be bound by it, the Protocol shall enter into force on the first day of the month following the expiration of a period of two months after the date of the deposit of the instrument of ratification, acceptance or approval.

Article 10 - Depositary functions

The Secretary General of the Council of Europe shall notify all the member States of the Council of Europe of:

a any signature;

b the deposit of any instrument of ratification, acceptance or approval;

c any date of entry into force of this Protocol in accordance with Articles 6 and 9;

d any other act, notification or declaration relating to this Protocol.

In witness whereof the undersigned, being duly authorised thereto, have signed this Protocol. Done at Strasbourg, this 22nd day of November 1984, in English and French, both texts being equally authentic, in a single copy which shall be deposited in the archives of the Council of Europe. The Secretary General of the Council of Europe shall transmit certified copies to each member State of the Council of Europe.

Protocol No. 12 to the Convention for the Protection of Human Rights and Fundamental Freedoms
Rome, 4.XI.2000

The member States of the Council of Europe signatory hereto,

Having regard to the fundamental principle according to which all persons are equal before the law and are entitled to the equal protection of the law;

Being resolved to take further steps to promote the equality of all persons through the collective enforcement of a general prohibition of discrimination by means of the Convention for the Protection of Human Rights and Fundamental Freedoms signed at Rome on 4 November 1950 (hereinafter referred to as 'the Convention');

Reaffirming that the principle of non-discrimination does not prevent States Parties from taking measures in order to promote full and effective equality, provided that there is an objective and reasonable justification for those measures,

Have agreed as follows:

Article 1 - General prohibition of discrimination

1 The enjoyment of any right set forth by law shall be secured without discrimination on any ground such as sex, race, colour, language, religion, political or other opinion, national or social origin, association with a national minority, property, birth or other status.

2 No one shall be discriminated against by any public authority on any ground such as those mentioned in paragraph 1.

Article 2 - Territorial application

1 Any State may, at the time of signature or when depositing its instrument of ratification, acceptance or approval, specify the territory or territories to which this Protocol shall apply.

2 Any State may at any later date, by a declaration addressed to the Secretary General of the Council of Europe, extend the application of this Protocol to any other territory specified in the declaration. In respect of such territory the Protocol shall enter into force on the first day of the month following the expiration of a period of three months after the date of receipt by the Secretary General of such declaration.

3 Any declaration made under the two preceding paragraphs may, in respect of any territory specified in such declaration, be withdrawn or modified by a notification addressed to the Secretary General of the Council of Europe. The withdrawal or modification shall become effective on the first day of the month following the expiration of a period of three months after the date of receipt of such notification by the Secretary General.

4 A declaration made in accordance with this article shall be deemed to have been made in accordance with paragraph 1 of Article 56 of the Convention.

5 Any State which has made a declaration in accordance with paragraph 1 or 2 of this article may at any time thereafter declare on behalf of one or more of the territories to which the declaration relates that it accepts the competence of the Court to receive applications from individuals, non-governmental organisations or groups of individuals as provided by Article 34 of the Convention in respect of Article 1 of this Protocol.

Article 3 – Relationship to the Convention

As between the States Parties, the provisions of Articles 1 and 2 of this Protocol shall be regarded as additional articles to the Convention, and all the provisions of the Convention shall apply accordingly.

Article 4 – Signature and ratification

This Protocol shall be open for signature by member States of the Council of Europe which have signed the Convention. It is subject to ratification, acceptance or approval. A member State of the Council of Europe may not ratify, accept or approve this Protocol without previously or simultaneously ratifying the Convention. Instruments of ratification, acceptance or approval shall be deposited with the Secretary General of the Council of Europe.

Article 5 – Entry into force

1 This Protocol shall enter into force on the first day of the month following the expiration of a period of three months after the date on which ten member States of the Council of Europe have expressed their consent to be bound by the Protocol in accordance with the provisions of Article 4.

2 In respect of any member State which subsequently expresses its consent to be bound by it, the Protocol shall enter into force on the first day of the month following the expiration of a period of three months after the date of the deposit of the instrument of ratification, acceptance or approval.

Article 6 – Depositary functions

The Secretary General of the Council of Europe shall notify all the member States of the Council of Europe of:

a   any signature;
b   the deposit of any instrument of ratification, acceptance or approval;
c   any date of entry into force of this Protocol in accordance with Articles 2 and 5;
d   any other act, notification or communication relating to this Protocol.

In witness whereof the undersigned, being duly authorised thereto, have signed this Protocol.

Done at Rome, this 4th day of November 2000, in English and in French, both texts being equally authentic, in a single copy which shall be deposited in the archives of the Council of Europe. The Secretary General of the Council of Europe shall transmit certified copies to each member State of the Council of Europe.

Protocol No. 13 to the Convention for the Protection of Human Rights and Fundamental Freedoms, concerning the abolition of the death penalty in all circumstances
[Vilnius, 3.V.2002]

The member States of the Council of Europe signatory hereto,

Convinced that everyone's right to life is a basic value in a democratic society and that the abolition of the death penalty is essential for the protection of this right and for the full recognition of the inherent dignity of all human beings;

Wishing to strengthen the protection of the right to life guaranteed by the Convention for the Protection of Human Rights and Fundamental Freedoms signed at Rome on 4 November 1950 (hereinafter referred to as 'the Convention');

Noting that Protocol No. 6 to the Convention, concerning the Abolition of the Death Penalty, signed at Strasbourg on 28 April 1983, does not exclude the death penalty in respect of acts committed in time of war or of imminent threat of war;

Being resolved to take the final step in order to abolish the death penalty in all circumstances,

Have agreed as follows:

Article 1 – Abolition of the death penalty

The death penalty shall be abolished. No one shall be condemned to such penalty or executed.

Article 2 – Prohibition of derogations

No derogation from the provisions of this Protocol shall be made under Article 15 of the Convention.

Article 3 – Prohibition of reservations

No reservation may be made under Article 57 of the Convention in respect of the provisions of this Protocol.

Article 4 – Territorial application

1   Any State may, at the time of signature or when depositing its instrument of ratification, acceptance or approval, specify the territory or territories to which this Protocol shall apply.

2   Any State may at any later date, by a declaration addressed to the Secretary General of the Council of Europe, extend the application of this Protocol to any other territory specified in the declaration. In respect of such territory the Protocol shall enter into force on the first day of the month following the expiration of a period of three months after the date of receipt of such declaration by the Secretary General.

3   Any declaration made under the two preceding paragraphs may, in respect of any territory specified in such declaration, be withdrawn or modified by a notification addressed to the Secretary General. The withdrawal or modification shall become effective on the first day of the month following the expiration of a period of three months after the date of receipt of such notification by the Secretary General.

Article 5 – Relationship to the Convention

As between the States Parties the provisions of Articles 1 to 4 of this Protocol shall be regarded as additional articles to the Convention, and all the provisions of the Convention shall apply accordingly.

Article 6 – Signature and ratification

This Protocol shall be open for signature by member States of the Council of Europe which have signed the Convention. It is subject to ratification, acceptance or approval. A member State of the Council of Europe may not ratify, accept or approve this Protocol without previously or simultaneously ratifying the Convention. Instruments of ratification, acceptance or approval shall be deposited with the Secretary General of the Council of Europe.

Article 7 – Entry into force

1   This Protocol shall enter into force on the first day of the month following the expiration of a period of three months after the date on which ten member States of the Council of Europe have expressed their consent to be bound by the Protocol in accordance with the provisions of Article 6.

2   In respect of any member State which subsequently expresses its consent to be bound by it, the Protocol shall enter into force on the first day of the month following the expiration of a period of three months after the date of the deposit of the instrument of ratification, acceptance or approval.

Article 8 – Depositary functions

The Secretary General of the Council of Europe shall notify all the member States of the Council of Europe of:

a   any signature;
b   the deposit of any instrument of ratification, acceptance or approval;
c   any date of entry into force of this Protocol in accordance with Articles 4 and 7;
d   any other act, notification or communication relating to this Protocol.

In witness whereof the undersigned, being duly authorised thereto, have signed this Protocol. Done at Vilnius, this 3rd day of May 2002, in English and in French, both texts being equally authentic, in a single copy which shall be deposited in the archives of the Council of Europe. The Secretary General of the Council of Europe shall transmit certified copies to each member State of the Council of Europe.

Members of the Council of Europe and Convention ratifications

I: MEMBERS OF THE COUNCIL OF EUROPE, as at 1 January 2009
(with date of joining)

Albania (13.7.1995)
Andorra (10.10.1994)
Armenia (25.1.2001)
Austria (16.4.1956)
Azerbaijan (25.1.2001)
Belgium (5.5.1949)
Bosnia and Herzegovina (24.4.2002)
Bulgaria (7.5.1992)
Croatia (6.11.1996)
Cyprus (24.5.1961)
Czech Republic (30.6.1993)
Denmark (5.5.1949)
Estonia (14.5.1993)
Finland (5.5.1989)
France (5.5.1949)
Georgia (27.4.1999)
Germany (13.7.1950)
Greece (9.8.1949)
Hungary (6.11.1990)
Iceland (9.3.1950)
Ireland (5.5.1949)
Italy (5.5.1949)
Latvia (10.2.1995)
Liechtenstein (23.11.1978)

Lithuania (14.5.1993)
Luxembourg (5.5.1949)
Macedonia (former Yugoslav Republic)
  (9.11.1995)
Malta (29.4.1965)
Moldova (13.7.1995)
Monaco (5.10.2004)
Montenegro (11.5.2007)
Netherlands (5.5.1949)
Norway (5.5.1949)
Poland (29.11.1991)
Portugal (22.9.1976)
Romania (7.10.1993)
Russian Federation (28.2.1996)
San Marino (16.11.1988)
Serbia (3.4.2003)
Slovakia (30.6.1993)
Slovenia (14.5.1993)
Spain (24.11.1977)
Sweden (5.5.1949)
Switzerland (6.5.1963)
Turkey (9.8.1949)
Ukraine (9.11.1995)
United Kingdom (5.5.1949)

State Candidate for Membership
Belarus (applied 12.3.1993; Special Guest status suspended 13.1.1997)

Observers to the Committee of Ministers
Canada (29.5.1996)
Holy See (7.3.1970)
Japan (20.11.1996)
Mexico (1.12.1999)
United States of America (10.1.1996)

Observers to the Parliamentary Assembly
Canada (28.5.1997)
Israel (2.12.1957)
Mexico (4.11.1999)

Map showing Members of the Council of Europe

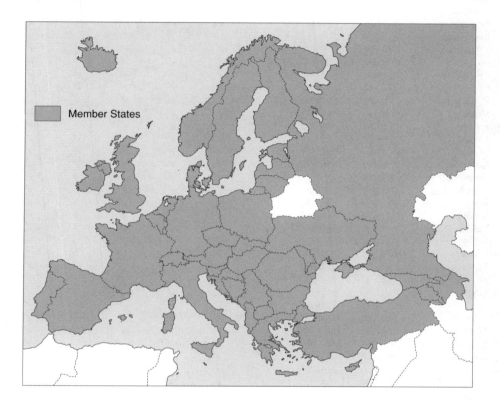

Member States

II: Ratifications of Convention Protocols, as at March 2009

This table lists which States have signed up to which of the Protocols that add substantive rights to the Convention; none of the other Protocols are still in effect, except the 11th, which has amended the procedure and has been ratified by all parties to the Convention; Protocol 14, further amending the procedure, is being delayed by Russia's refusal to ratify.

(Key: ✓ – ratified and in force; S – signed but not ratified)

Member State	Signature of Convention	Entry into force of Convention	1st Protocol	4th Protocol	6th Protocol	7th Protocol	12th Protocol	13th Protocol
Albania	13/07/95	02/10/96	✓	✓	✓	✓	✓	✓
Andorra	10/11/94	22/01/96	✓	✓	✓	✓	✓	✓
Armenia	25/01/01	26/04/02	✓	✓	✓	✓	✓	S
Austria	13/12/57	03/09/58	✓	✓	✓	✓	S	✓
Azerbaijan	25/01/01	15/04/02	✓	✓	✓	✓	S	–
Belgium	04/11/50	14/06/55	✓	✓	✓	S	S	✓
Bosnia and Herzegovina	24/04/02	12/07/02	✓	✓	✓	✓	✓	✓
Bulgaria	07/05/92	07/09/92	✓	✓	✓	✓	–	✓
Croatia	06/11/96	05/11/97	✓	✓	✓	✓	✓	✓
Cyprus	16/12/61	06/10/62	✓	✓	✓	✓	✓	✓
Czech Republic	21/02/91	01/01/93	✓	✓	✓	✓	S	✓
Denmark	04/11/50	03/09/53	✓	✓	✓	✓	–	✓
Estonia	14/05/93	16/04/96	✓	✓	✓	✓	S	✓
Finland	05/05/89	10/05/90	✓	✓	✓	✓	✓	✓
France	04/11/50	03/05/74	✓	✓	✓	✓	–	✓
Georgia	27/04/99	20/05/99	✓	✓	✓	✓	✓	✓
Germany	04/11/50	03/09/53	✓	✓	✓	S	S	✓
Greece	28/11/50	28/11/74	✓	–	✓	✓	S	✓
Hungary	06/11/90	05/11/92	✓	✓	✓	✓	S	✓
Iceland	04/11/50	03/09/53	✓	✓	✓	✓	S	✓
Ireland	04/11/50	03/09/53	✓	✓	✓	✓	S	✓
Italy	04/11/50	26/10/55	✓	✓	✓	✓	S	S
Latvia	10/02/95	27/06/97	✓	✓	✓	✓	S	S
Liechtenstein	23/11/78	08/09/82	✓	✓	✓	✓	S	✓
Lithuania	14/05/93	20/06/95	✓	✓	✓	✓	–	✓
Luxembourg	04/11/50	03/09/53	✓	✓	✓	✓	✓	✓
Macedonia	09/11/95	10/04/97	✓	✓	✓	✓	✓	✓
Malta	12/12/66	23/01/67	✓	✓	✓	✓	–	✓
Moldova	13/07/95	12/09/97	✓	✓	✓	✓	S	✓
Monaco	5/10/04	30/11/05	S	✓	✓	✓	–	✓
Montenegro	03/04/03	03/03/04	✓	✓	✓	✓	✓	✓
Netherlands	04/11/50	31/08/54	✓	✓	✓	S	✓	✓
Norway	04/11/50	03/09/53	✓	✓	✓	✓	S	✓
Poland	26/11/91	19/01/93	✓	✓	✓	✓	–	S
Portugal	22/09/76	09/11/78	✓	✓	✓	✓	S	✓
Romania	07/10/93	20/06/94	✓	✓	✓	✓	✓	✓
Russia	28/02/96	05/05/98	✓	✓	S	✓	S	–
San Marino	16/11/88	22/03/89	✓	✓	✓	✓	✓	✓
Serbia	03/04/03	03/03/04	✓	✓	✓	✓	✓	✓
Slovakia	21/02/91	01/01/93	✓	✓	✓	✓	S	✓
Slovenia	14/05/93	28/06/94	✓	✓	✓	✓	S	✓
Spain	24/11/77	04/10/79	✓	S	✓	S	✓	S
Sweden	28/11/50	03/09/53	✓	✓	✓	✓	–	✓
Switzerland	21/12/72	28/11/74	S	–	✓	✓	–	✓
Turkey	04/11/50	18/05/54	✓	S	✓	S	S	✓
Ukraine	09/11/95	11/09/97	✓	✓	✓	✓	✓	✓
United Kingdom	04/11/50	03/09/53	✓	S	✓	–	–	✓
Total parties (signed but not ratified)		47(0)	45(2)	42(3)	46(1)	41(5)	17(20)	40(5)
Entered into force		03/09/53	18/05/54	02/05/68	01/03/85	01/11/88	01/04/05	01/07/03

The Universal Declaration of Human Rights

Preamble

Whereas recognition of the inherent dignity and of the equal and inalienable rights of all members of the human family is the foundation of freedom, justice and peace in the world,
Whereas disregard and contempt for human rights have resulted in barbarous acts which have outraged the conscience of mankind, and the advent of a world in which human beings shall enjoy freedom of speech and belief and freedom from fear and want has been proclaimed as the highest aspiration of the common people,
Whereas it is essential, if man is not to be compelled to have recourse, as a last resort, to rebellion against tyranny and oppression, that human rights should be protected by the rule of law,
Whereas it is essential to promote the development of friendly relations between nations,
Whereas the peoples of the United Nations have in the Charter reaffirmed their faith in fundamental human rights, in the dignity and worth of the human person and in the equal rights of men and women and have determined to promote social progress and better standards of life in larger freedom,
Whereas Member States have pledged themselves to achieve, in co-operation with the United Nations, the promotion of universal respect for and observance of human rights and fundamental freedoms,
Whereas a common understanding of these rights and freedoms is of the greatest importance for the full realization of this pledge,
Now, therefore, the General Assembly proclaims this Universal Declaration of Human Rights as a common standard of achievement for all peoples and all nations, to the end that every individual and every organ of society, keeping this Declaration constantly in mind, shall strive by teaching and education to promote respect for these rights and freedoms and by progressive measures, national and international, to secure their universal and effective recognition and observance, both among the peoples of Member States themselves and among the peoples of territories under their jurisdiction.

Article 1

All human beings are born free and equal in dignity and rights. They are endowed with reason and conscience and should act towards one another in a spirit of brotherhood.

Article 2

Everyone is entitled to all the rights and freedoms set forth in this Declaration, without distinction of any kind, such as race, colour, sex, language, religion, political or other opinion, national or social origin, property, birth or other status.

Furthermore, no distinction shall be made on the basis of the political, jurisdictional or international status of the country or territory to which a person belongs, whether it be independent, trust, non-self-governing or under any other limitation of sovereignty.

Article 3

Everyone has the right to life, liberty and security of person.

Article 4

No one shall be held in slavery or servitude; slavery and the slave trade shall be prohibited in all their forms.

Article 5

No one shall be subjected to torture or to cruel, inhuman or degrading treatment or punishment.

Article 6

Everyone has the right to recognition everywhere as a person before the law.

Article 7

All are equal before the law and are entitled without any discrimination to equal protection of the law. All are entitled to equal protection against any discrimination in violation of this Declaration and against any incitement to such discrimination.

Article 8

Everyone has the right to an effective remedy by the competent national tribunals for acts violating the fundamental rights granted him by the constitution or by law.

Article 9

No one shall be subjected to arbitrary arrest, detention or exile.

Article 10

Everyone is entitled in full equality to a fair and public hearing by an independent and impartial tribunal, in the determination of his rights and obligations and of any criminal charge against him.

Article 11

1   Everyone charged with a penal offence has the right to be presumed innocent until proved guilty according to law in a public trial at which he has had all the guarantees necessary for his defence.

442

2   No one shall be held guilty of any penal offence on account of any act or omission which did not constitute a penal offence, under national or international law, at the time when it was committed. Nor shall a heavier penalty be imposed than the one that was applicable at the time the penal offence was committed.

Article 12

No one shall be subjected to arbitrary interference with his privacy, family, home or correspondence, nor to attacks upon his honour and reputation. Everyone has the right to the protection of the law against such interference or attacks.

Article 13

1   Everyone has the right to freedom of movement and residence within the borders of each State.
2   Everyone has the right to leave any country, including his own, and to return to his country.

Article 14

1   Everyone has the right to seek and to enjoy in other countries asylum from persecution.
2   This right may not be invoked in the case of prosecutions genuinely arising from non-political crimes or from acts contrary to the purposes and principles of the United Nations.

Article 15

1   Everyone has the right to a nationality.
2   No one shall be arbitrarily deprived of his nationality nor denied the right to change his nationality.

Article 16

1   Men and women of full age, without any limitation due to race, nationality or religion, have the right to marry and to found a family. They are entitled to equal rights as to marriage, during marriage and at its dissolution.
2   Marriage shall be entered into only with the free and full consent of the intending spouses.
3   The family is the natural and fundamental group unit of society and is entitled to protection by society and the State.

Article 17

1   Everyone has the right to own property alone as well as in association with others.
2   No one shall be arbitrarily deprived of his property.

Article 18

Everyone has the right to freedom of thought, conscience and religion; this right includes freedom to change his religion or belief, and freedom, either alone or in community with others and in public or private, to manifest his religion or belief in teaching, practice, worship and observance.

Article 19

Everyone has the right to freedom of opinion and expression; this right includes freedom to hold opinions without interference and to seek, receive and impart information and ideas through any media and regardless of frontiers.

Article 20

1 Everyone has the right to freedom of peaceful assembly and association.
2 No one may be compelled to belong to an association.

Article 21

1 Everyone has the right to take part in the government of his country, directly or through freely chosen representatives.
2 Everyone has the right to equal access to public service in his country.
3 The will of the people shall be the basis of the authority of government; this will shall be expressed in periodic and genuine elections which shall be by universal and equal suffrage and shall be held by secret vote or by equivalent free voting procedures.

Article 22

Everyone, as a member of society, has the right to social security and is entitled to realization, through national effort and international co-operation and in accordance with the organization and resources of each State, of the economic, social and cultural rights indispensable for his dignity and the free development of his personality.

Article 23

1 Everyone has the right to work, to free choice of employment, to just and favourable conditions of work and to protection against unemployment.
2 Everyone, without any discrimination, has the right to equal pay for equal work.
3 Everyone who works has the right to just and favourable remuneration ensuring for himself and his family an existence worthy of human dignity, and supplemented, if necessary, by other means of social protection.
4 Everyone has the right to form and to join trade unions for the protection of his interests.

Article 24

Everyone has the right to rest and leisure, including reasonable limitation of working hours and periodic holidays with pay.

Article 25

1 Everyone has the right to a standard of living adequate for the health and well-being of himself and of his family, including food, clothing, housing and medical care and necessary social services, and the right to security in the event of unemployment, sickness, disability, widowhood, old age or other lack of livelihood in circumstances beyond his control.
2 Motherhood and childhood are entitled to special care and assistance. All children, whether born in or out of wedlock, shall enjoy the same social protection.

Article 26

1 Everyone has the right to education. Education shall be free, at least in the elementary and fundamental stages. Elementary education shall be compulsory. Technical and professional education shall be made generally available and higher education shall be equally accessible to all on the basis of merit.
2 Education shall be directed to the full development of the human personality and to the strengthening of respect for human rights and fundamental freedoms. It shall promote understanding, tolerance and friendship among all nations, racial or religious groups, and shall further the activities of the United Nations for the maintenance of peace.
3 Parents have a prior right to choose the kind of education that shall be given to their children.

Article 27

1 Everyone has the right freely to participate in the cultural life of the community, to enjoy the arts and to share in scientific advancement and its benefits.
2 Everyone has the right to the protection of the moral and material interests resulting from any scientific, literary or artistic production of which he is the author.

Article 28

Everyone is entitled to a social and international order in which the rights and freedoms set forth in this Declaration can be fully realized.

Article 29

1 Everyone has duties to the community in which alone the free and full development of his personality is possible.
2 In the exercise of his rights and freedoms, everyone shall be subject only to such limitations as are determined by law solely for the purpose of securing due recognition and respect for the rights and freedoms of others and of meeting the just requirements of morality, public order and the general welfare in a democratic society.
3 These rights and freedoms may in no case be exercised contrary to the purposes and principles of the United Nations.

Article 30

Nothing in this Declaration may be interpreted as implying for any State, group or person any right to engage in any activity or to perform any act aimed at the destruction of any of the rights and freedoms set forth herein.

Further reading

We have avoided citations of the academic literature in the text because this is designed as an introductory text to the rights and the law on them, rather than to the academic discussion concerning them. However, there is a great deal of material available for those who wish to learn more about any particular area covered. Thus we include some suggestions for further reading.

 ## GENERAL TEXTS ON THE ACT

There are a very large number of other books and articles on the Act and the Convention. The following are some of the leading general textbooks.

Clayton and Tomlinson, *The Law of Human Rights* (2nd edition, Oxford University Press, 2009)

Emmerson and Simor, *Human Rights Practice* (Sweet & Maxwell, looseleaf)

Lester, Pannick and Herberg, *Human Rights: Law and Practice* (3rd edition, LexisNexis, 2009)

There have also been a host of books, articles, collections of essays and case notes on various aspects of the Act. The following are some of those which are more general in their discussion:

Campbell, Ewing and Tomkins (eds), *Sceptical Essays on Human Rights* (Oxford University Press, 2001)

Fenwick, Philipson and Masterman (eds), *Judicial Reasoning under the UK Human Rights Act* (Cambridge University Press, 2007)

Gearty, *Principles of Human Rights Adjudication* (Oxford University Press, 2004)

Gearty, *Can Human Rights Survive? The 2005 Hamlyn Lectures* (Cambridge University Press, 2006) (especially on the dangers inherent in the Human Rights Act as regards the legal system's interaction with the judicial system; and on the dangers raised by anti-terrorist legislation). Response and discussion *Symposium* reported [2007] PL 209

Young, *Parliamentary Sovereignty and the Human Rights Act* (Hart, 2008)

The scope of the Act and the judicial response to it

Alder: *The Sublime and the Beautiful: Incommensurability and Human Rights* [2006] PL 697

Allan, *Human Rights and Judicial Review: A Critique of 'Due Deference'* [2006] 65 CLJ 671

Amos, *The Impact of the Human Rights Act on the UK's Performance before the European Court of Human Rights* [2007] PL 655

Arden, *The Changing Judicial Role: Human Rights, Community Law and the Intention of Parliament* [2008] CLJ 487

Craig, *The Courts, the Human Rights Act and Judicial Review* (2001) 117 LQR 589

Fredman, *Human Rights Transformed: Positive Duties and Positive Rights* [2006] PL 498

Hickman, *The Substance and Structure of Proportionality* [2008] PL 694

Hunt, *The Horizontal Effect of the Human Rights Act* [1998] PL 428

Klug, *A Bill of Rights: Do We Need One, or Do We Already Have One?* [2007] PL 701

Lewis, *The European Ceiling on Human Rights* [2007] PL 720

Morgan, *Questioning the 'true effect' of the Human Rights Act* (2002) 22 Legal Studies 259

Mowbray, *An Examination of the Work of the Grand Chamber of the European Court of Human Rights* [2007] PL 507

Nicol, *Law and Politics after the Human Rights Act* [2006] PL 722 (for a response, see: Hickman, *The Courts and Politics after the Human Rights Act: A Comment* [2008] PL 84)

Palmer, *Public, Private and the Human Rights Act 1998: An Ideological Divide* [2007] CLJ 559

Public authorities

Craig, *Contracting Out, the Human Rights Act and the Scope of Judicial Review* (2002) 118 LQR 551

Oliver, *Functions of a Public Nature under the Human Rights Act* [2004] PL 328

Quane, *The Strasbourg Jurisprudence and the Meaning of a 'Public Authority' under the Human Rights Act* [2006] PL 106

Procedure and remedies

Beyleveld, Kirkham and Townend, *Which Presumption? A critique of the House of Lords' reasoning on retrospectivity and the Human Rights Act* (2002) 22 Legal Studies 185

Lester and Beattie, *Note on the Commission for Equality and Human Rights* [2006] PL 197

Steele, *Damages in Tort and under the Human Rights Act: Remedial or Functional Separation?* [2008] CLJ 606

Article 2

Pedain, *The Human Rights Dimension of the Diane Pretty Case* [2003] CLJ 181

Article 6

Ashworth, *Criminal Proceedings after the Human Rights Act: The First Year* [2001] Criminal Law Review 855

Ashworth, *Social Control and 'Anti-Social Behaviour': the Subversion of Human Rights* (2004) 120 LQR 263

Beatson and Smith (eds), *The Human Rights Act and the Criminal Justice and Regulatory Process* (Hart, 1999)

Hamer, *The Presumption of Innocence and Reverse Burdens: A Balancing Act* [2007] CLJ 142

Article 8

Bainham, *Arguments about Parentage* [2008] CLJ 322

Goold, *Liberty v United Kingdom: A new chance for another missed opportunity* [2009] PL 5

Moreham, *Privacy in the Common Law: A Doctrinal and Theoretical Analysis* [2005] LQR 628 and *Privacy in Public Places* [2006] 65 CLJ 606

Article 9

Gibson, *Faith in the Courts: Religious Dress and Human Rights* [2007] CLJ 657

Hill and Sandberg, *Is Nothing Sacred? Clashing Symbols in a Secular World* [2007] PL 488

McGoldrick, *Human Rights and Religion: The Islamic Headscarf Debate in Europe* (Hart Publishing, 2006)

Article 10

Costigan, *Protection of Journalists' Sources* [2007] PL 464

Article 14

Finnis, *Nationality, Alienage and Constitutional Principle* (2007) 123 LQR 417
Fredman, *From Deference to Democracy: The Role of Equality under the Human Rights Act 1998* (2006) 122 LQR 53

Article 1-1

Hoffman, *The Law of Restitution and the Human Rights Act 1998* (2004) RLR 64

Article 1-3

Lewis and Cumper, *Balancing Freedom of Political Expression Against Equality of Political Opportunity: The Courts and the UK Broadcasting Ban on Political Advertising* [2009] PL 89

Terrorism

Arden, *Human Rights in the Age of Terrorism* [2005] 604
Chaskalson, *The Widening Gyre: Counter-terrorism, Human Rights and the Rule of Law* [2008] CLJ 69
Duffy, *The War on Terror and the Framework of International Law* (Cambridge University Press, 2005)
Ewing and Tham, *The Continuing Futility of the Human Rights Act* [2008] PL 668
Feldman, *Human Rights, Terrorism and Risk: The Roles of Politicians and Judges* [2006] PL 364
Ip, *The Rise and Spread of the Special Advocate* [2008] PL 717
The main law journals also include case notes on all the leading cases; we have not referred to these specifically, but they are useful further reading on specific topics.

 # SOME USEFUL WEBSITES

References to debates in Parliament are references to volumes of *Hansard*, the official record of Parliamentary proceedings, which are either HC (House of Commons) or HL (House of Lords). These can be found online at http://www.parliament.the-stationery-office.co.uk. This includes House of Lords' judicial decisions. Privy Council decisions can be found at http://www.privycouncil.org.uk.

Some other decisions can be found online at the Court Service website, http://www.courtservice. gov.uk, which also contains information should you wish to bring a claim under the Act. Another source of recent judicial decisions is BAILII, the British and Irish Legal Information Institute, which can be found at http://www.bailii.org.

More recent Acts of Parliament and Statutory Instruments (SI) can be found online at http://www.opsi.gov.uk, with a collection of all legislation to date at http://www.statutelaw.gov.uk/. The government's website, for other governmental information, which includes proposals for legislation, is http://www.direct.gov.uk/en/index.htm.

The Parliamentary Joint Committee on Human Rights considers human rights issues in the context of proposed legislation and reviews the government's response on human rights issues. Its reports can be found on its website at: http://www.parliament.uk/parliamentary_committees/joint_committee_on_human_rights.cfm.

The Council of Europe has a very full website at http://www.coe.int. In particular, it contains the full series of Council treaties, including the Convention, with the status of the various protocols, etc. at http://conventions.coe.int. The European Court's site can be found at: http://www.echr.coe.int.

A useful digest of the older European Court case law is Starmer, *Blackstone's Human Rights Digest* (Blackstone Press, 2001).

If you are interested more generally in human rights treaties, the most relevant website is the United Nations website: http://www.un.org/ which contains all the UN treaties.

The Law Commission, the government's law review and reform body, has published a number of reports which are relevant to this area, most especially Report 266 (2000), *Damages under the Human Rights Act 1998*, which is a comprehensive survey of this topic. Reports 267 (2001), *Double Jeopardy and Prosecution Appeals*, and 269 (2001), *Bail and the Human Rights Act 1998*, raise specific human rights issues, but this is now a routine consideration in all Law Commission reports and consultations. These, and their other reports, can be found online at http://www.lawcom.gov.uk/.

The Commission for Equality and Human Rights is now in operation and is charged with monitoring the protection of human rights generally, and campaigning for better protection where required. There are useful materials on its website at http://www.equalityhumanrights.com/.

 ## THEORY OF RIGHTS

There is, of course, a vast literature on the nature of rights within the disciplines of legal and political theory. Some of the key writers in the development of modern views of rights and their place in our law and constitution are mentioned in Chapter 3, such as Locke, Blackstone, Paine, Wollstonecraft, Dicey, etc. All we can really do here is acknowledge the main modern jurisprudential texts which underlie the discussion in Chapter 2 (and elsewhere). These are:

Hohfeld, *Fundamental Legal Conceptions as Applied in Judicial Reasoning* (Yale University Press, 1923), an influential analysis of rights which underpins the distinctions drawn between different uses of the word 'right' on p. 7.

Fuller, *The Morality of Law* (Yale University Press, 1964), is an important analysis of the rule of law; and one significant response was that of: Hart (1965) 78 Harvard Law Review 1281, reprinted in Hart, *Essays in Jurisprudence and Philosophy* (Oxford University Press, 1983). The debate has been continued, especially by Raz in *The Authority of Law* (Oxford University Press, 1979). See also Bingham, *The Rule of Law* [2007] CLJ 67.

For the general consideration of the interface between morality and law, we particularly recommend:

Hart, *The Concept of Law* (Oxford University Press, 1961, re-issued 1997)

Hart, *Law, Liberty and Morality* (Oxford University Press, 1963)

Finnis, *Natural law and Natural Rights* (Oxford University Press, 1980)

A useful introductory selection of material on the subject of rights, including some of the above, can be found in: Davies and Holdcroft, *Jurisprudence: Texts and Commentary* (Butterworths, 1991).

A recent analysis of the theory of human rights which is both incisive and concise is Harris, *Human Rights and Mythical Beasts* (2004) 120 LQR 428.

 ## HISTORY OF RIGHTS

For those interested in the history of rights in general, we recommend: Kelly, *A Short History of Western Legal Theory* (Oxford University Press, 1992). For the history of the precedents to, and genesis of, the Convention itself, we highly recommend: Simpson, *Human Rights and the End of Empire* (Oxford University Press, 2001); this was an invaluable source for our substantially more summary survey in Chapter 3.

For a more general history of English law, the best overview is: Baker, *An Introduction to English Legal History* (4th edition, Oxford University Press, 2002).

 ## CONSTITUTIONAL AND ADMINISTRATIVE LAW

Our discussion of the United Kingdom constitution, of the field of administrative law, which is primarily the law of judicial review, and of the relationship between Parliament and the courts, is necessarily limited. For more detail in these areas, some leading textbooks are:
Craig, *Administrative Law* (Sweet & Maxwell, 2008)
Wade and Forsyth, *Administrative Law* (Oxford University Press, 2009)
Forsyth (ed), *Judicial Review and the Constitution* (Hart, 2000)
Heuston, *Essays in Constitutional Law* (Stevens, 1964)
A provocative analysis of the recent wave of constitutional reform is Bogdanor, *Our New Constitution* (2004) LQR 242.

 ## CASE REFERENCES

Recent cases have a neutral citation (the year, plus e.g. UKHL for House of Lords, EWCA for Court of Appeal, etc.). We have provided these as, where cases are unreported, they can be used to find cases on online reporting sites such as BAILII, Lawtel, etc.

The following abbreviations used in the text refer to series of law reports. The leading series of reports referred to are:

EHRR	European Human Rights Reports: European Court cases
DR, CD	European Commission decisions
AC	Appeal Cases (House of Lords and Privy Council decisions)
QB/KB	Queen's Bench/King's Bench Reports
Ch	Chancery Division Reports
Fam	Family Division Reports
All ER	All England Law Reports
WLR	Weekly Law Reports

Reports of Court of Appeal and High Court decisions (QB/KB, Ch, Fam)

Other general series of law reports cited are:

BHRC	Butterworths Human Rights Cases
CAR	Criminal Appeal Reports
Crim LR	Criminal Law Review
EHRLR	European Human Rights Law Review
FLR	Family Law Reports
FSR	Fleet Street Reports
IRLR	Industrial Relations Law Reports
LGR	Local Government Reports
LTL	Lawtel Law Reports (online at http://www.lawtel.co.uk)
RTR	Road Traffic Reports
Times	The Times Law Reports
UKHRR	United Kingdom Human Rights Reports
US	United States report

Journal abbreviations used in the Further Reading section

CLJ   Cambridge Law Journal
LQR   Law Quarterly Review
PL   Public Law
RLR   Restitution Law Review

Index

pport with study and revision
you ever thought possible ...

EDWIN SHORTS AND CLAIRE DE THAN

> UNDERSTAND QUICKLY
> REVISE EFFECTIVELY
> TAKE EXAMS WITH CONFIDENCE

HUMAN RIGHTS

UNRIVALLED REVISION SUPPORT INCLUDES EVEN MORE ONLINE!
> Personalised study plan > Interactive quizzes > Full Q&A support
> Flashcards > Revision podcasts > Exam marking insight

ISBN: 978-1-4058-5963-9 | £10.99*

> 'You really feel that someone is trying to help you: 'you're not alone'! The tone is approachable, reader-friendly and empathises with the student. It really is a helping hand.'
>
> **Sarah Bainbridge, law student**

Law Express: Understand quickly. Revise effectively. Take exams with confidence.

Other titles are available in this series.

For further information or to order these books, please visit:

www.pearsoned.co.uk/law

PEARSON
Longman